Clause 8 Publishing

Intellectual Property in the New Technological Age: 2023

Volume I: Perspectives, Trade Secrets & Patents

Peter S. Menell
UC Berkeley School of Law

Mark A. Lemley
Stanford Law School

Robert P. Merges
UC Berkeley School of Law

Shyamkrishna Balganesh
Columbia Law School

ISBN-13: 978-1-945555-24-4 (Clause 8 Publishing)

For Claire, Dylan and Veronica, and Noah and Taylor

P.S.M.

For Rose, as always

M.A.L.

For my brothers, Bruce, Paul, and Matt

R.P.M.

For Irene and Marky

S.B.

Q PREFACE

When we embarked on this project more than two decades ago, we envisioned many things, but not that it would lead to self-publishing a casebook.

A lot has changed since we began collaborating. At the time that we launched this project, most intellectual property courses were taught along particular mode of protection lines: patent law, copyright law, trademark law, and trade secret law. From our research and real world experience, we recognized that digital technology blurred the traditional doctrinal lines. We set out to design a book for the emerging technological age. We built the book around core philosophical frameworks, broad integrated coverage, and a pedagogical model that emphasizes problem-solving.

Over the ensuing years, our insight and framing proved enduring. Nearly all manner of enterprise and organization—from high technology start-ups to traditional manufacturing and media companies, government agencies, and even educational institutions—came to confront a broad range of intellectual property issues spanning the full spectrum of protection modes. The survey intellectual property course became a core subject at our law schools and many others across the United States and around the world. That much we had at least dreamed of.

But we did not foresee entering the publishing business. During the formative stage of our careers, we were thrilled to gain the interest of established publishers. Our book hit the market just as the Internet was gaining traction. The IP field expanded rapidly and we found ourselves churning out new editions every two or three years to keep pace with the increasing velocity of IP law. Little, Brown's law book division was acquired by Aspen, which was then acquired by Wolters Kluwer. The market for our book continued to grow.

Yet as advances in digital technology reshaped the world around us—from Internet search to online publishing—we, and our adopters and students, saw relatively little change in our publishing market. Prices continued to rise each year. Publishing schedules remained rigid. The publishing of our book seemed suspended in time. Most frustratingly, our students were paying $250 for a book that generated just $15 in total author royalties. This pattern conflicted with the thrust of our book and scholarship. Advances in digital technology and competition should have been driving prices down, not up. Our frustration grew.

These issues came to a head in September 2014. When our publisher indicated that we missed the deadline for getting our book into the summer 2015 catalog, we dusted off our original publishing contract from December 1993. In checking the revision clause, we recognized that we held the copyright in the work *and* retained the right to prepare derivative works.

Once we realized that we had the right to shift to self-publishing, we faced a choice: stay with a leading publisher or take on the start-up costs and day-to-day operations of self-publishing. Peter had been writing about disintermediation in the media industries and strongly believed the time was ripe to branch out on our own. He posed a simple question: how would we view this choice ten years down the road? A quick review of self-publishing options indicated that we could substantially reduce the cost of our book while providing students with more convenient access—both digital versions and print-on-demand. We could also move to annual editions and take control over the production pipeline. This would ensure that our book was always current. Although striking out on our own involved some risk and additional tasks, failing to take this path would perpetuate an obsolete and unjustifiably costly burden on students at a time when they can ill afford it. We decided to take the plunge.

After reviewing options, we decided to begin our self-publishing experiment with Amazon. (We retain copyright ownership and hence flexibility to try other platforms as the marketplace evolves, an important lesson from various media markets.) Amazon's publishing platform imposes size limits that required us to divide our book into two volumes: Volume I covering Philosophical Perspectives, Trade Secrets, and Patent Law (we also included the patent preemption cases from Chapter VI for those interested in studying those materials in conjunction with the trade secret and patent law chapters); Volume II covering Copyright Law, Trademark Law, and State Law IP Protections (including the preemption materials). The volumes are available as eBooks and through Amazon's on-demand publishing platform. This has the virtues of reducing the weight of what students need to carry around on a daily basis and creating more modular teaching options. We also distribute Chapters I and II on SSRN so that students can sample the book before committing to the class.

Which brings us to what we hope is a New Publishing Age for all manner of academic publishing. In addition to releasing IPNTA2--- (we plan to designate new editions by publication year rather than volume number), we launched Clause 8 Publishing, a new publishing venture to "promote Progress" in intellectual property education (and possibly more). We plan to introduce a series of complementary products, enhancements, supplementary texts, multimedia, and other resources for adopters and students—at low cost and with easy accessibility. You will be able to learn about these resources at IPNTA.com and Clause8Publishing.com.

Peter has managed the transition of our book to a self-publishing model and has taken the lead on establishing this platform. Those interested in adopting our book (or anything else about the project) should contact him at pmenell@law.berkeley.edu. (Please include "IPNTA" or "Clause 8" in the subject line.) IPNTA2016, the first self-published edition of "Intellectual Property in the New Technological Age," more than exceeded our hopes. Sales for IPNTA increased above the highest sales of prior editions, resulting in savings to students of over $1 million in the first year. IPNTA2017 through IPNTA 2020 continued on this path. We added Shyamkrishna Balganesh to this project in 2020. IPNTA2023 updates the text to reflect the most recent developments in this rapidly evolving field of law.

In retrospect, the subject matter covered by our original edition—philosophical perspectives on intangible resources, promoting progress in technology and creative expression, and competition policy—set us on the path to DIY/New Age publishing. Copyright law seeks to harness market forces to encourage creative expression and widespread dissemination. It builds bridges between creators and those who value their work. Digital technology and the Internet enhance these powerful forces by lowering the costs of creation and providing the virtual dissemination bridges. We feel fortunate to have liberated our book and very much look forward to working with law professors and students in building a more productive marketplace and community for IP teaching materials.

Peter S. Menell	Mark A. Lemley	Robert P. Merges	Shyamkrishna Balganesh

July 2023

♀ NEW FEATURES

Rapid advances in digital and life sciences technology continue to spur the evolution of intellectual property law. As professors and practitioners in this field know all too well, Congress and the courts continue to develop intellectual property law and jurisprudence at a rapid pace. For that reason, we have significantly augmented and revised our text.

The 2023 volumes reflect the following principal developments:

• **Trade Secrets**: Congress passed the Defend Trade Secrets Act of 2016, one of the most momentous changes in the history of trade secret protection. We have updated this chapter to reflect its growing influence.

• **Patent Law**: The past several years have witnessed some of the most significant developments in U.S. patent history and technological change. This edition weaves generative AI into various parts of the chapter, including a new section on inventorship featuring the Federal Circuit's decision in *Thaler v. Vidal*. It also revamps the enablement section in light of the Supreme Court's *Amgen* decision.

• **Copyright Law**: This chapter substantially reworks coverage of fair use law in the aftermath of the Supreme Court's momentous decision in *The Andy Warhol Foundation v. Goldsmith*. It also weaves generative AI into various sections, including a new section on authorship.

• **Trademark Law**: This chapter revises coverage of trademark defenses—particularly the role of the First Amendment and parody—in light of the Supreme Court's decision in *Jack Daniel's Properties v. VIP Products*.

• **Other State IP Protections**: This chapter expands the section on the right of publicity to encompass the emergence of name, image, and likeness (NIL) policy in the college sports marketplace. It also includes a problem highlighting ramifications of generative AI for recording artists.

ABOUT Clause 8 Publishing

Clause 8 Publishing is a digital publishing venture founded and managed by Peter Menell. Mark Lemley, Robert Merges, and Shyamkrishna Balganesh serve on the Editorial Board. Inspired by Article I, Section 8, Clause 8 of the U.S. CONSTITUTION, Clause 8 Publishing seeks to promote production and dissemination of the highest quality and most up-to-date educational resources at fair prices and in a way that ensures that much of the revenue flows to authors. It aims to streamline the publishing process, take full advantage of evolving digital platforms and print-on-demand functionality, and develop innovative educational resources.

Clause 8 Publishing plans to produce annual editions of INTELLECTUAL PROPERTY IN THE NEW TECHNOLOGICAL AGE.

Over the coming years, Clause 8 Publishing aims to support a series of complementary products (statutory supplement, primers, problem sets, multi-media presentations) and resources for intellectual property professors, students, judges, and policy makers. It aspires to lead the academy toward more productive and just publishing models. More information will be available at Clause8Publishing.com and IPNTA.com.

💡 ACKNOWLEDGMENTS

We are indebted to a great many people who have helped us since this project began in 1991. We would like to thank our many colleagues who reviewed earlier drafts of the book and provided helpful guidance. While many of these reviews were anonymous, we have also benefitted from the advice of Lynn Baker, Paul Heald, Tom Jorde, and Pam Samuelson, each of whom read several different drafts of the book as it made its way through the editorial process. We gratefully acknowledge the research assistance of Evelyn Findeis, Edwin Flores, Ryan Garcia, Shari Heino, Toni Moore Knudson, Christopher Leslie, and Barbara Parvis. We would also like to thank Michele Co for exceptional secretarial and administrative assistance in completing the original text.

We are grateful to many colleagues for providing suggestions for improving this book over the years. In particular, we would like to thank Fred Abbott, Amit Agarwal, John Allison, BJ Ard, Ann Bartow, Andrew Chin, Julie Cohen, Ken Dam, Robin Feldman, Terry Fisher, James Gibson, Scott Hemphill, Michael Jacobs, Patricia Judd, Dmitry Karshtedt, Marshall Leaffer, Jake Linford, Glynn Lunney, Ron Mann, David McGowan, Chuck McManis, Roberta Morris, David Nimmer, Tyler Ochoa, Ruth Okediji, Lucas Osborn, Lisa Ouellette, Malla Pollack, Peggy Radin, Lisa Ramsey, Jerry Reichmann, Eva Subotnik, Sharon Sandeen, Paul Schwartz, Jacob Sherkow, Lon Sobel, Harry Surden, Allan Sternstein, Mark Thurmon, and Ty Trejo. We have also benefitted greatly from the research assistance and proofreading of Alex Barata, Adam Blankenheimer, Will Buckingham, Amber Burroff, Brian Carver, Concord Cheung, Colleen Chien, Sarah Craven, Louise Decoppet, Will Devries, Amit Elazari, Tom Fletcher, Ryan Garcia, Ines Gonzalez, David Grady, Andrea Hall, Jade Jurdi, Robert Damion Jurrens, Victoria H. Kane, Jeffrey Kuhn, Michelle A. Marzahn, Megan McKnelly, Selena R. Medlen, David Moore, Roberta Morris, Pilar Ossorio, Ryan Owens, Stephanie N.-P. Pham-Quang, Laura Quilter, John Sasson, Michael Sawyer, Shannon Scott, Michael Liu Su, Allison Watkins, Joel Wallace, Reid Whitaker, Emily Wohl, and Tarra Zynda.

We thank Amit Elazari for production assistance and Israel Vela for design and website development assistance.

SUMMARY OF CONTENTS

I. INTRODUCTION

II. TRADE SECRET LAW

III. PATENT LAW

IV. COPYRIGHT LAW

V. TRADEMARK LAW

VI. STATE IP PROTECTIONS

TABLE OF CONTENTS

EDITORIAL NOTE

We have selectively omitted citations and footnotes from cases without the uses of ellipses or other indications. All footnotes are numbered consecutively within each chapter, except that footnotes in cases and other excerpts correspond to the actual footnote numbers in the published reports. Many of the problems in this text are taken from actual cases. In many instances, we have altered the facts and the names of the parties for pedagogical purposes. In a few cases, however, particularly in the trademark chapter, we felt that it was important to the problem to use the name of a product or company with which the reader would be familiar. Readers should understand that the problems are hypothetical in nature and that we do not intend them to represent the actual facts of any case or situation.

CHAPTER I:
INTRODUCTION

The concept of property is among the oldest institutions of human civilization. It is widely recognized that people may own real property and tangible objects. The common law and the criminal law protect private property from interference by others. The Fifth Amendment to the U.S. Constitution protects private property against takings by the government for public use without just compensation. The philosophical bases for protection of private property are well entrenched in most societies: Private property results when labor is applied to nature, as an incentive for discovery, as an essential part of personhood, and as a foundation for an ordered economic system.

Ideas and information, by definition, are less tangible. They exist in the mind and work of humans. Legal protection for intellectual work evolved much later in the development of human society than did protection for tangible property. The protection of such "intellectual property" raises complex philosophical questions. Should the first person to discover a way of performing an important task—for example, a procedure for closing a wound—be entitled to prevent others from using this procedure? Should the first person to pen a phrase or hum a melody be entitled to prevent others from copying such words or singing the song? Should such "intellectual property rights" be more limited than traditional property rights (i.e., the fee simple)? This book explores the legal institutions and rules that have developed to protect intellectual property.

This chapter has two principal purposes. It first explores the principal philosophical foundations for the protection of intellectual property. Understanding the reasons why we protect intellectual property—and how those reasons differ from the justifications for real and other forms of tangible property—motivates the many legal rules that will follow in this book. The second section provides a comparative overview of the principal modes of intellectual property protection: trade secret, patent, copyright, and trademark/trade dress. Understanding the intellectual property landscape requires thinking about each form of intellectual property not just in isolation but as it interacts with the others. The remainder of this book explores these areas in detail, highlighting their logic and interplay in promoting progress in technology and the arts.

A. PHILOSOPHICAL PERSPECTIVES

Philosophical accounts of intellectual property fall into two broad categories. In the first and more common one, theories that have previously been used to justify tangible property are applied and extended to intangible resources. By contrast, in the second, the theories focus less on trying to think of intellectual property as a form of "property," and instead emphasize the specific type of behavior (e.g., copying, counterfeiting) that the intellectual property regime seeks to curtail. Locke's labor theory and Hegel's personhood account exemplify the first category, while Kant's autonomy-based theory remains the best-known justification within the second.

Property-based justifications for intellectual property protection, whether economic or moral, must contend with a fundamental difference between intangible and tangible property. Tangible property, whether land or chattels, is composed of atoms, physical things that can occupy only one place at any given time. This means that possession of a physical thing is necessarily "exclusive"—if I have it, you don't. Indeed, the core of property lies in the right granted to the "owner" of a thing or a piece of land to exclude others from certain uses of it. Settled ownership rights in land and goods are thought to prevent both disputes over who can use the property for what purpose, and the overuse of property that would result if everyone had common access to it.

Intangibles, though, do not have this characteristic of excludability. If I know a particular piece of information, and I tell it to you, you have not deprived me of it. Rather, we both possess it. The fact that the possession and use of intangibles such as information is largely "nonrivalrous" is critical to intellectual property theory because it means that the traditional economic justification for tangible property does not fit intellectual property. In the state of nature, there is no danger of overusing or overdistributing information, and no danger of fighting over who gets to use it. Everyone can use the information without diminishing its value. *See generally* Peter S. Menell & Suzanne Scotchmer, *Intellectual Property Law*, in 2 HANDBOOK OF LAW AND ECONOMICS 1474 (A. Mitchell Polinsky & Steven Shavell eds., 2007).

Theorists have therefore turned elsewhere to justify exclusive rights in intangibles. Over the course of human history, numerous theories have been put forth to explain intellectual property protection. The principal basis for such protection in the United States is the utilitarian or economic incentive framework. Nonetheless, other theories— most notably the natural rights and personhood justifications—have been important in understanding the development and scope of intellectual property law, both here and abroad. The four sections that follow examine different philosophical theories. In reading them, consider how each might apply to the creation of rights and ownership interests in intangibles.

1. The Natural Rights Perspective

JOHN LOCKE
TWO TREATISES ON GOVERNMENT
Third Edition, 1698

Though the earth and all inferior creatures be common to all men, yet every man has a "property" in his own "person." This nobody has any right to but himself. The "labour" of his body and the "work" of his hands, we may say, are properly his. Whatsoever, then, he removes out of the state that Nature hath provided and left it in, he hath mixed his labor with it, and joined to it something that is his own, and thereby makes it his property. It being by him removed from the common state Nature placed it in, it hath by this labour something annexed to it that excludes the common right of other men. For this "labour" being the unquestionable property of the labourer, no man but he can have a right to what that is once joined to, at least where there is enough, and as good left in common for others.

He that is nourished by the acorns he picked up under an oak, or the apples he gathered from the trees in the wood, has certainly appropriated them to himself   That labour put a distinction between them and common   And will any one say he had no right to those acorns or apples he thus appropriated because he had not the consent of all mankind to make them his? Was it a robbery thus to assume to himself what belonged to all in common? If such a consent as that was necessary, man had starved, notwithstanding the plenty God had given him. We see in commons, which remain so by compact, that it is the taking any part of what is common, and removing it out of the state Nature leaves it in, which begins the property, without which the common is of no use. And the taking of this or that part does not depend on the express consent of all the commoners. . . .

It will, perhaps, be objected to this, that if gathering the acorns or other fruits, of the earth, etc., makes a right to them, then any one may engross as much as he will. To which I answer, Not so. The same law of Nature that does by this means give us property, does also bound that property too   As much as any one can make use of to any advantage of life before it spoils, so much he may by his labor fix his property in. Whatever is beyond this is more than his share, and belongs to others. . . .

As much land as a man tills, plants, improves, cultivates, and can use the product of, so much is his property. He by his labor does, as it were, enclose it from the common. . . . Nor was this appropriation of any parcel of land, by improving it, any prejudice to any other man, since there was still enough and as good left, and more than the yet unprovided could use. So that, in effect, there was never the less left for others because of his enclosure for himself. For he that leaves as much as another can make use of does as good as take nothing at all.

COMMENTS AND QUESTIONS

1. How do Locke's theories of real property apply to intellectual property? Should we treat the two as the same for ownership purposes? What would Locke say about the exclusive rights granted by the patent laws, to prevent others from using the claimed invention for up to 20 years, whether or not they discovered the invention on their own? Surely if Locke considered the working of land and raw materials to be "labor" that justified ownership of the resulting product, he would have considered labor toward the creation of a new *idea*—the "sweat of the brow"—to be equally deserving of protection. Or do the differences between real and intellectual property mean that Locke's arguments shouldn't apply to intellectual property?

Should it matter whether Locke's hypothetical creator was the only one likely to come up with his particular invention or discovery? If others would have discovered the same phenomenon a few years (or a few weeks) later, does Locke's argument for property rights lose its force? We might distinguish between a Lockean theory of copyright, which prevents copying, and an effort to justify patent law, which precludes even independent invention and therefore restricts the labor of others.

For illumination on these and related points, *see* Edwin C. Hettinger, *Justifying Intellectual Property*, 18 PHIL. & PUB. AFF. 31 (1989). Hettinger critiques the major theories of intellectual property rights. As to Lockean labor theory, Hettinger observes:

> [A]ssuming that labor's fruits are valuable, and that laboring gives the laborer a property right in this value, this would entitle the laborer only to the value she added, and not to the *total* value of the resulting product. Though exceedingly difficult to measure, these two components of value (that attributable to the object labored on and that attributable to the labor) need to be distinguished. . .
>
> .
>
> Property rights in the thing produced are . . . not a fitting reward if the value of these rights is disproportional to the effort expended by the laborer. "Effort" includes (1) how hard someone tries to achieve a result, (2) the amount of risk voluntarily incurred in seeking this result, and (3) the degree to which moral considerations played a role in choosing the result intended. The harder one tries, the more one is willing to sacrifice, and the worthier the goal, the greater are one's deserts.

Id. at 37, 41-42. Robert Nozick made the first point by means of *reductio ad absurdum:* he asks whether the owner of a can of tomato juice who dumps it into the ocean can thereafter claim ownership of all the high seas. *See* ROBERT NOZICK, ANARCHY, STATE AND UTOPIA 175 (1984).

Doesn't Locke justify taking something if you can make productive use of it? How can that explain giving a right to prevent anyone from using it? Many patent suits today are filed by "non-practicing entities" who don't make products themselves, but sue those who do. Should a Lockean approach to IP require that the owner make productive use of the right?

2. An application of the Lockean approach with an especially detailed consideration of the Lockean "proviso" (i.e., that "as much and as good" be left for others after appropriation) can be found in Wendy J. Gordon, *A Property Right in Self-Expression: Equality and Individualism in the Natural Law of Intellectual Property*, 102 YALE L.J. 1533 (1993). The proviso poses a problem we will see throughout the course: how to delimit the rights of a creator in the face of claims by consumers and other members of the public at large.

More particularly, Professor Gordon challenges the extreme view taken by some commentators that a creator's rights should be absolute. The absolutist view proceeds from the idea that since the creator is solely responsible for the creation, no one is harmed if the creation is withheld from the public entirely. And since the creator can withhold it entirely, he or she can naturally restrict its availability in any manner, including a high price or conditions on its purchase. *See, e.g.*, JOHN STUART MILL, PRINCIPLES OF POLITICAL ECONOMY 142 (1872); Steven N.S. Cheung, *Property Rights and Invention*, in 8 RESEARCH IN LAW AND ECONOMICS: THE ECONOMICS OF PATENTS AND COPYRIGHTS 5, 6 (John Palmer & Richard O. Zerbe, Jr. eds., 1986). Through the examination of various examples—such as the Church of Scientology's efforts to restrain books critical of its teachings, West Publishing's suit to enjoin Lexis from offering page numbers corresponding to West's case reports, and Disney's efforts to prevent bawdy parodies of its images that ridicule sanitized popular culture—Gordon suggests that, sometimes at least, the public can be worse off if a creation is offered and then limited in its use than it would have been had the creation never been made.

For detailed discussions of the "Lockean proviso," *see* Jeremy Waldron, *Enough and as Good Left for Others*, 29 PHIL. Q. 319 (1979); ROBERT NOZICK, ANARCHY, STATE AND UTOPIA 175–82 (1984); DAVID GAUTHIER, MORALS BY AGREEMENT 190–232 (1986). For more detailed treatment of another problem addressed by Gordon—the follow-on creator who builds on a preexisting work—*see* Lawrence C. Becker, *Deserving to Own Intellectual Property*, 68 CHI.-KENT L. REV. 609 (1993). For insightful historical analysis of Locke's theory and its application to intellectual property, *see* Justin Hughes, *Copyright and Incomplete Historiographies: Of Piracy, Propertization, and Thomas Jefferson*, 79 S. CAL. L. REV. 993 (2006). If labor or effort is the key to property claims under Locke, how should we handle situations where numerous dispersed people accumulate their labor to produce something useful? *See* Robert P. Merges, *Locke for the Masses*, 36 HOFSTRA L. REV. 1179 (2008).

3. Nozick's ANARCHY, STATE AND UTOPIA offers a different philosophical perspective on intellectual property rooted in the libertarian tradition. It is not clear how libertarians should think of intellectual property rights. On the one hand, ownership of property seems necessary to the market exchange that is at the heart of the libertarian model of society. On the other hand, one might view the free flow of information unfettered by property rights as the norm, and view government-enforced intellectual property rights as an unnecessary aberration. For a libertarian approach that is decidedly hostile to intellectual property, *see* John Perry Barlow, *The Economy of Ideas*, 2.03 WIRED 84 (Mar. 1994); *cf.* Peter S. Menell, *The Property Rights Movement's Embrace*

of Intellectual Property: True Love or Doomed Relationship?, 34 ECOL. L.Q. 713 (2007).

4. Natural rights are strongly emphasized in the continental European justifications for intellectual property. Those justifications to some extent parallel Locke's arguments, but there are important differences. Continental scholars emphasize the importance of reputation and noneconomic aspects of intellectual property, factors that lead them to support moral rights in copyright law. Professor Alfred Yen presents a thorough account of the role of natural rights in American copyright law. *See* Alfred Yen, *Restoring the Natural Law: Copyright as Labor and Possession*, 51 OHIO ST. L.J. 517 (1990). For a detailed comparison of efficiency, natural rights, and other foundational theories of intellectual property law, *see* ROBERT P. MERGES, JUSTIFYING INTELLECTUAL PROPERTY (2011).

5. Professor Mala Chatterjee argues that even if Locke's theory is problematic as a defense of property that is extended to intellectual property, it nevertheless becomes more plausible when applied directly to copyright. *See* Mala Chatterjee, *Lockean Copyright Versus Lockean Property*, 12 J. LEG. ANALYSIS 136 (2020). In this view, intangible resources such as expression are both non-rival and transformable, which allows Locke's labor-based justification to account for a minimalist copyright regime. Do you agree? Should one's labor be protected only against exact duplication?

PROBLEM I-1

You are a botanist exploring a remote region of a small tropical country. You stumble across a field of strange flowers that you have never encountered before. The tribespeople tell you that they use the flower to heal various ailments by rubbing its petals on the skin and chanting a healing prayer. You pluck one of the flowers and when you return to your campsite that night, you show it to a fellow explorer who is an expert in biochemistry. The biochemist smells the flower and says that it is vaguely reminiscent of Substance P. Substance P is a medicine widely used to treat a variety of serious diseases. She tells you that Substance P is easy to detect: It turns bright yellow when exposed to intense heat. That evening, you put the flower over the campfire and, sure enough, it turns bright yellow. When you return home, you work for months to isolate the active ingredient in the flower. It is not Substance P, but a close structural analog. In chemical experiments, the extract shows great promise for fighting many of the diseases that Substance P can treat without Substance P's dreaded side effects.

What rights, if any, should you have in this discovery and research? Should those rights prevent anyone else from going back to the tropical country, finding the flower, and isolating the chemical you have discovered?

You make a profit selling your medicine throughout the world, including to the native tribespeople of the tropical country. John, a chemist in your company, is angered by this policy. Your formula is a carefully guarded secret, but John publishes it in THE NEW ENGLAND JOURNAL OF MEDICINE. A nonprofit organization begins producing the medicine and selling your product to the native tribespeople at a discount. The organization advertises that it is selling your medicine for pennies a year. Should you be able to stop them from selling your medicine? Should you be able to stop them from using the name of your medicine in their ads?

You have named your medicine "Tropicurical." To advertise the product, one of the employees in your advertising department writes a song based on the very distinctive sounds of the wind in the inland coves of the country mixed with the native birds' calls. The tribespeople of the tropical country have a song that sounds remarkably similar to your advertising tune. The song is important to their tribal identity, and they argue that it is inappropriate to use their distinctive tribal song to commercialize your product. They ask you to stop using it. Should they be able to stop you from using the name or song?

When you refuse to stop using the Tropicurical song to advertise your product, the tribespeople write a new version of their song entitled "Tropicursical" with angry lyrics claiming that your product destroys culture. Should you be able to stop them from singing the song? NATIONAL GEOGRAPHIC records the tribespeople singing "Tropicursical." The recording plays as part of the news report on their television show. It is also available for download on NATIONAL GEOGRAPHIC's website. Individuals download copies of the song and e-mail it to their friends. It spreads like wildfire over the Internet, and eventually popular radio stations play it over the air. Should you be able to stop these copies and performances?

2. The Personhood Perspective

Margaret Jane Radin
Property and Personhood
34 Stanford Law Review 957 (1982)

This article explores the relationship between property and personhood, a relationship that has commonly been both ignored and taken for granted in legal thought. The premise underlying the personhood perspective is that to achieve proper self-development—to be *a person*—an individual needs some control over resources in the external environment. The necessary assurances of control take the form of property rights. Although explicit elaboration of this perspective is wanting in modern writing on property, the personhood perspective is often implicit in the connections that courts and commentators find between property and privacy or between property and liberty. In addition to its power to explain certain aspects of existing schemes of property entitlement, the personhood perspective can also serve as an explicit source of values for making moral distinctions in property disputes and hence for either justifying or criticizing current law. . . .

In what follows I shall discuss the personhood perspective as Hegel developed it in *Philosophy of Right,* trace some of its later permutations and entanglements with other perspectives on property, and try to develop a contemporary view useful in the context of the American legal system. . . .

I. Property for Personhood: An Intuitive View

Most people possess certain objects they feel are almost part of themselves. These objects are closely bound up with personhood because they are part of the way we constitute ourselves as continuing personal entities in the world. They may be as different as people are different, but some common examples might be a wedding ring, a portrait, an heirloom, or a house.

One may gauge the strength or significance of someone's relationship with an object by the kind of pain that would be occasioned by its loss. On this view, an object is closely related to one's personhood if its loss causes pain that cannot be relieved by the object's replacement. If so, that particular object is bound up with the holder. For instance, if a wedding ring is stolen from a jeweler, insurance proceeds can reimburse the jeweler, but if a wedding ring is stolen from a loving wearer, the price of a replacement will not restore the status quo—perhaps no amount of money can do so.

The opposite of holding an object that has become a part of oneself is holding an object that is perfectly replaceable with other goods of equal market value. One holds such an object for purely instrumental reasons. The archetype of such a good is, of course, money, which is almost always held only to buy other things. A dollar is worth no more than what one chooses to buy with it, and one dollar bill is as good as another. Other examples are the wedding ring in the hands of the jeweler, the automobile in the hands of the dealer, the land in the hands of the developer, or the apartment in the hands of the commercial landlord. I shall call these theoretical opposites—property that is bound up with a person and property that is held purely instrumentally—personal property and fungible property respectively. . . .

III. Hegel, Property, and Personhood

A. Hegel's Philosophy of Right

. . . Because the person in Hegel's conception is merely an abstract unit of free will or autonomy, it has no concrete existence until that will acts on the external world. . . .

Hegel concludes that the person becomes a real self only by engaging in a property relationship with something external. Such a relationship is the goal of the person. In perhaps the best-known passage from this book, Hegel says:

> The person has for its substantive end the right of placing its will in any and every thing, which thing is thereby mine; [and] because that thing has no such end in itself, its destiny and soul take on my will. [This constitutes] mankind's absolute right of appropriation over all things.

Hence, "property is the first embodiment of freedom and so is in itself a substantive end.". . .

Hegel seems to make property "private" on the same level as the unit of autonomy that is embodying its will by holding it. He argues that property is private to individuals when discussing it in the context of the autonomous individual will and that it is essentially common within a family, when discussing it in the context of the autonomous family unit. He does not make the leap to state property, however, even though his theory of the state might suggest it. For Hegel, the properly developed state (in contrast to civil society) is an organic moral entity. . . . and individuals within the state are subsumed into its community morality. . . .

B. Hegel and Property for Personhood

[A] theory of personal property can build upon some of Hegel's insights. First, the notion that the will is embodied in things suggests that the entity we know as a person cannot come to exist without both differentiating itself from the physical environment and yet maintaining relationships with portions of that environment. The idea of embodied will, cut loose from Hegel's grand scheme of absolute mind, reminds us that people and things have ongoing relationships which have their own ebb and flow, and that these relationships can be very close to a person's center and sanity. If these relationships justify ownership, or at least contribute to its justification, Hegel's notion that ownership requires continuous embodiment of the will is appealing.

Second, Hegel's incompletely developed notion that property is held by the unit to which one attributes autonomy has powerful implications for the concept of group development and group rights. Hegel thought that freedom (rational self-determination) was only possible in the context of a group (the properly organized and fully developed state). Without accepting this role for the state, one may still conclude that in a given social context certain groups are likely to be constitutive of their members in the sense that the members find self-determination only within the groups. This might have political consequences for claims of the group on certain resources of the external world (i.e., property).

Third, there may be an echo of Hegel's notion of an objective community morality in the intuition that certain kinds of property relationships can be presumed to bear close bonds to personhood. If property in one's body is not too close to personhood to be considered property at all, then it is the clearest case of property for personhood. The property/privacy nexus of the home is also a relatively clear case in our particular history and culture. . . .

[T]he personhood theory helps us understand the nature of the right dictating that discrete units [i.e., an undivided, individual asset] ought to be protected.

An argument that discrete units are more important than total assets takes the following form. A person cannot be fully a person without a sense of continuity of self over time. To maintain that sense of continuity over time and to exercise one's liberty or autonomy, one must have an ongoing relationship with the external environment, consisting of both "things" and other people. One perceives the ongoing relationship to the environment as a set of individual relationships, corresponding to the way our perception separates the world into distinct "things." Some things must remain stationary if anything is to move; some points of reference must be constant or thought and action is not possible. In order to lead a normal life, there must be some continuity in relating to "things." One's expectations crystallize around certain "things," the loss of which causes more disruption and disorientation than does a simple decrease in aggregate wealth. For example, if someone returns home to find her sofa has disappeared, that is more disorienting than to discover that her house has decreased in market value by 5%. If, by magic, her white sofa were instantly replaced by a blue one of equal market value, it would cause no loss in net worth but would still cause some disruption in her life.

This argument assumes that all discrete units one owns and perceives as part of her continuing environment are to some degree personal. If the white sofa were totally fungible, then magically replacing it with a blue one would cause no disruption. In fact, neither would replacing it with money. . . .

But the theory of personal property suggests that not all object-loss is equally important. Some objects may approach the fungible end of the continuum so that the justification for protecting them as specially related to persons disappears. They might just as well be treated by whatever general moral rules govern wealth-loss at the hands of the government. If the moral rules governing wealth-loss correspond to Michelman's utilitarian suggestion—government may take whatever wealth is necessary to generate higher welfare in which the individual can confidently expect to share—then the government could take some fungible items without compensation. In general, the moral inquiry for whether fungible property could be taken would be the same as the moral inquiry for whether it is fair to impose a tax on this particular person.

On the other hand, a few objects may be so close to the personal end of the continuum that no compensation could be "just." That is, hypothetically, if some object were so bound up with me that I would cease to be "myself" if it were taken, then a government that must respect persons ought not to take it. If my kidney may be called my property, it is not property subject to condemnation for the general public welfare. Hence, in the context of a legal system, one might expect to find the characteristic use of standards of review and burdens of proof designed to shift risk of error away from protected interests in personal property. For instance, if there were reason to suspect that some object were close to the personal end of the continuum, there might be a prima facie case against taking it. That prima facie case might be rebutted if the government could show that the object is not personal, or perhaps that the object is not "too" personal compared with the importance to the government of acquiring that particular object for social purposes.

COMMENTS AND QUESTIONS

1. How well does Professor Radin's theory of real property apply to intellectual property? Can an individual be so "bound up" in their inventions or works of authorship that their loss would occasion more than economic damage? Does it affect your answer that intellectual property can be used simultaneously by many people without depleting its functional value to anyone—so that an author's "loss" is not the physical deprivation of stolen chattels, but the less personal fact that someone else has copied her work? Is this more like giving blood than donating a kidney?

It may be that the investment of "personhood" in intellectual property varies greatly, both with the type of intellectual property at issue and with the time and effort the owner put into developing it. For example, an author may feel more connected to a novel on which she has worked for several years than to a massive software program for navigating a jumbo jet or a company's customer list. Should the law take account of these differences, giving greater protection to more personal works?

For applications of Radin's "personhood" ideas in the context of intellectual property, *see* Neil W. Netanel, *Copyright Alienability Restrictions and the Enhancement of Author Autonomy: A Normative Evaluation*, 24 RUTGERS L.J. 347 (1993); Steven Cherensky, Comment, *A Penny for Their Thoughts: Employee-Inventors, Preinvention Assignment Agreements, Property, and Personhood*, 81 CAL. L. REV. 595, 641 (1993). Cherensky argues, using personhood theory and the related idea of market-inalienability, that employee-inventors should retain greater property interests in their inventions than they typically do under conventional employee assignment contracts. On market-inalienability, i.e., things which should not be subject to market exchange at all, *see* Margaret Jane Radin, *Market-Inalienability*, 100 HARV. L. REV. 1849 (1987). *Cf.* Justin Hughes, *The Philosophy of Intellectual Property*, 77 GEO. L.J. 287, 350–53 (1988) (suggesting various strains of the personhood justification in American copyright law). Professor Roberta Kwall offers a related "moral" basis for legal protection emphasizing the dignity, honor, self-worth, and autonomy of the author. *See* ROBERTA KWALL, THE SOUL OF CREATIVITY: FORGING A MORAL RIGHTS LAW FOR THE UNITED STATES 37 (2009). For more on control over one's economic situation—i.e., economic autonomy—and its role in contemporary intellectual property debates, *see* Robert P. Merges, *The Concept of Property in the Digital Era*, 45 HOUS. L. REV. 1239 (2008). For a detailed explication of Hegel's approach to property, *see* JEREMY WALDRON, THE RIGHT TO PRIVATE PROPERTY (1988).

2. For a critique of Radin's broader personhood perspective, *see* Stephen J. Schnably, *Property and Pragmatism: A Critique of Radin's Theory of Property and Personhood*, 45 STAN. L. REV. 347 (1993) (challenging Radin's appeal to consensus and arguing that this focus obscures issues of power and the like). For further elaboration and defense of the personhood perspective, *see* MARGARET JANE RADIN, REINTERPRETING PROPERTY (1993) (a collection of related essays); A. JOHN SIMMONS, THE LOCKEAN THEORY OF RIGHTS (1992); JEREMY WALDRON, THE RIGHT TO PRIVATE PROPERTY (1991) (comparing Lockean and Hegelian property rights theories); Symposium, *Property Rights*, 11 SOC. PHIL. & POL'Y 1–286 (1994).

3. Personhood theories of IP rights focus on the connection between the creator's identity and the thing created. But consumers too may identify with creative works; indeed, Radin's example of the couch suggests that buyers too have an identity interest bound up with the things they own (or, perhaps, read). How should the law take that interest into account? Does it suggest that we need to give broader scope for user-generated content like fan fiction and videos that incorporate literary characters or songs? Or might it suggest the opposite—that consumers have an interest in the purity of their iconic works, free from the unauthorized modification of those works by others? *See* Justin Hughes, *"Recoding" Intellectual Property and Overlooked Audience Interests*, 77 TEX. L. REV. 923 (1999).

Creators are often motivated as much if not more by attribution and fairness than by the prospect of money. *See* JESSICA SILBEY, THE EUREKA MYTH: CREATORS,

INVENTORS, AND EVERYDAY INTELLECTUAL PROPERTY (2014); Jeanne Fromer, *Expressive Incentives in Intellectual Property*, 98 VA. L. REV. 1745 (2012).

4. Drawing on deconstructive literary criticism, several scholars have questioned a core intellectual property premise: the concept of *"the* author" herself. *See* MARTHA WOODMANSEE & PETER JASZI EDS., THE CONSTRUCTION OF AUTHORSHIP: TEXTUAL APPROPRIATION IN LAW AND LITERATURE (1994); Peter Jaszi, *Toward a Theory of Copyright: The Metamorphoses of "Authorship,"* 1991 DUKE L.J. 455; James Boyle, *A Theory of Law and Information: Copyright, Spleens, Blackmail and Insider Trading*, 80 CAL. L. REV. 1413 (1992). This critique challenges the application of personhood theory to intellectual property protection. These scholars suggest that the concept of authorship is so malleable, contingent, and "socially constructed" that we should be wary about identifying a creative work too closely with a particular author, let alone her personality. According to this view, all creations derive from communal forces. Dividing the stream of intellectual discourse into discrete units—each owned by and closely associated with a particular author—is therefore a logically incoherent exercise subject more to the political force of asserted authors' groups than to recognition of inherent claims of "personhood."

If authorship is an incoherent concept, is there any role at all for copyright law? How can one protect the rights (natural, moral, or economic) of the author if there is, in fact, no author? Does the literary critique answer the charge that authors will not create in the absence of economic reward? Or is it directed only at personality-based theories of intellectual property?

5. Consider the observations of philosopher Lawrence Becker:

So if property-as-personality [à la Hegel] again turns out to be a dead end, perhaps we should dispense with the search for a deep justification for property rights (from metaphysics, moral psychology, sociobiology, or whatever) and focus on the behavioral surface: the observed, persistent, robust behavioral connections between various property arrangements and human well-being, broadly conceived. This may provide a foundation for egalitarian arguments that is more secure than speculative metaphysics, and a foundation for private property that is more stable than a pluralistic account of the standard array of bedrock justifications for it.

Lawrence Becker, *Too Much Property*, 21 PHIL. & PUB. AFF. 196, 206 (1992).

3. Distributive and Social Justice

More recently, the idea of distributive justice has entered the fray in theoretical discussions of intellectual property. While it is rarely offered up as a standalone justification, it is usually discussed in the construction and application of different intellectual property regimes. Put simply, "[p]rinciples of distributive justice" are seen as:

[P]roviding moral guidance for the political processes and structures that affect the distribution of benefits and burdens in societies, and any principles which do offer this kind of moral guidance on distribution, regardless of the terminology they employ, should be considered principles of distributive justice.Julian Lamont & Christi Favor, *Distributive Justice, in* THE STANFORD ENCYCLOPEDIA OF PHILOSOPHY (Edward N. Zalta ed., Winter 2017), https://plato.stanford.edu/cgi-bin/encyclopedia/archinfo.cgi?entry=justice-distributive.

At its root, distributive justice derives from a strong commitment to equality. In A THEORY OF JUSTICE (1971)—probably the most influential work of political philosophy written in the past century—John Rawls offers an "ideal contractarian" theory of distributive shares. To determine the just allocation of the benefits and burdens of social life, he asks what distributive principles suitably disinterested persons would choose. To ask what selfish people would want, or what social contract would actually result from a convocation of all members of society, Rawls argues, would ensure that the naturally smart or strong, or people who shared a particular race, nationality, religion, or ideology, dominated the rest, if any agreement could be reached at all. Rawls rejects this construction of the "original position" for choosing social rules—which more libertarian philosophers, such as David Gauthier, come closer to favoring—because he finds this consequence intuitively unacceptable. He assumes instead that the resources and opportunities a person should have available should not depend primarily on how fortunate he or she was in the natural lottery of talents and parents, or in what group that person happens to be born.

Rawls, therefore, tries to determine principles that rational people behind a "veil of ignorance" would choose. Rawls contends that the veil must be quite opaque. It must, for example, exclude from the minds of those choosing principles of justice all knowledge of their own abilities, desires, parentage, and social stratum.

Rawls concludes that people behind the veil of ignorance would adopt what he calls the "difference principle." They would agree, he says, that the fundamental institutions of society should be arranged so that the distribution of "primary goods"—not only wealth, income, and opportunities for work or leisure, but also what Rawls terms the "bases of self-respect"—is to the maximal advantage of a representative member of the least advantaged social class. Defining the least advantaged class and the proper set of primary goods is difficult and contentious. In POLITICAL LIBERALISM (1993), Rawls refines his theory of distributive justice in the following passage:

> [M]easures are required to assure that the basic needs of all citizens can be met so that they can take part in political and social life.

> About this last point, the idea is not that of satisfying needs as opposed to mere desires and wants; nor is it that of redistribution in favor of greater equality. The constitutional essential here is rather that below a certain level of material and social well-being, and of training and education, people simply cannot take part in society as citizens, much less equal citizens.

Id. at 166.

Within intellectual property, distributive justice ideals are often used to determine the allocation of rights, liabilities and immunities among different actors. Distributive justice principles here ordinarily operate by identifying a particular class of actors who require a specific kind of rule, independent of the rules that affect society more generally. An example here is the additional protection that copyright law offers the authors and their heirs by way of its rules relating to termination of transfers. Here, the motivating idea is that authors and their heirs may require additional financial protection multiple decades (thirty-five years) after the initial transfer.

Closely related to—but somewhat distinct from—distributive justice is the idea of "social justice" that some scholars have used to describe the commitment to equality and fairness in the working of intellectual property regimes. While this idea is inchoate and less structured, it is more expansive and of wide application. Legal scholars Lateef Mtima and Steven Jamar describe the idea as follows:

> Social justice is a protean concept that varies with circumstances. It includes the aspirational ideal of substantive equality as well as the relatively easily addressable procedural equality. Social justice includes at least some aspects of individual liberty (e.g., autonomy) as well as incorporating some communitarian liberty values such as religious association, pursuit of legitimate group interests, and civic virtues such as voting. Social justice includes not only access to, but also inclusion in, the social, cultural, and economic life of the country. Indeed, it extends beyond inclusion in social, cultural, and economic life to full participation in and ability to affect the direction of civil society in all its manifestations. Social justice thus rests upon the core values of equality, liberty, and advancing the general welfare enshrined in the Declaration of Independence and Preamble to the U.S. Constitution.
>
> ...
>
> In the field of intellectual property, social justice includes the ability to enjoy the fruits of others at some base level of procedural equality (equal access to the works of others) and, to a lesser but important extent, the ability to have some base level of substantive equality in the beneficial impact of intellectual property created by others. Even more importantly, social justice in the area of intellectual property extends beyond mere access and beyond mere passive observation or enjoyment of others' works (e.g., listening to a recording or seeing a movie): it includes the ability to participate in the creation and exploitation of intellectual property both in a procedurally fair way and a substantively significant way.

Lateef Mtima & Steven D. Jamar, *Fulfilling the Copyright Social Justice Promise: Digitizing Textual Information*, 55 N.Y.L.S.L. REV. 77, 83–84 (2010).

COMMENTS AND QUESTIONS

1. Do you agree with Rawls that people behind the veil of ignorance would agree that the fundamental institutions of society should be arranged so that the distribution of "primary goods"—including property—is to the maximal advantage of a representative member of the least advantaged social class? Would you agree to this principle if you were behind a veil of ignorance?

Consider political scientist James Q. Wilson's critique:

[E]verybody in Rawls's universe is averse to risk; each wants to make certain that, if he winds up on the bottom of the heap, the bottom is as attractive as possible.

But many people are in fact not averse to risk, they are risk takers; to them, a just society would be one in which inequalities in wealth were acceptable provided that the people at the top of the heap got there as a result of effort and skill. And even people who are not risk takers may endorse this position because they think it fair that rewards should be proportional to effort, even if some people lose out entirely. (These same people might also expect their church or government to take care of those who lost out.) They have this view of fairness because they recognize that people differ in talent, energy, temperament, and interests; that conflicts among such people are inevitable; and that matching, as best one can, rewards to contributions is the best way of handling that conflict.

. . .

Equality is a special and, as it turns out, rare and precarious case of equity. Settled living, and in particular the accumulation of private property, makes equality of outcomes impossible because inequality of contributions become manifest. The task of settled societies is to devise ways of assuring that outcomes are proportional to worth, reasonably defined.

JAMES Q. WILSON, THE MORAL SENSE 73–76 (1993); *see also* ERIC RAKOWKSI, EQUAL JUSTICE (1991) (advocating a more meritocratic "equality of fortune" that affords all members of society a just initial distribution of resources but tolerates inequalities resulting from exercise of free will—notably, occupational preferences, wise business decisions, and diligence in school, training, and work).

2. What do Rawls' principles of distributive justice imply for the rights in intellectual property? Doesn't the essential mechanism of intellectual property protection—rewarding time-limited monopoly power in exchange for advancing society's knowledge base—inexorably produce inequality?

3. *Justifying Intellectual Property?* At a basic level, technological advance produces higher standards of living. It enables society to accomplish more with fewer resources and therefore increases productivity. Furthermore, no one is required to purchase IP-protected goods. Therefore, in an exchange economy, only those who value such goods more than their cost will purchase the goods. Moreover, patent and copyright protection eventually expire. At a coarse level of granularity, modern societies have the benefit of all manner of innovation and creativity—from sanitation technologies that support safe drinking water to telecommunications and modern medicines. As such, innovation tends to reduce poverty and raise standards of living in an absolute sense over the long run (but as John Maynard Keynes famously observed, "In the long run we are all dead"). Professor Merges argues that a Rawlsian perspective can therefore justify IP rights in broad brush. *See* ROBERT P. MERGES, JUSTIFYING INTELLECTUAL PROPERTY (2011). He also identifies a series of "mid-level principles"—nonremoval from the public domain, proportionality of IP rights to value or significance of the work covered by the right, economic efficiency, and respect for the dignity of the author—that seek to

balance the interests of creators and users of IP. *See also* Peter S. Menell, *Intellectual Property and Social Justice: Mapping the Next Frontier,* in STEVEN D. JAMAR AND LATEEF MTIMA (EDS), HANDBOOK OF INTELLECTUAL PROPERTY AND SOCIAL JUSTICE: ACCESS, INCLUSION, EMPOWERMENT (Cambridge University Press) (2023).

4. *Access to Medicine.* The argument that intellectual property protection increases productivity and eventually becomes available to all affords little solace to those who cannot afford to purchase patented, life-saving medicines. Should the patent rights give way for life-saving medicines and treatments? To what extent would such a rule undermine the race to discover cures for disease? Is unequal access to medicine best addressed through social insurance institutions? *Cf.* Amy Kapczynski, *Access to Knowledge Mobilization and the New Politics of Intellectual Property*, 117 YALE L.J. 804 (2008); William W. Fisher & Talha Syed, *Global Justice in Healthcare: Developing Drugs for the Developing World*, 40 U.C. DAVIS L. REV. 581 (2007).

5. *Access to Culture and Cumulative Creativity.* We can also see distributive values in the broadening of expressive opportunities for authors and artists. Since expression often builds on and reacts to prior expressive works, such distributive values can run counter to the provision of exclusive rights. Limiting doctrines and the fair use privilege implicitly cross-subsidizes cumulative creators. Such freedom to build on the work of others can, however, adversely affect authors' moral and dignitary interests. *See* Molly Shaffer Van Houweling, *Distributive Values in Copyright*, 83 TEX. L. REV. 1535 (2005); *see also* Peter S. Menell, *Adapting Copyright for the Mashup Generation*, 164 U. PA. L. REV. 441 (2016).

6. *IP and Inequality.* While the digital revolution has provided especially rapid technological advance, it has also contributed to skewing of wealth distribution. Like the technological advances of the Industrial Revolution, the Digital Revolution of the past several decades—characterized by scalability of information technologies, network effects, and displacement of labor by smart machines—has produced a new Gilded Age. *See* Menell, *Property, Intellectual Property, and Social Justice*, 5 BRIGHAM-KANNER PROPERTY CONFERENCE JOURNAL at 190–93; ERIK BRYNJOLFSSON & ANDREW MCAFEE, RACE AGAINST THE MACHINE: HOW THE DIGITAL REVOLUTION IS ACCELERATING INNOVATION, DRIVING PRODUCTIVITY, AND IRREVERSIBLY TRANSFORMING EMPLOYMENT AND THE ECONOMY (2011). Many of the wealthiest people in the world are technology entrepreneurs. The sports and entertainment professions, which depend critically upon copyright, trademark, and publicity right protections, also contribute to high wealth for a relatively small "superstar" class.

7. *Gender and Racial Equality.* The concentration of wealth and economic leverage that intellectual property produces places vast power in the hands of a relatively small group of entrepreneurs and their representatives. The class of venture capitalists, corporate titans, and Hollywood moguls reflect historical gender and race biases. *See* Menell, *Property, Intellectual Property, and Social Justice,* 5 BRIGHAM-KANNER PROPERTY CONFERENCE JOURNAL at 190–93; K.J. Greene, *Intellectual Property at the Intersection of Race and Gender: Lady Sings the Blues*, 16 AM. U. J. GENDER, SOC. POL'Y & L. 365 (2008). Yet copyright protection has been especially effective in

providing whatever limited "equality of opportunity" Black people in America have enjoyed in the United States. Indeed, copyright has been the most important form of property for many of the wealthiest black families, *see* Justin Hughes & Robert P. Merges, *Copyright and Distributive Justice*, 92 NOTRE DAME L. REV. 513 (2016). At the same time, IP raises the cost of music and other content, and that disadvantages the poor, who are disproportionately non-white.

Moreover, adequately funded and well-produced film, art, music, and literature play an inestimable role in promoting social and cultural understanding and tolerance. As much as lawyers emphasize the role of legal advocacy in shifting the law, the television series *Will and Grace* likely had more influence in shifting the nation's and Supreme Court's views on gay marriage than anything that lawyers argued. Similarly, works such as TO KILL A MOCKINGBIRD and THE HELP powerfully communicated the indignity of the Jim Crow South. The public's gradual embrace of R&B, jazz, and gospel—what was once referred to as "race music"—played a critical role in building a more cohesive and inclusive nation. *See* K.J. Greene, "Copynorms," *Black Cultural Protection, and the Debate over African-American Reparations*, 25 CARDOZO ARTS & ENT. L.J. 1179 (2008). At the same time, art and literature can also reinforce stereotypes. The ability to challenge, rework, and criticize canons of literature may be critical to interrogating and undermining those stereotypes.

8. *IP and the Environment*. While motivating the development of better environmental technologies, the patent system potentially constrains the diffusion of technological advances that seek to ameliorate environmental harms. Even if advances in wind turbine and solar technologies dramatically lowered the cost of producing electricity, distributing that energy to consumers depends critically upon a grid infrastructure that can move decentralized sources of electricity to market. Moreover, such energy must compete with harmful alternatives. Without fees to internalize those harmful effects, renewable sources of energy face a competitive disadvantage. Thus, intellectual property cannot be the sole policy to address problems like pollution and climate change. Prizes, subsidies, and externality-internalizing fees on fossil fuels offer complementary tools for balancing the R&D appropriability problem, the environmental externalities of fossil fuel consumption, and the geopolitical distortions of reliance on oil. *See generally* PETER S. MENELL & SARAH M. TRAN, INTELLECTUAL PROPERTY, INNOVATION AND THE ENVIRONMENT (2014).

9. *IP and Colonialism*. Locke and Hegel reflect a classical European view of the world as a set of raw materials ready to be harvested, worked, and owned by the enlightened colonists. In real property, that view produced an era of colonial empires that few would want to replicate today. Is there an analogous problem with asserting dominion over the intangible resources of the commons? Several scholars have argued that there is something wrong with taking traditional knowledge from the developing world and turning it into an IP right owned by those in the developed world who "discovered" it. *See* EVANA WRIGHT, PROTECTING TRADITIONAL KNOWLEDGE: LESSON FROM GLOBAL CASE STUDIES (2020); Srividhya Ragavan, *Protection of Traditional Knowledge*, 2 MINN. INTELL. PROP. REV. 1 (2001); VANDANA SHIVA,

BIOPIRACY: THE PLUNDER OF NATURE AND KNOWLEDGE (1997). Perhaps ironically, many of those scholars argue for IP rights in traditional knowledge to permit local peoples to engage in appropriation of their own. *See* Stephen R. Munzer & Kal Raustiala, *The Uneasy Case for Intellectual Property Rights in Traditional Knowledge*, 27 CARDOZO ARTS & ENT. L.J. 37 (2009).

4. Autonomy

The eighteenth-century German philosopher Immanuel Kant developed the most nuanced and influential account of human autonomy, from which he explained the working of various private legal rights. *See* ARTHUR R. RIPSTEIN, FORCE AND FREEDOM: KANT'S LEGAL AND POLITICAL PHILOSOPHY (2009). In a 1785 essay, Kant deployed some of these insights to copyright protection. Immanuel Kant, *On the Wrongfulness of Unauthorized Publication of Books, in* PRACTICAL PHILOSOPHY 27, 29–35 (Mary J. Gregor ed. & trans., Cambridge 1996) (1785). Drawing on an autonomy-driven theory that is independent of property, Kant contends that unauthorized publication of another's work is morally problematic and therefore legitimately the basis of a private action (i.e., for copyright infringement). *See* ROBERT P. MERGES, JUSTIFYING INTELLECTUAL PROPERTY 78 (2011).

According to Kant, when an author expresses herself in a book, that expression is more than just a commodity. It is instead a form of communication, something he terms a "speech act." Control over the speech act is distinct from the ownership of the book. When a publisher prints a book, that publisher is purporting to act on behalf of the author by speaking in her name publicly. Such behavior is unproblematic when authorized by the author, since the publisher is then the legitimate voice of the author. When the publication is altogether unauthorized, however, the publisher is now speaking as the author without her consent. This in turn forces the author to commit a speech act against her own will by either acknowledging the existence of such speech or taking responsibility for it. Such unauthorized publication therefore interferes with the individual autonomy of the author as a moral agent to speak on her own terms, rendering it wrongful and thus potentially actionable. Copyright law, in this understanding, exists to safeguard an author's autonomy as speaker interacting with the public.

Kant's emphasis on autonomy arguably extends far beyond the right to prevent counterfeiting. *See* MERGES, JUSTIFYING INTELLECTUAL PROPERTY, at 81 (explaining that "full realization of [Michelangelo's] autonomy interest in [a] statue includes the right to make a living from carving and selling it. His plan or purpose extends not just to possessing and carving a piece of marble, but well beyond. It includes a desire to develop his talent, to earn a reputation as an artist, and ultimately to make a living as an artist."). There are, naturally, limits to these broader aspects of autonomy. *See id.*, at 87 ("Kant is no absolutist when it comes to property. As with Locke, significant limits on property are not just sprinkled on top of a theory of initial appropriation; instead, they are baked in, as a basic ingredient. Kant locates the legal rights of ownership in a broad web of duties that apply to all citizens.").

COMMENTS AND QUESTIONS

1. Does Kant's autonomy-based theory have any applicability beyond the domain of copyright law? While Kant focused most immediately on copyright law, could his idea be extended to other forms of intellectual property rights that implicate the individual self, such as rights of publicity? For an account along these lines, see Alice Haemmerli, *Whose Who? The Case for a Kantian Right of Publicity*, 49 DUKE L.J. 383 (1999).

Even within the domain of copyright law, does Kant's theory sufficiently explain the full extent of modern copyright doctrine? Are performances, displays, and distributions—forms of infringement today—equally forms of speech under Kant's account? *See* ABRAHAM DRASSINOWER, WHAT'S WRONG WITH COPYING? (2015).

2. One of the most notable features of Kant's theory is that it purports to justify copyright without reference to the consequences of the regime and its effects, i.e., consequentialism. In other words, it develops a defense for the regime from within by focusing on the irreducibility of human autonomy as a value. This form of justification is often referred to as an "immanent" defense of the system. *See* Shyamkrishna Balganesh, *The Immanent Rationality of Copyright Law*, 115 MICH. L. REV. 1047 (2017) (reviewing Drassinower's account). Are other intellectual property regimes besides copyright capable a similar immanent defense? Is there an autonomy right to one's own name and likeness, for instance? *See* Chapter VI(D).

3. Does the notion of author autonomy suggest that intellectual property and privacy concerns are related? Should intellectual property regimes such as copyright give greater weight to an individual's desire to have their expression stay out of public scrutiny? *Compare* Shyamkrishna Balganesh, *Privative Copyright*, 73 VAND. L. REV. 1 (2020) (arguing that copyright law does and should continue to recognize the role of privacy concerns) *with* Eric Goldman & Jessica Silbey, *Copyright's Memory Hole*, 2019 BYU L. REV. 929 (2020) (arguing for a more limited recognition of privacy concerns within copyright).

4. Copyright cases often feature not just rote copying, but defendants who engage in their own speech modifying or commenting on the copyright owner's expression. Do those defendants have autonomy rights in their speech too? If the autonomy right is morally defensible regardless of consequence, how are we to balance those interests?

5.   The Utilitarian/Economic Incentive Perspective

Utilitarian theory and the economic framework built upon it have long provided the dominant paradigm for analyzing and justifying the various forms of intellectual property protection. *See generally* Peter S. Menell & Suzanne Scotchmer, *Intellectual Property Law*, in 2 HANDBOOK OF LAW AND ECONOMICS 1474, 1525 (A. Mitchell Polinsky & Steven Shavell eds., 2007); WILLIAM M. LANDES & RICHARD A. POSNER, THE ECONOMIC STRUCTURE OF INTELLECTUAL PROPERTY LAW (2003). For purposes of exploring the economic dimensions of the intellectual property field, it is important to distinguish between two quite distinct functions. The principal objective of much of intellectual property law is the promotion of new and improved works—whether technological or expressive. This purpose encompasses patent, copyright, and trade secret law, as well as several more specialized protection systems (for mask works (semiconductor chip layouts), databases, and designs). Trademark and related bodies of unfair competition law focus primarily on a very different economic problem—ensuring the integrity of the marketplace.

i.   *Promoting Innovation and Creativity*

Both the United States Constitution and judicial decisions emphasize incentive theory in justifying intellectual property. The Constitution expressly conditions the grant of power in the patent and copyright clause on a particular end, namely "to Promote the Progress of Science and useful Arts." U.S. CONST., ART. I, §8, CL. 8. As the Supreme Court explained in *Mazer v. Stein*, 347 U.S. 201 (1954):

> The copyright law, like the patent statutes, makes reward to the owner a "secondary consideration." *United States v. Paramount Pictures*, 334 U.S. 131, 158. However, it is "intended definitely to grant valuable, enforceable rights to authors, publishers, etc., without burdensome requirements: 'to afford greater encouragement to the production of literary [or artistic] works of lasting benefit to the world.'" *Washington Pub. Co. v. Pearson*, 306 U.S. 30. The economic philosophy behind the clause empowering Congress to grant patents and copyrights is the conviction that it is the best way to advance public welfare through the talents of authors and inventors in "Science and useful Arts." Sacrificial days devoted to such creative activities deserve rewards commensurate with the services rendered.

To understand why the Framers thought exclusive rights in inventions and creations would promote the public welfare, consider what might happen absent any intellectual property protection. Invention and creation require the investment of resources—the time of an author or inventor, and often expenditures on facilities, prototypes, supplies, etc. In a private market economy, individuals will not invest in invention or creation unless the expected return from doing so exceeds the cost of doing so—that is, unless they can reasonably expect to make a profit from the endeavor. To profit from a new idea or work of authorship, the creator must be able either to sell it to others or to put it to some use that provides her with a comparative advantage in a market, such as by reducing the cost of producing goods.

But ideas (and writings, for that matter) are notoriously hard to control. Even if the idea is one that the creator can use herself, for example, to boost productivity in her business, she will sometimes reap a reward from that idea only to the extent that her competitors don't find out about it. A creator who depends on secrecy for value, therefore, lives in constant peril of discovery and disclosure. Competitors may steal the idea or learn of it from an ex-employee. They may be able to figure it out by watching the creator's production process or by examining the products she sells. Finally, they may come upon the idea on their own or discover it in the published literature. In all of these cases, the secrecy value of the idea will be irretrievably lost.

The creator who wants to sell her idea is in an even more difficult position. Selling information requires disclosing it to others. Once the information has been disclosed outside a small group, however, it is extremely difficult to control. Information has the characteristics of what economists call a "public good"—it may be "consumed" by many people without depletion, and it is difficult to identify those who will not pay and prevent them from using the information. *See* Kenneth J. Arrow, *Economic Welfare and the Allocation of Resources for Invention*, in THE RATE AND DIRECTION OF INVENTIVE ACTIVITY: ECONOMIC AND SOCIAL FACTORS 609, 614–16 (Nat'l Bureau of Economic Research ed., 1962). Once the idea of the intermittent windshield wiper is disclosed, others can imitate its design relatively easily. Once a book is published, others can copy it at low cost. It is difficult to exclude nonpurchasers from sharing in the benefits of the idea. Ideas and information can also be used by many without depleting the enjoyment of others. Unlike an ice cream cone, a good story or the concept of intermittent windshield wipers can be enjoyed by many without diminishing enjoyment of these creations by others.[1] If we assume that it is nearly costless to distribute information to others—an assumption that was once unrealistic, but now has become much more reasonable with advances in digital technology (including the Internet)—it will prove virtually impossible to charge for information over the medium run in the absence of effective intellectual property or some other means of protection (such as technological protection measures). If the author of a book charges more than the cost of distribution, hoping to recover some of her expenditures in writing the work, competitors will quickly jump in to offer the book at a lower price. Competition will drive the price of the book toward its marginal cost—in this case, the cost of producing and distributing one additional copy. In such a competitive market, the author will be unable to recoup the fixed cost of writing the book. More to the point, if this holds true generally, authors may be expected to leave the profession in droves, since they cannot make any money at it. The result, according to economic theory, would be an underproduction of books and other works of invention and creation with similar public goods characteristics.

Information is not the only example of a public good. Economists generally offer lighthouses and national defense as examples of public goods, since it is virtually impossible to provide the benefits of either one only to paying clients. It is impossible to exclude some ships and not others from the benefits of a lighthouse. Furthermore, the use of the lighthouse by one ship does not deplete the value of its hazard warning to others. As a result, it would be inefficient to exclude nonpayers from using the lighthouse's warning system even if we could, since consumption of this good is "nonrivalrous" (meaning that everyone can benefit from it once it is produced). For

---

[1] To some extent this statement oversimplifies the problem by ignoring possible second-order distorting effects. In practice, if you taught several hundred million people to fish, the result might be depletion of a physical resource (fish) that would otherwise not have occurred. Similarly, wide dissemination of some information may have particular effects on secondary markets.

these reasons, the market will in theory undersupply such goods because producers cannot reap the marginal (incremental) value of their investment in providing them.[2]

Can you see why broadcast television signals, beautiful gardens on a public street, and national defense are also public goods?

By contrast, markets for pure private goods, such as ice cream cones, feature exclusivity and rivalrous competition—the ice cream vendor provides the good only to those who pay the price, and the consumer certainly depletes the amount of the good available to others. Thus, the market system provides adequate incentives for the creation of ice cream cones: sellers can exact their cost of production, and the value of the product is fully enjoyed by the purchaser.

In the case of national defense (and most lighthouses), we avoid the underproduction that would result from leaving provision of the good to the market by having the government step in and pay for the public good. For a variety of reasons, we have not gone that route with many forms of information. Instead, the government has created time-limited intellectual property rights over technological inventions and expressive creativity to encourage inventors and authors to invest in the development of new ideas and works of authorship. Thus, the economic justification for intellectual property lies not in rewarding creators for their labor but in ensuring that they (and other creators) have appropriate incentives to engage in innovative and creative activities.

Unfortunately, this approach comes at a cost. Granting inventors and authors rights to exclude others from using their inventions, discoveries, and expression limits the diffusion of those ideas and so prevents some others from benefiting from and building upon these advances, at least for the duration of intellectual property protection. In economic terms, intellectual property rights prevent competition in the sale of the particular invention or expressive work covered by those rights, and therefore allows the intellectual property owner to raise the price of that work above the marginal cost of reproducing it. This means that fewer people will acquire the work than if it were distributed on a competitive basis, and they will pay more for access. A fundamental principle of our economic system is the proposition that free market competition will ensure an efficient allocation of resources, absent market failures. In fact, the principal thrust of the antitrust laws serves precisely this goal. In this limited sense, then, intellectual property rights appear to run counter to free market competition: they limit the ability of competitors to copy or closely imitate the intellectual efforts of the first person to develop an idea. These rights enable those possessing intellectual property rights to charge monopoly prices or to otherwise limit competition, such as by controlling the use of the intellectual work in subsequent products.

---

[2] Ronald Coase questioned the contention that lighthouses must be publicly provided. *See* Ronald H. Coase, *The Lighthouse in Economics*, in THE FIRM, THE MARKET, AND THE LAW (1988); *but see* David E. Van Zandt, *The Lessons of the Lighthouse: "Government" or "Private" Provision of Goods*, 22 J. LEGAL STUDIES 47 (1993) (reporting that lighthouses relying on voluntary payments failed and that government support played a critical role in their provision); Elodie Bertrand, *The Coasean Analysis of Lighthouse Financing: Myths and Realities*, 30 CAMBRIDGE J. ECON. 389 (2006).

Because intellectual property rights impose social costs on the public, the intellectual property laws can be justified by the public goods argument only to the extent that they do on balance encourage enough creation and dissemination of new works to offset those costs. One of the reasons that intellectual property rights are limited in scope, duration, and effect is to balance these costs and benefits. For example, the limited term of intellectual property rights ensures that inventions will be freely available after that fixed term. The key to economic efficiency lies in balancing the social benefit of providing economic incentives for creation and the social costs of limiting the diffusion of knowledge. We will encounter this critical trade-off throughout our study of intellectual property. The two examples below highlight some of the major issues.

a.   *Economic Incentive Benefit*

Intellectual property protection is necessary to encourage inventors, authors, and artists to invest in the process of creation. Without such protection, others could copy or otherwise imitate the intellectual work without incurring the costs and effort of creation, thereby inhibiting the original creators from reaping a reasonable return on their investment. Consider the following example:

> After years of effort and substantial expense, Earnest Inventor develops the Mousomatic, a significantly better mousetrap. Not only does it catch mice better than the competition's trap, but it also neatly packages the dead mice in disposable sanitary bags. Consumers are willing to pay substantially more for this product than for its competitors. The Mousomatic catches the attention of Gizmo Gadget Incorporated. Gizmo copies the basic design of the Mousomatic and offers its version of the Mousomatic at a substantial discount. (Gizmo can still earn a profit at this lower price because it had minimal research and development expense.) To stay in business, Earnest is forced to lower his price. Market competition pushes the price down to the cost of production and distribution. In the end, Earnest is unable to recover his cost of research and development and suffers a loss. Although he has numerous other interesting ideas, he decides that they are not worth pursuing because Gizmo, or some other company, will simply copy them if they turn out well.

The existence of intellectual property rights encourages Earnest and other inventors to pursue their creative efforts. If Earnest can obtain the right to prevent others from copying his inventions, then he stands a much better chance to reap a profit. Hence, he will be much more inclined to make the initial investment in research and development. In the end, not only will Earnest be wealthier, but the public will be enriched by the new and better products brought forth by intellectual property protection.

b.   *Costs of Limiting Diffusion*

Legal protection for ideas and their expression prevents others from using those works to develop similar works that build upon them. Knowledge in society is cumulative. In the words of Sir Isaac Newton, "If I have seen further [than others], it is by standing on the shoulders of giants." Hence, society at large can be harmed by intellectual property protection to the extent that it unnecessarily raises the cost of acquiring a product (through monopoly pricing by the right holder) and limits others from making further advances. Consider the following scenario:

> Professor Lee conducts research on drug treatments at University College. Grants from the federal government fund her laboratory. For the past decade, Professor Lee has competed with colleagues at other laboratories to discover the cure for a prevalent form of cancer. It is likely that the first person to discover the cure will win a Nobel Prize, as well as numerous other financial and professional rewards. In early 1995, Professor Lee hits upon the Alpha drug, which cures the disease. She files for and receives a patent. Professor Hu, a researcher at another research institution, independently discovers the identical cure a few months later. With patent in hand, Professor Lee starts selling Alpha for a price 100 times the cost of production. Because Alpha is a life-saving cure, those stricken with the disease who can afford the treatment are more than willing to pay the price. Then, to relieve the suffering of millions, Professor Hu begins selling Alpha at the cost of production. Moreover, she has developed an improvement on the Alpha drug, Alpha+, that reduces the side effects of the treatment. Professor Lee quickly obtains an injunction preventing Hu from selling either version of Alpha for the life of the patent.

This example raises serious questions about whether intellectual property protection is desirable, at least for this class of invention. Professor Lee does not bear significant risk in pursuing the invention because the government and university generously fund her research. Furthermore, the potential for a Nobel Prize, expanded research funding, and professional recognition provide substantial encouragement for Professor Lee to pursue a cure whether or not she gains financially from sales of Alpha. Moreover, other researchers were poised to make the same discovery at about the time that Professor Lee made her discovery. Yet she has the right not only to block sales of Alpha by competitors, but also to block sales of improvements such as Alpha+. Does such a system benefit society? One must also consider that without the financial incentive of a patent, there would perhaps have been less competition to discover and market any cure for cancer. Problems such as this one have led some scholars to question the economic efficiency of the patent system in particular circumstances. *See* F. M. SCHERER, INDUSTRIAL MARKET STRUCTURE AND ECONOMIC PERFORMANCE 445–55 (2d ed. 1980).

Similar problems can arise in the copyright domain. In 1936, Margaret Mitchell published her epic novel GONE WITH THE WIND. The plot revolves around Scarlett O'Hara, a hard-working and ambitious Southern woman who lives through the American Civil War and Reconstruction. GONE WITH THE WIND quickly became one of the most popular books ever written, eventually selling more than 30 million copies throughout the world. Ms. Mitchell would receive a Pulitzer Prize, and the novel would become the basis for one of the most successful movies ever.

Sixty-five years later, Alice Randall, an African-American historian, set out to tell the history of the Civil War-era South from another viewpoint. She invented the character of Cynara, a slave on Scarlett's plantation who also happened to be Scarlett's half-sister. Although Mitchell's novel did not depict a character named Cynara, many other characters in Randall's novel mimic characters in the original. Randall's THE WIND DONE GONE depicts the mistreatment and suffering of slaves in their vernacular dialect. Randall believed that GONE WITH THE WIND, as the lens through which millions viewed the deep South during the Civil War era, provided a unique vehicle for communicating the racial injustice of American history. Margaret Mitchell's estate sued Randall for copying GONE WITH THE WIND without authorization, obtaining a preliminary injunction. Although Randall eventually prevailed on appeal under the fair use doctrine, *Suntrust Bank v. Houghton Mifflin Co.*, 268 F.3d 1257 (11th Cir. 2001), this controversy illustrates how strong copyright protection can potentially inhibit cumulative creativity.

In applying a utilitarian framework, we must balance the economic incentive benefits of intellectual property rights against the costs of limiting diffusion of knowledge. A critical issue in assessing the need for intellectual property protection is whether innovators have sufficient means to appropriate an adequate return on investment in research and development. In this regard, the market itself often provides means by which inventors can realize sufficient rewards to pursue innovation without formal intellectual property rights beyond contract law. The first to introduce a product can in many contexts earn substantial and long-lived advantages in the market. In many markets, the costs or time required to imitate a product (for example, to reverse engineer a complex machine) are so great that the first to market a product has substantial opportunity for profit. Moreover, as we will see in Chapter II, inventors can often prevent imitation through contractual means, such as trade secrecy and licensing agreements with customers. Where the invention relates to a manufacturing process, the innovator may be able to maintain protection through secrecy even after the product is on the market. Alternatively, a producer may be able to bundle products with essential services and contracts for updates of the product. In addition, the producer may be able to spread the costs of research and development among a group of firms through research joint ventures.

In those areas in which economic incentives for innovation are inadequate, and the creation of intellectual property rights is the most efficacious way of encouraging progress, society must determine the appropriate requirements for, duration and scope of, and set of rights afforded intellectual property. Over the past several decades, economists have developed and refined models to assess the appropriate trade-off between the social benefits of providing economic incentives for innovation through intellectual property rights and the social costs of limiting diffusion of knowledge. Professor William Nordhaus developed the first formal model analyzing the optimal duration of intellectual property. His model of the innovative process assumed that investments in research produced a single independent innovation. WILLIAM NORDHAUS, INVENTION, GROWTH, AND WELFARE: A THEORETICAL TREATMENT OF TECHNOLOGICAL CHANGE 3–7 (1969). The principal policy implication of this model is that the term of intellectual property protection should be calibrated to balance the incentive benefits of protection against the deadweight loss of monopoly pricing and the resulting limitations on dissemination.

Since Nordhaus's important early work, economic historians and economic theorists have greatly enriched our understanding of the innovative process and the implications for public policy. Historical and industry studies of the innovation process find that inventions are highly interdependent: "Technologies . . . undergo a gradual, evolutionary development which is intimately bound up with the course of their diffusion." Paul David, *New Technology, Diffusion, Public Policy, and Industrial Competitiveness* 20 (Center for Economic Policy Research, Pub. No. 46, Apr. 1985). In fact, "secondary inventions"—including essential design improvements, refinements, and adaptations to a variety of uses—are often as crucial to the generation of social benefits as the initial discovery. *See, e.g.,* J.L. Enos, *A Measure of the Rate of Technological Progress in the Petroleum Refining Industry,* 6 J. INDUS. ECON. 180, 189 (1958); James Mak & Gary Walton, *Steamboats and the Great Productivity Surge in River Transportation,* 32 J. ECON. HIST. 619, 625 (1972). Economic theorists have developed models of the innovative process incorporating concepts of rivalrous and cumulative innovation, *see* Suzanne Scotchmer, *Standing on the Shoulders of Giants: Cumulative Research and the Patent Law,* 5 J. ECON. PERSPECTIVES 29 (1991); Robert P. Merges & Richard Nelson, *On the Complex Economics of Patent Scope,* 90 COLUM. L. REV. 839 (1990); Peter S. Menell, *Tailoring Legal Protection for Computer Software,* 39 STAN. L. REV. 1329 (1987), uncovering a range of important effects. Most notably, excessive protection for first-generation innovation can impede later innovations if licensing is costly. More generally, these models cast doubt on the notion that society can perfectly calibrate intellectual property rewards for each innovation.

As is increasingly evident, the range of innovative activity and creative expression in our society is vast and ever changing. As the materials in this book highlights, the intellectual property institutions and rules that have evolved to promote technology and the arts are intricate. It will be the challenge of future generations of policymakers, judges, and lawyers to refine the ability of the intellectual property system to enhance the public welfare.

COMMENTS AND QUESTIONS

1. One significant difference between the natural rights perspective and the utilitarian perspective relates to who is entitled to the fruits of productive labor. In the natural rights framework, the inventor or author is entitled to the social benefits produced by his or her efforts. In the utilitarian framework, reward to the inventor or author is a secondary consideration; the principal objective is to enrich the public at large. Which view is more compelling? Consider in this regard the optimal division of

benefits from the invention of Alpha among Professor Lee, Professor Hu, and the public at large. Is Professor Lee entitled to all or even a lion's share of the benefits?

2. In 1966, the REPORT OF THE PRESIDENT'S COMMISSION ON THE PATENT SYSTEM identified four major economic justifications for the patent laws. First, a patent system provides an incentive to invent by offering the possibility of reward to the inventor and to those who support him. This prospect encourages the expenditure of time and private risk capital in research and development efforts. Second, and complementary to the first, a patent system stimulates the investment of additional capital needed for the further development and marketing of the invention. In return, the patent owner is given the right, for a limited period, to exclude others from making, using, or selling the invented product or process. Third, by affording protection, a patent system encourages early public disclosure of technological information, some of which might otherwise be kept secret. Early disclosure reduces the likelihood of duplication of effort by others and provides a basis for further advances in the technology involved. Fourth, a patent system promotes the beneficial exchange of products, services, and technological information across national boundaries by providing protection for industrial property of foreign nationals.

While directed specifically at the patent system, many of these arguments have application to all forms of intellectual property.

Are these incentives necessary to invention and creation? Using cost and other data from publishing companies, Professor (later Justice) Stephen Breyer contended that lead time advantages and the threat of retaliation reduce the cost advantages of copiers, thus obviating if not eliminating the need for copyright protection for books. *See* Stephen Breyer, *The Uneasy Case for Copyright: A Study in Copyright of Books, Photocopies and Computer Programs*, 84 HARV. L. REV. 281 (1970). *Cf.* Barry W. Tyerman, *The Economic Rationale for Copyright Protection for Published Books: A Reply to Professor Breyer*, 18 UCLA L. REV. 1100 (1971); Stephen Breyer, *Copyright: A Rejoinder*, 20 UCLA L. REV. 75 (1972). This debate took place decades ago. Have advances in technology strengthened or weakened Breyer's argument?

3. *Intellectual Property as Property*. It is tempting to view intellectual property through a tangible property lens. *See* Richard Epstein, *The Disintegration of Intellectual Property? A Classical Liberal Response to a Premature Obituary*, 62 STAN. L. REV. 455 (2010). After all, intellectual property draws on tangible property concepts of first-in-time, exclusivity, and transferability, and scholars have explored the philosophy of tangible property rules and institutions for centuries. However, simplistic Blackstonian conceptions of land and other tangible resources miss a lot of the most important economic and social concerns relating to protecting intangible resources. *See* Peter S. Menell, *Governance of Intellectual Resources and Disintegration of Intellectual Property in the Digital Age*, 26 BERKELEY TECH. L.J. 1523 (2011); Mark A. Lemley, *Property, Intellectual Property, and Free Riding*, 83 TEX. L. REV. 1031 (2005). Nonetheless, tangible property law and institutions dealing with more complex resources (such as water, wild animals, oil and natural gas) and circumstances (control of the dead hand, shared use of resources) offer valuable insights into the design of

intellectual property rules and institutions. *Cf.* Molly Shaffer Van Houweling, *Intellectual Property as Property*, in RESEARCH HANDBOOK ON THE ECONOMICS OF INTELLECTUAL PROPERTY LAW (Peter S. Menell & Ben Depoorter eds., forthcoming 2018).

4. *Comparative Institutional Analysis*. Numerous institutional mechanisms exist for addressing the public goods problem inherent in the production of ideas and information—direct government funding of research, government research subsidies, promotion of joint ventures, and prizes. The case for intellectual property rights ideally compares all of these options. *See* Daniel J. Hemel & Lisa Larrimore Ouellette, *Beyond the Patents-Prizes Debate*, 92 TEX. L. REV. 303 (2013). Intellectual property rights have the advantage of limiting the government's role in allocating resources to a finite set of decentralized decisions: whether particular inventions are worthy of a fixed period of protection. The market then serves as the principal engine of progress. Decentralized consumers generate demand for products and competing decentralized sellers produce them. By contrast, most other incentive systems, especially large-scale research funding, require central planning on a mass scale. Most economists place more confidence in the former means of allocating resources. The case for intellectual property rights, then, is based more on a generalized perception of institutional choice than on strong direct evidence of the superiority of intellectual property rights relative to the alternatives.

Is the market the best way of allocating resources to inventions in all cases? Claire Xue and Lisa Ouellette have argued that the patent system undersupplies vaccines because preventing a disease is frequently less profitable than treating it, even though society would be better off with prevention. *See* Claire Xue & Lisa Ouellette, *Innovation Policy and the Market for Vaccines*, 7 J. L. & BIOSCIENCES 1 (2020).

5. *The Open Source Movement*. The emergence of cooperative working environments for the development of software has raised questions about the core precept underlying the utilitarian/economic perspective: that exclusive property rights represent the most effective means for promoting creative enterprise. *See generally* STEVEN WEBER, THE SUCCESS OF OPEN SOURCE (2004); Yochai Benkler, *Coase's Penguin, or Linux and the Nature of the Firm*, 112 YALE L.J. 369 (2002); David McGowan, *The Legal Implications of Open Source Software*, 2001 U. ILL. L. REV. 241. Open source software traces its origins to the early 1970s and the culture of collaborative research on computer software that existed in many software research environments. To perpetuate that model in the face of increasingly proprietary software, Richard Stallman, a former researcher in MIT's Artificial Intelligence Laboratory, established the Free Software Foundation (FSF) to promote users' rights to use, study, copy, modify, and redistribute computer programs. Open source programs such as GNU/Linux have become widely used throughout the computing world. In the process, they have spawned a large community of computer programmers and service organizations committed to the principles of open source development. The growth and success of Linux has brought the open source movement into the mainstream computer software industry. Today, a variety of vendors, such as Red Hat, Caldera, and Ubuntu, distribute open source software, and it has tens of millions of users worldwide. Does this experience

refute the logic underlying the property rights paradigm or merely broaden the range of viable governance structures?

6. Drawing upon Thomas Jefferson's natural rights insight that "ideas should freely spread from one to another over the globe, for the moral and mutual instruction of man, and improvement of his condition, seems to have been peculiarly and benevolently designed by nature," ANDREW A. LIPSCOMB & ALBERT ELLERY BERGH EDS., THE WRITINGS OF THOMAS JEFFERSON, vol. 13: 333–35 (Writings (document 12): letter from Thomas Jefferson to Isaac McPherson, 13 Aug. 1813) (1905), John Perry Barlow's essay "The Economy of Ideas" has emerged as a manifesto for a new libertarianism that resists intellectual property protection online. John Perry Barlow, *The Economy of Ideas*, 2.03 WIRED 84 (Mar. 1994). Barlow questions whether a right of property can or should exist in a medium (digital networks) lacking physical structure or any significant cost of distribution. This approach resonates with many in the computer hacker community who believe that "information wants to be free." Professor Lawrence Lessig explores and expands upon this perspective in his books FREE CULTURE: HOW BIG MEDIA USES TECHNOLOGY AND THE LAW TO LOCK DOWN CULTURE AND CONTROL CREATIVITY (2004) and THE FUTURE OF IDEAS: THE FATE OF THE COMMONS IN A CONNECTED WORLD (2001), although his focus is not on eliminating intellectual property but on preserving spaces free of such property. For historical analysis of Jefferson's thinking and its application to intellectual property, *see* Adam Mossoff, *Who Cares What Thomas Jefferson Thought About Patents? Reevaluating the Patent Privilege in Historical Context*, 92 CORNELL L. REV. 953 (2007); Justin Hughes, *Copyright and Incomplete Historiographies—of Piracy, Propertization, and Thomas Jefferson*, 79 S. CAL. L. REV. 993 (2006).

What is likely to happen if we abolish the concept of ownership of information on the Internet? In general? Consider the implications for particular works of authorship: musical compositions, sound recordings, software, movies, databases. Will people stop producing these works? Or will other types of incentives and appropriation mechanisms (e.g., encryption, secrecy) continue to encourage invention and creativity? What are the advantages and disadvantages of these alternative mechanisms? Are people intrinsically motivated to create certain types of works, whether or not they get paid? For a controversial argument that we don't need IP at all, *see* MICHELE BOLDRIN & DAVID LEVINE, AGAINST INTELLECTUAL MONOPOLY (2007).

7. The rapid growth of generative AI has resulted in the creation of vast numbers of new works of art, music, and writing. Does an AI need the incentive of copyright to create? Should anyone own new works that are generated in a matter of seconds from a simple prompt?

ii.   *Ensuring Integrity of the Marketplace*

Unlike patent and copyright, trademark law does not protect innovation or creativity directly. Rather, it aims to protect the integrity of the marketplace by prohibiting the use of marks associated with particular manufacturers in ways that would cause confusion as to the sources of the goods. In so doing, trademark law reduces consumer confusion and enhances incentives for firms to invest in activities (including R&D) that improve brand reputation. This function, however, is part of a larger framework of laws and institutions that regulate the quality of information in the marketplace. *See generally* Peter S. Menell & Suzanne Scotchmer, *Intellectual Property Law*, in 2 HANDBOOK OF LAW AND ECONOMICS 1474, 1536–56 (A. Mitchell Polinsky & Steven Shavell eds., 2007).

The efficiency of the marketplace depends critically upon the quality of information available to consumers. In markets in which the quality of goods is uniform or easily inspected at the time of purchase, consumers can determine the attributes themselves and no information problem arises. In many markets, however—such as used automobiles, computers, watches, as well as designer handbags—an information asymmetry exists: sellers typically have better information about their products or services than buyers can uncover without buying the product. *See* George A. Akerlof, *The Market for "Lemons": Quality Uncertainty and the Market Mechanism*, 84 Q.J. ECON. 488 (1970). Unscrupulous sellers will be tempted to make false or misleading product claims or copy the trademark of a rival producer known for superior quality. It is often easier to copy a trademark than to duplicate production techniques, quality assurance programs, and the like. For example, two watches that look the same on the outside may have very different mechanical features, manufacturing quality, and composition of materials used.

Proliferation of unreliable information in the marketplace increases consumers' costs of search and distorts the provision of goods. Consumers will have to spend more time and effort inspecting goods, researching the product market, and testing products. Manufacturers will have less incentive to produce quality goods as others will be able to free-ride on such reputations. In markets for products where quality is costly to observe, high-quality manufacturers might not be able to survive without effective mechanisms for policing the source of products and the accuracy of claims relating to unobservable product characteristics.

Trademarks, as concise and unequivocal indicators of the source (e.g., Apple) and nature (e.g., iPhone) of particular goods, counteract the "market for lemons" problem by communicating to consumers the enterprise responsible for the goods and, in some cases, the specifications of the goods. The brand name Coca-Cola, for example, informs the consumer of the maker of the soft drink beverage as well as the taste that they can expect. If the product meets or exceeds expectations, then the trademark owner gains a loyal customer who will be willing to pay a premium in future transactions; if the product disappoints, then the trademark owner will have more difficulty making future sales to that consumer (or will have to offer a discount to attract their business). In this way, trademarks implicitly communicate unobservable characteristics about the quality of branded products, thereby fostering incentives for firms to invest in product quality, even when such attributes are not directly observable prior to a purchasing decision. Sellers who enter the high-quality segment of the market must initially invest in building a strong reputation. Only after consumers become acquainted with the attributes of their brand can they recoup these costs. As this process unfolds, high-quality items can sell for a premium above their costs of production, since consumers will expect them to be of high quality. Trademarks also facilitate efficient new business models, such as franchising, which generate economies of scale and scope in marketing and facilitate rapid business diffusion across vast geographic areas.

The marking of products also creates incentives for disreputable sellers to pass off their own wares as the goods of better-respected manufacturers. Trademark law (as well as false advertising and unfair competition laws more generally) harnesses the incentives of sellers in the marketplace to police the use of marks and advertising claims of competitors. Sellers often have the best information about the quality of products in the marketplace; they also have a direct stake in preventing competitors from free-riding on their brand, reputation, and consumer loyalty. By creating private causes of action, trademark and false advertising law take advantage of this informational base and incentive structure as well as the vast, decentralized enforcement resources of trademark owners to regulate the informational marketplace, effectively in the name of consumers.

As with patent and copyright law, the creation of intellectual property rights in words, phrases, logos, and other identifying product features can entail several types of costs. Protection of descriptive terms as trademarks can increase search costs and impair competition by raising the marketing costs of competitors. For example, if a cookie manufacturer were to obtain a trademark on the word "cookie," then other companies interested in selling cookies would have a much more difficult time communicating the nature of their goods to consumers. If, however, the trademark was to "Mrs. Fields Cookies" and any protection for "cookies" was disclaimed, then potential competitors would be able to describe their products in the most easily recognized manner and would be able to develop their own marks—such as "ACME Cookies." At a minimum, trademark protection for descriptive terms significantly reduces the effective range of terms that others can use commercially.

More generally, trademark protection for descriptive terms can impede competition. Gaining control over the most effective term for describing a product raises the costs of potential competitors seeking to sell in that marketplace. By not being able to use a term or means of communication most easily understood by the consuming public, the entrant must bear higher marketing costs. Limitations on the use of trademarked terms for purposes of comparative advertising would also impede vigorous competition.

Trademark protection can also interfere with both communicative and creative expression. Broad exclusive trademark rights would limit the ability of others (including non-competitors) to comment on and poke fun at trademarks and their owners. As we will see, various doctrines limit such adverse effects. But as trademark protection has expanded beyond the traditional core—for example, to encompass a broad conception of connection to, sponsorship of, and affiliation with a trademark owner—it becomes more difficult to assess the boundaries, leading film and television production companies, for example, to tread carefully (and increasingly incur the costs of licensing transactions) in the use of trademarks in their works.

COMMENTS AND QUESTIONS

1. *Comparative Institutional Analysis.* In addition to private rights of action for trademark infringement and false advertising, several other mechanisms are available to provide and regulate market information, such as deceit and fraud common law causes of action and privately enforced consumer protection statutes, public regulation and public enforcement of unfair competition laws, and industry self-regulation and certification organizations. How do these institutions compare with trademark protection? Should they supplement or substitute for trademark protection? *See* Dan L. Burk & Brett McDonnell, *Trademarks and the Theory of the Firm*, 51 WM. & MARY L. REV. 345 (2009).

2. *Status Goods.* Some trademarks also serve a more ambiguous function: signaling status or identity for some consumers. Some have referred to such commodities as "Veblen" goods, reflecting Thorstein Veblen's theory of conspicuous consumption. *See* THORSTEIN VEBLEN, THE THEORY OF THE LEISURE CLASS: AN ECONOMIC STUDY OF INSTITUTIONS (1899). This theory posits that unlike normal goods, demand for status goods increases with their price. Purchasers of such goods may be interested in being associated with a particular brand—such as a Rolex watch, a t-shirt with the name and colors of a particular university, or a corporate brand—possibly apart from whether it is authentic or the quality associated with the authentic good. Some purchasers of such goods may well prefer a less expensive, counterfeit version. They presumably would not be confused when purchasing such goods (e.g., a Rolex watch sold on a street corner for $10). Of course, where both buyers and sellers are aware of the difference between cheap imitations of a luxury good and the genuine article, things might be different. It could be that cheap imitations in some ways promote sales of the luxury good. *See* Jonathan Barnett, *Shopping for Gucci on Canal Street: Status Consumption, Intellectual Property and the Incentive Thesis*, 91 VA. L. REV. 1381 (2005).

The marketing of less expensive, lower quality imitations of status goods creates the possibility of separate harm to the sellers and purchasers of authentic goods. The availability of counterfeit articles could well divert some consumers who would otherwise purchase the authentic article, although this effect is likely to be relatively small due to the large price differential and the availability of the authentic goods for those who are interested. The lower quality of the counterfeit goods could, however, erode the goodwill associated with the authentic manufacturer through post-sale confusion—on-lookers who mistake the shoddier counterfeit good for the authentic good and are thereby less inclined to purchase the authentic version, thereby reducing sales by the trademark owner. In addition, due to the proliferation of non-easily recognized "fakes," prior and potential purchasers of the authentic "status" goods may be less interested in owning a much less rare commodity. The value of ownership may be sullied. In essence, status goods exhibit a negative network externality, whereby proliferation of such goods erodes the value to prior purchasers. Should trademark law be concerned with this effect?

B.   OVERVIEW OF INTELLECTUAL PROPERTY

Intellectual property law has traditionally been taught along doctrinal lines. Separate courses have covered patent, copyright, and trademarks, with trade secrets often lost between the gaps. Yet the practice of intellectual property law increasingly cuts across these lines. Computer technology companies, for example, frequently require lawyers to address trade secret, copyright, patent, trademark, and antitrust issues simultaneously. Moreover, from a purely practical standpoint, clients are ultimately interested in appropriating a return from their investments, not in how many patents, copyrights, or trademarks their lawyers can obtain. Thus, intellectual property lawyers must possess an integrated understanding of these various fields to provide sound advice.

With this objective in mind, our book integrates the various modes of intellectual property in a functional manner. Before we begin this more detailed study, however, a brief survey of the overall landscape of intellectual property is in order. The following section sketches the elements of each of the principal modes of intellectual property protection in a comparative framework. These elements are summarized in Table 1-1. As an initial exploration, we conclude the chapter with a problem highlighting the integrated nature of intellectual property law and the challenges of applying its many branches to a real-world problem.

TABLE 1-1

Principal Modes of Legal Protection for Intellectual Work

	Trade secret	*Utility Patent*	*Design Patent*	*Copyright*	*Trademark/dress*
Underlying Theory	Freedom of contract; protection against unfair means of competition	Limited monopoly to encourage production of utilitarian works in exchange for immediate disclosure and ultimate enrichment of the public domain	Limited monopoly to encourage production of ornamental designs for articles of manufacture to encourage expressive creativity	Limited (although relatively long-lived) monopoly to encourage the authorship of expressive works; developed initially as a means of promoting publishing	Perpetual protection for distinctive nonfunctional names and dress to improve the quality of information in the marketplace
Source of Law	Federal statute (Defend Trade Secrets Act); State statutes (Uniform Trade Secrets Act); common law	Patent Act (federal)	Patent Act (federal)	Copyright Act (federal); common law (limited)	Lanham Act (federal); common law (unfair competition)
Subject Matter	Formula, pattern, compilation, program, device, method, technique, process	Process, machine, manufacture, or composition of matter; plants (asexually reproducing)— *excluding*: abstract ideas, laws of nature, natural phenomena	Surface ornamentation and three-dimensional shapes—*excluding*: functional features	Works of authorship *limited by* idea/expression dichotomy (no protection for ideas, systems, methods, procedures); no protection for facts/research	Trademarks; service marks; certification marks; collective marks; trade dress—*excluding* generic terms, functional features

	Trade secret	*Utility Patent*	*Design Patent*	*Copyright*	*Trademark/dress*
Standard for Protection	Information not generally known or available; reasonable efforts to maintain secrecy; commercial value	Novelty; non-obviousness; utility (distinctiveness for plant patents)	Novelty, originality, ornamentality	Originality; authorship; fixation in a tangible medium	Distinctiveness; secondary meaning (for descriptive and geographic marks); use in commerce; famous mark (for dilution protection)
Scope of Protection	Protection against misappropriation—acquisition by improper means or unauthorized disclosure	Exclusive rights to make, use, sell, offer to sell, or import innovation; extends to "equivalents"	Exclusive rights to make, use, sell, offer to sell, or import innovation	Rights of reproduction, adaptation, distribution, performance, and display; limited protection for attribution and integrity afforded some works of visual art; protection against circumvention of technical protection measures	Exclusive rights in U.S. if likelihood of confusion; false designation of origin (§ 43(a)); dilution (for famous marks)
Period of Protection	Until becomes public knowledge	20 years from filing (utility); extensions up to 5 years for drugs, medical devices and additives	15 years from grant	Life of author + 70 years; "works for hire": minimum of 95 years after publication or 120 years after creation	Perpetual, subject to abandonment

	Trade secret	Utility Patent	Design Patent	Copyright	Trademark/dress
Disclosure	Loss of protection (unless sub rosa)	Right to patent lost if disclosure more than one year before filing; full disclosure is required in patent application; marking enhances damages	Right to patent lost if disclosure more than one year before filing; full disclosure in patent application; marking enhances damages	© notice and publication no longer required, but confers benefits	® notice optional, but confers benefits
Rights of Others	Independent discovery; reverse engineering; whistleblower immunity	Only if licensed; can request reexamination by Patent Office	Only if licensed; can request reexamination by Patent Office	Fair use; compulsory licensing for musical compositions, cable TV, et al.; independent creation	Truthful indication of source; fair and nominative use (e.g., comment)
Costs of Protection	Security expenses; personnel dissatisfaction; litigation costs	Filing, issue, and maintenance fees; litigation costs	Filing and issue fees	None (protection attaches upon fixation); publication requires notice; suit requires registration	Registration search; marking product (optional)
Remedies	Civil suit; damages (potentially double); injunctive relief; criminal prosecution	Injunctive relief and damages (potentially treble); attorney fees (in exceptional cases)	Injunctive relief and damages (total profit; attorney fees (in exceptional cases)	Injunction; destruction of infringing articles; damages (actual or profits); statutory ($200–$150,000); attorney fees (within court's discretion); criminal prosecution	Injunction; destruction of infringing articles; disgorgement; damages; attorney fees (in exceptional cases); criminal prosecution

1.   Trade Secret

Trade secret protection emerged from common law doctrines that protect against the misappropriation of confidential information that is the subject of reasonable efforts to maintain secrecy. As such, they are more akin to traditional tort and contract law than to patent or copyright law. While protection for trade secrets has long been a part of the common law, most states today protect trade secrets by statute. The federal government has taken a growing interest in protecting trade secrets as concerns about international espionage and hacking have grown. The passage of the Defend Trade Secrets Act of 2016 added federal protection for trade secrets.

The purpose of protecting trade secrets is to prevent "theft" of information by unfair or commercially unreasonable means. In essence, trade secret law is a form of *private* intellectual property law under which creators establish contractual limitations or build legal "fences" that afford protection from misappropriation.

The definition of subject matter eligible for protection is broad: business or technical information of any sort. To be protected by trade secret laws, the information must be a secret. However, only relative and not absolute secrecy is required. In addition, the owner of a trade secret must take reasonable steps to maintain its secrecy. Trade secrets have no definite term of protection but may be protected only as long as they are secret. Once a trade secret is disclosed, protection is lost.

There is no state agency that "issues" (or even registers) trade secrets. Rather, any information that meets the above criteria can be protected. Courts will find misappropriation of trade secrets in two circumstances: (1) where the secrets were obtained by theft or other improper means; or (2) disclosed in violation of an express or implied agreement to keep the information secret. However, trade secret laws do not protect against independent discovery or invention. Nor do they prevent competitors from "reverse engineering" a legally obtained product to determine the secrets contained inside. Moreover, federal trade secret law protects employees and contractors reporting suspected illegal activity to the government or discussing their concerns with counsel if done confidentially. Violations of trade secret law entitle the owner to damages and, in some cases, injunctions against use or further disclosure.

2.   Utility Patent

Patent law is the classic example of an intellectual property regime modeled on the utilitarian framework. Following the constitutional authorization to promote progress in the "useful Arts," what we would today call technology and scientific discovery, patent law offers the possibility of a limited period of exclusive rights to encourage research and development aimed at discovering new processes, machines, articles of manufacture, and compositions of matter, and improvements thereof. The public benefits directly through the spur to innovation and disclosure of new technology. After the term of the patent expires, the innovation becomes part of the public domain, freely available to all.

To obtain a utility patent, an inventor must submit an application to the Patent and Trademark Office (PTO) that meets five requirements: patentable subject matter, usefulness, novelty, nonobviousness, and disclosure sufficient to enable others skilled in the art to make and use the invention. While the threshold for usefulness is low, the novelty and non-obviousness standards are substantial, and the PTO conducts an independent review of the application to ensure that it meets these requirements. If the PTO grants the patent, the inventor obtains exclusive rights to make, use, and sell the innovation for a term of up to 20 years from the application filing date. The patent grant is nearly absolute, barring even those who independently develop the invention from practicing its art. Infringement will be found where the accused device, composition, or process embodies all of the elements of a valid patent claim (or accomplishes substantially the same function in substantially the same way to achieve the same result).

3. Design Patent

As the industrial revolution unfolded in the early 19th century, advances in iron casting processes, textile manufacturing, and other consumer product industries paved the way for mass producing decorative goods. As patents on these processes and products expired, competition shifted toward the decorative features. Ornamentation of useful articles did not, however, fit easily within utility patent or copyright protection. Although advances in the production processes and casting machinery were eligible for utility patents, the particular designs resulting from such processes and machinery did not qualify for utility patent protection. And copyright protection extended only to books, maps, charts, and prints, not to three-dimensional works.

England's more developed manufacturing economy had already confronted these issues through the enactment of a copyright-based design protection regime. Drawing on England's precedent, a successful American stove manufacturer, along with other industrialists and designers, petitioned Congress to enact design protection modeled on the British legislation. The Commissioner of Patents advocated the legislation in 1841, but under the "design patent" label and the Patent Office's authority. The design patent regime remains today, although copyright protection now extends to useful articles.

To obtain a design patent, a designer must submit an application to the PTO illustrating the design that satisfies four requirements: novelty, originality, ornamentality, and nonobviousness. The ornamentality requirement was intended to exclude design patent protection for functional features. Design patents have a term of 15 years from the grant date.

4. Copyright

Although the copyright and patent laws flow from the same constitutional basis and share the same general approach—statutorily created monopolies to foster progress—they feature different elements and rights, reflecting the very different fields of human ingenuity that they seek to encourage. In general, copyrights are easier to secure and last substantially longer than patents, although the scope of protection afforded copyrights is narrower and less absolute than that given to patents.

Copyright law covers the broad range of literary and artistic expression—including books, poetry, song, dance, dramatic works, computer programs, movies, sculpture, and paintings. Ideas themselves are not copyrightable, but the author's particular expression of an idea is protectable. A work must exhibit a modicum of originality and be fixed in a "tangible medium of expression" to receive protection. Copyright protection attaches as soon as a work is fixed. There is no examination by a governmental authority, although the Copyright Office registers copyrightable works. Such registration is no longer required for validity, but U.S. authors must register their works prior to filing an infringement suit. A copyright lasts for the life of the author plus 70 years or a total of 95 years in the case of entity authors.

The breadth and ease of acquisition of copyright protection are balanced by the more limited rights that copyright law confers. Ownership of a valid copyright protects a copyright holder from unauthorized copying, public performance, and display, and it entitles the holder to make derivative works and to control sale and distribution of the work. These rights, however, are limited in a number of ways. Others may make "fair use" of the material in certain circumstances. The Copyright Act also establishes compulsory licensing for musical compositions and cable television. A limited set of moral rights protects against misattribution or destruction of a narrow class of works of visual art.

Copyright law protects only against *copying* of protected expression. Independent creation of a copyrighted work does not violate the Copyright Act, nor does copying the unprotected elements of a work. Therefore, copyright law must have some mechanism for determining when a work has been copied illegally. While in rare cases direct proof of copying may be available, usually it is not. In its place, courts infer copying from proof that the defendant has had *access* to the plaintiff's work combined with evidence that the two works are *similar*. Even if copying is established, it must be further shown that the defendant's work is *substantially similar* to protected elements (e.g., excluding ideas) of the plaintiff's work.

With the proliferation of digital technology, Congress has augmented traditional copyright protection by prohibiting the circumvention of technical protection measures intended to prevent unauthorized use and distribution of copyrighted works and alteration of copyright management information. These new rights are subject to various exceptions and limitations.

5.   Trademark/Trade Dress

Trademarks are also protected by state statute and common law as well as federal statute, although the source of constitutional authority is different from that of the Patent and Copyright Acts. Rather than deriving from a specific grant of constitutional power, federal power to regulate trademarks and unfair competition is based on the Commerce Clause, which authorizes Congress to regulate foreign and interstate commerce. Unlike patent and copyright protection, trademark law did not evolve from a desire to stimulate particular types of economic activity. Rather, its original purpose was to protect consumers from unscrupulous sellers attempting to fly under the banner of someone else's logo or identifying symbol. Trademark law has more recently embraced incentive and natural rights rationales. The Lanham Act (the federal trademark statute) protects words, symbols, and other attributes that serve to identify the nature and source of goods or services. Examples of marks protectable under the Lanham Act include corporate and product names, symbols, logos, slogans, pictures and designs, product configurations, colors, and even smells. Not all such marks are protectable, however. To receive trademark protection, a mark need not be new or previously unused, but it must represent to consumers the source of the good or service identified. It cannot be merely a description of the good itself or a generic term for the class of goods or services offered. Further, the identifying mark may not be a functional element of the product itself but must serve a purely identifying purpose. Since 1996, famous marks also receive federal protection against "dilution" by blurring or tarnishment. Finally, trademark protection is directly tied to the use of the mark to identify goods in commerce. Trademarks do not expire on any particular date but continue in force until they are "abandoned" by their owner or become unprotectable.

The PTO examines trademark applications and issues trademark registrations that confer significant benefits upon the registrants, including prima facie evidence of validity; constructive notice to others of the claim of ownership; federal subject matter jurisdiction; incontestability after five years, which confers exclusive right to use the mark; authorization to seek treble damages and attorney fees; and the right to bar importation of goods bearing the infringing mark. Federal trademark registration, however, is not necessary to obtain trademark protection. A trademark owner who believes that another is using the same or a similar mark to identify competing goods can bring suit for trademark infringement. Infringement turns on whether consumers are likely to be confused as to the origin of the goods or services. If so, the trademark owner is entitled to an injunction against the confusing use, damages for past infringement, and in some cases the seizure and destruction of infringing goods.

PROBLEM I-2

MEMORANDUM

To: Associate
From: Senior Partner
Re: HEALTHWARE Inc.

Janet Peterson called me yesterday about a new venture that she plans to try to get off the ground. As you may know, Janet is a computer programmer and a registered nurse. She has an interesting idea for a new venture and would like our advice on how she might structure the business to have the best potential for success.

She would like to call the venture Healthware. Janet believes that she can tap into the diet/health/environmental/mobile device craze by developing a user-friendly app that would monitor the user's diet and fitness activity. The user would input information on his or her health (e.g., age, weight, medical history, dietary restrictions). Each day, the program would collect information on the user's diet and physical exercise. An accelerometer built into the user's smartphone would collect exercise information. The user could manually enter their food consumption, or could use a Quick Response Code (a matrix barcode) reader to scan dietary information on a growing array of packaged and restaurant foods. The software would periodically provide an analysis of the user's health, as well as suggestions for achieving the user's goals, whether weight reduction, better fitness, or general health. In addition, the program would compile a record of the user's activities which they could bring to annual physicals. Other subroutines would be available for pregnant and lactating women, children, the elderly, diabetics, vegetarians, triathletes, etc. Over time, Healthware would compile data from users for developing an AI-driven health, exercise, and diet predictive model for improving the software's efficacy.

Janet thinks that she could put together the diverse people necessary to pull this project off: programmers, a nutritionist, a physician, a fitness consultant. She is concerned, however, that one of these people could, after they are familiar with the product, develop a competing program.

What are the options for structuring Healthware? What problems do you foresee in structuring this venture? Assuming that the product is popular, what are the major risks to Healthware's success? How can we structure Healthware so as to overcome these problems?

CHAPTER II:
TRADE SECRET LAW

A. INTRODUCTION

1. Historical Background

The idea that information should be protected against "theft" (which may include the physical taking of tangible goods containing information or simply the copying or memorization of data) is a venerable one in the law. One scholar traces the earliest legal protection against "misappropriation of trade secrets" to the Roman empire. *See* A. Arthur Schiller, *Trade Secrets and the Roman Law: The* Actio Servi Corrupti, 30 COLUM. L. REV. 837 (1930).[1] The Roman courts created a cause of action called "actio servi corrupti"—literally, an action for corrupting a slave. According to Schiller, the actio servi corrupti was used to protect slave owners from third parties who would "corrupt" slaves (by bribery or intimidation) into disclosing their owners' confidential business information. The law made such third parties liable to the slave owner for twice the damages he suffered as a result of the disclosure.

While scholarship has cast some doubt on the enforcement of trade secret protection in the Roman empire, *see* Alan Watson, *Trade Secrets and Roman Law: The Myth Exploded*, 11 TUL. EUR. & CIV. L.F. 19 (1996), the concept that so-called business or "trade secrets" were entitled to legal protection spread rapidly throughout the world. As early as the Renaissance, most European nation-states had laws that protected businesses (notably, the guild cartels) from those who used their secret processes and ideas without permission.

In preindustrial economies, craftsmen passed along their knowledge of the trade to their apprentice with the understanding that the know-how would be kept secret during the apprenticeship period. *See* Catherine L. Fisk, *Working Knowledge: Trade Secrets, Restrictive Covenants in Employment, and the Rise of Corporate Intellectual Property, 1800–1920*, 52 HASTINGS L.J. 441, 450–51 (2001). After this training, the apprentice was free to practice the trade. These protections were reinforced by custom, trade guilds, and close-knit communities. *See* CARLO M. CIPOLLA, BEFORE THE INDUSTRIAL REVOLUTION: EUROPEAN ECONOMY AND SOCIETY 1000–1700 (2d ed. 1980).

This informal system, governed principally through social norms and restrictions on apprentice mobility through mandatory periods of service, eroded as industrialization shifted production to factories and labor mobility increased in the early nineteenth century. Factories operated on a far larger scale than traditional craft enterprises and without the social and guild constraints on the dissemination of proprietary techniques and know-how. While patents afforded protection for larger, discrete advances, smaller-bore, incremental know-how was more vulnerable to misappropriation in the impersonal, specialized factory setting. Factory owners in England pressed for a broader form of protection for workplace trade secrets. The know-how behind industrial processes gradually gained recognition and enforcement by common law courts. *See Newbery v.*

---

[1] Trade secrets may have existed before this time, albeit in unusual forms. *See* Mark C. Suchman, *Invention and Ritual: Notes on the Interrelation of Magic and Intellectual Property in Preliterate Societies*, 89 COLUM. L. REV. 1264, 1274 (1989).

James, 35 Eng. Rep. 1011, 1011–12 (Ch.) (1817); Fisk, *supra*, at 450–88. The practice spread to the United States by the mid-nineteenth century and developed rapidly in the common law. *See Vickery v. Welch*, 36 Mass. (19 Pick.) 523, 525–27 (1837).

Trade secret protection could encompass information that was not generally known to the public so long as the employer undertook reasonable precautions to preserve secrecy. This latter requirement brought non-disclosure agreements ("NDAs") into common practice. Failure to guard against disclosure of trade secrets by employees and contractors would jeopardize trade secret protection.

The emerging law of trade secrets was collected in the RESTATEMENT OF TORTS, published in 1939. The RESTATEMENT protected as a trade secret any information "used in one's business" that gives its owner "an opportunity to obtain an advantage over competitors who do not know or use it," so long as the information was in fact a secret. When the RESTATEMENT (SECOND) OF TORTS was published in 1979, the authors omitted the trade secrets provisions on the grounds that the law of trade secrets had developed into an independent body of law that no longer relied on general principles of tort law. Nonetheless, the original RESTATEMENT has remained influential because so many judicial decisions have relied on it, and statutes and other key sources have integrated its tenets.

By the mid-twentieth century, "the body of state and federal law that ha[d] traditionally coped with [industrial espionage] languish[ed] in a deepening maze of conflict and confusion." *See* Note, *Theft of Trade Secrets: The Need for a Statutory Solution*, 120 U. PA. L. REV. 378 (1971). Recognizing this doctrinal muddle and the growing economic importance of trade secret protection, the American Bar Association established a special committee to investigate the drafting of a uniform trade secret act to harmonize protection among the states in 1968. Over the course of the next decade, that committee drafted and refined the Uniform State Trade Secrets Act (UTSA), which the National Commission on Uniform State Laws promulgated in 1979. The UTSA has since been adopted by every state except New York. In the 1990s, the American Law Institute integrated trade secret law into the RESTATEMENT (THIRD) OF UNFAIR COMPETITION. In 2016, Congress enacted the Defend Trade Secrets Act, which brought uniformity of federal law without significantly changing the rules that have developed under state law. Before turning to these modern sources of trade secret protection, it will useful to examine the principles undergirding trade secret protection.

2. Theoretical Justifications for Trade Secrets

Trade secret law has long been justified on two distinct grounds: property rights and unfair competition grounded in tort.

i. *Property (and Intellectual Property) Rights*

Some jurists have conceptualized "intellectual property" as a species of the broader concept of "property." In addressing whether government disclosure of proprietary information constituted a taking under the Fifth Amendment to the U.S. Constitution, the

Supreme Court held that trade secrets constituted a form of property. *Ruckelshaus v. Monsanto Co.*, 467 U.S. 986, 1001–04 (1984). In holding that trade secrets were "property," the court reasoned in part that "[t]rade secrets have many of the characteristics of more tangible forms of property. A trade secret is assignable. A trade secret can form the res of a trust, and it passes to a trustee in bankruptcy." *Id.* at 1002–04.

Courts routinely characterize trade secrets as "property"[2] and grant injunctive relief to prevent their disclosure. The nature of the "property" interest is, however, limited by the relational character of trade secrets. *See* Robert G. Bone, *A New Look at Trade Secret Law: Doctrine in Search of Justification*, 86 CAL. L. REV. 241, 251–60 (1998). As the court in *Peabody v. Norfolk*, 98 Mass. 452, 458 (1868), noted, if a party "invents or discovers and keeps secret a process of manufacture, whether a proper subject for a patent or not, he has not indeed an exclusive right to it as against the public, or against those who in good faith acquire knowledge of it, but he has property in it which a court of chancery will protect against one who, in violation of contract and breach of confidence, undertakes to apply it to his own use, or to disclose it to third persons." The court explained that courts of equity would intervene to "prevent such a breach of trust, when the injury would be irreparable and the remedy at law inadequate, is well established by authority." Thus, injunctions were available for breaches of trust "in the course of confidential employment."

Treatment of trade secrets as property rights vested in the trade secret "owner" is consistent with a view of trade secrets law as providing an additional incentive to innovate beyond that provided by patent law.

Professor Mark Lemley argues that trade secrets make sense not so much as real property, but as *intellectual* property—that is, as government policy designed to promote innovation and, ironically, to encourage efficient disclosure of secrets. Mark A. Lemley, *The Surprising Virtues of Treating Trade Secrets as IP Rights*, 61 STAN. L. REV. 311 (2008). The idea is that without a legal mechanism to protect secrets, companies will either forgo investment in new innovation or go to unnecessary efforts to hide those innovations—building fences, hiring less-qualified but trusted friends and family members instead of strangers, refusing to share the secret with business partners, and so on. Trade secret law, on this view, encourages both more innovation and more disclosure than we would get without it.

The *Kewanee Oil* opinion similarly recognized an IP-related goal of trade secret protection: encouragement of research and development:

> Certainly the patent policy of encouraging invention is not disturbed by the existence of another form of incentive to invention. In this respect the two systems are not and never would be in conflict. . . .

---

[2] *See, e.g.*, Tabor v. Hoffman, 118 N.Y. 30, 23 N.E. 12 (1889) (holding that "independent of copyright or letters patent, an inventor or author has, by the common law, an exclusive property in his invention or composition, until by publication it becomes the property of the general public").

Trade secret law will encourage invention in areas where patent law does not reach, and will prompt the independent innovator to proceed with the discovery and exploitation of his invention. Competition is fostered and the public is not deprived of the use of valuable, if not quite patentable, invention.

Kewanee Oil Co. v. Bicron Corp., 416 U.S. 470, 481–85 (1974). The Court recognized that

even though a discovery may not be patentable, that does not destroy the value of the discovery to one who makes it, or advantage the competitor who by unfair means, or as the beneficiary of a broken faith, obtains the desired knowledge without himself paying the price in labor, money, or machines expended by the discoverer.

Id. at 482 (quoting *A. O. Smith Corp. v. Petroleum Iron Works Co.*, 73 F.2d 531, 539 (6th Cir. 1934). The Court emphasized "the importance of trade secret protection to the subsidization of research and development and to increased economic efficiency within large companies through the dispersion of responsibilities for creative developments." *See id.* (citing *Wexler v. Greenberg*, 399 Pa. 569, 578–79, 160 A.2d 430, 434–435 (Penn. S. Ct. 1960)). This aligns with Justice Gray's declaration, in a seminal case, that "it is the policy of the law, for the advantage of the public, to encourage and protect invention and commercial enterprise." *Peabody v. Norfolk*, 98 Mass. at 458.

ii.   *Tort Law*

An alternate explanation for much of trade secrets law is what might be described as a "duty-based" theory, or what Melvin Jager calls "the maintenance of commercial morality." 1 MELVIN JAGER, TRADE SECRETS LAW §1.03 (2013), at 1–4. Justice Oliver Wendell Holmes questioned the "property" view of trade secrets in *E.I. du Pont & Co. v. Masland*, 244 U.S. 100, 102 (1917), preferring to characterize these rights in relational terms.

[T]he word 'property' as applied to . . . trade secrets is an unanalyzed expression of certain secondary consequences of the primary fact that the law makes some rudimentary requirements of good faith. Whether the plaintiffs have any valuable secret or not, the defendant knows the facts, whatever they are, through a special confidence that he accepted. The property may be denied, but the confidence cannot be. Therefore, the starting point for the present matter is not property or due process of law, but that the defendant stood in confidential relations with the plaintiffs.

E.I. duPont de Nemours Powder Co. v. Masland, 244 U.S. 100, 102 (1917).[3]

Trade secret law has long been grounded in what has been termed "commercial morality." *See* MELVIN F. JAGER, TRADE SECRETS LAW §1:3 (2013) ("[t]he Anglo-

---

[3] The *Monsanto* Court distinguished *Masland* by observing that "Justice Holmes did not deny the existence of a property interest; he simply deemed determination of the existence of that interest irrelevant to the resolution of the case." *Monsanto*, 467 U.S. 1004 n.9.

American common law . . . began to develop protection for business secrets to enhance commercial morality and good-faith dealings in business"); Bone, 86 CAL. L. REV. at 244 ("Trade secret law is grounded in "relationally specific duties," such as "disloyal employees who use or disclose their employers' secrets in violation of a duty of confidence stemming from the employer-employee relationship").

The *Eastman* case illustrates the principle in action. *See Eastman Co. v. Reichenbach*, 20 N.Y.S. 110, 110, 116 (N.Y. Sup. Ct. 1892), *aff'd sub nom. Eastman Kodak Co. v. Reighenbach*, 29 N.Y.S. 1143 (N.Y. Gen. Term 1894). In the late nineteenth century, Eastman (Kodak), a pioneering developer of photographic technology, brought suit against former high-level employees who departed to start a competing business using secret information that they helped develop at Eastman. They had executed assignment agreements covering all inventions, discoveries, and improvements in photography that they might make, discover, or invent while at Eastman and agreed to maintain company secrets in strict confidence and not to disclose or make improper use of them. The court enjoined defendants' competing venture on the ground that

> [t]his is not legitimate competition, which it is always the policy of the law to foster and encourage, but it is *contra bonos mores* [against good morals], and constitutes a breach of trust which a court of law, and much less a court of equity, should not tolerate.

20 N.Y.S. at 116.

This theme pervades trade secret law. As the Supreme Court recognized in *Kewanee Oil Co. v. Bicron Corp.*, 416 U.S. 470 (1974), its landmark decision holding that federal patent law does not preempt state trade secret protection, "[t]he maintenance of standards of commercial ethics and the encouragement of invention are the broadly stated policies behind trade secret law. 'The necessity of good faith and honest faith dealing is the very life and spirit of the commercial world.'" *Id.* at 481–82 (1974) (quoting *National Tube Co. v. Eastern Tube Co.*, 3 Ohio Cir. Ct. R., N.S., 459, 462 (1902), *aff'd*, 69 Ohio St. 560, 70 N.E. 1127 (1903)).

By contrast to the property view, the commercial morality concern aims to deter wrongful acts and is therefore sometimes described as a tort theory. Here the aim of trade secret law is to punish and prevent illicit behavior and even to uphold reasonable standards of commercial behavior. Under the tort theory trade secret protection is not explicitly about encouraging investments. It is plain, however, that one consequence of deterring wrongful behavior would be to encourage investment in trade secrets. Hence, despite their conceptual differences, the tort and property/incentive approaches to trade secrets may well push in the same direction.

One significant difference, though, is that the tort view focuses first and foremost on the question of infringement – did the defendant do something wrong? The property and IP views, by contrast, first ask whether there is a property right at all to be protected.

iii. Contracts

While trade secrets protect against theft of a secret by third parties, many trade secret cases arise out of a "duty" explicitly stated in a contract, such as a technology license or an employment agreement. The tort-based breach of duty theory merges in those cases with a standard common law action for breach of contract. *Cf.* Robert G. Bone, *A New Look at Trade Secret Law: Doctrine in Search of Justification*, 86 CAL. L. REV. 241 (1998) (questioning any distinct theoretical justification for trade secret law and arguing that contract and tort doctrines provide a proper foundation).

Trade secrets may be valuable because they give parties something to transact over. In so doing, they solve what has been called "Arrow's Information Paradox." People won't pay money for ideas unless they know what those ideas are, so they can decide if the idea is valuable. But without legal protection, disclosing the idea to a potential buyer would destroy its value. Parties sometimes sign "nondisclosure agreements" promising not to use information disclosed so it can be evaluated. Trade secret law can establish a right to protect that information against misuse once it is disclosed even in the absence of an express contract.

3. Overview of Modern Trade Secret Protection

Today, every one of the United States protects trade secrets. Improper use or disclosure of a trade secret was traditionally a common law tort. The Uniform Trade Secrets Act has come to unify trade secret protection notwithstanding its predominately state law foundation. The RESTATEMENT OF TORTS, §§757, 758 as well as the RESTATEMENT (THIRD) OF UNFAIR COMPETITION also serve as valuable sources for navigating trade secret protection.

Only New York has not adopted the UTSA, although some states, like North Carolina, adopted a modified version of the UTSA. New York protects trade secrets under common law, applying the Restatement of Torts framework. Because of the Uniform Act's importance, we reproduce its primary provisions here.

Uniform Trade Secrets Act, with 1985 Amendments

§1. Definitions

As used in this [Act], unless the context requires otherwise:

(1) "Improper means" includes theft, bribery, misrepresentation, breach or inducement of a breach of a duty to maintain secrecy, or espionage through electronic or other means;

(2) "Misappropriation" means:

(i) acquisition of a trade secret of another by a person who knows or has reason to know that the trade secret was acquired by improper means; or

(ii) disclosure or use of a trade secret of another without express or implied consent by a person who

(A) used improper means to acquire knowledge of the trade secret; or

(B) at the time of disclosure or use, knew or had reason to know that his knowledge of the trade secret was

    (I) derived from or through a person who had utilized improper means to acquire it;

    (II) acquired under circumstances giving rise to a duty to maintain its secrecy or limit its use; or

    (III) derived from or through a person who owed a duty to the person seeking relief to maintain its secrecy or limit its use; or

(C) before a material change of his [or her] position, knew or had reason to know that it was a trade secret and that knowledge of it had been acquired by accident or mistake. . . .

(4) "Trade secret" means information, including a formula, pattern, compilation, program, device, method, technique, or process, that:

(i) derives independent economic value, actual or potential, from not being generally known to, and not being readily ascertainable by proper means by, other persons who can obtain economic value from its disclosure or use, and

(ii) is the subject of efforts that are reasonable under the circumstances to maintain its secrecy.

The federal Defend Trade Secrets Act, enacted in 2016, was "modeled on the Uniform Trade Secrets Act," H. REP. NO. 114-529, 114th CONG., 2D SESS., DEFEND TRADE SECRETS ACT OF 2016 (2016). It defines trade secret misappropriation using the language of the UTSA. The DTSA augments the UTSA by defining "improper means":

(A) includes theft, bribery, misrepresentation, breach or inducement of a breach of a duty to maintain secrecy, or espionage through electronic or other means; and

(B) does not include reverse engineering, independent derivation, or any other lawful means of acquisition.

The federal definition of secrecy, while still broad, is narrower than the UTSA, limiting the reach of the law to certain types of information:

the term "trade secret" means all forms and types of financial, business, scientific, technical, economic, or engineering information, including patterns, plans, compilations, program devices, formulas, designs, prototypes, methods, techniques, processes, procedures, programs, or codes, whether tangible or intangible, and whether or how stored, compiled, or memorialized physically, electronically, graphically, photographically, or in writing if—

(A) the owner thereof has taken reasonable measures to keep such information secret; and

(B) the information derives independent economic value, actual or potential, from not being generally known to, and not being readily ascertainable through proper means by, another person who can obtain economic value from the disclosure or use of the information.

18 U.S.C. §1839(3).

Is there any practical difference between these definitions? Texas took the adoption of the federal law as evidence of *disuniformity*, modifying its version of the UTSA in 2017 to adopt the definition of a trade secret in the DTSA (itself held over from the Economic Espionage Act) rather than conforming to the laws of other states.

* * * * *

A trade secret claim can be broken down into three essential elements. First, the subject matter involved must qualify for trade secret protection: it must be the type of knowledge or information that trade secret law was meant to protect, and it must not be generally known to all. On eligible subject matter, the current trend, exemplified by the UTSA, is to protect as a trade secret any valuable information so long as the information is capable of adding economic value to the owner. The requirement that the information not be generally known follows from the label trade "secret." The requirement is meant to ensure that no one claims intellectual property protection for information commonly known in a trade or industry.

The second element is that the holder of the trade secret took *reasonable precautions* under the circumstances to prevent its disclosure. Courts have varied in their rationale for this requirement. Some view it as evidence that the trade secret is valuable enough to bother litigating; others reason that where the plaintiff has taken reasonable precautions, the defendant likely acquired the trade secret wrongfully. Whatever the justification, it is clear that no one may let information about products and operations flow freely to competitors at one time and then later claim that competitors have wrongfully acquired valuable trade secrets. To establish the right, one must be diligent in protecting information. As always, however, the presence of the term "reasonable" ensures close cases and difficult line-drawing for courts, a theme reflected in several of the cases that follow.

Finally, a trade secret plaintiff must prove that the defendant acquired the information wrongfully—in a word, that the defendant *misappropriated* the trade secret. Just because a person's information is valuable does not make it wrong for another to use it or disclose it. But use or disclosure is wrongful when the information is acquired through deception, skullduggery, or outright theft. Close cases abound because of competitors' ingenuity in rooting out information about their rivals' businesses and products.

Most trade secret cases arise not from skullduggery by outsiders but from breach of an obligation to the trade secret holder not to disclose or appropriate the trade secret. Such an obligation can arise by *express contract* or an *implied duty*. Even in the absence of an express contract, most employees are held to have a duty to protect their employers' interests in their secret practices and information. Even where the duty arises by explicit contract, however, public policy limitations on the scope and duration of the agreement will often come into play, in some cases resulting in substantial judicial modification of the explicit obligations laid out in the contract.

The Defend Trade Secrets Act of 2016 added an important limitation on trade secret protection: an express immunity from suit for whistleblowers, employees and contractors who disclose suspected illegal activity to the government and their attorney confidentially. *See* 18 U.S.C. §1833(b). This limitation on trade secret protection promotes the social interest in rooting out and deterring corporate fraud and other forms of illegal activity.

The United States pioneered modern trade secret law, and other countries have followed suit. The EU Trade Secrets Directive, for instance, largely tracks the UTSA definitions of secrecy, reasonable efforts, and misappropriation. *See* Council Directive 2016/943, art. 2–5, 2016 O.J. (L 157/1) 1 (EC).

B.   SUBJECT MATTER

1.   Defining Trade Secrets

Mallet and Company Inc. v. Lacayo
United States Court of Appeals for the Third Circuit
16 F.4th 364 (3d Cir. 2021))

JORDAN, CIRCUIT JUDGE.

Behind the breads, cakes, and other treats on our grocery store shelves, there is a ferociously competitive market for baking supplies, and that is the setting for this trade secret and unfair competition case.

In 2019, Mallet and Company Inc. ("Mallet") learned that Russell T. Bundy Associates, Inc., doing business as Bundy Baking Solutions ("Bundy"), was becoming its newest competitor in the sale of baking release agents. Release agents are lubricants that allow baked goods to readily separate from the containers in which they are made. Bundy was already well-known for other products it offered to the commercial baking industry when it decided to launch a new subsidiary, Synova LLC ("Synova"), to sell baking release agents. Synova hired two of Mallet's employees, both of whom had substantial access to Mallet's proprietary information. Taking some of that information with them from Mallet to Synova, they helped Synova rapidly develop, market, and sell release agents to Mallet's customers. Mallet sued, saying such progress would have taken years to accomplish but for the misappropriation of its trade secrets. Agreeing with Mallet, the District Court issued the preliminary injunction now challenged on appeal, restraining Bundy, Synova, and those employees (collectively, "the Defendants") from competing with Mallet.

While we appreciate the challenges inherent in disputes involving trade secrets and requests for preliminary relief, the injunction at issue is flawed and must be vacated. For the reasons that follow, we will remand for further consideration of what, if any, equitable relief is warranted . . .

I. BACKGROUND

A. Factual Background

1. *Mallet and the Defendant Employees*

For over eighty years, Mallet has been in the business of developing, manufacturing, and selling baking release agents as well as the equipment used to apply such agents. Release agents are applied to commercial baking pans to ensure the consistent release of baked goods over hundreds of uses. They thus play a crucial role in large-scale baking operations. While the ingredients used to create them—mineral oils, vegetable oils, and lecithin—are commonly known, developing a successful release agent is not as simple as knowing a few of its components. There are "a wide range of factors that have to be considered when formulating a release agent," including product performance, stability, application, cost, availability, and packaging. And the efficacy of a release agent can greatly depend on the customer's product, pan condition, storage conditions, and machinery used to apply the agent. As a result, there are different kinds of release agents, each with unique properties that may be further tailored to maximize performance when used in the production of certain goods. Still, competitors in the release agent market often manufacture and sell identical or similar products.

. . . Prior to 2018, [Mallet] manufactured about fifty different release agents, including its "Vegalube Super P" ("Super P"), which it calls "the premier and best-performing baking release agent product in the market." Mallet contends that it has "take[n] substantial time, research, and effort" to formulate and perfect its release agents, including Super P. After developing a product in the laboratory, additional work is needed to bring that product to scale and optimize its performance at a customer's facility   To safeguard that competitive advantage, Mallet has put in place several measures to protect its information, including nondisclosure and noncompetition agreements with its employees, restricted access to its lab and formulas, and password protection for its computer network.

Along with its release agent "formulas and [the] processes used to make them[,]" Mallet considers the following information to be its "confidential, proprietary, trade secret information":

> specific products sold to customers or purchased from suppliers; all information pertaining to Mallet's business with its customers and its suppliers; Mallet's sales data and cost data; the body of knowledge about the development, production, and application of Mallet's release agents and equipment, including the tailoring of release agents and equipment for specific customer challenges; information about the internal business affairs of any customers, suppliers, dis-

tributors, agents and contractors doing business with Mallet; pricing information; strategies; marketing information; and exclusive relationships with certain suppliers of release agent ingredients.

Mallet's Proposed Findings of Fact. According to Mallet, "the trade secret in question
here is the overall body of knowledge that connects . . . the development, production,
application and implementation of the release agent . . . coupled with Mallet's proprietary equipment, which go hand in hand with [a] formulated solution."

As sweeping as that statement is, Mallet does recognize some limits on what it can
claim as a trade secret. For example, it does not consider its "product data sheets" to be
trade secret information, since those specification sheets are "produced and provided to
consumers of its products[.]" It also agrees that some ingredients in baking release
agents . . . have been common knowledge in the industry for more than thirty years, and
that the components for release agents are published in product data sheets, articles, and
company websites, and are therefore public knowledge, though the precise ratios and
processes for combining them are not. . . .

Mallet further recognizes that its own patents disclose "various formulas for the
creation of the lubricants[,]" ""examples of blends and blend ratios[,]" and a "series of
different formulated release agents[.]" Those patents publicize some properties of each
formulated release agent "based on various tests that Mallet . . . had conducted," including "viscosity, stability, texture and other releasing characteristics." While seeming to
concede that information in patents cannot—at least by itself—constitute trade secrets,
Mallet . . . distinguishes the "particular formulation[s]" that its patents cover from the
"know-how" that Mallet has developed over its eighty-year presence in the marketplace
and that it continues to utilize on an ongoing basis for the "formulation, application[,]
and implementation of [its] release agents for customers." According to Mallet, that
know-how is a trade secret. And two of its former employees, Ada Lacayo and William
Bowers, had substantial access to it.

a. Lacayo's Employment with Mallet

[Lacayo worked at Mallet for 20 years] Lacayo's job responsibilities spanned all
aspects of Mallet's release agent business, from product development and quality control to customer-specific applications and technical support. Through her director positions, she obtained extensive access to Mallet's technical information. That information
allowed her to analyze ingredient interactions, create over two dozen new product formulas and processing methods, and perform "economic justifications and case studies
to substantiate improvements." In addition, Lacayo played a key role in quality control,
running onsite tests for customers, troubleshooting issues, and recommending changes
to improve product performance. Along with educating individual customers, Lacayo
promoted Mallet's products, solutions, and machinery more generally. She "wrote and
designed manuals, instructional programs, marketing materials, [and] presentations,"
which she "delivered . . . to diverse audiences in English and Spanish." She also participated in trade shows, "[m]anaged the Latin American machinery and product introduction program," and "[c]onducted seminars on product lines." . . . And as a result of her

extensive exposure to all sides of Mallet's business and the "know-how [she] gleaned from Mallet over decades[,]" she was widely known by "the customer base of the baking industry[.]"

. . .

2. Bundy, Synova, and the Baking Release Agent Industry

. . .

Synova was formally "created on April 27, 2017 and launched on May 15, 2019 to manufacture and distribute external baking release agents and oils." Between its creation and its launch, Synova's President, Robert A. Bundy, was "engaged in business development[,] ... looking for as much information on as many topics as [he] could get" on the baking release agent industry. Along the way, he sought information from and recruited Lacayo and Bowers.

. . .

Although Lacayo secretly interviewed and accepted a position with Synova on January 22, 2018, she remained employed with Mallet until February 12, 2018. When she did finally announce that she was leaving Mallet, Lacayo concealed her employment with Synova and informed Mallet that she was instead leaving to take care of her mother.

Just three days before her interview with Synova, on January 19, 2018, Lacayo copied 1,748 files onto a USB drive. Those "bulk copied files were stored across four main (root) folders" titled: "Mallet Lab Methods, MRO Project, Supplier Approval Program, and Supplier Information." She also emailed information, including screenshots of two formulas, from Mallet's files to her private Gmail account. On February 28, 2018, when she was no longer employed with Mallet, Lacayo emailed to herself a spreadsheet with technical data from Mallet's research.

. . .

During discovery in this case, "over 1,000 documents" containing "metadata associated with Mallet" were found on Lacayo's Synova computer, with 649 of those documents having "a Mallet logo ... [branded] on the face of the document." Digital forensic evidence indicates that Lacayo not only copied those documents but also used them, including a Mallet release agent formula and associated pricing information, while working for Synova.

The purloined documents, however, are not the whole of the problem Mallet has with Lacayo. It says that "the value she brings [to a competitor] goes far beyond any particular formula she may have provided" or any documents she may have stolen. "It's really the know-how that she brings" to Synova that Mallet says it is worried about. After "work[ing] for Mallet for" so long, Lacayo "has quite a lot of know-how that went with her to the Bundy organization[,]" including information about "the formulation, application and implementation of release agent" products that Mallet had "developed over the course of its 80 years." And that know-how, it says, "would be impossible to erase from her mind."

In January 2018, Synova was in the earliest stages of its existence, and while "[t]he development of the release agents had already begun," it had not completed a final product. Synova had "identified the archetypes of ingredients that would be required and broadly [knew] the ratios of those ingredients." But it was still in the research and development process and had not yet conducted "any internal product testing on a release agent." As Mr. Bundy explained, "that was part of the reason to hire someone with a good science background[,]" like Lacayo. Less than ten months after joining Synova, Lacayo had formulated a lineup of release agents, which Synova marketed as direct replacements for Mallet's release agents. Indeed, in internal correspondence it explicitly described its new formulas as "Synova=Mallet." Lacayo provided oil blend recipes to Synova, built Synova's processes and programs, and touted her ability to match a Mallet product for a customer.

. . .

B. Procedural Background

. . . [T]he District Court found that "[a]t least some of the Mallet information in question, possessed by Defendants, satisfies the trade secret definition(s)," including, "among other things, highly sensitive details about how Mallet produces, markets and sells its release agents[.]" The Court listed thirteen categories of Mallet information it deemed "protected materials," as follows:

> Mallet's formulas; customer purchase orders demonstrating Mallet's pricing; identification of customers experiencing difficulty with Mallet's products; internal discussions of "actual major problems" at customer locations; internal discussions of how Mallet would address issues with its products; internal discussions of customers' preferences and complaints; Mallet's completed organic certifications; identification of Mallet's supply source for product ingredients; Mallet's internal manuals and procedures showing how Mallet's lab is operated; pricing and volume data; information about Mallet's equipment; Mallet's training materials showing how Mallet markets and sells its products; and a compilation of Mallet's product specification sheets.

. . .

II. DISCUSSION

. . . We fully appreciate the challenges inherent in expedited proceedings. Nevertheless, when an injunction lacks sufficient specificity to permit meaningful appellate review, there needs to be another effort at crafting the contours of the order. Because the District Court did not identify with specificity the information it found to be Mallet's trade secrets, we are not in a position to make an informed decision as to whether Mallet is likely to prevail on its trade secret misappropriation claims. . . .

We will accordingly vacate the injunction order and remand for reconsideration. In doing so, we outline a few matters to be considered when identifying allegedly misappropriated trade secrets. We also discuss the permissible scope of an injunction and the limits of a district court's discretion when determining the associated amount of a bond.

A. A preliminary injunction predicated on trade secret misappropriation must adequately identify the allegedly misappropriated trade secrets.

. . .

For a federal trade secret misappropriation claim, [plaintiff must show]: "(1) the existence of a trade secret . . . (2) that 'is related to a product or service used in, or intended for use in, interstate or foreign commerce[,]' and (3) the misappropriation of that trade secret[.]" *Oakwood Labs. LLC v. Thanoo*, 999 F.3d 892, 905 (3d Cir. 2021). And, of course, each of those elements is predicated on an adequate identification of what the plaintiff contends to be its trade secret. *See id.* ("To plead the existence of a trade secret in a misappropriation claim . . ., [a plaintiff] must sufficiently identify the information it claims as a trade secret[.]").

The Defend Trade Secrets Act ("DTSA") defines a trade secret as information that "the owner thereof has taken reasonable measures to keep . . . secret" and that "derives independent economic value, actual or potential, from not being generally known to, and not being readily ascertainable through proper means by, another person who can obtain economic value from the disclosure or use of the information[.]" 18 U.S.C. §1893(3). We cannot evaluate whether a plaintiff is likely to succeed on any element of a trade secret misappropriation claim until the plaintiff has sufficiently described those trade secrets. *See Porous Media Corp. v. Midland Brake Inc.*, 187 F.R.D. 598, 600 (D. Minn. 1999) ("Failure to identify the trade secrets with sufficient specificity renders the Court powerless to enforce any trade secret claim."). It follows that a district court's injunction order must first adequately identify the information to which it accords trade secret status. Otherwise, the injunction order lacks the foundation necessary for holding a plaintiff likely to prevail on its misappropriation claim. Without that information, the injunction order fails to comply with Rule 65(d), and it must be vacated.

The District Court determined that "[a]t least some of the Mallet information in question" constitutes protectable trade secrets, "includ[ing], among other things, highly sensitive details about how Mallet produces, markets and sells its release agents[.]" Absent from the District Court's high-level description, however, are any specifics of what those "highly sensitive details" are. Rather, we are left with a list of thirteen broad categories of Mallet information which the District Court deemed "protected materials":

> Mallet's formulas; customer purchase orders demonstrating Mallet's pricing; identification of customers experiencing difficulty with Mallet's products; internal discussions of "actual major problems" at customer locations; internal discussions of how Mallet would address issues with its products; internal discussions of customers' preferences and complaints; Mallet's completed organic certifications; identification of Mallet's supply source for product ingredients; Mallet's internal manuals and procedures showing how Mallet's lab is operated; pricing and volume data; information about Mallet's equipment; Mallet's training materials showing how Mallet markets and sells its products; and a compilation of Mallet's product specification sheets.

While some information falling within those categories may very well include trade secrets, there is a fair probability that many of the categories—and perhaps all of them—also include information that does not qualify for trade secret protection.

The injunction order's statement of protected material is better characterized as a list of general categories of business and technical information, a list that could be used to describe documents found in any number of corporations. *See A&P Tech., Inc. v. Lariviere*, No. 1:17-cv-534, 2017 WL 6606961, at *10 (S.D. Ohio Dec. 27, 2017) ("Terms such as 'engineering,' 'research and development procedures and materials,' and 'marketing materials' could be applied to almost any corporation in existence, and do not in any way allow Defendants to properly craft a defense around the alleged misappropriation of trade secrets."). The generic list thus falters against the standard for specifying a trade secret. At a minimum, "the subject matter of the trade secret must be described 'with sufficient particularity to separate it from matters of general knowledge in the trade or of special knowledge of those persons who are skilled in the trade, and to permit the defendant to ascertain at least the boundaries within which the secret lies.'" *Oakwood* , 999 F.3d at 906) (quoting *Diodes, Inc. v. Franzen*, 260 Cal.App.2d 244, 67 Cal. Rptr. 19, 24 (1968) (describing the minimum specificity threshold to survive a motion to dismiss). That is especially the case where, as here, the record suggests that those boundaries may not be particularly clear.[4]

For example, Mallet recognizes that its own patents publicly disclose some of its formulas, but it appears to contend that even formulas thus publicly disclosed are part of its trade secrets. (*See* Mallet Depo.) ("What I am saying is while these formulations were developed here, it doesn't necessarily mean that the exact formula in one of these [patent] tables is at question as a trade secret. These are examples only. They form a part of the examples of the patent   *They are part of a trade secret.*") (emphasis added).) If that is really its position—and it is hard for us to tell—then it is hard to take entirely seriously. A formula disclosed in a patent is, by definition, not a secret. Nevertheless, "[w]hile the precise information provided within or directly ascertainable from a patent cannot constitute a trade secret, patent holders are not necessarily precluded from cultivating trade secrets that go beyond the corpus of the patent or that refine the patent's process in some proprietary way." *AutoTrakk, LLC v. Auto. Leasing Specialists,*

---

[4] Mallet contends that its trade secrets are adequately identified because of the following series of steps: (1) the District Court's order granting an injunction was based on the Court's Findings of Fact, Conclusions of Law & Order deciding a preliminary injunction was warranted; (2) the Court's Finding of Fact ¶8—stating that "Lacayo had access to, and was intimately familiar with, Mallet's protectable information."; (3) those seventeen paragraphs in Mallet's Proposed Findings of Fact—the contents of which summarized broadly that Lacayo had access to and knowledge of trade secret information; (4) all of those exhibits are declarations and excerpts of deposition testimony that themselves attach exhibits; and (5) somewhere in there are trade secrets. At oral argument, Mallet cited a range of documents as proof that it had specified its trade secrets. Circumstances such as access to trade secrets, unusually accelerated or low-cost development of a competing product, and relative lack of prior expertise, may, in combination, establish a likelihood of success on the element of misappropriation, *see Oakwood* , 999 F.3d 908, 911-12. But they do not establish that likelihood for the element on which we focus here: the existence of a trade secret that has been identified "with sufficient particularity." *Id.* at 906

Inc., No. 4:16-cv-1981, 2017 WL 2936730, at *5 (M.D. Pa. July 10, 2017). Problematically, though, Mallet fails to explain how we or anyone else is to distinguish between what is generally known or available information and what it contends to be protectable trade secrets. With a wave of the hand, it declares everything to be secret know-how. (*See* Mallet Depo. ("The issue at hand is not so much that the formula might be the same or different. What is at hand is that the know-how that Ms. Lacayo took from Mallet, and is applying within Bundy, is all about delivering the performance, the quality, and those other factors I mentioned to the customer to provide them the solution. That know-how was developed by Mallet over 80 years.").)

When the breadth of a trade secret description is so far-reaching that it includes publicly available information (like patent disclosures) and admitted industry knowledge, that information is not specific enough to be accorded trade secret sta- tus. *DeRubeis v. Witten Techs., Inc.*, 244 F.R.D. 676, 689 (N.D. Ga. 2007) ("If the list is too general, it will encompass material that the defendant will be able to show cannot be trade secret." (citation omitted)). While we recognize the difficulty inherent in articulating what trade secrets Lacayo and Bowers may have misappropriated—and it certainly appears they took things that may qualify as trade secrets—"care must [still] be taken to not allow a plaintiff in a trade secret misappropriation case to make generalized claims that leave a defendant wondering what the secrets at issue might be[.]" *Oakwood*, 999 F.3d at 907.

The District Court, in effect, recapitulated Mallet's own broadly stated categories of information. But, like Mallet, it did not identify which formulas it referred to, nor did it describe any characteristics or properties contributing specific competitive value to Mallet that could serve as a marker for separating Mallet's formulas from publicly available information or generally known formulas in the industry. The District Court also concluded that "pricing and volume data" and "Mallet's training materials showing how [it] markets and sells its products" are trade secrets. But those trade secret descriptions fare no better than Mallet's assertion that "pricing information[,] strategies[, and] marketing information" are trade secrets. Specific examples are needed and, if provided, could very well suffice to support injunctive relief.[5]

---

[5] Though our decision relies on the District Court's findings of fact, we note that on remand the Court is not bound by its initial findings and should again carefully assess the evidentiary record, weighing all conflicting evidence. We offer two examples of findings that give us pause, at least as presently explained. First, extensive evidence was introduced showing that many of both Mallet's and Synova's products were single ingredient oils, some of which were simply repackaged for sale. Given that, we hesitate to agree with the District Court that the testimony relating to unformulated pure oils is a "red herring" and immaterial to Mallet's right to relief. As of December 7, 2020, repackaged mineral oils constituted approximately half of Synova's Supra and Primo series. Further, we wonder whether a single naturally occurring ingredient can be repackaged as a product and then be considered a formula warranting trade secret protection, but we leave that for consideration in the first instance on remand.

Second, the Court found that "Mallet's evidence establishes that the formulation of its relevant products takes substantial time, sometime years" and that "Lacayo's testimony, to the effect that formulating such products is 'very easy,' was not credible." But those findings make no mention of other evidence that supported Lacayo's claim about the ease of developing some formulas. Two other witnesses—including

. . . [I]t is first and foremost the plaintiff's burden to specifically identify what it contends to be its trade secrets and to demonstrate with record evidence a "significantly better than negligible" chance, of establishing the existence of those trade secrets. If a plaintiff fails to meet that burden, the district court faces the same problem we now have on appeal, and a preliminary injunction for trade secret misappropriation ought not issue.

While we are persuaded that some of Mallet's information—such as that contained in its patents—cannot legitimately have the protected status that it may have been afforded by the District Court, we lack the information necessary to decide anything more about what allegedly does have that protected status and Mallet's likelihood of success in establishing misappropriation of that specific information. So, instead, we share two observations for consideration on remand.

First, information will not necessarily be deprived of protection as a trade secret because parts of it are publicly available. A confidential compilation and organization of public information can amount to a trade secret. "Courts have long recognized that 'a trade secret can exist in a combination of characteristics and components, each of which, by itself, is in the public domain, but the unified process, design and operation of which, in unique combination, affords a competitive advantage and is a protectable secret.'" *AirFacts, Inc. v. de Amezaga*, 909 F.3d 84, 96 (4th Cir. 2018) (quoting *Imperial Chem. Indus. v. Nat'l Distillers & Chem. Corp.*, 342 F.2d 737, 742 (2d Cir. 1965)). Similarly, "[w]hile the precise information provided within or directly ascertainable from a patent [or other published document] cannot constitute a trade secret," that does not, as noted earlier, mean that a patentee is "precluded from cultivating trade secrets that go beyond the corpus of the patent or that refine the patent's process in some proprietary way." *AutoTrakk, LLC*, 2017 WL 2936730, at *5.

Second, an employee's general know-how should be distinguished from the particular secrets held by an employer. In other words, while an employee's general know-how does not constitute trade secret information, employers remain free to identify and protect their particular proprietary information. Admittedly, the line distinguishing between the two—an employee's general knowledge or skill and an employer's protectable trade secrets—may often be difficult to draw. Thus, in exercising its equitable discretion, a district court need not draw the line with precision, but the plaintiff has to provide something better than sweeping generalities for the court to work with. It is the trade secret owner that bears the burden of demonstrating its claimed secrets are protectable and are not general industry knowledge. Just how much specificity a court should require of the plaintiff-owner is again a context-specific matter. We cannot provide a bright-line rule. The best we can do is say that Mallet's very general description

---

Mallet's own witness, Roja Ergun—acknowledged that some basic release agents were in fact easy to make. . . . Further insight into the District Court's weighing of such conflicting evidence will assist us in providing meaningful appellate review.

of categories does not "sufficiently identify the information it claims as a trade se- cret," *Oakwood*, 999 F.3d at 905, and thus does not suffice to justify the sweeping in- junction the District Court issued.

. . .

COMMENTS AND QUESTIONS

1. *The Often Fuzzy Line between General Skill and Trade Secrets*. Trade secret law aims to protect valuable information while at the same time not interfering with labor mobility and robust competition. How might Mallet have better identified its trade se- crets to sustain the preliminary injunction? What risks would it have faced by providing greater specificity? Was the plaintiff's problem in *Mallet* just a failure to specify the secrets? Or is the claim that all its formulas and business know-how are trade secrets a sign that it can't identify secrets that meet the standards of the DTSA?

2. *Secrecy*. While information must not be generally known or readily ascertainable in order to be a secret, the plaintiff can still disclose the secret for business purposes. As one court put it:

> Although the law requires secrecy, it need not be absolute. Public revelation would, of course, dispel all secrecy, but the holder of a secret need not remain totally silent:
>
>> He may, without losing his protection, communicate to employees involved in its use. He may likewise communicate it to others pledged to secrecy   Nevertheless, a substantial element of secrecy must exist, so that except by the use of improper means, there would be difficulty in acquiring the information.

RESTATEMENT OF TORTS, §757 Comment *b* (1939). We conclude that a holder may divulge his information to a limited extent without destroying its status as a trade secret. To hold otherwise would greatly limit the holder's ability to profit from his secret. If disclosure to others is made to further the holder's economic interests, it should, in appropriate circumstances, be considered a limited disclo- sure that does not destroy the requisite secrecy. The only question is whether we are dealing with a limited disclosure here. . . .

> Looking . . . to the policy considerations involved, we glean two reasons why Metallurgical's disclosures to others are limited and therefore insufficient to extinguish the secrecy Metallurgical's other evidence has suggested. First, the disclosures were not public announcements [such as disclosures in an issued pa- tent]; rather, Metallurgical divulged its information to only two businesses with whom it was dealing   Second, the disclosures were made to further Metal- lurgical's economic interests. Disclosure to Consarc was made with the hope that Consarc could build the second furnace. A long-standing agreement gave La Floridienne the right, as a licensee, to the information in exchange for royalty

payments. Metallurgical therefore revealed its discoveries as part of business transactions by which it expected to profit.

Metallurgical Indus. v Fourtek, 790 F.2d 1195, 1200 (5th Cir. 1986). Should the fact that neither Consarc or Floridienne signed NDAs doom Metallurgical's trade secret misappropriation lawsuit against Fourtek, a consultant who had signed an NDA? What if Metallurgical had sold the furnace technology to the general public? *Cf. Turret Labs v. CargoSprint, LLC*, 2022 WL 701161 (2d Cir. Mar. 9, 2022) (holding that the failure to obtain a confidentiality agreement from business partners showed that the plaintiff did not take reasonable efforts to protect its secrets).

3. *Compilations of Unprotectable Information.* The categories of information eligible for protection as trade secrets are expansive. As *Mallet* makes clear, they include secret combinations of items which by themselves can be publicly known. They also include both scientific and technical information and business information, such as customer lists and business plans. As we will see throughout our study of IP law, the protection of compilations of elements that are themselves unprotectable is a major theme.

Courts have frequently held certain basic ideas or concepts incapable of protection as secrets because they were too well known to derive value from secrecy. *See Buffets, Inc. v. Klinke*, 73 F.3d 765 (9th Cir. 1996) (holding that the plaintiff could not claim its relatively straightforward recipes for barbecued chicken and macaroni and cheese as trade secrets); *Bimbo Bakeries USA v. Sycamore*, 39 F.4th 1250, 1259–64 (3d Cir. 2022) (finding bread recipe unprotectable because the individual elements were sufficiently obvious); *but cf. Camp Creek Hospitality Inns v. Sheraton Franchise Corp.*, 139 F.3d 1396 (11th Cir. 1997) (holding that a hotel could protect information about its prices, discounts, and occupancy levels as a trade secret where it was closely guarded information in the industry); *Nextdoor.com, Inc. v. Abhyanker*, 2013 WL 3802526 (N.D. Cal. July 19, 2013) (finding that the decision to test a new neighborhood-oriented social network in a particular neighborhood could be a trade secret where the plaintiff did substantial investigation to select the most appropriate neighborhood to launch the network).

3 *Novelty.* Courts have made it clear that trade secrets need not be entirely new to receive trade secret protection. The idea may have occurred to someone before; it may even be in use by another. But if it is not *generally known* or *readily ascertainable* to the competitors in an industry, it may still qualify for trade secret protection. One widely cited decision described the standard for protectable ideas as follows:

> [U]niqueness in the patent law sense is not an essential element of a trade secret, for the patent laws are designed to encourage invention, whereas trade secret law is designed to protect against a breach of faith. However, the trade secret must "possess at least that modicum of originality which will separate it from everyday knowledge." *Cataphote Corporation v. Hudson*, 444 F.2d 1313, 1315 (5th Cir. 1971). As stated in an authoritative treatise on this subject:

> As distinguished from a patent, a trade secret need not be essentially new, novel or unique; therefore, prior art is a less effective defense in a trade secret case than it is in a patent infringement case. The idea need not be complicated; it may be intrinsically simple and nevertheless qualify as a secret, unless it is in common knowledge and, therefore, within the public domain.

2 CALLMAN, UNFAIR COMPETITION, TRADEMARKS AND MONOPOLIES §52.1 (3d ed. 1968).

Forest Laboratories v. The Pillsbury Co., 425 F.2d 621, 624 (7th Cir. 1971). Some courts have gone even further, suggesting that "[a] trade secret may be no more than 'merely a mechanical improvement that a good mechanic can make.'" *SI Handling Systems, Inc. v. Heisley*, 753 F.2d 1244, 1256 (3d Cir. 1985). And information may not be generally known or even readily ascertainable to people in one industry even if it is well-known in a completely different field. *Masimo v. True Wearables*, 2022 WL 205485 (Fed. Cir. Jan. 24, 2022). By contrast, "[i]nformation in published patents or patent applications is readily ascertainable by proper means." *Olaplex Inc. v. L'Oreal USA*, 855 F. Appx. 701 (Fed. Cir. 2021).

Why not require novelty in order to protect a trade secret? That is, why should the law protect the "secrecy" of a piece of information if others have already discovered it?

4. Why should we bother to protect secrets that were stumbled upon with little or no investment in research but that happen to have "value"? Does the economic rationale for intellectual property suggest that such secrets will be underproduced absent protection?

5. Why is secrecy required at all? Trade secrets are not misappropriated unless information is taken by improper means or from a confidential relationship. Why aren't those tortious elements enough? It is certainly possible to envision a "misappropriation" tort that punishes diversion of information, whether or not it is secret. Indeed, some cases discussed in Chapter VI(B) and VI(C) have created just such a common law tort.

One possible objection to such a scheme is that it would chill the legitimate acquisition of information from competitors. But the only information protected by a misappropriation tort that is not also protected by trade secret law is public information. Since it is publicly available, the need for competitors to acquire it directly from another company or through dubious means is presumably low.[6]

But there may be a gray area between "secret" information and "public" information. If three large companies all use the same process but guard it closely, is it a

---

[6] Another reason for limiting common law protection to secret information may be concern over preemption of state common law by the federal intellectual property laws. Federal courts have generally held that state laws that create property rights in public information are preempted by the patent and copyright laws. There are two rationales for such preemption. First, federal laws reflect a judgment that unpatentable inventions ought to belong to the public. Second, preemption "channels" inventions into one or another form of protection. We focus on federal preemption in in Chapters II(H), III(K), and VI(A).

secret? If a company guards a process closely as a secret, but an account of the process is available in an obscure published source, does the company have a protectable trade secret?

6. *Known vs. Knowable.* Does it matter how obscure the published source is if the defendant in fact obtains the information from the plaintiff rather than going to the publicly available source? What theory of trade secrets would support a finding of liability in such a case?

Many courts following the RESTATEMENT OF TORTS took the view that if the defendant in fact got the information from the plaintiff, it must be a secret. Thus, in *Rohm & Haas Co. v. Adco Chemical Co.*, 689 F.2d 424 (3d Cir. 1982), defendant Harvey was a former Rohm & Haas employee who was hired by Adco to duplicate a process for producing "paint delivery vehicles," the chemicals added to paint that allow it to be applied to surfaces easily. There seems no question in the case that Harvey did, in fact, memorize the plaintiff's formula and take it to Adco. In their defense, the defendants offered evidence that a series of prior publications had, in fact, disclosed Rohm & Haas's process. The court nonetheless concluded that it was a protectable trade secret, in part because the defendants *did not in fact* obtain the information from those publications.

This view gives broad scope to trade secret protection, because it allows a plaintiff to protect information that could have been acquired properly but in fact was not. It also underscores the unfair competition rationale for trade secret protection—the problem is not that the defendant acquired the information, but the way in which the defendant acquired it.

In a significant break with the RESTATEMENT OF TORTS rule, the UTSA provides that information is not a trade secret if it is "generally known" or "readily ascertainable by proper means."[7] Under this view, once a secret is readily available through public sources, it loses all trade secret protection. At this point, the defendant is free to obtain the information from the public source *or from the plaintiff herself. See* RESTATEMENT (THIRD) OF UNFAIR COMPETITION §39, Comment *f*, at 433 ("When the information is readily ascertainable from such [public] sources, however, actual resort to the public domain is a formality that should not determine liability.").

Even jurisdictions that follow the RESTATEMENT OF TORTS view place limit what can qualify for trade secret protection. If information is generally known to the public, or even within a specialized industry, it does not qualify for protection. No company can claim that "$E=mc^2$" is a trade secret, for example, even if it keeps the formula under lock and key, and even if the defendant steals it from the company rather than obtaining it elsewhere. *See, e.g., Spring Indus. v. Nicolozakes*, 58 U.S.P.Q.2d 1794 (Ohio Ct. App.

---

[7] California, by contrast, treats ready ascertainability as a defense, not part of the plaintiff's case. *See* Cal. Civ. Code § 3426.1(d)(1); *ABBA Rubber Co. v. Seaquist*, 286 Cal. Rptr. 518 (Ct. App. 1991).

2000) (information on gravel mining not a trade secret despite efforts to keep it confidential). We consider the rather different issue of whether two parties could *agree* to treat the formula as a secret in Section D.

7. *Identification of Trade Secrets*. Because the definition of trade secrets is so broad and amorphous, courts typically require the plaintiff to identify the particular trade secrets as at issue. As the First Circuit explained:

> Most forms of intellectual property have boundaries that are defined before the commencement of litigation. . . . To be sure, there may be and often are disputes as to scope, but the outer bounds are defined in advance so that competitors can tailor their conduct accordingly. Trade secrets are different. There is no requirement of registration and, by definition, there is no public knowledge of the trade secret in advance of litigation. Even the defendant is not necessarily on notice of the trade secret before litigation. This raises the possibility that the trade secret owner will tailor the scope of the trade secret in litigation to conform to the litigation strategy.

TLS Mgmt & Mktng Serv. v. Rodríguez-Toledo, 966 F.3d 46, 51–52 (1st Cir. 2020).

Some states require trade secret plaintiffs to identify the secrets in question with specificity as part of the early case management. *See, e.g.*, CAL. CODE OF CIV. PRO. §2019.210 (requiring "the party alleging the misappropriation [to] identify the trade secret with reasonable particularity"); *SL Montevideo Tech., Inc. v. Eaton Aerospace, LLC*, 491 F.3d 350, 354 (8th Cir. 2007) (observing that "[s]imply to assert that a trade secret resides in some combination of otherwise known data is not sufficient, as the combination itself must be delineated with some particularity in establishing its trade secret status"); *Quintara Biosciences v. Ruifeng Biztech*, 2021 WL 2166880 (N.D. Cal. May 27, 2021) (requiring the trade secret claimants in a DTSA case to submit a statement identifying the particular trade secrets at issue). Courts have cautioned, however, that "identifying a trade secret is not intended to be a mini-trial on the merits but is instead a preliminary step before reaching the merits." *Brescia v. Angelin*, 172 Cal. App. 4th 135, 144 (Cal. Ct. App. 2009).

8. Mallet offered strong evidence that the defendants surreptitiously absconded with much of the knowledge that Mallet developed over decades of building its business, yet its failure to specifically identify the trade secrets barred effective relief. Is that result unfair? Are some trade secrets too broad and amorphous to garner effective protection? Does the court's concern for free competition justify its complete overturning of the preliminary injunction? Would Mallet have been better served by seeking an early trial on the merits rather than pursuing preliminary relief?

PROBLEMS

Problem II-1. Company *X* possesses a valuable piece of information about the process for making its product. That information is not known at all outside company *X*. Suppose *X* discloses the information to two companies, *A* and *B*. *A* receives the information in confidence, and subject to a written agreement that it will not use or disclose the information outside the bounds of the relationship. *B* receives the information without any restrictions whatever on its use. Does *X* have a protectable trade secret that it can assert against *A*? Against *B*? Against *C*, who steals the information from *X*'s computer network?

Does your answer change if *X*, *A*, *B*, and *C* are the only companies in the industry?

Problem II-2. StartUp, Inc., is the only participant in a new market. The market is based on a product for which StartUp has a non-exclusive license from the inventor; that is, StartUp cannot prevent others from obtaining a similar license. Nonetheless, StartUp has exhaustively researched the demand for the product, has concluded that a market exists, and has worked to stimulate demand. As a result, it has both "made" a market for the product and developed a comprehensive list of customers.

Thaddeus, a sales representative for StartUp, leaves to found his own company. He gets a license to make the product from its inventor. He takes with him from StartUp the customer list he worked with as an employee, his personal knowledge of and con- tacts with specific customers, and StartUp's knowledge of the market. StartUp sues Thaddeus for misappropriation of trade secrets. What result?

Problem II-3. Research Co. is a major pharmaceutical company working on a cure for certain types of cancer. Derek is a molecular biologist employed by Research. After several years on the job, Derek leaves Research for Conglomerate, Inc., another pharmaceutical company, which has decided to work on the same cancer cure. At the time Derek leaves, Research has not been successful in finding a cancer cure. However, as a result of his work at Research, Derek is able to help Conglomerate avoid several unproductive avenues of research. Aided in part by this knowledge, Conglomerate (using scientists other than Derek) develops a cancer cure before Research. Research sues Conglomerate, alleging misappropriation of trade secrets. Does Research have a case?

Problem II-4. The Church of True Belief is a religious group founded around a set of closely guarded scriptural materials supposedly handed down to Church's elders from Church's deity. After a bitter theological dispute, a group of adherents leaves the church to form the House of Absolute Belief. They take with them a copy of Church's confidential scriptures, which they rely on in gaining adherents and founding the new House. Church sues House for misappropriation of trade secrets.

At trial, the issue is whether the scriptures qualify as a trade secret. The evidence indicates that the scriptures had never before been removed from the confines of Church, that both Church and House are tax-exempt nonprofit organizations which rely on do-nations for their funding, and that Church (but not House) rations access to the scriptures in proportion to the size of an adherent's donation.

Can the scriptures qualify as a trade secret? Does your answer depend on whether the governing law is the UTSA, the RESTATEMENT OF TORTS, or the RESTATEMENT (THIRD) OF UNFAIR COMPETITION?

Problem II-5. Pear Computer Corporation, known for its obsessive secrecy, pass-word protects all its files. Can the password itself be a trade secret? Does it matter whether the UTSA or the Restatement applies?

2. Reasonable Efforts to Maintain Secrecy

Besides the existence of a trade secret, plaintiffs must show under the Uniform Act that they have taken "reasonable measures" to protect the secrecy of their idea. Cer-tainly, a plaintiff cannot publicly disclose the secret and still expect to protect it. But precautions must go further than that. Generally, they must include certain efforts to prevent theft or use of the idea by former employees.

Rockwell Graphic Systems, Inc. v. DEV Industries, Inc.
United States Court of Appeals for the Seventh Circuit
925 F.2d 174 (7th Cir. 1991)

POSNER, CIRCUIT JUDGE:

This is a suit for misappropriation of trade secrets. Rockwell Graphic Systems, a manufacturer of printing presses used by newspapers, and of parts for those presses, brought the suit against DEV Industries, a competing manufacturer, and against the president of DEV, who used to be employed by Rockwell. . . .

When we said that Rockwell manufactures both printing presses and replacement parts for its presses—"wear parts" or "piece parts," they are called—we were speaking approximately. Rockwell does not always manufacture the parts itself. Sometimes when an owner of one of Rockwell's presses needs a particular part, or when Rockwell antic-ipates demand for the part, it will subcontract the manufacture of it to an independent machine shop, called a "vendor" by the parties. When it does this it must give the vendor a "piece part drawing" indicating materials, dimensions, tolerances, and methods of manufacture. Without that information the vendor could not manufacture the part. Rock-well has not tried to patent the piece parts. It believes that the purchaser cannot, either by inspection or by "reverse engineering" (taking something apart in an effort to figure out how it was made), discover how to manufacture the part; to do that you need the piece part drawing, which contains much information concerning methods of manufacture, alloys, tolerances, etc. that cannot be gleaned from the part itself. So Rock-well tries—whether hard enough is the central issue in the case—to keep the piece part drawings secret, though not of course from the vendors; they could not manufacture the parts for Rockwell without the drawings. DEV points out that some of the parts are for presses that Rockwell no longer manufactures. But as long as the presses are in service—which can be a very long time—there is a demand for replacement parts.

Rockwell employed Fleck and Peloso in responsible positions that gave them access to piece part drawings. Fleck left Rockwell in 1975 and three years later joined DEV as its president. Peloso joined DEV the following year after being fired by Rockwell when a security guard caught him removing piece part drawings from Rockwell's plant. This suit was brought in 1984, and pretrial discovery by Rockwell turned up 600 piece part drawings in DEV's possession, of which 100 were Rockwell's. DEV claimed to have obtained them lawfully, either from customers of Rockwell or from Rockwell vendors, contrary to Rockwell's claim that either Fleck and Peloso stole them when they were employed by it or DEV obtained them in some other unlawful manner, perhaps from a vendor who violated his confidentiality agreement with Rockwell. Thus far in the litigation DEV has not been able to show which customers or vendors lawfully supplied it with Rockwell's piece part drawings.

The defendants persuaded the magistrate and the district judge that the piece part drawings weren't really trade secrets at all, because Rockwell made only perfunctory efforts to keep them secret. Not only were there thousands of drawings in the hands of the vendors; there were thousands more in the hands of owners of Rockwell presses, the customers for piece parts. The drawings held by customers, however, are not relevant. They are not piece part drawings, but assembly drawings. . . . An assembly drawing shows how the parts of a printing press fit together for installation and also how to integrate the press with the printer's other equipment. Whenever Rockwell sells a printing press it gives the buyer assembly drawings as well. These are the equivalent of instructions for assembling a piece of furniture. Rockwell does not claim that they contain trade secrets. It admits having supplied a few piece part drawings to customers, but they were piece part drawings of obsolete parts that Rockwell has no interest in manufacturing and of a safety device that was not part of the press as originally delivered but that its customers were clamoring for; more to the point, none of these drawings is among those that Rockwell claims DEV misappropriated.

. . . DEV's main argument is that Rockwell was impermissibly sloppy in its efforts to keep the piece part drawings secret.

On this, the critical, issue, the record shows the following. (Because summary judgment was granted to DEV, we must construe the facts as favorably to Rockwell as is reasonable to do.) Rockwell keeps all its engineering drawings, including both piece part and assembly drawings, in a vault. Access not only to the vault, but also to the building in which it is located, is limited to authorized employees who display identification. These are mainly engineers, of whom Rockwell employs 200. They are required to sign agreements not to disseminate the drawings, or disclose their contents, other than as authorized by the company. An authorized employee who needs a drawing must sign it out from the vault and return it when he has finished with it. But he is permitted to make copies, which he is to destroy when he no longer needs them in his work. The only outsiders allowed to see piece part drawings are the vendors (who are given copies, not originals). They too are required to sign confidentiality agreements, and in addition each drawing is stamped with a legend stating that it contains proprietary material. Vendors, like Rockwell's own engineers, are allowed to make copies for internal working purposes, and although the confidentiality agreement that they sign requires the vendor to return the drawing when the order has been filled, Rockwell does not enforce this requirement. The rationale for not enforcing it is that the vendor will need the drawing if Rockwell reorders the part. Rockwell even permits unsuccessful bidders for a piece part contract to keep the drawings, on the theory that the high bidder this round may be the low bidder the next. But it does consider the ethical standards of a machine shop before making it a vendor, and so far as appears no shop has ever abused the confidence reposed in it.

The mere fact that Rockwell gave piece part drawings to vendors—that is, disclosed its trade secrets to "a limited number of outsiders for a particular purpose"—did not forfeit trade secret protection. On the contrary, such disclosure, which is often necessary to the efficient exploitation of a trade secret, imposes a duty of confidentiality on the part of the person to whom the disclosure is made. But with 200 engineers checking out piece part drawings and making copies of them to work from, and numerous vendors receiving copies of piece part drawings and copying them, tens of thousands of copies of these drawings are floating around outside Rockwell's vault, and many of these outside the company altogether. Although the magistrate and the district judge based their conclusion that Rockwell had not made adequate efforts to maintain secrecy in part at least on the irrelevant fact that it took no efforts at all to keep its assembly drawings secret, DEV in defending the judgment that it obtained in the district court argues that Rockwell failed to take adequate measures to keep even the piece part drawings secret. Not only did Rockwell not limit copying of those drawings or insist that copies be returned; it did not segregate the piece part drawings from the assembly drawings and institute more secure procedures for the former. So Rockwell could have done more to maintain the confidentiality of its piece part drawings than it did, and we must decide whether its failure to do more was so plain a breach of the obligation of a trade secret owner to make reasonable efforts to maintain secrecy as to justify the entry of summary judgment for the defendants.

The requirement of reasonable efforts has both evidentiary and remedial significance . . .

[T]he plaintiff must prove that the defendant obtained the plaintiff's trade secret by a wrongful act, illustrated here by the alleged acts of Fleck and Peloso in removing piece part drawings from Rockwell's premises without authorization, in violation of their employment contracts and confidentiality agreements, and using them in competition with Rockwell. Rockwell is unable to prove directly that the 100 piece part drawings it got from DEV in discovery were stolen by Fleck and Peloso or obtained by other improper means. But if it can show that the probability that DEV could have obtained them otherwise—that is, without engaging in wrongdoing—is slight, then it will have taken a giant step toward proving what it must prove in order to recover under the first theory of trade secret protection. The greater the precautions that Rockwell took to maintain the secrecy of the piece part drawings, the lower the probability that DEV obtained them properly and the higher the probability that it obtained them through a wrongful act; the owner had taken pains to prevent them from being obtained otherwise.

. . . If Rockwell expended only paltry resources on preventing its piece part drawings from falling into the hands of competitors such as DEV, why should the law, whose machinery is far from costless, bother to provide Rockwell with a remedy? The information contained in the drawings cannot have been worth much if Rockwell did not think it worthwhile to make serious efforts to keep the information secret.

The remedial significance of such efforts lies in the fact that if the plaintiff has allowed his trade secret to fall into the public domain, he would enjoy a windfall if permitted to recover damages merely because the defendant took the secret from him, rather than from the public domain as it could have done with impunity. It would be like punishing a person for stealing property that he believes is owned by another but that actually is abandoned property. If it were true, as apparently it is not, that Rockwell had given the piece part drawings at issue to customers, and it had done so without requiring the customers to hold them in confidence, DEV could have obtained the drawings from the customers without committing any wrong. The harm to Rockwell would have been the same as if DEV had stolen the drawings from it, but it would have had no remedy, having parted with its rights to the trade secret. . . .

It is easy to understand therefore why the law of trade secrets requires a plaintiff to show that he took reasonable precautions to keep the secret a secret. If analogies are needed, one that springs to mind is the duty of the holder of a trademark to take reasonable efforts to police infringements of his mark, failing which the mark is likely to be deemed abandoned, or to become generic or descriptive (and in either event be unprotectable). The trademark owner who fails to police his mark both shows that he doesn't really value it very much and creates a situation in which an infringer may have been unaware that he was using a proprietary mark because the mark had drifted into the public domain, much as DEV contends Rockwell's piece part drawings have done.

But only in an extreme case can what is a "reasonable" precaution be determined on a motion for summary judgment, because the answer depends on a balancing of costs and benefits that will vary from case to case and so require estimation and measurement by persons knowledgeable in the particular field of endeavor involved. On the one hand, the more the owner of the trade secret spends on preventing the secret from leaking out, the more he demonstrates that the secret has real value deserving of legal protection, that he really was hurt as a result of the misappropriation of it, and that there really was misappropriation. On the other hand, the more he spends, the higher his costs. The costs can be indirect as well as direct. The more Rockwell restricts access to its drawings, either by its engineers or by the vendors, the harder it will be for either group to do the work expected of it. Suppose Rockwell forbids any copying of its drawings. Then a team of engineers would have to share a single drawing, perhaps by passing it around or by working in the same room, huddled over the drawing. And how would a vendor be able to make a piece part—would Rockwell have to bring all that work in house? Such reconfigurations of patterns of work and production are far from costless; and therefore perfect security is not optimum security.

There are contested factual issues here, bearing in mind that what is reasonable is itself a fact for purposes of Rule 56 of the civil rules. Obviously Rockwell took some precautions, both physical (the vault security, the security guards—one of whom apprehended Peloso in flagrante delicto) and contractual, to maintain the confidentiality of its piece part drawings. Obviously it could have taken more precautions. But at a cost, and the question is whether the additional benefit in security would have exceeded that cost. . . .

Reversed and remanded.

COMMENTS AND QUESTIONS

1. Contrast *Rockwell* with the Minnesota Supreme Court's decision in *Electro-Craft Corp. v. Controlled Motion, Inc.*, 332 N.W.2d 890 (Minn. 1983), a case that also involved information taken by former employees and used in starting a competing company. The court found that the information the employees took was not generally known or readily ascertainable in the industry. However, it found that the information did not constitute a trade secret:

(c) Reasonable efforts to maintain secrecy. It is this element upon which [plaintiff Electro-Craft Corp., or "ECC"]'s claim founders. The district court found that, even though ECC had no "meaningful security provisions," ECC showed an intention to keep its data and processes secret. This finding does not bear upon the statutory requirement that ECC use "efforts that are reasonable under the circumstances to maintain . . . secrecy." Minn. Stat. §325C.01, subd. 5(ii). . . . [E]ven under the common law, more than an "intention" was required—the plaintiff was required to show that it had manifested that intention by making some effort to keep the information secret.

This element of trade secret law does not require maintenance of absolute secrecy; only partial or qualified secrecy has been required under the common law. What is actually required is conduct which will allow a court acting in equity to enforce plaintiff's rights. . . .

In the present case, even viewing the evidence most favorably to the findings below, we hold that ECC did not meet its burden of proving that it used reasonable efforts to maintain secrecy as to [the subject matter of the suit, a product called the ECC 1125]. We acknowledge that ECC took minimal precautions in screening its Handbook and publications for confidential information and by requiring some of its employees to sign a confidentiality agreement, but these were not enough.

First, ECC's physical security measures did not demonstrate any effort to maintain secrecy. By "security" we mean the protection of information from discovery by outsiders. Security was lax in this case. For example, the main plant had a few guarded entrances, but seven unlocked entrances existed without signs warning of limited access. Employees were at one time required to wear badges, but that system was abandoned by the time of the events giving rise to this case. The same was generally true of the Amery, Wisconsin plant where ECC 1125 and brushless motors were manufactured. One sign was posted at each plant, however, marking the research and development lab at Hopkins and the machine shop at Amery as restricted to "authorized personnel." Discarded drawings and plans for motors were simply thrown away, not destroyed. Documents such as motor drawings were not kept in a central or locked location, although some design notebooks were kept locked.

The relaxed security by itself, however, does not preclude a finding of reasonable efforts by ECC to maintain secrecy. Other evidence did not indicate that industrial espionage is a major problem in the servo motor industry. There- fore, "security" measures may not have been needed, and the trial court could have found trade secrets if ECC had taken other reasonable measures to pre- serve secrecy.

However, ECC's "confidentiality" procedures were also fatally lax, and the district court was clearly in error in finding ECC's efforts to be reasonable. By "confidentiality" in this case we mean the procedures by which the employer signals to its employees and to others that certain information is secret and should not be disclosed. Confidentiality was important in this case, for testimony demonstrated that employees in the servo motor business frequently leave their employers in order to produce similar or identical devices for new employers. ECC has hired many employees from other corporations manufacturing similar products.[8] If ECC wanted to prevent its employees from doing the same thing, it had an obligation to inform its employees that certain information was secret.

ECC's efforts were especially inadequate because of the non-intuitive nature of ECC's claimed secrets here. The dimensions, etc., of ECC's motors are not trade secrets in as obvious a way as a "secret formula" might be. ECC should have let its employees know in no uncertain terms that those features were secret.

Instead, ECC treated its information as if it were not secret. None of its technical documents were marked "Confidential," and drawings, dimensions and parts were sent to customers and vendors without special marking. Employee access to documents was not restricted. ECC never issued a policy statement outlining what it considered secret. Many informal tours were given to

---

[8] One ECC employee actually prided himself on the information he had brought with him from his former employer. One day, just before that employee left ECC to join another company, the president of ECC found him copying documents after hours. ECC never questioned the employee or warned him or his new employer that certain information was confidential.

vendors and customers without warnings as to confidential information. Further, two plants each had an "open house" at which the public was invited to observe manufacturing processes. . . .

In summary, ECC has not met its burden of proof in establishing the existence of any trade secrets. The evidence does not show that ECC was ever consistent in treating the information here as secret.

Given that the information in question was not in fact known at all outside ECC, why shouldn't ECC be able to prevent its employees from using the information they acquired there? Should the laxity of ECC's precautions matter if no one other than the defendants, in fact, took advantage of it?

2. There is an intuitive relationship between the existence of a secret and reasonable efforts to protect a secret. After all, if something is not a secret, there would not seem to be any point to protecting it. And the fact that an idea is well protected may be evidence that it is, in fact, a secret. Nonetheless, the requirements are conceptually distinct. Information in the public domain cannot be turned into a secret merely by treating it as a secret. This distinction is made clear in the UTSA, which defines a trade secret as information that is both "not generally known" *and* the subject of reasonable efforts to maintain secrecy. UTSA §1(4).

Consider whether the opinion in *Rockwell* conflates these two into a single requirement. The court seems to emphasize the evidentiary significance of the precautions Rockwell took in proving misappropriation. Since it was clear (to the court, at least) that the DEV employees did, in fact, take the information from Rockwell, the court did not consider the precautions to be that important.

3. In *Rockwell,* the court apparently assumed that the manufacturer was in a confidential relationship with the subcontractors to which it sent drawings. Is it reasonable to assume that there was an implied confidential relationship in the absence of an express agreement? In *IMAX Corp. v. Cinema Technologies*, 152 F.3d 1161, 1169–70 (9th Cir. 1998), the court reversed a grant of summary judgment in favor of a company that had gained access to IMAX's technology through an IMAX theater operator who had entered into an agreement to keep IMAX's technology confidential. By contrast, the court in *Entertainment Research Group v. Genesis Creative Group*, 122 F.3d 1211, 1227–28 (9th Cir. 1997), found no confidential relationship existed between a manufacturer of inflatable costumes and the marketing firm hired to distribute them where the plaintiff had marketed the costumes—and hence disclosed the designs—prior to the defendants' entering into a confidential disclosure agreement. Can you reconcile these decisions?

4. How much effort should be required of trade secret owners? Obviously, the best way to protect a secret is not to tell anyone at all. In the modern commercial world, however, this is normally impractical. Companies with trade secrets must tell the secret to their employees, their business partners, and often their distributors and customers as well. But the risk of *inadvertent* use or disclosure can be reduced in a number of ways: for example, by requiring employees, licensees, and even customers to sign

confidentiality agreements; by investing in physical security measures against theft, such as fences, safes, and guards; and by designing products themselves so that they do not reveal their secrets upon casual (or even detailed) inspection. The First Circuit has held that "affirmative steps" to protect secrecy, not merely "ordinary discretion," are required. *Incase Inc. v. Timex Corp.*, 488 F.3d 46 (1st Cir. 2007).

5. Will reasonable precautions always be a question of fact? Or are certain activities (publishing a secret formula, for example) so inconsistent with trade secret protection that they automatically preclude a successful trade secret suit? *See* Section B(3) (discussing disclosure of trade secrets).

6. If the idea is to encourage investment in trade secrets, why require any degree of "reasonable precautions" at all? One sometimes hears in this regard that *all* "fencing" expenditures are inefficient. *Cf.* Edmund W. Kitch, *The Law and Economics of Rights in Valuable Information*, 9 J. LEGAL STUD. 683 (1980) (arguing that reasonable precautions make sense only as evidence of the existence of a trade secret). Why not simply require explicit notice—large neon signs, stamps on all documents, or publication of a secrecy policy—in place of physical precautions? For a suggestion that proceeds along these lines to some extent, *see* J.H. Reichman, *Legal Hybrids Between the Patent and Copyright Paradigms*, 94 COLUM. L. REV. 2432 (1994).

Are prospective trade secret thieves actually encouraged by the reasonable precautions argument to steal ideas when they observe a lapse in security, and does this rule give them an incentive to search out such lapses? Professor Kitch asks the related question of why these expenses should be required in addition to the expense of bringing a trade secret lawsuit. Some scholars contend that a trade secret cause of action which yields a legal remedy ought to be available when it is cheaper than the physical precautions that would be necessary to protect a piece of information. *See* David Friedman, William Landes & Richard Posner, *Some Economics of Trade Secret Law*, 5 J. ECON. PERSPECTIVES 61, 67 (1991). They note further that where "the social costs of enforcing secrecy through the legal system would be high, the benefits of shared information are likely to exceed the net benefits of legal protection."

What value is there in a legal rule that requires investment in precautions up to the level that would be rational in the absence of the legal rule? Should it be a defense to a trade secret action that the plaintiff could more easily have protected the secret through physical precautions?

Professor Kitch notes by way of analogy that we do not prohibit criminal complaints for larceny just because a property owner was careless. (On the other hand, many states reduce recovery in tort suits for "comparative negligence.") He also suggests that reasonable precautions are required only to put prospective infringers on notice about the existence of a right and to serve as evidence of the fact that the secret is worth protecting legally. The fencing thus serves a notice function, akin to "marking" products with patent numbers, copyright symbols, or trademark symbols. Kitch, *supra*, at 698.

The Court in *duPont & Co. v. Christopher*, 431 F.2d 1012 (5th Cir. 1970), pays significant attention to the role of fencing costs in trade secrets suits. We will return to that case when we consider misappropriation of trade secrets. *See* Section C.

One might imagine other rationales for requiring reasonable protection. For example, one might treat the requirement of reasonable precautions as serving a gatekeeper function that helps to weed out frivolous trade secret claims by requiring evidence of investment by the plaintiff in protecting the secret.

PROBLEMS

Problem II-6. Smith, a bar owner in rural Alabama, develops by accident one night the relatively simple formula for a new alcoholic beverage. The drink is simply a mixture of three common ingredients. Smith begins selling the drink, which he calls "Mobile Mud," in his bar. However, he instructs his bartenders not to reveal the formula to anyone and has them premix "Mud" in the back of the bar, out of sight of customers. Smith is outraged when he learns that Jimmy Dean, an international distributor of alcoholic beverages, has copied his formula and is marketing it under a different name. At trial, Dean employees and independent experts unanimously testify that it is possible for someone with experience in the beverage industry to determine the formula for Mud by looking at, smelling and tasting the drink.

Has Smith taken reasonable precautions? What more could he have done to protect the "secret formula" of Mobile Mud? Is the secret so obvious to consumers that selling the product on the open market destroys protection? Does your opinion of the case change if you learn that Dean's representative went to Smith's bar and bribed a bartender to disclose the formula?

Problem II-7. MidContinent is a small manufacturer of signs and decals. It has only five employees, two of whom are father and son and two more of whom are family friends. The company describes itself as having a "relaxed, congenial" working atmosphere. In order to avoid what the president considers excessive formality, the employees have never been required to sign confidentiality agreements, and documents kept within the company aren't stamped confidential. The company has never conducted "exit interviews" or instructed its employees about trade secrecy. According to the company president, "we trust our employees, and that trust has never been misplaced." On the other hand, the company does take certain steps to keep outsiders from accessing its customer lists and its adhesive manufacturing process. And there is little history of economic espionage in the decal-manufacturing business. Has MidContinent taken reasonable efforts to protect its secrets? Should it matter whether the party accused of stealing those secrets is an employee or an outsider?

3.   Disclosure of Trade Secrets

It is axiomatic that public disclosure of a trade secret destroys the "secret," and therefore ends protection. The corollary to this rule is that as long as a trade secret remains secret, it is protectable. Thus, trade secrets do not last for a specific term of years but continue indefinitely until the occurrence of a particular event—the public disclosure of the secret. Disclosure of a once-protected trade secret can occur in several ways:

i.   *Voluntary Disclosure by the Trade Secret Owner*

When a trade secret owner publishes the secret, whether in an academic journal or any other public forum, secrecy is lost so long as he publication is accessible to those interested in the subject matter. This loss might reasonably be considered a substantial disincentive to publication of scientific or technical advances. But publication of secret information regularly occurs, either because inventors have not thought through the consequences of their actions or because the value or prestige of first publication is deemed to outweigh the potential loss of commercial trade secret protection.

One common form of disclosure is the publication of an issued patent. Because (as we shall see) patent law requires the public disclosure of an invention with sufficient specificity to enable one of ordinary skill in the art to make it, obtaining a patent on an invention destroys trade secret protection. *See Tewari De-Ox Sys. v. Mountain States*, 637 F.3d 604 (5th Cir. 2011); *Ferroline Corp. v. General Aniline & Film Corp.*, 207 F.2d 912 (7th Cir. 1953). Thus, an inventor must "elect" either patent or trade secret protection, for the two cannot protect the same invention simultaneously.

The Federal Circuit applied a notable exception to this seemingly absolute rule in *Rhone-Poulenc Agro v. DeKalb Genetics Corp.*, 272 F.3d 1335 (Fed. Cir. 2001). In that case, the defendant had stolen the plaintiff's trade secrets and published them in its own patent application. The court concluded that the trade secret owner never had the opportunity to "elect" to give up trade secret protection, and so ruled that the publication of the defendant's patent had not disclosed plaintiff's trade secrets. This result seems equitable to the inventor. But does it really comport with the principle that information must be secret to be protected? For a contrary rule, *see Evans v. General Motors*, 125 F.3d 1448 (Fed. Cir. 1997) (holding that publication by a thief started the one-year clock running for patenting an invention, and reasoning that because the trade secret owner knew of the theft he could have acted to seek patent protection within a reasonable time period).

What about patent applications? Until 1999, patent applications were kept secret by the U.S. Patent Office unless and until the patent issued. If a patent application was not actively prosecuted, or if the patent did not issue, it was declared abandoned by the Patent Office. *See* 37 C.F.R. §1.114 (1995). Abandoned applications were not available to the public. In fact, the application itself was destroyed after 20 years.

In 1999, Congress changed U.S. law to require that some (but not all) patent applications be published after 18 months. *See* 35 U.S.C. §122. Since it takes approximately three years on average for a patent to issue, many applicants face an election not between patent and trade secret protection, but between the *prospect* of future patent protection and trade secret protection.

The notion of an "election" between trade secret and patent protection assumes that the patent application actually describes all the details of an invention. For more on this issue—known as the "enablement" requirement in patent law—*see* 35 U.S.C. §112, discussed in Chapter III(B)(4)(i). Some firms pursue patent protection in a way that withholds valuable know-how from the public. *See* Peter S. Menell & Michael J. Meurer, *Notice Failure and Notice Externalities*, 5 J. LEGAL ANALYSIS 1, 32–34 (2013) (noting that the quality of patent disclosure varies widely); HENRY PETROSKI, THE PENCIL 114–15 (1990) (describing how the family of Henry David Thoreau kept its pencil-making technology secret rather than disclose it by obtaining a patent). For example, in *Life Spine, Inc. v. Aegis Spine, Inc.*, 8 F.4th 531 (7th Cir. 2021), the court held that plaintiff had a protectable trade secret in the exact dimensions of a patented spinal implant device because the patent did not disclose those dimensions.

ii. *Distributing a Product that Embodies the Trade Secret to the Public*

Selling or distributing a product embodying a trade secret to the public may jeopardize the secret if the secret becomes readily accessible. As one court explained, both the RESTATEMENT OF TORTS and the UTSA "necessarily compel the conclusion that a trade secret is protectable only so long as it is kept secret by the party creating it. If a so-called trade secret is fully disclosed by the products produced by use of the secret then the right to protection is lost." *Vacco Indus. v. Van den Berg*, 6 Cal. Rptr. 2d 602, 611 (Ct. App. 1992) (citations omitted). Further, disclosure may occur even without sale of the product itself, if the secret is disclosed freely and without restriction during the manufacturing or development processes.

However, sales of a product to the public do not necessarily disclose a trade secret simply because the product embodies the trade secret. Rather, the question is whether the secret is apparent from the product. Secrets that are apparent to the buyers of a product are disclosed by the product, but secrets contained in undecipherable form within the product (such as object code in a computer program) are considered secret even when the product is sold.

In *Data General Corp. v. Digital Computer Controls, Inc.*, 297 A.2d 433 (Del. Ct. Ch. 1971), *aff'd*, 297 A.2d 437 (Del. S. Ct. 1972), Data General sold mainframe computers (the Nova 1200) to sophisticated business customers. Data General supplied logic drawings along with the computer to any customers who requested this information so as to enable them to repair or customize them. Digital Computer Controls acquired a Nova 1200 on the open market along with the design drawings. When it launched a business repairing and maintaining Data General Nova 1200 computers, Data General sued for misappropriation of the secrets reflected in the design drawings. The court held that Data General had not forfeited secrecy merely by selling the computers:

> Defendants insist, however, that plaintiff has not maintained that degree of secrecy which will preserve its right to relief, either by publicly selling an article

alleged to contain a trade secret, or by failing to restrict access to the design drawings for its device, arguing that matters of common knowledge in an industry may not be claimed as trade secrets.

It has been recognized in similar cases that even though an unpatented article, device or machine has been sold to the public, and is therefore subject to examination and copying by anyone, the manner of making the article, device or machine may yet constitute a trade secret until such a copy has in fact been made, *Schulenburg v. Signatrol, Inc.*, 33 Ill. 2d 379, 212 N.E.2d 865, and *Tabor v. Hoffman*, N.Y., 118 N.Y. 30, 23 N.E. 12.

Defendants contend, however, that the issuance by plaintiff of copies of design drawings to its customers was made without safeguards designed properly to maintain the secrecy requisite to the existence of a trade secret. In other words, it is contended that plaintiff's attempts to maintain secrecy merely consisted of (1) not giving copies of the design drawings to those customers who did not need them for maintenance of their computer, (2) obtaining agreements not to disclose the information from those customers who were given copies of the drawings, and (3) printing a legend on the drawings which contained the allegedly confidential information which identified the drawing as proprietary information, the use of which was restricted. Plaintiff argues, however, that disclosure of the design drawings to purchasers of the computer is necessary properly to maintain its device, that such disclosure was required by the very nature of the machine, and that reasonable steps were taken to preserve the secrecy of the material released. I conclude at this preliminary stage of the case that it cannot be held as a matter of law that such precautions were inadequate, a factual dispute as to the adequacy of such precautions having clearly been raised. Defendants' motion for summary judgment must accordingly be denied.

Id.

Selling products that embody a secret may or may not disclose the secret. Whether it does so depends on how easy it is to discern the secret from the product. Coca-Cola can protect its secret formula even while selling millions of cans of Coke so long as buyers cannot tell what's in it. *See Data General Corp. v. Grumman Systems Support Corp.*, 825 F. Supp. 340, 359 (D. Mass. 1993) ("Even those who obtained MV/ADEX and were able to *use* MV/ADEX were unable to discover its trade secrets because MV/ADEX was distributed only in its object code form, which is essentially unintelligible to humans."). By contrast, the inventor of the wheel can't protect the idea that it is round once the world can see that for themselves. As we shall see, however, customers who buy a product on the open market are entitled to break it apart to see how it works. This process is called "reverse engineering" the product. Trade secret law does not protect owners against legitimate purchasers who discover the secret through reverse engineering, absent a valid nondisclosure agreement. But while the person who does the reverse engineering is free to do what they want with the secret they discovered, the possibility that a product might be reverse engineered does not automatically foreclose *any* trade secret protection, even against people who have not actually reverse engineered the product.

Of what relevance is the motivation behind the disclosure of a secret? Recall that in *Metallurgical Industries,* the court found the fact that Metallurgical had disclosed its secrets only for profit to weigh in favor of trade secret status. Why should this be the case? On the one hand, licensing is evidence that a secret has value and is worth protecting. On the other hand, one could argue that the fact that a secret holder has sold its information for profit suggests that it is not trying to keep this information secret at all but rather is attempting to profit from its disclosure. Which of these arguments you find persuasive may depend on your view of the reasons for trade secret protection.

iii. *Public Disclosure by a Third Party*

Trade secrets may be publicly disclosed (through publication or the sale of a product) by someone other than the trade secret owner. Commonly, this occurs when someone other than the trade secret owner has independently developed or discovered the secret. Call the first trade secret "owner" *A,* and the independent developer *B. A* has no control over what *B* does with her independent discovery; if she chooses to publish the secret, she defeats not only her rights to trade secret protection, but *A*'s rights as well. Suppose *B* did not develop the secret independently of *A* but in fact stole it from *A.* What happens if *B* publishes the secret? Can *A* still protect it? If so, what happens to *C,* who began using the secret after reading *B*'s publication? This issue was addressed in *Religious Technology Center v. Lerma*, 908 F. Supp. 1362 (E.D. Va. 1995). In that case, the Church of Scientology sued (among others) the Washington Post, which had quoted from part of its confidential scriptures. The court concluded that the fact that the scriptures were posted on a Usenet newsgroup for ten days defeated any claim of trade secrecy:

> [For ten days, the documents] remained potentially available to the millions of Internet users around the world.

> As other courts who have dealt with similar issues have observed, "posting works to the Internet makes them generally known" at least to the relevant people interested in the newsgroup. Once a trade secret is posted on the Internet, it is effectively part of the public domain, impossible to retrieve. Although the person who originally posted a trade secret on the Internet may be liable for trade secret misappropriation, the party who merely downloads Internet information cannot be liable for misappropriation because there is no misconduct involved in interacting with the Internet.

908 F. Supp. at 1368; *accord American Red Cross v. Palm Beach Blood Bank Inc.*, 143 F.3d 1407 (11th Cir. 1998) (Red Cross donor list lost trade secret status because it was posted on a publicly accessible computer bulletin board). *But see Silicon Image Inc. v. Analogix Semiconductor Inc.*, 2008 WL 166950 (N.D. Cal. Jan. 17, 2008) (presence of

information on the Internet does not destroy secrecy absent evidence that competitors knew about it).

Should the obscurity of the Web site matter? What if it is not indexed in a search engine? In *DVD Copy Control Ass'n v. Bunner*, 116 Cal. App. 4th 241, 10 Cal. Rptr. 3d 185 (Ct. App. 2004), the court found disclosure of a secret on the Internet only because it was "quickly and widely republished to an eager audience," and cautioned that it did not assume that the secrets were lost merely because they were put on the Internet.

Because of the risk of loss of trade secrecy through Internet posting, companies have been more aggressive in suing individuals who post information they consider confidential. *See O'Grady v. Superior Court*, 44 Cal. Rptr. 3d 72 (Ct. App. 2006); *Ford v. Lane*, 67 F. Supp. 2d 745 (E.D. Mich. 1999). In some of these cases, notably *O'Grady*, the company knows only that the information has been disclosed, and not who has done so. Do such lawsuits present First Amendment issues? Several defendants have asserted that they were reporting legitimate news. *See* Franklin B. Goldberg, Ford Motor Co. v. Lane, 16 BERKELEY TECH. L.J. 271 (2001). And *O'Grady* held that bloggers who disclosed Apple's trade secrets were entitled to First Amendment protection as reporters, so their identity could not be disclosed by subpoena.

For an argument that disclosure on the Internet should not destroy a secret irrevocably, *see* Elizabeth A. Rowe, *Introducing a Takedown for Trade Secrets on the Internet*, 2007 WIS. L. REV. 1042; Elizabeth A. Rowe, *Saving Trade Secret Disclosures on the Internet Through Sequential Preservation*, 42 WAKE FOREST L. REV. 1 (2007).

iv. *Inadvertent Disclosure*

Trade secrets may be disclosed inadvertently (for example, by being left on a train or elsewhere in public view). While the case law on this issue is sparse, it seems reasonable to argue that a truly accidental disclosure should not defeat trade secret protection if reasonable precautions have been taken. On the other hand, if the inadvertent disclosure is widespread, it would seem unfair (as well as impracticable) to require the public as a whole to "give back" the secret. Note that §1(2)(ii)(C) of the Uniform Trade Secrets Act provides that it is misappropriation for someone to disclose a secret that they have reason to know has been acquired "by accident or mistake." THE RESTATEMENT (THIRD) OF UNFAIR COMPETITION §40(b)(4) takes the same position, "unless the [acci- dental] acquisition was the result of the [trade secret owner]'s failure to take reasonable precautions to maintain the secrecy of the information." *See also Williams v. Curtis-Wright Corp.*, 681 F.2d 161 (3d Cir. 1982) (user of secrets disclosed by mistake was liable for misappropriation because he had constructive notice of the secrecy of the information). But in *DVD Copy Control Ass'n v. Bunner*, 116 Cal. App. 4th 241, 10 Cal. Rptr. 3d 185 (Ct. App. 2004), the court rejected the idea that "once the information became *publicly* available everyone else would be liable under the trade secret laws simply because they knew about its unethical origins." "This," the court said, "is not what trade secret law is designed to do."

v. *Government Disclosure*

Government agencies sometimes require the disclosure of trade secrets by private parties in order to serve some other social purpose. *See Corn Products Refining Co. v. Eddy*, 249 U.S. 427 (1919) (requiring a food manufacturer to label its product with an accurate list of ingredients). Health and environmental concerns are a very common reason for the government to require disclosure of product contents. For example, the Federal Insecticide, Fungicide and Rodenticide Act (FIFRA), 7 U.S.C. §§136 et seq., requires disclosure of the contents of pesticides as well as a great deal of other information. FIFRA makes two concessions to trade secret protection, however. First, it limits public disclosure of information concerning manufacturing processes and inert (as opposed to active) contents. Second, it provides for compensation to be paid to the inventors of trade secrets which the government appropriates by public disclosure. *See also Ruckelshaus v. Monsanto Co.*, 467 U.S. 986 (1984) (holding that a federal requirement that private parties disclose trade secrets may constitute a taking under the Fifth Amendment); *Philip Morris Inc. v. Reilly*, 312 F.3d 24 (1st Cir. 2002) (en banc) (holding that a Massachusetts law requiring labeling of cigarette ingredients was a taking of tobacco companies' trade secrets); *but see* Amy Kapczynski, *The Public History of Trade Secrets*, 55 U.C. DAVIS L. REV. 1367, 1431–35 (2022) (discussing "forgotten" cases upholding state statutes requiring the disclosure of the ingredients of "patent medicines"—proprietary nonprescription elixirs that were not the subject of utility patents and often had questionable medical benefits—and fertilizers); *cf. Lyft, Inc. v. City of Seattle*, 418 P.3d 102, 105 (Wash. 2018) (finding plaintiffs' zip code information likely a trade secret, but determining that it should be disclosed to the public under state Public Records Act; court did not consider the takings issue).

COMMENTS AND QUESTIONS

1. The plaintiff in *Data General* sold over 500 Nova computers to the general public. Data General provided any buyer who requested the "confidential" design drawings with a copy. Why are these drawings still considered secret? Does widespread disclosure compromise the secrecy claim at some point, even though all disclosures are made under an agreement of confidentiality? This issue often arises in the software industry. As computers have become ubiquitous, the numbers of "secret" programs in circulation may be counted in the millions rather than the hundreds. *Data General* implicitly concludes that even a relatively widespread disclosure to customers does not compromise the secrecy of the computer design. For cases addressing this issue in the context of computer software, compare *Management Science of America v. Cyborg Sys., Inc.*, 1977-1 Trade Cas. (CCH) ¶61,472 (N.D. Ill. 1977) (holding that distribution of 600 copies of a program under a confidentiality agreement did not destroy secrecy) with *Young Dental Mfg. Co. v. Q3 Special Prods., Inc.*, 891 F. Supp. 1345 (E.D. Mo. 1995) (characterizing as "completely frivolous" plaintiff's claim that its publicly sold software was a trade secret).

A closely related question involves attempts by the owners of information to "contract around" the requirement of secrecy. If the parties agree to treat a piece of information as secret, is the licensee bound not to use or disclose the information under contract principles regardless of whether or not it is in fact in the public domain? This issue is a recurring one in intellectual property law, and a problem that has never adequately been addressed. Under what circumstances does the sale of a commercial product embodying a trade secret destroy the secret? Is the answer different for a commercially available product produced by a secret manufacturing process? In this regard, computer software may present a special case. While a particular computer program may be widely distributed, in fact all that is sold to the consumer is a disk containing object code. Object code is virtually impossible for humans to read without machine assistance.[9] Because of this, computer software is in some sense unlike a physical product whose design is evident to the casual observer. Even after it is publicly distributed, object code is meaningless to the casual observer. Only a complex process of reverse engineering (sometimes called "disassembly" or "decompilation") can enable the user to decipher the source code that was originally written for the program.

Should it matter that a computer program is distributed only in object code form? Consider the following case, in which the defendant was accused of misappropriating a computer program in object code form:

> The source code can and does qualify as a trade secret. . . .

> Whether the object code is a trade secret is a more difficult question.[7] Atkinson first contends that the object code cannot be a trade secret because it does not derive independent economic value from its secrecy, and therefore fails the first definitional requirement of a trade secret. This argument has no merit. Trandes generates most of its revenues by providing computer services. . . . Armed with a copy of the object code, an individual would have the means to offer much the same engineering services as Trandes. . .

> Atkinson next argues that the object code cannot be a trade secret because Trandes did not keep it secret   Atkinson asserts that the Tunnel System has been widely disclosed as a mass-marketed product and that its existence and its abilities are not secret. [The court concluded that the object code remained secret because it had only been distributed to two customers, and both of them signed licenses agreeing to keep the program a secret.]

---

[9] It is possible to "reverse engineer" object code in some cases to create a kind of rough estimate of what must have been in the original source code. The process, however, is demanding and time consuming even for expert programmers.

[7] This case presents an unusual set of facts. In the ordinary case, the owner of trade secret computer software will maintain the secrecy of the source code but freely distribute the object code. *See, e.g., Q-Co Indus. v. Hoffman*, 625 F. Supp. 608, 617 (S.D.N.Y. 1985) (program secret where source code secret, even though object code not secret). In such cases, the owner of the software cannot claim trade secret protection for the object code because its disclosure to the public destroyed its secrecy. In this case, however, Trandes maintained the secrecy of the source code and the object code, as we explain below.

Trandes Corp. v. Guy F. Atkinson Co., 996 F.2d 655, 663–64 (4th Cir. 1993). Consider the court's footnote. Can object code be a trade secret if it can easily be duplicated (whether or not the copier understands what he is copying)? Is the plaintiff in this case really trying to leverage copyright protection out of a trade secret claim? In many cases, the alleged trade secret at issue is not the source or object code of the computer program itself but certain high-level design features of the program (its "architecture"). *See Integrated Cash Management Services, Inc. v. Digital Transactions, Inc.*, 920 F.2d 171, 173 (2d Cir. 1990). Suppose that, rather than using what they had learned of the architecture of the program while employed by the company, ICM's former employees had copied the object code of the program altogether. (Leave aside for a moment questions of copyright infringement, and consider only the trade secret issue.) Would they be liable for misappropriating the trade secrets contained in the program architecture on the grounds that copying the program in its entirety necessarily copied the architecture? Or would the fact that the object code was publicly disclosed protect them from liability? *See Silvaco Data Sys. v. Intel Corp.*, 109 Cal. Rptr. 3d 27 (Cal. Ct. App. 2010) (holding that one "does not, by executing machine-readable software, 'use' the underlying source code; nor does one acquire the requisite knowledge of any trade secrets embodied in that code."); *Beacon Wireless Solutions Inc. v. Garmin Int'l*, 894 F. Supp. 2d 727 (W.D. Va. 2012). How would the courts in *Trandes* and the *Data General* cases answer this question? Does the answer suggest a problem with relying on trade secrecy to protect computer programs?

2. To what extent does the incorporation of a secret in a public governmental record preclude trade secret protection? *See Frazee v. U.S. Forest Service*, 97 F.3d 367 (9th Cir. 1996) (information was not a trade secret because it could be obtained from the government under the Freedom of Information Act); *Weygand v. CBS, Inc.*, 43 U.S.P.Q.2d 1120 (C.D. Cal. 1997) (depositing a work with the U.S. Copyright Office destroys trade secrecy).

3. Can a trade secret ever be abandoned by its owner through non-use? For an argument that unused secrets should be treated as abandoned, allowing others to use them, see Camilla Hrdy & Mark A. Lemley, *Abandoning Trade Secrets*, 73 STAN. L. REV. 1 (2021).

C. MISAPPROPRIATION OF TRADE SECRETS

Not all uses of another's trade secrets constitute misappropriation. Acquisition or use of a trade secret is illegal only in two basic situations: where it is done through improper means, or where it involves a breach of confidence. UTSA § 1; RESTATEMENT (THIRD) OF UNFAIR COMPETITION § 40.

1. Improper Means

 E. I. du Pont deNemours & Co. v. Christopher
United States Court of Appeals for the Fifth Circuit
431 F.2d 1012 (5th Cir. 1970)

GOLDBERG, CIRCUIT JUDGE:

This is a case of industrial espionage in which an airplane is the cloak and a camera the dagger. The defendants-appellants, Rolfe and Gary Christopher, are photographers in Beaumont, Texas. The Christophers were hired by an unknown third party to take aerial photographs of new construction at the Beaumont plant of E.I. duPont deNemours & Company, Inc. Sixteen photographs of the DuPont facility were taken from the air on March 19, 1969, and these photographs were later developed and delivered to the third party.

DuPont employees apparently noticed the airplane on March 19 and immediately began an investigation to determine why the craft was circling over the plant. By that afternoon the investigation had disclosed that the craft was involved in a photographic expedition and that the Christophers were the photographers. DuPont contacted the Christophers that same afternoon and asked them to reveal the name of the person or corporation requesting the photographs. The Christophers refused to disclose this information, giving as their reason the client's desire to remain anonymous.

Having reached a dead end in the investigation, DuPont subsequently filed suit against the Christophers, alleging that the Christophers had wrongfully obtained photographs revealing DuPont's trade secrets which they then sold to the undisclosed third party. DuPont contended that it had developed a highly secret but unpatented process for producing methanol, a process which gave DuPont a competitive advantage over other producers. This process, DuPont alleged, was a trade secret developed after much expensive and time-consuming research, and a secret which the company had taken special precautions to safeguard. The area photographed by the Christophers was the plant designed to produce methanol by this secret process, and because the plant was still under construction parts of the process were exposed to view from directly above the construction area. Photographs of that area, DuPont alleged, would enable a skilled person to deduce the secret process for making methanol. DuPont thus contended that the Christophers had wrongfully appropriated DuPont trade secrets by taking the photographs and delivering them to the undisclosed third party. In its suit DuPont asked for damages to cover the loss it had already sustained as a result of the wrongful disclosure of the trade secret and sought temporary and permanent injunctions prohibiting any further circulation of the photographs already taken and prohibiting any additional photographing of the methanol plant. . . .

. . . [T]he Christophers argue that for an appropriation of trade secrets to be wrongful there must be a trespass, other illegal conduct, or breach of a confidential relationship. We disagree.

It is true, as the Christophers assert, that the previous trade secret cases have contained one or more of these elements. However, we do not think that the Texas courts would limit the trade secret protection exclusively to these elements. On the contrary, in *Hyde Corporation v. Huffines*, 1958, 158 Tex. 566, 314 S.W.2d 763, the Texas Supreme Court specifically adopted the rule found in the Restatement of Torts which provides:

> One who discloses or uses another's trade secret, without a privilege to do so, is liable to the other if
>
> > (a) he discovered the secret by improper means, or
> >
> > (b) his disclosure or use constitutes a breach of confidence reposed in him by the other in disclosing the secret to him. . . .

RESTATEMENT OF TORTS §757 (1939). Thus, although the previous cases have dealt with a breach of a confidential relationship, a trespass, or other illegal conduct, the rule is much broader than the cases heretofore encountered. Not limiting itself to specific wrongs, Texas adopted subsection (a) of the RESTATEMENT which recognizes a cause of action for the discovery of a trade secret by any "improper" means. . . .

The question remaining, therefore, is whether aerial photography of plant construction is an improper means of obtaining another's trade secret. We conclude that it is and that the Texas courts would so hold. The Supreme Court of that state has declared that "the undoubted tendency of the law has been to recognize and enforce higher standards of commercial morality in the business world." *Hyde Corporation v. Huffines, supra,* 314 S.W.2d at 773. That court has quoted with approval articles indicating that the proper means of gaining possession of a competitor's secret process is "through inspection and analysis" of the product in order to create a duplicate. *K & G Tool & Service Co. v. G & G Fishing Tool Service,* 1958, 158 Tex. 594, 314 S.W.2d 782, 783, 788. Later another Texas court explained:

> The means by which the discovery is made may be obvious, and the experimentation leading from known factors to presently unknown results may be simple and lying in the public domain. But these facts do not destroy the value of the discovery and will not advantage a competitor who by unfair means obtains the knowledge without paying the price expended by the discoverer.

Brown v. Fowler, Tex. Civ. App. 1958, 316 S.W.2d 111, 114, *writ ref'd n.r.e.*

We think, therefore, that the Texas rule is clear. One may use his competitor's secret process if he discovers the process by reverse engineering applied to the finished product; one may use a competitor's process if he discovers it by his own independent research; but one may not avoid these labors by taking the process from the discoverer without his permission at a time when he is taking reasonable precautions to maintain its secrecy. To obtain knowledge of a process without spending the time and money to discover it independently is improper unless the holder voluntarily discloses it or fails to take reasonable precautions to ensure its secrecy.

In the instant case the Christophers deliberately flew over the DuPont plant to get pictures of a process which DuPont had attempted to keep secret. The Christophers delivered their pictures to a third party who was certainly aware of the means by which they had been acquired and who may be planning to use the information contained therein to manufacture methanol by the DuPont process. The third party has a right to use this process only if he obtains this knowledge through his own research efforts, but thus far all information indicates that the third party has gained this knowledge solely by taking it from DuPont at a time when DuPont was making reasonable efforts to preserve its secrecy. In such a situation DuPont has a valid cause of action to prohibit the Christophers from improperly discovering its trade secret and to prohibit the undisclosed third party from using the improperly obtained information.

We note that this view is in perfect accord with the position taken by the authors of the RESTATEMENT. In commenting on improper means of discovery the savants of the RESTATEMENT said:

> *f. Improper means of discovery.* The discovery of another's trade secret by improper means subjects the actor to liability independently of the harm to the interest in the secret. Thus, if one uses physical force to take a secret formula from another's pocket, or breaks into another's office to steal the formula, his conduct is wrongful and subjects him to liability apart from the rule stated in this Section. Such conduct is also an improper means of procuring the secret under this rule. But means may be improper under this rule even though they do not cause any other harm than that to the interest in the trade secret. Examples of such means are fraudulent misrepresentations to induce disclosure, tapping of telephone wires, eavesdropping or other espionage. A complete catalogue of improper means is not possible. In general they are means which fall below the generally accepted standards of commercial morality and reasonable conduct.

RESTATEMENT OF TORTS §757, Comment *f* at 10 (1939).

In taking this position we realize that industrial espionage of the sort here perpetrated has become a popular sport in some segments of our industrial community. However, our devotion to free-wheeling industrial competition must not force us into accepting the law of the jungle as the standard of morality expected in our commercial relations. Our tolerance of the espionage game must cease when the protections required to prevent another's spying cost so much that the spirit of inventiveness is dampened.

Commercial privacy must be protected from espionage which could not have been reasonably anticipated or prevented. We do not mean to imply, however, that everything not in plain view is within the protected vale, nor that all information obtained through every extra optical extension is forbidden. Indeed, for our industrial competition to remain healthy there must be breathing room for observing a competing industrialist. A competitor can and must shop his competition for pricing and examine his products for quality, components, and methods of manufacture. Perhaps ordinary fences and roofs must be built to shut out incursive eyes, but we need not require the discoverer of a trade secret to guard against the unanticipated, the undetectable, or the unpreventable methods of espionage now available.

In the instant case DuPont was in the midst of constructing a plant. Although after construction the finished plant would have protected much of the process from view, during the period of construction the trade secret was exposed to view from the air. To require DuPont to put a roof over the unfinished plant to guard its secret would impose an enormous expense to prevent nothing more than a school boy's trick. We introduce here no new or radical ethic since our ethos has never given moral sanction to piracy. The market place must not deviate far from our mores. We should not require a person or corporation to take unreasonable precautions to prevent another from doing that which he ought not do in the first place. Reasonable precautions against predatory eyes we may require, but an impenetrable fortress is an unreasonable requirement, and we are not disposed to burden industrial inventors with such a duty in order to protect the fruits of their efforts. "Improper" will always be a word of many nuances, determined by time, place, and circumstances. We therefore need not proclaim a catalogue of commercial improprieties. Clearly, however, one of its commandments does say "thou shall not appropriate a trade secret through deviousness under circumstances in which countervailing defenses are not reasonably available." . . .

COMMENTS AND QUESTIONS

1. Improper means has a substantial basis in other torts. *See* Comment *f* to THE RESTATEMENT, cited in *duPont,* and the RESTATEMENT (THIRD) OF UNFAIR COMPETITION §43 (defining improper means as including "theft, fraud, unauthorized interception of communications, inducement of or knowing participation in a breach of confidence, and other means either wrongful in themselves or wrongful under the circumstances of the case.").

DuPont provides an example of conduct prohibited by trade secret law that is probably not otherwise tortious. Should otherwise legitimate conduct be prohibited because it will disclose a trade secret? As Judge Posner noted in *Rockwell,* misappropriation of trade secrets is largely redundant if it does not reach any further than other torts. Nonetheless, the reach of the case is troubling. Consider the last sentence of the *duPont* opinion. What is wrong with "deviousness"? And why should "countervailing defenses" enter the picture?

2. There is general agreement that "reverse engineering"—that is, legally obtaining a product and taking it apart to see how it works—is not a misappropriation of a trade secret Is reverse engineering (which is legal) any less devious than aerial photography? While it may be easy to reverse engineer a product, reverse engineering manufacturing processes can be especially difficult. Are there realistic alternatives to the sort of espionage condemned in *duPont* for those who seek to understand a process? Should there be some legally protected way of discovering a competitor's process?

3. Note how the decision in *duPont* dovetails with the discussion of precautions in II(B)(2). DuPont could have protected itself against aerial photography by building a roof over its plant area before beginning internal construction. The Fifth Circuit rejected this alternative because it would "impose an enormous expense to prevent nothing more than a school boy's trick." On the other hand, the courts are clearly willing to put duPont to *some* expense to protect its secrets from prying eyes. If duPont had allowed its engineers to leave copies of the plant blueprints on subways, the result of the case might be very different.

How much expense is duPont required to incur to protect itself? The uniform answer of the courts is that only "reasonable" precautions must be taken. While this is not a terribly helpful answer, it may be a fairly practical one in any given industry, where companies can protect themselves by taking those precautions that are customary in that industry.

On the other hand, consider the Second Circuit's statement in *Franke v. Wiltschek*, 209 F.2d 493, 495 (2d Cir. 1953):

> It matters not that the defendants could have gained their knowledge from a study of the expired patent and plaintiff's publicly marketed product. The fact is they did not. Instead they gained it from plaintiffs via their confidential relationship, and in doing so incurred a duty not to use it to plaintiff's detriment. This duty they have breached.

Is this consistent with the UTSA?

4. An interesting case involving only circumstantial evidence of misappropriation is *Pioneer Hi-Bred International v. Holden Foundation Seeds, Inc.*, 35 F.3d 1226, 31 U.S.P.Q.2d 1385 (8th Cir. 1994). Plaintiff Pioneer could not establish a specific act of misappropriation, but it did show (through the use of three sophisticated scientific tests) that it was highly unlikely that defendant's hybrid seeds had been developed independently of plaintiff's seeds. Instead, due to genetic similarities, Pioneer showed that it was much more likely that those seeds were "derived from" a popular Pioneer hybrid. Pioneer was found to have maintained reasonable measures to guard against disclosure, including putting experimental seeds in bags marked with a secret code, allowing seeds to be grown only under strict nondisclosure arrangements, and leaving unmarked the fields in which the seeds had been planted. Pioneer was awarded $46.7 million in damages.

By contrast, the Fourth Circuit in *Othentec Ltd. v. Phelan*, 526 F.3d 135 (4th Cir. 2008), made it clear that speculation of theft based on the defendant's speed in entering the market was not enough. The court required "actual objective evidence" of misappropriation.

5. When does someone "acquire" a trade secret? The issue sometimes arises when an employee leaves an employer with trade secrets in its possession and starts work at a new company. The employee obtained the secrets lawfully. Is continuing to possess them a misappropriation? Has the new employer acquired the secrets by hiring the employee? *See Six Dimensions, Inc. v. Perficient, Inc.*, 969 F.3d 219 (5th Cir. 2020) (company never acquired trade secrets where new employee possessed the secrets but never communicated them to the new employer). Using or disclosing the secrets, by contrast, would be unlawful, as we will see in the next section.

6. Can it ever be improper to obtain information in public view? In *Compulife Software, Inc. v. Newman*, 959 F.3d 1288 (11th Cir. 2020), the Eleventh Circuit held that the defendant could be liable for using a bot to scrape the data from plaintiff's website for price information, sending millions of queries to receive price quotes. While the public was free to access the site to get price quotes, the court nonetheless concluded that the aggregation of the price information on the site was still a secret and that sending automated requests was improper.

PROBLEMS

Problem II-8. Suppose that, at trial in the *duPont* case, the Christophers proved that they could have discovered the secrets contained in the layout of the duPont plant by careful viewing of images available on Google Earth. Are the Christophers then relieved from liability for misappropriation of trade secrets? Would your answer change if they had in fact obtained the photos by sneaking onto the duPont property on the ground?

Problem II-9. Prior to baseball games, catchers and pitchers agree on a set of hand signal codes that the catcher will use to coordinate pitch type—e.g., fast ball, curve ball, slider, change up—and location. During the game, catchers propose pitches using these signals. Pitchers nod in the affirmative when then agree, and then deliver the pitches.

With the advent of replay and other video technologies, Major League Baseball issued a series of memoranda warning teams that they may not use electronic equipment to communicate with each other during games, especially for the purpose of stealing signs.

During the 2017 season, the Houston Astros implemented video surveillance equipment to learn competing teams' signs. The technology quite possibly contributed to the Astros success in beating the Los Angeles Dodgers in the World Series. Suppose that the Los Angeles Dodgers sued the Astros for trade secret misappropriation. At trial, the Astros contended that catcher-pitcher hand signals are not trade secrets. Furthermore, the Astros introduced former Major League players and coaches who testified that sign stealing has long been considered part of baseball. A baseball historian stated that "sign stealing was something of an art form which is tolerated, even admired." How should court rule?

2. Confidential Relationship

The most common allegation of trade secret misappropriation involves breach of a confidential relationship. *See* David S. Almeling et al., *A Statistical Analysis of Trade Secret Litigation in State Courts*, 46 GONZ. L. REV. 57, 59 (2011) (reporting that 93 percent of all trade secret cases are between parties who know each other). The RE-STATEMENT (THIRD) OF UNFAIR COMPETITION §41 explains that a confidential relationship is established in the following circumstances:

(a) the person made an express promise of confidentiality prior to the disclosure of the trade secret; or

(b) the trade secret was disclosed to the person under circumstances in which the relationship between the parties to the disclosure or the other facts surrounding the disclosure justify the conclusions that, at the time of the disclosure,

(1) the person knew or had reason to know that the disclosure was intended to be in confidence, and

(2) the other party to the disclosure was reasonable in inferring that the person consented to an obligation of confidentiality.

Smith v. Dravo Corp.
United States Court of Appeals for the Seventh Circuit
203 F.2d 369 (7th Cir. 1953)

LINDLEY, J.

Plaintiffs appeal from a judgment for defendant entered at the close of a trial by the court without a jury. The complaint is in four counts: 1 and 2 charge an unlawful appropriation by defendant of plaintiffs' trade secrets relating to the design and construction and selling and leasing of freight containers; 3 and 4 aver infringement of plaintiffs' patents Nos. 2,457,841 and 2,457,842. . . .

In the early 1940s Leathem D. Smith, now deceased, began toying with an idea which, he believed, would greatly facilitate the ship and shore handling and transportation of cargoes. As he was primarily engaged in the shipbuilding business, it was quite natural that his thinking was chiefly concerned with water transportation and dock handling. Nevertheless his overall plan encompassed rail shipping as well. He envisioned construction of ships especially designed to carry their cargo in uniformly sized steel freight containers. These devices (which, it appears, were the crux of his idea) were: equipped with high doors at one end; large enough for a man to enter easily; weather and pilfer proof; and bore collapsible legs, which (1) served to lock them (a) to the deck of the ship by fitting into recesses in the deck, or (b) to each other, when stacked, by reason of receiving sockets located in the upper four corners of each container, and (2) allowed sufficient clearance between deck and container or container and container for the facile insertion of a fork of a lift tractor, and (3) were equipped with lifting eyelets, which, together with a specially designed hoist, made possible placement of the containers upon or removal from a ship, railroad car or truck, while filled with cargo. The outer dimensions of the devices were such that they would fit compactly in standard gauge North American railroad cars, or narrow gauge South American trains, and in the holds of most water vessels.

[At the end of World War II, Smith's company—Safeway Containers—had some success building and selling such containers.]

On June 23, 1946, Smith died in a sailing accident. The need for cash for inheritance tax purposes prompted his estate to survey his holdings for disposable assets. It was decided that the container business should be sold. Devices in process were completed but no work on new ones was started.

Defendant was interested in the Safeway container, primarily, it appears, for use by its subsidiary, the Union Barge Lines. In October 1946 it contacted Agwilines [one of Smith's customers] seeking information. It watched a loading operation in which Agwilines used the box. At approximately the same time, defendant approached the ship-building company and inquired as to the possibility of purchase of a number of the containers. It was told to communicate with Cowan, plaintiffs' eastern representative. This it did, and, on October 29, 1946, in Pittsburgh, Cowan met with defendant's officials to discuss the proposed sale of [containers]. But, as negotiations progressed, defendant demonstrated an interest in the entire container development. Thus, what started as a meeting to discuss the purchase of individual containers ended in the possible foundation for a sale of the entire business.

Based upon this display of interest, Cowan sent detailed information to defendant concerning the business. This included: (1) patent applications for both the "knock-down" and "rigid" crates; (2) blue prints of both designs; (3) a miniature Safeway container; (4) letters of inquiry from possible users; (5) further correspondence with prospective users. In addition, defendant's representatives journeyed to Sturgeon Bay, Wisconsin, the home of the shipbuilding company, and viewed the physical plant, inventory and manufacturing operation.

Plaintiffs quoted a price of $150,000 plus a royalty of $10 per unit. This was rejected. Subsequent offers of $100,000 and $75,000 with royalties of $10 per container were also rejected. Negotiations continued until January 30, 1947, at which time defendant finally rejected plaintiffs' offer.

On January 31, 1947 defendant announced to Agwilines that it "intended to design and produce a shipping container of the widest possible utility" for "coastal steamship application . . . [and] use . . . on the inland rivers and . . . connecting highway and rail carriers." Development of the project moved rapidly, so that by February 5, 1947 defendant had set up a stock order for a freight container which was designed, by use of plaintiffs' patent applications, so as to avoid any claim of infringement. One differing feature was the use of skids and recesses running the length of the container, rather than legs and sockets as employed in plaintiffs' design. However, Agwilines rejected this design, insisting on an adaptation of plaintiffs' idea. In short defendant's final product incorporated many, if not all, of the features of plaintiffs' design. So conceived, it was accepted by the trade to the extent that, by March 1948, defendant had sold some 500 containers. Many of these sales were made to firms who had shown considerable prior interest in plaintiffs' design and had been included in the prospective users disclosed to defendant.

One particular feature of defendant's container differed from plaintiffs: its width was four inches less. As a result plaintiffs' product became obsolete. Their container could not be used interchangeably with defendant's; they ceased production. Consequently the prospects of disposing of the entire operation vanished.

The foregoing is the essence of plaintiffs' cause of action. Stripped of surplusage, the averment is that defendant obtained, through a confidential relationship, knowledge of plaintiffs' secret designs, plans and prospective customers, and then wrongfully breached that confidence by using the information to its own advantage and plaintiffs' detriment.

[The court found that, notwithstanding certain disclosures of information during the operation of Safeway, plaintiffs' information about how to design its containers remained a trade secret.]

(3) Was Defendant in a Position of Trust and Confidence at the Time of the Disclosure?

Mr. Justice Holmes once said that the existence of the confidential relationship is the "starting point" in a cause of action such as this. *E.I. DuPont de Nemours Powder Co. v. Masland*, 244 U.S. 100, 102 [1917]. While we take a slightly different tack, there is no doubt as to the importance of this element of plaintiffs' case.

Certain it is that a non-confidential disclosure will not supply the basis for a law suit. Plaintiffs' information is afforded protection because it is secret. Promiscuous disclosures quite naturally destroy the secrecy and the corresponding protection. But this is not true where a confidence has been reposed carrying with it communication of an idea.

It is clear that no express promise of trust was exacted from defendant. There is, however, the further question of whether one was implied from the relationship of the parties. Pennsylvania has not provided us with a decision precisely in point but *Pressed Steel Car Co. v. Standard Car Co.*, 210 Pa. 464, 60 A. 4, furnishes abundant guideposts. There plaintiff delivered its blue prints to customers in order that they might acquaint themselves more thoroughly with the railroad cars they were purchasing; from these customers, defendant obtained the drawings. In holding that the customers held the plans as a result of a confidence reposed in them by plaintiff, and that the confidence was breached by delivery of the blue prints to defendant, the court said, 60 A. at page 10: "While there was no expressed restriction placed on the ownership of the prints, or any expressed limitation as to the use to which they were to be put, it is clear . . . that the purpose for which they were delivered by the plaintiff was understood by all parties   "

The quoted language is applicable and determinative. Here plaintiffs disclosed their design for one purpose, to enable defendant to appraise it with a view in mind of purchasing the business. There can be no question that defendant knew and understood this limited purpose. Trust was reposed in it by plaintiffs that the information thus transmitted would be accepted subject to that limitation. "[T]he first thing to be made sure of is that the defendant shall not fraudulently abuse the trust reposed in him. It is the usual incident of confidential relations. If there is any disadvantage in the fact that he knew the plaintiffs' secrets, he must take the burden with the good." *E.I. DuPont de Nemours Powder Co. v. Masland*, 244 U.S. 100,102.

Nor is it an adequate answer for defendant to say that the transactions with plaintiffs were at arm's length. So, too, were the overall dealings between plaintiffs and defendants in *Booth v. Stutz Motor Car Co.*, 7 Cir., 56 F.2d 962; *Allen-Qualley Co. v. Shellmar Products Co.*, D.C., 31 F.2d 293, affirmed, 7 Cir., 36 F.2d 623 and *Schavoir v. American Rebonded Leather Co.*, 104 Conn. 472, 133 A. 582. That fact does not detract from the conclusion that but for those very transactions defendant would not have learned, from plaintiffs, of the container design. The implied limitation on the use to be made of the information had its roots in the "arms-length" transaction.

(4) The Improper Use by Defendant of the Secret Information

Defendant's own evidence discloses that it did not begin to design its container until after it had access to plaintiffs' plans. Defendant's engineers admittedly referred to plaintiffs' patent applications, as they said, to avoid infringement. It is not disputed that, at the urging of Agwilines, defendant revised its proposed design to incorporate the folding leg and socket principles of plaintiffs' containers. These evidentiary facts, together with the striking similarity between defendant's and plaintiffs' finished product, were more than enough to convict defendant of the improper use of the structural information obtained from plaintiffs.

COMMENTS AND QUESTIONS

1. Since the shipping containers were available on the open market, couldn't Dravo have argued that they were not a trade secret? Did Smith's agent, Cowan, disclose anything that was *not* readily apparent from inspection of the containers? For more on the history of containerization, *see* MARC LEVINSON, THE BOX: HOW THE SHIPPING CONTAINER MADE THE WORLD SMALLER AND THE WORLD ECONOMY BIGGER (2008) (mentioning Dravo Corporation container as early precursor of containerization).

2. In *Van Prods. Co. v. General Welding & Fabricating Co.*, 213 A.2d 769, 779–80 (Pa. 1965), the Pennsylvania Supreme Court criticized *Smith* for focusing on the existence of a confidential relationship to the exclusion of whether there was a trade secret at all. The court said: "The starting point in every case of this sort is not whether there was a confidential relationship, but whether, in fact, there was a trade secret to be misappropriated." But where there is a secret, a company that receives the secret in a business negotiation and then uses it without paying is guilty of misappropriating that secret. *See Altavion Inc. v. Konica Minolta Sys. Lab. Inc.*, 171 Cal. Rptr. 3d 714 (Cal. Ct. App. 2014).

3. Compare *Smith v. Dravo* with *Omnitech Int'l v. Clorox Co.*, 29 U.S.P.Q.2d 1665 (5th Cir. 1994), where the court held that it was not an actionable "use" of a trade secret for the defendant to *evaluate* it in the course of trying to decide whether to (a) acquire the company or (b) take a license to use the trade secret. A finding of no liability here makes sense, because it allows the potential licensee to make an informed judgment and therefore promotes efficient licensing. But how far does it extend? Is the potential licensee entitled to replicate the research or build models in an effort to evaluate it? Are there special limits that should be placed on companies engaged in a "make or buy" decision—that is, who are considering *either* licensing the plaintiff's technology *or* entering the market themselves?

Smith and *Omnitech* both involved disclosures in the course of licensing negotiations. Cases such as these form part of the amorphous law of "precontractual liability." *See* E. Allen Farnsworth, *Precontractual Liability and Preliminary Agreements: Fair Dealing and Failed Negotiations*, 87 COLUM. L. REV. 217 (1987). Both the *Smith* and *Omnitech* cases present the problem of Arrow's Information Paradox. What the plaintiff has to sell to the defendant is information that is valuable only because it is secret. If there is no legal protection and if the plaintiff discloses the secret to the defendant, its value will be lost. But the defendant cannot be expected to pay for information unless it can see the information to determine its value. Thus, absent some form of legal protection for confidential disclosures, sale or licensing of trade secrets may not occur. Note that this problem does not arise in other areas of intellectual property, such as patent law, since the inventions being licensed are already publicly disclosed.

5. The court in *Bateman v. Mnemonics, Inc.*, 79 F.3d 1532 (11th Cir. 1996), indicated that it was "wary" of trade secret claims based on implied confidential relationships because such claims were subject to abuse. The court rejected Bateman's allegation that such a relationship existed because Bateman had not "made it clear to the parties involved that there was an expectation and obligation of confidentiality." Thus, the court seemed to create a standard of actual knowledge on the part of the recipient of confidential information that the discloser of such information intended the disclosure to be confidential. At the other extreme, the Fifth Circuit in *Phillips v. Frey*, 20 F.3d 623, 631–32 (5th Cir. 1994) found an implied confidential relationship to exist in the course of negotiations over the sale of a business despite the fact that the disclosing party never even requested that the information remain confidential.

Which approach makes more sense? Who is in the best position to clarify the question, the discloser or the recipient?

Is there any way for a potential licensee to prevent the formation of a confidential relationship in such a situation?

6. The defendant in *Smith* actually sold a device that was not identical to the plaintiff's. Under what circumstances can a defendant be liable for misappropriation without literally copying the trade secret? In *Mangren Res. & Dev. Corp. v. National Chem. Co.*, 87 F.3d 1339 (7th Cir. 1996), the court defined improper "use" broadly, stating that "the user of another's trade secret is liable even if he uses it with modifications or improvements upon it effected by his own efforts, so long as the substance of the process used by the actor is derived from the other's secret   If trade secret law were not flexible enough to encompass modified or even new products that are substantially derived from the trade secrets of another, the protections that the law provides would be hollow indeed." To similar effect as *Mangren* is *Texas Tanks Inc. v. Owens-Corning Fiberglas Corp.*, 99 F.3d 740 (5th Cir. 1997). In *Texas Tanks,* the Fifth Circuit held that any improper "exercise of control and domination" over a secret constituted a commercial use of that secret. It rejected the defendant's argument that it could not be liable for taking a secret unless the secret was actually incorporated in a commercial product. The court noted that Owens Corning's awareness of the secret would likely influence the development of its own competing product, and that this was enough to demonstrate improper "use" of the secret. And in *Collelo v. Geographic Servs., Inc.*, 283 Va. 56 (2012), the Virginia Supreme Court held that a party could be liable for trade secret misappropriation even though it did not compete with the plaintiff so long as the plaintiff could show injury. *See* Mark A. Lemley, *The Fruit of the Poisonous Tree in IP Law*, 103 IOWA L. REV. 245, 250–53 (2017).

7. *Use of a Trade Secret Without Consent.* There are three ways to establish misappropriation under the DTSA: improper acquisition, disclosure, or use of a trade secret without consent. 18 U.S.C. §1839(5). In *Oakwood Laboratories LLC v. Thanoo*, 999 F.3d 892 (3d Cir. 2021), the Third Circuit construed the DTSA expansively, as covering

> any exploitation of the trade secret that is likely to result in injury to the trade secret owner or enrichment to the defendant[.]   Thus, marketing goods that embody the trade secret, employing the trade secret in manufacturing or production, relying on the trade secret to assist or accelerate research or development, or soliciting customers through the use of information that is a trade secret . . . all constitute 'use.'"

Based on this broad definition, the court overturned the district court's dismissal of a trade secret complaint for failure to state a cause of action on the ground that the plaintiff had not sufficiently alleged use of a trade secret. The Third Circuit faulted the district court for requiring that Oakwood explain how defendants used the trade secrets and equating "use" of a trade secret with "replication" of the trade secret process or technology. It was sufficient Oakwood to allege that Dr. Thanoo—who had served for an extensive period as the Oakwood's Vice President of Product Development during the time that it developed a costly, labor-intensive, two-decade long bioequivalent research project—joined a company that developed a comparable project in just a few years. While there was no direct allegation that the defendants used any of plaintiff's secrets, the court held that use could be inferred from the circumstances. Taking the allegations of the complaint as true, the Third Circuit noted that "use" of Oakwood's trade secret information could readily be understood from the timing of Dr. Thanoo's employment with the competitor Aurobindo, Dr. Thanoo's deception in informing Oakwood about the work he would engage in at Aurobindo, Aurobindo's lack of experience in the highly specialized field of microsphere technology, Aurobindo's access to Oakwood's trade secret information, its rapid success in developing four microsphere products, and the comparatively insignificant financial investment Aurobindo put into that development.

The Third Circuit also faulted the district court for holding that Oakwood had not adequately pled harm: "Defendants have not launched any products . . . Oakwood has not yet suffered any harm from missed partnerships or investment opportunities." The Third Circuit ruled that "trade secret misappropriation is harm. *See* 18 U.S.C. §§1839(3), (5)."

8. *Accident or Mistake.* In a high-profile incident, an Apple employee left an early prototype of the new iPhone in a bar, where it was found by a reporter. Is the reporter free to write about the new prototype? Would it matter if it was found by a competitor? *See* Greg Sandoval & Declan McCullagh, *Apple Loses Another Unreleased iPhone (exclusive)*, CNET (Aug, 31, 2011) (noting that California imposes liability for theft upon any person who finds lost and appropriates property if the person knows who the owner is likely to be).

The UTSA extends liability to anyone who uses or discloses a trade secret that they knew or should have known was acquired by "accident or mistake."

PROBLEMS

Problem II-10. Solomon, a regular customer of ToolCo's products, comes up with an idea for a new tool. He sends the idea to ToolCo, suggesting that they manufacture it. ToolCo does in fact produce and sell the new tool. Is Solomon entitled to compensation for ToolCo's use of his idea? Does it make any difference if (1) ToolCo actively solicited the idea from Solomon? (2) Solomon sent the suggestion to ToolCo along with a letter saying he wanted to open negotiations over a possible licensing arrangement to use the idea? (3) ToolCo has in the past had an informal, unwritten policy of compensating inventors who submit good ideas?

Problem II-11. VenCo, a venture capitalist in the business of financing start-up companies, investigates TechCo in an effort to decide whether or not to finance it. To aid in its investigation, VenCo asks for and receives confidential information about TechCo's products and *market* position. VenCo eventually decides not to finance

TechCo because of concerns about its management, but it does finance a start-up competitor of TechCo in the same field. Are VenCo or the start-up liable to TechCo? What obligations, if any, does VenCo undertake as a result of its exposure to TechCo's secrets?

Problem II-12. Falcon Systems employs Kotva as a sales representative. In the course of her work for Falcon, Kotva comes into contact with a large number of actual and potential customers. Some are leads provided by Falcon, while others she develops on her own. To manage her connections, she uses LinkedIn, which allows people to record and build business connections. Kotva uses LinkedIn for all her connections, business as well as personal.

When Kotva leaves Falcon to take a job with a competitor, Falcon argues that her LinkedIn "connections" are effectively a customer list and belong to the company. They insist that she delete her LinkedIn account, or alternatively eliminate any job-related contacts from the site. How should the court rule?

D. PROPER MEANS AND IMMUNITY

Although the UTSA does not contain any express exceptions to trade secret liability, the definition of misappropriation requires the trade secret owner to prove that the defendant acquired the trade secret by improper means. Independent discovery or reverse engineering are not improper. Thus, to the extent that a defendant can show that it reverse engineered or independently developed trade secret information, it can avoid liability. *See Raytheon Co. v. Indigo Sys. Corp.*, 895 F.3d 1333 (Fed. Cir. 2018) (crediting evidence of independent invention by a former employee after he left plaintiff's employ). The DTSA expressly provides that reverse engineering and independent invention are not improper means of acquiring a trade secret. DTSA 18 U.S.C. §1839(6)(B).

Furthermore, courts have long recognized that trade secret protection can "implicate the interest in freedom of expression or advance another significant public interest." *See* RESTATEMENT (THIRD) OF UNFAIR COMPETITION, §40, comment *c*. The DTSA expressly immunizes whistleblowers—those who disclose trade secrets to the government or an attorney for purposes of reporting or investigating suspected illegal activity—from trade secret liability.

1. Independent Discovery and Reverse Engineering

Not all use or disclosure of a trade secret is actionable misappropriation. Rather, as the commissioners who drafted the Uniform Trade Secrets Act noted, there are several categories of "proper means" of obtaining a trade secret. These "proper means" do not directly deny the existence of a trade secret or the defendant's use of that secret. Rather, they are *legitimate* uses of trade secrets by a competitor.

UTSA Comment to §1 explains that:

One of the broadly stated policies behind trade secret law is "the maintenance of standards of commercial ethics." THE RESTATEMENT OF TORTS, Section 757,

Comment (f), notes: "A complete catalogue of improper means is not possible," but Section 1(1) includes a partial listing.

Proper means include:

1. Discovery by independent invention;

2. Discovery by "reverse engineering," that is, by starting with the known product and working backward to find the method by which it was developed. The acquisition of the known product must, of course, also be by a fair and honest means, such as purchase of the item on the open market, for reverse engineering to be lawful;

3. Discovery under a license from the owner of the trade secret;

4. Observation of the item in public use or on public display;

5. Obtaining the trade secret from published literature.

See also RESTATEMENT (THIRD) OF UNFAIR COMPETITION §43 ("Independent discovery and analysis of publicly available products or information are not improper means of acquisition.").

Kadant, Inc. v. Seeley Machine, Inc.
United States District Court for the Northern District of New York
244 F. Supp. 2d 19 (N.D.N.Y. 2003)

HURD, DISTRICT JUDGE.

. . .

II.　Facts

Kadant is a publicly traded corporation with yearly sales eclipsing $100 million. Kadant AES ("AES") is a division of Kadant located in Queensbury, New York. For twenty-eight years, AES has manufactured and sold to customers worldwide products that clean and condition papermaking machines and filter water used in the papermaking process. "There are three main products areas of the business of AES: shower and spray devices and nozzles; foil blades to remove water from the paper during the papermaking process; and structures that hold foils and filters for straining water utilized in the papermaking process so that it can be reused." . . . Plaintiff occupies a dominant place in the national papermaking market.

Corlew was hired by AES in July of 1995 as a machinist. Nearly three years later, in April of 1998, he was promoted to a position in the engineering department. In that capacity, Corlew would be provided with a refined customer order, made by an AES engineer and a customer, and it was his job to create a "manufacturing drawing (with instructions and a bill of materials—i.e., the 'recipe') for the order." In order to create such a drawing, Corlew used a computer assisted drawing machine. The computer assisted drawing machine contained "the recipes for the AES products and generate[d] drawings and bills of materials." Plaintiff contends that AES took steps to protect the secrecy of the information contained in the computer assisted drawing machine. In June of 1999, Corlew was promoted again and now had the responsibility to assist the engineers in designing customer orders. Corlew was terminated in the summer of 2001.

During his tenure at AES, Corlew had access to plaintiff's "recipes" ("design specifications") for its products and to plaintiff's computerized database of prospective customers, which includes "names, addresses, and e-mails for all potential customers in the papermaking industry, including the names of individuals key to these companies' purchasing orders." Plaintiff contends that one of Corlew's final assignments while at AES was to coordinate this database with the database containing information on all current AES customers and their purchasing histories. Corlew had access to AES's entire computer system, which apparently included both databases as well as the computer assisted drawing machine containing the design specifications. At the end of his employment, Corlew's access to AES's computer system was terminated, and his laptop was wiped clean of AES information, and/or access thereto. Throughout his employment with AES, Corlew was subject to a signed confidentiality agreement, in which he agreed not to disclose or use to his benefit any confidential information, including information about AES customers.

. . .

Near the end of April of 2002, Corlew began working for Seeley, "developing and marketing a new line of Seeley products for sale to the pulp and papermaking industry." According to defendants, "[t]he products comprising this new line were reverse-engineered from existing products, freely available in the public domain and unprotected by published patent applications, in-force patents or trade secrets." According to plaintiff, the only way defendants could have developed and put out for sale this new line of products in so short of time is not by reverse engineering, which it alleges is time consuming, expensive, and requiring technical skill, but by Corlew's theft of AES's trade secrets—its design specifications and the customer databases—and infringement of its trademark.

Specifically, claims plaintiff, using as a frame of reference defendants' own expert, it would take defendants 1.7 years to reverse engineer all of plaintiff's nozzles. Defendants maintain, however, that only a small fraction, not all, of plaintiff's products were reverse engineered. The parties also dispute how much time would be associated with the manufacturing process. . . .

III. Discussion

Plaintiff has moved for preliminary injunctive relief pursuant to Fed. R. Civ. P. 52(a). . . .

In order for plaintiff to successfully move for a preliminary injunction, it must demonstrate: 1) a likelihood of irreparable harm if the injunction is not granted; and 2) either a likelihood of success on the merits of its claims, or the existence of serious questions going to the merits of its claims plus a balance of the hardships tipping decidedly in its favor. *Bery v. City of New York*, 97 F.3d 689, 693–94 (2d Cir. 1996). Because the issuance of a preliminary injunction is a drastic remedy, plaintiff is required to make a "clear showing" of these requirements. *See Mazurek v. Armstrong*, 520 U.S. 968, 972 (1997). . . .

B. TRADE SECRET THEFT/MISAPPROPRIATION

. . .

1. Likelihood of Success on the Merits

To establish misappropriation of a trade secret, a plaintiff must prove: 1) that "it possessed a trade secret; and 2) that defendants are using that trade secret in breach of an agreement, confidence, or duty, or as a result of discovery by improper means." *Integrated Cash Management Services, Inc. v. Digital Transactions, Inc.*, 920 F.2d 171, 173 (2d Cir. 1990); *see also Carpetmaster of Latham v. Dupont Flooring Systems*, 12 F. Supp. 2d 257, 261 (N.D.N.Y. 1998). . . .

b. Design Specifications

Secrecy again takes center stage and is dispositive when determining whether plaintiff's product design specifications are entitled to trade secret protection for the purposes of obtaining preliminary injunctive relief. If secrecy is lost when a product is placed on the market, there is no trade secret protection. *See LinkCo*, 230 F. Supp. 2d at 498–99 (collecting cases). The primary issue with respect to this alleged trade secret is whether plaintiff's products could be reverse engineered in the time span between Corlew's hiring at Seeley and defendants' marketing and putting out their products for sale.[10] As will be shown, *infra*, the parties disagree about every material fact that goes toward resolving this debate."

Trade secret law . . . does not offer protection against discovery by . . . so-called reverse engineering[.]" *Kewanee Oil Co. v. Bicron Corp.*, 416 U.S. 470, 476 (1974). However, "the term 'reverse engineering' is not a talisman that may immunize the theft of trade secrets." *Telerate Systems, Inc. v. Caro*, 689 F. Supp. 221, 233 (S.D.N.Y. 1988). The relevant inquiry is whether the means to obtain the alleged trade secret were proper or "honest," as opposed to being obtained by virtue of a confidential relationship with an employer. *See Franke v. Wiltschek*, 209 F.2d 493, 495 (2d Cir. 1953); *Telerate*, 689 F. Supp. at 233. Reverse engineering a product to determine its design specifications is, therefore, permissible so long as the means used to get the information necessary to reverse engineer is in the public domain, and not through the confidential relationship established with the maker or owner of the product.

One court, not satisfied with this distinction, has held that even where a product is out in the public domain, and was thus subject to being reverse engineered by a purchaser, trade secret status remains intact because the defendant's former employment with the plaintiff was the only basis for the defendants being "able to select particular

---

[10] "Reverse engineering is the process by which an engineer takes an already existing product and works backward to re-create its design and/or manufacturing process." *United Technologies Corp. by Pratt & Whitney v. F.A.A.*, 102 F.3d 688, 690 n.1 (2d Cir. 1996).

items from a vast sea of public information." *See Monovis, Inc. v. Aquino*, 905 F. Supp. 1205, 1228 (W.D.N.Y. 1994). This view of the law would effectively eviscerate any benefit reverse engineering would provide in the preliminary injunction analysis as applied to trade secrets, forestall healthy notions of commercial competitiveness, and heavily contribute to an inert marketplace where products can only be developed and sold under an impenetrable cloak of originality. It is therefore rejected.

Plaintiff has presented no evidence that the means used by defendants to obtain the alleged trade secret were improper or dishonest. In short, it has no evidence Corlew actually stole the design specifications. It instead necessarily relies upon an inference— that the only way defendants could develop, market, and sell their products in so short of time is if Corlew stole the design specification information—that is, as far as the evidence to this point shows, is [sic] unjustified. Plaintiff does not seem to argue that reverse engineering is impossible, just that it would take a great deal of time, skill, and expense, and that the lack thereof demonstrates that the design specifications must have been stolen. Defendants have argued that the plaintiff's products were simple, consisting of non-technical and few parts, that reverse engineering would take little time, and that, in any event, they only reverse engineered a small fraction, not all, of plaintiff's products. Plaintiff has not sufficiently rebutted these contentions. Thus, because plaintiff has failed to make a clear showing that defendants improperly obtained and reverse-engineered its products, trade secret protection at this stage of the litigation is improper. *See, e.g., Bridge C.A.T. Scan Associates v. Technicare Corp.*, 710 F.2d 940, 946–47 (2d Cir. 1983) (lack of evidence that means to receive information that plaintiff claimed was trade secret were improper mandated denying preliminary injunctive relief).

COMMENTS AND QUESTIONS

1. Why is reverse engineering lawful? If, as the UTSA Commissioners suggested, one purpose of trade secret law is to promote standards of commercial ethics, doesn't there seem to be something wrong with taking apart a competitor's product in order to figure out how to copy it? Does reverse engineering benefit only those competitors who are not smart enough to develop ideas or products for themselves?

In *Chicago Lock Co. v. Fanberg*, 676 F.2d 400 (9th Cir. 1982), the manufacturer of cylindrical locks sued a locksmith who compiled a list of master key codes for the plaintiff's locks by soliciting information from those who had picked the locks on behalf of their clients. The court rejected the claim, holding that the owners of the individual locks had the right to open them, and therefore to authorize others to reverse engineer the key codes:

> A lock purchaser's own reverse-engineering of his own lock, and subsequent publication of the serial number-key code correlation, is an example of the independent invention and reverse engineering expressly allowed by trade

secret doctrine.[4] Imposing an obligation of nondisclosure on lock owners here would frustrate the intent of California courts to disallow protection to trade secrets discovered through "fair and honest means." *See id.* Further, such an implied obligation upon the lock owners in this case would, in effect, convert the Company's trade secret into a state-conferred monopoly akin to the absolute protection that a federal patent affords. Such an extension of California trade secrets law would certainly be preempted by the federal scheme of patent regulation.

Appellants, therefore, cannot be said to have procured the individual locksmiths to breach a duty of nondisclosure they owed to the Company, for the locksmiths owed no such duty.

Isn't protection of lock codes often in the public interest? As we will see in Chapter IV(D)(1)(iv)(b), the Digital Millennium Copyright Act prohibits circumvention of digital locks (and "trafficking" in lock codes) to protect copyrighted works from unauthorized distribution.

2. Consider the recurring question of whether the parties can agree to override trade secret law. Suppose that the owner of a trade secret includes in a license or sale contract a provision prohibiting the buyer from reverse engineering the product. Is that contractual provision enforceable? The courts are split. *Compare SAS Institute v. World Programming Ltd.*, 874 F.3d 370 (4th Cir. 2017) (enforcing contract that barred reverse engineering, albeit between sophisticated businesses), *and K & G Oil Tool & Serv. Co. v. G & G Fishing Tool Serv.*, 158 Tex. 94, 314 S.W.2d 782, 785–86 (1958) (contract preventing disassembly of tools to protect trade secrets was enforceable), *with Vault Corp. v. Quaid Software Ltd.*, 847 F.2d 255, 265–67 (5th Cir. 1988) (contract provision prohibiting reverse engineering of software void as against public policy); *Aqua Connect, Inc. v. Code Rebel, Inc.*, 2012 WL 469737 (C.D. Cal. Feb. 13, 2012) ("the mere presence of the EULA does not convert reverse engineering into an 'improper means' within the definition of California trade secret law.").

3. Trade secret law does not protect owners against legitimate purchasers who discover the secret through reverse engineering. But does the possibility that a product might be reverse engineered foreclose *any* trade secret protection? Recall *Data General Corp. v. Grumman Systems Support Corp.*, 825 F. Supp. 340 (D. Mass. 1993), where the court upheld a jury's verdict that Grumman had misappropriated trade secrets contained in object code form in Data General's computer program, despite the fact that many copies of the program had been sold on the open market. The court reasoned:

> With the exception of those who lawfully licensed or unlawfully misappropriated MV/ADEX, Data General enjoyed the exclusive use of MV/ADEX. Even those who obtained MV/ADEX and were able to *use* MV/ADEX were unable

---

[4] If a group of lock owners, for their own convenience, together published a listing of their own key codes for use by locksmiths, the owners would not have breached any duty owed to the Company. Indeed, the Company concedes that a lock owner's reverse engineering of his own lock is not "improper means."

to discover its trade secrets because MV/ADEX was distributed only in its object code form, which is essentially unintelligible to humans.

Id. at 359 (emphasis in original). The court noted that Data General took significant steps to preserve the secrecy of MV/ADEX, requiring that all users of the program sign licenses agreeing not to disclose the program to third parties. Under this decision, a defendant may have to prove that they had some sort of legitimate access to the plaintiff's information—for example, by demonstrating that they reverse engineered it from a publicly available product—even though the product containing the secret is widely distributed.

Similarly, in *Reingold v. Swiftships*, 126 F.3d 645 (5th Cir. 1997), the court rejected a claim that a boat hull mold could not be a trade secret because it could readily be reverse engineered. While reverse engineering may protect one who engages in it, the court held, it does not protect those who actually acquire the secret by improper means. Should ease of reverse engineering be a measure of whether information is "readily ascertainable"? Should it matter whether the reverse engineering is very difficult or easy enough that any competitor could do it? how many firms have actually reverse engineered the product? If reverse engineering is sufficiently easy, it may be that there is simply no secret to protect. In that case, not only the reverse engineer but anyone who obtains the secret would not face trade secret liability, even if they obtained it by improper means.

The *Data General* cases suggest that reasonable efforts to protect the secrecy of an idea contained in a commercial product—such as locks, black boxes, or the use of unreadable code—may suffice to maintain trade secret protection even after the product itself is widely circulated. Does this result make sense? For a different approach, *see Videotronics v. Bend Electronics*, 564 F. Supp. 1471, 1476 (D. Nev. 1983) (holding that software cannot be a trade secret if it is publicly distributed and can be readily copied).

4. If a company is looking for a piece of information—say, the solution to a given technical problem—the company should be allowed free access to information in the public domain. The reason is that minimizing the search costs of the company is a social good, consistent with some level of protection for the prior investment of others. In a similar vein, suppose the costs of obtaining that information from the public domain are very high, but the costs (to the company) of stealing it from a competitor are very low. Should society punish—and therefore deter—the theft? Wouldn't that simply create an inefficiency, since the company could get the information but would have to incur greater search costs? *Cf.* David Friedman, William Landes & Richard Posner, *Some Economics of Trade Secret Law*, 5 J. ECON. PERSPECTIVES 61, 62 (1991) (arguing that trade secret law prohibits only costly means of obtaining competitors' information, while encouraging cheaper forms of obtaining information such as reverse engineering). Are there other considerations that militate in favor of requiring such a search?

6. *Clean Rooms and Independent Creation.* In *Snapkeys Ltd. v. Google LLC*, 539 F.Supp.3d 1040, 1052 (N.D. Cal. 2021), the court rejected a claim that Google took the

plaintiff's code for a smartwatch keyboard. The court found that Google "presents un-disputed evidence of independent creation. Google engineers who worked on the code for Google's keyboard application for smartwatches never saw the two smart- watches." *See also Mann v. Columbia Pictures*, 128 Cal. App. 3d 628, 650 (1982) (in- dependent creation was a defense because there was no evidence defendant screenwrit- ers had seen the plaintiff's script).

PROBLEMS

Problem II-13. Atech and Alpha both manufacture complex medical devices used in diagnosing a variety of ailments. These devices are sold almost exclusively to hospitals since they cost in excess of $100,000 each. There are several hundred Atech devices currently in use in hospitals throughout the country. Atech, which claims a trade secret in the internal workings of its device, carefully monitors the purchasers of its device. Alpha pays a third party to buy a device from Atech without disclosing that it will be given to Alpha. Once it has obtained the device, Alpha disassembles it and stud-ies it in order to compare it to Alpha's own device. In the course of opening it up, Al-pha's engineers pick two internal padlocks on the Atech device. When Atech discovers that Alpha has obtained the device, it demands the unit's return, offering to refund the purchase price. Alpha refuses, and Atech sues for misappropriation of trade secrets.

a) Assume that Atech's trade secrets were worth $5 million. Assume further that the padlocks cost $5 each, and that it costs $100 per lock to pick these padlocks. Has Atech taken reasonable precautions to preserve its secrets? What other security measures must Atech take—and at what cost—both to deter Alpha (and others) from reverse engineering and to preserve its secrecy? Does Atech's sale of the products on the open market automatically preclude a finding of secrecy?

b) Assume Atech has presented the buyer of the machine with a contract that li-censes (rather than sells) the machine, subject to the following restrictions: (a) the buyer is prohibited from disclosing anything she learns during the course of using the machine; (b) the buyer is prohibited from reselling the machine; and (c) the buyer is liable for Atech's damages in the event that any third party learns of Atech's secrets from the buyer or the buyer's machine. Is such an agreement enforceable? Would you advise a client thinking of licensing an Atech machine to sign this contract? How would you redraft the agreement to protect the buyer?

c) Assume that after Alpha's engineers picked the padlocks, they gained access to the inner workings of the machine. Assume further that they discovered numerous flaws in the imaging mechanism that caused potentially serious defects in the images (and hence the diagnoses) *stemming* from the Atech machine. Finally, assume that Alpha's engineers not only fixed these problems but significantly improved on Atech's design and hence the reliability of the machine. Should these facts affect Alpha's liability? Atech's remedy?

Problem II-14. Bonnie Bluenote, a world-famous blues guitarist, is noted for her distinctive sound, which she gets by tuning her guitar specially every time before she plays. Although the *guitar* itself is a standard professional model, Bonnie's adjustments of settings on the guitar, amplifier, and sound system combine to produce a distinctive sound. Because the sound is so important to her image, Bonnie guards it carefully. While she is tuning her guitar, only band members and close associates are allowed in the room. When she records in a new studio, she has the sound engineers sign nondisclosure agreements.

One day Freddie Fender-Rhodes, a big fan of Bonnie's and a budding bluesman himself, is hanging around outside the studio where Bonnie is recording her newest album. He happens to see an ID tag, worn by all guests in the studio, in the wastebasket. He fills in his name and walks into the studio. The band members and recording engineers, seeing the tag, let Freddie stay. He observes how Bonnie tunes her guitar, sees the soundboard settings, and makes extensive mental notes.

Five months later, Bonnie is shocked to see in a record store a CD by Freddie titled "The Bonnie Bluenote Sound." Then she discovers that Freddie is planning to publish an article in Blues Guitar magazine revealing the secrets to Bonnie's sound. Does she have any recourse against Freddie? What additional precautions should she have taken?

2. Public Policy Limitation

Courts have long recognized that trade secret protection can "implicate the interest in freedom of expression or advance another significant public interest," RESTATEMENT (THIRD) OF UNFAIR COMPETITION, §40, comment c, and recognized a limited privilege to disclose trade secrets. *See* DAVID W. QUINTO & STUART H. SINGER, 1 TRADE SECRETS: LAW AND PRACTICE §3.02; 1 MELVIN JAGER, TRADE SECRETS LAW §3:14.

The RESTATEMENT provides that the exception

depends upon the circumstances of the particular case, including the nature of the information, the purpose of the disclosure, and the means by which the actor acquired the information. A privilege is likely to be recognized, for example, in connection with the disclosure of information that is relevant to public health or safety, or to the commission of a crime or tort, or to other matters of substan- tial public concern.

§40, comment *c*.

This framing of a public policy exception, however, offers relatively little clarity or solace to those who seek to report corporate wrongdoing. *See* Peter S. Menell, *Tailoring a Public Policy Exception to Trade Secret Protection*, 105 CAL. L. REV. 1, 31–36 (2017). Nearly all businesses require their employees to sign NDAs as a condition of employment. Such agreements are essential to being able to establish the reasonable precautions necessary to secure trade secret protection. They are also broad and strict. What if an employee uncovers evidence of regulatory violations, fraud, or even criminal violations at their company? Do they violate their NDA by consulting an attorney or disclosing documents revealing the illegal activity to the government?

At first blush, RESTATEMENT (THIRD) OF UNFAIR COMPETITION, §40, comment *c*, appears to provide some leeway to report the illegal activity. The murky contours of the public policy limitation, however, would give a potential whistleblower pause. How can the employee evaluate "the circumstances of the particular case, including the nature of the information, the purpose of the disclosure, and the means by which the actor acquired the information" without consulting an attorney? At a minimum, its characterization as a defense that turns on a case-by-case balancing of potentially subjective factors means that an employee or contractor who divulges proprietary information to the government could be sued for their breach of an NDA. The prospective whistleblower would likely have to consult an attorney, with the attendant costs, and the very act of discussing the allegedly illegal activity with the lawyer could create exposure for violating the NDA. More generally, many prospective whistleblowers might not even be aware of the public policy exception to their NDA.

Cafasso v. Gen. Dynamics C4 Sys., 637 F.3d 1047 (9th Cir. 2011), illustrates the Catch-22 that existed for whistleblowers prior to enactment of the DTSA. While working as a Chief Scientist at a government aerospace contractor, Mary Cafasso became aware of corporate decisions that she believed to be in violation of the company's obligations under its government contracts. Her reporting of these concerns internally went unheeded. Upon learning that her position was being eliminated, she hurriedly downloaded numerous confidential files that she believed could support her suspicion. She subsequently filed a False Claims Act action against her former employer. Her employer learned of Cafasso's removal of proprietary documents and filed suit against her in state court for breach of contract, misappropriation of trade secrets, and conversion. Notwithstanding that Cafasso never disclosed the confidential files to anyone other than her counsel and the government under seal, the court ultimately determined that Cafasso was not immunized by a public policy limitation and ordered her to pay $300,000 in attorneys' fees for the breach of contract action.

On appeal, the Ninth Circuit declined to adopt a public policy exception in a case involving "vast and indiscriminate appropriation" of confidential files, even for the purpose of reporting allegedly illegal activity to her attorney and the government. The court emphasized the overbreadth of the document retrieval, notwithstanding that Cafasso was under substantial time pressure in gathering the documents. The court expressed concern about the sensitivity of the information, despite the facts that it was all infor- mation to which Cafasso was authorized to view and that she limited disclosure to her attorney (who was also duty-bound to protect the information) and the government through a sealed court filing.

Given the exigency surrounding whistleblower situations, how many employees are willing to run the risk and exposure of a trade secret suit? Whistleblowers jeopardize their career, financial security, emotional stability, health insurance, and social community. Many struggle to find other positions in their field. *See* Menell, 105 CAL. L. REV. at 36–44. As the authors of an empirical study examining corporate fraud at large U.S. companies note, "[t]he surprising part [of whistleblowing] is not that most employees do not talk; it is that some talk at all." Alexander Dyck, Adair Morse & Luigi Zingales, *Who Blows the Whistle on Corporate Fraud?*, 65 J. FIN. 2213, 2245 (2010).

Congress addressed these concerns as part of the DTSA. Section 7 expressly immunizes whistleblowers from trade secret liability so long as they limit disclosure to trusted intermediaries (attorneys and the government through confidential channels). The legislative history explains that the provision aims to counteract the concern that corporations can "bully" and deter potential whistleblowers through the mere threat of costly trade secret litigation. *See* 162 CONG. REC. S1636 (2016). Furthermore, Congress included a requirement that trade secret owners provide notice of this immunity in non-disclosure agreements with employees and contractors.

(B) IMMUNITY FROM LIABILITY FOR CONFIDENTIAL DISCLOSURE OF A TRADE SECRET TO THE GOVERNMENT OR IN A COURT FILING

(1) IMMUNITY.—An individual shall not be held criminally or civilly liable under any Federal or State trade secret law for the disclosure of a trade secret that—

(A) is made—

(i) in confidence to a Federal, State, or local government official, either directly or indirectly, or to an attorney; and

(ii) solely for the purpose of reporting or investigating a suspected violation of law; or

(B) is made in a complaint or other document filed in a lawsuit or other proceeding, if such filing is made under seal.

(2) USE OF TRADE SECRET INFORMATION IN ANTI-RETALIATION LAWSUIT.—An individual who files a lawsuit for retaliation by an employer for reporting a suspected violation of law may disclose the trade secret to the attorney of the individual and use the trade secret information in the court proceeding, if the individual—

(A) files any document containing the trade secret under seal; and

(B) does not disclose the trade secret, except pursuant to court order.

(3) NOTICE.—

(A) IN GENERAL.—An employer shall provide notice of the immunity set forth in this subsection in any contract or agreement with an employee that governs the use of a trade secret or other confidential information.

(B) POLICY DOCUMENT.—An employer shall be considered to be in compliance with the notice requirement in subparagraph (A) if the employer provides a cross-reference to a policy document provided to the employee that sets forth the employer's reporting policy for a suspected violation of law.

(C) NON-COMPLIANCE.—If an employer does not comply with the notice requirement in subparagraph (A), the employer may not be awarded exemplary damages or attorney fees under subparagraph (C) or (D) of section 1836(b)(3) in an action against an employee to whom notice was not provided.

(D) APPLICABILITY.—This paragraph shall apply to contracts and agreements that are entered into or updated after the date of enactment of this subsection.

(4) EMPLOYEE DEFINED.—For purposes of this subsection, the term 'employee' includes any individual performing work as a contractor or consultant for an employer.

(5) RULE OF CONSTRUCTION.—Except as expressly provided for under this subsection, nothing in this subsection shall be construed to authorize, or limit liability for, an act that is otherwise prohibited by law, such as the unlawful access of material by unauthorized means.

DTSA §7, *codified at* 18 U.S.C. §1833.

COMMENTS AND QUESTIONS

1. Professor Menell contends that this express immunity properly focuses trade secret protection on commercial morality and promoting legitimate competition, not shielding illegal activity. Do you agree? Could someone who wishes to steal a trade secret abuse this protection? How?

2. The DTSA immunity provision is built upon the idea that lawyers and the government can serve as "trusted intermediaries." *See* Menell, *Tailoring a Public Policy Exception to Trade Secret Protection,* 105 CAL. L. REV. at 48–55. Federal law provides that

> Whoever, being an officer or employee of the United States or . . . any person acting [as an agent thereof including an employee of a private sector organization who is assigned to a government agency] publishes, divulges, discloses, or makes known in any manner or to any extent not authorized by law any . . . trade secrets . . . shall be fined under this title, or imprisoned not more than one year, or both; and shall be removed from office or employment.

18 U.S.C. §1905. This provision is essential to the operation of the federal courts and many agencies, such as the Food and Drug Administration and the Patent and Trademark Office, which routinely handle confidential information.

3. Would the DTSA immunity provision have assisted Edward Snowden in his effort to blow the whistle on the National Security Agency's surveillance activities? As Menell cautions, the sealed disclosure/trusted intermediary safe harbor depends critically upon the trustworthiness of government officials to whom illegal activity is reported. Corrupting forces can influence government as well as private actors. President

Nixon approved the bugging of his political rivals. Contractors can develop cozy relationships with the agencies with whom they work. The revolving door of hiring government officials as well as lobbying can undermine an agency's objectivity. Various anti-corruption laws, such as the Ethics in Government Act of 1978, counteract those forces. *See generally* ROBERT G. VAUGHN, THE SUCCESSES AND FAILURES OF WHISTLE-BLOWER LAWS (2012). Nonetheless, a government agency can be the source of the misconduct. The sealed disclosure/trusted intermediary safe harbor is ill-equipped to address such challenges, although it contributes to general awareness of whistleblowing and anti-corruption policies.

4. *Construing Whistleblower Immunity.* The first court to apply the whistleblower immunity provision treated the safe harbor as an affirmative defense. *See Unum Corp. v. Loftus*, 220 F. Supp.3d 143 (D. Mass. 2016). Without providing any specific evidence that Loftus sought to use the trade secret information for any purpose other than to report or investigate a suspected violation of law, Unum Group challenged Loftus's invocation of immunity and propounded costly discovery into a wide range of issues. The court declined Loftus's motion to dismiss the trade secret misappropriation claim, holding that discovery was required to determine whether the information was taken only for permissible purposes. In so doing, the court exposed Loftus to the full discovery and other burdens and risks of trade secret litigation—the very precarious circumstance that Congress sought to avoid. *See. Saucier v. Katz*, 533 U.S. 194 (2001) (stating that immunity is not a "mere defense" to liability but an "immunity from suit," and stressing that immunity issues must be resolved as early as possible based on the public policies animating the grant of immunity). It also undermined government investigatory policies. The False Claims Act, for example, authorizes whistleblowers to file lawsuits in the name of the government under seal so as to enable the government to conduct its investigation of false claims without tipping off the targets of the investigation. as to protect the confidentiality of the government's investigation. *See* 31 U.S.C. §3730(b)(2); *State Farm Fire & Cas. Co. v. United States ex rel. Rigsby*, 580 U.S. 26, 34–35 (2016). *See* Peter S. Menell, *Misconstruing Whistleblower Immunity Under the Defend Trade Secrets Act*, 1 NEV. L. REV. F. 92, 97 (2017) (contending that where an employee asserts under oath that they disclosed company documents to government officials or an attorney in confidence solely for the purpose of reporting or investigating a suspected violation of law, the DTSA whistleblower regime requires the employer to come forward with concrete evidence that the employee has shared trade secret information outside of the protected categories or for an impermissible purpose; and that absent such evidence, the court should dismiss the trade secret case without prejudice).

Is there a risk that the mere assertion of whistleblowing could provide cover to an employee who actually intended to misuse trade secrets? Are there countervailing considerations that militate against this risk? How should the burden of proof be allocated where a defendant invokes the whistleblower immunity provision? In *First Energy Corp. v. Pircio*, 524 F.Supp.3d 732 (N.D. Ohio 2021), the court dismissed the trade secret suit where the pleadings showed that the defendant only shared confidential information with his counsel and a government agency. *See id.* at 738 (explaining that "discovery is not a fishing expedition, and Plaintiffs' speculation about what discovery may reveal does not suffice to raise the right to relief they claim above the speculative level," citing *Twombly*, 550 U.S. at 555, and *Iqbal*, 556 U.S. at 678–79). But how should courts handle situations where the defendant seeks to invoke the immunity provision without explaining the details? *See* PETER S. MENELL, ET AL., TRADE SECRET CASE MANAGEMENT JUDICIAL GUIDE §3.5.2.2 (2023).

5. Should the whistleblower immunity be broader, allowing for *public disclosure* of trade secrets in some circumstances? David Levine argues that some enterprises, like companies that make voting machines, are so important to the public that the way they work should be transparent. *See* David S. Levine, *Secrecy and Unaccountability: Trade Secrets in Our Public Infrastructure*, 59 FLA. L. REV. 135 (2007).

6. Deepa Varadarajan argues for a broader right to make beneficial uses of a secret, for instance, to improve on the original product or to protect public health. *See* Deepa Varadarajan, *Trade Secret Fair Use*, 83 FORDHAM L. REV. 1401 (2014). Would such a regime be feasible?

7. *Breach of Non-Disclosure Agreement to Report Allegedly Illegal Activity and the Public Policy Bar on Contract Enforcement*. Notwithstanding the general enforceability of NDAs, a breach of NDA action against a person who reports allegedly illegal information to the government (or consults with an attorney regarding such matters) fits squarely within the public policy exception to contract enforcement. Courts generally bar enforcement of contracts and contract terms that are contrary to public policy and a growing list of statutes and agency rulings make the enforcement—or in some cases, even the inclusion of such terms in contracts—unlawful. *See* RESTAT. (SECOND) CONTRACTS §178. The DTSA whistleblower immunity provision as well as whistleblower statutes (such as the False Claims Act) and state public policies provide a strong foundation for whistleblowers to defend breach of NDA cause of actions targeting reporting of suspected illegal activity on the ground that such lawsuits are against public policy. *See, e.g.,* CAL. LABOR CODE §1102.5(b) (forbidding retaliation against an employee who discloses "information to a government or law enforcement agency, where the employee has reasonable cause to believe that the information discloses a violation of state or federal statute, or a violation or noncompliance with a state or federal rule or regulation"); *See* PETER S. MENELL, ET AL., TRADE SECRET CASE MANAGEMENT JUDICIAL GUIDE §2.8.1.1 (2023).

PROBLEMS

Problem II-15. Amalia Garcia has worked over the past three years as a software engineer at AutoDrive, a software company based in Mountain View, California, that is developing artificial intelligence software for autonomous vehicles. When she joined the company in 2018, she signed the following employment agreement:

Nondisclosure Agreement: During the time of my employment by AutoDrive, I will not disclose or use any Confidential Information except to the extent I am required to disclose or use such Confidential Information in the performance of my assigned duties; and I will use my best efforts to safeguard the Confidential Information and protect it against disclosure, misuse, espionage, loss and theft. After the termination of my employment at AutoDrive, I will not use any Confidential Information or disclose any Confidential Information to any person or entity who is not specifically authorized by AutoDrive to receive it.

AutoDrive employs strict controls over access to its facilities, servers, and software. As part of Amalia's work, she had access to AutoDrive's proprietary source code, database for developing its autonomous driving software, and testing data.

Soon after Amalia was hired, the U.S. Department of Defense entered into a contract with AutoDrive to develop software for military vehicles. The contract required that AutoDrive meet quarterly safety tests on a series of obstacle road tests intended to show the progression of AutoDrive's military vehicle autonomous driving software's performance. Amalia became aware that managers fabricated some of the testing data to inflate the efficacy of the software and to avoid the military withholding progress payments. She raised this concern with her bosses, who told her not to worry because the senior engineers on the team were confident that they could improve the software sufficiently to meet the final testing criteria at the conclusion of the contract. Her bosses instructed her to keep quiet about the problem.

Amalia became increasingly worried about AutoDrive's dishonesty and how it might reflect on her if this deception were revealed. She debated whether to report this problem to the government.

Her anxiety was somewhat alleviated last week when Tesla reached out to her and offered her a position on its autonomous driving team. She had interviewed with Tesla before she was hired by AutoDrive, but was not offered a job at that time. Amalia accepted the Tesla position and tendered her resignation from AutoDrive.

Before she exited AutoDrive, Amalia copied the AutoDrive software and testing data onto a memory storage device and has kept the device secure at her home. AutoDrive detected her copying of its source code and data just prior to her departure. The company filed a trade secret complaint against her alleging trade secret misappropriation and violation of her employment agreement. She comes to you for advice.

(a) Does Amalia's employment agreement comply with the Defend Trade Secrets Act? Why or why not? If not, what are the ramifications?

(b) Can AutoDrive succeed in a suit against her for trade secret misappropriation?

(c) What other advice would you provide her about minimizing her legal exposure and opposing AutoDrive's lawsuit?

Problem II-16. Sarah Kopple works at Complex Systems Inc. (CSI), a software forensics company that develops expert artificial intelligence software programs for law enforcement agencies. These tools, which purport to predict recidivism rates of criminal defendants, are routinely used in criminal sentencing recommendations and parole hearings. Sarah is concerned that this software is prone to disparate racial impacts due to the limitations of the demographic data and models used. CSI carefully guards this software and data as trade secrets. All CSI employees have signed nondisclosure agreements.

Sarah comes to you for legal advice about her concerns that CSI software might inadvertently produce disparate impacts in violation of civil rights laws. Can she share CSI's proprietary software and data with you and the government in an effort to determine whether these programs violate civil rights? What if you were defending a client being sentenced using the CSI software? Can she or you bring this information to the attention of newspaper reporters?

E. AGREEMENTS TO KEEP SECRETS

As we have seen, trade secret law imposes certain limitations on the owner of a trade secret. To qualify for trade secret protection, information must not be generally known, must be valuable, and must not be disclosed. But can an owner of information avoid those restrictions by requiring others to *agree* to keep the information secret, whether or not the information meets the requirements for protection? The question is fundamental in intellectual property law.

Licenses are generally considered good from an economic standpoint because they promote efficiency. The company (or individual) that develops a new product might not be in the best position to market it, particularly if the invention has uses in several different fields. Without the ability to license the technology, the inventor would either have to sell the product directly, use it incompletely or inefficiently, enter a new field itself, or forgo commercializing the technology. Private contracting allows the market to reorder itself efficiently and still determine the appropriate reward for invention. But can or should a trade secret licensing agreement continue to be enforceable after the trade secret has become public through no fault of the licensee?

 Warner-Lambert Pharmaceutical Co. v. John J. Reynolds, Inc.
United States District Court for the Southern District of New York
178 F. Supp. 655 (S.D.N.Y. 1959)

BRYAN, DISTRICT JUDGE.

Plaintiff sues under the Federal Declaratory Judgment Act, 28 U.S.C. §§2201 and 2202, for a judgment declaring that it is no longer obligated to make periodic payments to defendants based on its manufacture or sale of the well known product "Listerine," under agreements made between Dr. J. J. Lawrence and J. W. Lambert in 1881, and between Dr. Lawrence and Lambert Pharmacal Company in 1885. Plaintiff also seeks to recover the payments made to defendants pursuant to these agreements since the commencement of the action.

Plaintiff is a Delaware corporation which manufactures and sells Listerine, among other pharmaceutical products. It is the successor in interest to Lambert and Lambert

Pharmacal Company which acquired the formula for Listerine from Dr. Lawrence under the agreements in question. Defendants are the successors in interest to Dr. Lawrence. . . .

For some seventy-five years plaintiff and its predecessors have been making the periodic payments based on the quantity of Listerine manufactured or sold which are called for by the agreements in suit. The payments have totaled more than twenty-two million dollars and are presently in excess of one million five hundred thousand dollars yearly. . . .

[J.J. Lawrence developed the formula for Listerine in 1880. He licensed the secret formula exclusively to Lambert (later Warner-Lambert) in 1881 under a contract which provided that

> I, Jordan Lambert, hereby agree for myself, my heirs, executors and assigns to pay monthly to Dr. Lawrence, his heirs, executors or assigns, the sum of twenty dollars for each and every gross of said Listerine hereafter sold by my-self, my heirs, executors or assigns.

The amount was reduced by subsequent agreement to $6.00 per gross.]

The agreements between the parties contemplated, it is alleged, "the periodic pay-ment of royalties to Lawrence for the use of a trade secret, to wit, the secret formula for" Listerine. After some modifications made with Lawrence's knowledge and approval, the formula was introduced on the market. The composition of the compound has re-mained the same since then and it is still being manufactured and sold by the plaintiff.

It is then alleged that the "trade secret" (the formula for Listerine) has gradually become a matter of public knowledge through the years following 1881 and prior to 1949, and has been published in the United States Pharmacopo[e]ia, the National For-mulary and the Journal of the American Medical Association, and also as a result of proceedings brought against plaintiff's predecessor by the Federal Trade Commission. Such publications were not the fault of plaintiff or its predecessors. . . .

(1)

The plaintiff seems to feel that the 1881 and 1885 agreements are indefinite and unclear, at least as to the length of time during which they would continue in effect. I do not find them to be so. These agreements seem to me to be plain and unambigu- ous. . . .

The obligation to pay on each and every gross of Listerine continues as long as this preparation is manufactured or sold by Lambert and his successors. It comes to an end when they cease to manufacture or sell the preparation   The plain meaning of the language used in these agreements is simply that Lambert's obligation to pay is co-extensive with manufacture or sale of Listerine by him and his successors. . . .

(3)

However, plaintiff urges with vigor that the agreement must be differently construed because it involved the conveyance of a secret formula. The main thrust of its argument is that despite the language which the parties used the court must imply a limitation upon Lambert's obligation to pay measured by the length of time that the Listerine for- mula remained secret.

To sustain this theory plaintiff relies upon a number of cases involving the obliga- tions of licensees of copyrights or patents to make continuing payments to the owner or licensor, and argues that these cases are controlling here. . . .

. . . [A]ll [these cases hold] is that when parties agree upon a license under a patent or copyright the court will assume, in the absence of express language to the contrary, that their actual intention as to the term is measured by the definite term of the underly- ing grant fixed by statute.

It is quite plain that were it not for the patent and copyright features of such license agreements the term would be measured by use. . . .

In the patent and copyright cases the parties are dealing with a fixed statutory term and the monopoly granted by that term. This monopoly, created by Congress, is de- signed to preserve exclusivity in the grantee during the statutory term and to release the patented or copyrighted material to the general public for general use thereafter. This is the public policy of the statutes in reference to which such contracts are made and it is against this background that the parties to patent and copyright license agreements con- tract.

Here, however, there is no such public policy. The parties are free to contract with respect to a secret formula or trade secret in any manner which they determine for their own best interests. A secret formula or trade secret may remain secret indefinitely. It may be discovered by someone else almost immediately after the agreement is entered into. Whoever discovers it for himself by legitimate means is entitled to its use.

But that does not mean that one who acquires a secret formula or a trade secret through a valid and binding contract is then enabled to escape from an obligation to which he bound himself simply because the secret is discovered by a third party or by the general public. I see no reason why the court should imply such a term or condition in a contract providing on its face that payment shall be co-extensive with use. To do so here would be to rewrite the contract for the parties without any indication that they intended such a result. . . .

One who acquires a trade secret or secret formula takes it subject to the risk that there be a disclosure. The inventor makes no representation that the secret is non-dis- coverable. All the inventor does is to convey the knowledge of the formula or process which is unknown to the purchaser and which in so far as both parties then know is unknown to any one else. The terms upon which they contract with reference to this subject matter are purely up to them and are governed by what the contract they enter into provides.

If they desire the payments or royalties should continue only until the secret is dis- closed to the public it is easy enough for them to say so. But there is no justification for implying such a provision if the parties do not include it in their contract, particularly where the language which they use by fair intendment provides otherwise. . . .

COMMENTS AND QUESTIONS

1. The term of trade secret protection *is* limited, not by a fixed term of years but by the length of time the information remains secret. Indeed, trade secrets become a part of the public domain once secrecy is lost, and their owner cannot prevent even direct copying. It seems odd that contract law would require royalty payments from Warner-Lambert for 80 years (or indeed 160 or more years, as Listerine is still sold commercially), while every other competitor can copy the formula for free.[11] Are there sound reasons for such a rule?

One such reason might be the economic value of freedom of contract. If a party agrees to pay based on something other than an IP right for as long as it uses a product, it is free to do so. *See Nova Chem., Inc. v. Sekisui Plastics Co.*, 579 F.3d 319, 329 (3d Cir. 2009) ("Here, in contrast [to *Warner-Lambert*], nothing in the License Agreement suggests that the parties intended any ongoing obligations with respect to trade secrets after the 1995 termination of NOVA's obligation to maintain the secrecy of Sekisui's technical information."). Presumably, the amount of the royalty payments as well as their duration will reflect the value of the secret to the buyer, discounted by the likelihood of public disclosure. But the obligation to pay for a patent or copyright expires with the IP right. That is not simply a default rule, as the court suggests. Rather, extending the payment obligation beyond expiration constitutes misuse. *See Meehan v. PPG Indus.*, 802 F.2d 881, 886 (7th Cir. 1986); *Boggild v. Kenner Prods.*, 776 F.2d 15, 1320–21 (6th Cir. 1985). Why does contract law allow a party to extend the duration of a trade secret beyond the loss of protection?

2. The *Warner-Lambert* result is controversial. The RESTATEMENT (THIRD) OF UNFAIR COMPETITION takes the position that "[a] promise to refrain from the use or disclosure of commercial information is ordinarily unenforceable unless the information is sufficiently secret to justify the restraint." *See* §41, Comment *d*. Further, the Restatement notes that "because of the public interest in preserving access to information that is in the public domain, such an agreement will not ordinarily estop a defendant from contesting the existence of a trade secret." §39, Comment *d*. A number of cases support this view, which seems at odds with *Warner-Lambert*. *See, e.g., Gary Van Zeeland Talent, Inc. v. Sandas*, 267 N.W.2d 242 (Wis. 1978); *Sarkes Tarzian, Inc. v. Audio Devices, Inc.*, 166 F. Supp. 250 (S.D. Cal. 1958), *aff'd*, 283 F.2d 695 (9th Cir. 1960).

On the other hand, the Federal Circuit has seemingly endorsed the *Warner-Lambert* approach, holding that the issuance of a patent did not extinguish the confidentiality obligation imposed by a nondisclosure agreement, even though the issuance of the pa-

---

[11] In 2020, the right to continue to receive royalties under the contract sold for $561,000. *See* Ryan Davis, *Rare Listerine Royalty Auction Tied To 1881 Contract Flub*, LAW360 (Jul. 21, 2020) (noting that contract generated $32,000 in royalty payments for 2019).

tent destroyed the trade secret that was the basis for the agreement. *Celeritas Technologies v. Rockwell Int'l Corp.*, 150 F.3d 1354 (Fed. Cir. 1998). The equities in that case might be thought to favor the plaintiff: the patent was held invalid, and so offered the plaintiff no relief against a theft of its technology. *Cf. Aronson v. Quick Point Pencil Co.*, 440 U.S. 257 (1979) (holding that the contract obligated licensee to continue paying (reduced) royalties on an invention even though licensor's patent application had been rejected). But isn't that the risk a trade secret owner takes in deciding to patent (and therefore disclose) her invention? The Seventh Circuit has held that courts had no power to review business nondisclosure agreements for reasonableness, even though employee agreements were subject to a reasonableness requirement. *IDX Systems v. Epic Systems*, 285 F.3d 581 (7th Cir. 2002). And in *Bernier v. Merrill Air Engineers*, 770 A.2d 97 (Me. 2001), the Maine Supreme Court held that an employee violated a nondisclosure agreement by disclosing information that did not qualify as a trade secret.

3. Should such restrictions be governed by intellectual property law—making them unenforceable—or by contract law, which presumably would enforce them? The answer to that question will determine whether intellectual property laws (including trade secret laws) constitute binding governmental rules balancing competing interests or merely "default" rules that parties may opt to change. In practice, the courts have walked a hazily defined middle line, refusing to hold that intellectual property statutes preempt contracts which alter their terms, but also refusing to enforce certain contracts that go "too far" in upsetting the balance the intellectual property laws have struck. In *Aqua Connect, Inc. v. Code Rebel, Inc.*, 2012 WL 469737 (C.D. Cal. Feb. 13, 2012), Aqua Connect alleged that Code Rebel misappropriated its trade secrets by reverse engineering in violation of an End User License Agreement (EULA) which prohibited reverse engineering. The court dismissed the claim on the ground that California UTSA provides that reverse engineering "shall not be considered improper means." The court noted that although a breach of the EULA may support a cognizable breach of contract claim, it concluded that "the mere presence of the EULA does not convert reverse engineering into an 'improper means' within the definition of California trade secret law."

4. What remedies are appropriate in a case in which a court enforces a contract that extends beyond the scope of trade secret law?

F.   THE CASE OF DEPARTING EMPLOYEES

Many of the thorniest issues in trade secret (and contract) law arise when employees leave a company in order either to start their own business or to take a job elsewhere. Such cases present a fundamental clash of rights between an employee's mobility and ability to pursue gainful employment and a former employer's protection of its trade secrets. Judge Adams captures the tradeoff in the following excerpt from *SI Handling Systems v. Heisley*, 753 F.2d 1244, 1266–69 (3d Cir. 1985) (Adams, J., concurring):

> When deciding the equitable issues surrounding the request for a trade secret injunction, it would seem that a court cannot act as a pure engineer or scientist, assessing the technical import of the information in question. Rather, the

court must also consider economic factors since the very definition of "trade secret" requires an assessment of the competitive advantage a particular item of information affords to a business. Similarly, among the elements to be weighed in determining trade secret status are the value of the information to its owner and to competitors, and the ease or difficulty with which the information may be properly acquired or duplicated.

While the majority may be correct in suggesting that the trial court need not always "engage in extended analysis of the public interest," the court on occasion must apply the elements of sociology. This is so since trade secret cases frequently implicate the important countervailing policies served on one hand by protecting a business person from unfair competition stemming from the usurpation of trade secrets, and on the other by permitting an individual to pursue unhampered the occupation for which he or she is best suited. "Trade secrets are not . . . so important to society that the interests of employees, competitors and competition should automatically be relegated to a lower position whenever trade secrets are proved to exist." Robison, *The Confidence Game: An Approach to the Law About Trade Secrets*, 25 ARIZ. L. REV. 347, 382 (1983).

These observations take on more force, I believe, when a case such as the present one involves the concept of "know-how." Under Pennsylvania law an employee's general knowledge, skill, and experience are not trade secrets. Thus in theory an employer generally may not inhibit the manner in which an employee uses his or her knowledge, skill, and experience—even if these were acquired during employment. When these attributes of the employee are inextricably related to the information or process that constitutes an employer's competitive advantage—as increasingly seems to be the case in newer, high-technology industries—the legal questions confronting the court necessarily become bound up with competing public policies.

It is noteworthy that in such cases the balance struck by the Pennsylvania courts apparently has favored greater freedom for employees to pursue a chosen profession. The courts have recognized that someone who has worked in a particular field cannot be expected to forego the accumulated skills, knowledge, and experience gained before the employee changes jobs. Such qualifications are obviously very valuable to an employee seeking to sell his services in the marketplace. A person leaving one employer and going into the marketplace will seek to compete in the area of his or her greatest aptitude. In light of the highly mobile nature of our society, and as the economy becomes increasingly comprised of highly skilled or high-tech jobs, the individual's economic interests will more and more be buffeted by competitive advantage. Courts must be cautious not to strike a balance that unduly disadvantages the individual worker.

. . .

In my view a proper injunction necessarily would impose the minimum restraint upon the free utilization of employee skill consistent with denying unfaithful employees an advantage from misappropriation of information. Thus, as I see it, the district court, on remand, should fashion an injunction that extends only so long as is essential to negate any unfair advantage that may have been gained by the appellants.

The majority opinion in *SI Handling* partially upheld a finding that two former employees had misappropriated trade secrets, but it vacated an injunction against them in order for the district court to reconsider its scope.

Professor Camilla Hrdy argues that excluding "general knowledge, skill, and experience" from the scope of trade secrets in departing employee cases is an important protection "intended to preserve an employee's right to improve her skills on the job and thereafter transfer those skills to a different job." *See* Camilla Hrdy, *The General Knowledge, Skill, and Experience Paradox*, 60 B.C. L. REV. 1 (2019). She notes that this requires a balancing not present in other trade secrets cases. It's not enough to decide whether information is generally known to the world at large. If that information is part of an employee's learning of skills, the employee should be free to use it even if others don't know it.

Departing employee cases constitute over two-thirds of all trade secret cases. *See* David S. Almeling, et al., *A Statistical Analysis of Trade Secret Litigation in State Courts*, 46 GONZ. L. REV. 57, 60 (2011). This section explores the thorny issues surrounding departing issues. Section 1 discusses restrictions on disclosure of a company's information (trade secret and otherwise) following employment. Section 2 addresses ownership of employee inventions. Section 3 examines the enforceability of nonsolicitation agreements. Section 4 discusses the enforceability of noncompetition agreements.

1. Confidentiality and Use of Trade Secrets

Nearly all companies require their employees to sign a confidentiality (or nondisclosure) agreement. These agreements generally recite that the employee will receive confidential information during their employment, and that they undertake to keep such information secret and not to use it for anyone other than the employer. Such agreements are essential to the establishment of trade secret protection—serving as a relatively low-cost effort to prevent disclosure—and are generally enforceable against current and former employees. Thus, there is a confidential relationship in most employee cases.

Even if there is no express nondisclosure agreement, some courts imply one. In *Winston Research Corp. v. 3M Co.*, 350 F.2d 134 (9th Cir. 1965), the court dismissed an argument that an employee owed no obligation of confidentiality in his own inventions:

Winston argues that information is protected from disclosure only if communicated to the employee by the employer who is seeking protection, and that the information involved in this case was not disclosed by [3M] to the employees subsequently hired by Winston, but rather was developed by these employees themselves, albeit while employed by [3M].

We need not examine the soundness of the rule for which Winston contends, or its applicability to a case such as this in which a group of specialists engaged in related facets of a single development project change their employer. . . . [A]n obligation not to disclose may arise from circumstances other than communication in confidence by the employer. It may also rest upon an express or implied agreement. In the present case, an agreement not to dis- close might be implied from [3M]'s elaborate efforts to maintain the secrecy of its development program, and the employees' knowledge of those efforts and participation in them. In any event, [3M] and its employees entered into express written agreements binding the latter not to disclose confidential information, and these agreements did not exclude information which the employee himself contributed.

Id. at 140.

Employers sometimes attempt to limit an employee's use of information that does not constitute a trade secret. This issue parallels the problem of restrictive license provisions raised in Section E—are employers limited by the intellectual property laws to protecting only trade secrets or are they free to impose additional restrictions on their employees? Courts struggle with this issue, with the majority concluding that "reasonable" contract restrictions on use or disclosure of information by employees are enforceable even in the absence of a protectable trade secret. *See Bernier v. Merrill Air Engineers*, 770 A.2d 97 (Me. 2001); 12 ROGER MILGRIM, MILGRIM ON TRADE SECRETS §3.05[1][a], at 3-209 to 3-210. Many such restrictions, however, are subject to the public policy limits discussed below. And several courts have invalidated nondisclosure agreements that purport to prohibit disclosure of information that is not in fact confidential. *See, e.g., TLS Mgmt. & Mktg. Servs. v. Rodriguez-Toledo*, 966 F.3d 46 (1st Cir. 2020); *Brown v. TGS Mgmt. Co.*, 271 Cal. Rptr. 303 (Ct. App. 2020); *Nagler v. Garcia*, 370 F.Appx. 678, 681 (6th Cir. 2010); *Assured Partners v. Schmitt*, 44 N.E.3d 463, 475-76 (Ill. Ct. App. 2015). As part of its effort to ban non-compete agreements, the Federal Trade Commission has also targeted overboard NDAs, providing that "[a] non-disclosure agreement between an employer and a worker that is written so broadly that it effectively precludes the worker from working in the same field after the conclusion of the worker's employment with the employer [might be] a de facto non-compete clause." *See* Federal Trade Commission, *FTC Proposes Rule to Ban Noncompete Clauses, Which Hurt Workers and Harm Competition* §910.1(b)(2)(1) (Jan. 5, 2023), https://www.ftc.gov/news-events/news/press-releases/2023/01/ftc-proposes-rule-ban-noncompete-clauses-which-hurt-workers-harm-competition

2. Ownership of Employee Inventions

i.   *The Common Law Obligation to Assign Inventions*

At common law, if there is no contract, ownership of inventions—including ownership of patent rights—was determined according to an employee's status under a long line of common law employee invention cases. In general, employees fall into one of three categories: (1) employees "hired to invent," which results in employer ownership of the invention; (2) employees who invent on the employer's time or using its resources, which results in a limited, nonexclusive "shop right" on the part of the employer to practice the invention; and (3) an employee's "independent invention," in which case the employee owns the invention. *See generally United States v. Dubilier Condenser Corp.*, 289 U.S. 178 (1933); John C. Stedman, *Employer-Employee Relations*, in FREDRIK NEUMEYER, THE EMPLOYED INVENTOR IN THE UNITED STATES 30, 40–41 (1971).

The first category is relatively straightforward: if the employee was hired to invent, what else would the employer be buying except the resulting inventions? It seems logical to extend this treatment to consultants and others who are not "employees" in the strict sense. Robert P. Merges, *Intellectual Property and the Costs of Commercial Exchange: A Review Essay*, 93 MICH. L. REV. 1570 (1995) (highlighting the role of intellectual property in structuring non-employment-based organizations, such as consulting companies and joint ventures).

Category (2) reflects situations where employers have less than a complete claim to the invention, but where the employer's facilities or resources are combined with the inventor's talent and industry to produce the invention. The employee owns it, but the employer is compensated by receiving a limited right to practice the invention. *Cf. McElmurry v. Arkansas Power & Light Co.*, 27 U.S.P.Q.2d 1129, 1135 n.15 (Fed. Cir. 1993) (upholding shop right in employer where inventor/patentee was a consultant); Notably, however, that shop right does not include the right to sell the invention to others. *Beriont v. GTE Labs., Inc.*, 535 F. App'x 919 (Fed. Cir. 2013).

An employee's obligation to refrain from using an employer's trade secrets looks more onerous when it is the employee who came up with the secret. In *Wexler v. Greenberg*, 160 A.2d 430 (Pa. 1960), the Pennsylvania Supreme Court concluded that a departing employee was entitled to take formulas he had developed at his prior employer to work for a competitor. Despite the fact that the employee, Greenberg, was the chief chemist at the plaintiff, the court concluded that he was not in fact "hired to invent" and therefore owned the inventions he made.

The *Wexler* result, while it may seem fair, is not the majority rule. Even in Pennsylvania, *Wexler* is not always followed. *See Healthcare Affiliated Services v. Lippancy*, 701 F. Supp. 1142, 1155 (W.D. Pa. 1988) (rejecting *Wexler* analysis, emphasizing that although defendant developed inventions on his own, he did so using knowledge and information made available by the plaintiff employer); *but see Fidelity Fund v. DiSanto*, 500 A.2d 431 (Sup. Ct. Pa. 1985) (denying recovery against ex-employee salesman partly on the basis that he developed client contacts himself during employment).

Category (3) covers cases where the employee invents on his or her own time, outside the field of employment. *See Dubilier, supra.* As the next section explains, employers sometimes seek to own such inventions through assignment agreements.

ii. Assignment Agreements

Many companies require their employees to assign inventions made during their employment to the employer. These agreements are generally enforceable with regard to inventions made within the scope of employment. This means that the common law rules just discussed rarely apply today.

In some cases, assignment agreements extend to all inventions made by an employee, whether or not at the employer's facilities, during work hours, or within the scope of employment. Several states forbid such broad assignments. CALIFORNIA LABOR CODE §2870 prohibits employers from requiring assignment of "invention[s] that the employee developed entirely on his or her own time without using the employer's equipment, supplies, facilities, or trade secret information" unless the invention relates to the employer's current or demonstrably anticipated business. Other states have similar "freedom to create" limitations on employer assignment agreements. *See, e.g.*, MINN. STAT. ANN. §181.78 (1980); N.C. GEN. STAT. §66–57.1 to 57.2 (1981); WASH. REV. CODE ANN. §49.44.140 (1987). By contrast, NEVADA REVISED STATUTES §600.500 automatically assigns inventions to an employer provided they were developed in the course of employment and relate to the scope of the employee's work, whether or not the employee signs an invention assignment agreement.

COMMENTS AND QUESTIONS

1. *Encouraging Employee Inventions Through Bonuses, Stock Options, and Other Rewards.* Some companies afford employed inventors a bonus or financial share in inventions that they develop. *See* Richard S. Gruner, *Corporate Patents: Optimizing Organizational Responses to Innovation Opportunities and Invention Discoveries*, 10 MARQ. INTELL. PROP. L. REV. 1, 30–31, 30 n.83 (2006) (describing bonus award systems); JULIE L. DAVIS & SUZANNE S. HARRISON, EDISON IN THE BOARDROOM: HOW LEADING COMPANIES REALIZE VALUE FROM THEIR INTELLECTUAL ASSETS 29 (2002) (discussing patent incentive systems). Nonetheless, commentators argue that overbroad assignment agreements dull innovation incentives and undermine economic growth. *See* ORLY LOBEL, TALENT WANTS TO BE FREE (2014) (arguing for an open market for labor); Henrik D. Parker, *Reform for Rights of Employed Inventors*, 57 S. CAL. L. REV. 603 (1984) (calling for federal legislation granting employed inventors greater control over, and interests in, their inventions); *but see* Robert P. Merges, *The Law and Economics of Employee Inventions*, 13 HARV. J.L. & TECH. 1 (1999) (defending employer ownership of inventions).

2. *Can Former Employees Challenge Assigned Patents?* Under the patent assignor estoppel doctrine, which we address in Chapter III(F)(1), courts have long barred someone who sells a patent or patent application from attacking the validity of the assigned patents in a subsequent patent infringement litigation absent exceptional circumstances.

That meant that employees who signed assignment agreements and later moved to a competing company or started their own could not later claim that patents on the inventions they made at their prior employer were invalid. In *Minerva Surgical, Inv., v. Hologic, Inc.*, 141 S.Ct. 2298 (2021), the Supreme Court substantially cabined the assignor estoppel doctrine, holding that it should not apply to a patent assignor who has not explicitly or implicitly represented the validity of an assigned patent. Another other limits on the doctrine, the Court specifically noted that employee inventors should not later be barred from challenging their own patents based on assignor estoppel where they assign future inventions to an employer as part of a standard invention assignment agreement.

3. *Confirmatory Assignment Agreements.* In the aftermath of *Minerva*, companies will likely require employee inventors to sign confirmatory assignment agreements at the time that patents based on the employee's work issue or prior to the employee's departure representing that the issued patent(s) or inventions made during their employment are valid. Will this practice largely nullify the effects of the *Minerva* decision? Is an employee "conveying something for value" if they sign a form "confirmation" that the employer already owns their invention? Does the need for such agreements afford departing employees bargaining leverage? Should Congress eliminate or trim the assignor estoppel doctrine so as to ensure that invalid patents are not insulated from attack?

4. *Abandonment for Trade Secret Nonuse?* Professors Camilla Hrdy and Mark Lemley argue that employees should be able to take their own inventions to a new company if their employer does not use them. *See* Camilla Hrdy & Mark A. Lemley, *Abandoning Trade Secrets*, 73 STAN. L. REV. 1 (2021). Should abandonment apply to assigned patents as well? How would the former employees know if and how their prior inventions are being used by their former employer? What about negative trade secrets, such as the knowledge that a chemical composition does not cure a disease?

PROBLEM II-17

In 2010, Dr. Oscar Livingston and Dr. Tina Fenton were working for Bio-Fab. Each of them signed an agreement that provided:

(a) Employee agrees to disclose promptly to the Company [Bio-Fab] the full details of any and all ideas, processes, recipes, trademarks and service marks, works, inventions, discoveries, marketing and business ideas, and improvements or enhancements to any of the foregoing ("IP"), that Employee conceives, develops, creates, or reduces to practice alone or with the aid of others during the term of Employee's employment with the Company. . . .

(b) Employee shall assign to the Company, without further consideration, Employee's entire right to any IP described in the preceding subsection, which shall be the sole and exclusive property of the Company whether or not patentable.

Drs. Livingston and Fenton left Bio-Fab in April 2012, and together they formed 1000X Genomics in July 2012. By August 2012, 1000X filed the first of several provisional patent applications that focused on using microcapsules in capsule partitions or droplet partitions (referred to as capsule-in-capsule and capsule-in-droplets architecture, respectively) for DNA barcoding, a method of identification using a short section of DNA from a specific gene or genes. By January 2013, the 1000X inventors had conceived of a different architecture: "gel bead in emulsion" (GEM). The GEM architecture involves "partitioning nucleic acids, DNA or RNA, in droplets together with gel beads that are used to deliver the barcodes into the droplet," where the "barcodes are released from the gel beads using a stimulus."

In 2018, 1000X asserted these patents against Bio-Fab. As part of its defense, Bio-Fab argued that it co-owns the 1000X patents asserted against it because Drs. Livingston and Fenton conceived of the ideas embodied in the patents while they were still employed by Bio-Fab.

The evidence at trial showed that Drs. Livingston and Fenton worked chiefly on droplet-in-droplet architecture while at Bio-Fab and that this architecture is different from the GEM architecture that 1000X patented, but their GEM architecture was inspired by the work they did at Bio-Fab and so were based on work done in the scope of their employment.

How should a court rule on the patent ownership issue? What considerations inform your determination? Does it matter if the language of the patent extends beyond the new GEM architecture to cover droplet-in-droplet microcapsules?

iii.   Trailer Clauses

An employee's obligation to assign inventions normally ends when employment ceases. *See Appleton v. Bacon*, 67 U.S. 699 (1862) ("Parties engaging the services of an inventor under an agreement . . . can lay no claim to improvements conceived by him after the expiration of such agreement."). To discourage employees from withholding inventions made during their employment, employers sometimes require employees to agree to a "trailer clause" assigning the employee's inventions for a period of time after they depart. Trailer clauses are enforceable in many states to the extent that they are "reasonable." They cannot, however, be enforced in most circumstances in California, which (as we will see) bans agreements not to compete. *See Whitewater West Indus. v. Alleshouse*, 981 F.3d 1045 (Fed. Cir. 2020) (holding that California law barred a trailer clause); *Applied Materials, Inc. v. Advanced Micro-Fabrication Equipment (Shanghai) Co.*, 630 F. Supp. 2d 1084 (N.D. Cal. 2009) (rejecting one-year trailer clause as an invalid noncompete agreement).

Clauses of particularly long or indefinite duration can be held unenforceable even in states that enforce trailer clauses and can even run afoul of the antitrust laws. *See United Shoe Machinery Co. v. La Chapelle*, 212 Mass. 467, 99 N.E. 289 (1912). One court expressed the requirement of reasonableness as follows:

Hold-over clauses are simply a recognition of the fact of business life that employees sometimes carry with them to new employers inventions or ideas so related to work done for a former employer that in equity and good conscience the fruits of that work should belong to that former employer. In construing and applying hold-over clauses, the courts have held that they must be limited to *reasonable times . . .* and to *subject matter* which an employee worked on or had knowledge of during his employment   Unless expressly agreed otherwise, an employer has no right under a holdover clause to inventions made outside the scope of the employee's former activities, and made on and with a subsequent employer's time and funds.

Dorr-Oliver, Inc. v. United States, 432 F.2d 447, 452 (Ct. Cl. 1970). Courts are skeptical of restrictions that are broader in scope. This is particularly true of large conglomerates that attempt to require the assignment of any invention related to their (diverse) fields of business. *See Ingersoll-Rand Co. v. Ciavatta*, 110 N.J. 609, 542 A.2d 879, 896 n.6 (1988).

In addition to controlling inventions made shortly after departure, employers might be able to lay claim to ideas conceived while the defendant was employed, even if those ideas aren't put into practice until years after the defendant leaves her job. *See Motorola Inc. v. Lemko Corp.*, 2012 WL 74319 (N.D. Ill. Jan. 10, 2012) (employment agreement that required assignment of "ideas" as well as "inventions" could cover an idea developed at a former employer that wasn't turned into a patent application until five years later).

Even if an employer uses an enforceable trailer clause, there is always the risk that the former employee will simply wait out the duration of the term and then conveniently announce the discovery after the trailer clause's expiration date. Courts are sometimes called upon to evaluate the credibility of such invention dates. In *General Signal Corp. v. Primary Flow Signal, Inc.*, the former employee asserted that his breakthrough occurred invention just five days after the expiration of the six months specified in the trailer clause:

> The perfection of a flow meter proved to be a painstakingly intricate process involving extensive testing. It is therefore difficult to believe that after a long and distinguished career with Plaintiff, Mr. Halmi in his musing five days after the trailer clause expired for the first time came up with the idea for the NTV. Although the word "Eureka!" has allegedly been uttered by more than one inventor over the years, the concept at issue does not lend itself to such sudden discovery. The court finds that the concept of the '434 patent must have existed in Mr. Halmi's mind before his employment with GSC ended. Mr. Halmi therefore violated his agreement with GSC.

General Signal Corp. v. Primary Flow Signal, Inc., 1987 U.S. Dist. LEXIS 6929, at *10 (D.R.I. Jul. 27, 1987).

3. Nonsolicitation Agreements

Soliciting employees. Employers worry that departing employees will take colleagues with them. Just the publicity of a mass defection can undermine a successful business. But is it illegal? In *Diodes, Inc. v. Franzen*, 260 Cal. App. 2d 244, 67 Cal. Rptr. 19 (1968), the president and vice-president of Diodes left to form a competing company, called Semtech. Before they left, the officers solicited a number of Diodes employees to join them. Diodes sued the departing employees, alleging a number of claims centering on unfair competition and breach of fiduciary duty. The court dismissed the complaint, stating:

> As a general principle, one who unjustifiably interferes with an advantageous business relationship to another's damage may be held liable therefor. The product is bottled under a variety of labels, including unfair competition, interference with advantageous relations, contract interference, and inducing breach of contract.
>
> Even though the relationship between an employer and his employee is an advantageous one, no actionable wrong is committed by a competitor who solicits his competitor's employees or who hires away one or more of his competitor's employees who are not under contract, so long as the inducement to leave is not accompanied by unlawful action. In the employee situation the courts are concerned not solely with the interests of the competing employers, but also with the employee's interest. The interests of the employee in his own mobility and betterment are deemed paramount to the competitive business interests of the employers, where neither the employee nor his new employer has committed any illegal act accompanying the employment change.

67 Cal. Rptr. at 25–26 (citations omitted). *See also Reeves v. Hanlon*, 33 Cal. 4th 1140 (2004) (a competitor who uses only lawful means to solicit at-will employees does not tortiously interfere with economic advantage). If it is legal for an employee to change jobs, why should it be illegal for someone to invite them to do so? *See* ORLY LOBEL, TALENT WANTS TO BE FREE (2014) (arguing against the enforcement of nonsolicitation agreements); *see also* ORLY LOBEL, YOU DON'T OWN ME: HOW MATTEL V. MGA ENTERTAINMENT EXPOSED BARBIE'S DARK SIDE (2018) (telling the extraordinary story of how Mattel Corporation sought to use employment agreements and copyright law to prevent a former employee from marketing the Bratz, a sassy, bratty, multi-racial doll ensemble).

Can employers change this result by forcing their employees to sign "nonsolicitation agreements" that prevent a departing employee from soliciting other employees to join him? Drawing on the California Supreme Court's decision in *Edwards v. Arthur Anderson LLP*, 81 Cal. Rptr. 3d 282 (2008), the California Court of Appeal held in *AMN Healthcare, Inc. v. Aya Healthcare Services, Inc.*, 28 Cal. App. 5th 923, 936–39 (2018), that the broad nonsolicitation provision of the employment agreement at issue—barring employees from either "directly or indirectly" soliciting or recruiting, or causing others to solicit or induce, any AMN employee for a period of at least one year after termination of employment with AMN—was void under CALIFORNIA BUSINESS AND PROFESSIONS CODE §16600. The court emphasized California's strong public policy of protecting the right of its citizens to pursue any lawful employment and enterprise of their choice.

Are a group of employees departing together more likely to misappropriate trade secrets? In *Suzhou Angela Online Game Tech. v. Snail Games USA*, 2022 WL 326725 (C.D. Cal. Jan. 31, 2022), the court inferred misappropriation from the hiring of 60 employees from the plaintiff in the course of one year.

A related issue involves "no-poach" agreements in which companies agree not to hire each other's employees. Those agreements are unlawful under the antitrust laws. In *Pittsburgh Logistics Sys. v. Beemac Trucking*, (Pa. April 29, 2021), the Pennsylvania Supreme Court held that a no-poach agreement could not be justified as a legitimate restraint on solicitation ancillary to an otherwise valid business agreement. For an argument that no-poach clauses are part of a broader effort to restrain the free movement of labor, see Orly Lobel, *Gentlemen Prefer Bonds: How Employers Fix the Talent Market*, 59 SANTA CLARA L. REV. 663 (2020).

Soliciting clients. Sometimes departing employees try to bring clients rather than co-workers with them when they leave. A common case is the departing sales representative who "takes" a list of customers (either a written list or one that they have memorized) in order to call on those customers for a competitor.[12] Customer lists are generally protectable as trade secrets, but enjoining employees from calling on customers with whom they have had long-standing relationships raises serious concerns about employee mobility.

RESTATEMENT (THIRD) OF UNFAIR COMPETITION §41, Comment *d* states:

> The reasonableness of an agreement that merely prohibits the use or disclosure of particular information depends primarily upon whether the information protected by the agreement qualifies as a trade secret. If the information qualifies for protection under the rule stated in §39, a contract prohibiting its use or disclosure is generally enforceable according to its terms. Although in some cases courts have enforced nondisclosure agreements directed at information found ineligible for protection as a trade secret, many of these decisions merely reflect a more narrow definition of trade secret than that adopted in §39. However, a nondisclosure agreement that encompasses information that is generally known or in which the promisee has no protectable interest, such as a former

---

[12] Merely memorizing a trade secret rather than taking physical documents will not preclude a finding of misappropriation, though it may make misappropriation harder to detect. *See Ed Nowogroski Ins. Inc. v. Rucker*, 971 P.2d 936 (Wash. 1999). In *Stampede Tool Warehouse Inc. v. May*, 651 N.E.2d 209 (Ill. Ct. App. 1995), for example, the plaintiff alleged that former employees who started a competing business had misappropriated its trade secrets by memorizing a list of plaintiff's customers and soliciting those customers. The court found the defendants liable, reasoning that "memorization is one method of misappropriation." But if the case involved merely a former employee contacting those she knew from experience to be potential customers, rather than explicitly attempting to memorize a list of customers, it would be hard to fault the employee's conduct.

employee's promise not to use information that is part of the employee's general skill and training (*see* §42, Comment *d*), may be unenforceable as an unreasonable restraint of trade. Agreements that deny the promisor the right to use information that is in the public domain are ordinarily enforceable only if justified on the basis of interests other than the protection of confidential information.

Where should the line be drawn between permissible work and impermissible use of "secret" lists of customers? To whom does the value inherent in personal relationships belong?

A nonsolicitation agreement precludes sales reps from calling on customers with whom they have an existing relationship even in the absence of a trade secret. Many courts uphold these agreements, though they may restrict their scope. *See ADP, LLC v. Kusins*, 215 A.3d 924 (App. Div. N.J. 2019) (enforcing nonsolicitation agreement, but "blue-penciling" it to limit it to existing rather than prospective clients). Courts that have allowed agreements preventing the solicitation of customers have nonetheless made it clear that it is only affirmative solicitation of the customer that is forbidden; a departing employee does not need to cut off all contact with clients, *In re Document Techs. Litig.*, 275 F. Supp. 3d 454, 465 (S.D.N.Y. 2017), and is free to work for a former customer who approaches them. *See Paramount Tax v. H&R Block*, 683 S.E.2d 141 (Ga. App. 2009); *Moss, Adams & Co. v. Shilling*, 179 Cal. App. 3d 124 (1986) (drawing a line between an employee announcing her departure to start a competing company and then responding to client inquiries, which is permissible, and actively soliciting old clients to follow her, which is not); *Reeves v. Hanlon*, 33 Cal. 4th 1140 (2004) ("the UTSA does not forbid an individual from announcing a change of employment, even to clients on a protected trade secret list."). More recently, California courts have punished solicitation of clients only if it was done using a secret customer list. *Ret. Grp. v. Galante*, 176 Cal. App. 4th 1226 (2009). Courts have also rejected alleged violations of the agreement based on speculation. *See GE Betz, Inc. v. Moffitt-Johnston*, 885 F.3d 318 (5th Cir. 2018) (requiring direct evidence of solicitation). Merely connecting with former customers or co-workers on LinkedIn, for instance, is not solicitation. *Bankers Life & Cas. Co. v. Am. Senior Benefits LLC*, 2017 Ill. App. 160687 (Ill. App. Ct. 2017).

Should the dominance of the employer in the industry matter? In *Wood v. Acordia of W. Va., Inc.*, 618 S.E.2d 415 (2005), the court upheld a two-year agreement preventing insurance agents from soliciting any of Acordia's current, former, or prospective customers. In dissent, Justice Starcher pointed out that Acordia was so dominant in the West Virginia insurance market that "every prospect in the market has been spoken for by an Acordia salesman." The agreement at issue thus effectively prevents all competition.

4. Noncompetition Agreements

Another way of reducing the risk that trade secrets will find their way into the hands of competitors is to limit departing employees' ability to compete with their former employer at all. Employees develop personal relationships with vendors, customers, and others that are immensely useful in business. Noncompetition agreements seek to prevent employees from competing with their former employer for a set period of time or within a particular geographic scope. Such agreements, however, directly impinge upon labor mobility and the ability to pursue gainful employment. Employees' livelihoods often depend on their ability to market their skills and know-how, thereby raising critical public policy and social justice questions. States vary in their approach to enforcing such agreements.

Edwards v. Arthur Andersen LLP
Supreme Court of California
81 Cal. Rptr. 3d 282 (Cal. 2008)

CHIN, J.

We granted review to address the validity of noncompetition agreements in California and the permissible scope of employment release agreements. We limited our review to the following issues: To what extent does Business and Professions Code section 16600 prohibit employee noncompetition agreements. . . .

We conclude that section 16600 prohibits employee noncompetition agreements unless the agreement falls within a statutory exception   We therefore affirm in part and reverse in part the Court of Appeal judgment.

Facts

In January 1997, Raymond Edwards II (Edwards), a certified public accountant, was hired as a tax manager by the Los Angeles office of the accounting firm Arthur Andersen LLP (Andersen). Andersen's employment offer was made contingent upon Edwards's signing a noncompetition agreement, which prohibited him from working for or soliciting certain Andersen clients for limited periods following his termination. The agreement was required of all managers, and read in relevant part: "If you leave the Firm, for eighteen months after release or resignation, you agree not to perform professional services of the type you provided for any client on which you worked during the eighteen months prior to release or resignation. This does not prohibit you from accepting employment with a client. For twelve months after you leave the Firm, you agree not to solicit (to perform professional services of the type you provided) any client of the office(s) to which you were assigned during the eighteen months preceding release or resignation. You agree not to solicit away from the Firm any of its professional personnel for eighteen months after release or resignation." Edwards signed the agreement.

Between 1997 and 2002, Edwards continued to work for Andersen, moving into the firm's private client services practice group, where he handled income, gift, and estate tax planning for individuals and entities with large incomes and net worth. Over this period he was promoted to senior manager and was on track to become a partner. In March 2002, the United States government indicted Andersen in connection with the investigation into Enron Corporation, and in June 2002, Andersen announced that it would cease its accounting practices in the United States. In April 2002, Andersen began selling off its practice groups to various entities. In May 2002, Andersen internally announced that HSBC USA, Inc. (a New York-based banking corporation), through a new subsidiary, Wealth and Tax Advisory Services (WTAS), would purchase a portion of Andersen's tax practice, including Edwards's group.

In July 2002, HSBC offered Edwards employment. Before hiring any of Andersen's employees, HSBC required them to execute a "Termination of Non-compete Agreement" (TONC) in order to obtain employment with HSBC. Among other things, the TONC required employees to, inter alia, (1) voluntarily resign from Andersen; (2) release Andersen from "any and all" claims, including "claims that in any way arise from or out of, are based upon or relate to Employee's employment by, association with or compensation from" defendant; (3) continue indefinitely to preserve confidential information and trade secrets except as otherwise required by a court or governmental agency; (4) refrain from disparaging Andersen or its related entities or partners; and (5) cooperate with Andersen in connection with any investigation of, or litigation against, Andersen. In exchange, Andersen would agree to accept Edwards's resignation, agree to Edwards's employment by HSBC, and release Edwards from the 1997 noncompetition agreement.

. . .

Edwards signed the HSBC offer letter, but he did not sign the TONC. In response, Andersen terminated Edwards's employment and withheld severance benefits. HSBC withdrew its offer of employment to Edwards.

Procedural History

. . . In the published part of its opinion, the Court of Appeal held: (1) the noncompetition agreement was invalid under section 16600, and requiring Edwards to sign the TONC as consideration to be released from it was an independently wrongful act for purposes of the elements of Edwards's claim for intentional interference with prospective economic advantage. . . .

Discussion

A. Section 16600

Under the common law, as is still true in many states today, contractual restraints on the practice of a profession, business, or trade, were considered valid, as long as they were reasonably imposed. (*Bosley Medical Group v. Abramson* (1984) 161 Cal. App. 3d 284, 288, 207 Cal. Rptr. 477.) This was true even in California. (*Wright v. Ryder* (1868) 36 Cal. 342, 357 [relaxing original common law rule that all restraints on trade were invalid in recognition of increasing population and competition in trade].) However, in 1872 California settled public policy in favor of open competition, and rejected the common law "rule of reasonableness," when the Legislature enacted the Civil Code. Today in California, covenants not to compete are void, subject to several exceptions discussed briefly below.

Section 16600 states: "Except as provided in this chapter, every contract by which anyone is restrained from engaging in a lawful profession, trade, or business of any kind is to that extent void." The chapter excepts noncompetition agreements in the sale or dissolution of corporations (§16601), partnerships (§16602), and limited liability corporations (§16602.5). In the years since its original enactment as Civil Code section 1673, our courts have consistently affirmed that section 16600 evinces a settled legislative policy in favor of open competition and employee mobility. (*See D'sa v. Playhut, Inc.* (2000) 85 Cal. App. 4th 927, 933, 102 Cal. Rptr. 2d 495.) The law protects Californians and ensures "that every citizen shall retain the right to pursue any lawful employment and enterprise of their choice." (*Metro Traffic Control, Inc. v. Shadow Traffic Network* (1994) 22 Cal. App. 4th 853, 859, 27 Cal. Rptr. 2d 573.) It protects "the important legal right of persons to engage in businesses and occupations of their choosing." (*Morlife, Inc. v. Perry* (1997) 56 Cal. App. 4th 1514, 1520, 66 Cal. Rptr. 2d 731.)

. . .

Under the statute's plain meaning, therefore, an employer cannot by contract restrain a former employee from engaging in his or her profession, trade, or business unless the agreement falls within one of the exceptions to the rule. (§16600.) Andersen, however, asserts that we should interpret the term "restrain" under section 16600 to mean simply to "prohibit," so that only contracts that totally prohibit an employee from engaging in his or her profession, trade, or business are illegal. It would then follow that a mere limitation on an employee's ability to practice his or her vocation would be permissible under section 16600, as long as it is reasonably based.

Andersen contends that some California courts have held that section 16600 (and its predecessor statutes, Civil Code former sections 1673, 1674, and 1675) are the statutory embodiment of prior common law, and embrace the rule of reasonableness in evaluating competitive restraints. (*See, e.g., South Bay Radiology Medical Associates v. Asher* (1990) 220 Cal. App. 3d 1074, 1080, 269 Cal. Rptr. 15 (*South Bay Radiology*) [§16600 embodies common law prohibition against restraints on trade]; *Vacco Industries, Inc. v. Van Den Berg* (1992) 5 Cal. App. 4th 34, 47–48, 6 Cal. Rptr. 2d 602 (*Vacco*) [§16600 is codification of common law reasonable restraint rule].) Andersen claims that these cases show that section 16600 "prohibits only broad agreements that prevent a person from engaging entirely in his chosen business, trade or profession. Agreements that do not have this broad effect—but merely regulate some aspect of post-employment conduct, e.g., to prevent raiding [employer's personnel]—are not within the scope of [s]ection 16600."

As Edwards observes, however, the cases Andersen cites to support a relaxation of the statutory rule simply recognize that the statutory exceptions to section 16600 reflect the same exceptions to the rule against noncompetition agreements that were implied in the common law. . . .

We conclude that Andersen's noncompetition agreement was invalid. As the Court of Appeal observed, "The first challenged clause prohibited Edwards, for an 18-month period, from performing professional services of the type he had provided while at Andersen, for any client on whose account he had worked during 18 months prior to his termination. The second challenged clause prohibited Edwards, for a year after termination, from 'soliciting,' defined by the agreement as providing professional services to any client of Andersen's Los Angeles office." The agreement restricted Edwards from performing work for Andersen's Los Angeles clients and therefore restricted his ability to practice his accounting profession. (*See Thompson v. Impaxx, Inc.* (2003) 113 Cal. App. 4th 1425, 1429, 7 Cal. Rptr. 3d 427 [distinguishing "trade route" and solicitation cases that protect trade secrets or confidential proprietary information].) The noncompetition agreement that Edwards was required to sign before commencing employment with Andersen was therefore invalid because it restrained his ability to practice his profession. (*See Muggill, supra*, 62 Cal. 2d at pp. 242–243, 42 Cal. Rptr. 107, 398 P.2d 147.)

B. Ninth Circuit's Narrow-Restraint Exception

Andersen asks this court to adopt the limited or "narrow-restraint" exception to section 16600 that the Ninth Circuit discussed in *Campbell v. Trustees of Leland Stanford Jr. Univ.* (9th Cir. 1987) 817 F.2d 499 (*Campbell*), and that the trial court relied on in this case in order to uphold the noncompetition agreement. In *Campbell*, the Ninth Circuit acknowledged that California has rejected the common law "rule of reasonableness" with respect to restraints upon the ability to pursue a profession, but concluded that section 16600 "only makes illegal those restraints which preclude one from engaging in a lawful profession, trade, or business." (*Campbell, supra*, 817 F.2d at p. 502.) The court remanded the case to the district court in order to allow the employee to prove that the noncompetition agreement at issue completely restrained him from practicing his "profession, trade, or business within the meaning of section 16600." (*Campbell*, at p. 503.)

The confusion over the Ninth Circuit's application of section 16600 arose in a paragraph in *Campbell*, in which the court noted that some California courts have excepted application of section 16600 "'where one is barred from pursuing only a small or limited part of the business, trade or profession.'" (*Campbell, supra*, 817 F.2d at p. 502.) . . .

Andersen is correct, however, that *Campbell* has been followed in some recent Ninth Circuit cases to create a narrow-restraint exception to section 16600 in federal court. . . .

Contrary to Andersen's belief, however, California courts have not embraced the Ninth Circuit's narrow-restraint exception. Indeed, no reported California state court decision has endorsed the Ninth Circuit's reasoning, and we are of the view that California courts "have been clear in their expression that section 16600 represents a strong public policy of the state which should not be diluted by judicial fiat." (*Scott v. Snelling and Snelling, Inc.* (N.D. Cal. 1990) 732 F. Supp. 1034, 1042.) Section 16600 is unambiguous, and if the Legislature intended the statute to apply only to restraints that were unreasonable or overbroad, it could have included language to that effect. We reject Andersen's contention that we should adopt a narrow-restraint exception to section

16600 and leave it to the Legislature, if it chooses, either to relax the statutory restrictions or adopt additional exceptions to the prohibition-against-restraint rule under section 16600. . . .

DISPOSITION

We hold that the noncompetition agreement here is invalid under section 16600, and we reject the narrow-restraint exception urged by Andersen. Noncompetition agreements are invalid under section 16600 in California even if narrowly drawn, unless they fall within the applicable statutory exceptions of sections 16601, 16602, or 16602.5. . . .

We therefore affirm in part and reverse in part the Court of Appeal judgment, and remand the matter for proceedings consistent with the views expressed above.

In *Comprehensive Technologies Int'l v. Software Artisans, Inc.*, 3 F.3d 730 (4th Cir. 1993), CTI brought suit for copyright infringement and misappropriation of trade secrets against a group of former employees who left the company to form a competing company which shortly thereafter came out with a new product. The court concluded that the departing employees had not infringed CTI's copyrights or misappropriated any CTI trade secrets. Nonetheless, the court enforced an agreement signed by one of the employees, Dean Hawkes. The agreement provided that for a period of twelve months after he left CTI, Hawkes would not

> engage directly or indirectly in any business within the United States (financially as an investor or lender or as an employee, director, officer, partner, independent contractor, consultant or owner or in any other capacity calling for the rendition of personal services or acts of management, operation or control) which is in competition with the business of CTI. For purposes of this Agreement, the "business of CTI" shall be defined as the design, development, marketing, and sales of CLAIMS EXPRESS- and EDI LINK-type PC-based software with the same functionality and methodology. . . .

The court stated the general legal standard governing covenants not to compete:

> Virginia has established a three-part test for assessing the reasonableness of restrictive employment covenants. Under the test, the court must ask the following questions:
>
> 1. Is the restraint, from the standpoint of the employer, reasonable in the sense that it is no greater than is necessary to protect the employer in some legitimate business interest?
>
> 2. From the standpoint of the employee, is the restraint reasonable in the sense that it is not unduly harsh and oppressive in curtailing his legitimate efforts to earn a livelihood?
>
> 3. Is the restraint reasonable from the standpoint of a sound public policy?

Blue Ridge Anesthesia & Critical Care, Inc. v. Gidick, 239 Va. 369, 389 S.E.2d 467, 469 (Va. 1990). If a covenant not to compete meets each of these standards of reasonableness, it must be enforced. As a general rule, however, the Virginia courts do not look favorably upon covenants not to compete, and will strictly construe them against the employer. The employer bears the burden of demonstrating that the restraint is reasonable.

The court found that Hawkes's agreement, which prevented him from competing with CTI anywhere in the United States, was reasonable because CTI had offices, clients, or prospects in many (though not all) states throughout the country. Further, the court noted:

> . . . As the individual primarily responsible for the design, development, marketing and sale of CTI's software, Hawkes became intimately familiar with every aspect of CTI's operation, and necessarily acquired information that he could use to compete with CTI in the marketplace. When an employee has access to confidential and trade secret information crucial to the success of the employer's business, the employer has a strong interest in enforcing a covenant not to compete because other legal remedies often prove inadequate. It will often be difficult, if not impossible, to prove that a competing employee has misappropriated trade secret information belonging to his former employer. On the facts of this case, we conclude that the scope of the employment restrictions is no broader than necessary to protect CTI's legitimate business interests.

COMMENTS AND QUESTIONS

1. The California rule set out in §16600 is the minority rule, but it is gaining broader acceptance. Other states, including Alabama, Oklahoma, Louisiana, Minnesota, Montana, North Dakota, and the District of Columbia, also forbid noncompetition agreements. Several states have enacted or are considering restrictions on noncompete agreements. Massachusetts, for example, requires advance notice of a noncompete before starting work, limits noncompetes to 12 months duration, bans their use for certain categories of employees, including hourly workers and those fired or laid off, and requires the employer to pay "garden leave" to former employees who can't work. A growing number of states, including Illinois, Washington, Oregon, Nevada, New Hampshire, and Colorado, ban noncompetes applied to "low-wage workers." *See, e.g.,* 820 ILCS §90; COLO. REV. STAT. §8-2-113. Still other states, including Colorado, Delaware, Massachusetts, and Tennessee, forbid them in professional settings but allow them in other contexts. *See, e.g., Murfreesboro Med. Clinic v. Udom*, 166 S.W.3d 674 (Tenn. 2005). In 2023, the Federal Trade Commission proposed to ban most noncompete agreements nationwide. *See* Federal Trade Commission, *FTC Proposes Rule to Ban Noncompete Clauses, Which Hurt Workers and Harm Competition* §910.1(b)(2)(1) (Jan. 5, 2023), https://www.ftc.gov/news-events/news/press-releases/2023/01/ftc-proposes-rule-ban-noncompete-clauses-which-hurt-workers-harm-competition

Most states apply an overarching requirement of "reasonableness" to covenants not to compete, as the Virginia court did in *CTI*. *See* MICH. COMP. LAWS §445.774a (non-competition agreements enforceable if the agreement is "reasonable as to its duration, geographical area, and type of employment or line of business"). As a general matter that means the majority of states enforce noncompetes are long as they are reasonably limited. *See ADP, LLC v. Kusins*, 215 A.3d 924 (App. Div. N.J. 2019) (enforcing non-compete against sales reps limited to geographic region they served). They may disagree, however, on what restrictions are reasonable. In *Gateway 2000 Inc. v. Kelley*, 9 F. Supp. 2d 790 (E.D. Mich. 1998), the court invalidated an agreement that was similar to the one upheld in *CTI*. The court relied in part on the fact that the company had later adopted a less restrictive noncompetition provision, suggesting that the older, broader provision was not necessary to protect its interests. And the Virginia Supreme Court has held unreasonable a noncompetition agreement that prevented the defendant from working for a competitor in any capacity, rather than specifying particular positions the defendant could not take. *Modern Environments, Inc. v. Stinnett*, 561 S.E.2d 694 (Va. 2002).

Some courts have limited the enforcement of noncompetition agreements to situations where trade secrets are likely to be used or disclosed if an employee is allowed to compete. The New York Court of Appeals, for example, took the following view:

> Undoubtedly judicial disfavor of these covenants is provoked by "powerful considerations of public policy which militate against sanctioning the loss of a man's livelihood" (*Purchasing Assoc. v. Weitz. . . .*) Indeed, our economy is premised on the competition engendered by the uninhibited flow of services, talent and ideas. Therefore, no restrictions should fetter an employee's right to apply to his own best advantage the skills and knowledge acquired by the overall experience of his previous employment. This includes those techniques which are but "skillful variations of general processes known to the particular trade" (RESTATEMENT, AGENCY 2d, §396 Comment *b*).

> Of course, the courts must also recognize the legitimate interest an employer has in safeguarding that which has made his business successful and to protect himself against deliberate surreptitious commercial piracy. Thus restrictive covenants will be enforceable to the extent necessary to prevent the disclosure or use of trade secrets or confidential customer information. In addition injunctive relief may be available where an employee's services are unique or extraordinary and the covenant is reasonable. This latter principle has been interpreted to reach agreements between members of the learned professions.

Reed Roberts Assocs. v. Strauman, 40 N.Y.2d 303, 353 N.E.2d 590 (Ct. App. 1976). Does the *Reed Roberts* approach in essence hold noncompetition agreements unenforceable, since it allows them to operate only when trade secret laws also provide relief? Are there sound reasons to enforce an employer-employee agreement that prevents the employee from competing after termination? State statutes which address the issue have generally been interpreted to allow such "reasonable" employee agreements, regardless of how the statutes themselves are worded.

What agreements are "reasonable" is far from clear in this context and is the subject of considerable litigation. Many states enforce at least some noncompetes. Nonetheless, even those states have invalidated some noncompetition agreements on the ground that they were unreasonable. *See, e.g., Mutual Service Casualty Ins. Co. v. Brass*, 625 N.W.2d 648 (Wis. Ct. App. 2001); *Brentlinger Enters. v. Curran*, 752 N.E.2d 994 (Ohio Ct. App. 2001); *Harvey Barnett, Inc. v. Shidler*, 143 F. Supp. 2d 1247 (D. Colo. 2001); *Mertz v. Pharmacists Mutual Ins.*, 625 N.W.2d 197 (Neb. 2001); *City Slickers, Inc. v. Douglas*, 40 S.W.3d 805 (Ark. Ct. App. 2001); *Intertek Testing Servs. v. Eastman*, 2023 WL 2544236 (Del. Ch. Mar. 16, 2023) (refusing to enforce three-year noncompete against co-founder who had sold the business). The confusion in this area is demonstrated by comparing *Paramount Termite Control Co. v. Rector*, 380 S.E.2d 922 (Va. 1989) (upholding a two-year noncompete) *with Home Paramount Pest Control v. Shaffer*, 718 S.E.2d 762 (Va. 2011) (striking down the *identical* noncompete agreement).

If a noncompetition agreement is overbroad, should the courts refuse to enforce it at all, or should they narrow it to make it enforceable? *Compare Coleman v. Retina Consultants*, 687 S.E.2d 457 (Ga. 2009) (refusing to reform unenforceable agreement) *and* NEV. REV. STAT. §613.200 (barring judicial reformation of problematic noncompete agreements) *with ADP, LLC v. Rafferty*, 923 F.3d 113 (3d Cir. 2019) (holding that overbroad agreements should be "blue-penciled": edited by the courts to make them reasonable).

2. There seems to be no question in the *CTI* court's mind that none of the defendants misappropriated any CTI trade secrets, infringed any copyrights, or otherwise "took" anything belonging to CTI in starting Software Artisans. Why doesn't that dispose of the case? What social purpose is served by enjoining former employees from pursuing their livelihood? In *ADP, LLC v. Rafferty*, 923 F.3d 113 (3d Cir. 2019), the court held that "the preservation of client relationships and goodwill" was a legitimate business justification for preventing competition by departing employees.

3. California courts have interpreted BUSINESS & PROFESSIONS CODE §16600 to bar noncompetition agreements altogether in employee contracts but to permit such agreements if they are ancillary to the sale of a business, so long as the terms of the agreement are "reasonable." *See Ixchel Pharma, LLC v. Biogen, Inc.*, 9 Cal.5th 1130 (2020); *Monogram Indus., Inc. v. SAR Indus., Inc.*, 64 Cal. App. 3d 692, 134 Cal. Rptr. 714, 718 (1976). Further, while California courts will not enforce a noncompetition agreement, they will prevent departing employees from using or disclosing their former employer's trade secrets. *See State Farm Mutual Automobile Ins. Co. v. Dempster*, 344 P.2d 821 (Cal. Ct. App. 1959); *Gordon v. Landau*, 49 Cal. 2d 690, 321 P.2d 456 (Cal. 1958). And §16600 does not prevent an employer from barring current employees from moonlighting for a competitor while still employed. *Techno Lite Inc. v. Emcod LLC*, 44 Cal.App.5th 462 (2020).

4. The strength of California's commitment to the free movement of employees was demonstrated in *The Application Group, Inc. v. The Hunter Group, Inc.*, 72 Cal. Rptr. 2d 73 (Ct. App. 1998). There, the California Court of Appeals held that §16600 precluded the enforcement of a noncompetition agreement entered into in Maryland between a Maryland employer and employee, where the employee subsequently left to take a job telecommuting from Maryland for a California company. Despite the fact that Maryland courts would enforce the agreement, the California court concluded that California's interests were "materially stronger" than Maryland's in this case. *See also D'Sa v. Playhut, Inc.*, 85 Cal. App. 4th 927, 102 Cal. Rptr. 2d 495 (2000) (disregarding choice of law provision in holding a noncompete agreement unenforceable); *Nuvasive, Inc. v. Alphatec Holdings*, 2019 WL 40108 (Del. Ct. Chan. Aug. 26, 2019) (finding that California's interest in barring noncompetes substantially outweighs Delaware's interest in a case involving a California employee; refusing to enforce Delaware choice of law clause in contract). California reinforced its policy in 2017 by enacting CAL. LABOR CODE §925, which prevents companies from sending noncompete cases to arbitration.

California's strong public policy has led to conflicts with other states. The most notable example is *Advanced Bionics v. Medtronic*, 87 Cal. App. 4th 1235 (2001), in which both California and Minnesota courts asserted that their law should control, with the Minnesota court enjoining the departing employee and the California court enjoining the employer from proceeding with the suit. The California Supreme Court ultimately reversed, not because it didn't consider the policy of employee mobility important but because it thought the specter of conflicting judgments unseemly. *Advanced Bionics v. Medtronic*, 29 Cal. 4th 697, 128 Cal. Rptr. 2d 172 (2002). But the California court's deference to a sister court may simply subjugate California's policy to the law of any other state that would enforce a noncompete agreement, even if the employee doesn't work in that state. *See IBM Corp. v. Bajorek*, 191 F.3d 1033 (9th Cir. 1999) (applying New York law to enjoin competition against New York company by employee in California, and disregarding California policy to the contrary); *Amazon.com, Inc. v. Powers*, 2012 WL 6726538 (W.D. Wash. Dec. 27, 2012) (enforcing Washington choice of law clause in noncompete contract against employee who left Amazon.com to work for Google in California). For a contrary ruling giving nationwide effect to a refusal to enforce a noncompete agreement under Georgia law, *see Palmer & Cay v. Marsh & McLennan*, 404 F.3d 1297 (11th Cir. 2005).

Is there a reasoned way to resolve such conflicts in public policy? Or will the inevitable result be a "race to the courthouse"? After *Advanced Bionics*, California enacted CAL. LABOR CODE §925, which prohibits employers from requiring California-based employees to agree to litigate their noncompetes outside the state. That suggests California remains strongly committed to protecting its employees against noncompetes.

5. What are the competing policy interests at stake in noncompetition clauses? On the one hand, it seems unfair to employers to simply allow their employees to do whatever they want upon leaving. Particularly where the employees were in positions of im-

portance, their knowledge of the employer's trade secrets may leave the former employer at a competitive disadvantage. In a competitive industry, preventing the disclosure of trade secrets is far preferable to suing for misappropriation after the trade secrets have already been disclosed, and employers may see a noncompetition agreement as a way to short-circuit any risk of trade secret misappropriation.

On the other hand, such restrictions seem onerous burdens to impose on employees. *See* Viva Moffat, *The Wrong Tool for the Job: The IP Problem with Non-Competition Agreements*, 52 WM. & MARY L. REV. 873 (2010). Imagine how you would feel as an attorney if you left a firm only to find that you were prevented from practicing law in the same field or geographic region for the next two years. (In this regard, it is significant that *Reed Roberts* expressed the view that the "learned professions" were properly subject to noncompetition agreements.) *See Central Indiana Podiatry PC v. Krueger*, 882 N.E.2d 723 (Ind. 2008) (noncompete agreement enforceable against physician if reasonable). In addition, it is not completely clear that such provisions benefit companies in the long run. Strauman, the defendant in *Reed Roberts,* came to Reed Roberts after having worked for a competitor for four years. He was hired in part because of his valuable experience in the industry. What if Strauman's former employer had required him to sign an enforceable noncompete agreement? For scholarly criticism of enforcing noncompetes, *see* Charles Tait Graves, *Analyzing the Non-Competition Covenant as a Category of Intellectual Property Regulation*, 3 HASTINGS SCI. & TECH. L.J. 69 (2010).

Some scholars have suggested that there is a more practical economic motivation for precluding such noncompetition agreements. They argue that the relative success of California's Silicon Valley compared to Boston's Route 128 is directly attributable to the prevalence of noncompetition agreements in Route 128 companies, which prevented the free movement of employees and therefore discouraged start-up companies. *See* ORLY LOBEL, TALENT WANTS TO BE FREE: WHY WE SHOULD LEARN TO LOVE LEAKS, RAIDS, AND FREE RIDING (2015) (citing numerous empirical studies that noncompetes restrict innovation); Ronald J. Gilson, *The Legal Infrastructure of High Technology Industrial Districts: Silicon Valley, Route 128, and Covenants Not to Compete*, 74 N.Y.U. L. REV. 575 (1999); ANNALEE SAXENIAN, REGIONAL ADVANTAGE: CULTURE AND COMPETITION IN SILICON VALLEY AND ROUTE 128 (1994); *but see* Jonathan Barnett & Ted M. Sichelman, *The Case for Noncompetes*, 86 U. CHI. L. REV. 953 (2020) (calling into question the role of noncompete agreements in the emergence of Silicon Valley over Route 128 and the larger empirical literature questioning noncompetes, and concluding that the common law's reasonableness standard likely represents the best approach).

6. When a firm requires an existing employee to sign an employment agreement containing a covenant not to compete, the employee is giving up something substantial. What is the employer giving up? Some cases have raised the issue of consideration (in the contract law sense) in such an agreement on the part of the employer; they generally conclude that there is consideration, on one theory or another. *See, e.g., Central Adjust-*

ment Bureau v. Ingram, 678 S.W.2d 28 (Tenn. 1984) (consideration in the form of continuous employment over a long period of time); *Alex Sheshunoff Mgmt. Servs. v. Johnson*, 209 S.W.3d 644, 646 (Tex. 2006) (same; rejecting prior Texas case law); *Lake Land Emp. Grp. v. Columber*, 804 N.E.2d 27 (Ohio 2004) (consideration in the form of continuing to employ an at-will employee; three Justices dissented).

Why not require, out of fairness, that an employer who insists on such a covenant must pay the employee's salary during the term of the noncompete provision? Several other nations follow this approach:

- *Germany*: The German Commercial Code requires that an employer compensate the employee for the complete duration of time that the covenant is in effect up to a maximum duration of two years. *See* WENDI S. LAZAR & GARY R. SINISCALCO (EDS.), RESTRICTIVE COVENANTS AND TRADE SECRETS IN EMPLOYMENT LAW: AN INTERNATIONAL SURVEY, Vol. I, 17-5 (2010) (GERMAN COMMERCIAL CODE §74(a)(1)). Compensation must be at least half of the employee's pay during the previous 12 months of employment.

- *China*: In 2008, China adopted a similar regime. *See* PRC LABOR CONTRACT LAW OF 1 JANUARY 2008, Articles 23–24 (2008). Employers may include noncompete restrictions of no more than two years in employment agreements with senior technicians, senior managers, and other employees who have access to trade secrets. Under the law, the employer must compensate the employee throughout the post-employment noncompete period, although the law does not specify the compensation level. It is unclear whether the compensation must be at the prior level or can be as low as minimum wage.

- *United Kingdom*: The UK employs a "garden leave" policy, under which the employee must provide the employer with a long notice period before changing employment. The employer is required to pay full salary and benefits during this period, but cannot force the employee to work. (The employee can stay at home and tend his or her garden.) The garden leave period must be reasonable under the circumstances of the employment.

Some U.S. companies have adopted such approaches on a voluntary basis. *See Marcam Corp. v. Orchard*, 885 F. Supp. 294 (D. Mass. 1995) (enforcing a contractual provision preventing Orchard from working for any competitor in the country for one year, provided that Marcam paid 110 percent of the salary offered by the competitor). *See* Sonya P. Passi, *Compensated Injunctions: A More Equitable Solution to the Problem of Inevitable Disclosure*, 27 BERKELEY TECH. L.J. 927 (2012) (suggesting such an approach). Is the employee likely to be satisfied by that approach? How employable will he be after sitting idle for two years?

7. Does the reasonableness of a noncompete agreement depend on the likelihood of trade secret misappropriation? In *Zodiac Records, Inc. v. Choice Envt'l Servs.*, 112

So.2d 587 (Fla. Ct. App. 2013), the court held that a three-year noncompete was unreasonable and violated due process where the plaintiff stipulated that it could not show that the defendant would use its trade secrets unless the agreement was enforced.

8. Can an employer avoid state laws restricting noncompetition agreements by requiring the employee to sign an agreement that does not forbid employment, but calls for the payment of a "liquidated damage" penalty if the employee goes to work for a competitor? Is such a monetary penalty effectively the same as enforcing a noncompete? What if the employer doesn't forbid employment, but conditions the grant of stock options on not going to work for a competitor? *See ADP, LLC v. Rafferty*, 923 F.3d 113 (3d Cir. 2019) (upholding such a condition). Note that it is common in high-tech industries to grant employees stock options that "vest" over a period of years, giving the employee an incentive not to leave and abandon the unvested options. Those provisions are legal.

9. Despite their unenforceability, many employers in California require employees to sign noncompete agreements. *See* J.J. Prescott et al., *Understanding Noncompetition Agreements: the 2014 Noncompete Survey Project*, 2016 MICH. ST. L. REV. 369. Employees who do not know that the agreements are unenforceable might be deterred from going to work for a competitor or starting their own business. Should employers that knowingly require unenforceable agreements face some penalty for doing so? Legislation pending in California in 2023 would create such a penalty. *See* Assembly Bill No. 747 §5 (Feb. 13, 2023), https://legiscan.com/CA/text/AB747/id/2769444

10. States that enforce noncompetes nonetheless allow departing employees to "prepare to compete" during the term of the agreement, "because restraining such acts would have the effect of extending the term of the covenant." *In re Document Techs. Litig.*, 275 F. Supp. 3d 454, 464 (S.D.N.Y. 2017).

Are there circumstances in which an employee's use or disclosure of trade secrets is "inevitable," so that the only way to avoid misappropriation of the secret is to preclude employment altogether? Consider the following case:

PepsiCo, Inc. v. Redmond
United States Court of Appeals for the Seventh Circuit
54 F.3d 1262 (7th Cir. 1995)

Flaum, J.:

[The district court ordered the issuance of a preliminary injunction preventing Quaker Oats Co. from employing Redmond, a former general manager for PepsiCo North America. Redmond was general manager of PepsiCo's California business unit for ten years until, in 1994, he accepted Quaker's offer to become the chief operating officer of its Gatorade and Snapple Co. divisions. The court held that Redmond would inevitably be forced to use PepsiCo trade secrets for his new employer.]

PepsiCo asserts that Redmond cannot help but rely on PCNA [PepsiCo North America] trade secrets as he helps plot Gatorade and Snapple's new course, and that these secrets will enable Quaker to achieve a substantial advantage by knowing exactly how PCNA will price, distribute, and market its sports drinks and new age drinks and being able to respond strategically. This type of trade secret problem may arise less often, but it nevertheless falls within the realm of trade secret protection under the present circumstance.

Quaker and Redmond assert that they have not and do not intend to use whatever confidential information Redmond has by virtue of his former employment. They point out that Redmond has already signed an agreement with Quaker not to disclose any trade secrets or confidential information gleaned from his earlier employment. They also note with regard to distribution systems that even if Quaker wanted to steal information about PCNA's distribution plans, they would be completely useless in attempting to integrate the Gatorade and Snapple beverage lines.

The defendants' arguments fall somewhat short of the mark. Again, the danger of misappropriation in the present case is not that Quaker threatens to use PCNA's secrets to create distribution systems or coopt PCNA's advertising and marketing ideas. Rather, PepsiCo believes that Quaker, unfairly armed with knowledge of PCNA's plans, will be able to anticipate its distribution, packaging, pricing, and marketing moves. Redmond and Quaker even concede that Redmond might be faced with a decision that could be influenced by certain confidential information that he obtained while at PepsiCo. In other words, PepsiCo finds itself in the position of a coach, one of whose players has left, playbook in hand, to join the opposing team before the big game. Quaker and Redmond's protestations that their distribution systems and plans are entirely different from PCNA's are thus not really responsive. . . .

Quaker and Redmond do not assert that the confidentiality agreement is invalid; such agreements are enforceable when supported by adequate consideration.[10] Rather, they argue that "inevitable" breaches of these contracts may not be enjoined. The case on which they rely, however, *R. R. Donnelley & Sons Co. v. Fagan*, 767 F. Supp. 1259 (S.D.N.Y. 1991) (applying Illinois law), says nothing of the sort. The *R. R. Donnelley* court merely found that the plaintiffs had failed to prove the existence of any confidential information or any indication that the defendant would ever use it. *Id.* at 1267. The threat of misappropriation that drives our holding with regard to trade secrets dictates the same result here.

. . . In *Teradyne* [v. Clear Communications Corp., 707 F. Supp. 353 (N.D. Ill. 1989)], Teradyne alleged that a competitor, Clear Communications, had lured employ- ees away from Teradyne and intended to employ them in the same field. In an insightful

---

[10] The confidentiality agreement is also not invalid for want of a time limitation. *See* 765 ILCS 1065/8(b)(1) ("[A] contractual or other duty to maintain secrecy or limit use of a trade secret shall not be deemed to be void or unenforceable solely for lack of durational or geographic limitation on the duty."). Nor is there any question that the confidentiality agreement covers much of the information PepsiCo fears Redmond will necessarily use in his new employment with Quaker.

opinion, Judge Zagel observed that "threatened misappropriation can be enjoined under Illinois law" where there is a "high degree of probability of inevitable and immediate . . . use of . . . trade secrets." *Teradyne,* 707 F. Supp. at 356. Judge Zagel held, however, that Teradyne's complaint failed to state a claim because Teradyne did not allege "that defendants have in fact threatened to use Teradyne's secrets or that they will inevitably do so." [The *Teradyne* court held]:

> the defendants' claimed acts, working for Teradyne, knowing its business, leav-
> ing its business, hiring employees from Teradyne and entering the same field
> (though in a market not yet serviced by Teradyne) do not state a claim of threat-
> ened misappropriation. All that is alleged, at bottom, is that defendants could
> misuse plaintiff's secrets, and plaintiffs fear they will. This is not enough. It
> may be that little more is needed, but falling a little short is still falling short.

Id. at 357.

In *AMP* we affirmed the denial of a preliminary injunction on the grounds that the plaintiff AMP had failed to show either the existence of any trade secrets or the likeli-hood that defendant Fleischhacker, a former AMP employee, would compromise those secrets or any other confidential business information. AMP, which produced electrical and electronic connection devices, argued that Fleischhacker's new position at AMP's competitor would inevitably lead him to compromise AMP's trade secrets regarding the manufacture of connectors. *AMP,* 823 F.2d at 1207. In rejecting that argument, we em-phasized that the mere fact that a person assumed a similar position at a competitor does not, without more, make it "inevitable that he will use or disclose . . . trade secret infor-mation" so as to "demonstrate irreparable injury." *Id.*

The ITSA, *Teradyne,* and *AMP* lead to the same conclusion: a plaintiff may prove a claim of trade secret misappropriation by demonstrating that defendant's new employ-ment will inevitably lead him to rely on the plaintiff's trade secrets. *See also* 1 Jager, . . . §7.02[2][a] at 7-20 (noting claims where "the allegation is based on the fact that the disclosure of trade secrets in the new employment is inevitable, whether or not the for-mer employee acts consciously or unconsciously"). . . .

PepsiCo presented substantial evidence at the preliminary injunction hearing that Redmond possessed extensive and intimate knowledge about PCNA's strategic goals for 1995 in sports drinks and new age drinks. The district court concluded on the basis of that presentation that unless Redmond possessed an uncanny ability to compart-mentalize information, he would necessarily be making decisions about Gatorade and Snapple by relying on his knowledge of PCNA trade secrets. It is not the "general skills and knowledge acquired during his tenure with" PepsiCo that PepsiCo seeks to keep from falling into Quaker's hands, but rather "the particularized plans or processes de-veloped by [PCNA] and disclosed to him while the employer-employee relationship existed, which are unknown to others in the industry and which give the employer an advantage over his competitors." *AMP,* 823 F.2d at 1202. The Teradyne and AMP plain-tiffs could do nothing more than assert that skilled employees were taking their skills elsewhere; PepsiCo has done much more.

COMMENTS AND QUESTIONS

1. What Pepsi trade secrets are threatened by Redmond's "defection" to Quaker? The information Redmond possesses includes: (1) new flavor and product packaging information; (2) pricing strategies; (3) Pepsi's "attack plans" for specific markets; and (4) Pepsi's new distribution plan, being pilot tested in California. What advantages would Quaker obtain by knowing this information? How long would it take Quaker to find out about each in the absence of inside knowledge from Redmond? If all these items would become readily apparent the moment Pepsi's plans were implemented, does this circumstance suggest a limit on the appropriate remedy?

Assuming that Quaker will learn of Pepsi's strategies from Redmond unless enjoined, how expensive would it be for Pepsi to develop a new marketing strategy? Could the new strategy take advantage of the fact that Quaker *thinks* it knows what Pepsi will do? How would this possibility affect Quaker's use of the information?

2. Assume that the market for sports and new age drinks is increasingly concentrated in the hands of two companies, Pepsi and Quaker. Should this affect the outcome of the case? Given the court's decision, what can one predict about future salary and benefits negotiations in this industry for employees like Redmond?

3. Is it fair to preclude former employees from doing any work for a competitor simply because they would be incapable of not using the information they obtained from their former employer? Note that the Seventh Circuit upheld an injunction against Redmond's employment for only six months. At the same time, the court issued a permanent injunction against the disclosure of Pepsi's trade secrets. Does this result make sense? If the theory of inevitable disclosure is that Redmond *must* use Pepsi's secrets in his employment, could he go to work for Quaker at the end of six months without violating the permanent injunction? Perhaps the court was implicitly seeking to balance Redmond's interests in employment mobility, reasoning that the business secrets would be less important after that time.

4. Is there any way that that employee can "keep separate" the ideas and projects he was working on for his old employer from the ideas and projects he will be asked to develop for his new employer? If not, should the employer be entitled to prevent the employee from competing even if it cannot show that the employee *intends* to use its trade secrets? *Cf. Al Minor & Assocs. v. Martin*, 881 N.E.2d 850 (Ohio 2008) (holding that the fact that a defendant had the plaintiff's secrets in his memory rather than on a disk or document did not preclude a finding of misappropriation).

Several cases have followed *PepsiCo* and enjoined employment absent either proof of trade secret misappropriation or an enforceable noncompetition agreement. *See Uncle B's Bakery v. O'Rourke*, 920 F. Supp. 1405 (N.D. Iowa 1996) (citing *PepsiCo* with approval and enjoining former plant manager at a bagel manufacturer from working for any competing business within a 500-mile radius); *see also Nat'l Starch & Chem. Corp. v. Parker Chem. Corp.*, 530 A.2d 31 (N.J. Super. Ct. App. Div. 1987). By contrast, one court has adopted what might be called a "partial inevitable disclosure" injunction. *See*

Merck & Co. v. Lyon, 941 F. Supp. 1443 (M.D.N.C. 1996) (enjoining a pharmaceutical marketing director from discussing his former employer's products or pricing for a period of two years, but declining to enjoin him from competing employment altogether absent a "showing of bad faith"); *Novell Inc. v. Timpanogos Research Grp.*, 46 U.S.P.Q.2d 1197 (D. Utah 1998) (applying the doctrine, but limiting injunction duration to nine months because the secrets at risk would turn stale over time).

5. *Doctrine or Evidentiary Showing of "Threatened Missappropriation."* One court notes that in discussing "inevitable disclosure doctrine" that "calling a line of reasoning a 'doctrine' poses the risk of ossifying the 'factors' into a rigid test." *Molon Motor & Coil Cor. v. Nidec Motor Corp.*, 2017 WL 1954531, at *5 n.13 (N.D. Ill. May 11, 2017). The "inevitable disclosure" language is used by many courts to summarize evidentiary showings pointing to an ongoing imminent risk of "threatened misappropriation." *See* PETER S. MENELL, ET AL., TRADE SECRET CASE MANAGEMENT JUDICIAL GUIDE §§2.6.1.1, 5.2, 5.8 (2023) (collecting cases and discussing factual showings pointing toward and away from a finding of imminent threatened misappropriation sufficient to support a claim for pre-trial injunctive relief); Stacey Dogan & Felicity Slater, *The Long Shadow of Inevitable Disclosure*, 30 GEO. MASON L. REV. 3 (2023) (noting that only a handful of jurisdictions have adopted the most extreme form of the doctrine and even those states rarely apply it to limit employee mobility). These showings are almost always based in on improper acts and not simply information that an individual knows.

6. Other jurisdictions reject the inevitable disclosure doctrine altogether. California's strict policy favoring employee mobility is the clearest example. *See* CAL. BUS. & PROF. CODE §16600. Some jurisdictions have rejected injunctions barring employment based on inevitable disclosure, although they have indicated that a noncompetition agreement could achieve such a result. *See Campbell Soup Co. v. Giles*, 47 F.3d 467 (1st Cir. 1995) (noting that public policy "counsels against unilateral conversion of non-disclosure agreements into non-competitive agreements"); *Carolina Chem. Equip. Co. v. Muckenfuss*, 471 S.E.2d 721 (S.C. Ct. App. 1996) (agreement entitled "Covenant Not to Divulge Trade Secrets" was an overbroad and unenforceable covenant not to compete, because the definition of trade secrets in the agreement effectively prevented any competition); *Del Monte Fresh Produce Co. v. Dole Food Co.*, 148 F. Supp. 2d 1326, 1337–39 (S.D. Fla. 2001) (same); *see also Holton v. Physician Oncology Servs.*, 742 S.E.2d 702, 705–06 (Ga. 2013) (holding that "the inevitable disclosure doctrine is not an independent claim under which a trial court may enjoin an employee from working for an employer or disclosing trade secrets"; such relief is only available upon a showing of actual or threatened misappropriation); *LeJeune v. Coin Acceptors*, 849 A.2d 451, 469–71 (Md. 2004); *FMC Corp. v. Cyprus Foote Mineral Co.*, 899 F. Supp. 1477, 1483 (W.D.N.C. 1995) (stating that North Carolina's "courts would refuse to enjoin an employee from working for its former employer's competitor under the doctrine of 'inevitable discovery' absent some showing of bad faith, underhanded dealing, or employment by an entity so plainly lacking comparable technology that misappropriation can be inferred").

7. The federal Defend Trade Secrets Act, enacted in 2016, acknowledges the conflicts between the states but declines to adopt an inevitable disclosure rule that would override the public policy of California and other states favoring employee mobility. *See* S. REP., NO. 114-220, 114TH CONG., 2D SESS., DEFEND TRADE SECRETS ACT OF 2016 12 n.12 (2016). To avoid doing so, the DTSA requires that proof of threatened future misappropriation be based on evidence of conduct and intent and not simply inferred from the employee's position or knowledge. 18 U.S.C. §1836(b)(3)(A)(i). That section provides that a court may:

(A) grant an injunction

(i) to prevent any actual or threatened misappropriation described in paragraph (1) on such terms as the court deems reasonable, provided the order does not

(I) prevent a person from entering into an employment relationship, and that the conditions placed on such employment shall be based on evidence of threatened misappropriation and not merely on the information the person knows; or

(II) otherwise conflict with an applicable State law prohibiting restraints on the practice of a lawful profession, trade, or business.

The SENATE REPORT notes that "[t]hese limitations on injunctive relief were included to protect employee mobility, as some have expressed concern that the injunctive relief authorized under the bill could override State-law limitations that safeguard employee mobility and thus could be a substantial departure from existing law in those states." S. REP., S. 1890 at 12. Thus, inevitable disclosure is not a viable theory under the DTSA. *See Idexx Labs. v. Bilbrough*, 2022 WL 3042966 (D. Me. Aug. 2, 2022); *CAE Integrated v. Moov Techs., Inc.*, 44 F.4th 257, 262–63 (5th Cir. 2022) (holding that where an employee had discarded all customer lists before moving to a new firm, the DTSA did not prohibit him from taking the job even if he still knew the customer information because doing so would impermissibly be based on his knowledge and not his behavior).

At the same time, the DTSA does not preempt state laws that apply the inevitable disclosure doctrine.

8. How inevitable must the disclosure be? In *Bimbo Bakeries v. Botticella*, 613 F.3d 102 (3d Cir. 2010), the court affirmed an injunction preventing a senior executive of Bimbo Bakeries, the maker of Thomas' English Muffins, from going to work for competitor Hostess. Botticella was one of only seven people at Bimbo who knew the formula for the muffins. Notably, the court did not find that it was "virtually impossible" for Botticella to do his job at Hostess without disclosing the formula. Instead, the court found it sufficient that there was a "substantial threat" of misappropriation. Does this result make sense? If the defendant denies any intent to deliver the secret to his new employer, what evidence should a court require before preventing him from going to work? Some courts seek to strike a middle ground, holding that where misappropriation is merely threatened rather than actual, the plaintiff must demonstrate "a high degree of

probability of inevitable disclosure   Mere knowledge of a trade secret is not enough, even where the person with such knowledge takes a comparable position with a competitor." *Katch, LLC v. Sweetser*, 2015 WL 6942132 (D. Minn. Nov. 10, 2015); *see also Archer Daniels Midland Co. v. Sinele*, 139 N.E.3d 1036, 1046 (Ill. Ct. App. 2019) (distinguishing *PepsiCo* where a sales manager went to a broker rather than to a competing seller); *Prime Therapeutics v. Beatty*, 354 F. Supp. 3d 957 (D. Minn. 2018) (no inevitable disclosure when employee's job for a competitor is somewhat different than the old job).

9. Even states like California that do not recognize the inevitable disclosure doctrine will sometimes enjoin departing employees from working at a new company, but only on a showing that the employee or the new employer actually engaged in conduct making trade secret misappropriation likely. Thus, in the high-profile lawsuit between Google (Waymo) and Uber over self-driving cars, Anthony Levandowski, the former head of Waymo's self-driving car division, was ordered not to work at Uber on the same parts of the project he worked on for Waymo and was eventually fired. *See* Aaron Marxhall, *Uber and Waymo Abruptly Settle For $245 Million*, WIRED (Feb. 9, 2019). The court ordered Levandowski to pay $179 million and the U.S. Attorney filed criminal trade secret and other charges. Levandowski ultimately pled guilty. *See* Reed Albergotti, *Ex-Uber executive Anthony Levandowski pleads guilty to trade-secret theft*, WASH. POST (Mar. 19, 2020).

PROBLEM 11-18

You have been offered a position with a high-technology start-up company. They ask you to sign the following agreement. Do you sign it? Is it enforceable?

EMPLOYMENT, CONFIDENTIAL INFORMATION, AND INVENTION AS-
SIGNMENT AGREEMENT

As a condition of my employment with Science Company, its subsidiaries, affiliates, successors, or assigns (together the "Company"), and in consideration of my employment with the Company and my receipt of the compensation now and hereafter paid to me by the Company, I agree to the following:

1. Confidential Information

(a) *Company Information.* I agree at all times during the term of my employment and thereafter, to hold in strictest confidence, and not to use, except for the benefit of the Company, or to disclose to any person, firm, or corporation without written authorization of the Board of Directors of the Company, any Confidential Information of the Company. I understand that "**Confidential Information**" means any Company proprietary information, technical data, trade secrets or know-how, including, but not limited to, research, product plans, products, services, customer lists and customers (including, but not limited to, customers of the Company on whom I called or with whom I became acquainted during the term of my employment), markets, software, developments, inventions, processes, formulas, technology, designs, drawings, engineering, hardware configuration information, marketing, finances, or other business information disclosed to me by the Company either directly or indirectly in writing, orally, or by drawings or observation of parts or equipment. I further understand that Confidential Information does not include any of the foregoing items which has become publicly known and made generally available through no wrongful act of mine or of others who were under confidentiality obligations as to the item or items involved.

(b) *Third Party Information.* I recognize that the Company has received and in the future will receive from third parties their confidential or proprietary information subject to a duty on the Company's part to maintain the confidentiality of such information and to use it only for certain limited purposes. I agree to hold all such confidential or proprietary information in the strictest confidence and not to disclose it to any person, firm, or corporation or to use it except as necessary in carrying out my work for the Company consistent with the Company's agreement with such third party.

2. Inventions

I agree that I will promptly make full written disclosure to the Company, will hold in trust for the sole right and benefit of the Company, and hereby assign to the Company, or its designee, all my right, title, and interest in and to any and all inventions, original works of authorship, developments, concepts, improvements or trade secrets, whether or not patentable or registrable under copyright or similar laws, which I may solely or jointly conceive or develop or reduce to practice, or cause to be conceived or developed or reduced to practice (collectively referred to as "Inventions"), during the period of time I am in the employ of the Company and for three months thereafter, except as provided below. I further acknowledge that all original works of authorship which are made by me (solely or jointly with others) within the scope of and during the period of my employment with the Company and which are protectable by copyright are "works made for hire," as that term is defined in the United States Copyright Act.

3. Conflicting Employment

I agree that, during the term of my employment with the Company and for a period of one year thereafter, I will not engage in any other employment, occupation, consulting, or other business activity in competition with or directly related to the business in which the Company is now involved or becomes involved during the term of my employment, nor will I engage in any other activities that conflict with my obligations to the Company.

4. Returning Company Documents

I agree that at the time of leaving the employ of the Company, I will deliver to the Company (and will not keep in my possession, recreate or deliver to anyone else) any and all devices, records, data, notes, reports, proposals, lists, correspondence, specifications, drawings, blueprints, sketches, materials, equipment, other documents or property, or reproductions of any aforementioned items developed by me pursuant to my employment with the Company or otherwise belonging to the Company, its successors or assigns.

5. *Notification to New Employer*

In the event that I leave the employ of the Company, I hereby grant consent to notification by the Company to my new employer about my rights and obligations under this Agreement.

6. *Solicitation of Employees*

I agree that for a period of twelve (12) months immediately following the termination of my relationship with the Company for any reason, whether with or without cause, I shall not either directly or indirectly solicit, induce, recruit or encourage any of the Company's employees to leave their employment, or take away such employees, or attempt to solicit, induce, recruit, encourage, or take away employees of the Company, either for myself or for any other person or entity.

G. REMEDIES

As might be expected given the widely varying circumstances surrounding trade secret misappropriation, trade secret law affords courts a broad range of options and discretion for tailoring appropriate remedies. The Uniform Trade Secrets Act sets forth the following remedies for misappropriation:

Section 2

(a) Actual or threatened misappropriation may be enjoined. Upon application to the court, an injunction shall be terminated when the trade secret has ceased to exist, but the injunction may be continued for an additional reasonable period of time in order to eliminate commercial advantage that otherwise would be derived from the misappropriation.

(b) If the court determines that it would be unreasonable to prohibit future use, an injunction may condition future use upon payment of a reasonable royalty for no longer than the period of time the use could have been prohibited.

(c) In appropriate circumstances, affirmative acts to protect a trade secret may be compelled by court order.

Section 3

(a) In addition to or in lieu of injunctive relief, a complainant may recover damages for the actual loss caused by misappropriation. A complainant also may recover for the unjust enrichment caused by misappropriation that is not taken into account in computing damages for actual loss.

(b) If willful and malicious misappropriation exists, the court may award exemplary damages in an amount not exceeding twice any award made under subsection (a).

Section 4

If (i) a claim of misappropriation is made in bad faith, (ii) a motion to terminate an injunction is made or resisted in bad faith, or (iii) willful and malicious misappropriation exists, the court may award reasonable attorney's fees to the prevailing party.

What motivates this range of remedial measures? As we shall see in the chapters to come, most intellectual property statutes operate on the basis of "property rules." That is, as in cases involving real property, the owner of the intellectual property right is entitled to judicial assistance in protecting the right from future interference. Normally, this assistance comes in the form of injunctive relief. By contrast, most tort and contract cases do not involve injunctive relief but rather damages designed to make the plaintiff "whole" in the sense of restoring her to the position she occupied before the tort, or to the position she expected to occupy if the contract had been performed.

Section 2 of the Uniform Trade Secrets Act seems to entitle trade secret plaintiffs to property-like protection, at least so long as their secret remains a secret. But §2(b) holds open the possibility that courts may refuse to grant such an injunction, settling instead for a reasonable "royalty" (presumably a court's attempt to approximate what the parties might have agreed to pay in a licensing transaction). This provision casts some doubt on the "property entitlement" a trade secret owner might expect.

Similar doubt pervades the provisions on damages. Concepts like "reasonable royalty," "lost profits," and limited-time injunctions designed to "eliminate commercial advantage" all sound like measures aimed at making the plaintiff whole after a loss without necessarily punishing or deterring the defendant. But further provisions permit trade secret plaintiffs to recover for "unjust enrichment" on the part of defendants, and to recover treble damages and attorney fees in the case of willful misappropriation. Those provisions are more focused on deterring defendants. And in some circumstances misappropriation of trade secrets can be a criminal offense, an idea that is certainly more consistent with a property entitlement rule than a tort or contract rule.

1. Injunctions

Injunctions are commonly ordered in trade secret cases, although their scope and duration are typically tailored based on the circumstances. Since injunctions offer only prospective relief, however, damages for preinjunction activities may also be collected. Since, unlike patents and copyrights, trade secrets have no definite term, the length of the injunction is often a difficult issue. The following case illustrates the use of one important measure of trade secret injunctions, the "head start" theory.

Winston Research Corp. v. 3M Corp.
United States Court of Appeals for the Ninth Circuit
350 F.2d 134 (9th Cir. 1965)

BROWNING, Circuit Judge:

For some uses of precision tape recorder/reproducers, the time interval between coded signals must be recorded and reproduced with great accuracy. To accomplish this, the tape must move at as constant a speed as possible during both recording and reproduction, and any changes in tape speed during recording must be duplicated as nearly as possible during reproduction. The degree to which a particular tape recorder/reproducer accomplishes, this result is measured by its "time-displacement error."

An electronic device known as a "servo" system is commonly used to reduce time-displacement error by detecting fluctuations in tape speed and immediately adjusting the speed of the motor. Machines prior to the Mincom machine employed a flywheel to inhibit fluctuation in tape speed by increasing the inertia of the system. However, the flywheel reduced the effectiveness of the servo system since the increased inertia prevented rapid adjustments in the speed of the motor.

The effectiveness of the servo system in prior machines was also reduced by resonances created by the moving parts. The range of sensitivity of the servo system was limited to exclude the frequencies of the interfering resonances. This had the disadvantage of limiting the capacity of the servo system to respond to a full range of variations in the speed of the tape.

To solve these problems Mincom eliminated the flywheel and reduced the mass of all other rotating parts. This reduced the inertia of the tape transport system, permitting rapid adjustments in tape speed. Interfering resonances were eliminated by mechanical means. This permitted use of a servo system sensitive to a wide range of frequencies, and hence capable of rapid response to a wide range of variations in tape speed. After four years of research and development based upon this approach, Mincom produced a successful machine with an unusually low time-displacement error.

In May 1962, when Mincom had substantially completed the research phase of its program and was beginning the development of a production prototype, Johnson, who was in charge of Mincom's program, left Mincom's employment. He joined Tobias, who had previously been discharged as Mincom's sales manager, in forming Winston Research Corporation. In late 1962, Winston contracted with the government to develop a precision tape reproducer. Winston hired many of the technicians who had participated in the development of the Mincom machine to work on the design and development of the Winston machine.

In approximately fourteen months, Winston completed a machine having the same low time-displacement error as the Mincom machine.

Conflicting policy considerations come into play in deciding what limitations should be imposed upon an employee in the use and disclosure of information acquired in the course of a terminated employment relationship—or, conversely, what protection should be extended to the former employer against use and disclosure of such information.

On the one hand, restrictions upon the use and disclosure of such information limit the employee's employment opportunities, tie him to a particular employer, and weaken his bargaining power with that employer. Such restrictions interfere with the employee's movement to the job in which he may most effectively use his skills. They inhibit an employee from either setting up his own business or from adding his strength to a competitor of his employer, and thus they diminish potential competition. Such restrictions impede the dissemination of ideas and skills throughout industry. The burdens that they impose upon the employee and society increase in proportion to the significance of the employee's accomplishments, and the degree of his specialization.

On the other hand, restrictions upon an employee's disclosure of information that was developed as a result of the employer's initiative and investment, and which was entrusted to the employee in confidence, are necessary to the maintenance of decent standards of morality in the business community. Unless protection is given against unauthorized disclosure of confidential business information by employees, employee-employer relationships will be demoralized; employers will be compelled to limit communication among employees with a consequent loss in efficiency; and business, espionage, deceit, and fraud among employers will be encouraged. . . .

. . . [S]tate law protecting trade secrets cannot be based "on a policy of rewarding or otherwise encouraging the development of secret processes or devices. The protection is merely against breach of faith and reprehensible means of learning another's secret." RESTATEMENT, TORTS §757, comment b.

The district court found, and Winston concedes, that Johnson and the other former Mincom employees based Winston's development program upon the same approach to the problem of achieving a low time-displacement error as they had pursued in developing the Mincom machine. The district court further found that this general approach was not a trade secret of Mincom's. Finally, the district court found that the particular embodiment of these general concepts in the Mincom machine was Mincom's trade secret, and had been improperly utilized by the former Mincom employees in developing the Winston machine.

[The court affirmed the district court's finding that Winston had misappropriated Mincom's trade secrets.]

The district court enjoined Winston Research Corporation, Johnson, and Tobias from disclosing or using Mincom's trade secrets in any manner for a period of two years from the date of judgment. The court also required the assignment of certain patent applications to Mincom. No damages were awarded   Mincom argues that the injunction should have been permanent, or at least for a substantially longer period. Winston contends that no injunctive relief was appropriate.

Mincom was, of course, entitled to protection of its trade secrets for as long as they remained secret. The district court's decision to limit the duration of injunctive relief was necessarily premised upon a determination that Mincom's trade secrets would shortly be fully disclosed, through no fault of Winston, as a result of public announcements, demonstrations, and sales and deliveries of Mincom machines. Mincom has not seriously challenged this implicit finding, and we think the record fully supports it. . . .

We think the district court's approach was sound. A permanent injunction would subvert the public's interest in allowing technical employees to make full use of their knowledge and skill and in fostering research and development. On the other hand, denial of any injunction at all would leave the faithless employee unpunished where, as here, no damages were awarded; and he and his new employer would retain the benefit of a headstart over legitimate competitors who did not have access to the trade secrets until they were publicly disclosed. By enjoining use of the trade secrets for the approximate period it would require a legitimate Mincom competitor to develop a successful machine after public disclosure of the secret information, the district court denied the employees any advantage from their faithlessness, placed Mincom in the position it would have occupied if the breach of confidence had not occurred prior to the public disclosure, and imposed the minimum restraint consistent with the realization of these objectives upon the utilization of the employees' skills. . . .

Winston also challenges the district court's determination that "knowledge of the reasons for" the particular specifications of the Mincom machine, and "knowledge of what not to do . . . and how not to make the same mistakes" as Mincom had made in arriving at these specifications, were Mincom trade secrets.   Although we agree with the district court's conclusion that such "negative know-how" is a trade secret, in the circumstances of this case we can see no way to prohibit Mincom's former employees from using such knowledge without prohibiting them from using their general knowledge and experience at the same time. In an appropriate case, this kind of knowledge can be protected by an injunction or even an award of damages, but this is not such a case. . . .

Mincom argues that the district court should have awarded money damages as well as injunctive relief. We think the district court acted well within its discretion in declining to do so. Since Winston sold none of its machines, it had no profits to disgorge. The evidence as to possible future profits was at best highly speculative. To enjoin future sales and at the same time make an award based on future profits from the prohibited sales would result in duplicative and inconsistent relief, and the choice that the district court made between these mutually exclusive alternatives was not an unreasonable one. There was evidence that Winston would probably sell its machine and realize profits after the injunction expired, but these sales and profits, as we have seen, would not be tainted by breach of confidence, since Winston could by that time have developed its machine from publicly disclosed information. . . .

[Judgment affirmed.]

COMMENTS AND QUESTIONS

1. The general rule in IP law does not make injunctions automatic, but applies a four-factor balancing test that asks whether the plaintiff will be irreparably injured absent an injunction, whether the grant or denial of an injunction would impose more hardship, and where the public interest lies. *See eBay, Inc. v. MercExchange LLC*, 547 U.S. 388 (2006). Because the public disclosure of a trade secret can destroy the secret altogether, courts and commentators have traditionally thought injunctions appropriate to prevent an injury that truly is irreparable. But in the wake of *eBay* some courts have denied injunctive relief. *See, e.g., Faiveley Transport Malmo AB v. Wabtec Corp.*, 559 F.3d 110 (2d Cir. 2009); *First Western Capital v. Malamed*, 874 F.3d 1136 (10th Cir. 2017) (no presumption of irreparable injury, and no preliminary injunction without proof of irreparable injury); *Am. Airlines, Inc. v. Imhof*, 620 F. Supp. 2d 574 (S.D.N.Y. 2009) (refusing to presume irreparable injury; plaintiff did not show that the defendant was likely to disclose the documents he took to his new employer).

Should there be a presumption that injunctive relief is appropriate? Such a presumption is typical of cases involving real property, but no such rule exists in most tort cases, and certainly not in typical contract cases. Are damages sufficient to protect trade secret owners? It would seem not, since trade secrets are often hard to value, and misappropriation by one party can destroy the secret altogether. On the other hand, the parties in most states could contract for injunctive relief, at least in employment cases, using non-competition or confidentiality agreements. Should the law impose obligations the parties have not undertaken voluntarily? *See East v. Aqua Gaming Inc.*, 805 So. 2d 932 (Fla. Dist. Ct. App. 2001) (affirming injunction against use of trade secrets, but vacating injunction that prevented competition in the absence of an enforceable noncompete agreement).

One problem with such "automatic" injunctive relief is that it is difficult—and costly—to enforce. Is it an appropriate use of judicial resources to supervise employer-employee relationships on an ongoing basis? Is there a more cost-effective alternative to such supervision?

2. "Head-start injunctions" like the one in *Winston* are available to plaintiffs who have published or otherwise disclosed their secret at some point after it was misappropriated. Suppose Anne possesses a secret that she is in the process of commercializing. Suppose further that it takes Anne two years after developing the secret to bring the product to market, at which point the secret is disclosed. If Benjamin steals Anne's idea during the development process (say, after one year), Benjamin will be able to get to market one year earlier than if he had waited until the information became public. In such a case, courts will issue a "head-start" injunction for a period of one year, putting Benjamin in the same position he would have been in without the secret. *See, e.g., Verigy US Inc. v. Mayder*, 2008 WL 564634 (N.D. Cal. Feb. 29, 2008) (granting a five-month injunction to account for the lag time defendant would have faced in getting to market absent misappropriation).

3. Should the idea of "head start" injunctions apply to noncompete agreements as well as trade secret misappropriation? In *EMC Corp. v. Arturi*, 655 F.3d 75 (1st Cir. 2011), Justice Souter, sitting by designation, held that the plaintiff could not extend a noncompete agreement beyond its expiration date, even if the court had not enforced the agreement pending litigation by issuing a preliminary injunction.

If an employee agrees not to compete for a year, and it takes more than a year for the court to decide that agreement is enforceable, what is the plaintiff's remedy? How would damages be calculated in such a case?

4. In *Kewanee Oil Co. v. Bicron Corp.*, 416 U.S. 470, 473 (1974), the former employees had signed confidentiality agreements. The Court upheld the district court's granting of a permanent injunction against the disclosure or use by respondents of 20 of the 40 claimed trade secrets until such time as the trade secrets had been released to the public, had otherwise generally become available to the public, or had been obtained by respondents from sources having the legal right to convey the information. *Id.* at 473–74. *See also Henry Hope X-Ray Prods., Inc. v. Marron Carrel, Inc.*, 674 F.2d 1336, 1342 (9th Cir. 1982) (the limitation on confidential information contains the implicit temporal limitation that information may be disclosed when it ceases to be confidential).

Most courts have held that an indefinite injunction that extends beyond the head start period is inappropriate. *See Texas Advanced Optoelectronic v. Renesas Elecs. Am.*, 888 F.3d 1322, 1336 (Fed. Cir. 2018); *Howard Schultz & Assocs. v. Broniec*, 239 Ga. 181, 236 S.E.2d 265, 270 (1977) ("The nondisclosure covenant here contains no time limitation and hence it is unenforceable"); *Gary Van Zeeland Talent, Inc. v. Sandas*, 54 Wis. 2d 202, 267 N.W.2d 242, 250 (1978) (unlimited duration of agreement not to disclose trade secret customer list makes the agreement per se void). The Eighth Circuit in *Sigma Chemical Co. v. Harris*, 794 F.2d 371, 375 (8th Cir. 1986) explained, in the course of rejecting a "temporally unlimited" injunction, the rationale for limiting injunctions in time:

> [E]xtending the injunction beyond the time needed for independent development would give the employer "a windfall protection and would subvert the public interest in fostering competition and in allowing employees to make full use of their knowledge and ability."

> We believe the part of the injunction prohibiting disclosure of trade secrets must be limited in duration and, accordingly, reverse in part and remand the case to the district court for consideration of the time it would take a "legitimate competitor" to independently reproduce the information contained in the product and vendor files. On remand, the district court should also modify the language of the injunction to expressly state that Harris may use that information which is already in the public domain.

But see Halliburton Energy Servs., Inc. v. Axis Techs., LLC, 444 S.W.3d 251 (Tex. App. 2014) (ordering a perpetual injunction and opining that such perpetual injunctions were the norm). *Halliburton* represents a decidedly minority view among courts to consider the duration of injunctions. *See* Richard F. Dole, Jr., *Permanent Injunctive Relief for Trade Secret Misappropriation Without an Express Limit upon Its Duration: The Uniform Trade Secrets Act Reconsidered,* 17 B.U. J. SCI. & TECH. L. 173, 191–98 (2011) (collecting cases). The Federal Circuit held in *Texas Advanced* that the Texas Supreme Court would not apply such a rule.

In addition to limits on time, courts also refuse to grant general "obey the law" injunctions against any misappropriation, instead enjoining only the use or disclosure of specific, identified trade secrets. Fed. R. Civ. P. 65(d); *Corning, Inc. v. PicVue Elecs.,* 365 F.3d 156, 157–58 (2d Cir. 2004). Thus, courts have reversed overbroad injunctions that prevented the defendant from using any information obtained from the plaintiff without determining whether the information was in fact a trade secret or merely represented general skill and knowledge the defendant gained on the job. *See, e.g.,,Mallet & Co. v. Lacayo,* 16 F.4th 364 (3d Cir. 2021).

5. Who should be enjoined? Several courts have refused to hold the new employer liable for an employee's malfeasance where they were unaware of it. *See Infinity Prods. v. Quandt,* 810 N.E.2d 1028 (Ind. 2004) (no respondeat superior liability for trade secret law); *BEA Sys. v. WebMethods, Inc.,* 595 S.E.2d 87 (Ga. Ct. App. 2004).

6. Ex Parte *Seizure Orders.* While most requests for early equitable relief in trade secret disputes are made on notice pursuant to FED. R. CIV. P. 65, Congress enacted as part of the DTSA a self-contained "civil seizure" provision, patterned on similar language in the Lanham Act, permitting the trade secret owner to seek an *ex parte* seizure order without notice to the other side to prevent the "propagation or dissemination" of the trade secret in "extraordinary circumstances." 18 U.S.C. §1836(b)(2)(A). This portion of the DTSA was also the issue most heavily debated and redrafted in the years leading up to its enactment.

This provision reflects Congress's concerns about cybersecurity and foreign hacking of websites. "The ex parte seizure provision is expected to be used in instances in which a defendant is seeking to flee the country or planning to disclose the trade secret to a third party immediately or is otherwise not amenable to the enforcement of the court's orders." S. Rep. No. 114-220, 114th Cong., 2d Sess., Defend Trade Secrets Act of 2016 9–10 (2016).

The DTSA permits *ex parte* seizures of trade secret information and evidence of misappropriation where there is some risk that the secrets would be disclosed or the evidence destroyed before a court could enjoin it during normal legal processes. Such *ex parte* seizures are subject to a number of conditions, limitations, and safeguards, including proof not only that the plaintiff is likely to win the case and meet the requirements for an injunction but also that the normal process of a temporary restraining order is inadequate because the defendant will not comply with it and that the defendant would destroy or hide the evidence if she were given notice of the proposed seizure. *See* 18 U.S.C. §1836(b)(A)(ii). If seizure is granted, the seizure order must "provide for the narrowest seizure of property necessary" to achieve the purposes of the order and to minimize any interruption of the business operations of third parties and, to the extent possible, the legitimate business operations of the person accused of misappropriation of the trade secret. The party seeking the *ex parte* seizure order "shall" be required to post security to pay damages that any person may be entitled to recover as a result of a wrongful or excess seizure or attempted seizure. The statute includes additional detailed safeguards, including protecting the party against whom an order is directed from publicity about the order and seizure at the behest of the person obtaining the order, protecting the seized storage medium, protecting the confidentiality of seized materials that are unrelated to the seized trade secret information and, where appropriate, appointing a special master and technical experts not controlled by or associated with the moving party or its counsel to assist in taking control of the seized material. *See* 18 U.S.C. §1836(b)(2)(C)–(D).

2. Damages and Disgorgement

The UTSA provides for damages adequate to compensate for infringement, and in addition for the disgorgement of defendant's profits from misappropriation to the extent they are not taken into account in the damages award. Both damages and profits must, however, be limited to losses suffered during the head start period, before the defendant could have lawfully obtained or developed the secret. *See Texas Advanced Optoelectronic v. Renesas Elecs. Am.*, 888 F.3d 1322, 1336 (Fed. Cir. 2018).

Damages. A plaintiff is entitled to recover as damages any economic losses they suffer as a result of the infringement. Those may include lost sales to a competitor or the loss of the value of the secret itself. But the plaintiff must prove that harm; it is not enough to speculate that the plaintiff would have succeeded in a new market but for the infringer's competition. *See Geometwatch Corp. v. Behunin*, 38 F.4th 1183, 1205 (10th Cir. 2022). While the plaintiff whose secret is disclosed and therefore destroyed by the defendant can recover the value of the secret as a whole, plaintiff can recover the value of the trade secret only if the defendant's acts destroyed the secret. *Syntel Sterling Best Shores Mauritius Ltd. v. The Trizetto Group*, 2023 WL 3236674 (2d Cir. May 25, 2023); *Airfacts, Inc. v. Amezaga*, 30 F.4th 359 (4th Cir. 2022).

Disgorgement. Plaintiffs can also obtain disgorgement of the defendant's gains from misappropriation to the extent they aren't already counted in plaintiff's losses. Disgorgement is designed to deter misappropriation by depriving the defendant of ill-gotten gains, even if those gains exceed what the plaintiff itself could have made. By contrast, New York, which follows the Restatement rather than the UTSA, has held that disgorgement of defendant's profits from infringement is not an available remedy. *See E.J. Brooks Co. v. Cambridge Security Seals*, 31 N.Y.3d 441 (Ct. App. N.Y. 2018).

A jury trial may be available on the damages claim, but disgorgement is an equitable remedy that is decided by a judge. *See id.* at 1337–44.

Royalties. Even if an injunction is impossible and the plaintiff can't show lost profits, courts may allow the defendant to continue using the former secret but require them to pay a "reasonable royalty.". The reasonable royalty is set by the court in an effort to approximate the royalty the trade secret owner might have charged in a voluntary transaction. That in turn is based on the value the defendant obtained from using the secret. *PPG Indus. Inc. v. Jiangsu Tie Mao Glass Co.*, 47 F.4th 156, 162 (3d Cir. 2022).

Is a reasonable royalty a fair solution in such a situation? *See Mid-Michigan Comp. Sys. v. Marc Glassman Inc.*, 416 F.3d 505 (6th Cir. 2005) (basing damages for misappropriation of computer software on a reasonable royalty). At least one commentator has suggested that such a remedy "is peculiarly inappropriate to redress a situation where injunctive relief ought to be applied." *See* 12 ROGER MILGRIM, MILGRIM ON TRADE SECRETS §1.01[2][a], at 1–36 n.20 (citing a district court decision concluding that limiting relief to a reasonable royalty invites misappropriation).

Is a reasonable royalty always appropriate in the absence of an injunction, even if there is no evidence that the plaintiff lost money (or the defendant gained it) as a result of the misappropriation? In *Ajaxo Inc. v. E*Trade Fin. Corp.*, 115 Cal. Rptr. 3d 168 (Ct. App. 2010), the court held that it was error to refuse to award a reasonable royalty where the plaintiff could not prove damages or unjust enrichment. And in *Bianco v. Globus Medical, Inc.*, 53 F. Supp. 3d 929 (E.D. Tex. 2014), the court treated a reasonable royalty as the normal remedy for use of a trade secret when the parties are not in competition, just as it is in patent cases. Notably, the *Bianco* court concluded that the royalty should be paid for fifteen years, well after the secret would have been discovered by independent means, reasoning that when the trade secret owner licensed ideas voluntarily it often signed contracts that required ongoing royalties. *See also Airfacts, Inc. v. Amezaga*, 30 F.4th 359 (4th Cir. 2022) (holding that a reasonable royalty should be awarded even though the defendant made no commercial use of the secret and merely put it on his resume).

The Seventh Circuit holds that treble damages for misappropriation of trade secrets are unconstitutional, extending a line of tort cases that limits the ratio of punitive to actual damages. *See Epic Sys. v. Tata Consultancy Servs.*, 980 F.3d 1117 (7th Cir. 2020). The court held that punitive damages could not exceed the amount of actual damages (thus permitting doubling but not trebling the award).

3. State Criminal Trade Secret Statutes

Misappropriation of trade secrets is not only a tort; in some circumstances, it is a crime. A series of well-publicized criminal prosecutions of computer executives accused of taking trade secrets to their new employers have raised the consciousness of industry professionals about trade secrets. The prosecutions have also raised ethical and political questions about the propriety of trade secret prosecutions "engineered" by the real parties in interest, often major companies such as Intel or Borland.

Criminal trade secret cases differ from civil ones in several respects. The complaining party is the government, rather than the injured company. However, the injured companies are the "real parties in interest" and usually have some presence in the case.

Even though they are not parties to the criminal proceeding, they at least supply a significant number of the witnesses and enjoy a high level of communication with the district attorney.

The burden of proof is higher than in a civil case. Some cases that could be won by the plaintiffs as civil cases will be lost in criminal court. This situation is even more likely because several states have definitions of trade secrets in their criminal laws that are more limited than their civil counterparts. For example, CAL. PENAL CODE §499c, which governs theft of trade secrets, historically limited the definition of a trade secret to "scientific or technical" information. (The constitutionality of this definition of trade secrets was upheld against a vagueness attack in *People v. Serrata*, 133 Cal. Rptr. 144 (Ct. App. 1976).) But in 1996, the California legislature amended its criminal trade secret statute to be coextensive with the broader definition of trade secrets in the Uniform Trade Secrets Act.

Defendants accused of stealing trade secrets may be charged with other offenses as well. For example, defendants who acquire a secret through improper means, as opposed to acquisition in a confidential relationship, may be guilty of larceny, receiving stolen property, or a host of similar crimes. *See People v. Gopal*, 217 Cal. Rptr. 487, 493–94 (Ct. App. 1985). Further, the growth of computer technology has expanded the federal role in prosecuting theft of trade secrets, since data taken over a computer network is considered to cross state lines. *See United States v. Riggs*, 739 F. Supp. 414 (N.D. Ill. 1990) (allowing indictment of computer hackers who published data from a Bell South computer text file for wire fraud and interstate transportation of stolen property).

The prosecution of a criminal (rather than civil) trade secret case has other effects on the parties involved. First, criminal trade secret courtrooms are the scene of constant battles over the publication of information. The real parties in interest will naturally oppose the disclosure in a public courtroom of the very secrets the defendant is accused of stealing. This concern runs headlong into the defendant's constitutional right to a public trial.[13] Second, civil cases are generally stayed pending the outcome of a criminal prosecution. Thus, a criminal prosecution may actually delay injunctive relief—the kind of remedy a civil plaintiff is often most interested in.

COMMENTS AND QUESTIONS

1. Given the stay imposed on a parallel civil action and the higher burden of proof in a criminal case, why would a civil plaintiff ever seek a criminal prosecution?

---

[13] There is no such right in civil cases. To avoid the very real danger that a misappropriation action will result in disclosure of the very secrets the plaintiff seeks to protect, civil trade secret actions will almost invariably include protective orders limiting the disclosure of information produced in discovery. Such orders are usually agreed to by the parties but may sometimes be imposed by the court. They will sometimes go so far as to prevent the parties themselves (as opposed to the attorneys and hired experts) from reviewing the other side's documents. In such a case, should in-house counsel be given access to discovery documents? *See Brown Bag Software v. Symantec Corp.*, 960 F.2d 1465, 1470 (9th Cir. 1992).

2. Should theft of trade secrets be a criminal offense? Does the presence of criminal sanctions have any effect on the optimal level of deterrence provided in damages suits, and therefore on the damages that should be awarded in a civil suit?

Do you see any problems with California's inclusion of business information in the criminal trade secret statute? Are there reasons to treat theft of scientific information more harshly than theft of business information?

4. Federal Criminal Trade Secret Liability

The Economic Espionage Act, enacted in 1996, imposes criminal liability for trade secret misappropriation. The EEA is divided into two sections: one focused on foreign espionage and the other applying generally. Section 1831 punishes the theft or misappropriation of a trade secret when undertaken by anyone "intending or knowing that the offense will benefit any foreign government, foreign instrumentality or foreign agent." 18 U.S.C. §1831(a). This prohibition targets foreign business espionage. To establish a violation of §1831, the government must prove that: (1) the defendant stole or without authorization of the owner, obtained, possessed destroyed, or conveyed information; (2) the defendant knew this information was proprietary; (3) the information was in fact a trade secret; and (4) the defendant intended or knew that the offense would "benefit" a "foreign government, foreign instrumentality or foreign agent."

Section 1832 is a general criminal trade secrets provision and applies to anyone who knowingly engages in any misappropriation of a trade secret. To establish a violation of §1832, the government must prove:

> (1) that the defendant intended to convert proprietary information to the economic benefit of anyone other than the owner; (2) that the proprietary information was a trade secret; (3) that the defendant knowingly stole, copied, possessed or received trade secret information; (4) that the defendant intended or knew the offense would injure the owner of the trade secret; and (5) that the trade secret was included in a product that is placed in interstate commerce.

United States v. Wen Chyu Liu, 716 F.3d 159, 169 (5th Cir. 2013).

By contrast to civil trade secret liability but in line with nearly all criminal statutes, both §1831(a)(4) and §1832(a)(4) also prohibit "attempts to commit any offense described in any of paragraphs (1) through (3)." *See United States v. Lange*, 312 F.3d 263 (7th Cir. 2002) (affirming guilty verdict on defendant even if he did not have real trade secrets in his possession because he thought that he did and took a substantial affirmative act (attempted sale) toward completion of the offense).

H. FEDERAL PREEMPTION

The Supremacy Clause of the U.S. CONSTITUTION provides that

> This Constitution, and the Laws of the United States which shall be made in Pursuance thereof; and all Treaties made, or which shall be made, under the Authority of the United States, shall be the supreme Law of the Land; and the

Judges in every State shall be bound thereby, any Thing [sic] in the Constitution or Laws of any State to the Contrary notwithstanding

U.S. CONSTITUTION, ART. VI, CL. 2. Thus, the Supremacy Clause nullifies state law attempts to duplicate or interfere with federal intellectual property protection. More difficult cases involve state laws that do not directly conflict with federal authority but instead address interstitial gaps within the federal regime. Courts must grapple with whether Congress intended to leave such gaps unfilled, thereby precluding state protection, or simply allowed state law to fill these voids. The following case addressed the interplay of federal patent law and state trade secret protection.

Kewanee Oil Co. v. Bicron Corp.
Supreme Court of the United States
416 U.S. 470 (1974)

MR. CHIEF JUSTICE BURGER delivered the opinion of the Court.

We granted certiorari to resolve a question on which there is a conflict in the courts of appeals: whether state trade secret protection is pre-empted by operation of the federal patent law. In the instant case the Court of Appeals for the Sixth Circuit held that there was preemption. The Courts of Appeals for the Second, Fourth, Fifth, and Ninth Circuits have reached the opposite conclusion. . . .

Petitioner brought this diversity action in United States District Court for the Northern District of Ohio seeking injunctive relief and damages for the misappropriation of trade secrets. The district Court, applying Ohio trade secret law, granted a permanent injunction against the disclosure or use by respondents of 20 of the 40 claimed trade secrets until such time as the trade secrets had been released to the public, had otherwise generally become available to the public, or had been obtained by respondents from sources having the legal right to convey the information.

The Court of Appeals for the Sixth Circuit held that the findings of fact by the District Court were not clearly erroneous, and that it was evident from the record that the individual respondents appropriated to the benefit of Bicron secret information on processes obtained while they were employees at Harshaw. Further, the Court of Appeals held that the District Court properly applied Ohio law relating to trade secrets. Nevertheless, the Court of Appeals reversed the District Court, finding Ohio's trade secret law to be in conflict with the patent laws of the United States. The Court of Appeals reasoned that Ohio could not grant monopoly protection to processes and manufacturing techniques that were appropriate subjects for consideration under 35 U.S.C. §101 for a federal patent but which had been in commercial use for over one year and so were no longer eligible for patent protection under 35 U.S.C. §102(b).

We hold that Ohio's law of trade secrets is not preempted by the patent laws of the United States, and accordingly, we reverse. . . .

III.

The first issue we deal with is whether the States are forbidden to act at all in the area of protection of the kinds of intellectual property which may make up the subject matter of trade secrets.

Article I, §8, cl. 8, of the Constitution grants to the Congress the power

> [t]o promote the Progress of Science and useful Arts, by securing for limited Times to Authors and Inventors the exclusive Right to their respective Writings and Discoveries. . . .

In the 1972 Term, in *Goldstein v. California*, 412 U.S. 546 (1973), we held that the cl. 8 grant of power to Congress was not exclusive and that, at least in the case of writings, the States were not prohibited from encouraging and protecting the efforts of those within their borders by appropriate legislation. The States could, therefore, protect against the unauthorized rerecording for sale of performances fixed on records or tapes, even though those performances qualified as "writings" in the constitutional sense and Congress was empowered to legislate regarding such performances and could pre-empt the area if it chose to do so. This determination was premised on the great diversity of interests in our Nation—the essentially nonuniform character of the appreciation of intellectual achievements in the various States. Evidence for this came from patents granted by the States in the 18th century. 412 U.S., at 557.

Just as the States may exercise regulatory power over writings so may the States regulate with respect to discoveries. States may hold diverse viewpoints in protecting intellectual property relating to invention as they do in protecting the intellectual property relating to the subject matter of copyright. The only limitation on the States is that in regulating the area of patents and copyrights they do not conflict with the operation of the laws in this area passed by Congress, and it is to that more difficult question we now turn.

IV.

The question of whether the trade secret law of Ohio is void under the Supremacy Clause involves a consideration of whether that law "stands as an obstacle to the accomplishment and execution of the full purposes and objectives of Congress." *Hines v. Davidowitz*, 312 U.S. 52, 67 (1941). *See Florida Avocado Growers v. Paul*, 373 U.S. 132, 141 (1963). We stated in *Sears, Roebuck & Co. v. Stiffel Co.*, 376 U.S. 225, 229 (1964), that when state law touches upon the area of federal statutes enacted pursuant to constitutional authority, "it is 'familiar doctrine' that the federal policy 'may not be set at naught, or its benefits denied' by the state law. *Sola Elec. Co v. Jefferson Elec. Co.*, 317 U.S. 173, 176 (1942). This is true, of course, even if the state law is enacted in the exercise of otherwise undoubted state power." . . .

The stated objective of the Constitution in granting the power to Congress to legislate in the area of intellectual property is to "promote the Progress of Science and useful Arts." The patent laws promote this progress by offering a right of exclusion for a limited period as an incentive to inventors to risk the often enormous costs in terms of time, research, and development. . . .

The maintenance of standards of commercial ethics and the encouragement of invention are the broadly stated policies behind trade secret law. "The necessity of good faith and honest, fair dealing, is the very life and spirit of the commercial world." . . .

As we noted earlier, trade secret law protects items which would not be proper subjects for consideration for patent protection under 35 U.S.C. §101. As in the case of the recordings in *Goldstein v. California*, Congress, with respect to nonpatentable subject matter, "has drawn no balance; rather, it has left the area unattended, and no reason exists why the State should not be free to act." *Goldstein v. California, supra,* at 570 (footnote omitted).

Since no patent is available for a discovery, however useful, novel, and nonobvious, unless it falls within one of the express categories of patentable subject matter of 35 U.S.C. §101, the holder of such a discovery would have no reason to apply for a patent whether trade secret protection existed or not. Abolition of trade secret protection would, therefore, not result in increased disclosure to the public of discoveries in the area of nonpatentable subject matter. . . .

Congress has spoken in the area of those discoveries which fall within one of the categories of patentable subject matter of 35 U.S.C. §101 and which are, therefore, of a nature that would be subject to consideration for a patent. Processes, machines, manufactures, compositions of matter, and improvements thereof, which meet the tests of utility, novelty, and nonobviousness are entitled to be patented, but those which do not, are not. The question remains whether those items which are proper subjects for consideration for a patent may also have available the alternative protection accorded by trade secret law.

Certainly the patent policy of encouraging invention is not disturbed by the existence of another form of incentive to invention. In this respect the two systems are not and never would be in conflict. Similarly, the policy that matter once in the public domain must remain in the public domain is not incompatible with the existence of trade secret protection. By definition a trade secret has not been placed in the public do- main.
. . .

. . . Trade secret law will encourage invention in areas where patent law does not reach, and will prompt the independent innovator to proceed with the discovery and exploitation of his invention. Competition is fostered and the public is not deprived of the use of valuable, if not quite patentable, invention. . . .

The final category of patentable subject matter to deal with is the clearly patentable invention, i.e., that invention which the owner believes to meet the standards of patentability. It is here that the federal interest in disclosure is at its peak. . . .

Trade secret law provides far weaker protection in many respects than the patent law. While trade secret law does not forbid the discovery of the trade secret by fair and honest means, e.g., independent creation or reverse engineering, patent law operates "against the world," forbidding any use of the invention for whatever purpose for a significant length of time. The holder of a trade secret also takes a substantial risk that the secret will be passed on to his competitors, by theft or by breach of a confidential relationship, in a manner not easily susceptible of discovery or proof. *Painton & Co. v. Bourns, Inc.*, 442 F.2d, at 224. Where patent law acts as a barrier, trade secret law functions relatively as a sieve. The possibility that an inventor who believes his invention meets the standards of patentability will sit back, rely on trade secret law, and after one year of use forfeit any right to patent protection, 35 U.S.C. §102(b), is remote indeed.

Nor does society face much risk that scientific or technological progress will be impeded by the rare inventor with a patentable invention who chooses trade secret protection over patent protection. The ripeness-of-time concept of invention, developed from the study of the many independent multiple discoveries in history, predicts that if a particular individual had not made a particular discovery others would have, and in probably a relatively short period of time. If something is to be discovered at all very likely it will be discovered by more than one person. . . .

. . . Trade secret law and patent law have co-existed in this country for over one hundred years. Each has its particular role to play, and the operation of one does not take away from the need for the other. . . . Congress, by its silence over these many years, has seen the wisdom of allowing the States to enforce trade secret protection. Until Congress takes affirmative action to the contrary, States should be free to grant protection to trade secrets. . . .

Mr. Justice DOUGLAS, with whom Mr. Justice BRENNAN concurs, dissenting.

Today's decision is at war with the philosophy of *Sears, Roebuck & Co. v. Stiffel Co.*, 376 U.S. 225, and *Compco Corp. v. Day-Brite Lighting, Inc.*, 376 U.S. 234. Those cases involved patents—one of a pole lamp and one of fluorescent lighting fixtures— each of which was declared invalid. The lower courts held, however, that though the patents were invalid the sale of identical or confusingly similar products to the products of the patentees violated state unfair competition laws. We held that when an article is unprotected by a patent, state law may not forbid others to copy it, because every article not covered by a valid patent is in the public domain. Congress in the patent laws decided that where no patent existed, free competition should prevail; that where a patent is rightfully issued, the right to exclude others should obtain for no longer than 17 years, and that the States may not "under some other law, such as that forbidding unfair competition, give protection of a kind that clashes with the objectives of the federal patent laws," 376 U.S., at 231. . . .

The conflict with the patent laws is obvious. The decision of Congress to adopt a patent system was based on the idea that there will be much more innovation if discoveries are disclosed and patented than there will be when everyone works in secret. Society thus fosters a free exchange of technological information at the cost of a limited 17-year monopoly. . . .

A suit to redress theft of a trade secret is grounded in tort damages for breach of a contract—a historic remedy, *Cataphote Corp. v. Hudson*, 422 F.2d 1290. Damages for breach of a confidential relation are not pre-empted by this patent law, but an injunction against use is pre-empted because the patent law states the only monopoly over trade secrets that is enforceable by specific performance; and that monopoly exacts as a price full disclosure. A trade secret can be protected only by being kept secret. Damages for breach of a contract are one thing; an injunction barring disclosure does service for the protection accorded valid patents and is therefore pre-empted. . . .

COMMENTS AND QUESTIONS

1. The rule set forth by *Sears, Roebuck & Co v. Stiffel Co.*, 376 U.S. 225 (1964), was fairly clear: patent law reflects a compromise between the goal of promoting innovation and the danger of condoning monopoly. Supplementing the scope of patent law may upset that balance, and is therefore prohibited. Supplementing *enforcement* of the federal intellectual property laws was condoned in dictum at the end of *Compco Corp. v. Day-Brite Lighting, Inc.*, 376 U.S. 234 (1964), a companion case, and in Justice Harlan's concurrence in both cases. After these cases, state law served a very limited function in the scheme of intellectual property protection. States could work to further the goals of federal protection, but they had to work within the parameters set down by federal law. As a result, both *Sears* and *Compco* struck down state statutes providing design protection to unpatentable utilitarian articles.

The *Kewanee* opinion takes a remarkably different tack. Chief Justice Burger's opinion for the Court emphasizes only one of the two policies shaping the patent laws: the goal of promoting innovation. The opinion does not discuss the dangers intellectual property protection poses for free competition. As a result, the *Kewanee* Court finds no problem with trade secret protection that extends beyond the scope of the patent laws. Note that the Court seems to approve not only of state laws that protect nonpatentable subject matter (an area in which it could be argued that the federal government has no interest),[14] but also the protection of inventions not patentable for some other reason (i.e., suppression, misuse, lack of novelty, or obviousness).

Is *Kewanee* reconcilable with *Sears*? The *Kewanee* court did not overrule *Sears* or *Compco*; indeed, it cited them in support of its holding. Thus state laws preventing copying were treated differently from trade secret laws after *Kewanee*. The latter, although broader in scope (they prevented far more than just outright copying of products), were permissible; the former were not. *See* Paul Goldstein, Kewanee Oil Co. v. Bicron Corp.: *Notes on a Closing Circle*, 1974 SUP. CT. REV. 81 (1974) (arguing that *Kewanee* "closed the circle" on the open-ended preemption analysis of *Sears* and *Compco*); Camilla A. Hrdy, *State Patents as a Solution to Underinvestment in Innovation*, 62 U. KAN. L. REV. 487 (2013) (arguing that state patents, which preceded the adoption of the Constitution in 1789, are still possible and in some cases desirable despite federal nature of patent law).

---

[14] Even in this area, though, a federal interest may be discerned. If Congress has declared some subject matter unpatentable, that could reflect a federal determination that that matter is unworthy of protection, a determination that state law should not be allowed to upset.

2. Is preemption a good idea? That depends on what you think of the balance the federal laws have struck. If you are more concerned about injury to competition by conferring monopoly rights on patentees, you are likely to favor the result in *Sears*. If, on the other hand, you think that innovation is under-rewarded, it is reasonable to oppose federal preemption. One way to reconcile these cases may be to read *Sears* and *Compco* as expressing a federal policy in favor of reverse engineering of products in the public domain. If that is the overarching federal goal, it is logical to strike down the laws in *Sears* and *Compco* but not *Kewanee,* since trade secrets statutes (unlike the unfair competition laws we have discussed) generally allow reverse engineering. This result is also consistent with the reading of trade secret laws as merely an application of tort and contract principles.

CHAPTER III:
PATENT LAW

A. INTRODUCTION

This chapter explores patent law. After a brief survey of the historical origins and an overview of the main contours, we turn to the elements of patentability. Patent law establishes relatively high thresholds for granting what can be extremely valuable exclusive rights. We then turn to claim construction, the delineation of the scope of patent claims. This provides a bridge to examining patent enforcement: infringement, defenses, and remedies. Thereafter, we turn to the increasingly important and controversial area of design patents, which as we will see in Chapters IV and V, overlaps copyright and trade dress protection. We then summarize international patent treaties and institutions. We conclude the chapter by exploring federal preemption of state laws aimed at protecting technology.

1. Historical Background

The first regular administrative apparatus for granting patents—the first real patent "system"—arose during the Renaissance. The term *patent*—from the Latin *patere* (to be open), referring to an open letter of privilege from the sovereign—originated in this period. The Venetian Senate's 1474 Act established the first regularized patent system:

> Be it enacted that, by the authority of this Council, every person who shall build any new and ingenious device in this City, not previously made in this Commonwealth, shall give notice of it to the office of our General Welfare Board when it has been reduced to perfection so that it can be used and operated. It being forbidden to every other person in any of our territories and towns to make any further device conforming with and similar to said one, without the consent and license of the author, for the term of 10 years. And if anybody builds it in violation hereof, the aforesaid author and inventor shall be entitled to have him summoned before any Magistrate of this City, by which Magistrate the said infringer shall be constrained to pay him one hundred ducats; and the device shall be destroyed at once.

Giulio Mandich, *Venetian Patents (1450–1550)*, 30 J. PAT. & TRADEMARK OFF. SOC'Y 166, 177 (1948).

The Venetian Act lays out all the essential features of modern patent protection. It covers "devices"; states that they must be registered with a specific administrative agency; says that they must be "new and ingenious," "reduced to perfection," and "not previously made in this Commonwealth"; provides a fixed term of ten years; and sets forth a procedure to determine infringement, as well as a remedy.

The opening of trade in Europe ensured that the new Venetian concept would spread. As Italian craftsmen—particularly glassworkers—fanned out across Europe, they brought with them the idea of legal protection for inventions.

Patents came to Great Britain by this route in the middle of the sixteenth century. The chief minister under Elizabeth I, William Cecil (Lord Burghley), used patent grants to induce foreign artisans to introduce continental technologies into England. Thus, what later became the Anglo-American patent system originated as a mercantilist instrument—what today would be called a "strategic international trade" policy. The idea was to lure immigrants who had desirable skills and know-how with the promise of an exclusive privilege. Ironically, by the mid-eighteenth century, Britain began to show concern over the reverse problem—leakage of its technical prowess to overseas rivals, including the American colonies. *See* DAVID JEREMY, TRANSATLANTIC INDUSTRIAL REVOLUTION 36–49 (1981).

With the accession of James I in England in the early seventeenth century, patents became less an incentive for inventors of new arts and more a royal favor dispensed to well-placed courtiers. Under this rubric, "patents" were granted to such enterprises as running ale-houses. Parliament, whose members represented many trades injured by these special privileges, was displeased. Thus arose the Statute of Monopolies of 1624, which forbade all grants of exclusive privilege except those described in the famous Section 6:

> [B]e it declared and enacted that any declaration before mentioned shall not extend to any letters patent and grants of privilege for the term of fourteen years or under, hereafter to be made, of the sole working or making of any manner of new manufactures within this realm, to the true and first inventor and inventors of such manufacture, which others at the time of making such letters patent shall not use, so as also they be not contrary to law, nor mischievous to the State, by raising prices of commodities at home, or hurt of trade, or generally inconvenient; the said fourteen years to be accounted from the date of the first letters patents, or grant of such privilege hereafter to be made. . . .

This statute called on the common law courts to review all privileges granted by the crown and outlawed all but those based on true inventions. The Statute of Monopolies, with its general ban on exclusive rights to manufacture and sell goods, and its limited exception for the purpose of fostering new inventions, is an early example of both antitrust laws and the complex economic interaction between a desire for competition and a desire for new inventions.

Patents were among the many British legal concepts introduced to the American colonies. State patents were granted in most of the original thirteen colonies, beginning with a Massachusetts patent in 1641. Even after the Revolution, under the Articles of Confederation, the individual states continued to issue patents.

Conflicts began to arise between the states—most notably over steamboat patents, which were issued to two different inventors during this period. With this problem (among others) in mind, the Constitutional Convention of 1789 resolved to create a national patent system rooted in the Constitution itself. Thus the provision of Article I, Section 8, Clause 8 authorizing Congress to award exclusive rights for a limited time to authors and inventors "for their respective writings and discoveries." The first U.S. patent statute was passed in 1790, in the very early days of the first Congress (reflecting the importance of this matter), and the first patent was issued shortly thereafter—to Samuel Hopkins of Pittsford, Vermont, for a process for making potash from wood ashes. Although there may be some limited scope for individual states to issue patents, for all intents and purposes patent law is and has been exclusively federal since 1790. *See* Camilla A. Hrdy, *State Patent Laws in the Age of Laissez Faire*, 28 BERKELEY

TECH. L.J. 45, 45 (2013); Camilla A. Hrdy, *State Patents As A Solution to Underinvestment in Innovation*, 62 U. KAN. L. REV. 487 (2013).

The story of Thomas Jefferson's involvement in the early national patent system has often been told. He was a significant contributor to the original statute, and he helped to administer the patent system established in 1790. *See* Edward C. Walterscheid, *The Use and Abuse of History: The Supreme Court's Interpretation of Thomas Jefferson's Influence on the Patent Law*, 39 IDEA 195 (1999); Adam Mossoff, *Who Cares What Thomas Jefferson Thought about Patents? Reevaluating the Patent "Privilege" in Historical Context*, 92 CORNELL L. REV. 953 (2007). Despite this, the strong federal flavor, as well as the emphasis on promotion of industrial technology, owes at least as much to the influence of Alexander Hamilton and other Federalist founders. *See* ALEXANDER HAMILTON, REPORT ON MANUFACTURERS (1791), *reprinted* in 3 ANNALS OF CONG. 971, 980–81 (Dec. 5, 1791), http://www.constitution.org/ah/rpt_manufactures.pdf (emphasizing the value of promoting specialization in invention relating to machinery).

The nation's first patent act set forth terse general standards for protection, duration, rights, and remedies, but few details. This original institutional structure of the U.S. patent system was, however, short-lived for several reasons. It called upon the Secretary of State (Thomas Jefferson), the Secretary for the Department of War, and the Attorney General to examine patents, which, in light of their other responsibilities, proved untenable. Second, inventors were displeased with the high and vague threshold for protection: that inventions be deemed "sufficiently useful and important."

As a result, in 1793, Congress replaced the examination process with a registration system, leaving the evaluation of patentability entirely to the courts. The Patent Act of 1793 retained a terse standard for patentability: an inventor could patent "any new and useful art, machine, manufacture or composition of matter, or any new and useful improvement on any art, machine, manufacture or composition of matter, not known or used before the application." Patent Act of Feb. 21, 1793, ch. 11, §1, 1 Stat. 318. The inventor was still required to provide a written description of the invention and the manner of use "in such full, clear and exact terms, as to distinguish the same from all other things before known, and to enable any person skilled in the art or science, of which it is a branch, or with which it is most nearly connected, to make, compound, and use the same." *See id.*, §3.

The courts fleshed out this lean statute. In the early years, they filled its gaps with English case law. *See* On the Patent Laws, 16 U.S. (3 Wheat.) App. 13–29 (1818) (Justice Joseph Story). In his first patent law opinion, Justice Story, sitting as a Circuit Justice, distinguished between unpatentable elements of motion and "the modus operandi, the peculiar device or manner of producing any given effect." The opinion recognized an experimental use defense based on the inference that "it could never have been the intention of the legislature to punish a man, who constructed such a machine merely for philosophical experiments, or for the purpose of ascertaining the sufficiency of the machine to produce its described effects." *See Whittemore v. Cutter*, 29 F.Cas. 1120, 1121–24 (C.C.D. Mass. 1813). In 1829, Justice Story interpreted the novelty requirement of "not known or used before the application" to pertain only to knowledge or use "by the public." *See Pennock v. Dialogue*, 27 U.S. 1, 19 (1829). The courts also established standards for disclosure, requiring that the patent document identify the patented invention with specificity and distinguish it from the prior art. *See Lowell v. Lewis*, 15 F. Cas. 1018, No. 8568 (C.C.D. Mass. 1817); *Evans v. Eaton*, 20 U.S. 356, 434–35 (1822).

While the patent system got on its feet under Jefferson and was fleshed out by jurists, it did not grow to its full stature until the 1836 revision, when a formal system of examination, with professional examiners, was substituted for the pro forma registration system of the 1793 Act. The lack of an examination system eroded faith in the patent system due to the proliferation of "unrestrained and promiscuous grants of patent privileges." *See* John Ruggles, SELECT COMMITTEE REPORT ON THE STATE AND CONDITION OF THE PATENT OFFICE, S. Doc. No. 24-338, at 4 (1836). The SENATE REPORT ACCOMPANYING THE PATENT ACT OF 1836 lamented that "[a] considerable portion of all the patents granted are worthless and void, as conflicting with, and infringing upon one another," the country had become "flooded with patent monopolies, embarrassing to bona fide patentees, whose rights are thus invaded on all sides," and that the "interference and collision of patents and privileges" had produced ruinous vexatious litigation. *See* Senate Report Accompanying Senate Bill No. 239, 24th Cong., 1st Sess. (April 28, 1836). At the same time, Congress recognized the importance of patent protection for the developing U.S. industrial economy.

> Whoever imagines that, because so many inventions and so many improvements in machinery have been made, there remains little else to be discovered, has but a feeble conception of the infinitude and vastness of mechanical powers, or of the unlimited reach of science. Much as has been discovered, infinitely more remains unrevealed. The ingenuity of man is exploring a region without limits, and delving in a mine whose treasures are exhaustless. 'Neither are all the mysteries of nature unfolded, nor the mind tired in the pursuit of them.'

Id. The 1836 Act aimed to establish a reliable system of patent examination. It marked the transition from the early era of patents as "privileges" to the more modern conception of regularized, individual property rights or statutory grants. *See* OREN BRACHA, OWNING IDEAS: THE INTELLECTUAL ORIGINS OF AMERICAN INTELLECTUAL PROPERTY 1790–1909, 208–09 (2016).

Since 1836 the patent system has grown dramatically by any standard—number of patents issued, number of cases litigated, or number of significant inventions patented. As greater demands were placed on it, the patent system developed new rules. For example, the requirement that an invention be more than novel, that it reveal an "inventive step," or what is now called nonobviousness, developed in the mid-nineteenth century to limit the number of patents that were being issued. Late in the nineteenth century the bureaucratic structure of the Patent Office as we know it began to take shape as well. *See* ROBERT P. MERGES, AMERICAN PATENT LAW: A BUSINESS AND ECONOMIC HISTORY Ch. 3, 4, 5 (2023) (describing how patents supported different business organizations over time, such as exclusive regional franchising, and later, in-house research and development).

The patent system was a well-accepted feature of the economic landscape by the beginning of the twentieth century. Key patents on the light bulb, the telephone system, the basic design of the automobile, and the first airplanes symbolized the technical virtuosity and dynamism of the age. *See* B. ZORINA KHAN, THE DEMOCRATIZATION OF INVENTION (2009) (extensive history of U.S. patent law in the nineteenth century); CHRISTOPHER BEAUCHAMP, INVENTED BY LAW: ALEXANDER GRAHAM BELL AND THE PATENT THAT CHANGED AMERICA (2015) (exploring the impact of the telephone patent wars on the formation of the Bell System in the U.S.). As the scale of industry grew, research and development departments began to appear in the larger companies. *See* THOMAS P. HUGHES, AMERICAN GENESIS: A CENTURY OF INVENTION AND TECHNOLOGICAL ENTHUSIASM 1870–1970, 150–80 (1989); CATHERINE L. FISK, WORKING KNOWLEDGE: EMPLOYEE INNOVATION AND THE RISE OF CORPORATE INTELLECTUAL PROPERTY, 1800–1930 (reissue ed., 2014). Patents were not only a valuable output of these departments; they helped measure the productivity of the departments and served to justify their importance.

The history of the U.S. patent system in the twentieth century reflects swings between greater and lesser protection. Following the trust-busting era at the turn of the century, some policymakers and jurists came to believe that large companies with patent portfolios were *too* powerful. Spurred in part by a series of anticompetitive acts by large companies whose patents dominated their respective industries, courts became less willing to enforce patent rights and more willing to punish patentees for exceeding the scope of their patent grant. Apart from the years of World War II, the Supreme Court for the most part placed strict limits on patent rights during the mid 20th century. By the time the War was over, patent professionals converged on Congress in an effort to quietly undo some of the Supreme Court's patent-limiting campaign. The 1952 Patent Act, the first major revision of the patent code since the nineteenth century, marked a rejection of the most limiting elements of Supreme Court doctrine. It was in some ways a return to the principles of that century in many respects. *See* Robert P. Merges, *One Hundred Years of Solicitude: Intellectual Property Law, 1900–2000*, 88 CAL. L. REV. 2187 (2000).

Despite the new statute, the patent system in some ways reached a low-water mark during the 1960s and into the 1970s. *See* ROBERT P. MERGES, AMERICAN PATENT LAW: A BUSINESS AND ECONOMIC HISTORY Ch. 6 (2023). This period found the American public losing some of its enthusiasm for new technologies—in part a response to the environmental pollution that was becoming so evident as a consequence of a century of industrialization. Patent law reflected the spirit of the time. It was difficult in this era to get a patent upheld in many federal circuit courts, and the circuits diverged widely both as to doctrine and basic attitudes toward patents. As a consequence, much of industry downplayed the significance of patents.

Things began to change in the late 1970s. The rising Japanese economy forced policymakers to notice that U.S. "competitiveness" lagged in many important industries, especially autos and consumer electronics. After Ronald Reagan's election in 1980, both Congress and the Executive Branch prioritized reinvigoration of the U.S. R&D system. Using an array of levers—ranging from tax policy to relaxed antitrust enforcement, university ownership of patents, and strengthening IP rights—the federal government moved to stimulate investment, invention and innovation.

In 1982 Congress passed the Federal Courts Improvement Act, creating the new Court of Appeals for the Federal Circuit. *See* Rochelle Dreyfuss, *The Federal Circuit: A Case Study in Specialized Courts*, 64 N.Y.U. L. REV. 1, 25–26 (1989). The Federal Circuit handles several important types of cases, but from the beginning one of its primary functions has been to hear all appeals involving patents. While the Federal Circuit was ostensibly formed strictly to unify patent doctrine, it was hoped by some (and expected by others) that the new court would make subtle alterations in the doctrinal fabric, with an eye toward expanding the scope of patent protection.

That is exactly what happened over the Federal Circuit's first two decades. *See* John R. Allison & Mark A. Lemley, *Empirical Evidence on the Validity of Litigated Patents*, 26 AM. INTELL. PROP. L. ASS'N Q.J. 185 (1998). The Federal Circuit expanded the scope of patentable subject matter (until the Supreme Court stepped in to narrow it again) and strengthened patent rights across many dimensions. The Federal Circuit's emergence paralleled a number of related developments that heightened interest in patents and thus in the work of the new court. Exciting new industries such as biotechnology, digital networks, high-capacity computers, and "green technologies" (fuel conservation, alternative energy, etc.) brought their patents before the court. Patents were found valid more often as compared to the days just preceding the Federal Circuit. Damage awards increased, moving patents into visibility at higher levels of many companies. Venture capitalists showed interest in some cases in patent protection as a prerequisite to startup financing. One result of this greater interest and stronger protection was a proliferation of low-quality business method and software patents in the late 1990s and early 2000 period. That in turn fully awakened the Supreme Court, which has issued numerous influential decisions since 2006 tightening patent standards and generally weakening patent protection. The Federal Circuit has followed suit, narrowing patent protection in the past several years. And Congress passed the America Invents Act in 2011, adding Patent Office administrative patent challenges to the landscape of U.S. patent law. Nonetheless, the growth of the patent system continues apace, with record numbers of patent applications and patent grants. *See* Mark A. Lemley, *The Surprising Resilience of the Patent System*, 95 TEX. L. REV. 1 (2016). The emergence of generative AI technology begins a new chapter in the patent story.

2. An Overview of the Patent System

It is important to appreciate some basic attributes of the patent system before delving into the cases. This is a complex body of law with its own terminology and tradition, and one must become acquainted with the rudiments before diving into the details.

i. Requirements for Patentability

The Patent and Trademark Office (PTO) reviews each patent application to see if it meets five requirements:

1. *Patentable Subject Matter §101*: The claimed invention fits within one of the four statutory categories ("process, machine, manufacture, or composition of matter") or "improvement thereof" and is not excluded by judicial doctrines barring patents on laws of nature, natural phenomena, and abstract ideas. Patents nonetheless cover inventive applications of these ineligible concepts.

2. *Utility §101*: The claimed invention must be useful in two respects: (1) credible utility—it must work for its intended purpose; and (2) specific and substantial utility—it must serve a particular practical purpose. Today, a patent will not be withheld even though the invention works only in an experimental setting and has no proven use in the field or factory. But it must serve *some* purpose. The possibility that it might be used later is not enough.

3. *Novelty §102*: The invention has not been preceded in identical form in the public "prior art" – the record of prior work in the field. Novelty is evaluated based on technical rules aimed at determining whether the claimed invention was in the prior art. U.S. patent law underwent significant reform of its novelty regime in 2013. For applications filed prior to March 16, 2013, U.S. patent law favors the first to invent so long as the invention was timely filed. For applications filed on or after March 16, 2013, U.S. patent favors the first applicant to have filed, subject to a grace period for prior publication.

4. *Nonobviousness §103*: It represents a nontrivial extension of what was known. This is the most important requirement; it has been called "the ultimate condition of patentability." The reason is that nonobviousness attempts to measure an even more abstract quality than novelty or utility: the *technical accomplishment* reflected in an invention. This requirement asks whether an invention is a big enough technical advance over the prior art. Even if an invention is new and useful, it will still not merit a patent if it represents merely a trivial step forward in the art.

5. *Disclosure §112*: The patent specification must convey to a person having ordinary skill in the art: (1) written description—the inventor gave a detailed account of the invention that demonstrated "possession" as of the time of filing the application; and (2) enablement—that the specification enable a person having ordinary skill in the art to make and use the invention. The disclosure requirements ensure that the patentee has fulfilled the social bargain underlying the patent grant—that those "skilled in the art" of the invention can read and understand the inventor's contribution, and that after the patent expires they will be able to make and use the invention themselves.

ii.   *Rights Conferred by a Patent*

The "specification" is the text of the patent. It describes the invention. It names all the parts or components of the invention, describes how they work, and illustrates how they work together to perform the invention's function. Most patents also have one or more drawings. Only at the end of the specification does the inventor (or, more usually, her patent lawyer) state the precise legal definition of the invention. These are the claims.

"Claims" are the heart of patent law. Claims define the boundaries of the property right that the patent confers. (Innumerable patent cases therefore analogize claims to the "metes and bounds" of a real property deed.)

The claims section of a patent commonly begins with the broadest claim, which is then "qualified" in a series of dependent claims. This is typically followed by a narrower independent claim, which may itself be qualified by a series of dependent claims. In this way, the general structure of a patent often resembles an inverted pyramid: the broadest claims are first, the narrowest last, and the scope of the claims generally "tapers" from the first to the last.

Here are a few examples of claims:

1.   Element 95.
2.   A composition comprising
     a.   a solid selected from the group consisting of
          i.   sodium chloride,
          ii.   potassium chloride and
          iii.   lithium chloride;
     b.   a liquid selected from the group consisting of
          i.   sulfuric acid,
          ii.   nitric acid. . . .
3.   The material wrought tungsten, having a specific gravity of approximately 19 or greater, and capable of being forged and worked.
4.   A windmill comprising a wind-catching device, directed to face the oncoming wind force, said device turning a shaft, said shaft acting on gears or another device to change the direction of said wind force, so as to operate a pump that pumps water.
5.   A windmill according to claim 4 wherein the force-changing device is a set of gears.
6.   A method for treating baldness comprising applying to the scalp an aqueous solution of the compound minoxidil.
7.   An apparatus for playing record albums comprising a cartridge or stylus made from at least 40 percent graphite by weight, a tone arm on which said cartridge or stylus is mounted, a turntable on which said record albums are

placed for playing, and means for turning said turntable at appropriate speeds for the playing of said record albums.

Note that all the claims except claim 5 are examples of *independent claims;* they do not refer to any other claim or claims. This is in contrast to a *dependent claim.* You can tell that claim 5 is a dependent claim because it begins with the phrase "A windmill according to claim 4 wherein . . ." A dependent claim incorporates all the limitations of the independent claim on which it depends.

Note also that claim 6 is a claim to a process or method rather than a device, and that the last element of claim 7 is stated in "means plus function" format: the element is not described in detail but is merely listed as "a means" for accomplishing some goal. The importance of this specialized claim format will be discussed in Chapter III(E)(4).

Following a preamble (such as "A composition"), patent claims use a transitional phrase to indicate how the claim limitations define the claim. The phrase "comprising" is an "open" transition: claims using this terminology cover devices that include all the listed elements *plus* any additional elements. The phrase "consisting of," by contrast, is closed: it does not cover devices that include additional elements. "Consisting essentially of" limits the scope of a claim to the specified materials or steps "and those that do not *materially* affect the *basic* and *novel* characteristic(s)" of the claimed invention. *In re Herz*, 537 F.2d 549, 551–52 (CCPA 1976) (emphasis in original).

A patent confers the right to exclude others from making, using, selling, offering for sale, or importing the claimed invention for 20 years from the filing of the patent application. Unlike trade secrets, independent invention is not a defense. Indeed, most patent suits are not against those who copied from the patentee.

The exclusionary right is in a sense a negative right, for two reasons. First, a patent does not automatically grant an affirmative right to do anything; patented pharmaceuticals, for instance, must still pass regulatory review at the Food and Drug Administration to be sold legally. Second, a patented invention may itself be covered by a preexisting patent. For instance, a broad "pioneering" patent on a product or process may cover later-developed inventions, themselves patented as improvements. In such a case the holder of an improvement patent has the right to exclude everyone from her improvement—including the holder of the broad patent—while at the same time being barred from use of the improvement herself unless the holder of the broad patent authorizes such use. Patents so related are said to be "blocking patents."

iii.   *Patent Prosecution*

The process of obtaining a patent from the Patent Office is known as "prosecution." The time and effort required to prosecute a patent varies immensely from case to case. A few applications are reviewed quickly and issued within a year of the application date. Others languish in the PTO for years and, especially when several inventors claim they were the first to produce a particular invention, even decades. The "average" prosecution takes approximately three to four years. By paying an additional fee, applicants can "fast-track" their patent applications, which reduces pendency to about 14 months. The typical application receives only 18 total hours of attention over the course of prosecution. *See* John R. Allison & Mark A. Lemley, *Who's Patenting What? An Empirical Exploration of Patent Prosecution*, 53 VAND. L. REV. 2099 (2000). There are, however, significant variations in the length of time and quality of patent examination.

Prosecution begins with the filing of a patent application. Although an inventor or his or her lawyer or patent agent[1] may file a temporary "placeholder" application, called a provisional application, it must be converted into a standard, full-blown "non-provisional" application within one year if it is ever to issue as a patent. *See* §111(b). The basics of an application are: (1) the specification, including a summary of the invention and drawings in most cases; (2) one or more claims, at the end of the specification; (3) an oath, declaring the inventor(s) actually invented what is described in the specification; and (4) applicable filing fees.

New applications are assigned to one of the main examining groups, then to a specific "art unit" that specializes in the relevant technology, and ultimately to one of the roughly 9,000 patent examiners employed at the Patent Office. Applicants may file additional papers, such as an information disclosure statement (IDS), describing prior art known to the applicant at the time of filing, 37 C.F.R. §§1.97, 1.98 (2002). Examiners usually make an initial review of the application, which includes a search of the prior art. The most common office action following this initial review is a rejection of most of the claims in the application, often on grounds of lack of novelty or obviousness. The examiner must state the reasons for each rejection, together with information and references to aid the applicant in judging the desirability of continuing prosecution or overcoming the rejection. §132. The examiner has the burden to show why an application should not issue as a patent. In response, the applicant can either contest (or "traverse," as patent lawyers say) the rejection or acquiesce in it.

Applications can be amended during prosecution. The most common reason for an amendment is to respond to a rejection or other office action. But applicants can also correct mistakes, add or change drawings, and even update the disclosure portion of the specification (though for amendments of this latter type, newly disclosed material does not enjoy the benefit of the initial filing date). Standard amendments are usually permitted up to the time when an examiner issues a final rejection, which may be as early as the second office action.

The label "final rejection" is a misnomer. An applicant can respond to a final rejection in a number of ways, most typically by a continuation or amendment after final rejection under 37 C.F.R. §1.116. (If the applicant feels continued prosecution would not be worthwhile, e.g., because there are clear disagreements with the examiner, he or she may file an appeal to the Patent Trial and Appeal Board (PTAB), an administrative tribunal within the PTO.) A continuation is basically a new version of the application, though continuations come in several flavors. Filing a continuation resets the

---

[1] Lawyers or non-lawyers with the requisite technical training (science or engineering degree) must pass the Patent Bar Examination administered by the U.S. PTO in order to prosecute patents and participate as lead counsel in Patent Trial and Appeal Board proceedings.

examination process. A simple continuation application retains the benefit of the initial application's filing date; it therefore may serve much the same role as an amendment. A continuation-in-part ("CIP"), by contrast, adds new matter to the specification. This new matter does not retain the benefit of the earlier filing date, though any information carried over from the original filing does.

Applicants may employ a variation on the continuation theme when the examiner has decided to allow some claims but has issued a final rejection as to others. Typical prosecution strategy is to take the bird in the hand and fight over the contested claims separately. To achieve this, the applicant can file an amendment after final rejection canceling the rejected claims. This puts the remaining claims in condition for allowance. Meanwhile, the rejected claims may be carried over into a separate continuation application. Then the battle over these claims can be joined again; in the meantime, the acceptable claims will become enforceable as soon as the original, slimmed-down application is allowed to issue as a patent.

In addition to these various filings, applicants can communicate with patent examiners by phone or in person, through what is called an examiner interview. Any notes made during these communications become part of the prosecution history of the patent.

Prior to 2001, U.S. patent applications were not published. They were held in secrecy until the issue date. Long-pending applications were referred to as "submarine patents" for this reason: they traveled under the surface and could pop up to surprise a mature industry. These abuses, together with the goal of harmonizing U.S. practice with that of Japan and Europe, led to the publication of patent applications under the American Inventors Protection Act of 1999 ("AIPA"), §122(b). Under the AIPA, most applications are published eighteen months after their filing date.[2] After publication but before the patent issues, the applicant has certain limited legal rights in the invention. So long as the infringer has actual notice of the published patent application, and so long as the claims in the published application are "substantially identical" to the claims in the patent when issued, the applicant/patentee can recover a reasonable royalty from the infringer. Unlike an issued patent, rights in a published application cannot be enforced with an injunction. §154(d).

Interested third parties—in particular, competitors of the applicant—sometimes (although not always) read their competitors' published applications. Significant third party participation is now permitted under various administrative procedures initiated in the America Invents Act (AIA) of 2011, which we discuss below.

Prosecution ends when the patent is granted or the application is abandoned. About three-fourths of all applications end up granted as patents, and about half the remainder are abandoned for business reasons, not because the PTO rejected them. *See* Mark A. Lemley & Bhaven Sampat, *Is the Patent Office a Rubber Stamp?*, 58 EMORY L.J. 181 (2008). The optimal grant rate is a matter of great interest to scholars, though there is

---

[2] Applicants that only seek protection in the United States can sometimes keep their applications secret until issued. This maintains trade secret protection if their application never issues.

no easy way to know for sure exactly how many patent applications should issue as patents. *See* Michael D. Frakes and Melissa F. Wasserman, *Does the U.S. Patent and Trademark Office Grant Too Many Bad Patents?: Evidence from a Quasi-Experiment*, 67 STAN. L. REV. 613 (2015).

Prosecution can in a sense continue after a patent has issued. A patentee who comes to believe that her patent claims are either too broad or too narrow can seek a reissue of the patent, so long as the deficiency in the original patent is the result of a bona fide error or omission. Reissues to broaden the scope of claims must be initiated within two years of the original issuance, however.

Once the patent issues, the patent owner can enforce the patent in federal court. Many of the cases that we examine in this chapter are the result of these proceedings. Some of the cases, however, are appeals of patent rejections to the Federal Circuit. Three other forms of patent litigation deserve brief mention here.

- *Post-Grant Review Proceeding*: Beginning in 1980 and now much expanded as result of the America Invents Act of 2011, the Patent Office (through the PTAB) affords patentees and challengers with several post-grant proceedings to ensure that the patent was properly issued. These post-grant proceedings can run in parallel with patent litigation in federal court, although it is common for district judges to stay cases involving patents that are being reviewed by the PTAB. We will discuss these proceedings in the final section on patent reform.

- *Declaratory Relief Action*: Companies that reasonably fear being sued for patent infringement (for example, because the patentee has threatened them with suit) can file declaratory judgment actions seeking to establish that the patent at issue is invalid, or that their conduct does not infringe the patent. Such declaratory judgment actions are typically met with counterclaims charging infringement; these proceed much as normal patent infringement suits.

- *Section 337 Investigation*: The International Trade Commission has jurisdiction to block the importation of products into the United States if they infringe U.S. patents and to block the importation of products made abroad by processes that are patented in the United States. Patent owners can complain to the ITC, which will bring "Section 337" actions against likely infringers. These actions have their own set of procedural rules that operate parallel to district court actions for patent infringement. *See generally* PETER S. MENELL, ET AL., SECTION 337 PATENT INVESTIGATION MANAGEMENT GUIDE (2012).

3. Theories of Patent Law

By contrast with trade secret law, which draws on a number of different (and sometimes contradictory) theoretical bases, the central theory behind patent law is relatively straightforward. This theory posits that inventions are public goods that are costly to make and that are difficult to control once they are released into the world. As a result, absent patent protection inventors will not have sufficient incentive to invest in creating, developing, and marketing new products. Patent law provides a market-driven incentive to invest in innovation, by allowing the inventor to appropriate some of the economic benefits of her invention. An alternative to classical incentive theory is the prospect theory of patents. *See* Edmund Kitch, *The Nature and Function of the Patent System*, 30 J.L. & ECON. 265 (1977). Kitch offers a property-based vision of patents as entitlements to innovate within a particular field, granted to those who have already started such innovation to encourage, not invention, but commercialization of technology. *See* Mark F. Grady & Jay I. Alexander, *Patent Law and Rent Dissipation*, 78 VA. L. REV. 305 (1992) (refining Kitch's approach using insights from political economy theory).

Other theories are sometimes advanced to explain intellectual property law. *See* ROBERT P. MERGES, JUSTIFYING INTELLECTUAL PROPERTY (2011) (synthesizing the landscape of philosophical perspectives); Adam Mossoff, *Rethinking the Development of Patents: An Intellectual History*, 1550–1800, 52 HASTINGS L.J. 1255 (2001) (emphasizing natural rights justifications); A. Samuel Oddi, *Un-Unified Economic Theories of Patents—The Not-Quite-Holy Grail*, 71 NOTRE DAME L. REV. 267, 274–77 (1996); Lawrence C. Becker, *Deserving to Own Intellectual Property*, 68 CHI.-KENT L. REV. 609 (1993) (arguing that entitlement-based rationales for patent law are intuitively appealing, but do not necessarily justify the scope of current patent doctrine); *cf.* Peter S. Menell, *Property, Intellectual Property, and Social Justice: Mapping the Next Frontier*, 5 BRIGHAM-KANNER PROPERTY CONFERENCE JOURNAL 147 (2016) (exploring social justice aspects).

Nonetheless, the utilitarian framework serves as the central framework for most patent scholarship. This reflects the utilitarian character of the U.S. Constitution's Intellectual Property Clause as well as the importance of promoting technological innovation for every nation that seeks to meet the needs of its citizens and to defend its sovereignty. It also reflects the patent system's market setting and the broad nature of the patent grant. Patents give the inventor the right to sue not only those who copy their invention, but those who reverse engineer it and even those who develop the same invention independently. The broad nature of this grant makes it difficult to speak of a "moral entitlement" to a patent. And in part the focus on utilitarian theory mirrors the subject matter of patents, which revolves around mechanical devices, chemical formulae, and the like. The "personality" invested in stamping machinery or pesticides is less obvious than in artistic works.

Although the economic incentive story is straightforward, it does not tell us very much about how to design a patent system to provide optimal incentives. For the reasons described in Chapter I, both overprotecting and underprotecting technology can impede innovation. Thus designing the proper economic incentive requires policymakers to balance the length of the patent term, the appropriate standard of invention, and the nature of the rights granted. Resolving these conflicts has occupied courts and legislators since the passage of the first patent statute in 1790. We will reexamine these issues at the end of the chapter.

B.   THE ELEMENTS OF PATENTABILITY

The systematic study of intellectual property regimes naturally begins with the requirements for or elements of protectability. This section investigates the five requirements of patentability. In prior editions, we began our coverage with patentable subject matter (§101), which states simply and broadly that

> Whoever invents or discovers any new and useful process, machine, manufacture, or composition of matter, or any new and useful improvement thereof, may obtain a patent therefor, subject to the conditions and requirements of this title.

Until 2008, with some exceptions (notably the brief period between 1978 and 1981), courts interpreted this language relatively expansively. And by the early 2000s, the Federal Circuit had pretty much lowered the patentable subject matter hurdle to a chalk line on the track. Even non-technological business methods qualified for patentability under *State St. Bank v. Signature Fin. Grp.*, 149 F.3d 1368, 1375 (Fed. Cir. 1998).

Thus, much of the challenge in understanding patentability related to novelty (§102), nonobviousness (§103), and, to a lesser extent, disclosure (§112). The Supreme Court's decisions in *Mayo Collaborative Servs. v. Prometheus Labs., Inc.*, 566 U.S. 66 (2012) and subsequent cases, however, significantly raised and complicated the patent eligibility standard, particularly as it relates to business methods, software, genetics, and medical diagnostic methods. This shift has intertwined the patent eligibility inquiry with the nonobviousness and disclosure inquiries. To comprehend nonobviousness, it is necessary to understand novelty. Therefore, we cover patentability in the following order: (1) novelty; (2) nonobviousness; (3) utility; (4) disclosure; and (5) subject matter. Please bear in mind, however, that courts have indicated that patentable subject matter is a threshold inquiry, and that it is generally decided before issues of novelty or nonobviousness are raised and without directly considering them.

1.   Novelty

The concept of novelty, at least as it relates to patent law, seems simple. All we need is a timeline. The first person to invent wins the race. Yet operationalizing this concept into an administrable and effective system of quasi-property rights in intangible resources raises some challenging policy choices. Even defining the moment of invention—what we call "conception"—introduces significant complications. And proving that moment adds evidentiary complexities.

For most of its history, the U.S. has operated under a first-to-invent system. The old law, Section 102 of the 1952 Patent Act, embodies the principle that only truly new inventions deserve patents, and that as between two claimants it is the first to invent who deserves protection. But even this system required some adaptations so as to encourage prompt filing of applications.

Most of the rest of the world, by contrast, has long operated under a first-to-file system, awarding the patent to the first person to bring the invention to the patent office. After decades of diplomacy, the U.S. significantly shifted toward the international standard through the enactment of the America Invents Act (AIA) of 2011. For all patent applications filed on or after March 16, 2013, the U.S. novelty regime is a variation on the international first-to-file system. We say variation because the AIA regime still permits an inventor a one year grace period under certain conditions. As a result, the U.S. regime still diverges from other first-to-file systems, but is much closer to regimes in other nations than it was under the 1952 Act.

Since part of the goal of the AIA was to both harmonize U.S. law with international law and to simplify the complex mechanics of the 1952 Act regime, you might think that your task in learning patent law is far simpler than prior generations of law students. Unfortunately, the opposite is true. Until at least 2033, patent lawyers must understand both the 1952 Act novelty regime (which governs patent applications filed prior to March 16, 2013) and the simpler AIA novelty regime, which governs all patents filed since that date.

The wording of specific prior art categories used in the AIA was carried over from the 1952 Act, and indeed, many phrases originate in even earlier versions of the Patent Act. Many crucial terms in this body of law carry with them extensive case law interpretations. It is generally understood, in patent law as elsewhere, that when Congress chooses to preserve legal language with an extensive body of interpretive case law behind it, that choice means that accepted case law interpretations are carried forward into the new legislative enactment. For purposes of the AIA, this general rule has some important consequences. One is that many older cases dealing with prior art will still be relevant when post-AIA patents begin to dominate patent litigation. Thus, many of the cases and principles we discuss in covering the 1952 regime will be important in understanding the AIA as well.

i.   The 1952 Regime

Under the 1952 Act, §102 sets forth two subsets of requirements for a patent to issue: (1) the invention is novel (subsections (a), (e), (f), and (g)); and (2) the application was filed in a timely manner, i.e., it is not subject to a "statutory bar" (subsections (b), (c), and (d)).

The first set of requirements, referred to as anticipation or lack of novelty, seeks to ensure that a patent issues only to the first inventor. This goal is accomplished by using the applicant's date of invention as the relevant baseline for analysis. Prior art—such as published articles (including publicly accessible websites), publicly known techniques, and marketed products—containing all elements of the claimed invention will anticipate, and thereby defeat, the patent claim. The same is true of patent applications filed by a third party before an inventor's application, as long as that earlier third party application is eventually published or issued as a patent.

The second set of requirements, known as statutory bars, promote timely filing by requiring that the patentee file an application within one year of various triggering events. In many cases, the bar arises because of something the inventor does. The classic example is publication of a scientific article. If an inventor fails to file a patent application within one year of the article's publication, she is barred from receiving a patent. She suffers a "loss of right."

Section 102 provides that "A person shall be entitled to a patent unless" various conditions set forth in subsections (a) through (g) stand in the way. Before turning to those conditions, which will occupy much of our study, it is worthwhile noting the evidentiary structure of this statutory provision. By stating that "[a] person shall be entitled to a patent *unless*" (emphasis added), Congress placed the burden of defeating patentability on the PTO. Thus, in rejecting a patent application, the PTO must establish the failure of one of the conditions of patentability.

The principal conditions of 102 are printed below, with bracketed insertions. Note that §102(a) is concerned with novelty, while the statutory bars are set forth in §102(b).

1952 Act: 35 U.S.C. §102. Conditions for Patentability; Novelty and Loss of Right to Patent

A person shall be entitled to a patent unless—

(a) [**Novelty**] the invention was known or used by others in this country, or patented or described in a printed publication in this or a foreign country, before the invention thereof by the applicant for patent, or

(b) [**Statutory Bars**] the invention was patented or described in a printed publication in this or a foreign country or in public use or on sale in this country, more than one year prior to the date of the application for patent in the United States, or

(c) [**Abandonment**] [the inventor] has abandoned the invention, or

(d) [**Late filing in the U.S.**] the invention was first patented or caused to be patented . . . by the applicant . . . in a foreign country prior to the date of the application for patent in this country on an application for patent . . . filed more than twelve months before the filing of the application in the United States, or

(e) [**Secret Prior Art: Previously-filed applications**] The invention was described in (1) [a published patent application] by another filed in the United States before the invention by the applicant for patent . . . or (2) a patent granted on an application for patent by another filed in the United States before the invention thereof by the applicant for patent . . . or

(f) [**Derivation**] he did not himself invent the subject matter sought to be patented, or

(g) [**First-to-Invent**] (1) [*inter partes* proceedings] during the course of an interference . . . , another inventor involved therein establishes, to the extent permitted in section 104. . .that before such person's invention thereof the invention was made by such other inventor and not abandoned, suppressed, or concealed, or (2) [*ex parte* prosecution/invalidity defense] before such person's invention thereof, the invention was made in this country by another inventor who had not abandoned, suppressed, or concealed it. In determining priority of invention under this subsection, there shall be considered not only the respective dates of conception and reduction to practice of the invention, but also the reasonable diligence of one who was first to conceive and last to reduce to practice, from a time prior to conception by the other.

ii.   *The Nature of Novelty*

Turning to the specific conditions that stand in the way of obtaining a patent, subsection a provides that

the invention was known or used by others in this country, or patented or described in a printed publication in this or a foreign country, before the invention thereof by the applicant for patent

What does it mean to be "known or used by others"?

Rosaire v. National Lead Co.
United States Court of Appeals for the Fifth Circuit
218 F.2d 72 (5th Cir. 1955)

TUTTLE, CIRCUIT JUDGE

In this suit for patent infringement there is presented to us for determination the correctness of the judgment of the trial court, based on findings of fact and conclusions of law, holding that the two patents involved in the litigation were invalid and void and that furthermore there had been no infringement by defendant.

The Rosaire and Horvitz patents relate to methods of prospecting for oil or other hydrocarbons. The inventions are based upon the assumption that gases have emanated from deposits of hydrocarbons which have been trapped in the earth and that these emanations have modified the surrounding rock. The methods claimed involve the steps of taking a number of samples of soil from formations which are not themselves productive of hydrocarbons, either over a horizontal area or vertically down a well bore, treating each sample, as by grinding and heating in a closed vessel, to cause entrained or absorbed hydrocarbons therein to evolve as a gas, quantitatively measuring the amount of hydrocarbon gas so evolved from each sample, and correlating the measurements with the locations from which the samples were taken.

Plaintiff claims that in 1936 he and Horvitz invented this new method of prospecting for oil. In due course the two patents in suit, Nos. 2,192,525 and 2,324,085, were issued thereon. Horvitz assigned his interest to Rosaire.

In view of the fact that the trial court's judgment that the patents were invalid, would of course dispose of [this infringement suit] if correct, we turn our attention to this issue. [Appellee argues] that work carried on by one Teplitz for the Gulf Oil Corporation invalidated both patents by reason of the relevant provisions of the patent laws which state that an invention is not patentable if it "was known or used by others in this country" before the patentee's invention thereof, 35 U.S.C.A. §102(a). Appellee contends that Teplitz and his coworkers knew and extensively used in the field the same alleged inventions before any date asserted by Rosaire and Horvitz.

On this point appellant himself in his brief admits that "Teplitz conceived of the idea of extracting and quantitatively measuring entrained or absorbed gas from the samples of rock, rather than relying upon the free gas in the samples. We do not deny that Teplitz conceived of the methods of the patents in suit." And further appellant makes the following admission: "We admit that the Teplitz-Gulf work was done before Rosaire and Horvitz conceived of the inventions. We will show, however, that Gulf did not apply for patent until 1939, did not publish Teplitz's ideas, and did not otherwise give the public the benefit of the experimental work."

The question as to whether the work of Teplitz was "an unsuccessful experiment," as claimed by appellant, or was a successful trial of the method in question and a reduction of that method to actual practice, as contended by appellee, is, of course, a question of fact. On this point the trial court made the following finding of fact:

I find as a fact that Abraham J. Teplitz and his coworkers with Gulf Oil Corporation and its Research Department during 1935 and early 1936, before any date claimed by Rosaire, spent more than a year in the oil fields and adjacent territory around Palestine, Texas, taking and analyzing samples both over an area and down drill holes, exactly as called for in the claims of the patents which Rosaire and Horvitz subsequently applied for and which are here in suit.

This Teplitz work was a successful and adequate field trial of the prospecting method involved and a reduction to practice of that method. The work was performed in the field under ordinary conditions without any deliberate attempt at concealment or effort to exclude the public and without any instructions of secrecy to the employees performing the work.

As we view it, if the court's findings of fact are correct then under the statute as construed by the courts, we must affirm the finding of the trial court that [appellant's] patents were invalid.

[T]here was sufficient evidence to sustain the finding of the trial court that there was more here than an unsuccessful or incomplete experiment. It is clear that the work was not carried forward, but that appears to be a result of two things: (1) that the geographical area did not lend itself properly to the test, and (2) that the "entire gas prospecting program was therefore suspended in September of 1936, in order that the accumulated information might be thoroughly reviewed." It will be noted that the program was not suspended to test the worth of the method but to examine the data that was produced by use of the method involved.

With respect to the argument advanced by appellant that the lack of publication of Teplitz's work deprived an alleged infringer of the defense of prior use, we find no case which constrains us to hold that where such work was done openly and in the ordinary course of the activities of the employer, a large producing company in the oil industry, the statute is to be so modified by construction as to require some affirmative act to bring the work to the attention of the public at large.

While there is authority for the proposition that one of the basic principles underlying the patent laws is the enrichment of the art, and that a patent is given to encourage disclosure of inventions, no case we have found requires a holding that, under the circumstances that attended the work of Teplitz, the fact of public knowledge must be shown before it can be urged to invalidate a subsequent patent.

COMMENTS AND QUESTIONS

1. The Federal Circuit considered a similar fact situation in *New Railhead Mfg., L.L.C. v. Vermeer Mfg. Co.*, 298 F.3d 1290 (Fed. Cir. 2002), a case raising a §102(b) statutory bar asserting that the claimed invention was in "public use" more than one year prior to the application filing date. Patentee New Railhead had tested a drill bit in underground drilling that occurred before the critical date for its patent. In response to the patentee's argument that its use was either nonpublic or experimental, the court followed the reasoning of *Rosaire* and invalidated the patent. In dissent, Judge Dyk noted that "[t]he use actually took place under public land, hidden from view, and there has been no showing whatsoever that the use was anything but confidential. To understand the method of using the drill bit a person at the job site would have to view the drill bit or see it in operation, and this was impossible to do while the drill bit was underground." *Id.* at 1300.

2. In *W.L. Gore & Assocs., Inc. v. Garlock, Inc.*, 721 F.2d 1540 (Fed. Cir. 1983), the Federal Circuit had this to say about "secret" prior use, where patentee Gore argued that prior use by another of a machine conforming to the elements of Gore's claim was nonpublic and therefore nonanticipatory:

> The nonsecret use of a claimed process in the usual course of producing articles for commercial purposes is a public use. Electric Storage Battery Co. v. Shimadzu, 307 U.S. 5, 20 (1939). . . . Thus it cannot be said that the district court erred in determining that the invention set forth in claim 1 of the '566 patent was known or used by others under §102(a), as evidenced by . . . operation of the '401 machine before Dr. Gore's asserted date of that invention.

By contrast, a use that is affirmatively kept secret is not prior art, and so will not bar a third party from later patenting the invention.

3. The very expansive view taken in *Rosaire* of what it means for a disclosure to be "public" was criticized by one scholar:

> The term "public" . . . seems merely to mean "not secret." It is unnecessary to show that the previous discovery was ever used commercially, that it was in fact observable by the public if such a process or device would not normally be so viewed, or that it was known to more than a few persons. This construction of the term "public" seems questionable, since it may result in the denial of a patent even though the subsequent inventor has conferred a benefit by filing the invention with the public records.

Comment, *Prior Art in the Patent Law*, 73 HARV. L. REV. 369, 373 (1959). The author goes on to propose a "higher standard of knowledge or use," arguing that

> an invention should be considered "known or used" only if it was so widely known or used that an ordinary skilled worker exercising reasonable diligence

to learn the state of the art would have discovered, recognized, and been able to construct the invention.

Id. at 373. In effect, this proposal would apply a trade secret standard of novelty to the patent law—an invention could be "new" even though it had been made before, as long as it was not in general knowledge or use. Are there any problems with applying this weaker standard of novelty to determine whether a patent should be issued? Can it be reconciled with the broad language of section 102(a), precluding patents on inventions that were previously "known or used by others in this country"?

In *Hall v. MacNeale*, 107 U.S. (17 Otto) 90 (1883), Hall had in 1866 received a patent on an improved design for the door and walls of burglar-proof safes. The question before the Court was whether the use of certain earlier-model safes before the critical date was *public* enough to create a statutory bar. The Court held:

> The construction and arrangement and purpose and mode of operation and use of the [hidden feature] in the safes were necessarily known to the workmen who put them in. They were, it is true, hidden from view, after the safes were completed, and it required a destruction of the safe to bring them into view. But this was no concealment of them or use of them in secret. They had no more concealment than was inseparable from any legitimate use of them.

In other words, the public use of a device starts the one-year clock running on that device even if the patented invention isn't evident on the face of the device.

4. One issue in *Rosaire* was the patentee's allegation that the Teplitz work was not prior art because it was incomplete, a mere "abandoned experiment." On this issue, consider *Picard v. United Aircraft Corp.*, 128 F.2d 632 (2d Cir. 1942) (L. Hand, J.):

> It is true that another's experiment, imperfect and never perfected, will not serve either as an anticipation or as part of the prior art, for it has not served to enrich it. The patented invention does not become "known" by such a use or sale, or by anything of which the art cannot take hold and make use as it stands. But the mere fact that an earlier "machine" or "manufacture," sold or used, was an experiment does not prevent its becoming an anticipation or a part of the prior art, provided it was perfected and thereafter became publicly known. Whether it does become so depends upon how far it becomes a part of the stock of knowledge of the art in question. Judged by that standard, the Curtiss engine [prior art reference] was not an "abandoned experiment"; it had been perfected; it had withstood a severer test than was necessary in use; it had been sold; it remained permanently accessible to the art, a contribution to the sum of knowledge so far as it went.

3. *Proof of Prior Use.* In *Woodland Trust v. Flowertree Nursery, Inc.*, 148 F.3d 1368 (Fed. Cir. 1998), defendant Flowertree argued the invalidity of the patent owned by Woodland based on prior use of a nursery watering system identical to that claimed in the patent:

> Under §102(a), Flowertree stated that the method was previously known and used by each of Joseph Burke and William Hawkins (an owner of

Flowertree) in the 1960s and 1970s at their nurseries in Florida, and was then discontinued by these users in 1976 and 1978. The district court found that Hawkins' system at Flowertree was reconstructed in 1988.

Four witnesses testified in support of the defense of prior knowledge and use: Mark Hawkins, Joseph Burke, Charles Hudson, and John Kaufmann. Mark Hawkins is the son of William Hawkins; he testified that his father's system, on which he worked as a child, was destroyed by a tornado in 1978, and was not reconstructed until 1988. Joseph Burke is a nursery owner who has known William Hawkins since the 1960s; he testified that he used the same system as shown in the patent, but tore it down in 1976 and did not rebuild it. Charles Hudson is a nursery owner who had worked for Joseph Burke, and John Kaufmann is a life-long friend of William Hawkins; they testified that they observed the patented system at the Burke or Hawkins nursery, before its use was discontinued.

148 F.3d at 1369. The Federal Circuit reviewed Supreme Court precedent laying down a stringent corroboration requirement, and then concluded:

This guidance, applied to this case, reinforces the heavy burden when establishing prior public knowledge and use based on long-past events. The Supreme Court's view of human nature as well as human recollection, whether deemed cynical or realistic, retains its cogency. This view is reinforced, in modern times, by the ubiquitous paper trail of virtually all commercial activity. It is rare indeed that some physical record (e.g., a written document such as notes, letters, invoices, notebooks, or a sketch or drawing or photograph showing the device, a model, or some other contemporaneous record) does not exist.

In this case, despite the asserted many years of commercial and public use, we take note of the absence of any physical record to support the oral evidence. The asserted prior knowledge and use by Hawkins and Burke was said to have begun approximately thirty years ago and to have continued for about a decade. Hawkins testified that his prior use was terminated in 1978, and the district court found that Hawkins' system was not reconstructed until 1988. The relationship of the witnesses and the fact that the asserted prior uses ended twenty years before the trial, and were abandoned until the defendant reportedly learned of the patentee's practices, underscore the failure of this oral evidence to provide clear and convincing evidence of prior knowledge and use. The district court did not rely on the two undated photographs, and indeed their lack of detail and clarity can not have provided documentary support.

With the guidance of precedent, whose cautions stressed the frailty of memory of things long past and the temptation to remember facts favorable to the cause of one's relative or friend, we conclude that this oral evidence, standing alone, did not provide the clear and convincing evidence necessary to invalidate a patent on the ground of prior knowledge and use under §102(a).

Id. at 1373.

Do you agree with the Federal Circuit's implication that in the absence of a strong corroboration requirement for prior public use evidence, there would be a temptation for competitors of a patentee to lie? Is it likely that the witnesses in *Woodland Trust* really made the whole thing up? Note that the alleged prior use was the defendant's own use, so in that particular case the defendant might have had an incentive to lie. With such a strong requirement of documentary evidence, is there much difference between public use evidence and proof that an invention appeared in a prior publication or patent?

6. *Inherency* – Section 102(a) provides that an applicant is not entitled to a patent if her invention was "known or used by others" prior to the date of the applicant's invention. The meaning of this phrase has been called into question in a series of cases involving unintended, "accidental" anticipation of an invention. Most of these cases involve the inherent, unintended production of a particular physical product. When an inventor later *intentionally* makes the product, presumably because she has some use for it, the prior unintended production of the product may be raised as prior art to the invention.

On the one hand, a venerable line of cases holds that where the first, accidental producer was not aware of the product and did not attempt to produce it, the first production did not bar a patent on the "invention" of the product. Thus, in *Tilghman v. Proctor*, 102 U.S. 707 (1880), the Supreme Court held that the accidental separation of fat acids from tallow during operation of a steam engine lubricated by tallow did not anticipate Tilghman's patent for a similar separation process. Of the prior production, the Court said:

> They revealed no process for the manufacture of fat acids. If the acids were accidentally and unwittingly produced, whilst the operators were in pursuit of other and different results, without exciting attention and without it even being known what was done or how it had been done, it would be absurd to say that this was an anticipation of Tilghman's discovery.

Id. at 711. On the other hand, an equally venerable line of cases holds that if a product is known in the art already, an inventor cannot obtain a patent *on the product* merely by putting it to a new use, "even if the new result had not before been contemplated." *Ansonia Brass & Copper Co. v. Elec. Supply Co.*, 144 U.S. 11 (1892). The inventor could obtain a patent on the new process using that product, however. For more on this distinction, *see Atlas Powder Co. v. Ireco, Inc.*, 190 F.3d 1342 (Fed. Cir. 1999).

Newer Federal Circuit cases have focused on whether an invention was present in the prior art in a way that provided a public benefit. The knowledge of those in the art has been de-emphasized as a factor. In *Schering Corp. v. Geneva Pharms., Inc.*, 339 F.3d 1373, 1377 (Fed. Cir. 2003), the court invalidated a claim to a compound that is necessarily produced in the human body whenever a person ingests the allergy medicine Claritin—even though the patentee Schering-Plough argued that no one knew about the claimed product until Schering characterized it. *See also Abbott Labs v. Geneva*

Pharmaceuticals, Inc., 182 F.3d 1315 (Fed. Cir. 1999) (distinguishing *Tilghman* in case where prior art product was appreciated and sold, even though party did not appreciate qualities of product). Another case is *Prima Tek II, L.L.C. v. Polypap, S.A.R.L.*, 412 F.3d 1284 (Fed. Cir. 2005), where the court invalidated a claim to a "potless" floral arrangement holder (see diagram). The claim included, among other things, the elements of (1) a band to hold the floral arrangement; (2) a sheet of decorative material covering the floral arrangement; and (3) "means for forming a crimped portion in the sheet of material." 412 F.3d 1284, 1287 n.1. Polypap, the accused infringer, argued that a published French patent application, the "Charrin reference," inherently anticipated the claim. The patentee Prima Tek countered with the argument that Charrin did not disclose the "crimping" limitation. The court agreed with Polypap, noting that in the drawing below Charrin clearly discloses a string along the top of the floral arrangement holder which necessarily creates crimping in the covering material:

In other words, the invention was already present in the prior art, because the decorative material would be crimped whenever the Charrin device was used, whether or not people recognized or intended that result. *See* Dan L. Burk & Mark A. Lemley, *Inherency*, 47 WM. & MARY L. REV. 371 (2005) (endorsing the move to public benefit, and making the point that if skilled artisans know about the prior use, then there is no need for an inherency doctrine at all).

iii.   Statutory Bars

Section 102(b) bars the granting of a patent where

> the invention was patented or described in a printed publication in this or a foreign country or in public use or on sale in this country, more than one year prior to the date of the application for patent in the United States.

Recall from the introduction to this section that one difference between statutory bars and novelty is that an inventor can create a statutory bar by her own actions (e.g., publication of an article), whereas she cannot destroy the novelty of her own inventions. In short, an inventor's own work cannot be cited against her (in general) under §102(a), but it is "fair game" under §102(b). Note, however, that the 1952 Act affords the inventor a one-year grace period for filing a patent application following one of the statutory bar triggers—patenting, printed publication, public, or public use in the U.S.

Notwithstanding this difference between novelty and statutory bars, subsections 102(a) and (b) are not appreciably different for many purposes. For example, courts interpret "publication"—a term common to both subsections—the same in both contexts. Thus, although the following case involves a §102(b) reference, the reasoning is equally applicable to §102(a).

In re Hall
United States Court of Appeals for the Federal Circuit
781 F.2d 897 (Fed. Cir. 1986)

BALDWIN, CIRCUIT JUDGE.

This is an appeal from the decision of the U.S. Patent and Trademark Office's (PTO) former Board of Appeals, adhered to on reconsideration by the Board of Patent Appeals and Interferences (board), sustaining the final rejection of claims 1–25 of [Hall's] reissue [a]pplication, based principally on a "printed publication" bar under 35 U.S.C. §102(b). The reference is a doctoral thesis. Because appellant concedes that his claims are unpatentable if the thesis is available as a "printed publication" more than one year prior to the application's effective filing date of February 27, 1979, the only issue is whether the thesis is available as such a printed publication. On the record before us, we affirm the board's decision.

A protest was filed during prosecution of appellant's reissue application which included in an appendix a copy of the dissertation "1,4-α-Glucanglukohydrolase ein amylotylisches Enzym . . ." by Peter Foldi (Foldi thesis or dissertation). The record indicates that in September 1977, Foldi submitted his dissertation to the Department of Chemistry and Pharmacy at Freiburg University in the Federal Republic of Germany, and that Foldi was awarded a doctorate degree on November 2, 1977. . . .

The examiner made a final rejection of the application claims. He said: "On the basis of the instant record it is reasonable to assume that the Foldi thesis was available (accessible) prior to February 27, 197[8]."

By letter, the PTO's Scientific Library asked Dr. Will whether the Foldi dissertation was made available to the public by being cataloged and placed in the main collection. Dr. Will replied in an October 20, 1983 letter, as translated: "Our dissertations, thus also the Foldi dissertation, are indexed in a special dissertations catalogue, which is part of the general users' catalogue. In the stacks they are likewise set apart in a special dissertation section, which is part of the general stacks."

In response to a further inquiry by the PTO's Scientific Library requesting (1) the exact date of indexing and cataloging of the Foldi dissertation or (2) "the time such procedures normally take," Dr. Will replied in a June 18, 1984 letter: "The Library copies of the Foldi dissertation were sent to us by the faculty on November 4, 1977.

Accordingly, the dissertation most probably was available for general use toward the beginning of the month of December, 1977."

The board held that the unrebutted evidence of record was sufficient to conclude that the Foldi dissertation had an effective date as prior art more than one year prior to the filing date of the appellant's initial application.

On appeal, appellant raises two arguments: (1) the §102(b) "printed publication" bar requires that the publication be accessible to the interested public, but there is no evidence that the dissertation was properly indexed in the library catalog prior to the critical date; and (2) even if the Foldi thesis were cataloged prior to the critical date, the presence of a single cataloged thesis in one university library does not constitute sufficient accessibility of the publication's teachings to those interested in the art exercising reasonable diligence.

The [printed publication] bar is grounded on the principle that once an invention is in the public domain, it is no longer patentable by anyone.

The statutory phrase "printed publication" has been interpreted to give effect to ongoing advances in the technologies of data storage, retrieval, and dissemination. Because there are many ways in which a reference may be disseminated to the interested public, "public accessibility" has been called the touchstone in determining whether a reference constitutes a "printed publication" bar under 35 U.S.C. §§102(b). The §§102 publication bar is a legal determination based on underlying fact issues, and therefore must be approached on a case-by-case basis. The proponent of the publication bar must show that prior to the critical date the reference was sufficiently accessible, at least to the public interested in the art, so that such a one by examining the reference could make the claimed invention without further research or experimentation.

[A]ppellant argues that the Foldi thesis was not shown to be accessible because Dr. Will's affidavits do not say when the thesis was indexed in the library catalog and do not chronicle the procedures for receiving and processing a thesis in the library.

[A]ppellant would have it that accessibility can only be shown by evidence establishing a *specific* date of cataloging and shelving before the critical date. While such evidence would be desirable, in lending greater certainty to the accessibility determination, the realities of routine business practice counsel against requiring such evidence. The probative value of routine business practice to show the performance of a specific act has long been recognized. *See, e.g.*, 1 WIGMORE, EVIDENCE §92 (1940); rule 406, FED. R. EVID. Therefore, we conclude that competent evidence of the general library practice may be relied upon to establish an approximate time when a thesis became accessible.

We agree with the board that the evidence of record consisting of Dr. Will's affidavits establishes a prima facie case for unpatentability of the claims under the §102(b) publication bar. It is a case which stands unrebutted.

Accordingly, the board's decision sustaining the rejection of appellant's claims is affirmed.

COMMENTS AND QUESTIONS

1. Note that the issue in this case could arise under either §102(a) or §102(b). If the publication had occurred before the *invention* of the subject matter by the applicant, §102(a) would apply. Section 102(b) applied in this case because the publication occurred more than one year before the applicant *filed* for a patent.

2. Compare the "publicness" standard in *Hall* to the rule in trade secret law (information must be "generally known or readily ascertainable" in an industry). Why is it so much easier to lose patent rights than trade secrets?

3. *Poster Sessions.* In general, a publication becomes public when it becomes available to at least one member of "the general public." In *In re Klopfenstein*, 380 F.3d 1345 (Fed. Cir. 2004), the Federal Circuit addressed whether temporary display of scientific research information at a conference "poster session" constituted publication under §102(b). The court held that the determination of whether the display constitutes a publication turns on a balancing of factors, including: (1) the length of time the display was exhibited; (2) the expertise of the target audience; (3) the existence (or lack thereof) of reasonable expectations that the material displayed would not be copied; and (4) the simplicity or ease with which the material displayed could have been copied. The audience, however, need not always be technically sophisticated. In *GoPro, Inc. v. Contour IP Holding, LLC*, 908 F.3d 690 (Fed. Cir. 2018), the Federal Circuit held that a sales catalog distributed at a trade show targeting marketers rather than engineers qualified as a printed publication because it was available to those *interested* in the art even if people *skilled* in the art were not at the trade show.

4. A magazine or technical journal is effective as of its date of publication, i.e., when someone first receives it, rather than the date a manuscript was sent to the publisher or the date the journal or magazine was mailed. *See In re Schlittler*, 234 F.2d 882 (C.C.P.A. 1956).

5. *Websites.* Is everything on the internet prior art? Does *In re Hall* provide any guidance? The Federal Circuit has held that an article posted on the Internet but not indexed in search engines can still be a printed publication, but not information in private, password-protected computer systems. *Voter Verified, Inc. v. Premier Election Solutions, Inc.*, 698 F.3d 1374 (Fed. Cir. 2012).

6. *Peer Review of Grant Proposals.* Is a grant proposal sent to a limited number of expert reviewers a publication under §102(a)? *See E. I. du Pont de Nemours & Co. v. Cetus Corp.*, 19 U.S.P.Q.2d (BNA) 1174 (N.D. Cal. 1990) (no).

PROBLEM III-1

In late 1967 the Navy encountered a problem with its new fighter plane. The Navy's aircraft—stationed on aircraft carriers—were more likely to suffer structural damage than Air Force planes of the same type that were positioned on land. Navy scientists concluded that the widespread problem of fuselage cracking, known as "stress corrosion," was attributable to the harsh marine environment. The Navy presented its problem to the aluminum industry, and Algol Corp. was awarded a research contract to develop a new alloy that would be more resistant to the phenomenon.

Pursuant to the terms of the defense contract, Algol would periodically report on its research results in "progress letters." The Navy drew up a distribution list of 33 designees to receive Algol's progress letters, and each letter bore the following "export control" notice: "This Document Is Subject to Special Export Controls and Each Transmittal to Foreign Governments or Foreign Nationals May Be Made Only with Prior Approval of the Naval Air Systems Command."

The designees included aluminum producers (including Algol's competitors), aircraft manufacturers, government agencies, branches of the military, and academic researchers. Several progress letters were mailed, the last on April 5, 1969. As of the last progress letter, Algol had succeeded in developing a high-strength, stress-corrosion-resistant alloy that met the Navy's needs. Algol successfully applied for a patent covering its process for aging and treating its new alloy on February 5, 1971.

When Algol refused to license the patent to its competitor Richards, the latter began to manufacture and sell a high-strength alloy using Algol's patented technology. Algol filed suit alleging infringement.

You are Senior Counsel for Intellectual Property Matters at Richards Aluminum. Your defense strategy is limited by the fact that if the Algol patent is valid, your company is undeniably engaged in infringement. Algol gathers evidence that the 33 designees who received Algol's progress reports treated them as highly confidential although they contained no express limitation on access other than the export control notice. Depositions of Richards' own executives reveal that your company kept its copies of the letters in a protected area, screened even from some of its own employees. Such procedures were typical in defense industry circles when a report bearing an export control notice was received. Nevertheless, the absence of any other access restrictions on the letters supports Richards' argument that Richards could have shared the report's contents with every American citizen.

Is the patent anticipated by Algol's prior "publication"? If so, under §102(a) or under §102(b)?

---

iv.   *Statutory Bars: Public Use and On Sale*

Egbert v. Lippmann
Supreme Court of the United States
104 U.S. 333 (1881)

MR. JUSTICE WOODS delivered the opinion of the court.

This suit was brought for an alleged infringement of the complainant's reissued letters-patent, No. 5216, dated Jan. 7, 1873, for an improvement in corset-springs.

The original letters were issued to Samuel H. Barnes. The reissue was made to the complainant, under her then name, Frances Lee Barnes, executrix of the original patentee.

The specification for the reissue declares:—

This invention consists in forming the springs of corsets of two or more metallic plates, placed one upon another, and so connected as to prevent them from sliding off each other laterally or edgewise, and at the same time admit of their playing or sliding upon each other, in the direction of their length or longitudinally, whereby their flexibility and elasticity are greatly increased, while at the same time much strength is obtained.

The bill alleges that Barnes was the original and first inventor of the improvement covered by the reissued letters-patent, and that it had not, at the time of his application for the original letters, been for more than two years in public use or on sale, with his consent or allowance.

The answer takes issue on this averment and also denies infringement. On a final hearing the court dismissed the bill, and the complainant appealed.

We have to consider whether the defence that the patented invention had, with the consent of the inventor, been publicly used for more than two years prior to his application for the original letters, is sustained by the testimony in the record.

[The patent statute] render[s] letters-patent invalid if the invention which they cover was in public use, with the consent and allowance of the inventor, for more than two years prior to his application.[3] Since the passage of the act of 1839 it has been strenuously contended that the public use of an invention for more than two years before such application, even without his consent and allowance, renders the letters-patent therefor void.

It is unnecessary in this case to decide this question, for the alleged use of the invention covered by the letters-patent to Barnes is conceded to have been with his express consent.

The evidence on which the defendants rely to establish a prior public use of the invention consists mainly of the testimony of the complainant.

She testifies that Barnes invented the improvement covered by his patent between January and May, 1855; that between the dates named the witness and her friend Miss Cugier were complaining of the breaking of their corset-steels. Barnes, who was present, and was an intimate friend of the witness, said he thought he could make her a pair that would not break. At their next interview he presented her with a pair of corset-steels which he himself had made. The witness wore these steels a long time. In 1858 Barnes made and presented to her another pair, which she also wore a long time. When the corsets in which these steels were used wore out, the witness ripped them open and took out the steels and put them in new corsets. This was done several times.

It is admitted, and, in fact, is asserted, by complainant, that these steels embodied the invention afterwards patented by Barnes and covered by the reissued letters-patent on which this suit is brought.

---

[3] [This has since been changed to one year.]

Joseph H. Sturgis, another witness for complainant, testifies that in 1863 Barnes spoke to him about two inventions made by himself, one of which was a corset-steel, and that he went to the house of Barnes to see them. Before this time, and after the transactions testified to by the complainant, Barnes and [the complainant] had intermarried. Barnes said his wife had a pair of steels made according to his invention in the corsets which she was then wearing, and if she would take them off he would show them to [Sturgis]. Mrs. Barnes went out, and returned with a pair of corsets and a pair of scissors, and ripped the corsets open and took out the steels. Barnes then explained to the witness how they were made and used.

The question for our decision is, whether this testimony shows a public use within the meaning of the statute.

We observe, in the first place, that to constitute the public use of an invention it is not necessary that more than one of the patented articles should be publicly used. The use of a great number may tend to strengthen the proof, but one well-defined case of such use is just as effectual to annul the patent as many. For instance, if the inventor of a mower, a printing press, or a railway-car makes and sells only one of the articles invented by him, and allows the vendee to use it for two years, without restriction or limitation, the use is just as public as if he had sold and allowed the use of a great number.

We remark, secondly, that, whether the use of an invention is public or private does not necessarily depend upon the number of persons to whom its use is known. If an inventor, having made his device, gives or sells it to another, to be used by the donee or vendee, without limitation or restriction, or injunction of secrecy, and it is so used, such use is public, even though the use and knowledge of the use may be confined to one person.

We say, thirdly, that some inventions are by their very character only capable of being used where they cannot be seen or observed by the public eye. An invention may consist of a lever or spring, hidden in the running gear of a watch, or of a rachet, shaft, or cog-wheel covered from view in the recesses of a machine for spinning or weaving. Nevertheless, if its inventor sells a machine of which his invention forms a part, and allows it to be used without restriction of any kind, the use is a public one. So, on the other hand, a use necessarily open to public view, if made in good faith solely to test the qualities of the invention, and for the purpose of experiment, is not a public use within the meaning of the statute.

Tested by these principles, we think the evidence of the complainant herself shows that for more than two years before the application for the original letters there was, by the consent and allowance of Barnes, a public use of the invention, covered by them. He made and gave to her two pairs of corset-steels, constructed according to his device, one in 1855 and one in 1858. They were presented to her for use. He imposed no obligation of secrecy, nor any condition or restriction whatever. They were not presented for the purpose of experiment, nor to test their qualities. No such claim is set up in her testimony. The invention was at the time complete, and there is no evidence that it was afterwards changed or improved. The donee of the steels used them for years for the purpose and in the manner designed by the inventor. They were not capable of any other use. She might have exhibited them to any person, or made other steels of the same kind, and used or sold them without violating any condition or restriction imposed on her by the inventor.

According to the testimony of the complainant, the invention was completed and put to use in 1855. The inventor slept on his rights for eleven years. Letters-patent were not applied for till March, 1866. In the mean time, the invention had found its way into general, and almost universal, use. A great part of the record is taken up with the testimony of the manufacturers and venders [sic] of corset-steels, showing that before he applied for letters-patent the principle of his device was almost universally used in the manufacture of corset-steels. It is fair to presume that having learned from this general use that there was some value in his invention, he attempted to resume, by his application, what by his acts he had clearly dedicated to the public.

We are of opinion that the defence of two years' public use, by the consent and allowance of the inventor, before he made application for letters-patent, is satisfactorily established by the evidence.

Decree affirmed.

MR. JUSTICE MILLER dissenting.

A private use with consent, which could lead to no copy or reproduction of the machine, which taught the nature of the invention to no one but the party to whom such consent was given, which left the public at large as ignorant of this as it was before the author's discovery, was no abandonment to the public, and did not defeat his claim for a patent. If the little steel spring inserted in a single pair of corsets, and used by only one woman, covered by her outer-clothing, and in a position always withheld from public observation, is a *public* use of that piece of steel, I am at a loss to know the line between a private and a public use.

COMMENTS AND QUESTIONS

1. In what sense was Frances Lee (later Barnes) using the corset steels (i.e., the springs) "publicly"? Why doesn't it matter how many people use the invention, for purposes of deciding if the use was public? Compare this holding to that of the court in *Rosaire* above.

2. The Court emphasizes that Ms. Barnes never entered into a confidentiality agreement with the inventor. But the Court also relates that the two later married. Does Barnes have a reasonable argument that although no *express* "injunction of secrecy" was made, nonetheless an *implied* requirement of secrecy could be inferred from the surrounding circumstances: i.e., an invention of an intimate nature, by a boyfriend (later husband), disclosed to few people? Justice Miller, in dissent, added: "It may well be imagined that a prohibition to the party so permitted [to use the springs] against her use of the steel spring to public observation, would have been supposed to be a piece of irony." 104 U.S. (14 Otto), at 339. Perhaps the embarrassment of asking was enough to keep Mr. Barnes from requesting that Frances Lee not show the invention to anyone.

See Kara W. Swanson, *Getting a Grip on the Corset: Gender, Sexuality, and Patent Law*, 23 YALE J.L. & FEMINISM (2011) (analyzing the invention and its social context).

3. Subsequent cases have not abandoned *Egbert,* but they have perhaps not read it as broadly as they could have. In particular, the Federal Circuit has focused on the nature and purpose of the use in deciding whether it was "public" or not. Use for a commercial purpose is generally a public use, even if it is secret and even if it only occurs once. Confidential, non-commercial uses do not implicate the 'extension of monopoly' rationale for a broad public use category of prior art. So they might not fall within the prior art.

A similar rule has developed with respect to the "on sale" prong of the §102(b) statutory bar. A single sale or offer to sell a product will start the clock running, whether or not it was made in secret. On the other hand, discussions that do not rise to the level of a definite offer to sell the invention will not bar a later patent on that invention.

4. The policy behind the statutory bars in §102(b) is to encourage inventors to file patent applications early. The inventor in *Egbert* did not do so. Was it reasonable to bar him from receiving a patent on his invention for this reason? Is anyone entitled to a patent on this invention?

5. *Inventor versus Third Party Use*: While "public use" and "on sale" bars frequently result from the inventor's own conduct, they do not have to. Indeed, sales of the invention by a third party can preclude the inventor from later obtaining a patent, even though the third party had stolen the invention from the inventor. *Evans Cooling Sys., Inc. v. General Motors*, 125 F.3d 1448 (Fed. Cir. 1997). The case arose out of inventor John Evans' demonstration of his aqueous reverse flow cooling system to GM engineers in the spring of 1989. GM, as early as June 13, 1991, received a binding order for sale of a Corvette model car incorporating the aqueous reverse flow cooling system. The district court agreed with GM that this sale created a statutory bar for Evans' subsequent patent application filed July 1, 1992. Evans appealed on two grounds: that no enforceable contract could have been formed in June of 1991 because GM had yet to clear certain requisite regulatory hurdles routinely required for sale of a new car model and that the theft of a trade secret ought to be considered an exception to the general statutory bar rule. The court disposed of the first ground by stating simply that "the mere fact that the offer for sale was illegal or ineffective does not remove it from the purview of the section 102(b) bar." *Id.* at 1452.

The court found the second ground—the "theft exception"—equally unpersuasive in light of existing case law. It wrote:

> While such a result may not seem fair, Evans is not without recourse if GM in fact misappropriated his invention. Evans would have an appropriate remedy in state court for misappropriation of a trade secret. We note as well that the facts Evans alleges in support of its misappropriation claim demonstrate that Evans knew GM stole the invention at the very time it was allegedly stolen because during the demonstration GM employees allegedly told Mr. Evans they intended to steal the invention and a sealed room was unsealed during the night

between the tests. Evans' patent rights would have nevertheless been protected if Mr. Evans had filed a patent application no more than one year from the date of the demonstration. This he did not do; instead Mr. Evans waited for more than two years after the demonstration and some six years after it was reduced to practice.

Id. at 1453–54. For a case involving both a close question of "public accessibility/confidentiality" as well as theft-of-idea issues as in *Evans Cooling, see Delano Farms Co. v. California Table Grape Comm'n*, 778 F.3d 1243, 1249 (Fed. Cir. 2015) (grape variety, stolen from plant patentee, was planted and subsequently transferred to another under conditions of secrecy; the grape vines were not visible to the public and were generally handled in "an environment of confidentiality"; held, not a public use that bars the patent). Other major patent systems exclude stolen information from being included in the prior art (or "state of the art") under the principle of "evident abuse of the [rightful] applicant." *See* ROBERT P. MERGES AND SEAGULL HAIYAN SONG, TRANSNATIONAL INTELLECTUAL PROPERTY LAW 95, 106 (2018) (discussing China and Europe).

6. *On-Sale Bar—Ready for Patenting.* Must an invention actually be completed and built before it can be sold or "offered for sale"? The Supreme Court has said no. *Pfaff v. Wells Elec., Inc.*, 525 U.S. 55 (1998). The Court reasoned that "invention" occurred when the inventor conceived of the product and did not require proof that the invention has actually been built. Indeed, it noted, many famous inventions (including Alexander Graham Bell's telephone) were patented before a prototype was ever built. *Id.* at 308–09. However, the Court did require evidence that the inventive concept itself was "complete, rather than merely . . . substantially complete":

> [T]he on-sale bar applies when two conditions are satisfied before the critical date. First, the product must be the subject of a commercial offer for sale. . . .
>
> Second, the invention must be ready for patenting. That condition may be satisfied in at least two ways: by proof of reduction to practice before the critical date; or by proof that prior to the critical date the inventor had prepared drawings or other descriptions of the invention that were sufficiently specific to enable a person skilled in the art to practice the invention. In this case the second condition of the on-sale bar is satisfied because the drawings Pfaff sent to the manufacturer before the critical date fully disclosed the invention.

Id. at 67. *See also Weatherchem Corp. v. J.L. Clark, Inc.*, 163 F.3d 1326 (Fed. Cir. 1998) (applying *Pfaff* to case where detailed drawings had been made in preparation of an offer for sale). Contrast *Pfaff* with *Micro Chem., Inc. v. Great Plains Chem. Co.*, 103 F.3d 1538 (Fed. Cir. 1997) ("Because Pratt was not close to completion of the invention at the time of the alleged offer and had not demonstrated a high likelihood that the invention would work for its intended purpose upon completion, his December 1984 'offer' could not trigger the on-sale bar.").

Several cases address the relationship between contract law and the "on sale" bar. In *Group One, Ltd. v. Hallmark Cards, Inc.*, 254 F.3d 1041 (Fed. Cir. 2001), the patentee and a third party had conducted correspondence and engaged in other interactions in connection with a later-patented technology. The Federal Circuit refused to find that this exploratory discussion placed the invention "on sale" under §102(b). Only a transaction which "rises to the level of a commercial offer for sale" under the Uniform Commercial Code triggers the on-sale bar, according to the court. 254 F.3d at 1047.

7. *Selling Method Claims.* One "sells" a method claim by performing the method in exchange for money, not by licensing the right to the invention itself. *In re Kollar*, 286 F.3d 1326 (Fed. Cir. 2002), concerned a licensing transaction involving a chemical process. The Federal Circuit refused to find that the transaction triggered the on-sale bar: "[L]icensing the invention," the court stated, "under which development of the claimed process would have to occur before the process is successfully commercialized, is not . . . a sale." *Id.*, at 1333. *Compare Elan Corp. v. Andrx Pharmaceuticals, Inc.*, 366 F.3d 1336 (Fed. Cir. 2004) (offer to supply potential licensee with limited quantities of bulk tablets not enough to constitute on-sale activity in what otherwise appeared to be a proposed licensing transaction), *with Minton v. National Ass'n of Secs. Dealers, Inc.*, 336 F.3d 1373, 1378 (Fed. Cir. 2003) (inventor's conveyance to lessee of fully operational computer program implementing and thus embodying method subsequently claimed in patent for interactive securities trading system, along with warranty of workability, enabled lessee to practice invention, and thus was "offer for sale" within meaning of on-sale bar).

Does this distinction make sense? Why should those who license a process invention be able to avoid the on-sale bar when those who sell a patented product cannot?

8. *On-Sale Activity Need Not Disclose the Manner in which the Patented Technology Functions.* According to an extensive body of case law, these prior art categories include material that can be quite confidential, or at any rate essentially undiscoverable by members of the general public. A consistent line of cases, for example, holds that confidential sales or offers places an invention "on sale" for purposes of novelty. *See, e.g., Buildex Inc. v. Kason Indus., Inc.*, 849 F.2d 1461, 1464 (Fed. Cir. 1988) (firm offer sent to prospective purchaser was an "on sale" event, even though the offer was marked "confidential"); *Pfaff v. Wells Elecs., Inc.*, 525 U.S. 55 (1998) (nowhere mentioning the need for information about a sale to be publicly available).

9. *Public Use—Informing versus Non-Informing (or Secret) Use/Patentee versus Third-Party Activity.* Although the 1952 Act makes no distinction based on whether a public use of a patented process reveals the patented invention, the courts have distinguished between patentee and third-party secret commercial uses. A patentee's secret commercial use is treated as a public use and therefore will bare them from later getting a patent, whereas a third party's is not. *Compare Metallizing Engineering Co. v. Kenyon Bearing & Auto Parts Co.*, 153 F.2d 516 (2d Cir.1946) (Hand, J.) (patentee's own secret use of machine to produce products for sale is an public use barring a patent

on the machine after a year) *with W.L. Gore & Associates, Inc. v. Garlock, Inc.*, 721 F.2d 1540 (1983) (third party secret sale of tape from tape-making machine did not bar a patent on the machine to an inventor who filed more than one year after that third party sale); *see generally Woodland Trust v. Flowertree Nursery*, 148 F.3d 1368, 1370–71 (Fed. Cir. 1998) (observing that "[s]ection 102(b), unlike §102(a), is primarily concerned with the policy that encourages an inventor to enter the patent system promptly"). This distinction is based on the policy concern that without such a limit, an inventor could keep his invention secret for years or even decades while profiting from its use, then file a patent application. Because that application was filed later, the patent would expire later, extending the effective life of the inventor's protection. This distinction lacks a textual basis, although it is well-established in Federal Circuit jurisprudence.

v.   *Statutory Bars: The Experimental Use Exception*

City of Elizabeth v. Pavement Company
Supreme Court of the United States
97 U.S. 126 (1877)

MR. JUSTICE BRADLEY delivered the opinion of the court.

This suit was brought by the American Nicholson Pavement Company against the city of Elizabeth, N.J., upon a patent issued to Samuel Nicholson, dated Aug. 20, 1867, for a new and improved wooden pavement, being a second reissue of a patent issued to said Nicholson Aug. 8, 1854. The reissued patent was extended in 1868 for a further term of seven years. . . . [I]n the specification, it is declared that the nature and object of the invention consists in providing a process or mode of constructing wooden block pavements upon a foundation along a street or roadway with facility, cheapness, and accuracy, and also in the creation and construction of such a wooden pavement as shall be comparatively permanent and durable, by so uniting and combining all its parts, both superstructure and foundation, as to provide against the slipping of the horses' feet, against noise, against unequal wear, and against rot and consequent sinking away from below.

The bill charges that the defendants infringed this patent by laying down wooden pavements in the city of Elizabeth, N.J., constructed in substantial conformity with the process patented, and prays an account of profits, and an injunction.

The defendants . . . averred that the alleged invention of Nicholson was in public use, with his consent and allowance, for six years before he applied for a patent, on a certain avenue in Boston called the Mill-dam; and contended that said public use worked an abandonment of the pretended invention. . . .

The next question to be considered is, whether Nicholson's invention was in public use or on sale, with his consent and allowance, for more than two years prior to his application for a patent, within the meaning of . . . the acts in force in 1854, when he obtained his patent. It is contended by the appellants that the pavement which Nicholson put down by way of experiment, on Mill-dam Avenue in Boston, in 1848, was publicly used for the space of six years before his application for a patent, and that this was a public use within the meaning of the law.

To determine this question, it is necessary to examine the circumstances under which this pavement was put down, and the object and purpose that Nicholson had in view. It is perfectly clear from the evidence that he did not intend to abandon his right to a patent. He had filed a *caveat* in August, 1847, and he constructed the pavement in question by way of experiment, for the purpose of testing its qualities. The road in which it was put down, though a public road, belonged to the Boston and Roxbury Mill Corporation, which received toll for its use; and Nicholson was a stockholder and treasurer of the corporation. The pavement in question was about seventy-five feet in length, and was laid adjoining to the toll-gate and in front of the toll-house. It was constructed by Nicholson at his own expense, and was placed by him where it was, in order to see the effect upon it of heavily loaded wagons, and of varied and constant use; and also to ascertain its durability, and liability to decay. Joseph L. Lang, who was toll-collector for many years, commencing in 1849, familiar with the road before that time, and with this pavement from the time of its origin, testified as follows:

Mr. Nicholson was there almost daily, and when he came he would examine the pavement, would often walk over it, cane in hand, striking it with his cane, and making particular examination of its condition. He asked me very often how people liked it, and asked me a great many questions about it. I have heard him say a number of times that this was his first experiment with this pavement, and he thought that it was wearing very well. The circumstances that made this locality desirable for the purpose of obtaining a satisfactory test of the durability and value of the pavement were: that there would be a better chance to lay it there; he would have more room and a better chance than in the city; and, besides, it was a place where most everybody went over it, rich and poor. It was a great thoroughfare out of Boston. It was frequently travelled by teams having a load of five or six tons, and some larger. As these teams usually stopped at the toll-house, and started again, the stopping and starting would make as severe a trial to the pavement as it could be put to.

This evidence is corroborated by that of several other witnesses in the cause; the result of the whole being that Nicholson merely intended this piece of pavement as an experiment, to test its usefulness and durability. Was this a public use, within the meaning of the law?

An abandonment of an invention to the public may be evinced by the conduct of the inventor at any time, even within the two years named in the law. The effect of the law is, that no such consequence will necessarily follow from the invention being in public use or on sale, with the inventor's consent and allowance, at any time within two years before his application; but that, if the invention is in public use or on sale prior to that time, it will be conclusive evidence of abandonment, and the patent will be void.

But, in this case, it becomes important to inquire what is such a public use as will have the effect referred to. That the use of the pavement in question was public in one sense cannot be disputed. But can it be said that the invention was in public use? The use of an invention by the inventor himself, or of any other person under his direction, by way of experiment, and in order to bring the invention to perfection, has never been regarded as such a use. CURTIS, PATENTS, § 381; *Shaw v. Cooper*, [32 U.S.] 7 Pet. 292 [1833].

Now, the nature of a street pavement is such that it cannot be experimented upon satisfactorily except on a highway, which is always public.

When the subject of invention is a machine, it may be tested and tried in a building, either with or without closed doors. In either case, such use is not a public use, within the meaning of the statute, so long as the inventor is engaged, in good faith, in testing its operation. He may see cause to alter it and improve it, or not. His experiments will reveal the fact whether any and what alterations may be necessary. If durability is one of the qualities to be attained, a long period, perhaps years, may be necessary to enable the inventor to discover whether his purpose is accomplished. And though, during all that period, he may not find that any changes are necessary, yet he may be justly said to be using his machine only by way of experiment; and no one would say that such a use, pursued with a *bona fide* intent of testing the qualities of the machine, would be a public use, within the meaning of the statute. So long as he does not voluntarily allow others to make it and use it, and so long as it is not on sale for general use, he keeps the invention under his own control, and does not lose his title to a patent.

It would not be necessary, in such a case, that the machine should be put up and used only in the inventor's own shop or premises. He may have it put up and used in the premises of another, and the use may inure to the benefit of the owner of the establishment. Still, if used under the surveillance of the inventor, and for the purpose of enabling him to test the machine, and ascertain whether it will answer the purpose intended, and make such alterations and improvements as experience demonstrates to be necessary, it will still be a mere experimental use, and not a public use, within the meaning of the statute.

Whilst the supposed machine is in such experimental use, the public may be incidentally deriving a benefit from it. If it be a grist-mill, or a carding-machine, customers from the surrounding country may enjoy the use of it by having their grain made into flour, or their wool into rolls, and still it will not be in public use, within the meaning of the law.

But if the inventor allows his machine to be used by other persons generally, either with or without compensation, or if it is, with his consent, put on sale for such use, then it will be in public use and on public sale, within the meaning of the law.

If, now, we apply the same principles to this case, the analogy will be seen at once. Nicholson wished to experiment on his pavement. He believed it to be a good thing, but he was not sure; and the only mode in which he could test it was to place a specimen of it in a public roadway. He did this at his own expense, and with the consent of the owners of the road. Durability was one of the qualities to be attained. He wanted to know whether his pavement would stand, and whether it would resist decay. Its character for durability could not be ascertained without its being subjected to use for a considerable time. He subjected it to such use, in good faith, for the simple purpose of ascertaining whether it was what he claimed it to be. Did he do anything more than the inventor of the supposed machine might do, in testing his invention? The public had the incidental use of the pavement, it is true; but was the invention in public use, within the meaning of the statute? We think not. The proprietors of the road alone used the invention, and used it at Nicholson's request, by way of experiment. The only way in which they could use it was by allowing the public to pass over the pavement.

Had the city of Boston, or other parties, used the invention, by laying down the pavement in other streets and places, with Nicholson's consent and allowance, then, indeed, the invention itself would have been in public use, within the meaning of the law; but this was not the case. Nicholson did not sell it, nor allow others to use it or sell it. He did not let it go beyond his control. He did nothing that indicated any intent to do so. He kept it under his own eyes, and never for a moment abandoned the intent to obtain a patent for it. . . .

It is sometimes said that an inventor acquires an undue advantage over the public by delaying to take out a patent, inasmuch as he thereby preserves the monopoly to himself for a longer period than is allowed by the policy of the law; but this cannot be said with justice when the delay is occasioned by a *bona fide* effort to bring his invention to perfection, or to ascertain whether it will answer the purpose intended. His monopoly only continues for the allotted period, in any event; and it is the interest of the public, as well as himself, that the invention should be perfect and properly tested, before a patent is granted for it. Any attempt to use it for a profit, and not by way of experiment, for a longer period than two years before the application, would deprive the inventor of his right to a patent.

COMMENTS AND QUESTIONS

1. Compare the facts in *City of Elizabeth* to those in *Egbert v. Lippmann, supra*, the corset case. How did Nicholson's actions in this case differ from those of Barnes in the *Egbert* case? What evidence did Nicholson have regarding his six-year prefiling period that Barnes did not have for his comparably long period?

2. Could Nicholson simply have filed a patent application at the end of year one and prosecuted it while conducting his continued test? Would a patent have been granted on such an application? Note that because Nicholson was able to delay filing his application for six years, he received a patent that expired later and was therefore arguably more valuable to him than the patent he would have received if he had applied at the end of one year.

3. *Factors to Be Considered.* In a 2002 decision, the Federal Circuit provides a list of 13 factors collected from prior cases that are relevant to a finding of experimental use:

(1) the necessity for public testing, (2) the amount of control over the experiment retained by the inventor, (3) the nature of the invention, (4) the length of the test period, (5) whether payment was made, (6) whether there was a secrecy obligation, (7) whether records of the experiment were kept, (8) who

conducted the experiment, (9) the degree of commercial exploitation during testing, (10) whether the invention reasonably requires evaluation under actual conditions of use, (11) whether testing was systematically performed, (12) whether the inventor continually monitored the invention during testing, and (13) the nature of contacts made with potential customers.

Allen Eng'g Corp. v. Bartell Indus., Inc., 299 F.3d 1336, 1353 (Fed. Cir. 2002). The jurisprudence, however, makes clear that even one factor can be decisive. *See Atlanta Attachment Co. v. Leggett & Platt, Inc.*, 516 F.3d 1361, 1366 (Fed. Cir. 2008) (observing that lack of control over the invention during the alleged experiment, while not always dispositive, may be so); *see also Clock Spring, L.P. v. Wrapmaster, Inc.*, 560 F.3d 1317 (Fed. Cir. 2009).

4. A 2005 Federal Circuit case applied the *City of Elizabeth* principles to a case involving "experimental sales." *Electromotive Div. of General Motors Corp. v. Transportation Systems Div. of General Elec. Co.*, 417 F.3d 1203 (Fed. Cir. 2005). In this case, the patentee (GM) claimed planetary compressor bearings for use in turbochargers for diesel train engines. Pursuant to its standard development and testing procedure, GM used prototypes of its new bearing design in numerous train engines before the critical date. It also agreed to supply some bearings covered by one of its patents as spares to one of its customers if it needed them. Defendant GE argued that the sale of the train engines containing the new bearings, and the agreement to supply them as spares, constituted "on sale" activity under §102(b). GM disagreed, and argued that because the bearings were part of its development and testing program, the customer's use of the engines with the bearings was covered by the "experimental use" of *City of Elizabeth*. The Federal Circuit sided with defendant GE:

When sales are made in an ordinary commercial environment and the goods are placed outside the inventor's control, an inventor's secretly held subjective intent to "experiment," even if true, is unavailing without objective evidence to support the contention. Under such circumstances, the customer at a minimum must be made aware of the experimentation:

We have generally looked to objective evidence to show that a pre-critical date sale was primarily for experimentation. . . . The length of the test period is merely a piece of evidence to add to the evidentiary scale. The same is true with respect to whether payment is made for the device, whether a user agreed to use secretly, whether records were kept of progress, whether persons other than the inventor conducted the asserted experiments, how many tests were conducted, how long the testing period was in relationship to tests of other similar devices. [*T.P. Laboratories, Inc. v. Professional Positioners, Inc.*, 724 F.2d 965 (Fed. Cir. 1984)], at 971–72.

We agree . . . that a customer's awareness of the purported testing in the context of a sale is a critical attribute of experimentation. If an inventor fails to communicate to a customer that the sale of the invention was made in pursuit of experimentation, then the customer, as well as the general public, can only view the sale as a normal commercial transaction. . . . Accordingly, we hold not only that customer awareness is among the experimentation factors, but also that it is critical.

Our precedent has treated control and customer awareness of the testing as especially important to experimentation. Indeed, this court has effectively made control and customer awareness dispositive. Accordingly, we conclude that control and customer awareness ordinarily must be proven if experimentation is to be found.

417 F.3d 1203, at 1212–15 (citations omitted).

vi.   *Priority Rules and First-to-Invent*

Having dealt with novelty, we turn now to the closely related topic of *priority*. Section 102(g) of the 1952 Act provides that "[a] person shall be entitled to a patent unless"

(1) [*inter partes* proceedings] during the course of an interference . . ., another inventor involved therein establishes, to the extent permitted in section 104 . . . that before such person's invention thereof the invention was made by such other inventor and not abandoned, suppressed, or concealed, or

(2) [*ex parte* prosecution/invalidity defense] before such person's invention thereof, the invention was made in this country by another inventor who had not abandoned, suppressed, or concealed it.

In determining priority of invention under this subsection, there shall be considered not only the respective dates of conception and reduction to practice of the invention, but also the reasonable diligence of one who was first to conceive and last to reduce to practice, from a time prior to conception by the other.

Because the 1952 Act was a first to invent system, the law needed a mechanism to decide who among competing inventors was the first to invent. Section 102(g) considers four issues in deciding who is first to invent: conception, reduction to practice, diligence, and abandonment.

Conception occurs when an inventor possesses a definite idea of a complete and operative invention as it is thereafter reduced to practice. Reduction to practice occurs when the inventor establishes that the claimed invention works for its intended purpose. This can be proven through laboratory experimentation, construction of a prototype, or drawings explaining the operative elements of the claimed invention. Filing a valid, enabling patent application constitutes a constructive reduction to practice.

As the following timeline illustrates, Inventor B is the first to conceive the claimed invention represented by the lightbulb above her head illuminating. She begins her experimentation soon thereafter and eventually reduces the invention to practice, as illustrated by her synthesis of the drug compound (Rx). Inventor A later independently conceives the same invention and reduces the invention to practice relatively quickly. In fact, he can establish reduction to practice before Inventor B.

Section 102(g) Timeline

As illustrated by the second timeline, notwithstanding that Inventor A is the first to reduce the invention to practice, the 1952 Patent Act grants Inventor B priority so long as she is reasonably diligent in her efforts to reduce the claimed invention to practice from a time prior to Inventor A's conception date, ultimately achieves a successful reduction to practice, and does not abandon, suppress, or conceal her invention.

An inventor "abandon[s], suppress[es] or conceal[s]" an invention by failing to pursue a patent or take steps to utilize or commercialize the invention. *See Dow Chem. Co. v. Astro-Valcour, Inc.,* 267 F.3d 1334, 1342 (Fed. Cir. 2001). Thus, a first inventor can lose priority if she fails to actively pursue her invention for a long enough time. *See, e.g., Peeler v. Miller,* 535 F.2d 647, 654 (C.C.P.A. 1976) (four-year delay between reduction to practice and filing of application constituted abandonment). Diligence concerns the inventor's conduct before reducing the invention to practice, while abandonment, suppression, or concealment only happen after an invention is reduced to practice.

Disputes over priority of invention arise in two contexts: (1) interference proceedings; or (2) as an invalidity defense. The same priority rule applies to both contexts. Section 102(g)(1) covers *interference proceedings*—formal priority contests between rival claimants who both want to patent the same subject matter. Such proceedings can take place at the PTO where an examiner or applicant determines that two pending patent applications cover the same invention. Subsection (2) covers the use of prior inventions as a source of prior art to defend against someone else's patent.

Besides the different contexts in which they arise, Sections 102(g)(1) and (2) differ in their territorial scope. The key phrases are "to the extent permitted in section 104" in (g)(1) and "in this country" in (g)(2). Section 104 allows proof of prior inventive activity in any country that is a signatory to the World Trade Organization (WTO). No proof of conception or reduction to practice in a non-WTO country can be entered in an interference, although this does not matter much since essentially all countries are in the WTO. (And even inventions from non-WTO countries may rely on their U.S. patent application filing date as their date of invention.) Contrast this with the language of (g)(2): only evidence of prior inventions made *in the U.S.* may be introduced.

Now you can understand why some interferences are so complex and can take so long to resolve. *See, e.g., Standard Oil Co. (Indiana) v. Montedison, S.P.A.,* 664 F.2d 356 (3d Cir. 1981) (1981 decision affirming findings of a PTO interference based on a patent application on polypropylene polymer filed in 1953); *U.S. Steel Corp. v. Phillips Petroleum Co.,* 865 F.2d 1247 (Fed. Cir. 1989) (validity of same patent upheld in litigation 36 years after patent was filed). You can also appreciate why Congress jettisoned the first to invent approach in favor of a "first-to-file" priority system in the America Invents Act.

In general, priority under the 1952 Act goes to the first inventor who can show reduction to practice (and who does not abandon, suppress or conceal by waiting too long). Often, this is also the same inventor who can show first conception. Priority in this case is easy: the first to conceive and first to reduce to practice wins, period. A more complicated case arises when one inventor is first to conceive but last to reduce to practice.

Such a case triggers application of the last sentence of §102(g), particularly the "reasonable diligence of one who was first to conceive but last to reduce to practice." In this special situation, as you will see in the following case, the first to conceive must prove an extra element to win priority—reasonable diligence.

Griffith v. Kanamaru
United States Court of Appeals for the Federal Circuit
816 F.2d 624 (Fed. Cir. 1987)

NICHOLS, SENIOR CIRCUIT JUDGE.

Owen W. Griffith (Griffith) appeals the decision of the Board of Patent Appeals and Interferences (board) that Griffith failed to establish a prima facie case that he is entitled to an award of priority against the filing date of Tsuneo Kanamaru, et al. (Kanamaru) for a patent on aminocarnitine compounds. We affirm.

Background

This patent interference case involves the application of Griffith, an Associate Professor in the Department of Biochemistry at Cornell University Medical College, for a patent on an aminocarnitine compound, useful in the treatment of diabetes, and a patent issued for the same invention to Kanamaru, an employee of Takeda Chemical Industries. The inventors assigned their rights to the inventions to the Cornell Research Foundation, Inc. (Cornell) and to Takeda Chemical Industries respectively.

Griffith had established conception by June 30, 1981, and reduction to practice on January 11, 1984. Kanamaru filed for a United States patent on November 17, 1982. The board found, however, that Griffith failed to establish reasonable diligence for a prima facie case of prior invention. . . .

The board . . . decided that Griffith failed to establish a prima facie case for priority against Kanamaru's filing date. This result was based on the board's conclusion that Griffith's explanation for inactivity between June 15, 1983, and September 13, 1983, failed to provide a legally sufficient excuse to satisfy the "reasonable diligence" requirement of 35 U.S.C. § 102(g). [The final sentence of 1952 Act §102(g) reads: "In determining priority of invention under this subsection, there shall be considered not only the respective dates of conception and reduction to practice of the invention, but also the reasonable diligence of one who was first to conceive and last to reduce to practice, from a time prior to conception by the other."] Griffith appeals on the issue of reasonable diligence.

Analysis

This is a case of first impression and presents the novel circumstances of a university suggesting that it is reasonable for the public to wait for disclosure until the most satisfactory funding arrangements are made. The applicable law is the "reasonable diligence" standard contained in 35 U.S.C. §102(g) and we must determine the appropriate role of the courts in construing this exception to the ordinary first-in-time rule. As a preliminary matter we note that, although the board focused on the June 1983 to September 1983 lapse in work, and Griffith's reasons for this lapse, Griffith is burdened with establishing a prima facie case of reasonable diligence from immediately before Kanamaru's filing date of November 17, 1982, until Griffith's reduction to practice on January 11, 1984. 35 U.S.C. §102(g).

On appeal, Griffith presents two grounds intended to justify his inactivity on the aminocarnitine project between June 15, 1983, and September 13, 1983. The first is that

. . . it is reasonable, and as a policy matter desirable, for Cornell to require Griffith and other research scientists to obtain funding from outside the university. The second reason Griffith presents is that he reasonably waited for Ms. Debora Jenkins to matriculate in the Fall of 1983 to assist with the project. He had promised her she should have that task which she needed to qualify for her degree. We reject these arguments and conclude that Griffith has failed to establish grounds to excuse his inactivity prior to reduction to practice.

The reasonable diligence standard balances the interest in rewarding and encouraging invention with the public's interest in the earliest possible disclosure of innovation. Griffith must account for the entire period from just before Kanamaru's filing date until his [i.e., Griffith's] reduction to practice. . . .

The board in this case was, but not properly, asked to pass judgment on the reasonableness of Cornell's policy regarding outside funding of research. The correct inquiry is rather whether it is reasonable for Cornell to require the public to wait for the innovation, given the well settled policy in favor of early disclosure. . . . A review of caselaw on excuses for inactivity in reduction to practice reveals a common thread that courts may consider the reasonable everyday problems and limitations encountered by an inventor. *See, e.g.,* . . . *Reed v. Tornqvist*, 436 F.2d 501 (C.C.P.A. 1971) (concluding it is not unreasonable for inventor to delay completing a patent application until after returning from a three week vacation in Sweden, extended by illness of inventor's father); . . . *De Wallace v. Scott*, 15 App. D.C. 157 (1899) (where applicant made bona fide attempts to perfect his invention, applicant's poor health, responsibility to feed his family, and daily job demands excused his delay in reducing his invention to practice).

. . . We first note that, in regard to waiting for a graduate student, Griffith does not even suggest that he faced a genuine shortage of personnel. He does not suggest that Ms. Jenkins was the only person capable of carrying on with the aminocarnitine experiment. We can see no application of precedent to suggest that the convenience of the timing of the semester schedule justifies a three-month delay for the purpose of reasonable diligence. Neither do we believe that this excuse, absent even a suggestion by Griffith that Jenkins was uniquely qualified to do his research, is reasonable.

Griffith's second contention that it was reasonable for Cornell to require outside funding, therefore causing a delay in order to apply for such funds, is also insufficient to excuse his inactivity. The crux of Griffith's argument is that outside funding is desirable as a form of peer review, or monitoring of the worthiness of a given project. He also suggests that, as a policy matter, universities should not be treated as businesses, which ultimately would detract from scholarly inquiry. Griffith states that these considerations, if accepted as valid, would fit within the scope of the caselaw excusing inactivity for "reasonable" delays in reduction to practice and filing.

Griffith's excuses sound more in the nature of commercial development, not accepted as an excuse for delay, than the "hardship" cases most commonly found and discussed *supra*. Delays in reduction to practice caused by an inventor's efforts to refine an invention to the most marketable and profitable form have not been accepted as sufficient excuses for inactivity.

. . . [I]t seems evident that Cornell has consciously chosen to assume the risk that priority in the invention might be lost to an outside inventor, yet, having chosen a noncommercial policy, it asks us to save it the property that would have inured to it if it had acted in single-minded pursuit of gain.

Although we agree with the board's conclusion, it is appropriate to go further and consider other circumstances as they apply to the reasonable diligence analysis of 35 U.S.C. §102(g). The record reveals that from the relevant period of November 17, 1982 (Kanamaru's filing date), to September 13, 1983 (when Griffith renewed his efforts towards reduction to practice), Griffith interrupted and often put aside the aminocarnitine project to work on other experiments. Between June 1982 and June 1983 Griffith admits that, at the request of the chairman of his department, he was primarily engaged in an unrelated research project. . . . Griffith also put aside the aminocarnitine experiment to work on a grant proposal on an unrelated project. . . . Griffith made only minimal efforts to secure funding directly for the aminocarnitine project.

The conclusion we reach from the record is that the aminocarnitine project was second and often third priority in laboratory research as well as the solicitation of funds. We agree that Griffith failed to establish a prima facie case of reasonable diligence or a legally sufficient excuse for inactivity to establish priority over Kanamaru.

COMMENTS AND QUESTIONS

1. What would the result in the interference have been if Professor Griffith had reduced the invention to practice on November 16, 1982? (Recall that Kanamaru's filing date—and therefore, in this case, his effective conception and reduction to practice dates—was November 17, 1982.)

If Griffith had reduced to practice on November 16, 1982, would it matter whether he was diligent between his conception date (June 30, 1981) and his reduction to practice? If not, why not? (Pay attention to the language: "there shall be considered not only the respective dates of conception and reduction to practice of the invention, but also the reasonable diligence of one who was first to conceive and last to reduce to practice." Note that reasonable diligence is mentioned *only in connection with* "one who was first to conceive and last to reduce to practice.").

Assume that Kanamaru introduced the following evidence: a conception date of January 1, 1982, and reduction to practice on November 1, 1982. Assume also, as actually happened, that Griffith's reduction to practice came after Kanamaru's. With Griffith the first to conceive of the invention, is Kanamaru's diligence an issue under the last sentence of §102(g)(1)? *Should* it be?

2. Since Takeda Chemical, Kanamaru's assignee, is based primarily in Japan, it is reasonable to conclude that Kanamaru did the research leading to his patent application in Japan. This would explain the exclusive reliance on the patent filing date in this priority contest. Before 1995, and thus at the time this case was decided, foreign inventors could not introduce evidence of foreign inventive activity (e.g., conception and reduction to practice). In 1994, however, as part of the legislative package implementing the Trade Related Aspects of Intellectual Property (TRIPs) portion of the

Uruguay Round negotiations under the GATT, Congress changed §104 to permit evidence of inventive activity taking place in any country that is a member of the World Trade Organization (the successor organization to the GATT) beginning in 1996. *See* Uruguay Round Agreements Act of 1994, P.L. 103–465, 108 Stat. 4809 (1994), at §531, codified at 35 U.S.C. §104.

3. *Corroboration of Invention Dates*. Due to the complexity of determining invention dates, the significant ramifications for patent ownership and validity, and the risk of fraud, courts require corroborating evidence of contemporaneous disclosure that would enable one skilled in the art to make the invention. *Mahurkar v. C.R. Bard*, 79 F.3d 1572, 1577 (Fed. Cir. 1996). This typically comes in the form of laboratory notebooks witnessed and signed by skilled artisans.

4. *Political Economy of First-to-Invent?* As noted at the outset of this section, most countries in the world have long based priority on application filing date—a far simpler and clearer system. The U.S. first-to-invent regime has been premised on a philosophical preference for rewarding true first inventors, not those (presumably large corporations) who have the resources to file quickly. In fact, small inventors were the major lobbying group opposed to international harmonization. Many questioned, however, whether this philosophical benefit outweighed the additional administrative cost, complexity, and lack of clarity about who will win a priority contest. For many years, it was thought that most interferences were predominantly won by senior parties anyway. That conventional wisdom didn't prove true. *See* Mark A. Lemley & Colleen V. Chien, *Are the U.S. Patent Priority Rules Really Necessary?*, 54 HASTINGS L.J. 1299 (2003) (finding that junior parties (second filers) have prevailed in 43% of interference proceedings resolved on priority grounds). Does this sway your thinking about the desirability of giving up the traditional U.S. "first to invent" standard? As we will see in the next section, the small inventors eventually lost this battle, but were able to retain a U.S. grace period.

5. *Prior User Rights*. Griffith and Kanamaru were well on their way to the same invention at roughly the same time. Under the Federal Circuit's decision, only Kanamaru gets a patent on the invention. What happens to Griffith? Not only is he not entitled to the exclusionary power of a patent on his idea, but Kanamaru can exclude *him* from using his own, independently developed idea. This result seems harsh, particularly where (as here) Griffith was working on his version of the invention long before the patent ever issued to Kanamaru.

To ameliorate this problem, Congress has since granted "prior user rights" to non-patentees if they could show that they were using the invention well before it was patented by someone else. *See* 35 U.S.C. §273 (2011). Under §273, a person who uses an invention commercially more than one year before another applies for a patent or commences the AIA grace period may continue to use the invention despite issuance of a patent to the other person. There are a number of technical restrictions on the new prior user right, including non-transferability. *See* §273(e)(1)(B) (restricting transfer of prior user right to sale of an entire company or line of business). So far the new prior rights provision has seen little use.

Are prior user rights a good idea? Do they unfairly weaken the patent grant? For an argument in favor of prior user rights, *see* Samson Vermont, *Independent Invention as a Defense to Patent Infringement*, 105 MICH. L. REV. 475 (2006). If a prior user is permitted to continue their use, should the patentee be compensated somehow—say, by receiving a compulsory licensing fee from the prior user? *See generally* Stephen Maurer & Suzanne Scotchmer, *The Independent Inventor Defense in Intellectual Property*, 69 ECONOMICA 535 (2002).

6. *A Simpler Approach . . . Eventually.* Under the AIA, all this complexity is swept away for patents filed on or after March 16, 2013. All that typically matters is who *files* first. The only exceptions are where the inventor publishes and files within a year of publication and where an invention is stolen or "derived" from the true inventor–as in the *Evans Cooling* case mentioned earlier. Even so, because the 1952 Act will continue to apply to patent applications filed prior to March 16, 2013, it is important to understand 1952 Act §102(g) until at least March 16, 2033.

vii. The America Invents Act Regime

Congress shifted the U.S. from the 1952 Act first-to-invent regime toward the international first-to-file standard. The U.S. did not, however, adopt a pure first-to-file system. Importantly, it retained a one-year grace period for inventors in certain cases. As a result, it might be more apt to characterize the AIA novelty regime as a modified first to file regime: a first to file or publish regime so long as that inventor files within a year of disclosure.

From a practical standpoint, the new regime makes the following changes: (1) the critical date for most purposes is now the date that a patent application is first filed; (2) the prior art relevant to a given patent claim now consists of all references available under the statute prior to the filing date rather than the invention date, subject to a one-year grace period for the inventor in some cases; and (3) priority contests between rival claimants to an invention will now be determined almost exclusively by looking to when each of the rivals filed their patent application. The discussion that follows elaborates these basic principles and describes how they compare to the operating rules that pertain to the old, 1952 Act, system of priority and novelty. We conclude this section with a series of problems that illustrate the differences between the 1952 Act and AIA regimes.

a. The AIA: A Simpler Structure

Overall, the AIA provides a simpler structure than the 1952 Act. The distinction between novelty, strictly speaking, and the statutory bars under the 1952 Act is gone. The AIA eliminates the 1952 Act's awkward structure, in which the related but distinct concepts of novelty and statutory bars appeared in successive subsections of §102. This means the end of the repetition of various categories or types of prior art under the two subsections, 1952 Act §102(a) and §102(b)–"patented, printed publications" etc. It also means that the concept of a grace period, which had been buried in the structure and wording of 1952 Act §102(b), is more apparent in the AIA.

The AIA integrates novelty and statutory bars into a unified provision, AIA §102, which first states the rule that prior art appearing before the critical date deprives the inventor of his or her entitlement to a patent; then defines all categories or types of references that qualify as prior art under the AIA (AIA §102(a)(1) and (2)); then defines the critical date as the inventor's filing date (last phrase of AIA §102(a)(1) and (2)); and then, finally, identifies the grace period concept as an exception to the general rule that prior art appearing earlier than an inventor's filing date precludes patentability for the inventor's claimed invention.

§102(a) NOVELTY; PRIOR ART. —

A person shall be entitled to a patent unless—

(1) the claimed invention was patented, described in a printed publication, or in public use, on sale, or otherwise available to the public before the effective filing date of the claimed invention; or

(2) the claimed invention was described in a patent issued [to another] . . . or in [another's] application for patent [that is] published . . . [and that] was effectively filed before the effective filing date of the claimed invention.

(b) EXCEPTIONS.—

(1) DISCLOSURES MADE 1 YEAR OR LESS BEFORE THE EFFECTIVE FILING DATE OF THE CLAIMED INVENTION. — disclosure made 1 year or less before the effective filing date of a claimed invention shall not be prior art to the claimed invention under subsection (a)(1) if —

(A) the disclosure was made by the inventor or joint inventor or by another who obtained the subject matter disclosed directly or indirectly from the inventor or a joint inventor; or

(B) the subject matter disclosed had, before such disclosure, been publicly disclosed by the inventor or a joint inventor or another who obtained the subject matter disclosed directly or indirectly from the inventor or a joint inventor.

(2) DISCLOSURES APPEARING IN APPLICATIONS AND PATENTS.—A disclosure shall not be prior art to a claimed invention under subsection (a)(2) if—

(A) the subject matter disclosed was obtained directly or indirectly from the inventor or a joint inventor;

(B) the subject matter disclosed had, before such subject matter was effectively filed under subsection (a)(2), been publicly disclosed by the inventor or a joint inventor or another who obtained the subject matter disclosed directly or indirectly from the inventor or a joint inventor; or

(C) the subject matter disclosed and the claimed invention, not later than the effective filing date of the claimed invention, were owned by the same person or subject to an obligation of assignment to the same person.

[Subsection (c), "COMMON OWNERSHIP UNDER JOINT RESEARCH AGREEMENTS," deems subject matter disclosed and claimed by members of a joint research team to be "owned by the same person" under §102(b)(2)(C) above.]

The phrase "effective filing date" generally refers to the filing of a patent application that establishes priority under U.S. law. This includes an application filed only in the U.S., or at least first in the U.S., and also certain applications filed first in foreign patent systems that are, by virtue of compliance with international treaties and U.S. law, granted the benefit of a U.S. filing date though initially filed elsewhere. *See* AIA §3, at (a)(2)(i) (adding definition of "effective filing date" to §100 of the Patent Act).

b. No Geographic Restrictions on Prior Art

The AIA continues a longstanding trend by eliminating geographic distinctions in the definition of prior art. Under the 1952 Act, certain types or categories of prior art are within the prior art regardless of where they occur. Patents and printed publications are the best examples. Whether a patent is issued in Germany, Japan, or China, it is still within the prior art; so too with publications. But under the 1952 Act other types of prior art have geographic limits; only "on sale" activities that occurred *within the U.S.*, for example, enter the prior art under the 1952 Act. Foreign sales are not within the prior art. The AIA eliminates geographic distinctions for all categories of prior art. Under the AIA, if an event or activity occurs that meets the definition of prior art, it is within the prior art for U.S. patent law–regardless of where it occurs.

c. Novelty vs. Priority

The AIA highlights the difference between priority and novelty. Strictly speaking, priority is a question of *who, as between two rival inventors, will obtain a patent for an identical invention.* Priority, in other words, is a matter of "inventor vs. inventor"; whichever of the two is first (under the relevant rule) wins the patent. Novelty is a different matter. Novelty is a question of *whether, as between an inventor and a piece of prior art, the inventor acts before or after the prior art enters the field.* Novelty, then, is a matter of "inventor vs. prior art": if an inventor can show that he or she did whatever is required before a reference enters the prior art, the inventor gets a patent.

The AIA's first-to-file rule eliminates the need to decide which of two rival inventors actually invented first. In most cases, the only relevant question under the AIA is which of the two rival inventors filed first. (One exception is where the first filer learned of or outright stole the invention from another person; when that other person files a rival application, the PTO can undertake a "derivation proceeding" to sort out who is the rightful owner of the invention.) This eliminates the need for the expensive and drawn-out priority contests under the 1952 Act known as patent interferences.

d. The AIA Grace Period

Calling the AIA a "first-to-file" regime is an oversimplification. Section 102(b)(1)(A) provides that an inventor is entitled to a one-year grace period if she discloses her invention first and then files within a year. This "inventor's own" grace period means that an inventor can do any of a number of acts before filing that would generally constitute prior art but still preserve the chance for a patent, as long as she files within a year. The §102(b)(1)(A) grace period is stated as an "exception" to the general rule that these acts would be prior art because they occur before the filing date. Note, however, that this grace period applies only to the inventor's own prior activity.

Section 102(b)(1)(B) provides a broader one year grace period if the inventor makes a "public disclosure"—as opposed to just a disclosure—that is good for purposes of the U.S. patent system against anyone else. Thus, it is akin to the grace period that patent applicants enjoyed under the 1952 Act. The rationale behind this more robust grace period is that if the applicant discloses her invention publicly before anyone else, there is no way to tell whether subsequent disclosers made and disclosed an independent invention or derived their disclosure from the patentee's publication. As a result, the law gives an inventor who is first to *publicly* disclose the invention a one year grace period against anyone else. Note, however, that the public disclosure will bar the inventor from obtaining a patent in most parts of the world.

Although the courts have yet to rule on what is a public disclosure, it is apparent that Congress intended some sort of distinction here. One reading is that "disclosure" under AIA §102 means any prior art reference as defined by the extensive case law under the 1952 Act. This includes some fairly obscure types of disclosure such as secret sales and items used in public but not in any way discernible by the general public. Another reading of "public disclosure" would mean only widely and freely available disclosures.

e. Scope of Prior Art: On Sale or in Public Use

As noted earlier, courts have drawn a distinction between patentee and third-party public uses depending on whether they are informing or non-informing/secret. Any public use of the patented technology by the patentee—whether informing or non-informing/secret—constitutes a public use, whereas only informing public uses by third parties qualifies as novelty-defeating public uses. This distinction puts added pressure on patentees to promptly disclose their technology through filing their patent application.

This distinction carries over into the AIA. Paralleling the 1952 Act, AIA §102(a) encompasses "on sale" and "public use" within the prior art references that defeat novelty. *Helsinn Healthcare S.A. v. Teva Pharm. USA, Inc.*, 139 S.Ct. 628 (2019). Writing for a unanimous court, Justice Thomas stressed the importance of carrying forward established meanings for statutory language in the absence of clear Congressional intent to change them:

> Congress enacted the AIA in 2011 against the backdrop of a substantial body of law interpreting [pre-AIA] §102's on-sale bar. . . .

> Although this Court has never addressed the precise question presented in this case, our precedents suggest that a sale or offer of sale need not make an invention available to the public. For instance, we held in *Pfaff* [v. *Wells Elec., Inc.*, 525 U.S. 55 (1998)] that an offer for sale could cause an inventor to lose

the right to patent, without regard to whether the offer discloses each detail of the invention. *E.g., id.*, at 67. Other cases focus on whether the invention had been sold, not whether the details of the invention had been made available to the public or whether the sale itself had been publicly disclosed . . . .

In light of this settled pre-AIA precedent on the meaning of "on sale," we presume that when Congress reenacted the same language in the AIA, it adopted the earlier judicial construction of that phrase. . . . The addition of "or otherwise available to the public" is simply not enough of a change for us to conclude that Congress intended to alter the meaning of the reenacted term "on sale."

139 S.Ct. at 633-34. The Court reasoned that Congress would not have overturned substantial precedent by subtly relying on the "associated-words canon" to imply a new limit to "on sale" stemming from the mere "catchall" phrase "otherwise available to the public." *Id.* at 634. While the specific issue in that case involved the term "on sale" and not "public use," it seems likely that the judicial interpretations of both terms from the 1952 Act apply with full force to the AIA given the Court's reasoning. Thus, the categories of prior art from the 1952 Act will have the same definition under the new statute. *See* Robert P. Merges, *Priority and Novelty Under the AIA*, 27 BERKELEY TECH. L. J. 1023 (2012); Mark A. Lemley, *Does "Public Use" Mean the Same Thing It Did Last Year?*, 93 TEX. L. REV. 1119 (2015) (both supporting this result).

PROBLEMS

Problem III-2.

a. Alma conceives of a compound (TAU) in December 2011. She synthesizes the compound in February 2012. Entirely independently of Alma, Edgar publishes an article in NATURE, a scientific journal, describing TAU on December 1, 2012. Alma files a U.S. patent application on April 1, 2013. Assuming that Alma's invention is useful, non-obvious, and adequately described, is her patent valid or invalid based on these facts in the United States?

b. Based on the facts in III-2a, suppose Edgar filed a patent application on April 2, 2013. Will he be able to get a patent?

c. Dylan conceives of a compound (UCB) in December 2011. He synthesizes the compound in February 2012. He publishes this research in SCIENCE, a scientific journal, on June 1, 2012. Entirely independently of Dylan, Katie publishes an article in NATURE describing UCB on December 1, 2012. Dylan files a U.S. patent application on April 1, 2013. Assuming that Dylan's invention is useful, non-obvious, and adequately described, is his patent valid or invalid based on these facts in the United States?

d. Stephanie conceives of a compound (QED) in December 2011. She synthesizes the compound in February 2012. Entirely independently of Stephanie, Klay publishes an article in NATURE describing QED on December 1, 2012. Stephanie files a U.S. patent application on February 1, 2013. Assuming that Stephanie's invention is useful, non-obvious, and adequately described, is her patent valid or invalid based on these facts in the United States?

e. Anna conceives of a compound (MIT) in December 2011. She synthesizes the compound in February 2012. Entirely independently of Anna, Noah places MIT on sale in Europe on December 1, 2012. Anna files a U.S. patent application on April 1, 2013. Assuming that Anna's invention is useful, non-obvious, and adequately described, is her patent valid or invalid based on these facts in the United States?

Problem III-3. Lisa invents a remarkable process for manufacturing circuit boards that reduces the cost by 20% without any diminution in quality. She promptly files a U.S. patent application on April 1, 2013. Much of the electronics industry licenses Lisa's patent. Lisa learns that Drago Corporation is using her patented technology without a license in the United States. She sues Drago for patent infringement. Drago does not deny that it learned of the technology from Lisa's patent. In its trial preparation, however, Drago learns that Mizuki, a small Japanese company, had developed the identical process and used it to manufacture a component of a video game controller that it sold in Japan in 2010. Mizuki has since gone out of business. Based on this information, Drago files a motion for summary judgment asserting that Lisa's patent is invalid for lack of novelty. How should a court decide? What is the basis for the decision?

Suppose instead that Lisa had filed her patent application on March 1, 2013. How should a court decide? Is the analysis any different?

2. Nonobviousness

Section 103(a) of the Patent Act provides that

A patent for a claimed invention may not be obtained, notwithstanding that the claimed invention is not identically disclosed as set forth in section 102, if the differences between the claimed invention and the prior art are such that the claimed invention as a whole would have been obvious before the effective filing date of the claimed invention to a person having ordinary skill in the art to which the claimed invention pertains. Patentability shall not be negated by the manner in which the invention was made.

The following case traces the history leading up to this requirement and establishes the modern framework for assessing this most important element of patentability.

Graham v. John Deere Co.
Supreme Court of the United States
383 U.S. 1 (1966)

MR. JUSTICE CLARK delivered the opinion of the Court.

After a lapse of 15 years, the Court again focuses its attention on the patentability of inventions under the standard of Art. I, §8, cl. 8, of the Constitution and under the conditions prescribed by the laws of the United States. Since our last expression on patent validity, *A. & P. Tea Co. v. Supermarket Corp.*, 340 U.S. 147 (1950), the Congress has for the first time expressly added a third statutory dimension to the two requirements of novelty and utility that had been the sole statutory test since the Patent

Act of 1793. This is the test of obviousness, i.e., whether "the subject matter sought to be patented and the prior art are such that the subject matter as a whole would have been obvious at the time the invention was made to a person having ordinary skill in the art to which said subject matter pertains. Patentability shall not be negatived by the manner in which the invention was made." §103 of the Patent Act of 1952, 35 U.S.C. §103 (1964 ed.).

The questions, involved in each of the companion cases before us, are what effect the 1952 Act had upon traditional statutory and judicial tests of patentability and what definitive tests are now required. We have concluded that the 1952 Act was intended to codify judicial precedents embracing the principle long ago announced by this Court in *Hotchkiss v. Greenwood*, 11 How. 248 [52 U.S.] (1851), and that, while the clear language of §103 places emphasis on an inquiry into obviousness, the general level of innovation necessary to sustain patentability remains the same.

I.

(a) *Graham v. John Deere Co.*, an infringement suit by petitioners, presents a conflict between two Circuits over the validity of a single patent on a "Clamp for vibrating Shank Plows." The invention, a combination of old mechanical elements, involves a device designed to absorb shock from plow shanks as they plow through rocky soil and thus to prevent damage to the plow. We granted certiorari. Although we have determined that neither Circuit applied the correct test, we conclude that the patent is invalid under §103. . . .

II.

At the outset it must be remembered that the federal patent power stems from a specific constitutional provision which authorizes the Congress "To promote the Progress of . . . useful Arts, by securing for limited Times to . . . Inventors the exclusive Right to their . . . Discoveries." Art. I, §8, cl. 8. The clause is both a grant of power and a limitation. This qualified authority, unlike the power often exercised in the sixteenth and seventeenth centuries by the English Crown, is limited to the promotion of advances in the "useful arts." It was written against the backdrop of the practices—eventually curtailed by the Statute of Monopolies—of the Crown in granting monopolies to court favorites in goods or businesses which had long before been enjoyed by the public. *See* MEINHARDT, INVENTIONS, PATENTS AND MONOPOLY, pp. 30–35 (London, 1946). The Congress in the exercise of the patent power may not overreach the restraints imposed by the stated constitutional purpose. Nor may it enlarge the patent monopoly without regard to the innovation, advancement or social benefit gained thereby. Moreover, Congress may not authorize the issuance of patents whose effects are to remove existent knowledge from the public domain, or to restrict free access to materials already available. Innovation, advancement, and things which add to the sum of useful knowledge are inherent requisites in a patent system which by constitutional command must "promote the Progress of . . . useful Arts." This is the standard expressed in the Constitution and it may not be ignored. And it is in this light that patent validity "requires reference to a standard written into the Constitution." *A. & P. Tea Co. v. Supermarket Corp.*, *supra*, at 154 (concurring opinion).

Within the limits of the constitutional grant, the Congress may, of course, implement the stated purpose of the Framers by selecting the policy which in its judgment best effectuates the constitutional aim. This is but a corollary to the grant to Congress of any Article I power. *Gibbons v. Ogden*, 9 Wheat. [22 U.S.] 1 [1824]. Within the scope established by the Constitution, Congress may set out conditions and tests for patentability. *McClurg v. Kingsland*, 1 How. [42 U.S.] 202, 206 [1843]. It is the duty of the Commissioner of Patents and of the courts in the administration of the patent system to give effect to the constitutional standard by appropriate application, in each case, of the statutory scheme of the Congress.

Congress quickly responded to the bidding of the Constitution by enacting the Patent Act of 1790 during the second session of the First Congress. It created an agency in the Department of State headed by the Secretary of State, the Secretary of the Department of War and the Attorney General, any two of whom could issue a patent for a period not exceeding 14 years to any petitioner that "hath . . . invented or discovered any useful art, manufacture, . . . or device, or any improvement therein not before known or used" if the board found that "the invention or discovery [was] sufficiently useful and important. . . ." 1 Stat. 110. This group, whose members administered the patent system along with their other public duties, was known by its own designation as "Commissioners for the Promotion of Useful Arts."

Thomas Jefferson, who as Secretary of State was a member of the group, was its moving spirit and might well be called the "first administrator of our patent system." *See* Federico, Operation of the Patent Act of 1790, 18 J. PAT. OFF. SOC. 237, 238 (1936). He was not only an administrator of the patent system under the 1790 Act, but was also the author of the 1793 Patent Act. In addition, Jefferson was himself an inventor of great note. His unpatented improvements on plows, to mention but one line of his inventions, won acclaim and recognition on both sides of the Atlantic. Because of his active interest and influence in the early development of the patent system, Jefferson's views on the general nature of the limited patent monopoly under the Constitution, as well as his conclusions as to conditions for patentability under the statutory scheme, are worthy of note.

Jefferson, like other Americans, had an instinctive aversion to monopolies. It was a monopoly on tea that sparked the Revolution and Jefferson certainly did not favor an equivalent form of monopoly under the new government. His abhorrence of monopoly extended initially to patents as well. From France, he wrote to Madison (July 1788) urging a Bill of Rights provision restricting monopoly, and as against the argument that limited monopoly might serve to incite "ingenuity," he argued forcefully that "the benefit even of limited monopolies is too doubtful to be opposed to that of their general suppression," V WRITINGS OF THOMAS JEFFERSON, at 47 (Ford ed., 1895).

His views ripened, however, and in another letter to Madison (Aug. 1789) after the drafting of the Bill of Rights, Jefferson stated that he would have been pleased by an express provision in this form: "Art. 9. Monopolies may be allowed to persons for their own productions in literature & their own inventions in the arts, for a term not exceeding ___ years but for no longer term & no other purpose." *Id.*, at 113. And he later wrote:

"Certainly an inventor ought to be allowed a right to the benefit of his invention for some certain time. . . . Nobody wishes more than I do that ingenuity should receive a liberal encouragement." Letter to Oliver Evans (May 1807), V WRITINGS OF THOMAS JEFFERSON, at 75–76 (Washington ed.).

Jefferson's philosophy on the nature and purpose of the patent monopoly is expressed in a letter to Isaac McPherson (Aug. 1813), a portion of which we set out in the margin.[2] He rejected a natural-rights theory in intellectual property rights and clearly recognized the social and economic rationale of the patent system. The patent monopoly was not designed to secure to the inventor his natural right in his discoveries. Rather, it was a reward, an inducement, to bring forth new knowledge. The grant of an exclusive right to an invention was the creation of society—at odds with the inherent free nature of disclosed ideas—and was not to be freely given. Only inventions and discoveries which furthered human knowledge, and were new and useful, justified the special inducement of a limited private monopoly. Jefferson did not believe in granting patents for small details, obvious improvements, or frivolous devices. His writings evidence his insistence upon a high level of patentability.

As a member of the patent board for several years, Jefferson saw clearly the difficulty in "drawing a line between the things which are worth to the public the embarrassment of an exclusive patent, and those which are not." The board on which he served sought to draw such a line and formulated several rules which are preserved in Jefferson's correspondence. Despite the board's efforts, Jefferson saw "with what slow progress a system of general rules could be matured." Because of the "abundance" of cases and the fact that the investigations occupied "more time of the members of the board than they could spare from higher duties, the whole was turned over to the judiciary, to be matured into a system, under which every one might know when his actions were safe and lawful." Letter to McPherson, *supra*, at 181, 182. Apparently

---

2

      Stable ownership is the gift of social law, and is given late in the progress of society. It would be curious then, if an idea, the fugitive fermentation of an individual brain, could, of natural right, be claimed in exclusive and stable property. If nature has made any one thing less susceptible than all others of exclusive property, it is the action of the thinking power called an idea, which an individual may exclusively possess as long as he keeps it to himself; but the moment it is divulged, it forces itself into the possession of every one, and the receiver cannot dispossess himself of it. Its peculiar character, too, is that no one possesses the less, because every other possesses the whole of it. He who receives an idea from me, receives instruction himself without lessening mine; as he who lights his taper at mine, receives light without darkening me. That ideas should freely spread from one to another over the globe, for the moral and mutual instruction of man, and improvement of his condition, seems to have been peculiarly and benevolently designed by nature, when she made them, like fire, expansible over all space, without lessening their density in any point, and like the air in which we breathe, move, and have our physical being, incapable of confinement or exclusive appropriation. Inventions then cannot, in nature, be a subject of property. Society may give an exclusive right to the profits arising from them, as an encouragement to men to pursue ideas which may produce utility, but this may or may not be done, according to the will and convenience of the society, without claim or complaint from any body.

VI WRITINGS OF THOMAS JEFFERSON 180–81 (H. A. Washington ed.).

Congress agreed with Jefferson and the board that the courts should develop additional conditions for patentability. Although the Patent Act was amended, revised or codified some 50 times between 1790 and 1950, Congress steered clear of a statutory set of requirements other than the bare novelty and utility tests reformulated in Jefferson's draft of the 1793 Patent Act.

III.

The difficulty of formulating conditions for patentability was heightened by the generality of the constitutional grant and the statutes implementing it, together with the underlying policy of the patent system that "the things which are worth to the public the embarrassment of an exclusive patent," as Jefferson put it, must outweigh the restrictive effect of the limited patent monopoly. The inherent problem was to develop some means of weeding out those inventions which would not be disclosed or devised but for the inducement of a patent.

This Court formulated a general condition of patentability in 1851 in *Hotchkiss v. Greenwood*, 11 How. 248 [52 U.S. (1851)]. The patent involved a mere substitution of materials—porcelain or clay for wood or metal in doorknobs—and the Court condemned it, holding:

> [Unless] more ingenuity and skill . . . were required . . . than were possessed by an ordinary mechanic acquainted with the business, there was an absence of that degree of skill and ingenuity which constitute essential elements of every invention. In other words, the improvement is the work of the skilful mechanic, not that of the inventor. At p. 267.

Hotchkiss, by positing the condition that a patentable invention evidence more ingenuity and skill than that possessed by an ordinary mechanic acquainted with the business, merely distinguished between new and useful innovations that were capable of sustaining a patent and those that were not. The *Hotchkiss* test laid the cornerstone of the judicial evolution suggested by Jefferson and left to the courts by Congress. The language in the case, and in those which followed, gave birth to "invention" as a word of legal art signifying patentable inventions. Yet, as this Court has observed, "[t]he truth is the word [invention] cannot be defined in such manner as to afford any substantial aid in determining whether a particular device involves an exercise of the inventive faculty or not." *McClain v. Ortmayer*, 141 U.S. 419, 427 (1891); *A. & P. Tea Co. v. Supermarket Corp., supra*, at 151. Its use as a label brought about a large variety of opinions as to its meaning both in the Patent Office, in the courts, and at the bar. The *Hotchkiss* formulation, however, lies not in any label, but in its functional approach to questions of patentability. In practice, *Hotchkiss* has required a comparison between the subject matter of the patent, or patent application, and the background skill of the calling. It has been from this comparison that patentability was in each case determined.

IV. The 1952 Patent Act

. . . The pivotal section around which the present controversy centers is §103. It provides:

> §103. Conditions for patentability; non-obvious subject matter

A patent may not be obtained though the invention is not identically disclosed or described as set forth in section 102 of this title, if the differences between the subject matter sought to be patented and the prior art are such that the subject matter as a whole would have been obvious at the time the invention was made to a person having ordinary skill in the art to which said subject matter pertains. Patentability shall not be negatived by the manner in which the invention was made.

The section is cast in relatively unambiguous terms. Patentability is to depend, in addition to novelty and utility, upon the "non-obvious" nature of the "subject matter sought to be patented" to a person having ordinary skill in the pertinent art. . . .

It is undisputed that this section was, for the first time, a statutory expression of an additional requirement for patentability, originally expressed in *Hotchkiss*. It also seems apparent that Congress intended by the last sentence of §103 to abolish the test it believed this Court announced in the controversial phrase "flash of creative genius," used in *Cuno Corp. v. Automatic Devices Corp.*, 314 U.S. 84 (1941).[7] . . .

V.

. . . While the ultimate question of patent validity is one of law, *A. & P. Tea Co. v. Supermarket Corp.*, *supra*, at 155, the §103 condition, which is but one of three conditions, each of which must be satisfied, lends itself to several basic factual inquiries. Under §103, the scope and content of the prior art are to be determined; differences between the prior art and the claims at issue are to be ascertained; and the level of ordinary skill in the pertinent art resolved. Against this background, the obviousness or nonobviousness of the subject matter is determined. Such secondary considerations as commercial success, long felt but unsolved needs, failure of others, etc., might be utilized to give light to the circumstances surrounding the origin of the subject matter sought to be patented. As indicia of obviousness or nonobviousness, these inquiries may have relevancy. *See* Note, Subtests of "Nonobviousness": A Nontechnical Approach to Patent Validity, 112 U. PA. L. REV. 1169 (1964).

This is not to say, however, that there will not be difficulties in applying the nonobviousness test. What is obvious is not a question upon which there is likely to be

---

[7] The sentence in which the phrase occurs reads: "[T]he new device, however useful it may be, must reveal the flash of creative genius, not merely the skill of the calling." At p. 91. Although some writers and lower courts found in the language connotations as to the frame of mind of the inventors, none were so intended. The opinion approved Hotchkiss specifically, and the reference to "flash of creative genius" was but a rhetorical embellishment of language going back to 1833. *Cf.* "exercise of genius," *Shaw v. Cooper*, 7 Pet. 292; "inventive genius," *Reckendorfer v. Faber*, 92 U.S. 347 (1876); *Concrete Appliances Co. v. Gomery*, 269 U.S. 177; "flash of thought," *Densmore v. Scofield*, 102 U.S. 375 (1880); "intuitive genius," Potts v. Creager, 155 U.S. 597 (1895). Rather than establishing a more exacting standard, *Cuno* merely rhetorically restated the requirement that the subject matter sought to be patented must be beyond the skill of the calling. It was the device, not the invention, that had to reveal the "flash of creative genius." *See* Boyajian, *The Flash of Creative Genius, An Alternative Interpretation*, 25 J. PAT. & TRADEMARK OFF. SOC'Y 776, 780, 781 (1943); *Pacific Contact Laboratories, Inc. v. Solex Laboratories, Inc.*, 209 F.2d 529, 533; *Brown & Sharpe Mfg. Co. v. Kar Engineering Co.*, 154 F.2d 48, 51–52; *In re Shortell*, 31 C.C.P.A. (Pat.) 1062, 1069, 142 F.2d 292, 295–96.

uniformity of thought in every given factual context. The difficulties, however, are comparable to those encountered daily by the courts in such frames of reference as negligence and scienter, and should be amenable to a case-by-case development. We believe that strict observance of the requirements laid down here will result in that uniformity and definiteness which Congress called for in the 1952 Act.

While we have focused attention on the appropriate standard to be applied by the courts, it must be remembered that the primary responsibility for sifting out unpatentable material lies in the Patent Office. To await litigation is—for all practical purposes—to debilitate the patent system. We have observed a notorious difference between the standards applied by the Patent Office and by the courts. While many reasons can be adduced to explain the discrepancy, one may well be the free rein often exercised by Examiners in their use of the concept of "invention." In this connection we note that the Patent Office is confronted with a most difficult task. Almost 100,000 applications for patents are filed each year. Of these, about 50,000 are granted and the backlog now runs well over 200,000. 1965 Annual Report of the Commissioner of Patents 13–14. This is itself a compelling reason for the Commissioner to strictly adhere to the 1952 Act as interpreted here. This would, we believe, not only expedite disposition but bring about a closer concurrence between administrative and judicial precedent.

We have been urged to find in §103 a relaxed standard, supposedly a congressional reaction to the "increased standard" applied by this Court in its decisions over the last 20 or 30 years. The standard has remained invariable in this Court. Technology, however, has advanced—and with remarkable rapidity in the last 50 years. Moreover, the ambit of applicable art in given fields of science has widened by disciplines unheard of a half century ago. It is but an evenhanded application to require that those persons granted the benefit of a patent monopoly be charged with an awareness of these changed conditions. The same is true of the less technical, but still useful arts. He who seeks to build a better mousetrap today has a long path to tread before reaching the Patent Office.

VI.

We now turn to the application of the conditions found necessary for patentability to the cases involved here:

A. The Patent in Issue in Graham v. John Deere Co.

This patent, No. 2,627,798 (hereinafter called the '798 patent) relates to a spring clamp which permits plow shanks to be pushed upward when they hit obstructions in the soil, and then springs the shanks back into normal position when the obstruction is passed over. The device . . . is fixed to the plow frame as a unit. The mechanism around which the controversy centers is basically a hinge. The top half of it, known as the upper plate, is a heavy metal piece clamped to the plow frame and is stationary relative to the plow frame. The lower half of the hinge, known as the hinge plate, is connected to the rear of the upper plate by a hinge pin and rotates downward with respect to it. The shank, which is bolted to the forward end of the hinge plate, runs beneath the plate and parallel to it for about nine inches, passes through a stirrup, and then continues backward for several feet curving down toward the ground. The chisel, which does the actual plowing, is attached to the rear end of the shank. As the plow frame is pulled forward, the chisel rips through the soil, thereby plowing it. In the normal position, the hinge plate and the shank are kept tight against the upper plate by a spring, which is atop the upper plate. A rod runs through the center of the spring, extending down through holes in both plates and the shank. Its upper end is bolted to the top of the spring while its lower end is hooked against the underside of the shank [see Figure 3-4].

When the chisel hits a rock or other obstruction in the soil, the obstruction forces the chisel and the rear portion of the shank to move upward. The shank is pivoted against the rear of the hinge plate and pries open the hinge against the closing tendency of the spring. This closing tendency is caused by the fact that, as the hinge is opened, the connecting rod is pulled downward and the spring is compressed. When the obstruction is passed over, the upward force on the chisel disappears and the spring pulls the shank and hinge plate back into their original position. The lower, rear portion of the hinge plate is constructed in the form of a stirrup which brackets the shank, passing around and beneath it. The shank fits loosely into the stirrup (permitting a slight up and down play). The stirrup is designed to prevent the shank from recoiling away from the hinge plate, and thus prevents excessive strain on the shank near its bolted connection. The stirrup also girds the shank, preventing it from fishtailing from side to side.

In practical use, a number of spring-hinge-shank combinations are clamped to a plow frame, forming a set of ground-working chisels capable of withstanding the shock of rocks and other obstructions in the soil without breaking the shanks.

Background of the Patent

Chisel plows, as they are called, were developed for plowing in areas where the ground is relatively free from rocks or stones. Originally, the shanks were rigidly attached to the plow frames. When such plows were used in the rocky, glacial soils of some of the Northern States, they were found to have serious defects. As the chisels hit buried rocks, a vibratory motion was set up and tremendous forces were transmitted to the shank near its connection to the frame. The shanks would break. Graham, one of the petitioners, sought to meet that problem, and in 1950 obtained a patent, U.S. No. 2,493,811 (hereinafter '811), on a spring clamp which solved some of the difficulties. Graham and his companies manufactured and sold the '811 clamps. In 1950, Graham modified the '811 structure and in 1951 filed for a patent. That patent, the one in issue, was granted in 1953. This suit against competing plow manufacturers resulted from charges by petitioners that several of respondents' devices infringed the '798 patent.

The Prior Art

Five prior patents indicating the state of the art were cited by the Patent Office in the prosecution of the '798 application. Four of these patents, 10 other United States patents and two prior-use spring-clamp arrangements not of record in the '798 file wrapper were relied upon by respondents as revealing the prior art. The District Court and the Court of Appeals found that the prior art "as a whole in one form or another contains all of the mechanical elements of the '798 Patent." One of the prior-use clamp devices not before the Patent Examiner—Glencoe—was found to have "all of the elements."

We confine our discussion to the prior patent of Graham, '811, and to the Glencoe clamp device, both among the references asserted by respondents. The Graham '811 and '798 patent devices are similar in all elements, save two: (1) the stirrup and the bolted connection of the shank to the hinge plate do not appear in '811; and (2) the position of the shank is reversed, being placed in patent '811 above the hinge plate, sandwiched between it and the upper plate. The shank is held in place by the spring rod which is hooked against the bottom of the hinge plate passing through a slot in the shank. Other differences are of no consequence to our examination. In practice the '811 patent arrangement permitted the shank to wobble or fishtail because it was not rigidly fixed to the hinge plate; moreover, as the hinge plate was below the shank, the latter caused wear on the upper plate, a member difficult to repair or replace.

Graham's '798 patent application contained 12 claims. All were rejected as not distinguished from the Graham '811 patent. The inverted position of the shank was specifically rejected as was the bolting of the shank to the hinge plate. The Patent Office examiner found these to be "matters of design well within the expected skill of the art and devoid of invention." Graham withdrew the original claims and substituted the two new ones which are substantially those in issue here. His contention was that wear was reduced in patent '798 between the shank and the heel or rear of the upper plate.[11] He also emphasized several new features, the relevant one here being that the bolt used to connect the hinge plate and shank maintained the upper face of the shank in continuing and constant contact with the underface of the hinge plate.

---

[11] In '811, where the shank was above the hinge plate, an upward movement of the chisel forced the shank up against the underside of the rear of the upper plate. The upper plate thus provided the fulcrum about which the hinge was pried open. Because of this, as well as the location of the hinge pin, the shank rubbed against the heel of the upper plate causing wear both to the plate and to the shank. By relocating the hinge pin and by placing the hinge plate between the shank and the upper plate, as in '798, the rubbing was eliminated and the wear point was changed to the hinge plate, a member more easily removed or replaced for repair.

Flex Comparison
Appendix to Opinion of the Court

Graham did not urge before the Patent Office the greater "flexing" qualities of the '798 patent arrangement which he so heavily relied on in the courts. The sole element in patent '798 which petitioners argue before us is the interchanging of the shank and hinge plate and the consequences flowing from this arrangement. The contention is that this arrangement—which petitioners claim is not disclosed in the prior art—permits the shank to flex under stress for its *entire* length. [W]hen the chisel hits an obstruction the resultant force (A) pushes the rear of the shank upward and the shank pivots against the rear of the hinge plate at (C). The natural tendency is for that portion of the shank between the pivot point and the bolted connection (i.e., between C and D) to bow downward and away from the hinge plate. The maximum distance (B) that the shank moves away from the plate is slight—for emphasis, greatly exaggerated in the sketches. This is so because of the strength of the shank and the short—nine inches or so—length of that portion of the shank between (C) and (D). On the contrary, in patent '811 the pivot point is the upper plate at point (c); and while the tendency for the shank to bow between points (c) and (d) is the same as in '798, the shank is restricted because of the underlying hinge plate and cannot flex as freely. In practical effect, the shank flexes only between points (a) and (c), and not along the entire length of the shank, as in '798. Petitioners say that this difference in flex, though small, effectively absorbs the tremendous forces of the shock of obstructions whereas prior art arrangements failed.

The Obviousness of the Differences

We cannot agree with petitioners. We assume that the prior art does not disclose such an arrangement as petitioners claim in patent '798. Still we do not believe that the argument on which petitioners' contention is bottomed supports the validity of the patent. The tendency of the shank to flex is the same in all cases. If free-flexing, as petitioners now argue, is the crucial difference above the prior art, then it appears evident that the desired result would be obtainable by not boxing the shank within the confines of the hinge. The only other effective place available in the arrangement was to attach it below the hinge plate and run it through a stirrup or bracket that would not disturb its flexing qualities. Certainly a person having ordinary skill in the prior art, given the fact that the flex in the shank could be utilized more effectively if allowed to run the entire length of the shank, would immediately see that the thing to do was what Graham did, i.e., invert the shank and the hinge plate.

Petitioners' argument basing validity on the free-flex theory raised for the first time on appeal is reminiscent of Lincoln Engineering Co. v. Stewart-Warner Corp., 303 U.S. 545 (1938), where the Court called such an effort "an afterthought. No such function . . . is hinted at in the specifications of the patent. If this were so vital an element in the functioning of the apparatus it is strange that all mention of it was omitted." At p. 550. No "flexing" argument was raised in the Patent Office. Indeed, the trial judge specifically found that "flexing is not a claim of the patent in suit . . ." and would not permit interrogation as to flexing in the accused devices. Moreover, the clear testimony of petitioners' experts shows that the flexing advantages flowing from the '798 arrangement are not, in fact, a significant feature in the patent.

We find no nonobvious facets in the '798 arrangement. The wear and repair claims were sufficient to overcome the patent examiner's original conclusions as to the validity of the patent. However, some of the prior art, notably Glencoe, was not before him. There the hinge plate is below the shank but, as the courts below found, all of the elements in the '798 patent are present in the Glencoe structure. Furthermore, even though the position of the shank and hinge plate appears reversed in Glencoe, the mechanical operation is identical. The shank there pivots about the underside of the stirrup, which in Glencoe is *above* the shank. In other words, the stirrup in Glencoe serves exactly the same function as the heel of the hinge plate in '798. The mere shifting of the wear point to the heel of the '798 hinge plate from the stirrup of Glencoe—itself a part of the hinge plate—presents no operative mechanical distinctions, much less nonobvious differences. . . .

The judgment of the Court of Appeals in [Graham v. John Deere] is affirmed. . . .

COMMENTS AND QUESTIONS

1. The Court states that it is proper in interpreting the Graham '798 claims to refer to the prosecution history (or "file wrapper") of the patent. We will see that this is an important tool in the law of infringement later in this chapter. For now, what is important is that the validity of the patent claims is only one part of a larger picture—"claim interpretation." Patentees not only want to have their patents upheld over the prior art, but they also want those patents to be interpreted broadly, to cover a wide range of potential infringements. Because these goals are in tension, it is important to keep them both in mind whenever you interpret the claims of a patent.

2. Without question, the plow design in *Graham* was new, i.e., novel under §102 of the patent code. What policy is served by the detailed inquiry into whether it is "new enough" to deserve a patent, i.e., nonobvious? What would be the effect of a patent system that only required novelty? *See* Robert P. Merges, *Uncertainty and the Standard of Patentability*, 7 HIGH TECH. L.J. 1 (1993). Arguably, §103 requires an "inventive leap" of some degree over what has been done before as a counterbalance to the strong rights given patentholders.

The test established in §103—whether the invention as a whole would be "obvious to one of ordinary skill in the art"—does not itself tell courts very much about how to decide what is obvious. Courts have developed a number of rules to assist in this determination. Two of the most important rules are discussed below.

i. Combining References

To anticipate a patent application under §102, a single prior art reference must disclose every element of what the patentee claims as his invention. If a prior art reference does not disclose all the parts of an invention, it does not "anticipate" the application. Under §103, however, a single reference need not disclose the entire invention to bar a patent. Thus §103 asks whether a researcher who is aware of all the prior art would think to create the claimed invention. In deciding the question of obviousness, it is sometimes permissible to analyze a combination of ideas from different sources of prior art (known as prior art "references").

KSR International Co. v. Teleflex Inc.
Supreme Court of the United States
550 U.S. 398 (2007)

JUSTICE KENNEDY delivered the opinion of the Court.

Teleflex Incorporated and its subsidiary Technology Holding Company—both referred to here as Teleflex—sued KSR International Company for patent infringement. The patent at issue, United States Patent No. 6,237,565 B1, is entitled "Adjustable Pedal Assembly With Electronic Throttle Control." The patentee is Steven J. Engelgau, and the patent is referred to as "the Engelgau patent." Teleflex holds the exclusive license to the patent.

Claim 4 of the Engelgau patent describes a mechanism for combining an electronic sensor with an adjustable automobile pedal so the pedal's position can be transmitted to a computer that controls the throttle in the vehicle's engine. When Teleflex accused KSR of infringing the Engelgau patent by adding an electronic sensor to one of KSR's previously designed pedals, KSR countered that claim 4 was invalid under the Patent Act, 35 U.S.C. §103, because its subject matter was obvious.

Section 103 forbids issuance of a patent when "the differences between the subject matter sought to be patented and the prior art are such that the subject matter as a whole would have been obvious at the time the invention was made to a person having ordinary skill in the art to which said subject matter pertains."

In *Graham v. John Deere Co. of Kansas City,* 383 U.S. 1 (1966), the Court set out a framework for applying the statutory language of §103, language itself based on the logic of the earlier decision in *Hotchkiss v. Greenwood,* 11 How. 248 (1851), and its progeny. *See* 383 U.S., at 15–17. The analysis is objective:

> Under §103, the scope and content of the prior art are to be determined; differences between the prior art and the claims at issue are to be ascertained; and the level of ordinary skill in the pertinent art resolved. Against this background the obviousness or nonobviousness of the subject matter is determined. Such secondary considerations as commercial success, long felt but unsolved needs, failure of others, etc., might be utilized to give light to the circumstances surrounding the origin of the subject matter sought to be patented.

Id., at 17–18.

While the sequence of these questions might be reordered in any particular case, the factors continue to define the inquiry that controls. If a court, or patent examiner, conducts this analysis and concludes the claimed subject matter was obvious, the claim is invalid under §103.

Seeking to resolve the question of obviousness with more uniformity and consistency, the Court of Appeals for the Federal Circuit has employed an approach referred to by the parties as the "teaching, suggestion, or motivation" test (TSM test), under which a patent claim is only proved obvious if "some motivation or suggestion to combine the prior art teachings" can be found in the prior art, the nature of the problem, or the knowledge of a person having ordinary skill in the art. *See, e.g., Al-Site Corp. v. VSI Int'l, Inc.,* 174 F.3d 1308, 1323–1324 (C.A. Fed. 1999). KSR challenges that test, or at least its application in this case. *See* 119 Fed. Appx. 282, 286–290 (C.A. Fed. 2005). Because the Court of Appeals addressed the question of obviousness in a manner contrary to §103 and our precedents, we granted certiorari. We now reverse.

I

A

In car engines without computer-controlled throttles, the accelerator pedal interacts with the throttle via cable or other mechanical link. The pedal arm acts as a lever rotating around a pivot point. In a cable-actuated throttle control the rotation caused by pushing down the pedal pulls a cable, which in turn pulls open valves in the carburetor or fuel injection unit. The wider the valves open, the more fuel and air are released, causing combustion to increase and the car to accelerate. When the driver takes his foot off the pedal, the opposite occurs as the cable is released and the valves slide closed.

In the 1990's it became more common to install computers in cars to control engine operation. Computer-controlled throttles open and close valves in response to electronic signals, not through force transferred from the pedal by a mechanical link. Constant, delicate adjustments of air and fuel mixture are possible. The computer's rapid processing of factors beyond the pedal's position improves fuel efficiency and engine performance.

For a computer-controlled throttle to respond to a driver's operation of the car, the computer must know what is happening with the pedal. A cable or mechanical link does not suffice for this purpose; at some point, an electronic sensor is necessary to translate the mechanical operation into digital data the computer can understand.

Before discussing sensors further we turn to the mechanical design of the pedal itself. In the traditional design a pedal can be pushed down or released but cannot have its position in the footwell adjusted by sliding the pedal forward or back. As a result, a driver who wishes to be closer or farther from the pedal must either reposition himself in the driver's seat or move the seat in some way. In cars with deep footwells these are imperfect solutions for drivers of smaller stature. To solve the problem, inventors, beginning in the 1970's, designed pedals that could be adjusted to change their location in the footwell. Important for this case are two adjustable pedals disclosed in U.S. Patent Nos. 5,010,782 (filed July 28, 1989) (Asano) and 5,460,061 (filed Sept. 17, 1993) (Redding). The Asano patent reveals a support structure that houses the pedal so that even when the pedal location is adjusted relative to the driver, one of the pedal's pivot points stays fixed. The pedal is also designed so that the force necessary to push the pedal down is the same regardless of adjustments to its location. The Redding patent reveals a different, sliding mechanism where both the pedal and the pivot point are adjusted.

We return to sensors. Well before Engelgau applied for his challenged patent, some inventors had obtained patents involving electronic pedal sensors for computer-controlled throttles. These inventions, such as the device disclosed in U.S. Patent No. 5,241,936 (filed Sept. 9, 1991) ('936), taught that it was preferable to detect the pedal's position in the pedal assembly, not in the engine. The '936 patent disclosed a pedal with an electronic sensor on a pivot point in the pedal assembly. U.S. Patent No. 5,063,811 (filed July 9, 1990) (Smith) taught that to prevent the wires connecting the sensor to the computer from chafing and wearing out, and to avoid grime and damage from the driver's foot, the sensor should be put on a fixed part of the pedal assembly rather than in or on the pedal's footpad.

In addition to patents for pedals with integrated sensors inventors obtained patents for self-contained modular sensors. A modular sensor is designed independently of a given pedal so that it can be taken off the shelf and attached to mechanical pedals of various sorts, enabling the pedals to be used in automobiles with computer-controlled throttles. One such sensor was disclosed in U.S. Patent No. 5,385,068 (filed Dec. 18, 1992) ('068). In 1994, Chevrolet manufactured a line of trucks using modular sensors "attached to the pedal support bracket, adjacent to the pedal and engaged with the pivot shaft about which the pedal rotates in operation." 298 F. Supp. 2d 581, 589 (E.D. Mich. 2003).

The prior art contained patents involving the placement of sensors on adjustable pedals as well. For example, U.S. Patent No. 5,819,593 (filed Aug. 17, 1995) (Rixon) discloses an adjustable pedal assembly with an electronic sensor for detecting the pedal's position. In the Rixon pedal the sensor is located in the pedal footpad. The Rixon pedal was known to suffer from wire chafing when the pedal was depressed and released.

This short account of pedal and sensor technology leads to the instant case.

B

KSR, a Canadian company, manufactures and supplies auto parts, including pedal systems. Ford Motor Company hired KSR in 1998 to supply an adjustable pedal system for various lines of automobiles with cable-actuated throttle controls. KSR developed an adjustable mechanical pedal for Ford and obtained U.S. Patent No. 6,151,976 (filed July 16, 1999) ('976) for the design. In 2000, KSR was chosen by General Motors Corporation (GMC or GM) to supply adjustable pedal systems for Chevrolet and GMC light trucks that used engines with computer-controlled throttles. To make the '976 pedal compatible with the trucks, KSR merely took that design and added a modular sensor.

Teleflex is a rival to KSR in the design and manufacture of adjustable pedals. As noted, it is the exclusive licensee of the Engelgau patent. Engelgau filed the patent application on August 22, 2000 as a continuation of a previous application for U.S. Patent No. 6,109,241, which was filed on January 26, 1999. He has sworn he invented the patent's subject matter on February 14, 1998. The Engelgau patent discloses an adjustable electronic pedal described in the specification as a "simplified vehicle control pedal assembly that is less expensive, and which uses fewer parts and is easier to package within the vehicle." Engelgau, col. 2, lines 2–5, Supplemental App. 6. Claim 4 of the patent, at issue here, describes:

A vehicle control pedal apparatus comprising:

a support adapted to be mounted to a vehicle structure;

an adjustable pedal assembly having a pedal arm moveable in for[e] and aft directions with respect to said support;

a pivot for pivotally supporting said adjustable pedal assembly with respect to said support and defining a pivot axis; and

an electronic control attached to said support for controlling a vehicle system;

   said apparatus characterized by said electronic control being responsive to said pivot for providing a signal that corresponds to pedal arm position as said pedal arm pivots about said pivot axis between rest and applied positions wherein the position of said pivot remains constant while said pedal arm moves in fore and aft directions with respect to said pivot.

Id., col. 6, lines 17–36 (diagram numbers omitted).

We agree with the District Court that the claim discloses "a position-adjustable pedal assembly with an electronic pedal position sensor attached to the support member of the pedal assembly. Attaching the sensor to the support member allows the sensor to remain in a fixed position while the driver adjusts the pedal." 298 F. Supp. 2d, at 586–587.

Before issuing the Engelgau patent the U.S. Patent and Trademark Office (PTO) rejected one of the patent claims that was similar to, but broader than, the present claim 4. The claim did not include the requirement that the sensor be placed on a fixed pivot point. The PTO concluded the claim was an obvious combination of the prior art disclosed in Redding and Smith, explaining:

> Since the prior ar[t] references are from the field of endeavor, the purpose disclosed . . . would have been recognized in the pertinent art of Redding. Therefore it would have been obvious . . . to provide the device of Redding with the . . . means attached to a support member as taught by Smith.

Id., at 595.

In other words Redding provided an example of an adjustable pedal and Smith explained how to mount a sensor on a pedal's support structure, and the rejected patent claim merely put these two teachings together.

Although the broader claim was rejected, claim 4 was later allowed because it included the limitation of a fixed pivot point, which distinguished the design from Redding's. *Ibid.* Engelgau had not included Asano among the prior art references, and Asano was not mentioned in the patent's prosecution. Thus, the PTO did not have before it an adjustable pedal with a fixed pivot point. The patent issued on May 29, 2001 and was assigned to Teleflex.

Upon learning of KSR's design for GM, Teleflex sent a warning letter informing KSR that its proposal would violate the Engelgau patent. "'Teleflex believes that any supplier of a product that combines an adjustable pedal with an electronic throttle control necessarily employs technology covered by one or more'" of Teleflex's patents. *Id.*, at 585. KSR refused to enter a royalty arrangement with Teleflex; so Teleflex sued for infringement . . .

C

The District Court granted summary judgment in KSR's favor. . . .

The District Court determined, in light of the expert testimony and the parties' stipulations, that the level of ordinary skill in pedal design was "'an undergraduate degree in mechanical engineering (or an equivalent amount of industry experience) [and] familiarity with pedal control systems for vehicles.'" The court then set forth the relevant prior art, including the patents and pedal designs described above.

[The district court found the claimed invention obvious in light of the Chevrolet and Asano references, and general trends in the field. The Federal Circuit reversed, pointing out that the district court failed to properly apply the Federal Circuit's requirement that there be a "teaching, suggestion, or motivation" (TSM) in the prior art to prove obviousness.]

II

A

We begin by rejecting the rigid approach of the Court of Appeals. Throughout this Court's engagement with the question of obviousness, our cases have set forth an expansive and flexible approach inconsistent with the way the Court of Appeals applied its TSM test here.

The principles underlying [our prior] cases are instructive when the question is whether a patent claiming the combination of elements of prior art is obvious. When a work is available in one field of endeavor, design incentives and other market forces can prompt variations of it, either in the same field or a different one. If a person of ordinary skill can implement a predictable variation, §103 likely bars its patentability. For the same reason, if a technique has been used to improve one device, and a person of ordinary skill in the art would recognize that it would improve similar devices in the same way, using the technique is obvious unless its actual application is beyond his or her skill.

Following these principles may be more difficult in other cases than it is here because the claimed subject matter may involve more than the simple substitution of one known element for another or the mere application of a known technique to a piece of prior art ready for the improvement. Often, it will be necessary for a court to look to interrelated teachings of multiple patents; the effects of demands known to the design community or present in the marketplace; and the background knowledge possessed by a person having ordinary skill in the art, all in order to determine whether there was an apparent reason to combine the known elements in the fashion claimed by the patent at issue. To facilitate review, this analysis should be made explicit. As our precedents make clear, however, the analysis need not seek out precise teachings directed to the specific subject matter of the challenged claim, for a court can take account of the inferences and creative steps that a person of ordinary skill in the art would employ.

B

When it first established the requirement of demonstrating a teaching, suggestion, or motivation to combine known elements in order to show that the combination is obvious, the Court of Customs and Patent Appeals captured a helpful insight. *See* Application of Bergel, 292 F.2d 955, 956–957 (1961). [A] patent composed of several elements is not proved obvious merely by demonstrating that each of its elements was, independently, known in the prior art. Although common sense directs one to look with care at a patent application that claims as innovation the combination of two known devices according to their established functions, it can be important to identify a reason that would have prompted a person of ordinary skill in the relevant field to combine the elements in the way the claimed new invention does. This is so because inventions in most, if not all, instances rely upon building blocks long since uncovered, and claimed discoveries almost of necessity will be combinations of what, in some sense, is already known.

Helpful insights, however, need not become rigid and mandatory formulas; and when it is so applied, the TSM test is incompatible with our precedents. The obviousness analysis cannot be confined by a formalistic conception of the words teaching, suggestion, and motivation, or by overemphasis on the importance of published articles and the explicit content of issued patents. The diversity of inventive pursuits and of modern technology counsels against limiting the analysis in this way. In many fields it may be that there is little discussion of obvious techniques or combinations, and it often may be the case that market demand, rather than scientific literature, will drive design trends. Granting patent protection to advances that would occur in the ordinary course without real innovation retards progress and may, in the case of patents combining previously known elements, deprive prior inventions of their value or utility.

C

The flaws in the analysis of the Court of Appeals relate for the most part to the court's narrow conception of the obviousness inquiry reflected in its application of the TSM test.

The first error of the Court of Appeals in this case was to foreclose this reasoning by holding that courts and patent examiners should look only to the problem the patentee was trying to solve. The question is not whether the combination was obvious to the patentee but whether the combination was obvious to a person with ordinary skill in the art. Under the correct analysis, any need or problem known in the field of endeavor at the time of invention and addressed by the patent can provide a reason for combining the elements in the manner claimed.

The second error of the Court of Appeals lay in its assumption that a person of ordinary skill attempting to solve a problem will be led only to those elements of prior art designed to solve the same problem. *Ibid.* The primary purpose of Asano was solving the constant ratio problem; so, the court concluded, an inventor considering how to put a sensor on an adjustable pedal would have no reason to consider putting it on the Asano pedal. *Ibid.* Common sense teaches, however, that familiar items may have obvious uses beyond their primary purposes, and in many cases a person of ordinary skill will be able to fit the teachings of multiple patents together like pieces of a puzzle. Regardless of Asano's primary purpose, the design provided an obvious example of an adjustable pedal with a fixed pivot point; and the prior art was replete with patents indicating that a fixed pivot point was an ideal mount for a sensor. The idea that a designer hoping to make an adjustable electronic pedal would ignore Asano because Asano was designed to solve the constant ratio problem makes little sense. A person of ordinary skill is also a person of ordinary creativity, not an automaton.

The same constricted analysis led the Court of Appeals to conclude, in error, that a patent claim cannot be proved obvious merely by showing that the combination of elements was "obvious to try." *Id.,* at 289 (internal quotation marks omitted). When there is a design need or market pressure to solve a problem and there are a finite number of identified, predictable solutions, a person of ordinary skill has good reason to pursue the known options within his or her technical grasp. If this leads to the anticipated success, it is likely the product not of innovation but of ordinary skill and common sense. In that instance the fact that a combination was obvious to try might show that it was obvious under §103.

The Court of Appeals, finally, drew the wrong conclusion from the risk of courts and patent examiners falling prey to hindsight bias. A factfinder should be aware, of course, of the distortion caused by hindsight bias and must be cautious of arguments reliant upon *ex post* reasoning. Rigid preventative rules that deny factfinders recourse to common sense, however, are neither necessary under our case law nor consistent with it.

What we hold is that the fundamental misunderstandings identified above led the Court of Appeals in this case to apply a test inconsistent with our patent law decisions.

III

When we apply the standards we have explained to the instant facts, claim 4 must be found obvious. We agree with and adopt the District Court's recitation of the relevant prior art and its determination of the level of ordinary skill in the field. As did the District Court, we see little difference between the teachings of Asano and Smith and the adjustable electronic pedal disclosed in claim 4 of the Engelgau patent. A person having ordinary skill in the art could have combined Asano with a pedal position sensor in a fashion encompassed by claim 4, and would have seen the benefits of doing so. . . .

B

The District Court was correct to conclude that, as of the time Engelgau designed the subject matter in claim 4, it was obvious to a person of ordinary skill to combine Asano with a pivot-mounted pedal position sensor. There then existed a marketplace that created a strong incentive to convert mechanical pedals to electronic pedals, and the prior art taught a number of methods for achieving this advance. The Court of Appeals considered the issue too narrowly by, in effect, asking whether a pedal designer writing on a blank slate would have chosen both Asano and a modular sensor similar to the ones used in the Chevrolet truckline and disclosed in the '068 patent.

In automotive design, as in many other fields, the interaction of multiple components means that changing one component often requires the others to be modified as well. Technological developments made it clear that engines using computer-controlled throttles would become standard. As a result, designers might have decided to design new pedals from scratch; but they also would have had reason to make pre-existing pedals work with the new engines. Indeed, upgrading its own pre-existing model led KSR to design the pedal now accused of infringing the Engelgau patent.

For a designer starting with Asano, the question was where to attach the sensor. The consequent legal question, then, is whether a pedal designer of ordinary skill starting with Asano would have found it obvious to put the sensor on a fixed pivot point. The prior art discussed above leads us to the conclusion that attaching the sensor where both KSR and Engelgau put it would have been obvious to a person of ordinary skill.

Like the District Court, finally, we conclude Teleflex has shown no secondary factors to dislodge the determination that claim 4 is obvious. Proper application of *Graham* and our other precedents to these facts therefore leads to the conclusion that claim 4 encompassed obvious subject matter. As a result, the claim fails to meet the requirement of §103.

We need not reach the question whether the failure to disclose Asano during the prosecution of Engelgau voids the presumption of validity given to issued patents, for claim 4 is obvious despite the presumption. We nevertheless think it appropriate to note that the rationale underlying the presumption—that the PTO, in its expertise, has approved the claim—seems much diminished here.

IV

A separate ground the Court of Appeals gave for reversing the order for summary judgment was the existence of a dispute over an issue of material fact. We disagree with the Court of Appeals on this point as well. To the extent the court understood the *Graham* approach to exclude the possibility of summary judgment when an expert provides a conclusory affidavit addressing the question of obviousness, it misunderstood the role expert testimony plays in the analysis. In considering summary judgment on that question the district court can and should take into account expert testimony, which may resolve or keep open certain questions of fact. That is not the end of the issue, however. The ultimate judgment of obviousness is a legal determination. *Graham*, 383 U.S., at 17. Where, as here, the content of the prior art, the scope of the patent claim, and the level of ordinary skill in the art are not in material dispute, and the obviousness of the claim is apparent in light of these factors, summary judgment is appropriate. Nothing in the declarations proffered by Teleflex prevented the District Court from reaching the careful conclusions underlying its order for summary judgment in this case.

* * *

We build and create by bringing to the tangible and palpable reality around us new works based on instinct, simple logic, ordinary inferences, extraordinary ideas, and sometimes even genius. These advances, once part of our shared knowledge, define a new threshold from which innovation starts once more. And as progress beginning from higher levels of achievement is expected in the normal course, the results of ordinary innovation are not the subject of exclusive rights under the patent laws. Were it otherwise patents might stifle, rather than promote, the progress of useful arts. *See* U.S. Const., Art. I, §8, cl. 8. These premises led to the bar on patents claiming obvious subject matter established in *Hotchkiss* and codified in §103. Application of the bar must not be confined within a test or formulation too constrained to serve its purpose.

KSR provided convincing evidence that mounting a modular sensor on a fixed pivot point of the Asano pedal was a design step well within the grasp of a person of ordinary skill in the relevant art. Its arguments, and the record, demonstrate that claim 4 of the Engelgau patent is obvious. In rejecting the District Court's rulings, the Court of Appeals analyzed the issue in a narrow, rigid manner inconsistent with §103 and our precedents. The judgment of the Court of Appeals is reversed, and the case remanded for further proceedings consistent with this opinion.

It is so ordered.

COMMENTS AND QUESTIONS

1. Consider the opinion's emphasis on predictability: "The combination of familiar elements according to known methods is likely to be obvious when it does no more than yield predictable results." What would it mean for a combination to yield an unpredictable result? *United States v. Adams,* 383 U.S. 39 (1966), offers an example. In

that case: (1) the prior art taught that batteries employing the elements claimed by the patentee would probably not work, and indeed might be dangerous; and (2) the claimed combination worked far better than was predicted in the prior art. How might you state an overall test of obviousness that employs "predictability" as its key term? *See generally* Robert P. Merges, *Uncertainty and the Standard of Patentability*, 7 [BERKELEY] HIGH TECH. L.J. 1, 2 (1992) ("The nonobviousness standard encourages researchers to pursue projects whose success appears highly uncertain at the outset. The standard insists that only the results from uncertain research should be rewarded with a patent.").

2. The Court also states: "Granting patent protection to advances that would occur in the ordinary course without real innovation retards progress and may, in the case of patents combining previously known elements, deprive prior inventions of their value or utility." Is there a danger that the Court's opinion may push too far in the opposite direction, awarding patent protection only to a few important and unpredictable innovations? What if the PHOSITA is herself an inventor? Does that mean that "ordinary inventions" are unpatentable? Does the opinion contain anything to alleviate this concern?

3. "The idea that a designer hoping to make an adjustable electronic pedal would ignore Asano because Asano was designed to solve the constant ratio problem makes little sense. A person of ordinary skill is also a person of ordinary creativity, not an automaton." In this passage, the Court rejects a narrow and formalistic notion of "teaching, motivation or suggestion." If you were a litigator seeking to invalidate a patent, how would you use this statement to build your case and structure your argument? Consider especially the Court's additional statements, (1) "When a work is available in one field of endeavor, design incentives and other market forces can prompt variations of it, either in the same field or a different one," and (2) "The proper question to have asked was whether a pedal designer of ordinary skill, facing the wide range of needs created by developments in the field of endeavor, would have seen a benefit to upgrading Asano with a sensor." What evidence would you introduce to establish (a) design incentives, (b) market forces, and (c) the wide range of needs created by developments in the field? How could patent examiners develop evidence of these things during prosecution? How will findings on these issues be handled on appeal? Recall that the Court found summary judgment on nonobviousness appropriate in this case because it is ultimately an issue of law.

4. *Pharmaceutical Patents*. Drug development is the process of taking a candidate drug from identification to marketing approval by the United States Food and Drug Administration. On average, the development of an approved drug takes ten to fifteen years and costs $1.5 billion. *See* Michael Enzo Furrow, *Pharmaceutical Patent Life-Cycle Management after* KSR v. Teleflex, 63 FOOD & DRUG L.J. 275, 278, 283 (2008). Therefore, patent protection plays a critical role in the pharmaceutical industry.

Courts assess the obviousness of chemical compounds by focusing on the identification of a lead compound, which is a compound in the prior art that would be "a natural choice for further development efforts." *Altana Pharma AG v. Teva Pharms.*

USA, Inc., 566 F.3d 999, 1008 (Fed. Cir. 2009). The Federal Circuit uses a three prong prima facie inquiry in assessing obviousness of chemical compounds:

(a) Whether an artisan of ordinary skill would have selected the asserted prior art as starting point or lead compound;

(b) Whether the prior art would have provided the PHOSITA with the motivation to alter the lead compound to obtain the claimed compound; and

(c) Whether the PHOSITA would have had a reasonable expectation of success in making the invention.

Takeda Chem. Indus., Ltd. v. Alphapharm Pty., Ltd., 492 F.3d 1350, 1357 (Fed. Cir. 2007). The first factor depends on the range and properties of potential compounds. The second factor looks to teachings in the prior art as well as structural similarities between the lead compound and the claimed compound. The third factor looks at predictability within the field, unexpected results, the extent to which the prior art teaches away from the compound, and obviousness to try. Should this test survive *KSR*?

What should happen if the invention is obvious to try, but the actual results of trying are unexpected? That often happens with follow-on pharmaceutical patents, for example when scientists follow established protocols to seek an expected variant of an existing chemical (called an "enantiomer") but that variant turns out to be more effective than expected. *See* Mark A. Lemley, *Expecting the Unexpected*, 92 NOTRE DAME L. REV. 1369 (2016) (collecting cases on both sides of the issue).

5. *AI and the Standard of Invention.* Section 103 requires that obviousness be evaluated from the perspective of one of skill in the art. Does the power of AI technology have relevance to the non-obviousness inquiry? Could the use of such technology to quickly "generate" inventions claimed by humans be used to find such inventions to be obvious? Generative AI has already solved problems that have vexed humans for years, such as figuring out how proteins are folded. If an invention is hard for a human of ordinary skill but can quickly be achieved by AI, is it obvious? *See* Ryan Abbott, *Everything is Obvious*, 66 UCLA L. REV. 2 (2018) (arguing yes).

PROBLEMS

Problem III-4. You are a patent lawyer who represents the Deco-Bag Company, a small company that has made a hit by selling decorative trash bags. The best-selling product for Deco-Bag is an orange trash bag, used for holding raked-up leaves and other lawn clippings, that has a traditional Jack-O-Lantern face stenciled onto it. At the same time that competitors have begun selling the bags in large numbers, Deco-Bag has just received an opinion of the Patent Trial and Appeal Board at the PTO. The Board has upheld a final rejection of all claims in a patent application on the bag with Jack-O-Lantern design. Deco-Bag officials are contemplating an appeal of the decision to the Federal Circuit; they have asked for your opinion on the wisdom of this course of action.

Dembiciczak Pumpkin

A representative claim from the application reads as follows:

74. A decorative bag for use by a user with trash filling material, the bag simulating the general outer appearance of an outer surface of a pumpkin having facial indicia thereon, comprising:

a flexible waterproof plastic trash or leaf bag having

an outer surface which is premanufactured orange in color for the user to simulate the general appearance of the outer skin of a pumpkin, and having

facial indicia including at least two of an eye, a nose and a mouth on the orange color outer surface for forming a face pattern on said orange color outer surface to simulate the general outer appearance of a decorative pumpkin with a face thereon,

said trash or leaf bag having first and second opposite ends, at least said second end having an opening extending substantially across the full width of said trash or leaf bag for receiving the trash filling material,

wherein when said trash or leaf bag is filled with trash filling material and closed, said trash or leaf bag takes the form and general appearance of a pumpkin with a face thereon.

The prior art cited by the examiner and the Board includes:

- MARY E. PLATTS, A HANDBOOK FOR TEACHERS OF ELEMENTARY ART 24–25 (1966), describing how to teach children to make a "Crepe Paper Jack-O-Lantern" out of a strip of orange crepe paper, construction paper cut-outs in the shape of facial features, and "wadded newspapers" as filling;

- VALERIE INDENBAUM & MARTHA SHAPIRO, THE EVERYTHING BOOK FOR TEACHERS OF YOUNG CHILDREN 73 (1985), describing a method of making a "paper bag pumpkin" by stuffing a bag with newspapers, painting it orange, and then painting on facial features with black paint;
- U.S. Patent No. 3,349,991 to Leonard Kessler, entitled "Flexible Container" ("Kessler"), describing a bag apparatus wherein the bag closure is accomplished by the use of folds or gussets in the bag material;
- Conventional plastic lawn or trash bags.

Based on this art, the PTAB affirmed the Examiner's final rejection of all the independent claims under §103, holding that they would have been obvious in light of the conventional trash bags in view of the Platts and Indenbaum/Shapiro references.

What advice would you give to Deco-Bag in this matter?

Problem III-5. You have drafted a patent application for a client claiming a lollipop in the shape of a human thumb. An examiner rejected the claims as obvious over a combination of numerous prior art references. You must now prepare an argument trying to overturn the examiner's decision by appeal to the Patent Trial and Appeal Board. The claimed invention consists of a lollipop filled with a plug of gum, chocolate or food-grade wax. A thumb-shaped elastomeric mold served as the product's internal wrapper, and after it was peeled from the candy, the user could wear the mold on his or her own thumb. The examiner relied on the following prior art references in rejecting claims to the thumb-shaped lollipop invention:

- Siciliano shows ice cream in a mold with a stick inserted. The removable mold also serves as the product's wrapper.
- Copeman shows candy lollipops in elastomeric molds taking "varying shapes, such as fruit or animals." The molds may be used as toy balloons after being removed.
- Harris shows a hollow, thumb-shaped lollipop into which the user's thumb is inserted.
- Webster shows a chewing gum entirely enclosing a liquid syrup product. This patent also suggests the greater appeal to consumers of providing two different components in the same confection.

Although some of the references cite at least one other reference, no reference explicitly suggests combining its teaching with that of any other reference. What is your basis for arguing that the invention is patentable?

ii. *"Secondary" Considerations*

In *Graham,* the Supreme Court stated that the "secondary factors" of commercial success, long-felt need, and so on "may have relevancy." 383 U.S. at 18. The Federal Circuit, by contrast, routinely speaks of these factors—under the rubric "objective evidence"—as a *required* fourth element in the §103 analysis. *See, e.g., Greenwood v. Haitori Seiko Co., Ltd.*, 900 F.2d 238, 241 (Fed. Cir. 1990):

> [C]ertain factual predicates are required before the legal conclusion of obviousness or nonobviousness can be reached. . . . The underlying factual determinations to be made are (1) the scope and content of the prior art, (2) the differences between the claimed invention and the prior art, (3) the level of ordinary skill in the art, and (4) objective evidence of non-obviousness, such as commercial success, long-felt but unsolved need, failure of others, copying, and unexpected results.

Secondary considerations may be useful at times to protect against hindsight bias. "[O]bjective evidence of nonobviousness . . . can often serve as insurance against the insidious attraction of the siren hindsight when confronted with a difficult task of evaluating the prior art." *Gore v. Garlock*, 721 F.2d 1540, 1553 (Fed. Cir. 1983). The Federal Circuit requires that there be a nexus between the proffered secondary consideration and the claimed invention.

Close adherence to this methodology is especially important in the case of less technologically complex inventions, where the very ease with which the invention can be understood may prompt one "to fall victim to the insidious effect of a hindsight syndrome wherein that which only the inventor taught is used against its teacher." *In re Dembiczak*, 175 F.3d 994, 999 (Fed. Cir. 1999) (citing *Gore v. Garlock*, 721 F.2d at 1553).

Secondary considerations include:

- Commercial success
- Long-felt need and failure by others
- Awards and praise
- Skepticism, "teaching away," and unexpected results
- Licensing activity
- Copying
- Advances in collateral technology
- Near-simultaneous invention

These "secondary considerations" may work as "plus factors," tipping the balance of obviousness one way or the other in a particular case. But the significance of each of these factors has been questioned.

> Th[e] use of secondary considerations is not new to the CAFC. Rather, these considerations were previously accorded little weight because their appearance can sometimes be attributed to factors other than nonobviousness. For instance, commercial success may be due to the dominant market position of the patentee before the introduction of the new invention; the sudden ability to meet long felt need could derive from other technological advances, unrelated to the inventor's contribution; acquiescence may be attributed to the relative cost of obtaining a license, as opposed to challenging the patent. Rather than reject

these considerations entirely, the CAFC has recognized their importance in making the law precise and instead has sought to minimize the extent to which they can be misused. Thus, the court has elaborated a "nexus" requirement, which requires that before secondary considerations can be used to demonstrate nonobviousness, a showing must be made that their appearance is attributable to the inventive characteristics of the discovery as claimed in the patent. . . . Since it is likely that the inconsistent treatment of such inventions was the most destabilizing element of the system, the CAFC has, in this area, made strides in achieving the appearance of precision.

Rochelle Dreyfuss, *The Federal Circuit: A Case Study in Specialized Courts*, 64 N.Y.U. L. REV. 1 (1989). Given the complex causal chain relating to commercial success and nonobviousness, it is important to be cautious in applying this factor.

Commercial success is a poor indicator of patentability because it depends for its effectiveness on a long chain of inferences, and because the links in the chain are often subject to doubt. This was one of the central insights of a seminal article on patentability, *Graham v. John Deere Co.: New Standards for Patents*, [1966 SUP. CT. REV. 293] written by Edmund Kitch in 1966. In it Kitch argued that commercial success was an unreliable indicator of nonobviousness. To make his point, Kitch identified four inferences a judge must make to work backward from evidence of market success to a conclusion of patentable invention:

First, that the commercial success is due to the innovation. Second, that . . . potential commercial success was perceived before its development. Third, the potential commercial success having been perceived, it is likely that efforts were made [by a number of firms] to develop the improvement. Fourth, the efforts having been made by men of skill in the art, they failed because the patentee was the first to reduce his development to practice.

With only this last event as a starting point, a court is asked to reconstruct a long series of events, and, more importantly, to decide how much of the final success is attributable to each factor introduced along the way. Each inference is weak, because there are almost always several explanations why a product was successful or why other firms missed a market opportunity. Only the *last* piece of the puzzle is indisputably established; the goal of the exercise is reached through a series of inferences that only begins with this last piece. It is an altogether extraordinary job of factual reconstruction, one that reveals the falsity of the term "objective evidence," which is often used by proponents of the secondary considerations.

Robert P. Merges, *Economic Perspectives on Innovation: Patent Standards and Commercial Success*, 76 CAL. L. REV. 803, 838 (1988). Professor Merges goes on to argue in favor of another "secondary consideration"—failure of others:

Unlike commercial success, the failure of others to make an invention proves directly that parallel research efforts were under way at a number of firms, and that one firm (the patentee) won the race to a common goal. So long as the race was long enough, and so long as there was a clear winner, it is difficult to find fault with such evidence as proof of patentability. In fact, since the failure of others is often one of the inferential steps underlying the commercial success doctrine, it makes sense for courts to adopt a rule of thumb requiring the patentee in most cases to prove failure of others before commercial success will be given substantial weight.

Should the inventor's cost of making the invention be considered in evaluating obviousness? The statute states that "[p]atentability shall not be negatived by the manner in which the invention was made." 35 U.S.C. §103(a). But perhaps the high cost of making the invention should count in favor of granting a patent even if cheap or serendipitous inventions don't count against granting a patent. *See* Robert P Merges, *Uncertainty and the Standard of Patentability*, 7 HIGH TECH. L.J. 1 (1992) (making this argument).

If failure of others is important evidence of nonobviousness, should the *success* of others be evidence of obviousness? One study found that a surprising number of the most prominent inventions in history were developed by multiple inventors at about the same time. *See* Mark A. Lemley, *The Myth of the Sole Inventor*, 110 MICH. L. REV. 709 (2012). Does that suggest those inventions were obvious? Or is there some other explanation?

Secondary considerations must have a nexus to the invention itself. *See Merck & Co., Inc. v. Teva Pharmaceuticals USA, Inc.*, 395 F.3d 1364 (Fed. Cir. 2005). In invalidating the patent as obvious, the court determined that the commercial success of the drug's once-weekly dosing claim resulted not from any technical advantage of the claimed invention—a weekly-dosing regimen for a known compound—but rather Merck's right to exclude others from practicing the claim based on a different patent covering the chemical compound and Merck's exclusive FDA approval to market any dosage of the drug for five years. As a result, there was no nexus between the patentee's commercial success and any technical advance. *See id.* at 1376-77; *see also Galderma Labs., L.P. v. Tolmar, Inc.*, 737 F.3d 731, 740 (Fed. Cir. 2013) (holding that commercial success does not support nonobviousness of the claimed invention where blocking patents prevented competitors from marketing the product earlier).

iii.   The AIA

The AIA version of §103 shifts the time for determining obviousness from a patent claimant's invention date (i.e., "at the time the invention was made") to the effective filing date ("before the effective filing date of the claimed invention"). This change is tied to the definition of novelty under AIA §102, and is one implication of the shift to a first inventor to file priority system. In theory, moving the relevant date from invention to filing may increase at least slightly the scope of prior art available for obviousness inquiries; but in reality, the change may not make too much difference, especially if inventors adapt their behavior and file soon after invention.

PROBLEM III-6

Suppose that researchers in a particular pharmaceutical field agree that there are roughly a dozen comparably plausible compounds for attacking a serious disease and that the cost of pursuing regulatory approval for these paths will run into the billions of dollars. Does this set of factors imply that the resulting drug may well be obvious? How can a pharmaceutical company sensibly evaluate this risk? Does this scenario suggest that patent protection is ill-suited for this type of innovation?

---

3. Utility

Section 101 provides that "[w]hoever invents or discovers any new and *useful* process, machine, manufacture, or composition of matter, or any new and *useful* improvement thereof, may obtain a patent therefor . . . ." This is the textual basis for the utility requirement.

At first glance, utility might seem a simple requirement to apply. After all, whether or not something is useful is typically easy to determine. Nonetheless, there are a few areas in which utility is questionable. Chemists often synthesize compounds that they believe might be useful someday but for which no particular use is known or a potential use is highly speculative at the time that they file their patent application. Should they be entitled to a patent before that utility is known?

 Brenner v. Manson
Supreme Court of the United States
383 U.S. 519 (1966)

MR. JUSTICE FORTAS delivered the opinion of the Court.

A Patent Office examiner denied Manson's application, and the denial was affirmed by the Board of Appeals within the Patent Office. The ground for rejection was the failure "to disclose any utility for" the chemical compound produced by the process. This omission was not cured, in the opinion of the Patent Office, by Manson's reference to an article in the November 1956 issue of the Journal of Organic Chemistry, 21 J. ORG. CHEM. 1333–1335, which revealed that steroids of a class which included the compound in question were undergoing screening for possible tumor-inhibiting effects in mice, and that a homologue[3] adjacent to Manson's steroid had proven effective in that role. Said the Board of Appeals, "It is our view that the statutory requirement of usefulness of a product cannot be presumed merely because it happens to be closely related to another compound which is known to be useful."

---

[3] "A homologous series is a family of chemically related compounds, the composition of which varies from member to member by CH2 (one atom of carbon and two atoms of hydrogen). . . . Chemists knowing the properties of one member of a series would in general know what to expect in adjacent members."

The Court of Customs and Patent Appeals (hereinafter CCPA) reversed[, stating] "where a claimed process produces a known product it is not necessary to show utility for the product," so long as the product "is not alleged to be detrimental to the public interest."

Our starting point is the proposition, neither disputed nor disputable, that one may patent only that which is "useful." [T]he concept of utility has maintained a central place in all of our patent legislation, beginning with the first patent law in 1790 and culminating in the present [§101] . . .

Respondent does not—at least in the first instance—rest upon the extreme proposition, advanced by the court below, that a novel chemical process is patentable so long as it yields the intended product and so long as the product is not itself "detrimental." Nor does he commit the outcome of his claim to the slightly more conventional proposition that any process is "useful" within the meaning of §101 if it produces a compound whose potential usefulness is under investigation by serious scientific researchers, although he urges this position, too, as an alternative basis for affirming the decision. Rather, he begins with the much more orthodox argument that his process has a specific utility which would entitle him to a declaration of interference even under the Patent Office's reading of §101. The claim is that the supporting affidavits, by reference to Ringold's 1956 article, reveal that an adjacent homologue of the steroid yielded by his process has been demonstrated to have tumor-inhibiting effects in mice, and that this discloses the requisite utility. We do not accept any of these theories as an adequate basis for overriding the determination of the Patent Office that the "utility" requirement has not been met.

Even on the assumption that the process would be patentable were respondent to show that the steroid produced had a tumor-inhibiting effect in mice, we would not overrule the Patent Office finding that respondent has not made such a showing. The Patent Office held that, despite the reference to the adjacent homologue, respondent's papers did not disclose a sufficient likelihood that the steroid yielded by his process would have similar tumor-inhibiting characteristics. Indeed, respondent himself recognized that the presumption that adjacent homologues have the same utility has been challenged in the steroid field because of "a greater known unpredictability of compounds in that field." In these circumstances and in this technical area, we would not overturn the finding of the Primary Examiner, affirmed by the Board of Appeals and not challenged by the CCPA.

The second and third points of respondent's argument present issues of much importance. Is a chemical process "useful" within the meaning of §101 either (1) because it works—i.e., produces the intended product? or (2) because the compound yielded belongs to a class of compounds now the subject of serious scientific investigation? These contentions present the basic problem for our adjudication. Since we find no specific assistance in the legislative materials underlying §101, we are remitted to an analysis of the problem in light of the general intent of Congress, the purposes of the patent system, and the implications of a decision one way or the other.

In support of his plea that we attenuate the requirement of "utility," respondent relies upon Justice Story's well-known statement that a "useful" invention is one "which may be applied to a beneficial use in society, in contradistinction to an invention injurious to the morals, health, or good order of society, or frivolous and insignificant"[20]—and upon the assertion that to do so would encourage inventors of new processes to publicize the event for the benefit of the entire scientific community, thus widening the search for uses and increasing the fund of scientific knowledge. Justice Story's language sheds little light on our subject. Narrowly read, it does no more than compel us to decide whether the invention in question is "frivolous and insignificant"—a query no easier of application than the one built into the statute. Read more broadly, so as to allow the patenting of any invention not positively harmful to society, it places such a special meaning on the word "useful" that we cannot accept it in the absence of evidence that Congress so intended. There are, after all, many things in this world which may not be considered "useful" but which, nevertheless, are totally without a capacity for harm.

Whatever weight is attached to the value of encouraging disclosure and of inhibiting secrecy, we believe a more compelling consideration is that a process patent in the chemical field, which has not been developed and pointed to the degree of specific utility, creates a monopoly of knowledge which should be granted only if clearly commanded by the statute. Until the process claim has been reduced to production of a product shown to be useful, the metes and bounds of that monopoly are not capable of precise delineation. It may engross a vast, unknown, and perhaps unknowable area. Such a patent may confer power to block off whole areas of scientific development, without compensating benefit to the public. The basic *quid pro quo* contemplated by the Constitution and the Congress for granting a patent monopoly is the benefit derived by the public from an invention with substantial utility. Unless and until a process is refined and developed to this point—where specific benefit exists in currently available form—there is insufficient justification for permitting an applicant to engross what may prove to be a broad field.

These arguments for and against the patentability of a process which either has no known use or is useful only in the sense that it may be an object of scientific research would apply equally to the patenting of the product produced by the process. Respondent appears to concede that with respect to a product, as opposed to a process, Congress has struck the balance on the side of nonpatentability unless "utility" is shown. Indeed, the decisions of the CCPA are in accord with the view that a product may not be patented absent a showing of utility greater than any adduced in the present case. We find absolutely no warrant for the proposition that although Congress intended that no patent be granted on a chemical compound whose sole "utility" consists of its potential role as an object of use-testing, a different set of rules was meant to apply to the process which yielded the unpatentable product. That proposition seems to us little more than

---

[20] *Note on the Patent Laws*, 3 Wheat. App. 13, 24. *See also* Justice Story's decisions on circuit in *Lowell v. Lewis*, 15 Fed. Cas. 1018 (No. 8568) (C.C.D. Mass.), and *Bedford v. Hunt*, 3 Fed. Cas. 37 (No. 1217) (C.C.D. Mass.).

an attempt to evade the impact of the rules which concededly govern patentability of the product itself.

This is not to say that we mean to disparage the importance of contributions to the fund of scientific information short of the invention of something "useful," or that we are blind to the prospect that what now seems without "use" may tomorrow command the grateful attention of the public. But a patent is not a hunting license. It is not a reward for the search, but compensation for its successful conclusion. "[A] patent system must be related to the world of commerce rather than to the realm of philosophy. . . ."

The judgment of the CCPA is Reversed.

MR. JUSTICE HARLAN, concurring in part and dissenting in part:

. . . Because I believe that the Court's policy arguments are not convincing and that past practice favors the respondent, I would reject the narrow definition of "useful" and uphold the judgment of the CCPA.

The Court's opinion sets out about half a dozen reasons in support of its interpretation. Several of these arguments seem to me to have almost no force. For instance, it is suggested that "[u]ntil the process claim has been reduced to production of a product shown to be useful, the metes and bounds of that monopoly are not capable of precise delineation" and "[i]t may engross a vast, unknown, and perhaps unknowable area." I fail to see the relevance of these assertions; process claims are not disallowed because the products they produce may be of "vast" importance nor, in any event, does advance knowledge of a specific product use provide much safeguard on this score or fix "metes and bounds" precisely since a hundred more uses may be found after a patent is granted and greatly enhance its value. . . .

More to the point, I think, are the Court's remaining, prudential arguments against patentability: namely, that disclosure induced by allowing a patent is partly undercut by patent-application drafting techniques, that disclosure may occur without granting a patent, and that a patent will discourage others from inventing uses for the product. How far opaque drafting may lessen the public benefits resulting from the issuance of a patent is not shown by any evidence in this case but, more important, the argument operates against all patents and gives no reason for singling out the class involved here. The thought that these inventions may be more likely than most to be disclosed even if patents are not allowed may have more force; but while empirical study of the industry might reveal that chemical researchers would behave in this fashion, the abstractly logical choice for them seems to me to maintain secrecy until a product use can be discovered. As to discouraging the search by others for product uses, there is no doubt this risk exists but the price paid for any patent is that research on other uses or improvements may be hampered because the original patentee will reap much of the reward. From the standpoint of the public interest the Constitution seems to have resolved that choice in favor of patentability.

What I find most troubling about the result reached by the Court is the impact it may have on chemical research. Chemistry is a highly interrelated field and a tangible benefit for society may be the outcome of a number of different discoveries, one discovery building upon the next. To encourage one chemist or research facility to invent and disseminate new processes and products may be vital to progress, although the product or process be without "utility" as the Court defines the term, because that discovery permits someone else to take a further but perhaps less difficult step leading to a commercially useful item. In my view, our awareness in this age of the importance of achieving and publicizing basic research should lead this Court to resolve uncertainties in its favor and uphold the respondent's position in this case.

COMMENTS AND QUESTIONS

1. Why does the majority claim that until an applicant shows an invention is useful, the inventor has not supplied the *quid pro quo* for a patent? What harm is there in granting a patent on an invention whose utility only becomes clear later? In granting a patent on a useless device? Who would be harmed by the granting of such a patent? Would granting the patent help the inventor attract investment that could help establish utility?

2. Cases following *Brenner* state that a claimed invention must have a specific and substantial utility that is credible. Asserted uses like "biological activity" or "useful for technical and pharmaceutical purposes" fail the requirement of specific utility; they are too vague. *See, e.g., In re Kirk*, 376 F.2d 936, 941 (C.C.P.A. 1967). The "substantial" utility standard requires proof that an invention serves some practical purpose, not merely that it is generally promising or promising enough to pursue further. "Simply put, to satisfy the 'substantial' utility requirement, an asserted use must show that that claimed invention has a significant and presently available benefit to the public." *Juicy Whip, Inc. v. Orange Bang, Inc.*, 185 F.3d 1364, 1366 (Fed. Cir. 1999).

The most common application of this requirement comes in chemical and biotechnology cases such as *Brenner* where a chemical compound is identified and is claimed to have utility as a pharmaceutical product. Although it is difficult to predict accurately how the human body will react to a specific compound, some evidence of basic effectiveness can establish utility. *See Ex parte Maas*, 9 U.S.P.Q.2d 1746 (Bd. Pat. App. & Int. 1987) (in vitro or animal test data that is reasonably predictive of utility must be accepted if one skilled in the art would find it predictive of utility).

The PTO presumes that claims to utility are credible. *In re Langer*, 503 F.2d 1380, 1391 (CCPA 1974). The only time the PTO questions utility, therefore, is when an invention presents a "fantastic claim" to utility such as a perpetual motion machine or cold fusion. *See Newman v. Quigg*, 681 F. Supp. 16 (D.D.C. 1988), *aff'd*, 877 F.2d 1575 (Fed. Cir. 1989) (perpetual motion machine); *In re Swartz*, 232 F.3d 862 (Fed. Cir. 2000) ("cold fusion"); *In re Huping Hu*, 848 Fed. Appx. 416 (Fed. Cir. 2021) (upholding rejection of patent application claiming the use of "quantum entanglement"—when fundamental particles such as photons or electrons interact and become linked—to alter gravity, pH values, and temperature at a distance for lack of experimental verification).

3. *Utility as a Limitation on Gun Jumping.* For the steroid compounds at issue in *Brenner*, a practical use was discovered after the patent application was filed—too late to save the patent. So utility might be thought of as a way to control the *timing* of the

patent grant. *See* Rebecca S. Eisenberg, *Analyze This: A Law and Economics Agenda for the Patent System*, 53 VAND. L. REV. 2081, 2087 (2000). Why do we require proof of practical utility at the time a patent application is filed? An analogy to land titling provides valuable insight. An early-stage researcher is akin to a "claim jumper" in the law of mining, or to someone who engages in a "land rush," racing to occupy real property simply to stake a claim, without making any real investment. Because these kinds of "racing behaviors" can be wasteful, the law often requires substantial investment before someone is awarded title. This discourages people from making large investments in running from claim to claim—which adds nothing to society's wealth in and of itself—and instead directs investment towards development of the resources in question. *See* David D. Haddock, *First Possession Versus Optimal Timing: Limiting the Dissipation of Economic Value*, 64 WASH. U. L.Q. 775 (1986); Terry L. Anderson & Peter J. Hill, *The Race for Property Rights*, 33 J.L. & ECON. 177, 184 (1990); Dean Lueck, *The Rule of First Possession and the Design of the Law*, 38 J.L. & ECON. 393 (1995).

4. *Use Patents*. Justice Harlan's dissent in *Brenner* highlights an anomaly of patent protection: an inventor who obtains a patent for a product, e.g., a particular molecule, has the right to exclude all others from making, using or selling that product for *any* and all purposes, including purposes that the inventor did not herself discover or invent. *See* Robert P. Merges & Richard Nelson, *On the Complex Economics of Patent Scope*, 90 COLUM. L. REV. 839, 902–03, 912–14 (1990). For example, a patented compound created for its use as a leather tanning agent might turn out to be an effective treatment for disease. *Cf. In re Thuau*, 135 F.2d 344 (C.C.P.A. 1943). If so, the patentee would have the right to prevent all others from selling the drug as a treatment—including the person who discovered that the leather tanning compound had therapeutic properties. Note that the utility requirement is met so long as the patentee shows any specific utility for the chemical when the patent is first filed—in our example, when the leather tanning property of the compound is discovered.

The discoverer of the new use can get their own patent on that use. Merges & Nelson, *supra*. In our example, the discoverer of the disease-fighting property of the leather tanning agent can obtain a *process* patent for "the process of using [the leather tanning compound] to treat disease." *See Rohm & Haas v. Roberts Chem. Co.*, 245 F.2d 693 (4th Cir. 1957) (upholding defendant's patent on a new use of a well-known product as a fungicide); 1 DONALD CHISUM, PATENTS §1.03[8] (collecting other cases on this point). This is in essence only an improvement patent; the discoverer would still have to obtain a license from the patentee to use the compound for the treatment of disease. But the reverse is also true; unlike the example outlined above, if the one who discovered the leather tanning agent's therapeutic properties obtained a process patent, the patentee would have to negotiate a license from the improver to have the right to use the compound to treat disease.

5. Utility for pharmaceutical products can generally be established by animal testing. *See* U.S. PATENT AND TRADEMARK OFFICE, MANUAL OF PATENT EXAMINING PROCEDURES §2107.01. In the past, the biotechnology industry sometimes had trouble

overcoming utility rejections without clinical data proving that a particular drug was effective *in humans,* despite Federal Circuit precedent holding that a showing of efficacy in a laboratory experiment was sufficient to establish the utility of a new drug. *Cross v. Iizuka,* 753 F.2d 1040, 1051 (Fed. Cir. 1985).

The Federal Circuit made it clear that human clinical trials are not necessary to prove the utility of a drug in *In re Brana,* 51 F.3d 1560 (Fed. Cir. 1995). The court held that the results of in vivo tests in mice were sufficiently probative of efficacy in humans to pass the utility threshold:

> The Commissioner, as did the Board, confuses the requirements under the law for obtaining a patent with the requirements for obtaining government approval to market a particular drug for human consumption. . . . FDA approval is not a prerequisite for finding a compound useful within the meaning of the patent laws. . . . Usefulness in patent law, and in particular in the context of pharmaceutical inventions, necessarily includes the expectation of further research and development. . . . Were we to require Phase II testing in order to prove utility, the associated costs would prevent many companies from obtaining patent protection on promising new inventions, thereby eliminating an incentive to pursue, through research and development, potential cures in many crucial areas such as the treatment of cancer.

Brana, 51 F.3d at 1567. On the other hand, in *In re Ziegler,* 992 F.2d 1197, 1203 (Fed. Cir. 1993), the Federal Circuit held that a patent applicant was not entitled to claim priority to a 1954 application for "polypropylene," since at the time of the 1954 application "at best, Ziegler was on the way to discovering a practical utility for polypropylene . . . but in that application Ziegler had not yet gotten there." Are these two cases distinguishable?

6. *Brenner* in many ways represents the high-water mark of the utility doctrine. Most applications of the doctrine have been limited in the hurdles they place before inventors. Certainly frivolous ideas are sometimes patented—such as a method of painting using a baby's bottom and a thumb-wrestling ring with stabilizing handle—suggesting that utility is not an effective mechanism for weeding out economically insignificant inventions. *See* Sean B. Seymore, *Making Patents Useful,* 98 MINN. L. REV. 1046 (2014) (proposing tightening of the utility requirement).

7. *PTO Utility Guidelines.* Drawing on *Brenner,* the PTO promulgated guidelines requiring that an asserted utility be "specific, credible, and substantial." The credibility element was well known; it is the basis of utility rejections for far-fetched inventions such as perpetual motion machines. The novel aspects of the guidelines were (1) the definition of a "specific" utility and (2) the addition of a new requirement of "substantial" utility. *See* Utility Examination Guidelines, 66 Fed. Reg. 1092 (Jan. 5, 2001).

8. *Specific Utility.* The PTO training materials based on the guidelines give as an example an asserted utility for a gene sequence, claimed to be useful to identify an unspecified disease. The Patent Office would now consider this not specific enough.

More detail—such as the *specific type* of disease sought to be identified—would be required. As regards "substantial" utility, the guidelines state that the "requirement excludes 'throw-away,' 'insubstantial,' or 'nonspecific' utilities, such as the use of a complex invention as landfill."

The *reason* that "throwaway" utilities are not acceptable is that they permit patents to issue on inventions whose greatest value has yet to be realized. This is particularly acute in the area of gene sequences. The raw sequence information is of only nominal value in itself. The real value lies in identifying the whole genes that include each sequence, and even more importantly, identifying which traits those genes code for. Only then can proteins be mass produced, diseases identified, and gene therapies devised. These are the very "downstream" uses that Heller and Eisenberg are at pains to protect from patent blockages, i.e., "anticommons." Michael A. Heller & Rebecca Eisenberg, *Can Patents Deter Innovation? The Anticommons in Biomedical Research*, 280 SCIENCE 698 (1998); *see also* Michael A. Heller, *The Tragedy of the Anticommons: Property in the Transition from Marx to Markets*, 111 HARV. L. REV. 622 (1998).

The Federal Circuit ruled in *In re Fisher*, 421 F.3d 1365 (Fed. Cir. 2005), that claims to "expressed sequence tags" (ESTs)—fragments of DNA nucleotide sequences—without identifying how they are useful do not satisfy the utility requirement. The court rejected the notion that sequence information is sufficiently useful as a research tool—such as a microscope—for better understanding the DNA puzzle. It reasoned that while any given DNA sequence could be used as a marker, none was more useful than any other, so they did not meet the requirement of utility specific to the claimed invention. As we examine in Section III(B)(5)(iii), the Supreme Court ruled that DNA sequences are not patent eligible because they are naturally occurring substances, but complementary DNA (cDNA) molecules or other modified DNA sequences are potentially patent-eligible.

NOTE ON MORAL UTILITY

The concept of immoral subject matter originated in dictum from a Joseph Story opinion. *Lowell v. Lewis*, 15 F. Cas. 1018 (No. 8568) (C.C.D. Mass. 1817). As examples of useless inventions, he cited patents to "poison people, or to promote debauchery, or to facilitate private assassination." This doctrine was often invoked in the late nineteenth century to deny patents on gambling devices. Some courts barred patents on inventions that were useful for things other than gambling if they could be used for gambling. *See, e.g., Schultz v. Holtz*, 82 F. 448 (N.D. Cal. 1897) (invalidating patent on coin return device for coin-operated machines because it had application to slot machines). Courts struck down patents on this basis well into the twentieth century. *See, e.g., Meyer v. Buckley Mfg. Co.*, 15 F. Supp. 640, 641 (N.D. Ill. 1936) (denying patent on "game of chance" vending machine where user inserted coin and tried to manipulate miniature steam shovel to scoop up a toy). By the 1970s, however, the courts were regularly upholding patents on gambling devices—both because gambling was no longer seen as a major moral issue and because courts had become warier of denying patents on the basis of an indeterminate moral standard. *See, e.g., Ex parte Murphy*, 200 U.S.P.Q. (BNA) 801, 803 (Bd. Pat. App. & Int. 1977) (upholding claim for "one-armed bandit").

The fight against immoral inventions was not limited to patents for gambling devices. Another line of cases denied patents for inventions that could be used only to defraud. In *Juicy Whip, Inc. v. Orange Bang, Inc.*, 185 F.3d 1364 (Fed. Cir. 1999), the inventor claimed a juice dispensing system that only appeared to circulate fresh juice. In actuality, it circulated an undrinkable liquid, while the tanks hidden underneath the glass bowl display dispensed the actual juice. The asserted utilities were this arrangement reduced maintenance costs and avoided contamination.

U.S. Patent No. 5,575,405

The defendant in *Juicy Whip*, who had infringed the design, took the remarkable position that the technology at issue was immoral in that it defrauded the public. We say remarkable, in that the defendant was, by infringing the technology, also defrauding the public on its theory. The Federal Circuit used the case to remove questions of morality from patent validity analysis. The court observed that "[t]he fact that one product can be altered to make it look like another is in itself a specific benefit sufficient to satisfy the statutory requirement of utility." The court gave the examples of cubic zirconium (designed to simulate a diamond), imitation gold leaf (designed to imitate real gold leaf), synthetic fabrics (designed to simulate expensive natural fabrics), and imitation leather (designed to look like real leather).

In each case, the invention of the product or process that makes such imitation possible has 'utility' within the meaning of the patent statute, and indeed there are numerous patents directed toward making one product imitate another. *See, e.g.,* U.S. Pat. No. 5,762,968 (method for producing imitation grill marks on food without using heat); U.S. Pat. No. 5,899,038 (laminated flooring imitating wood); U.S. Pat. No. 5,571,545 (imitation hamburger). Much of the value of such products resides in the fact that they appear to be something they are not. Thus, in this case the claimed post-mix dispenser meets the statutory requirement of utility by embodying the features of a post-mix dispenser while imitating the visual appearance of a pre-mix dispenser.

The fact that customers may believe they are receiving fluid directly from the display tank does not deprive the invention of utility. . . . [E]ven if the use of a reservoir containing fluid that is not dispensed is considered deceptive, that is not by itself sufficient to render the invention unpatentable. The requirement of 'utility' in patent law is not a directive to the Patent and Trademark Office or the courts to serve as arbiters of deceptive trade practices. Other agencies, such as the Federal Trade Commission and the Food and Drug Administration, are assigned the task of protecting consumers from fraud and deception in the sale of food products. *Cf. In re Watson,* 517 F.2d 465, 474–76 (CCPA 1975) (stating that it is not the province of the Patent Office to determine, under section 101, whether drugs are safe). As the Supreme Court put the point more generally, "Congress never intended that the patent laws should displace the police powers of the States, meaning by that term those powers by which the health, good order, peace and general welfare of the community are promoted." *Webber v. Virginia,* 103 U.S. (13 Otto) 344, 347–48 (1880).

Of course, Congress is free to declare particular types of inventions unpatentable for a variety of reasons, including deceptiveness. *Cf.* 42 U.S.C. §2181(a) (exempting from patent protection inventions useful solely in connection with special nuclear material or atomic weapons). Until such time as Congress does so, however, we find no basis in section 101 to hold that inventions can be ruled unpatentable for lack of utility simply because they have the capacity to fool some members of the public. The district court therefore erred in holding that the invention of the '405 patent lacks utility because it deceives the public through imitation in a manner that is designed to increase product sales.

COMMENTS AND QUESTIONS

1. *Patentable Subject Matter as a New Form of Moral Utility.* The AIA expressly excludes patents on specific subject matter categories, namely tax strategies and human organisms. *See* Pub. L. 112–29, §§14, 33, 125 Stat. 284 (2011). These exclusions reflect moral utility concerns. *See* Laura A. Keay, *Morality's Move Within U.S. Patent Law:*

From Moral Utility to Subject Matter, 40 AIPLA Q.J. 409 (2012) (describing a recent reemergence in U.S. patent law of the moral utility doctrine as a result of ethical debates surrounding biotechnologies such as human-animal chimeras and genetic diagnostics); Margo A. Bagley, *Patent First, Ask Questions Later: Morality and Biotechnology in Patent Law*, 45 WM. & MARY L. REV. 469 (2003) (arguing for just such a revival of the moral utility doctrine); Thomas A. Magnani, *The Patentability of Human-Animal Chimeras*, 14 BERKELEY TECH. L.J. 443 (1999).

2. *Moral Utility Abroad.* Other nations have integrated moral and ethical considerations more directly into their patent systems. *See* Convention on the Grant of European Patents, Oct. 5, 1973, 13 I.L.M. 268, Art. 53(a) (providing that "European patents shall not be granted in respect of: (a) inventions the publication or exploitation of which would be contrary to *ordre public* or morality"); Cynthia M. Ho, *Splicing Morality and Patent Law: Issues Arising from Mixing Mice and Men*, 2 WASH. U. J.L. & POL'Y 247 (2000) (discussing the controversy surrounding the patenting of the oncogene mouse and the differences between the U.S. and Europe). *See also* Patent Law of the People's Republic of China, 2008, at Article 5 ("Patent rights shall not be granted for invention-creations that violate the law or social ethics, or harm public interests.").

Should patent examiners serve as moral censors? Do such standards risk subjecting technological advance to special interest politics? *See* Benjamin D. Enerson, *Protecting Society from Patently Offensive Inventions: The Risk of the Moral Utility Doctrine*, 89 CORNELL L. REV. 685 (2004).

PROBLEM III-7

Worn Look, Inc. (WLI) is a fabric design company that specializes in designing jeans for the high-end fashion market. WLI develops a process for producing a "random shredded effect" on the fabric of new jeans, catering to the market for new jeans that appear to be pre-worn and partially torn. ALI seeks a patent not only on the process of treating the jeans to produce a random shredded effect but on jeans treated by this process. The patent examiner rejects the claim to pre-shredded jeans on the ground that they lack utility. Is this rejection proper? What test of utility does the patent examiner apply here?

---

4. Disclosure

A patent can be a potent right. In exchange for this government grant, an inventor must disclose the workings of the invention in enough detail to be informative to other people working in the same field. The sufficiency of the patentee's disclosure, and its relationship to the claims of a patent, are the topics we consider in this section.

The overall goal when drafting patent claims is to make them as broad as the Patent Office will allow. There are two constraints on the breadth of the claims you can draft: (a) the mass of publicly available information on your problem—"the prior art" that is essential to novelty and nonobviousness analysis; and (b) the actual work the inventor has done, in the sense that the inventor may not claim beyond what they have invented and described.

The disclosure requirement of the modern Patent Act provides:

§112(a) The specification shall contain a written description of the invention, and of the manner and process of making and using it, in such full, clear, concise, and exact terms as to enable any person skilled in the art to which it pertains, or with which it is most nearly connected, to make and use the same, and shall set forth the best mode contemplated by the inventor of carrying out his invention.

This provision comprises three requirements: (i) enablement; (ii) written description; and (iii) best mode. We take each of these sections up in turn. Sections 112(b)–(f) deal with how patents are claimed, as opposed to the adequacy of disclosure.[4] We will cover these issues in the section on claim construction.

i.   *Enablement*

Amgen Inc. v. Sanofi
Supreme Court of the United States
143 S.Ct. 1243 (2023)

JUSTICE GORSUCH delivered the opinion of the Court.

The development of antibody drugs has yielded life-changing therapies. Individuals across the world now rely on antibody drugs to treat conditions ranging from Crohn's disease to cancer. This case concerns patents covering antibodies that help reduce levels of low-density lipoprotein cholesterol, sometimes called LDL cholesterol (for the obvious reason) or bad cholesterol (because it can lead to cardiovascular disease, heart attacks, and strokes).

The case comes to us this way. Several years ago, petitioners (Amgen) obtained two patents. Together, these patents claim a monopoly over all antibodies that (1) bind to specific amino acids on a naturally occurring protein known as PCSK9, and (2) block PCSK9 from impairing the body's mechanism for removing LDL cholesterol from the bloodstream. Soon after receiving these patents, Amgen sued respondents (Sanofi) for infringement. In response, Sanofi argued that the patents were invalid under §112 of the Patent Act. That provision requires a patent applicant to describe its invention "in such full, clear, concise, and exact terms as to enable any person skilled in the art ... to make and use the [invention]." 35 U.S.C. §112(a). Sanofi contended that Amgen's patents failed to meet this standard because they sought to claim for Amgen's exclusive use potentially millions more antibodies than the company had taught scientists to make. In the end, both the district court and Federal Circuit sided with Sanofi. The question we face is whether to disturb their judgment.

---

[4] The 1952 Act presented Section 112 as six paragraphs. As a result, court decisions referred to subsections by paragraph number, *e.g.*, §112, ¶1. The AIA relabeled these subsections (a)–(f).

I

A

The immune system produces antibodies as a defense to foreign agents called antigens. When a particular antigen—a virus, for example—enters the body, the immune system generates antibodies to attack it. In a successful attack, the antibodies target and bind to the antigen, stopping it from causing harm to the body. *See* Brief for Sir Gregory Paul Winter et al. as *Amici Curiae* 8 (Winter Brief); M. Lemley & J. Sherkow, *The Antibody Patent Paradox*, 132 YALE L. J. 994, 1001-02 (2023).

Antibodies are incredibly diverse. Some scientists estimate that there may be as many unique antibodies as there are stars in the galaxy. *See id.,* at 1003; *see also* B. Briney, A. Inderbitzin, C. Joyce, & D. Burton, *Commonality Despite Exceptional Diversity in the Baseline Human Antibody Repertoire*, 566 NATURE 393, 397 (No. 7744, Feb. 2019) (estimating that the immune system could potentially generate up to a quintillion unique antibodies). This diversity shows up in both structure and function.

Start with structure. "When scientists refer to an antibody's 'structure,'" they may have in mind "several related concepts," each of which describes "what an antibody *is*." Winter Brief 10. Antibodies are made up of amino acids, and scientists commonly identify a particular antibody according to its specific sequence of amino acids—what they call an antibody's "'primary structure.'" But antibodies are not just linear chains of amino acids. As the atoms of the amino acids interact with each other, they create folds that result in complex three-dimensional shapes. *Ibid.* Scientists refer to an antibody's intricate topography as its "tertiary structure."

An antibody's structure does much to dictate its function—its ability to bind to an antigen and, in some instances, to block other molecules in the body from doing the same. "For an antibody to bind to an antigen, the two surfaces have to fit together and contact each other at multiple points." But just because an antibody can bind to an antigen does not mean that it can also block. To bind and block, the antibody must establish a sufficiently broad, strong, and stable bond to the antigen. See *ibid.* Different antibodies have different binding and blocking capacities based on the amino acids that compose them and their three-dimensional shapes.

Despite recent advances, aspects of antibody science remain unpredictable. For example, scientists understand that changing even one amino acid in the sequence can alter an antibody's structure and function. But scientists cannot always accurately predict exactly how trading one amino acid for another will affect an antibody's structure and function. ' As Amgen's expert testified at trial: "'[T]he way in which you get from sequence to that three-dimensional structure isn't fully understood today. It's going to get a Nobel Prize for somebody at some point, but translating that sequence into a known three-dimensional structure is still not possible.'"

B

While the immune system naturally produces an army of antibodies to protect us from various harms, scientists are now able to engineer antibodies to assist in treating diseases. Some of these lab-made antibodies target not foreign agents but the body's own proteins, receptors, and ligands. "While naturally occurring in our bodies, these [proteins, receptors, and ligands] can also be involved in inflammatory disorders, uncontrolled cell growth, or other biological pathways that may be associated with disease."

One part of this effort has focused on the creation of antibodies to treat patients with high LDL cholesterol. A silent killer, LDL cholesterol can contribute to the formation of plaque in the arteries that may lead to cardiovascular disease, heart attacks, and strokes. For many people with high LDL cholesterol, drugs called statins offer an effective treatment. For others, statins do not work well or come with unwelcome side effects. In those cases, a relatively new antibody-based treatment known as a PCSK9 inhibitor may be appropriate. See *Amgen Inc. v. Sanofi*, 872 F.3d 1367, 1371 (C.A. Fed. 2017).

. . .

Eventually, Amgen developed a PCSK9-inhibiting drug that it marketed under the name Repatha, and Sanofi produced one it labeled Praluent. Each drug employs a distinct antibody with its own unique amino acid sequence. In 2011, Amgen obtained a patent for the antibody employed in Repatha, and Sanofi received one covering the antibody used in Praluent. Each patent describes the relevant antibody by its amino acid sequence. Neither of these patents is at issue in this case.

Instead, our dispute focuses on two additional patents Amgen obtained in 2014 that relate back to the company's 2011 patent. See U. S. Patent No. 8,829,165 (Sept. 9, 2014); U. S. Patent No. 8,859,741 (Oct. 14, 2014). We refer to them as the '165 and '741 patents. In particular, this case revolves around claims 19 and 29 of the '165 patent and claim 7 of the '741 patent. See 987 F.3d 1080, 1082 (C.A. Fed. 2021). In these claims, Amgen did not seek protection for any particular antibody described by amino acid sequence. Instead, Amgen purported to claim for itself "the entire genus" of antibodies that (1) "bind to specific amino acid residues on PCSK9," and (2) "block PCSK9 from binding to [LDL receptors]." *Amgen*, 872 F.3d, at 1372.

As part of its submission to the patent office, Amgen identified the amino acid sequences of 26 antibodies that perform these two functions, and it depicted the three-dimensional structures of two of these 26 antibodies. 987 F.3d, at 1083. But beyond that, Amgen only offered scientists two methods to make other antibodies that perform the binding and blocking functions it described. The first method is what Amgen calls the "roadmap." At a high level, the roadmap directs scientists to: (1) generate a range of antibodies in the lab; (2) test those antibodies to determine whether any bind to PCSK9; (3) test those antibodies that bind to PCSK9 to determine whether any bind to the sweet spot as described in the claims; and (4) test those antibodies that bind to the sweet spot as described in the claims to determine whether any block PCSK9 from binding to LDL receptors. See *id.*, at 13–14. The second method is what Amgen calls "conservative substitution." *Id.*, at 14, 17. This technique requires scientists to: (1) start with an antibody known to perform the described functions; (2) replace select amino acids in the antibody with other amino acids known to have similar properties; and (3) test the resulting antibody to see if it also performs the described functions. *See id.*, at 14–15.

C

. . . While Amgen had identified the amino acid sequences of 26 antibodies that bind to PCSK9 and block it from binding to LDL receptors, Sanofi observed that Amgen's claims cover potentially millions more undisclosed antibodies that perform these same functions. And, Sanofi argued, neither of the two methods Amgen had outlined for generating additional antibodies with the same functions enable a person skilled in the art to do so reliably. Instead, Sanofi submitted, those methods require scientists to engage in little more than a trial-and-error process of discovery. *See id.*, at 1085.

[Two juries held that the claims were enabled]. The district court granted Sanofi judgment as a matter of law, concluding that the claims at issue "are not enabled." 2019 WL 4058927, *13 (D. Del., Aug. 28, 2019). The Federal Circuit affirmed. 987 F.3d, at 1088. . . .

II

The Constitution vests Congress with the power to "promote the Progress of Science and useful Arts, by securing for limited Times to Authors and Inventors the exclusive Right to their respective Writings and Discoveries." Art. I, §8, cl. 8. Right there in the text, one finds the outline of what this Court has called the patent "bargain." *Bonito Boats, Inc. v. Thunder Craft Boats, Inc.*, 489 U.S. 141, 150 (1989). In exchange for bringing "new designs and technologies into the public domain through disclosure," so they may benefit all, an inventor receives a limited term of "protection from competitive exploitation." *Id.*, at 151; *see also* THE FEDERALIST NO. 43, p. 272 (C. Rossiter ed. 1961) (J. Madison) (explaining that in such cases "[t]he public good fully coincides . . . with the claims of individuals").

Congress has exercised this authority from the start. The Patent Act of 1790 promised up to a 14-year monopoly to any applicant who "invented or discovered any useful art, manufacture, . . . or device, or any improvement therein not before known or used." Act of Apr. 10, 1790, §1, 1 Stat. 110. Reflecting the *quid-pro-quo* premise of patent law, the statute required the applicant to deposit with the Secretary of State a "specification ... so particular . . . as not only to distinguish the invention or discovery from other things before known and used, but also to enable a workman or other person skilled in the art or manufacture . . . to make, construct, or use the same." §2. The statute made clear that this disclosure would ensure "the public may have the full benefit [of the invention or discovery], after the expiration of the patent term.".

Even as Congress has revised the patent laws over time, it has left this "enablement" obligation largely intact. See 35 U.S.C. §§111, 112. Section 111 of the current Patent Act provides that a patent application "shall include . . . a specification as prescribed by section 112." §111(a)(2)(A). Section 112, in turn, requires a specification to include "a written description of the invention, and of the manner and process of making and using it, in such full, clear, concise, and exact terms as to enable any person skilled in the art ... to make and use the same." §112(a). So today, just as in 1790, the law secures for the public its benefit of the patent bargain by ensuring that, "upon the expiration of [the patent], the knowledge of the invention [i]nures to the people, who are thus enabled without restriction to practice it." *United States v. Dubilier Condenser Corp.*, 289 U.S. 178, 187 (1933); *see also Grant v. Raymond*, 6 Pet. 218, 247 (1832) (MARSHALL, C. J.) ("This is necessary in order to give the public, after the privilege shall expire, the advantage for which the privilege is allowed, and is the foundation of the power to issue a patent."); *Whittemore v. Cutter*, 29 F.Cas. 1120, 1122 (No. 17,600) (CC Mass. 1813) (STORY, J.) ("If therefore [the disclosure] be so obscure, loose, and imperfect, that this cannot be done, it is defrauding the public of all the consideration, upon which the monopoly is granted.").

This Court has addressed the enablement requirement on many prior occasions. *See, e.g., Wood v. Underhill*, 5 How. 1 (1846); *O'Reilly* v. *Morse*, 15 How. 62 (1854); *The Incandescent Lamp Patent*, 159 U.S. 465 (1895); *Minerals Separation, Ltd. v. Hyde*, 242 U.S. 261 (1916); *Holland Furniture Co. v. Perkins Glue Co.*, 277 U.S. 245 (1928). While the technologies in these older cases may seem a world away from the antibody treatments of today, the decisions are no less instructive for it.

Begin with *Morse*. While crossing the Atlantic Ocean in 1832 aboard a ship named *Sully*, Samuel Morse found himself in conversation with other passengers about "experiments and discoveries" around electromagnetism. 15 How. at 68. "In the course of this discussion, it occurred to [Morse] that, by means of electricity, signs representing figures, letters, or words, might be legibly written down at any distance." So clear was the idea in Morse's mind that, "[b]efore he landed in the United States, he had ... drawn out in his sketch book . . . the form of an instrument for an electro-magnetic telegraph." Immediately upon his arrival in New York, Morse showed his brothers his sketches. He spent the next few years refining his invention. The "great difficulty" he faced was that "the galvanic current, however strong in the beginning, became gradually weaker as it advanced on the wire[,] and was not strong enough to produce a mechanical effect, after a certain distance." By 1837, Morse had a solution: "combining two or more electric or galvanic circuits, with independent batteries for the purpose of overcoming the diminished force of electro-magnetism in long circuits." Morse demonstrated his telegraph the following year at the Franklin Institute in Philadelphia, and he displayed it soon after in Congress. He received a patent in 1840, which reissued in 1848.

The litigation that brought Morse before this Court concerned a telegraphic system that Henry O'Reilly had installed between Louisville and Nashville. Morse sued O'Reilly for infringement, alleging that O'Reilly's system was "identical with" Morse's own. O'Reilly mounted a number of defenses, including that Morse's patent was void because it lacked an adequate specification.

Morse's patent included eight claims, and this Court had no trouble upholding seven of them—those limited to the telegraphic structures and systems he had designed. But the Court paused on the eighth. That claim covered "the essence" of the invention, which Morse described as "the use of the motive power of the electric or galvanic current . . . however developed for marking or printing intelligible characters, signs, or letters, at any distances." Leaving no doubt about this claim's scope, Morse stated plainly: "'I do not propose to limit myself to the specific machinery or parts of machinery described in the foregoing specification and claims.'"

The Court held the eighth claim "too broad, and not warranted by law." The problem was that it covered *all* means of achieving telegraphic communication, yet Morse had not described how to make and use them all. *See id.*, at 113-17. "[I]f the eighth claim . . . can be maintained," the Court concluded, "there was no necessity for any specification, further than to say that he had discovered that, by using the motive power of electro-magnetism, he could print intelligible characters at any distance." 15 How. at 119. "[I]t will be admitted on all hands, that no patent could have issued on such a specification."

Consider, too, *Incandescent Lamp*. For much of the 19th century, gas lamps helped illuminate streets and supplemented candles inside homes, factories, offices, and theaters. But gas lighting had drawbacks. It took effort to ignite lamps each night and extinguish them each morning. Then there were the problems of soot and fumes. *See* R. STROSS, THE WIZARD OF MENLO PARK 84-85 (2007) (STROSS). By the 1870s, many had experimented with other forms of lighting, including incandescence and the arc light. 159 U.S., at 470. But these alternatives burned unreliably or with unbearable brightness. *See id.*, at 470-71. The latter problem in particular led one observer to lament this "new sort of urban star," which shines "horrible, unearthly, obnoxious" light. R. L. STEVENSON, A PLEA FOR GAS LAMPS, IN VIRGINIBUS PUERISQUE AND OTHER PAPERS 295 (1881).

Enter Thomas Edison. From his laboratory in Menlo Park, Edison and a team toiled to improve upon the prevailing method of incandescent lighting, which tended to employ carbon filaments. 159 U.S., at 471-73. The problem with carbon filaments was that they disintegrated rapidly. In a sense, "carbon contained in itself the elements of its own destruction." Seeking an alternative, Edison tinkered for a time with platinum, but it was expensive and difficult to bring to the point of incandescence without melting. STROSS 78, 82. Eventually, Edison dispatched men across the globe to collect specimens of bamboo. *Id.*, at 109-10. One sample from Japan worked brilliantly because "[its] fibres [ran] more nearly parallel than in other species of wood." Satisfied, Edison arranged to have a Japanese farmer supply all of the bamboo he would ever need. STROSS 110.

But there was a catch. William Sawyer and Albon Man had obtained a patent for an "'electric lamp'" with an "'incandescing conductor'" made of "'carbonized fibrous or textile material,'" which they claimed was an improvement over conductors made of "'mineral or gas carbon.'" 159 U.S., at 466, 468. Sawyer and Man's patent had not won them commercial success. They had designed a lamp with a conductor made of carbonized paper, but the lamp proved defective and quickly fell out of use. *See id.*, at 471-72. Still, their failure did not stop them from seeking to share in some of Edison's success. Sawyer and Man alleged that Edison's lamp infringed their patent because it "made use of a fibrous or textile material, covered by the patent." *Id.*, at 471. What was that offending material? Bamboo.

This Court sided with Edison. It held that Sawyer and Man's patent claimed much but enabled little. "Sawyer and Man supposed they had discovered in carbonized paper the best material for an incandescent conductor." *Id.*, at 472. But "[i]nstead of confining themselves to carbonized paper, as they might properly have done, and in fact did in their third claim, they made a broad claim for every fibrous and textile material." *Ibid.* Even that broad claim "might" have been permissible, the Court allowed, if Sawyer and Man had disclosed "a quality common" to fibrous and textile substances that made them "peculiarly" adapted to incandescent lighting. Had they done so, others would have known how to select among such materials to make an operable lamp. But the record showed that most fibrous and textile materials failed to work. Only through "painstaking experimentation" did Edison discover that bamboo "answered the required purpose." The Court summed up things this way: "[T]he fact that paper happens to belong to the fibrous kingdom did not invest [Sawyer and Man] with sovereignty over this entire kingdom."

The Court returned to these principles in *Holland Furniture*. There, the evidence indicated that animal glue has properties that have long made it excellent for wood veneering. *See* 277 U.S., at 247. Seeking a substitute, Perkins Glue Company had developed and patented a starch glue similar enough to animal glue that craftsmen could also use it for wood veneering. Yet Perkins's patent included a claim that went beyond the specific starch glue it manufactured. This claim covered all "starch glue which, [when] combined with about three parts or less by weight of water, will have substantially the same properties as animal glue." Perkins's specification instructed gluemakers to choose a "starch ingredient" with "such qualities" that it would yield a product "'as good as animal glue'" for wood veneering "when combined with three parts of water and with alkali."

The Court held this broad claim invalid for lack of enablement. The specification described the key input—the "starch ingredient"—in terms of its "use or function" rather than its "physical characteristics or chemical properties." And that left gluemakers in a bind. As the Court put it: "One attempting to use or avoid the use of Perkins' discovery as so claimed and described functionally could do so only after elaborate experimentation" with different starches. To be sure, the Court held, Perkins was entitled to its patent on the specific starch glue it had invented. The specification described that glue's "characteristic ingredient" with "particularity." But just as Morse could not claim all means of telegraphic communication, and Sawyer and Man could not claim all fibrous and textile materials for incandescence, Perkins could not claim all starch glues made from whatever starch happened to perform as well as animal glue. To hold otherwise, the Court said, "would extend the monopoly beyond the invention."

Our decisions in *Morse*, *Incandescent Lamp*, and *Holland Furniture* reinforce the simple statutory command. If a patent claims an entire class of processes, machines, manufactures, or compositions of matter, the patent's specification must enable a person skilled in the art to make and use the entire class. In other words, the specification must enable the full scope of the invention as defined by its claims. The more one claims, the more one must enable. *See* §112(a); *see also Continental Paper Bag Co. v. Eastern Paper Bag Co.*, 210 U.S. 405, 419 (1908) ("[T]he claims measure the invention.").

That is not to say a specification always must describe with particularity how to make and use every single embodiment within a claimed class. For instance, it may suffice to give an example (or a few examples) if the specification also discloses "some general quality . . . running through" the class that gives it "a peculiar fitness for the particular purpose." *Incandescent Lamp*, 159 U.S., at 475. In some cases, disclosing that general quality may reliably enable a person skilled in the art to make and use all of what is claimed, not merely a subset. *See id.*, at 475-76.[5]

Nor is a specification necessarily inadequate just because it leaves the skilled artist to engage in some measure of adaptation or testing. In *Wood*, a patent claimed a process for making bricks by mixing coal dust into clay. 5 How., at 4. The patent included "a general rule" about the proportion of dust and clay to use and offered two alternative proportions "where the clay has some peculiarity." The Court upheld the claim, recognizing that "some small difference in the proportions must occasionally be required" given the varieties of clay. Similarly, in *Minerals Separation*, the Court dismissed a challenge to a claimed process for separating metal from mineral ores. 242 U.S., at 270. The record showed that "preliminary tests" were required to adapt the process to any particular ore. Once more, the Court explained that "the certainty which the law requires in patents is not greater than is reasonable." And because the "composition of ores varies infinitely," it was "impossible to specify in a patent the precise treatment which would be most successful and economical in each case." *Id.*, at 271.[6]

Decisions such as *Wood* and *Minerals Separation* establish that a specification may call for a reasonable amount of experimentation to make and use a patented invention. What is reasonable in any case will depend on the nature of the invention and the underlying art. See *Minerals Separation*, 242 U.S., at 270-71; *see also Mowry v. Whitney*, 14 Wall. 620, 644 (1872) ("[T]he definiteness of a specification must vary with the nature of its subject. Addressed as it is to those skilled in the art, it may leave something to their skill in applying the invention."). But in allowing that much tolerance, courts cannot detract from the basic statutory requirement that a patent's specification describe the invention "in such full, clear, concise, and exact terms as to enable any person skilled in the art" to "make and use" the invention. §112(a). Judges may no more subtract from the requirements for obtaining a patent that Congress has

---

[5] *See also Béné v. Jeantet*, 129 U.S. 683, 684-86 (1889) (rejecting claim to method of shrinking coarse hair because the specification failed to give "one skilled in chemistry such an idea of the particular kinds and character of the chemicals, or combination of chemicals, with the relative proportions of each, as would enable him to use the invention without having to resort to experiments of his own to discover those ingredients"); *Corona Cord Tire Co. v. Dovan Chemical Corp.*, 276 U.S. 358, 385 (1928) (rejecting claims to process of treating rubber with "'a disubstituted guanidine' " because "between fifty and one hundred substances" fit that description and the specification did not disclose "any general quality common to disubstituted guanidines which makes them all effective").

[6] *See also, e.g., Ives v. Hamilton*, 92 U.S. 426, 429 (1876) (upholding claim "for an improvement in sawmills" based on "curved guides at the upper end of the saw," even though the specification did not "stat[e] the nature of the curve," because a "good mechanic acquainted with the construction of sawmills, and having the patent and diagram before him, would have no difficulty in adopting the improvement, and making suitable curves"); *Tilghman v. Proctor*, 102 U.S. 707, 732-33 (1881) (upholding claim for process of separating fats and oils even though the specification "suggests a trial . . . with different degrees of heat so as to ascertain that which is best for each particular kind of fat").

prescribed than they may add to them. *See Bilski v. Kappos*, 561 U.S. 593, 602-03, 612 (2010).

III

With these principles in mind, we return to claims 19 and 29 of the '165 patent and claim 7 of the '741 patent. In doing so, we do not doubt that Amgen's specification enables the 26 exemplary antibodies it identifies by their amino acid sequences. Even Sanofi concedes that description is enough to allow a person skilled in the art to make and use those embodiments. *See* Tr. of Oral Arg. 68. But the claims before us sweep much broader than those 26 antibodies. And we agree with the lower courts that Amgen has failed to enable all that it has claimed, even allowing for a reasonable degree of experimentation.

While the technology at the heart of this case is thoroughly modern, from the law's perspective Amgen's claims bear more than a passing resemblance to those this Court faced long ago in *Morse, Incandescent Lamp*, and *Holland Furniture*. Amgen seeks to monopolize an entire class of things defined by their function—every antibody that both binds to particular areas of the sweet spot of PCSK9 and blocks PCSK9 from binding to LDL receptors. The record reflects that this class of antibodies does not include just the 26 that Amgen has described by their amino acid sequences, but a "vast" number of additional antibodies that it has not. 987 F.3d, at 1085, 1088; see 2019 WL 4058927, *8 ("at least millions of candidates"); see also Tr. of Oral Arg. 52–53. Much as Morse sought to claim all telegraphic forms of communication, Sawyer and Man sought to claim all fibrous and textile materials for incandescence, and Perkins sought to claim all starch glues that work as well as animal glue for wood veneering, Amgen seeks to claim "sovereignty over [an] entire kingdom" of antibodies. *Incandescent Lamp*, 159 U.S., at 476.

That poses Amgen with a challenge. For if our cases teach anything, it is that the more a party claims, the broader the monopoly it demands, the more it must enable. That holds true whether the case involves telegraphs devised in the 19th century, glues invented in the 20th, or antibody treatments developed in the 21st. To be fair, Amgen does not dispute this much. It freely admits that it seeks to claim for itself an entire universe of antibodies. Still, it says, its broad claims are enabled because scientists can make and use every undisclosed but functional antibody if they simply follow the company's "roadmap" or its proposal for "conservative substitution."

We cannot agree. These two approaches amount to little more than two research assignments. The first merely describes step-by-step Amgen's own trial-and-error method for finding functional antibodies—calling on scientists to create a wide range of candidate antibodies and then screen each to see which happen to bind to PCSK9 in the right place and block it from binding to LDL receptors. The second isn't much different. It requires scientists to make substitutions to the amino acid sequences of antibodies known to work and then test the resulting antibodies to see if they do too— an uncertain prospect given the state of the art. Whether methods like a "roadmap" or "conservative substitution" might suffice to enable other claims in other patents— perhaps because, as this Court suggested in *Incandescent Lamp*, the inventor identifies a quality common to every functional embodiment—they do not here. They leave a scientist about where Sawyer and Man left Edison: forced to engage in "painstaking experimentation" to see what works. 159 U.S., at 475. That is not enablement. More nearly, it is "a hunting license." *Brenner v. Manson*, 383 U.S. 519, 536 (1966).

Think about it this way. "Imagine a combination lock with 100 tumblers, each of which can be set to 20 different positions." Brief for Intellectual Property Law Professors and Scholars as *Amici Curiae* 20. "Through trial and error, imagine that an inventor finds and discloses 26 different successful lock combinations." But imagine, too, "that the inventor tries to claim much more, namely all successful combinations," while instructing others "to randomly try a large set of combinations and then record the successful ones." Sure enough, that kind of "roadmap" would produce functional combinations. But it would not enable others to make and use functional combinations; it would instead leave them to "random trial-and-error discovery." Like many analogies, this one may oversimplify a bit, but it captures the gist of the problem.

Failing in its primary argument that it has enabled all of the antibodies it claims, Amgen tries a few alternative lines of attack. First, it suggests that the Federal Circuit erred by applying an enablement test unmoored from the statutory text. As Amgen sees it, that court conflated the question whether an invention is enabled with the question how long may it take a person skilled in the art to make every embodiment within a broad claim. We do not see it that way. While we agree with Amgen that enablement is not measured against the cumulative time and effort it takes to make every embodiment within a claim, we are not so sure the Federal Circuit thought otherwise. That court went out of its way to say that it "do[es] not hold that the effort required to exhaust a genus is dispositive." 987 F.3d, at 1088 (emphasis deleted). Instead, the court stressed, the problem it saw is the same problem we see: Amgen offers persons skilled in the art little more than advice to engage in "trial and error." . . . .

Finally, Amgen warns that an affirmance risks "destroy[ing] incentives for breakthrough inventions." But striking the proper balance between incentivizing inventors and ensuring the public receives the full benefit of their innovations is a policy judgment that belongs to Congress. Since 1790, Congress has included an enablement mandate as one feature among many designed to achieve the balance it wishes. Our only duty in this case lies in applying that mandate faithfully.

*

Section 112 of the Patent Act reflects Congress's judgment that if an inventor claims a lot, but enables only a little, the public does not receive its benefit of the bargain. For more than 150 years, this Court has enforced the statutory enablement requirement according to its terms. If the Court had not done so in *Incandescent Lamp*, it might have been writing decisions like *Holland Furniture* in the dark. Today's case may involve a new technology, but the legal principle is the same. The judgment is

Affirmed.

COMMENTS AND QUESTIONS

1. Genus claims have long been a feature of patent law. Upholding the claims to Alexander Graham Bell's patent on the telephone, the Supreme Court observed that "a patent for such a discovery is not to be confined to the mere means he improvised to prove the reality of his conception." *The Telephone Cases*, 126 U.S. 1, 539 (1888). "It is enough if [the patentee] describes his method with sufficient clearness and precision to enable those skilled in the matter to understand what the process is, and if he points out *some* practicable way of putting it into operation." *Id.* at 536 (emphasis added). Quoting from a leading patent law treatise, the Court explained in another opinion that "the principle of the invention is a unit, and invariably the modes of its embodiment in a concrete invention may be numerous and in appearance very different from each other." *Cont'l Paper Bag Co. v. E. Paper Bag Co.*, 210 U.S. 405, 419-20 (1908) (quoting 2 WILLIAM CALLYHAN ROBINSON, THE LAW OF PATENTS FOR USEFUL INVENTIONS §485 (1890)). As the Court said in *Tilghman v. Proctor*:

> Perhaps the process is susceptible of being applied in many modes and by the use of many forms of apparatus. The inventor is not bound to describe them all in order to secure to himself the exclusive right to the process, if he is really its inventor of discoverer. But he must describe some particular mode, or some apparatus, by which the process can be applied with at least some beneficial result, in order to show that it is capable of being exhibited and performed in actual experience.

102 U.S. 707, 728-29 (1880).

These cases recognize that genus claims are critical for meaningful patent protection. Without them, patentees face "the risk of an infringement being avoided" by a minor modification of the particular embodiments disclosed in the patent's specification.

Amgen required that patentees claiming broad genus claims enable the "full scope" of those claims. Is that likely to be possible for a genus that may encompass thousands or millions of examples? Several scholars have warned that genus claims are essentially impossible under the full scope standard, at least in the life sciences industries. *See, e.g.,* Dmitry Karshtedt, et al., *The Death of the Genus Claim*, 35 HARV. J. L. & TECH. 1 (2021). Should we be troubled by that? Perhaps that is just the cost of seeking broad claims. *MagSil Corp.*, 687 F.3d at 1381 ("[A] patentee chooses broad claim language at the peril of losing any claim that cannot be enabled across its full scope of coverage.").

Professor Jeffrey Lefstin argues that most patent claims today actually cover a potentially infinite set of potential objects, particularly ones not yet conceived of. Jeffrey Lefstin, *The Formal Structure of Patent Law and the Limits of Enablement,* 23 Berkeley Tech. L.J. 1141, 1168 (2008). Does that mean those claims all fail the enablement requirement? Logically the answer should be yes. But it seems more likely that courts will distinguish between claims like those in *Amgen* and *Holland Furniture* that are written in functional terms (that is, to cover anything that performs the desired function) and those that define a group by some other characteristic (like the structure of a chemical). That won't help patent claims to antibodies; as the court notes, they seem to have little relationship between structure and function. But it may mean that simpler terms like "fastener" or "chair" in better-understood technologies will be held enabled even though they could in theory encompass an unlimited number of not-yet-identified embodiments.

Justice Gorsuch reasoned that Amgen's "roadmap" was little different from "a combination lock with 100 tumblers, each of which can be set to 20 different positions. Through trial and error, imagine that an inventor finds and discloses 26 different successful lock combinations," but the inventor claims "all successful combinations." Do you think that this is an apt analogy? Does it move a field forward to simply report that there are at least some successful candidates out there? If the knowledge that "some within this set of possible candidates will work" is very valuable, and if the cost of working out which candidates work is not too high, perhaps there is an economic argument that the disclosure is enabling. On the other hand, if the initial finding does little to assist in discovery of other successful candidates—e.g., if each random trial is just as likely (or unlikely) to succeed after the initial disclosure, and if the initial disclosure does not lower the cost of testing the next random candidate—then perhaps the genus is not enabled.

2. *Person Having Ordinary Skill in the Art (PHOSITA) Standard.* As we saw in Section (B)(2) on nonobviousness, patent law employs a hypothetical person, like tort law's reasonable person, in evaluating patentability. As one court has noted:

> A patent specification is not addressed to judges or lawyers, but to those skilled in the art; it must be comprehensible to them, even though the unskilled may not be able to gather from it how to use the invention, and even if it is "all Greek" to the unskilled.

Gould v. Mossinghoff, 229 U.S.P.Q. 1 (D.D.C. 1985), *aff'd in part, vacated in part sub nom. Gould v. Quigg*, 822 F.2d 1074 (Fed. Cir. 1987).

3. *Undue Experimentation Standard.* How much would Sawyer and Man have to disclose to justify a patent on all vegetable and fibrous filaments in *Incandescent Lamp*? What if they had tested 100 filaments, and they had all worked about as well? The Federal Circuit in *In re Wands*, 858 F.2d 731 (Fed. Cir. 1988), established that enablement is tested by asking whether the person having ordinary skill in the art would be able to make and use all the species covered by the patent without "undue experimentation." The multi-factor test considers: (1) the quantity of experimentation necessary, (2) the amount of direction or guidance presented, (3) the presence or absence of working examples, (4) the nature of the invention, (5) the state of the prior art, (6) the relative skill of those in the art, (7) the predictability or unpredictability of the art, and (8) the breadth of the claims.

Sawyer and Man   **Edison**

Thus, if Sawyer and Man had tested multiple fibrous filaments and found that they generally worked, that might justify a claim to the genus, even though it turned out that some worked quite well and some did not work at all. The problem with their broad genus claim was two-fold: (1) they did not do that testing; and (2) if they had, it would not have shown that vegetable and fibrous material was a meaningful class of filaments with similar characteristics.

4. Of what relevance, if any, is it that Edison's research resulted in several patents of his own? Does the fact that inventor *A* received a patent suggest anything about whether *A*'s research results are enabled by the specification of a prior patent issued to *B*?

As a doctrinal matter, Edison's patents should be irrelevant to the validity of Sawyer and Man's. It is not only possible but common for *A* to invent something and for *B* to improve it. Think of the pencil, for example. The inventor of the pencil could patent that idea. A later inventor who comes up with the idea of attaching an eraser to the pencil would be entitled to their own patent on the pencil + eraser combination. Those patents are said to "block" each other; neither *A* nor *B* can make a pencil with an eraser without infringing the other's rights. On the economics of blocking patents, *see* Robert P. Merges, *Intellectual Property Rights and Bargaining Breakdown: The Case of Blocking Patents*, 62 TENN. L. REV. 75 (1994).

5. The *Amgen* Court devotes substantial attention to the Court's 1853 case involving Samuel F.B. Morse's invention of the telegraph. That patent included eight claims, the first seven of which—relating the particular machinery for propagating signals through electrical wires and Morse code—were not at issue. The Court's seminal enablement decision related to Morse's eighth claim:

I do not propose to limit myself to the specific machinery, or parts of machinery, described in the foregoing specifications and claims; the essence of my invention being the use of the motive power of the electric or galvanic current, which I call electro-magnetism, however developed, for making or printing intelligible characters, letters, or signs, at any distances, being a new application of that power, of which I claim to be the first inventor or discovered.'

Here is how the Court explained its rejection of the eighth claim:

It is impossible to misunderstand the extent of this claim. [Morse] claims the exclusive right to every improvement where the motive power is the electric or galvanic current, and the result is the marking or printing intelligible characters, signs, or letters at a distance.

If this claim can be maintained, it matters not by what process or machinery the result is accomplished. For aught that we now know, some future inventor, in the onward march of science, may discover a mode of writing or printing at a distance by means of the electric or galvanic current, without using any part of the process or combination set forth in the plaintiff's specification. His invention may be less complicated—less liable to get out of order—less expensive in construction, and in its operation. But yet if it is covered by this patent, the inventor could not use it, nor the public have the benefit of it, without the permission of this patentee.

Nor is this all; while he shuts the door against inventions of other persons, the patentee would be able to avail himself of new discoveries in the properties and powers of electro-magnetism which scientific men might bring to light. For he says he does not confine his claim to the machinery or parts of machinery which he specifies, but claims for himself a monopoly in its use, however developed, for the purpose of printing at a distance. New discoveries in physical science may enable him to combine it with new agents and new elements, and by that means attain the object in a manner superior to the present process and altogether different from it. And if he can secure the exclusive use by his present patent, he may vary it with every new discovery and development of the science, and need place no description of the new manner, process, or machinery upon the records of the patent office. And when his patent expires, the public must apply to him to learn what it is. In fine, he claims an exclusive right to use a manner and process which he has not described and indeed had not invented, and therefore could not describe when he obtained his patent. The court is of opinion that the claim is too broad, and not warranted by law.

O'Reilly v. Morse, 56 U.S. 62, 112-13 (1853).

The Court in *Morse* placed particular emphasis on *Neilson v. Harford*, a prominent English court decision involving another industrial revolution breakthrough: a method for improving the functioning of hot blast furnaces by heating air before injecting it into the receptacle. Like Morse, Neilson claimed this breakthrough in broad terms. But unlike in *Morse*, the Court of the Exchequer upheld the broad claim.

Neilson's Hot Blast Furnace (1829)

What distinguishes Morse's broad eighth claim, which the Court invalidated, from Neilson's broad claim, which the Court of Exchequer upheld?

Morse quotes Baron Parke stating that

It is very difficult to distinguish [Neilson's patent] from the specification of a patent for a principle, and this at first created in the minds of the court much difficulty, but after full consideration we think that the plaintiff does not merely claim a principle, but a machine embodying a principle, and a very valuable one. *We think the case must be considered as if, the principle being well known,* the plaintiff had first invented a mode of applying it by a mechanical apparatus to furnaces, and his invention then consists in this: by interposing a receptacle for heated air between the blowing apparatus and the furnace.

Neilson v. Harford, 1 Web. P. C. 295, 371 (1841) (emphasis added), quoted in *O'Reilly v. Morse,* 56 U.S. at 115. *Morse* then explains:

Neilson, in his specification, described his invention as one for the improved application of air to produce heat in fires, forges, and furnaces where a blowing apparatus is required. And it was to be applied as follows: the blast or current of air produced by the blowing apparatus was to be passed from it into an air vessel or receptacle made sufficiently strong to endure the blast, and through or from that vessel or receptacle by means of a tube, pipe, or aperture into the fire, the receptacle be kept artificially heated to a considerable temperature by heat externally applied. He then described in rather general terms the manner in which the receptacle might be constructed and heated and the air conducted through it to the fire, stating that the form of the receptacle was not material nor the manner of applying heat to it. In the action above-mentioned for the infringement of this patent, the defendant, among other defenses, insisted that the machinery for heating the air and throwing it hot into the furnace was not sufficiently described in the specification, and the patent void on that account—and also, that a patent for throwing hot air into the furnace instead of cold, and thereby increasing the intensity of the heat, was a patent for a principle, and that a principle was not patentable.

Undoubtedly, the principle that hot air will promote the ignition of fuel better than cold, was embodied in this machine. But the patent was not supported because this principle was embodied in it. He would have been equally entitled to a patent, if he had invented an improvement in the mechanical arrangements of the blowing apparatus, or in the furnace, while a cold current of air was still used. But his patent was supported, because he had invented a mechanical apparatus, by which a current of hot air, instead of cold, could be thrown in. And this new method was protected by his patent. The interposition of a heated receptacle, in any form, was the novelty he invented.

We do not perceive how the claim in the case before us, can derive any countenance from this decision. If the Court of Exchequer had said that Neilson's patent was for the discovery, that hot air would promote ignition better than cold, and that he had an exclusive right to use it for that purpose, there might, perhaps, have been some reason to rely upon it. But the court emphatically denied this right to such a patent. And his claim, as the patent was construed and supported by the court, is altogether unlike that of the patentee before us.

For Neilson discovered, that by interposing a heated receptacle between the blower and the furnace, and conducting the current of air through it, the heat in the furnace was increased. And this effect was always produced, whatever might be the form of the receptacle, or the mechanical contrivances for heating it, or for passing the current of air through it, and into the furnace.

But Professor Morse has not discovered, that the electric or galvanic current will always print at a distance, no matter what may be the form of the machinery or mechanical contrivances through which it passes. You may use electro-magnetism as a motive power, and yet not produce the described effect, that is, print at a distance intelligible marks or signs. To produce that effect, it must be combined with, and passed through, and operate upon, certain complicated and delicate machinery, adjusted and arranged upon philosophical principles, and prepared by the highest mechanical skill. And it is the high praise of Professor Morse, that he has been able, by a new combination of known powers, of which electro-magnetism is one, to discover a method by which intelligible marks or signs may be printed at a distance. And for the method or process thus discovered, he is entitled to a patent. But he has not discovered that the electro-magnetic current, used as motive power, in any other method, and with any other combination, will do as well.

Id. at 114-17.

Professor Jeffrey Lefstin explains why would the English Court treat Neilson's discovery as "being well known":

Considering the principle to have "an anterior existence"—being well known— was a way to rationalize dedicating the patentee's underlying discovery to the public. Baron Alderson was attempting to reconcile the legal doctrine that the abstract principle behind the invention was not patentable with the recognition that the discovery of the principle may have been the real 'invention' by the patentee. This is not a paradox for modern patent doctrine founded on the peripheral claim. The inventor's creation and the scope of patent protection are ontologically quite distinct. But in a time where 'invention' and 'scope of protection' were essentially synonymous, it was necessary to explain how an inventor who had discovered a new principle was nonetheless not entitled to claim it. Treating the principle as having an anterior existence was a way to assess whether the patentee was claiming a principle in the abstract or a mode of practically applying that principle.

Jeffrey A. Lefstin, *Inventive Application: A History*, 67 FLA. L. REV. 565, 583 (2015). As we will see in the section on patentable subject matter (Section B(5)), patent law has long excluded patents on laws of nature in the abstract. *Neilson* and *Morse* figure prominently in that jurisprudence.

Why was Morse's specification inadequate to support his eighth claim? What if he had also taught the use of electromagnetism to communicate sounds (as telephones do)? Would the claim still be too broad? What more would Morse have had to show to justify that claim? Is it even possible? And what of the fact that many uses of electromagnetism would not succeed in communicating at a distance? Morse had only developed a method of opening and closing an electrical circuit and amplifying the signal. Or is there nonetheless a sense in which the claim is too broad and abstract regardless of how many examples Morse taught? Do we really want someone—even a pioneering inventor like Morse—to own the concept of communication at a distance?

6. The *Amgen* Court treats *Morse* as an enablement case. But the Court has also treated *Morse* as involving unpatentable "abstract ideas" under the doctrine of patentable subject matter. At the time *Morse* was decided, the same statutory provision created both requirements. One way to think about the question is to ask whether the problem was just that Morse didn't teach enough to enable people to practice his invention or whether the problem is that the claim is too broad no matter what he taught. If the problem is the former, the issue is enablement, and presumably Morse could have given enough information to justify such a claim. If the issue is the latter, that may be better thought of as a limit on patentable subject matter.

PROBLEM III-8

Suppose William Schrafft received a patent claiming "all food-based flavors" of jelly beans. In his specification, he discloses his method for manufacturing lemon and raspberry varieties. Several years later, during the patent's life, the wizard Bertie Bott (from the Harry Potter series) was experimenting with confections when a pair of dirty socks fell into his concoction. Recognizing the sales potential of sweets that present a "risk with every mouthful," he introduces "Bertie Bott's Every Flavour Beans," which includes "Bogey," "Dirt," "Dirty Sock," "Earthworm," "Earwax," "Envelope Glue," "Phlegm," "Soap," and "Vomit," as well as a broad range of more appetizing flavors— including cherry, lemon, and kale (well, maybe not so appetizing). Can Bertie Bott successfully challenge or circumvent Schrafft's claim? How would you structure the analysis?

ii. *The Written Description Requirement*

In addition to the enablement requirement, a series of cases developed the notion that §112(a) added a "written description" requirement. Originally seen as a doctrine that applied only when claims were amended during prosecution, it has been expanded to form an integral component of the law of patent disclosure. The basic standard is stated clearly enough in the cases: as of the application filing date, the applicant must show the inventor was "in possession" of the invention as later claimed. Courts compare the original disclosure with the final claims of an issued patent and ask whether the applicant signified that the specific features and embodiments later claimed were in fact important aspects of the invention. As it has evolved, the doctrine has become a way to prevent applicants from claiming subject matter they were not themselves yet aware of, even if skilled artisans could have gleaned it from the patent specification.

The written description doctrine is more restrictive than the enablement requirement. That is, claims that meet the enablement test do not necessarily meet the written description test. *See, e.g., Amgen Inc. v. Hoechst Marion Roussel, Inc.*, 314 F.3d 1313, 1334 (Fed. Cir. 2003) ("The enablement requirement is often more indulgent than the written description requirement. The specification need not explicitly teach those in the art to make and use the invention; the requirement is satisfied if, given what they already know, the specification teaches those in the art enough that they can make and use the invention without 'undue experimentation.'"). For example, a patent's disclosure may teach about a certain group of embodiments sufficiently that they can be made without "undue experimentation" under *The Incandescent Lamp Patent*, and yet not single out a specific feature that later appears in a claim, thereby failing the written description requirement.

In recent years, courts have also used written description to test for claim overbreadth in a manner quite reminiscent of the classic enablement test. *See* Dennis Crouch, *An Empirical Study of the Role of the Written Description Requirement in Patent Examination*, 104 NW. U. L. REV. 1665, 1667-68 (2010) (citing studies showing that most written description cases could also be decided on enablement grounds, and finding that in patent appeals at the PTO, written description was almost never used as a ground of invalidity).

There are two classes of cases, however, where written description does additional work beyond enablement: (1) Opportunistic Claiming—where the patentee has filed an enabling continuation claim after seeing the competition's product; and (2) Gun-Jumping—where the patentee has filed an enabling patent claim before they have sufficient support.

The Gentry Gallery, Inc. v. The Berkline Corp.
United States Court of Appeals for the Federal Circuit
134 F.3d 1473 (Fed. Cir. 1998)

LOURIE, CIRCUIT JUDGE.

The Gentry Gallery appeals from the judgment of the United States District Court for the District of Massachusetts holding that the Berkline Corporation does not infringe U.S. Patent 5,064,244, and declining to award attorney fees for Gentry's defense to Berkline's assertion that the patent was unenforceable. . . . Berkline cross-appeals from the decision that the patent was not shown to be invalid. . . . [B]ecause the court clearly erred in finding that the written description portion of the specification supported certain of the broader claims asserted by Gentry, we reverse the decision that those claims are not invalid under 35 U.S.C. §112, ¶1 (1994).

Background

Gentry owns the '244 patent, which is directed to a unit of a sectional sofa in which two independent reclining seats ("recliners") face in the same direction. Sectional sofas are typically organized in an L-shape with "arms" at the exposed ends of the linear sections. According to the patent specification, because recliners usually have had adjustment controls on their arms, sectional sofas were able to contain two recliners only if they were located at the exposed ends of the linear sections. Due to the typical L-shaped configuration of sectional sofas, the recliners therefore faced in different directions. *See* '244 patent; col. 1, ll. 15–19. Such an arrangement was "not usually comfortable when the occupants are watching television because one or both occupants must turn their heads to watch the same [television] set. Furthermore, the separation of the two reclining seats at opposite ends of a sectional sofa is not comfortable or conducive to intimate conversation." *Id.* at col. 1, ll. 19–25.

The invention of the patent solved this supposed dilemma by, *inter alia,* placing a "console" between two recliners which face in the same direction. This console "accommodates the controls for both reclining seats," thus eliminating the need to position each recliner at an exposed end of a linear section. *Id.* at col. 1, ll. 36–37. Accordingly, both recliners can then be located on the same linear section allowing two people to recline while watching television and facing in the same direction. Claim 1, which is the broadest claim of the patent, reads in relevant part:

A sectional sofa comprising:

a pair of reclining seats disposed in parallel relationship with one another in a double reclining seat sectional sofa section being without an arm at one end . . . ,

each of said reclining seats having a backrest and seat cushions and movable between upright and reclined positions . . . ,

a fixed console disposed in the double reclining seat sofa section between the pair of reclining seats and with the console and reclining seats together comprising a unitary structure, said console including an armrest portion for each of the reclining seats; said arm rests remaining fixed when the reclining seats move from one to another of their positions, and

a pair of control means, one for each reclining seat, *mounted on the double reclining seat sofa section. . . .*

Id. at col. 4, line 68 to col. 5, ll. 1–27 (emphasis added to most relevant claim language). Claims 9, 10, 12–15, and 19–21 are directed to a sectional sofa in which the control means are specifically located on the console.

Patent drawing for the Gentry '244 patent.

In 1991, Gentry filed suit . . . alleging that Berkline infringed the patent by manufacturing and selling sectional sofas having two recliners facing in the same direction. In the allegedly infringing sofas, the recliners were separated by a seat which has a back cushion that may be pivoted down onto the seat, so that the seat back may serve as a tabletop between the recliners. . . . The district court granted Berkline's motion for summary judgment of non-infringement, but denied its motions for summary judgment of invalidity and unenforceability.

. . .

Discussion

. . .

B. Invalidity

. . .

Berkline . . . argues that claims 1–8, 11, and 16–18 are invalid because they are directed to sectional sofas in which the location of the recliner controls is not limited to the console. According to Berkline, because the patent only describes sofas having controls on the console and an object of the invention is to provide a sectional sofa "with a console . . . that accommodates the controls for both the reclining seats," '244 patent, col. 1, ll. 35–37, the claimed sofas are not described within the meaning of §112, ¶1. Berkline also relies on Sproule's testimony that "locating the controls on the console is definitely the way we solved it [the problem of building sectional sofa with parallel recliners] on the original group [of sofas]." Gentry responds that the disclosure represents only Sproule's preferred embodiment, in which the controls are on the console, and therefore supports claims directed to a sofa in which the controls may be located elsewhere. Gentry relies on *Ethicon Endo-Surgery, Inc. v. United States Surgical Corp.*, 93 F.3d 1572, 1582 n.7 (Fed. Cir. 1993), and *In re Rasmussen*, 650 F.2d 1212, 1214 (CCPA 1981), for the proposition that an applicant need not describe more than one embodiment of a broad claim to adequately support that claim.

We agree with Berkline that the patent's disclosure does not support claims in which the location of the recliner controls is other than on the console. Whether a specification complies with the written description requirement of §112, ¶1, is a question of fact, which we review for clear error on appeal from a bench trial. *See Vas-Cath Inc. v. Mahurkar*, 935 F.2d 1555, 1563 (Fed. Cir. 1991). To fulfill the written description requirement, the patent specification "must clearly allow persons of ordinary skill in the art to recognize that [the inventor] invented what is claimed." *In re Gosteli*, 872 F.2d 1008, 1012 (Fed. Cir. 1989). An applicant complies with the written description requirement "by describing *the invention,* with all its claimed limitations." *Lockwood v. American Airlines, Inc.*, 107 F.3d 1565, 1572 (Fed. Cir. 1997).

It is a truism that a claim need not be limited to a preferred embodiment. However, in a given case, the scope of the right to exclude may be limited by a narrow disclosure. For example, as we have recently held, a disclosure of a television set with a keypad, connected to a central computer with a video disk player did not support claims directed to "an individual terminal containing a video disk player." *See id.* (stating that claims directed to a "distinct invention from that disclosed in the specification" do not satisfy the written description requirement); *see also Regents of the Univ. of Cal. v. Eli Lilly & Co.*, 119 F.3d 1559, 1568 (Fed. Cir. 1997) (stating that the case law does "not compel the conclusion that a description of a species always constitutes a description of a genus of which it is a part").

In this case, the original disclosure clearly identifies the console as the only possible location for the controls. It provides for only the most minor variation in the location of the controls, noting that the control "may be mounted on top or side surfaces of the console rather than on the front wall . . . without departing from this invention." '244 patent, col. 2, line 68 to col. 3, line 3. No similar variation beyond the console is even suggested. Additionally, the only discernible purpose for the console is to house the controls. As the disclosure states, identifying the only purpose relevant to the console, "[a]nother object of the present invention is to provide . . . a console positioned between [the reclining seats] that accommodates the controls for both of the reclining seats." *Id.* at col. 1, ll. 33–37. Thus, locating the controls anywhere but on the console is outside the stated purpose of the invention. Moreover, consistent with this disclosure, Sproule's broadest original claim was directed to a sofa comprising, *inter alia,* "control means located upon the center console to enable each of the pair of reclining seats to move separately between the reclined and upright positions." Finally, although not dispositive, because one can add claims to a pending application directed to adequately described subject matter, Sproule admitted at trial that he did not consider placing the controls outside the console until he became aware that some of Gentry's competitors were so locating the recliner controls. Accordingly, when viewed in its entirety, the disclosure is limited to sofas in which the recliner control is located on the console.

Gentry's reliance on *Ethicon* is misplaced. It is true, as Gentry observes, that we noted that "an applicant . . . is generally allowed claims, when the art permits, which cover more than the specific embodiment shown." *Ethicon,* 93 F.3d at 1582 n.7 (quoting *In re Vickers*, 141 F.2d 522, 525 (CCPA 1944)). However, we were also careful to point out in that opinion that the applicant "was free to draft claim[s] broadly (within the limits imposed by the prior art) to exclude the lockout precise location as a limitation of the claimed invention" only because he "did not consider the precise location of the lockout to be an element of his invention." *Id.* Here, as indicated above, it is clear that Sproule considered the location of the recliner controls on the console to be an essential element of his invention. Accordingly, his original disclosure serves to limit the permissible breadth of his later-drafted claims.

Similarly, *In re Rasmussen* does not support Gentry's position. In that case, our predecessor court restated the uncontroversial proposition that "a claim may be broader than the specific embodiment disclosed in a specification." 650 F.2d at 1215. However, the court also made clear that "[a]n applicant is entitled to claims as broad as the prior art *and his disclosure* will allow." *Id.* at 1214 (emphasis added). The claims at issue in *Rasmussen,* which were limited to the generic step of "adheringly applying" one layer to an adjacent layer, satisfied the written description requirement only because "one skilled in the art who read [the] specification would understand that it is unimportant how the layers are adhered, so long as they are adhered." Here, on the contrary, one skilled in the art would clearly understand that it was not only important, but essential to Sproule's invention, for the controls to be on the console.

In sum, the cases on which Gentry relies do not stand for the proposition that an applicant can broaden his claims to the extent that they are effectively bounded only by the prior art. Rather, they make clear that claims may be no broader than the supporting disclosure, and therefore that a narrow disclosure will limit claim breadth. Here, Sproule's disclosure unambiguously limited the location of the controls to the console. Accordingly, the district court clearly erred in finding that he was entitled to claims in which the recliner controls are not located on the console. We therefore reverse the judgment that claims 1–8, 11, and 16–18, were not shown to be invalid.

COMMENTS AND QUESTIONS

1. Do you see why *Gentry Gallery* is an opportunistic claiming case? What would have happened if the patentee had filed its broader amended claim in the first place, before it ever saw the defendant's product?

2. *Critique of the Written Description Doctrine.* Does it make sense to have both an enablement requirement and a written description requirement? If the inventor must

teach one of ordinary skill in the art how to make and use the invention, why require them to write down the exact invention as well? *Cf. Moba v. Diamond Automation, Inc.,* 325 F.3d 1306, 1323 (Fed. Cir. 2003) (Rader, J., dissenting) ("Under Federal Circuit case law, [the plaintiff in this case] asked the jury to decide that the patent's disclosure can enable a skilled artisan to make and practice the entire invention, but still not inform that same artisan that the inventor was in possession of the invention. Perplexing."); *see* Harris A. Pitlick, *The Mutation on the Description Requirement Gene,* 80 J. PAT. & TRADEMARK OFF. SOC'Y 209, 222 (1998) (written description cases are "an unmitigated disaster"); Laurence H. Pretty, *The Recline and Fall of Mechanical Genus Claim Scope Under "Written Description" in the Sofa Case,* 80 J. PAT. & TRADEMARK OFF. SOC'Y 469 (1998). Can enablement do the work written description currently does? *See* Robert P. Merges, *Software and Patent Scope: A Report from the Middle Innings,* 85 TEX. L. REV. 1627 (2007) (describing *Gentry Gallery* as an example of "misappropriation by claim amendment," and suggesting that it could have been decided on enablement, not written description, grounds).

3. *Defense of the Written Description Doctrine.* The separate requirement of adequate written description has been defended on the ground that enablement doctrine is incapable of defining meaningful limits to claim scope. *See* Jeffrey A. Lefstin, *The Formal Structure of Patent Law and the Limits of Enablement,* 23 BERKELEY TECH. L.J. 1141 (2008). Professor Lefstin argues that almost every claim includes in theory an infinite number of embodiments, so that no specification actually teaches how to make all or substantially all claimed embodiments. Written description steps in at this point; its requirement that embodiments be actually described resolves the logical deficiencies of enablement doctrine. Written description, properly understood, is a doctrine of *definition.* One might respond that it is the rigid logic of contemporary enablement doctrine that creates this need, and that an alternative to written description is a relaxing of these doctrinal rigidities—a fix from "within" enablement, which would dispense with the need for a separate doctrine. But for Professor Lefstin, the problem is inherent in the effort to draft a claim to cover a universe of actual and potential embodiments.

4. *Biotechnology Claims and Gun-Jumping.* The application of the written description requirement to biotechnology claims has been a particularly controversial issue. A number of cases beginning in the late 1990s required inventors to disclose specific gene sequences to claim them, even when functional properties of a gene (such as the protein it codes for) were already known. *See Regents of the University of California v. Eli Lilly & Co.,* 119 F.3d 1559 (Fed. Cir. 1997) (claims covering gene sequence for human insulin invalidated under written description requirement, where specification disclosed only sequence of rat insulin); Janice M. Mueller, *The Evolving Application of the Written Description Requirement to Biotechnological Inventions,* 13 BERKELEY TECH. L.J. 615 (1998). If *Gentry Gallery* and its ilk were about late claiming —trying to change the patent to cover things the inventor had not in fact thought of— the biotechnology cases are about "gun-jumping" —leaving the gate before the starter has fired the pistol. The patent race motivates inventors to lay claim to an invention at the earliest possible moment, and sometimes before it is the inventor's grasp. As we

have seen, this same concern arises with regard to the utility requirement, discussed in Chapter III(B)(5).

5. *The Separate Written Description Requirement.* In *Ariad Pharmaceuticals, Inc. v. Eli Lilly & Co.*, 598 F.3d 1336 (Fed. Cir. 2010) (en banc), the Federal Circuit established unequivocally that the written description requirement of §112(a) is separate from enablement. The court based its analysis on a close but controversial textual reading analysis of §112(a), focusing on punctuation and the placement of "and" connectors, as well as precedent, *see Schriber-Schroth Co. v. Cleveland Trust Co.*, 305 U.S. 47, 56–57 (1938); *Vas-Cath Inc. v. Mahurkar*, 935 F.2d 1555, 1562–63 (Fed Cir. 1991).

Ariad clarifies application of the doctrine. The specification must clearly demonstrate to a PHOSITA that the inventor possessed what is claimed as of the filing date. It is a question of fact that depends on the context: nature and scope of the claims; complexity and predictability of relevant technology; extent and content of the prior art; maturity of the science or technology. The requirement has particular relevance to genus claims so as to ensure that the scope is commensurate with the invention. Notably, the Federal Circuit denied that "possession" itself was the touchstone for written description, though it did not articulate an alternative formulation.

The court's application of the test to a breakthrough biotechnology discovery emphasized the "gun-jumping" analysis. The invention at issue was made in a new and unpredictable field. And although Ariad had hypothesized three classes of molecules potentially capable of achieving its broad claim of reducing NF-κB (nuclear factor kappa-light-chain-enhancer of activated B cells) activity, the disclosure was more in the nature of a research plan: Ariad had not actually produced any of those molecules at the time it filed its patent application. Notwithstanding that Ariad's conjectures were ultimately borne out, the court ruled that Ariad was not adequately in possession of the necessary knowledge at the time that they filed their application. A key figure in the file which established the effects was not disclosed until two years after the application date. Ariad sought to salvage the patent by arguing that a PHOSITA could have achieved the result based on the original specification through experimentation. The court concluded, however, that "[i]n the context of this invention, a vague functional description and invitation for further research does not constitute written description of a specific inhibitor [molecule]."

iii.   Best Mode

The best mode requirement was established as a safeguard against incomplete disclosure of the most effective ways of practicing the invention. The requirement does not permit inventors to hold back their preferred method or embodiment from their disclosure. *In re Nelson*, 280 F.2d 172 (CCPA 1960).

The AIA substantially curtailed the significance of the best mode requirement by eliminating failure to disclose best mode as a basis for invalidating a patent claim. Nonetheless, the best mode requirement remains theoretically applicable in patent examination. *See* MANUAL OF PATENT EXAMINING PROCEDURE (MPEP) §2165. It is difficult, however, for an examiner to police this requirement.

PROBLEM

Problem III-9. Slice-O-Rama is a company that makes food preparation items, including cheese slicers. It owns a U.S. patent covering a cheese slicer with a novel twist: The cutting element is a wire, which can be stretched between an end point and a handle. The slicer is well-received by the public and is even the subject of a national design award. One element in the claim calls for "a cutting wire" stretched between a handle and a fixed point on the base of the cutting element arm.

Cheese Slicer Patent Drawing

OmniCorp is a large conglomerate with numerous divisions in various industries. One division, BigChem, Inc., is in the business of developing and manufacturing plastics. In the wake of research on new plastics, BigChem has come up with a plastic that is capable of holding a sharp cutting edge. Deemed "sharpylene," it can be manufactured in a variety of thicknesses, including a very thin version that looks like a wire or piece of string. As part of an internal initiative to encourage various divisions of OmniCorp to work more closely, Fran Fromage, product manager for the food processor and blender product lines in OmniCorp's FoodMulch division, comes across a sample of the BigChem plastic. Being familiar with the popularity of the Slice-O-Rama cheese slicer, she hits on the idea of substituting BigChem's new plastic in place of the metal wire. She believes that this cheese slicer would be an important addition to the FoodMulch product line. She is aware of the Slice-O-Rama patent, but as she puts it, "how can that patent stop us from selling blades made from plastic that *we invented*?! Those folks over at Slice-O-Rama have never even heard of sharpylene!"

You are a member of the patent department at OmniCorp. Assuming that the FoodMulch cheese slicer will meet all limitations other than the "cutting wire" element in the Slice-O-Rama patent, how would you advise Ms. Fromage?

5. Patentable Subject Matter

Section 101 protects "any" "process, machine, manufacture, or composition of matter" or "improvement thereof . . . subject to the conditions and requirements of this title." Essentially the same language has been part of U.S. patent law since 1790. Although the Patent Act has not expressly excluded any subject matter for much of U.S. history,[7] courts have long recognized that there are limits on the types of inventions that are eligible for patenting. These limits emerged during the early to mid-nineteenth century as Anglo-American common law-trained jurists fleshed out the relatively terse requirements for patent eligibility.

Thus, we find the contours of these doctrines not in the text of the Patent Act but in two centuries of jurisprudence that has ebbed and flowed with technological advances, perspectives on scientific discovery, and concerns about whether the patent system encourages or stifles new inventions. Patent eligibility doctrines began to lose salience in the early 1980s as the Federal Circuit substantially liberalized the scope of patentable subject matter. The Supreme Court was silent on patentable subject matter from 1981 until 2010. Since then, the Court has issued four opinions that have redrawn the boundaries of patent eligible subject matter and reinvigorated litigation in the area. *See Bilski v. Kappos*, 561 U.S. 593 (2010); *Mayo Collaborative Servs. v. Prometheus Labs., Inc.*, 566 U.S. 66 (2012); *Ass'n for Molecular Pathology v. Myriad Genetics, Inc.*, 569 U.S. 576 (2013); *Alice Corp. v. CLS Bank Int'l*, 134 S.Ct. 2347 (2014). Most patents in force today issued when the subject matter eligible for patent protection was broader. Consequently, the number of invalidations based on §101 has grown substantially since 2010.

Navigating the boundaries of patentable subject matter requires careful study of the Supreme Court's recent decisions as well as the history that led to these cases.

i. The Evolution of Patentable Subject Matter Limitations

Like the modern Patent Act, the nation's first patent statutes authorized granting of patents for a broad range of subject matter—"any new and useful art, machine, manufacture, or composition of matter"—without express limitations. Courts came to recognize that patentability of broad scientific principles and abstract claims created the need for patent eligibility and scope limitations—what we today consider §112 concerns. These concepts were intertwined in the early jurisprudence and continue to overlap today.

a. Early Development of Patent Eligibility Limitations

---

[7] The AIA, for the first time, expressly excludes specific subject matter categories, namely patents on tax strategies and human organisms. *See* Pub. L. 112–29, §§14, 33, 125 Stat. 284 (2011).

In the years following the nation's founding, English cases greatly influenced American jurisprudence. Intellectual property law followed English statutes and traditions particularly closely.

With the industrial revolution picking up steam (so to speak), courts on both sides of the Atlantic struggled to delineate claims for groundbreaking inventions, such as the steam engine, sewing machine, telegraph, and telephone. Scientific discoveries in metallurgy, chemistry, and electricity fueled the industrial revolution. Patenting of the hot blast process, which historians view as "the most important single innovation in the industry in the age of iron," would prove especially significant to patent eligibility doctrine. *See* ALAN BIRCH, THE ECONOMIC HISTORY OF THE BRITISH IRON AND STEEL INDUSTRY 1784–1879, 181 (1968).

Scottish inventor James Beaumont Neilson challenged the conventional wisdom that hot blast furnaces worked best if they were fed cold air. Instead, Neilson preheated the air entering a furnace which substantially reduced the fuel required and enabled the use of raw coal and lower quality ores. Neilson's patent provided few details. The specification declared broadly that the composition of the air vessel, the manner of applying heat, and "[t]he form or shape of the receptacle" are immaterial to the effect.

Neilson sued numerous ironmakers for patent infringement. The litigation led to the decision in the English Court of the Exchequer, *Neilson v. Harford* (1841), that still reverberates in U.S. patent jurisprudence today. The patent was attacked on the ground that a patent for injecting hot air into the furnace, instead of cold, and thereby increasing the intensity of the heat, was a patent for a principle, and that an abstract (unapplied) principle was not patentable. In upholding the patent, the court reasoned that since the principle worked regardless of the dimensions of the receptacle in which the air was preheated, Neilson's invention did not claim the principle itself but an application of the principle, if a broad one, and thus was patent-eligible.

U.S. courts followed the English approach. They barred protection for a mere "principle," "motive" force, or "new power" in the abstract, but allowed patents on applications of newly discovered laws of nature. The Supreme Court explained in *Le Roy v. Tatham*, where a patent claimed both improved machinery for manufacturing lead pipe and a new property (the manufacture of wrought pipe from solid lead under heat and pressure), that

> [a] principle, in the abstract, is a fundamental truth; an original cause; a motive; these cannot be patented, as no one can claim in either of them an exclusive right. Through the agency of machinery a new steam power may be said to have been generated. But no one can appropriate this power exclusively to himself, under the patent laws. The same may be said of electricity, and of any other power in nature, which is alike open to all, and may be applied to useful purposes by the use of machinery.
>
> In all such cases, the processes used to extract, modify, and concentrate natural agencies, constitute the invention. The elements of the power exist; the invention is not in discovering them, but in *applying* them to useful objects. . . .

55 U.S. (14 How.) 156, 175 (1853) (emphasis added).

As we saw earlier, the Supreme Court addressed *Neilson* again the following year in *O'Reilly v. Morse*, 56 U.S. (15 How.) 62 (1853). While endorsing the requirement that patents must apply a law of nature, the Court nonetheless distinguished Neilson's claim from Morse's final claim. Whereas the effect that Neilson claimed (improving the functioning of a hot blast furnace) produced the desired effect for "whatever might be the form of the receptacle, or the mechanical contrivances for heating it, or for passing the current of air through it, and into the furnace," Morse had "not discovered, that the electric or galvanic current will always print at a distance, no matter what may be the form of the machinery or mechanical contrivances through which it passes." *Id.* at 116–17.

By the end of the nineteenth century, American patent eligibility doctrine merely required that the patentee "carry the principle into effect, however simple and self-evident such means may be." *See* DAVID FULTON, THE LAW AND PRACTICE RELATING TO PATENTS, TRADE MARKS AND DESIGNS 41 (1902); *see also* ROBERT FROST, A TREATISE ON THE LAW AND PRACTICE OF LETTERS PATENT FOR INVENTIONS 36 (1891) ("Principles in a concrete form, together with a mode of applying them to a new and useful purpose, may form the subject of a grant of letters patent. . . . It is not necessary that the means, as well as the principle, should be new, for the novelty of the invention consists in applying the new principle by the means specified."). This view continued well into the twentieth century. *See* CAESAR & RIVISE, PATENTABILITY AND VALIDITY, §§33, 34 (1936) (observing that "[i]n the cases where the inventor was required to be also the discoverer of the law or force utilized, it appeared that the application or utilization of the law became self-evident as soon as the principle was formulated").

b. *Funk Brothers: The Emergence of Eligibility Skepticism*

The Supreme Court's decision in *Funk Brothers Seed Co. v. Kalo Inoculant Co.*, 333 U.S. 127 (1948), curtailed patent protection for natural products. The patentee in the case, Kalo Inoculant Company, claimed

> An inoculant for leguminous plants comprising a plurality of selected mutually non-inhibitive strains of different species of bacteria of the genus Rhizobium, said strains being unaffected by each other in respect to their ability to fix nitrogen in the leguminous plant for which they are selected.

Such bacteria promote plant growth. When the invention was made, it was known that bacteria of the genus *Rhizobium* naturally exist in symbiosis with leguminous plants, such as peas and beans. Farmers routinely mixed *Rhizobium* cultures with leguminous plants to fix nitrogen from the air into the soil. Unfortunately, particular species of the *Rhizobium* genus can colonize only particular legumes. Mixing different *Rhizobium* species into a single commercial product, however, proved unsuccessful. The bacteria species exert inhibitory effects on each other when mixed together. As a result, farmers needed to apply separate cultures to each leguminous crop, adding cost and complication. Kalo discovered that particular combinations of naturally occurring *Rhizobium* bacteria were not inhibitory and, therefore, could be packaged together into a product to be applied across leguminous plants more conveniently. He claimed, however, not a specific combination of bacteria but the idea of combining noninhibitory strains, whatever they turned out to be.

A divided Supreme Court invalidated the patent on eligibility grounds: it did "not disclose an invention or discovery within the meaning of the patent statutes." *Funk Bros.*, 333 U.S. at 132. The Court explained:

> [P]atents cannot issue for the discovery of phenomena of nature. The qualities of these bacteria, like the heat of the sun, electricity, or the quality of metals, are part of the storehouse of knowledge of all men. They are manifestations of laws of nature, free to all men and reserved exclusively to none. He who discovers a hitherto unknown phenomenon of nature has no claim to a monopoly of it which the law recognizes. If there is to be invention from such a discovery, it must come from the *application* of the law of nature to a new and useful end. . . .
>
> Discovery of the fact that certain strains of each species of these bacteria can be mixed without harmful effect to the properties of either is a discovery of their qualities of non-inhibition. It is no more than the discovery of some of the handiwork of nature and hence is not patentable. *The aggregation of select strains of the several species into one product is an application of that newly-discovered natural principle.* But however ingenious the discovery of that natural principle may have been, the application of it is hardly more than an advance in the packaging of the inoculants.

Id. at 131 (emphasis added). Justice Douglas acknowledged that the inventor had applied the law of nature, but nonetheless invalidated the claim as insufficiently inventive in its application of the newly-discovered natural principle. The Court noted that

> a product must be more than new and useful to be patented; it must also satisfy the requirements of invention or discovery. *Cuno Eng'g Corp. v. Automatic Devices Corp.*, 314 U.S. 84, 90, 91 (1941), and cases cited; 35 U.S.C. §31. The application of this newly-discovered natural principle to the problem of packaging of inoculants may well have been an important commercial advance. But once nature's secret of the non-inhibitive quality of certain strains of the species of Rhizobium was discovered, the state of the art made the production of a mixed inoculant a simple step. Even though it may have been the product of skill, it certainly was not the product of invention.

Id. at 131–32.

In a concurring opinion, Justice Frankfurter offered an alternate basis for invalidation reminiscent of the *Morse* decision. In his view, the patent was invalid not for unpatentable subject matter but rather for want of adequate identification of successful combinations of mutually non-inhibitory bacteria. *Funk Bros.*, 333 U.S. at 133. He went on to observe

It only confuses the issue . . . to introduce such terms as 'the work of nature' and the 'laws of nature.' For these are vague and malleable terms infected with too much ambiguity and equivocation. Everything that happens may be deemed 'the work of nature,' and any patentable composite exemplifies in its properties 'the laws of nature.' Arguments drawn from such terms for ascertaining patentability could fairly be employed to challenge almost every patent.

Id. at 134–35.[8]

c. *The New Technological Age*

The dawn of the digital age presented new patent eligibility issues for the Supreme Court. The inventor in *Gottschalk v. Benson*, 409 U.S. 63 (1972), claimed an algorithm for converting binary-coded decimal numerals into pure binary numerals. In upholding the PTO's rejection of the patent on subject matter grounds, a unanimous Court, drawing upon *Le Roy*, *Morse*, and *Funk Brothers*, articulated three principles for determining whether a process is patentable: (1) "[p]henomena of nature, though just discovered, mental processes, and abstract intellectual concepts are not patentable, as they are the basic tools of scientific and technological work," *id.* at 67; (2) "[t]ransformation and reduction of an article 'to a different state or thing' is the clue to the patentability of a process claim that does not include particular machines," *id.* at 70; and (3) algorithms may not be patented so as to avoid the practical effect of "wholly pre-empt[ing a] mathematical formula," *id.* at 71. Echoing concerns raised by various amicus briefs, the Court concluded by calling on Congress to take up the question of whether and to what extent computer programs ought to be patentable. *See id.* at 71–73.

Six years later in *Parker v. Flook*, 437 U.S. 584 (1978), the Supreme Court addressed whether a procedure for updating an alarm limit—measuring the present value of a process variable (such as temperature), using an algorithm to calculate an updated alarm-limit value, and adjusting the updated value—was eligible for patent protection. Writing for the majority in a sharply divided opinion, Justice Stevens expressly embraced an *inventive* application doctrine in upholding the PTO's rejection of the claim. The Court grounded the doctrine on the statement in *Neilson* that "'*the case must be considered as if the principle being well known, the plaintiff had first invented a mode of applying it . . .*'" *Flook*, 437 U.S. at 592 (quoting *Morse*, quoting *Neilson*). Based on this sentence from *Neilson*, the Supreme Court reasoned that "this case must also be considered as if the principle or mathematical formula were well known" and that patent eligibility required sufficient inventiveness beyond the application of the algorithm to be within the scope of patentable subject matter. *Id.* at 592, 594–95. The Court declared:

Even though a phenomenon of nature or mathematical formula may be well known, an *inventive application* of the principle may be patented. Conversely,

---

[8] Justices Burton and Jackson dissented, finding the product claims within the scope of patentable subject matter and adequately disclosed. *Funk Bros.*, at 136.

the discovery of such a phenomenon cannot support a patent unless there is some other inventive concept in its application.

Id. at 594 (emphasis added).

Query: Did the Court interpret *Neilson* (and *Morse*'s interpretation of *Neilson*) correctly?

Justice Stewart, with whom Chief Justice Burger and Justice Rehnquist joined, dissenting, did not see the patent at issue as pre-empting use of the algorithm, but rather as a potentially patentable application of it. *Id.* at 599. He criticized the majority opinion for excluding a process from the scope of patentable subject matter because "*one step in the process would not be patentable subject matter if considered in isolation.*" The dissent observed that "thousands of processes and combinations have been patented that contained one or more steps or elements that themselves would have been unpatentable subject matter." *Id.* (citation omitted; emphasis in original). The majority opinion responded to this contention by noting that the process is unpatentable "not because it contains a mathematical algorithm as one component, but because once that algorithm is assumed to be within the prior art, the application, considered as a whole, contains no patentable invention," *id.* at 594—the *inventive* application doctrine.

As the Court grappled with the patentability of computer software, it also confronted the patentability of genetically modified organisms. *See Diamond v. Chakrabarty*, 447 U.S. 303 (1980). The inventor claimed a self-replicating bacterium into which he had injected oil-degrading plasmids that could be used in dispersing oil spills. *Id.* at 305. The PTO rejected the claim on the grounds that microorganisms are "products of nature" and living things, both of which make them ineligible for patent protection under §101. *Id.* at 306. The Court of Customs and Patent Appeals reversed, upholding the claim under the standards set forth in *Flook*.

The Supreme Court affirmed the appellate court decision, opening the way for patent protection for genetically modified organisms. *Id.* at 318. Writing for the majority, Chief Justice Burger characterized the Constitution's grant of patent legislative authority and §101's text broadly. *Chakrabarty*, 447 U.S. at 307–08. While recognizing the unpatentability of "laws of nature, physical phenomena, and abstract ideas," the Court judged Chakrabarty's claim to a "nonnaturally occurring manufacture or composition of matter—a product of human ingenuity "having a distinctive name, character [and] use"—to "plainly" qualify for patent eligibility. *Id.* at 309–10 (quoting *Hartranft v. Wiegmann*, 121 U.S. 609, 615 (1887)). Drawing a contrast to *Funk Brothers*, the Court noted that Chakrabarty "has produced a new bacterium with markedly different characteristics from any found in nature and one having the potential for significant utility. His discovery is not nature's handiwork, but his own." *Id.* at 310.[9]

---

[9] Justice Brennan, joined by Justices White, Marshall, and Powell, dissented on the grounds that the 1930 and 1970 plant patent statutes indicate that that Congress did not believe that newly developed living organisms were patentable under §101. *Id.* at 320–21.

Moreover, *Chakrabarty* interpreted the scope of patent-eligible subject matter expansively, stressing that §101 encompasses any invention falling within the four designated categories. *Id.* at 308–09. The Supreme Court also looked to the legislative history of the 1952 Patent Act, from which it concluded that "Congress intended statutory subject matter to 'include anything under the sun that is made by man.'"[10] *Id.* at 309.

Propelled in part by *Chakrabarty*'s broad reading of patent eligibility, the pendulum swung decisively away from *Flook* the next year. Writing for the majority, Justice Rehnquist explained that processes have been eligible for patent protection since the 1793 Act and referenced the statement from *Benson* that "[t]ransformation and reduction of an article 'to a different state or thing' is the clue to the patentability of a process claim that does not include particular machines." *Diamond v. Diehr*, 450 U.S. 175, 184 (1981) (quoting *Benson*, 409 U.S. at 70). The Court concluded that "a physical and chemical process for molding precision synthetic rubber products falls within the §101 categories of possibly patentable subject matter." *Id.* Justice Rehnquist purported to distinguish *Benson* and *Flook* before proclaiming that "[o]ur earlier opinions lend support to our present conclusion that a claim drawn to subject matter otherwise statutory does not become nonstatutory simply because it uses a mathematical formula, computer program, or digital computer." *Id.* at 187. The Court emphasized that process claims are properly analyzed

> as a whole. It is inappropriate to dissect the claims into old and new elements and then to ignore the presence of the old elements in the analysis. This is particularly true in a process claim because a new combination of steps in a process may be patentable even though all the constituents of the combination were well known and in common use before the combination was made. The 'novelty' of any element or steps in a process, or even of the process itself, is of no relevance in determining whether the subject matter of a claim falls within the §101 categories of possibly patentable subject matter.

Id. at 188–89. In so holding, Justice Rehnquist seemed to overrule *Flook*'s requirement of *inventive* application. He reiterated, however, that "a mathematical formula as such" is not patentable nor is limiting the use of a formula to a particular technological environment, citing *Benson* and *Flook*. *Id.* at 191. The touchstone for patentability of a process embodying a mathematical formula, according to the majority opinion, is significant post-solution activity—i.e., "transforming or reducing an article to a different state or thing." *Id.* at 191–92.

---

[10] The full passage from which this quotation was taken is arguably less expansive. It reads "A person may have 'invented' a machine or a manufacture, which may include anything under the sun that is made by man, but it is not necessarily patentable under section 101 unless the conditions of the title are fulfilled." *See* Brief Amici Curiae of Professors Peter S. Menell and Michael J. Meurer In Support of Respondent, Bilski v. Kappos, U.S. S.Ct. No 08-964, at 19–22, http://papers.ssrn.com/sol3/papers.cfm?abstract_id=1482022.

Justice Stevens, joined by Justices Brennan, Marshall, and Blackmun, dissented, emphasizing that the majority eviscerated *Flook*'s inventive application requirement. To the dissenters, if the inventor's "method is regarded as an 'algorithm' as that term was used" in *Benson* and *Flook*, "and if no other inventive concept is disclosed in the patent application," then the claim falls outside the scope of patentable processes under §101. *Id.* at 213–14. Moreover, the dissenters contended that "the postsolution activity described in the *Flook* application was no less significant than the automatic opening of the curing mold involved in [*Diehr*]." *Id.* at 215.

d.   The Rise of the Federal Circuit and Dismantling of Patentable Subject Matter Limitations

In the ensuing three decades, the Federal Circuit gradually eroded patent eligibility limitations. Building off of *Diehr*, the Federal Circuit chipped away at the post-solution activity necessary to bring software-related claims within §101. *See, e.g.*, *In re Alappat*, 33 F.3d 1526 (Fed. Cir. 1994) (holding that the display of data on a computer screen could suffice). Similarly, the Federal Circuit endorsed the PTO's policy of permitting the patenting of isolated DNA molecules. *See Amgen, Inc. v. Chugai Pharm. Co.*, 927 F.2d 1200 (Fed. Cir. 1991). In a departure from prior jurisprudence—see *Hotel Sec. Checking Co. v. Lorraine Co.*, 160 Fed. 467, 469, 479 (2d Cir. 1908); WILLIAM ANTHONY DELLER, 1 WALKER ON PATENTS: DELLER'S EDITION, 62, 69 (1937)—the Federal Circuit "la[id the] ill-conceived [business method] exception to rest." *State St. Bank v. Signature Fin. Grp.*, 149 F.3d 1368, 1375 (Fed. Cir. 1998). At the time, the Supreme Court declined to weigh in on these controversies.

The Federal Circuit's loosening of patent eligibility standards expanded the range of patents being issued. The PTO shifted its position from skepticism about expansive patent eligibility to openness and even enthusiasm. Patents for software, DNA, and business methods flooded the PTO. Entrepreneurs and venture capitalists saw patenting as a valuable tool for developing (or at least claiming) Internet businesses. The late 1990s witnessed unprecedented growth of start-up businesses based on speculative initial public offerings secured, in part, on patent portfolios.

The bursting of the Internet (dot-com) stock bubble in 2000 produced a dramatic shake-out. Bankruptcies and subsequently, the auctioning and trading of Internet-related patents, became widespread. Entities whose sole purpose was to assert these patents emerged. Patent holding companies and non-practicing entities sought to monetize their Internet patents, purchased at fire sales. Lawsuits by patent assertion entities produced a tidal wave of patent validity challenges as well as calls by Silicon Valley companies, policymakers, and scholars for policy reform.

In the late 2000s the Federal Circuit issued several decisions that cautiously reintroduced limits on patent eligibility. *See, e.g.*, *In re Nuijten*, 500 F.3d 1346 (Fed. Cir. 2007) (holding that a watermarked electromagnetic signal does not fall into any of the four categories of patent-eligible subject matter); *In re Comiskey*, 499 F.3d 1365 (Fed. Cir. 2007), *amended by* 554 F.3d 967 (Fed. Cir. 2009) (affirming rejection of a business method patent under §101 as merely relying on mental steps). Most notably, the Federal Circuit, sitting en banc, attempted to clarify the boundaries of patentable subject matter under §101. *See In re Bilski*, 545 F.3d 943 (Fed. Cir. 2008) (en banc).

Bilski claimed a method of managing risk of commodity prices—a business method that a computer could implement:

> A method for managing the consumption risk costs of a commodity sold by a commodity provider at a fixed price comprising the steps of:
>
> (a) initiating a series of transactions between said commodity provider and consumers of said commodity wherein said consumers purchase said commodity at a fixed rate based upon historical averages, said fixed rate corresponding to a risk position of said consumer;
>
> (b) identifying market participants for said commodity having a counter-risk position to said consumers; and
>
> (c) initiating a series of transactions between said commodity provider and said market participants at a second fixed rate such that said series of market participant transactions balances the risk position of said series of consumer transactions.

Claim 1, U.S. Patent Application No. 08/833,892. In an effort to harmonize the Supreme Court's *Benson*, *Flook*, and *Diehr* precedents, the Federal Circuit articulated the "machine-or-transformation" (MoT) test "to determine whether a process claim is tailored narrowly enough to encompass only a particular application of a fundamental principle rather than to pre-empt the principle itself." Under the MoT test, a claimed process is patent-eligible under §101 if: "(1) it is tied to a particular machine or apparatus, or (2) it transforms a particular article into a different state or thing." The court concluded that the Bilski patent failed both prongs and hence was unpatentable: it was not tied to a "particular" machine. Further, the transformation of legal obligations or relationships, business risks, or other abstractions is not a tangible change, eligible for patent protection.

ii. The Supreme Court's Revival of Subject Matter Limitations

The Supreme Court opened a new chapter in patent eligibility jurisprudence with its grant of review in the *Bilski* case. The majority ruled that Bilski's broad independent claim to hedging was "an unpatentable abstract idea, just like the algorithms at issue in *Benson* and *Flook*. Allowing petitioners to patent risk hedging would pre-empt use of this approach in all fields, and would effectively grant a monopoly over an abstract idea." *Id.* at 611–12. The Court further rejected Bilski's narrower dependent claims as unpatentable by reference to *Flook*, which "established that limiting an abstract idea to one field of use or adding token postsolution components did not make the concept patentable." *Id.*

While affirming the Federal Circuit's decision holding Bilski's hedging patent application invalid, the Supreme Court rejected the MoT test as the sole test of patent eligibility of process claims. Nonetheless, the Supreme Court characterized the MoT test as a "useful and important clue, an investigative tool, for determining whether some claimed inventions are processes under §101," but too rigid given the broad statutory definition in §100(b) of "process." *Id.* at 603–04. While recognizing the jurisprudentially developed exclusions for laws of nature, natural phenomena, and abstract ideas, the Court nonetheless warned that the judiciary does not have "*carte blanche* to impose other limitations that are inconsistent with the text and the statute's purpose and design." *Id.* at 603. On similar grounds, the majority rejected the argument that business methods are categorically excluded from patent eligibility. *Id.* at 606–08.

Justice Stevens, joined by Justices Ginsburg, Breyer, and Sotomayor, concurred in the judgment, but contended that the Patent Act and jurisprudence have long categorically excluded business methods from patent eligibility. *Id.* at 613. The opinion grounded its conclusion in constitutional limits on legislative power. Article I, §8, cl. 8 authorizes Congress to grant patents for discoveries so as to promote "useful Arts." The "useful Arts" translate to "technology" in modern parlance. Justice Stevens did not believe that innovations in business methods fell within this domain. "During the 17th and 18th centuries, Great Britain saw innovations in business organization, business models, management techniques, and novel solutions to the challenges of operating global firms[, yet f]ew if any of these methods of conducting business were patented." *Id.* at 631 (footnotes omitted).

The Supreme Court then turned to patents on medical diagnostic processes.

Mayo Collaborative Services v. Prometheus Laboratories, Inc.
Supreme Court of the United States
566 U.S. 66 (2012)

JUSTICE BREYER delivered the opinion of the Court.

Section 101 of the Patent Act defines patentable subject matter. It says:

> Whoever invents or discovers any new and useful process, machine, manufacture, or composition of matter, or any new and useful improvement thereof, may obtain a patent therefor, subject to the conditions and requirements of this title.

The Court has long held that this provision contains an important implicit exception. "[L]aws of nature, natural phenomena, and abstract ideas" are not patentable. *Diamond v. Diehr,* 450 U.S. 175, 185 (1981); *Le Roy v. Tatham,* 14 How. 156, 175 (1853); *O'Reilly v. Morse,* 15 How. 62, 112–120 (1854); *cf. Neilson v. Harford,* Webster's Patent Cases 295, 371 (1841) (English case discussing same). Thus, the Court has written that "a new mineral discovered in the earth or a new plant found in the wild is not patentable subject matter. Likewise, Einstein could not patent his celebrated law that $E=mc^2$; nor could Newton have patented the law of gravity. Such discoveries are 'manifestations of . . . nature, free to all men and reserved exclusively to none.'" *Chakrabarty, supra,* at 309 (quoting *Funk Brothers Seed Co. v. Kalo Inoculant Co.,* 333 U.S. 127, 130 (1948)).

"Phenomena of nature, though just discovered, mental processes, and abstract intellectual concepts are not patentable, as they are the basic tools of scientific and technological work." *Gottschalk v. Benson,* 409 U.S. 63, 67 (1972). And monopolization of those tools through the grant of a patent might tend to impede innovation more than it would tend to promote it.

The Court has recognized, however, that too broad an interpretation of this exclusionary principle could eviscerate patent law. For all inventions at some level embody, use, reflect, rest upon, or apply laws of nature, natural phenomena, or abstract ideas. Thus, in *Diehr* the Court pointed out that "'a process is not unpatentable simply because it contains a law of nature or a mathematical algorithm.'" 450 U.S., at 187 (quoting *Parker v. Flook,* 437 U.S. 584, 590 (1978)). It added that "an *application* of a law of nature or mathematical formula to a known structure or process may well be deserving of patent protection." *Diehr, supra,* at 187. And it emphasized Justice Stone's similar observation in *Mackay Radio & Telegraph Co. v. Radio Corp. of America,* 306 U.S. 86 (1939):

> "'While a scientific truth, or the mathematical expression of it, is not a patentable invention, a novel and useful structure created with the aid of knowledge of scientific truth may be.'" 450 U.S., at 188 (quoting *Mackay Radio, supra,* at 94).

See also Funk Brothers, supra at 130 ("If there is to be invention from [a discovery of a law of nature], it must come from the application of the law of nature to a new and useful end").

Still, as the Court has also made clear, to transform an unpatentable law of nature into a patent-eligible *application* of such a law, one must do more than simply state the law of nature while adding the words "apply it." *See, e.g., Benson, supra,* at 71–72.

The case before us lies at the intersection of these basic principles. It concerns patent claims covering processes that help doctors who use thiopurine drugs to treat patients with autoimmune diseases determine whether a given dosage level is too low or too high. The claims purport to apply natural laws describing the relationships between the concentration in the blood of certain thiopurine metabolites and the likelihood that the drug dosage will be ineffective or induce harmful side-effects. We must determine whether the claimed processes have transformed these unpatentable natural laws into patent-eligible applications of those laws. We conclude that they have not done so and that therefore the processes are not patentable.

Our conclusion rests upon an examination of the particular claims before us in light of the Court's precedents. Those cases warn us against interpreting patent statutes in ways that make patent eligibility "depend simply on the draftsman's art" without reference to the "principles underlying the prohibition against patents for [natural laws]." *Flook, supra,* at 593. They warn us against upholding patents that claim processes that too broadly preempt the use of a natural law. *Morse, supra,* at 112–120; *Benson, supra,* at 71–72. And they insist that a process that focuses upon the use of a natural law also contain other elements or a combination of elements, sometimes referred to as an "inventive concept," sufficient to ensure that the patent in practice amounts to significantly more than a patent upon the natural law itself. *Flook, supra,* at 594; *see also Bilski, supra,* at 3218 ("[T]he prohibition against patenting abstract ideas 'cannot be circumvented by attempting to limit the use of the formula to a particular technological environment' or adding 'insignificant postsolution activity'" (quoting *Diehr, supra,* at 191–192)).

We find that the process claims at issue here do not satisfy these conditions. In particular, the steps in the claimed processes (apart from the natural laws themselves) involve well-understood, routine, conventional activity previously engaged in by researchers in the field. At the same time, upholding the patents would risk disproportionately tying up the use of the underlying natural laws, inhibiting their use in the making of further discoveries.

I

A

The patents before us concern the use of thiopurine drugs in the treatment of autoimmune diseases, such as Crohn's disease and ulcerative colitis. When a patient ingests a thiopurine compound, his body metabolizes the drug, causing metabolites to form in his bloodstream. Because the way in which people metabolize thiopurine compounds varies, the same dose of a thiopurine drug affects different people differently, and it has been difficult for doctors to determine whether for a particular patient a given dose is too high, risking harmful side effects, or too low, and so likely ineffective.

At the time the discoveries embodied in the patents were made, scientists already understood that the levels in a patient's blood of certain metabolites, including, in particular, 6-thioguanine and its nucleotides (6-TG) and 6-methyl-mercaptopurine (6-MMP), were correlated with the likelihood that a particular dosage of a thiopurine drug could cause harm or prove ineffective. *See* U.S. Patent No. 6,355,623, col.8, ll.37–40, 2 App. 10. ("Previous studies suggested that measurement of 6-MP metabolite levels can be used to predict clinical efficacy and tolerance to azathioprine or 6-MP" (citing Cuffari, Théorêt, Latour, & Seidman, *6–Mercaptopurine Metabolism in Crohn's Disease: Correlation with Efficacy and Toxicity,* 39 GUT 401 (1996))). But those in the field did not know the precise correlations between metabolite levels and likely harm or ineffectiveness. The patent claims at issue here set forth processes embodying researchers' findings that identified these correlations with some precision.

More specifically, the patents—U.S. Patent No. 6,355,623 ('623 patent) and U.S. Patent No. 6,680,302 ('302 patent)—embody findings that concentrations in a patient's blood of 6-TG or of 6-MMP metabolite beyond a certain level (400 and 7000 picomoles per 8×10^8 red blood cells, respectively) indicate that the dosage is likely too high for the patient, while concentrations in the blood of 6-TG metabolite lower than a certain level (about 230 picomoles per 8×10^8 red blood cells) indicate that the dosage is likely too low to be effective.

The patent claims seek to embody this research in a set of processes. Like the Federal Circuit we take as typical claim 1 of the '623 Patent, which describes one of the claimed processes as follows:

"A method of optimizing therapeutic efficacy for treatment of an immune-mediated gastrointestinal disorder, comprising:

"(a) administering a drug providing 6-thioguanine to a subject having said immune-mediated gastrointestinal disorder; and

"(b) determining the level of 6-thioguanine in said subject having said immune-mediated gastrointestinal disorder,

"wherein the level of 6-thioguanine less than about 230 pmol per 8x108 red blood cells indicates a need to increase the amount of said drug subsequently administered to said subject and

"wherein the level of 6-thioguanine greater than about 400 pmol per 8x108 red blood cells indicates a need to decrease the amount of said drug subsequently administered to said subject." '623 patent, col.20, ll.10–20, 2 App. 16.

For present purposes we may assume that the other claims in the patents do not differ significantly from claim 1. . . .

II

Prometheus' patents set forth laws of nature—namely, relationships between concentrations of certain metabolites in the blood and the likelihood that a dosage of a thiopurine drug will prove ineffective or cause harm. Claim 1, for example, states that if the levels of 6–TG in the blood (of a patient who has taken a dose of a thiopurine drug) exceed about 400 pmol per $8x10^8$ red blood cells, then the administered dose is likely to produce toxic side effects. While it takes a human action (the administration of a thiopurine drug) to trigger a manifestation of this relation in a particular person, the relation itself exists in principle apart from any human action. The relation is a consequence of the ways in which thiopurine compounds are metabolized by the body—entirely natural processes. And so a patent that simply describes that relation sets forth a natural law.

The question before us is whether the claims do significantly more than simply describe these natural relations. To put the matter more precisely, do the patent claims add enough to their statements of the correlations to allow the processes they describe to qualify as patent-eligible processes that apply natural laws? We believe that the answer to this question is no.

A

If a law of nature is not patentable, then neither is a process reciting a law of nature, unless that process has additional features that provide practical assurance that the process is more than a drafting effort designed to monopolize the law of nature itself. A patent, for example, could not simply recite a law of nature and then add the instruction "apply the law." Einstein, we assume, could not have patented his famous law by claiming a process consisting of simply telling linear accelerator operators to refer to the law to determine how much energy an amount of mass has produced (or vice versa). Nor could Archimedes have secured a patent for his famous principle of flotation by claiming a process consisting of simply telling boat builders to refer to that principle in order to determine whether an object will float.

What else is there in the claims before us? The process that each claim recites tells doctors interested in the subject about the correlations that the researchers discovered. In doing so, it recites an "administering" step, a "determining" step, and a "wherein" step. These additional steps are not themselves natural laws but neither are they sufficient to transform the nature of the claim.

First, the "administering" step simply refers to the relevant audience, namely doctors who treat patients with certain diseases with thiopurine drugs. That audience is a pre-existing audience; doctors used thiopurine drugs to treat patients suffering from autoimmune disorders long before anyone asserted these claims. In any event, the "prohibition against patenting abstract ideas 'cannot be circumvented by attempting to limit the use of the formula to a particular technological environment.'" *Bilski, supra* (quoting *Diehr*, 450 U.S., at 191–92).

Second, the "wherein" clauses simply tell a doctor about the relevant natural laws, at most adding a suggestion that he should take those laws into account when treating his patient. That is to say, these clauses tell the relevant audience about the laws while trusting them to use those laws appropriately where they are relevant to their decision making (rather like Einstein telling linear accelerator operators about his basic law and then trusting them to use it where relevant).

Third, the "determining" step tells the doctor to determine the level of the relevant metabolites in the blood, through whatever process the doctor or the laboratory wishes to use. As the patents state, methods for determining metabolite levels were well known in the art. '623 patent, col.9, ll.12–65, 2 App. 11. Indeed, scientists routinely measured metabolites as part of their investigations into the relationships between metabolite levels and efficacy and toxicity of thiopurine compounds. '623 patent, col.8, ll.37–40, *id.*, at 10. Thus, this step tells doctors to engage in well-understood, routine, conventional activity previously engaged in by scientists who work in the field. Purely "conventional or obvious" "[pre]-solution activity" is normally not sufficient to transform an unpatentable law of nature into a patent-eligible application of such a law. *Flook*, 437 U.S., at 590; *see also Bilski*, 130 S.Ct., at 3230 ("[T]he prohibition against patenting abstract ideas 'cannot be circumvented by' . . . adding 'insignificant post-solution activity'" (quoting *Diehr*, supra, at 191–92)).

Fourth, to consider the three steps as an ordered combination adds nothing to the laws of nature that is not already present when the steps are considered separately. *See Diehr, supra*, at 188 ("[A] new combination of steps in a process may be patentable even though all the constituents of the combination were well known and in common use before the combination was made"). Anyone who wants to make use of these laws must first administer a thiopurine drug and measure the resulting metabolite concentrations, and so the combination amounts to nothing significantly more than an instruction to doctors to apply the applicable laws when treating their patients.

The upshot is that the three steps simply tell doctors to gather data from which they may draw an inference in light of the correlations. To put the matter more succinctly, the claims inform a relevant audience about certain laws of nature; any additional steps consist of well-understood, routine, conventional activity already engaged in by the scientific community; and those steps, when viewed as a whole, add nothing significant beyond the sum of their parts taken separately. For these reasons we believe that the steps are not sufficient to transform unpatentable natural correlations into patentable applications of those regularities.

B

1

A more detailed consideration of the controlling precedents reinforces our conclusion. The cases most directly on point are *Diehr* and *Flook,* two cases in which the Court reached opposite conclusions about the patent eligibility of processes that embodied the equivalent of natural laws. The *Diehr* process (held patent eligible) set forth a method for molding raw, uncured rubber into various cured, molded products. The process used a known mathematical equation, the Arrhenius equation, to determine when (depending upon the temperature inside the mold, the time the rubber had been in the mold, and the thickness of the rubber) to open the press.

The Court pointed out that the basic mathematical equation, like a law of nature, was not patentable. But it found the overall process patent eligible because of the way the additional steps of the process integrated the equation into the process as a whole. Those steps included "installing rubber in a press, closing the mold, constantly determining the temperature of the mold, constantly recalculating the appropriate cure time through the use of the formula and a digital computer, and automatically opening the press at the proper time." *Id.,* at 187. It nowhere suggested that all these steps, or at least the combination of those steps, were in context obvious, already in use, or purely conventional. And so the patentees did not "seek to pre-empt the use of [the] equation," but sought "only to foreclose from others the use of that equation in conjunction with all of the other steps in their claimed process." *Ibid.* These other steps apparently added to the formula something that in terms of patent law's objectives had significance—they transformed the process into an inventive application of the formula.

The process in *Flook* (held not patentable) provided a method for adjusting "alarm limits" in the catalytic conversion of hydrocarbons. Certain operating conditions (such as temperature, pressure, and flow rates), which are continuously monitored during the conversion process, signal inefficiency or danger when they exceed certain "alarm limits." The claimed process amounted to an improved system for updating those alarm limits through the steps of: (1) measuring the current level of the variable, e.g., the temperature; (2) using an apparently novel mathematical algorithm to calculate the current alarm limits; and (3) adjusting the system to reflect the new alarm-limit values. 437 U.S., at 585–587.

The Court, as in *Diehr,* pointed out that the basic mathematical equation, like a law of nature, was not patentable. But it characterized the claimed process as doing nothing other than "provid[ing] a[n unpatentable] formula for computing an updated alarm limit." *Flook, supra,* at 586. Unlike the process in *Diehr,* it did not "explain how the variables used in the formula were to be selected, nor did the [claim] contain any disclosure relating to chemical processes at work or the means of setting off an alarm or adjusting the alarm limit." *Diehr, supra,* at 192, n. 14; *see also Flook,* 437 U.S., at 586. And so the other steps in the process did not limit the claim to a particular application. Moreover, "[t]he chemical processes involved in catalytic conversion of hydrocarbons[,] . . . the practice of monitoring the chemical process variables, the use of alarm limits to trigger alarms, the notion that alarm limit values must be recomputed and readjusted, and the use of computers for 'automatic monitoring-alarming'" were all "well known," to the point where, putting the formula to the side, there was no "inventive concept" in the claimed application of the formula. *Id.,* at 594. "[P]ost-solution activity" that is purely "conventional or obvious," the Court wrote, "can[not] transform an unpatentable principle into a patentable process." *Id.,* at 589, 590.

The claim before us presents a case for patentability that is weaker than the (patent-eligible) claim in *Diehr* and no stronger than the (unpatentable) claim in *Flook.* Beyond picking out the relevant audience, namely those who administer doses of thiopurine drugs, the claim simply tells doctors to: (1) measure (somehow) the current level of the relevant metabolite, (2) use particular (unpatentable) laws of nature (which the claim sets forth) to calculate the current toxicity/inefficacy limits, and (3) reconsider the drug dosage in light of the law. These instructions add nothing specific to the laws of nature other than what is well-understood, routine, conventional activity, previously engaged in by those in the field. And since they are steps that must be taken in order to apply the laws in question, the effect is simply to tell doctors to apply the law somehow when treating their patients. The process in *Diehr* was not so characterized; that in *Flook* was characterized in roughly this way.

2

Other cases offer further support for the view that simply appending conventional steps, specified at a high level of generality, to laws of nature, natural phenomena, and abstract ideas cannot make those laws, phenomena, and ideas patentable. This Court has previously discussed in detail an English case, *Neilson,* which involved a patent claim that posed a legal problem very similar to the problem now before us. . . .

[There], the claimed process included not only a law of nature but also several unconventional steps (such as inserting the receptacle, applying heat to the receptacle externally, and blowing the air into the furnace) that confined the claims to a particular, useful application of the principle.

In *Bilski* the Court considered claims covering a process for hedging risks of price changes by, for example, contracting to purchase commodities from sellers at a fixed price, reflecting the desire of sellers to hedge against a drop in prices, while selling commodities to consumers at a fixed price, reflecting the desire of consumers to hedge against a price increase. One claim described the process; another reduced the process to a mathematical formula. 130 S.Ct., at 3223–3224. The Court held that the described "concept of hedging" was "an unpatentable abstract idea." *Id.,* 130 S.Ct., 3239. That some claims limited hedging to use in commodities and energy markets and specified that "well-known random analysis techniques [could be used] to help establish some of the inputs into the equation" did not undermine this conclusion, for "*Flook* established that limiting an abstract idea to one field of use or adding token postsolution components did not make the concept patentable." *Id.*, 130 S.Ct., at 3231.

Finally, in *Benson* the Court considered the patentability of a mathematical process for converting binary-coded decimal numerals into pure binary numbers on a general purpose digital computer. The claims "purported to cover any use of the claimed method in a general-purpose digital computer of any type." 409 U.S., at 64. The Court recognized that "'a novel and useful structure created with the aid of knowledge of scientific truth'" might be patentable. *Id.*, at 673 (quoting *Mackay Radio*, 306 U.S., at 94). But it held that simply implementing a mathematical principle on a physical machine, namely a computer, was not a patentable application of that principle. For the mathematical formula had "no substantial practical application except in connection with a digital computer." *Benson, supra,* at 71. Hence the claim (like the claims before us) was overly broad; it did not differ significantly from a claim that just said "apply the algorithm."

3

The Court has repeatedly emphasized [the] concern that patent law not inhibit further discovery by improperly tying up the future use of laws of nature. Thus, in *Morse* the Court set aside as unpatentable Samuel Morse's general claim for "'the use of the motive power of the electric or galvanic current ... however developed, for making or printing intelligible characters, letters, or signs, at any distances,'" 15 How., at 86. The Court explained:

> "For aught that we now know some future inventor, in the onward march of science, may discover a mode of writing or printing at a distance by means of the electric or galvanic current, without using any part of the process or combination set forth in the plaintiff's specification. His invention may be less complicated—less liable to get out of order—less expensive in construction, and in its operation. But yet if it is covered by this patent the inventor could not use it, nor the public have the benefit of it without the permission of this patentee." *Id.,* at 113.

Similarly, in *Benson* the Court said that the claims before it were "so abstract and sweeping as to cover both known and unknown uses of the [mathematical formula]." 409 U.S., at 67, 68. In *Bilski* the Court pointed out that to allow "petitioners to patent risk hedging would pre-empt use of this approach in all fields." 130 S.Ct., at 3231. And in *Flook* the Court expressed concern that the claimed process was simply "a formula for computing an updated alarm limit," which might "cover a broad range of potential uses." 437 U.S., at 586.

These statements reflect that, even though rewarding with patents those who discover new laws of nature and the like might well encourage their discovery, those laws and principles, considered generally, are "the basic tools of scientific and technological work." *Benson, supra,* at 67. And so there is a danger that the grant of patents that tie up their use will inhibit future innovation premised upon them, a danger that becomes acute when a patented process amounts to no more than an instruction to "apply the natural law," or otherwise forecloses more future invention than the underlying discovery could reasonably justify. *See generally* Lemley, Risch, Sichelman, & Wagner, *Life After* Bilski, 63 STAN. L. REV. 1315 (2011) (hereinafter Lemley) (arguing that §101 reflects this kind of concern); *see also* C. BOHANNAN & H. HOVENKAMP, CREATION WITHOUT RESTRAINT: PROMOTING LIBERTY AND RIVALRY IN INNOVATION 112 (2012) ("One problem with [process] patents is that the more abstractly their claims are stated, the more difficult it is to determine precisely what they cover. They risk being applied to a wide range of situations that were not anticipated by the patentee"); W. LANDES & R. POSNER, THE ECONOMIC STRUCTURE OF INTELLECTUAL PROPERTY LAW 305–06 (2003) (The exclusion from patent law of basic truths reflects "both . . . the enormous potential for rent seeking that would be created if property rights could be obtained in them and . . . the enormous transaction costs that would be imposed on would-be users [of those truths].").

The laws of nature at issue here are narrow laws that may have limited applications, but the patent claims that embody them nonetheless implicate this concern. They tell a treating doctor to measure metabolite levels and to consider the resulting measurements in light of the statistical relationships they describe. In doing so, they tie up the doctor's subsequent treatment decision whether that treatment does, or does not, change in light of the inference he has drawn using the correlations. And they threaten to inhibit the development of more refined treatment recommendations (like that embodied in Mayo's test), that combine Prometheus' correlations with later discovered features of metabolites, human physiology or individual patient characteristics. The "determining" step too is set forth in highly general language covering all processes that make use of the correlations after measuring metabolites, including later discovered processes that measure metabolite levels in new ways.

We need not, and do not, now decide whether were the steps at issue here less conventional, these features of the claims would prove sufficient to invalidate them. For here, as we have said, the steps add nothing of significance to the natural laws themselves. Unlike, say, a typical patent on a new drug or a new way of using an existing drug, the patent claims do not confine their reach to particular applications of those laws. The presence here of the basic underlying concern that these patents tie up too much future use of laws of nature simply reinforces our conclusion that the processes described in the patents are not patent eligible, while eliminating any temptation to depart from case law precedent.

III

We have considered several further arguments in support of Prometheus' position. But they do not lead us to adopt a different conclusion. First, the Federal Circuit, in upholding the patent eligibility of the claims before us, relied on this Court's determination that "[t]ransformation and reduction of an article 'to a different state or thing' is *the clue* to the patentability of a process claim that does not include particular machines." *Benson, supra,* at 70–71 (emphasis added). It reasoned that the claimed processes are therefore patent eligible, since they involve transforming the human body by administering a thiopurine drug and transforming the blood by analyzing it to determine metabolite levels. 628 F.3d, at 1356–1357.

The first of these transformations, however, is irrelevant. As we have pointed out, the "administering" step simply helps to pick out the group of individuals who are likely interested in applying the law of nature. And the second step could be satisfied without transforming the blood, should science develop a totally different system for determining metabolite levels that did not involve such a transformation. Regardless, in stating that the "machine-or-transformation" test is an *"important and useful clue"* to patentability, we have neither said nor implied that the test trumps the "law of nature" exclusion. *Bilski,* 130 S.Ct., at 3225–3227 (emphasis added). That being so, the test fails here.

Second, Prometheus argues that, because the particular laws of nature that its patent claims embody are narrow and specific, the patents should be upheld. Thus, it encourages us to draw distinctions among laws of nature based on whether or not they will interfere significantly with innovation in other fields now or in the future. Brief for Respondent 42–46; *see also* Lemley 1342–1344 (making similar argument).

But the underlying functional concern here is a *relative* one: how much future innovation is foreclosed relative to the contribution of the inventor. A patent upon a narrow law of nature may not inhibit future research as seriously as would a patent upon Einstein's law of relativity, but the creative value of the discovery is also considerably smaller. And, as we have previously pointed out, even a narrow law of nature (such as the one before us) can inhibit future research.

In any event, our cases have not distinguished among different laws of nature according to whether or not the principles they embody are sufficiently narrow. *See, e.g., Flook,* 437 U.S. 584 (holding narrow mathematical formula unpatentable). And this is understandable. Courts and judges are not institutionally well suited to making the kinds of judgments needed to distinguish among different laws of nature. And so the cases have endorsed a bright-line prohibition against patenting laws of nature, mathematical formulas and the like, which serves as a somewhat more easily administered proxy for the underlying "building-block" concern.

Third, the Government argues that virtually any step beyond a statement of a law of nature itself should transform an unpatentable law of nature into a potentially patentable application sufficient to satisfy §101's demands. Brief for United States as Amicus Curiae. The Government does not necessarily believe that claims that (like the claims before us) extend just minimally beyond a law of nature should receive patents. But in its view, other statutory provisions—those that insist that a claimed process be novel, 35 U.S.C. §102, that it not be "obvious in light of prior art," §103, and that it be "full[y], clear[ly], concise[ly], and exact[ly]" described, §112—can perform this screening function. In particular, it argues that these claims likely fail for lack of novelty under §102.

This approach, however, would make the "law of nature" exception to §101 patentability a dead letter. The approach is therefore not consistent with prior law. The relevant cases rest their holdings upon section 101, not later sections.

We recognize that, in evaluating the significance of additional steps, the §101 patent-eligibility inquiry and, say, the §102 novelty inquiry might sometimes overlap. But that need not always be so. And to shift the patent-eligibility inquiry entirely to these later sections risks creating significantly greater legal uncertainty, while assuming that those sections can do work that they are not equipped to do.

What role would laws of nature, including newly discovered (and "novel") laws of nature, play in the Government's suggested "novelty" inquiry? Intuitively, one would suppose that a newly discovered law of nature is novel. The Government, however, suggests in effect that the novelty of a component law of nature may be disregarded when evaluating the novelty of the whole. *See* Brief for United States as Amicus Curiae 27. But §§102 and 103 say nothing about treating laws of nature as if they were part of the prior art when applying those sections. *Cf. Diehr,* 450 U.S., at 188 (patent claims "must be considered as a whole"). And studiously ignoring *all* laws of nature when evaluating a patent application under §§102 and 103 would "make all inventions unpatentable because all inventions can be reduced to underlying principles of nature which, once known, make their implementation obvious." *Id.,* at 189, n. 12. *See also* Eisenberg, *Wisdom of the Ages or Dead-Hand Control? Patentable Subject Matter for Diagnostic Methods After* In re Bilski, 3 CASE W. RES. J.L. TECH. & INTERNET 1, [62–63] (2012).

Section 112 requires only a "written description of the invention . . . in such full, clear, concise, and exact terms as to enable any person skilled in the art to make and use the same." It does not focus on the possibility that a law of nature (or its equivalent) that meets the[] [disclosure] conditions will nonetheless create [a] risk that a patent on the law would significantly impede future innovation.

These considerations lead us to decline the Government's invitation to substitute §§102, 103, and 112 inquiries for the better established inquiry under §101.

Fourth, Prometheus, supported by several amici, argues that a principle of law denying patent coverage here will interfere significantly with the ability of medical researchers to make valuable discoveries, particularly in the area of diagnostic research. That research, which includes research leading to the discovery of laws of nature, is expensive; it "ha[s] made the United States the world leader in this field"; and it requires protection. Brief for Respondent 52.

Other medical experts, however, argue strongly against a legal rule that would make the present claims patent eligible, invoking policy considerations that point in the opposite direction. [Various medical organizations] tell us that if "claims to exclusive rights over the body's natural responses to illness and medical treatment are permitted to stand, the result will be a vast thicket of exclusive rights over the use of critical scientific data that must remain widely available if physicians are to provide sound medical care." Brief for American College of Medical Genetics et al. as Amici Curiae 7.

We do not find this kind of difference of opinion surprising. Patent protection is, after all, a two-edged sword. On the one hand, the promise of exclusive rights provides monetary incentives that lead to creation, invention, and discovery. On the other hand, that very exclusivity can impede the flow of information that might permit, indeed spur, invention, by, for example, raising the price of using the patented ideas once created, requiring potential users to conduct costly and time-consuming searches of existing patents and pending patent applications, and requiring the negotiation of complex licensing arrangements. . . .

* * *

For these reasons, we conclude that the patent claims at issue here effectively claim the underlying laws of nature themselves. The claims are consequently invalid. And the Federal Circuit's judgment is reversed.

COMMENTS AND QUESTIONS

1. The Supreme Court summarized the representative patent claim at issue as comprising three components: (1) an administering step; (2) a determining step; and (3) a wherein clause. The Court declares that "to transform an unpatentable law of nature into a patent-eligible application of such a law, one must do more than simply state the law of nature while adding the words 'apply it.'" Could the patentee have cured its eligibility problem by claiming that the thiopurine dosage be modified based on the blood chemistry change, rather than merely "indicating" a change in the "wherein" clause? Would that have changed the claim from being merely a glorified observation of a natural fact into a true process that leads to actions that cause some effects? Why might the patentee have claimed its invention in such an oblique way?

In *Vanda Pharmaceuticals Inc. v. West-Ward Pharmaceuticals*, 887 F.3d 1117 (Fed. Cir. 2018), the Federal Circuit upheld the validity of a method for treating schizophrenia that, much like the claim in *Mayo*, based the dosage of a drug on how a patient metabolized the drug. The court distinguished *Mayo* on the ground that the claims there "were not directed to a novel method of treating a disease . . . but rather to a diagnostic method based on the 'relationships between concentrations of certain metabolites in the blood and the likelihood that a dosage of a thiopurine drug will prove ineffective or cause harm.'" *Id.* at 1134. The court emphasized that the representative claim in *Mayo* "*was not directed to* the application of a drug to treat a particular disease." *Id.* (emphasis added). By contrast, the claims at issue in *Vanda* are "directed to a method of using iloperidone to treat schizophrenia." *Id.* at 1135. The court noted that the inventors did not claim the relationship between the drug and its metabolization in the body, but rather "an application of that relationship." Thus, the claims are "'a new way of using an existing drug' that is safer for patients because it reduces [a particular] risk." *Id.* at 1135 (quoting *Mayo*). Chief Judge Prost dissented, explaining that the claimed invention "is no more than an optimization of an existing treatment of schizophrenia, just as the claims in *Mayo* concerned 'optimizing therapeutic efficacy' of thiopurine drugs." *Id*. at 1142 (Prost, C.J., dissenting). She noted that "*Mayo* warned against 'drafting effort[s] designed to monopolize the law of nature itself.'" *Id.*

2. *Inventive Application*. The decision revives the inventive application framework set forth in *Flook*, a test that appeared to have been overridden by *Diehr*. In so doing, the Court based the decision, as it did in *Flook*, on *Neilson v. Harford*, stating that "the claimed process [in *Neilson*] included not only a law of nature but also several *unconventional* steps (such as inserting the receptacle, applying heat to the receptacle externally, and blowing the air into the furnace) that confined the claims to a particular, useful application of the principle." (Emphasis added.) Did the *Mayo* Court interpret *Neilson* (and *Morse*'s interpretation of *Neilson*) correctly? What is unconventional about inserting a receptacle, applying heat to the receptacle externally, and blowing air into the furnace? The Court of Exchequer considered Neilson's application of discovery (preheating air prior to injection into the furnace) to be "perfectly well known." *Neilson v. Harford*, 1 Web. P. C. 295, 344 (1841).

So why would Baron Parke have said "[w]e think the case must be considered as if the principle being well known"? Professor Jeffrey Lefstin contends that the answer lies in the prior sentence: "we think that the plaintiff does not merely claim a principle, but a machine embodying a principle, and a very valuable one." The Court of Exchequer was drawing an analogy to *Minter v. Wells*, Carpmael's Patent Cases 622 (1834), which held that a broad claim to a reclining chair embodying a well-known scientific principle (the self-adjusting leverage) was drawn to a machine as opposed to merely claiming a principle of mechanics in the abstract. The *Neilson* decision was merely postulating a counter-factual scenario so as to analogize to *Minter*. The Exchequer concluded that Neilson's claim, like Minter's, was to a machine and not merely an abstract scientific principle. Neilson's discovery, that preheating air before injecting into a blast furnace would improve combustion over the prior art (injecting unheated air), was in fact new. *See* Jeffrey A. Lefstin, *Inventive Application: A History*, 67 FLA. L. REV. 565, 581-87 (2015) (arguing that both *Flook* and *Mayo* based the inventive application requirement on a profound misunderstanding of the *Neilson* case).

3. How does §101 patentable subject matter eligibility analysis compare with §103 nonobviousness analysis? How does determination of whether application of a law of nature is "well-understood, routine, conventional" compare with whether "the differences between the subject matter sought to be patented and the prior art are such that the subject matter as a whole would have been obvious at the time the invention was made to a person having ordinary skill in the art to which said subject matter pertains"?

4. *Inventions and Discoveries*. Art. I, §8, Cl. 8 of the U.S. CONSTITUTION grants Congress power to establish patent protection for "Discoveries." U.S. patent law has, since its inception in 1790, authorized the granting of patents for "inventions and discoveries," The Senate Report accompanying the Patent Act of 1836 leaves no doubt that Congress fully intended patent protection for practical applications of scientific discoveries:

Whoever imagines that, because so many inventions and so many improvements in machinery have been made, there remains little else to be discovered, has but a feeble conception of the infinitude and vastness of mechanical powers, or of the unlimited reach of science. Much as has been *discovered, infinitely more remains unrevealed.* The ingenuity of man is exploring a region without limits, and delving in a mine whose treasures are exhaustless. 'Neither are all the mysteries of nature unfolded, nor the mind tired in the pursuit of them.'

The first conceptions of ingenuity, like the first suggestions of science, are theories which require something of experiment and practical exemplification to perfect. . . .

SENATE REPORT ACCOMPANYING SENATE BILL NO. 239, 24th Cong., 1st Sess. (Apr. 28, 1836) (emphasis added). But what about protection for the scientific discovery itself? The 1952 Patent Act defines "invention" to mean "invention or discovery." §100(a). Does the judicially-established inventive application standard override legislative intent as reflected in the text of the patent acts? Under *Mayo*, are conventional applications of new discoveries patentable? The discoveries themselves? Professor Sean O'Connor contends that "discovery" in 1790 meant an important invention, not what it means today: the identification of an idea or scientific principle. *See* Sean O'Connor, *The Overlooked French Influence on the Intellectual Property Clause*, 82 U. CHI. L. REV. 733 (2015).

5. What does the Supreme Court mean by a "law of nature"? Is a mathematical algorithm the same as the relationship between blood-borne drug (or metabolite) levels and the efficacy of the drug? Is a formula such as the one in *Flook* the product of observation, such as the correlation in *Mayo*? Do mathematical relationships exist "in nature" where engineers and mathematicians discover them, or are they human creations? A more apt description of what the Court has in mind may be "facts about the world." The optimal metabolic level of thiopurine in the human body isn't a "law of nature" in a classical sense. But it is a fact to be discovered, not invented. That seems enough to bring it within the ambit of *Mayo*.

As for the algorithms in cases such as *Flook*, there is a longstanding tradition that sees mathematical relationships as preexisting facts about the world that are merely discovered, rather than invented. *See Platonism in the Philosophy of Mathematics*, STANFORD ENCYCLOPEDIA OF PHILOSOPHY, http://plato.stanford.edu/entries/platonism-mathematics/. On the other hand, there is an alternative tradition that sees mathematics as a very useful set of descriptive aids that are more properly described as inventions rather than pre-existing truths. *See* MARK BALAGUER, PLATONISM AND ANTI-PLATONISM IN MATHEMATICS (2001). In any event, computer software code can hardly be described as pure mathematics—it is written in a complex, human-invented programming language that is used to solve real-world problems. It would surprise most coders to be told that the complex piece of programming they worked on for three months was merely "discovered"!

One author has suggested that there are actually three types of "abstract ideas" under the Court's current cases:

- "laws of nature as such." This was what was at issue in cases like *Neilson*, and includes *Mayo*'s focus on facts about the world.

- mental steps and economic activity such as business methods and calculations that can be done in the human mind, even if they are in fact performed using a computer.

- a new output or function of a machine where the machine itself is not new.

Joseph Matal, *The Three Types of Abstract Ideas*, 30 Fed. Cir. B.J. 87 (2021). The Court's use of the term "abstract ideas" or "laws of nature" to refer to these very different concepts may help explain some of the doctrinal confusion in this area.

6. *The* Alice *Decision.* In *Alice Corp. v. CLS Bank International*, 573 U.S. 208 (2014), the Supreme Court addressed patent claims reminiscent of those at issue in *Bilski*. A representative claim stated:

A method of exchanging obligations as between parties, each party holding a credit record and a debit record with an exchange institution, the credit records and debit records for exchange of predetermined obligations, the method comprising the steps of:

(a) creating a shadow credit record and a shadow debit record for each stakeholder party to be held independently by a supervisory institution from the exchange institutions;

(b) obtaining from each exchange institution a start-of-day balance for each shadow credit record and shadow debit record;

(c) for every transaction resulting in an exchange obligation, the supervisory institution adjusting each respective party's shadow credit record or shadow debit record, allowing only these transactions that do not result in the value of the shadow debit record being less than the value of the shadow credit record at any time, each said adjustment taking place in chronological order, and

(d) at the end-of-day, the supervisory institution instructing on[e] of the exchange institutions to exchange credits or debits to the credit record and debit record of the respective parties in accordance with the adjustments of the said permitted transactions, the credits and debits being irrevocable, time invariant obligations placed on the exchange institutions.

U.S. Patent No. 5,970,479, Claim 33. The en banc Federal Circuit divided 5-5 on the interpretation of *Bilski* and *Mayo*. Writing for a unanimous Supreme Court, Justice Thomas reaffirmed the inventive application approach revived in *Mayo*. The decision characterized *Mayo* as a two-step inquiry:

Step 1: Is the patent "directed to" a patent-ineligible law of nature, natural phenomena, or abstract idea?

Step 2: If so, does the claim contain an inventive concept sufficient to transform the ineligible law of nature, natural phenomena, or abstract idea into a patent-eligible application of the ineligible subject matter?

The *Alice* decision characterized step two of this analysis as a search for an "inventive concept"—i.e., an element or combination of elements that is "sufficient to ensure that the patent in practice amounts to significantly more than a patent upon the [ineligible concept] itself." *Id.* at 218. Applying this framework, the Court concluded that the representative method claim does no more than implement the abstract idea of intermediated settlement on a generic computer and that the system and media claims add nothing of substance to the underlying abstract idea. *Id.* at 217-27. Echoing Justice Stevens' concurrence in *Bilski*, Justice Sotomayor, joined by Justices Ginsburg and Breyer, concurred in the holding based on the view that business methods do not qualify as a "process" under §101. *Id.* at 227; *see* Peter S. Menell, *Forty Years of Wondering in the Wilderness and No Closer to the Promised Land: Bilski's Superficial Textualism and the Missed Opportunity to Return Patent Law to its Technology Mooring*, 63 STAN. L. REV. 1289 (2011).

7. *Implementing the Mayo/Alice Framework.* The two-step *Alice* test has become the definitive test for patentable subject matter since 2014. Lower courts have struggled to apply the Supreme Court's decisions. *See DDR Holdings, LLC v. Hotels.com, L.P.*, 773 F.3d 1245 (Fed. Cir. 2014) (emphasizing under step 1 that the claim is "rooted in the computer technology" and hence not abstract; and basing step 2 analysis on a bald assertion that the claimed invention is "not merely the routine or conventional use of the Internet" without discussion of prior art); *Ultramercial, Inc. v. Hulu, LLC*, 772 F.3d 709, 715 (Fed. Cir. 2014) (noting that "[a]s the Court stated in *Alice*, '[a]t some level, "all inventions . . . embody, use, reflect, rest upon, or apply laws of nature, natural phenomena, or abstract ideas"").

Between 2014 and the end of 2017, district courts invalidated over 300 patents on §101 grounds. By contrast, courts invalidated fewer than 30 patents on §101 grounds over the prior decade. The Federal Circuit in particular invalidated more than 90% of the claims that reached it on §101 grounds between 2014 and 2019. But patentees have been gaining ground over time; the share of patentee wins is steadily increasing. *See* Mark A. Lemley & Samantha Zyontz, *Does Alice Target Patent Trolls?*, 18 J. EMPIRICAL LEGAL STUD. 47 (2021).

Mayo and *Alice* have had a substantial effect on Patent Office rejections, but only in some fields:

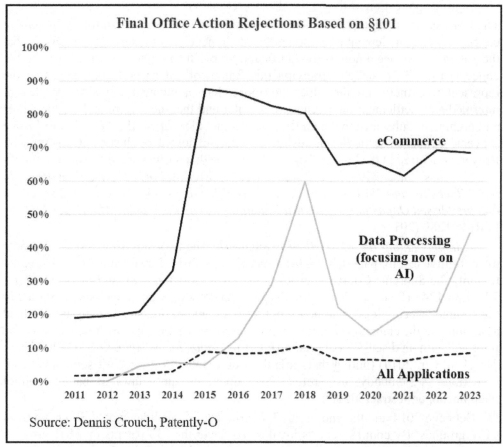

Source: Dennis Crouch, Patently-O

8. *Procedure.* In the wake of *Alice*, district courts began to invalidate patent claims at the pleading (FED. R. CIV. P. 12(b)(6) and 12(c)) and summary judgment stages, often without construing the claims. One rationale for addressing §101 invalidity contentions at an early stage of litigation is to afford courts a quick way to screen out weak patents, particularly abstract business method patents issued prior to the Supreme Court's *Bilski*, *Mayo*, and *Alice* decisions.

In a stark shift, the Federal Circuit ruled in 2018 that "[t]he question of whether a claim element or combination of elements is well-understood, routine and conventional to a skilled artisan in the relevant field is a question of fact" and hence is not amenable to summary adjudication unless there is no genuine disputed issue. *See Berkheimer v. HP Inc.*, 881 F.3d 1360, 1368 (Fed. Cir. 2018). Moreover, "[t]he mere fact that something is disclosed in a piece of prior art . . . does not mean it was well-understood, routine, and conventional." *Id.* at 1369. Furthermore, the Federal Circuit intimated in *Aatrix Software v. Green Shades Software*, 882 F.3d 1121, 1128, 1130 (Fed. Cir. 2018), that claim construction might be necessary in resolving whether a claim is invalid under §101.

The Federal Circuit's *Berkheimer* and *Aatrix* decisions will likely shift litigants and courts toward focusing on other grounds for invalidating patents. Are there other relatively efficient ways to dispose of unmeritorious cases? Perhaps. Moreover, the new administrative review procedures available under the AIA provide an additional avenue. *See* Chapter III(D). But patentable subject matter is a question of law, while most other invalidity doctrines are factual or mixed questions of law and fact, meaning that it is much harder to resolve them early in a case. That might be a good thing. *See* Dennis D. Crouch & Robert P. Merges, *Operating Efficiently Post-*Bilski *by Ordering Patent Doctrine Decision-Making*, 25 BERKELEY TECH. L.J. 1673 (2010) (arguing that §101 should be used only as a last resort). But it may also mean that plaintiffs with weak patents can coerce a settlement by pointing to the cost and uncertainty of litigation.

The policy question is whether changing §101, thereby increasing the cost of weeding out bad patents early in litigation, is worth the cost. Making §103 summary judgment the earliest occasion for eliminating weak patents adds settlement leverage for patent owners; letting them get to trial adds even more. That needs to be balanced against any extra cost incurred in applying the *Mayo-Alice* §101 test in cases in which no §101 analysis would have been necessary under the pre-*Mayo/Alice* cases, or would be necessary under a newly revised §101. *Mayo/Alice* added a §101 issue to many cases, adding to the cost of liitgation. Under the current test, some patent owners must defend a FED. R. CIV. P. 12(b)(6) motion that would not have been made under the old law. On the other hand, many patents that face a §101 challenge are invalidated on that ground. Does that suggest that the law is an efficient way to weed out weak claims?

9. *Preemption Rationale.* How does §101 patentable subject matter eligibility analysis compare with the §112(a) written description requirement? Citing *Morse*, the *Mayo* Court emphasizes that its limits on patent eligibility are based on concerns about preempting the use of a natural law, i.e., conferring overbroad monopoly power and interfering with cumulative creativity. Is *Morse* better understood as a case about overbroad claiming—the specification did not support a claim to all methods of communicating at a distance using electromagnetism—or about the abstract nature of Morse's audacious eighth claim? In *Dolbear v. Am. Bell Tel. Co.*, 126 U.S. 1, 535 (1888), the Supreme Court explained that an inventor's claim might practically preempt all of a discovery. Such breadth would "show []the great importance of [the] discovery, but it will not invalidate [the] patent." Does §112 provide sufficient tools for ensuring that patents do not extend beyond their proper scope? Or is there room for patentable subject matter to police patent overreaching? *See* Mark A. Lemley, et al., *Life After* Bilski, 63 STAN. L. REV. 1315 (2011) (arguing that the proper role for patentable subject matter is in policing overbreadth).

Recall Justice Frankfurter's concurrence in *Funk Brothers* that introducing "such terms as 'the work of nature' and the 'laws of nature'" only confuse the issue as "[a]rguments drawn from such terms for ascertaining patentability could fairly be employed to challenge almost every patent." 333 U.S. at 134–35.

How are patentees, the PTO, and lower courts to make sense of the inventive application doctrine? Aren't most innovations in the burgeoning field of personalized medicine—the determination of correlations between an individual's genetic makeup and the probabilities of his or her responsiveness to particular treatments such as chemotherapy—likely to fall within the "law of nature" exclusion? Is the Court suggesting that such application of breakthrough scientific discoveries—even though potentially life-saving and worthy of a Nobel Prize—are unpatentable because they risk "inhibit[ing] further discovery by improperly tying up the future use of laws of nature"? Wouldn't it better, as Justice Frankfurter suggested in his *Funk Bros.* concurrence, to address the preemption concern by policing claim breadth? Can §112 serve that purpose? How would a §112 challenge have fared in *Mayo*?

Subsequent decisions have made clear that while preemption is the concern that motivates the patentable subject matter cases, the legal test is not whether a law of nature or an abstract idea is preempted. Rather, the two-part *Mayo-Alice* test is the definitive test for all patentable subject matter inquiries. *Ariosa Diagnostics, Inc. v. Sequenom, Inc.*, 788 F.3d 1371 (Fed. Cir. 2015).

10. *Patent Policy and Promoting Advances in Personalized Medicine.* Is *Mayo* good patent policy? Is it good health care policy? On what does your answer depend? The cost of personalized medicine research? The riskiness of personalized medicine research? The extent to which it constrains medical practitioners and downstream innovators? Suppose that the costs of collecting and evaluating DNA, which are falling precipitously, drive the cost of personalized medicine research. Does that affect your view?

Suppose Congress were to decide that the determination of novel and non-obvious correlations between known drug treatments and individual responsiveness based on molecular biology research merited patent protection. Similarly, suppose Congress were to decide that the determination of novel and non-obvious algorithms merited patent protection. Could Congress amend §101 to include the following: "Applications of newly discovered laws of nature and algorithms shall be eligible for patent protection so long as the claimed invention is new, non-obvious, and useful when viewed as a whole." Would such an approach effectively eliminate the patentable subject matter inquiry? How would the claims in *Alice* and *Mayo* fare under that test?

11. *Medical and Surgical Procedure Patents and Political Economy.* In 1992, Dr. Samuel L. Pallin obtained U.S. Patent No. 5,080,111 on a method of making self-sealing incisions as part of cataract surgery. Prior to this patent, medical professionals did not generally seek patents on surgical procedures. After word of this patent spread, the American Medical Association ("AMA") unanimously adopted a resolution at its 1994 Annual Meeting "vigorously condemn[ing] the patenting of medical and surgical procedures and [vowing to] work with Congress to outlaw this practice." The uproar increased after Dr. Pallin sued another doctor for infringement. *See Pallin v. Singer*, 36 U.S.P.Q.2d 1050 (D. Vt. 1995). A broad coalition of medical associations successfully enlisted several legislators with medical backgrounds to block such patents. The biotechnology and pharmaceutical industry, in conjunction with patent law associations,

vigorously opposed any effort to restrict patent eligibility. The ultimate compromise left §101 unchanged. Instead, Congress added §287(c), which bars infringement actions against any medical practitioner or a related health care entity. The provision does not, however, bar lawsuits against makers of devices specially designed to infringe a medical procedure patent. *See* §271(c) (contributory infringement). As noted earlier, an analogous compromise led to the establishment of a prior user right for methods of doing business following the Federal Circuit's *State Street Bank* decision opening the way for business method patents. The political economy surrounding reforming patentable subject matter (and patent law more generally) is complicated by entrenched interests.

iii.   *Patenting of Molecular Biology/Biotechnology*

Path-breaking discoveries in the field of genetic engineering have posed substantial challenges for patent eligibility. As noted earlier, the Supreme Court held in *Diamond v. Chakrabarty*, 447 U.S. 303 (1980), that newly invented genetically modified organisms were patentable.

But this precedent did not resolve the question of whether isolated sequences of DNA are patentable. Since the late 19th century, following Gregor Mendel's discovery of the basic principles of heredity from plant experiments and Swiss physician Friedrich Miescher's discovery of a microscopic substance in the pus of discarded surgical bandages, scientists have suspected that chemical compounds in the nuclei of cells played a role in human biology. In 1953, James Watson and Francis Crick proposed the double-helix model of DNA structure. Within a few years, they and others had begun to unravel the relationship among DNA, RNA, and proteins that form the foundation of molecular biology.

Although this early basic research was not patented, methods for combining and replicating DNA were. Stanford University and the University of California patented the first gene splicing methods, invented by Professors Stanley Cohen and Herbert Boyer, in the early 1970s and licensed them broadly, earning more than $200 million for the universities. Boyer would go on to co-found Genentech, which became a major biotechnology company. The polymerase chain reaction (PCR) technique for amplifying a single copy of a piece of DNA, invented by Dr. Kary Mullis of Cetus Corporation was patented in the late 1980s, *see* U.S. Patent Nos. 4,683,202, 4,683,195, 4,965,188. It greatly expanded biotechnology research. These method patents fit well within the mold of traditional scientific process inventions and did not encounter serious patentable subject matter eligibility challenges.

The use of these and other techniques to map the human (and other) genomes and isolate regions of the DNA structure associated with particular traits and disease propensities generated significant controversy over the patenting of natural substances and life. Could scientists patent particular, isolated, naturally-occurring sequences of DNA?

To appreciate this question, we need to examine earlier jurisprudence relating to claims to isolated natural substances. In *American Wood-Paper Co. v. The Fibre Disintegrating Co.*, 90 U.S. (23 Wall.) 566 (1874), the patentee claimed "as a new article of manufacture" "a pulp suitable for the manufacture of paper, made from wood or other vegetable substances, by boiling the wood or other vegetable substance in an alkali under pressure, substantially as described." In essence, the patentee sought to patent the cellulose product (and not just the process) of a paper production technology. The Supreme Court rejected the claim, noting that "There are many things well known and valuable in medicine or in the arts which may be extracted from divers[e] substances. But the extract is the same, no matter from what it has been taken. A process to obtain it from a subject from which it has never been taken may be the creature of invention, but the thing itself when obtained cannot be called a new manufacture." *Id.* at 593–94.

Notwithstanding (and apparently unaware of) this decision, Judge Learned Hand issued a highly influential decision several decades later upholding a claim to purified adrenaline. *See Parke-Davis & Co. v. H.K. Mulford & Co.*, 189 F. 95 (C.C.S.D.N.Y. 1911) (Hand, J.), *aff'd in part, rev'd in part*, 196 F. 496 (2d Cir. 1912); Linda J. Demaine & Aaron Xavier Fellmeth, *Reinventing the Double Helix: A Novel and Nonobvious Reconceptualization of the Biotechnology Patent*, 55 STAN. L. REV. 303, 334–39 (2002). Judge Hand established a pragmatic test: "Takamine was the first to make [purified adrenaline] available for any use by removing it from the other gland-tissue. . . . [I]t became for every practical purpose a new thing commercially and therapeutically." 189 F. at 102–03.

With the advances in biotechnology following Watson and Crick's path-breaking discoveries, mapping the human genome became a realistic goal by the mid-1980s. In 1988, Congress funded the Department of Energy and the National Institutes of Health (NIH) to undertake the Human Genome Project. A private company also entered the competition, which quickly led to the filing of patent claims on sequences of cDNA called expressed sequence tags (ESTs). After reviewing the patent jurisprudence, the PTO issued a series of guidelines essentially following Judge Hand's approach. In its 2001 Utility Examination Guidelines, the PTO explained:

> An inventor can patent a discovery when the patent application satisfies the statutory requirements. The U.S. Constitution uses the word 'discoveries' where it authorizes Congress to promote progress made by inventors. . . .
>
> . . . Thus, an inventor's discovery of a gene can be the basis for a patent on the genetic composition isolated from its natural state and processed through purifying steps that separate the gene from other molecules naturally associated with it.

PTO, Utility Examination Guidelines, 66 Fed. Reg. 1092, 1092–93 (Jan. 5, 2001) (citing Parke-Davis and a patent issued to Louis Pasteur on a yeast used in beer brewing, U.S. Patent No. 141,072 (1873)). Patenting of isolated genetic compounds quickly took off, with the principal focus on the utility requirement, which we covered in Chapter III(B)(3).

The patentable subject matter question, however, was simmering and would come to a boil over a decade later over the patenting of genes associated with breast and ovarian cancer. In the early 1990s human gene discovery was incredibly challenging.

The human genome contains about 3 billion nucleotides and the average gene contains about 10,000–15,000 nucleotides making the search for a specific gene without a map akin to finding a needle in the haystack.

In 1990, a UC Berkeley team led by Professor Mary-Claire King made the first major step towards identifying the breast cancer 1 (BRCA1) gene by using linkage analysis[11] to locate BRCA1 to a 22-million nucleotide region on chromosome 17. *See* Mary-Claire King. *"The Race" to Clone BRCA1*, 343 SCIENCE 1462 (Mar. 28, 2014).

This region was too large to directly sequence or clone but set off a race between competing teams of scientists to pinpoint the exact location and sequence of BRCA1. Mark Skolnick, a population geneticist, assembled a team and co-founded Myriad Genetics to discover the BRCA1 gene. Myriad had two key advantages—strong ability to raise capital to undertake this labor-intensive work and access to the Utah Cancer registry and an extensive database of Mormon pedigrees living in Utah. These factors led Myriad to pinpoint the BRCA1 gene to a 600,000-nucleotide region, which was small enough for physical mapping. Myriad used several positional cloning strategies to map this region using libraries of random human genomic DNA fragments and cDNA. But others, including King, were also racing to sequence the BRCA1 and BRCA2 genes. In 1994, Myriad discovered the precise location of BRCA1, the BRCA1 cDNA sequence, and a partial sequence of BRCA1 genomic DNA. Myriad subsequently filed a patent containing composition and method claims stemming from this discovery including isolated DNA claims. A competing company, Oncor, also filed patents on the BRCA1 gene, and the two sued each other for infringement. Myriad published the gene sequence for BRCA2 in 1995, just one day before a competing group published partial sequence data for the same gene. *See* E. Richard Gold & Julia Carbone, *Myriad Genetics: In the Eye of the Policy Storm*, 12 GENET. MED. S39 (2010).

After over a decade of patients paying thousands of dollars to use Myriad's test for the gene, the Association for Molecular Pathology, a consortium of individuals from academic and community medical centers, government, and industry, challenged the patentability of DNA compounds.

Association for Molecular Pathology v. Myriad Genetics, Inc.
Supreme Court of the United States
569 U.S. 576 (2013)

THOMAS, J.

Respondent Myriad Genetics, Inc. (Myriad), discovered the precise location and sequence of two human genes, mutations of which can substantially increase the risks

---

[11] Genetic linkage analysis is based on the tendency for genes and other genetic markers to be inherited together because of their location near one another on the same chromosome. A gene is a functional physical unit of heredity that can be passed from parent to child. Because DNA segments that lie near each other on a chromosome tend to be inherited together, markers are often used as tools for tracking the inheritance pattern of a gene that has not yet been identified but whose approximate location is known. Linkage analysis uses statistical measures to estimate linkage of DNA and genetic traits.

of breast and ovarian cancer. Myriad obtained a number of patents based upon its discovery. This case involves claims from three of them and requires us to resolve whether a naturally occurring segment of deoxyribonucleic acid (DNA) is patent eligible under 35 U.S.C. §101 by virtue of its isolation from the rest of the human genome. We also address the patent eligibility of synthetically created DNA known as complementary DNA (cDNA), which contains the same protein-coding information found in a segment of natural DNA but omits portions within the DNA segment that do not code for proteins. For the reasons that follow, we hold that a naturally occurring DNA segment is a product of nature and not patent eligible merely because it has been isolated, but that cDNA is patent eligible because it is not naturally occurring. We, therefore, affirm in part and reverse in part the decision of the United States Court of Appeals for the Federal Circuit.

I

A

Genes form the basis for hereditary traits in living organisms. The human genome consists of approximately 22,000 genes packed into 23 pairs of chromosomes. Each gene is encoded as DNA, which takes the shape of the familiar "double helix" that Doctors James Watson and Francis Crick first described in 1953. Each "cross-bar" in the DNA helix consists of two chemically joined nucleotides. The possible nucleotides are adenine (A), thymine (T), cytosine (C), and guanine (G), each of which binds naturally with another nucleotide: A pairs with T; C pairs with G. The nucleotide cross-bars are chemically connected to a sugar-phosphate backbone that forms the outside framework of the DNA helix. Sequences of DNA nucleotides contain the information necessary to create strings of amino acids, which in turn are used in the body to build proteins. Only some DNA nucleotides, however, code for amino acids; these nucleotides are known as "exons." Nucleotides that do not code for amino acids, in contrast, are known as "introns."

Creation of proteins from DNA involves two principal steps, known as transcription and translation. In transcription, the bonds between DNA nucleotides separate, and the DNA helix unwinds into two single strands. A single strand is used as a template to create a complementary ribonucleic acid (RNA) strand. The nucleotides on the DNA strand pair naturally with their counterparts, with the exception that RNA uses the nucleotide base uracil (U) instead of thymine (T). Transcription results in a single strand RNA molecule, known as pre-RNA, whose nucleotides form an inverse image of the DNA strand from which it was created. Pre-RNA still contains nucleotides corresponding to both the exons and introns in the DNA molecule. The pre-RNA is then naturally "spliced" by the physical removal of the introns. The resulting product is a strand of RNA that contains nucleotides corresponding only to the exons from the original DNA strand. The exons-only strand is known as messenger RNA (mRNA), which creates amino acids through translation. In translation, cellular structures known as ribosomes read each set of three nucleotides, known as codons, in the mRNA. Each codon either tells the ribosomes which of the 20 possible amino acids to synthesize or provides a stop signal that ends amino acid production.

DNA's informational sequences and the processes that create mRNA, amino acids, and proteins occur naturally within cells. Scientists can, however, extract DNA from cells using well known laboratory methods. These methods allow scientists to isolate specific segments of DNA—for instance, a particular gene or part of a gene—which can then be further studied, manipulated, or used. It is also possible to create DNA synthetically through processes similarly well known in the field of genetics. One such method begins with an mRNA molecule and uses the natural bonding properties of nucleotides to create a new, synthetic DNA molecule. The result is the inverse of the mRNA's inverse image of the original DNA, with one important distinction: Because the natural creation of mRNA involves splicing that removes introns, the synthetic DNA created from mRNA also contains only the exon sequences. This synthetic DNA created in the laboratory from mRNA is known as complementary DNA (cDNA).

Changes in the genetic sequence are called mutations. Mutations can be as small as the alteration of a single nucleotide—a change affecting only one letter in the genetic code. Such small-scale changes can produce an entirely different amino acid or can end protein production altogether. Large changes, involving the deletion, rearrangement, or duplication of hundreds or even millions of nucleotides, can result in the elimination, misplacement, or duplication of entire genes. Some mutations are harmless, but others can cause disease or increase the risk of disease. As a result, the study of genetics can lead to valuable medical breakthroughs.

B

This case involves patents filed by Myriad after it made one such medical breakthrough. Myriad discovered the precise location and sequence of what are now known as the BRCA1 and BRCA2 genes. Mutations in these genes can dramatically increase an individual's risk of developing breast and ovarian cancer. The average American woman has a 12- to 13-percent risk of developing breast cancer, but for women with certain genetic mutations, the risk can range between 50 and 80 percent for breast cancer and between 20 and 50 percent for ovarian cancer. Before Myriad's discovery of the BRCA1 and BRCA2 genes, scientists knew that heredity played a role in establishing a woman's risk of developing breast and ovarian cancer, but they did not know which genes were associated with those cancers.

Myriad identified the exact location of the BRCA1 and BRCA2 genes on chromosomes 17 and 13. Chromosome 17 has approximately 80 million nucleotides, and chromosome 13 has approximately 114 million. Within those chromosomes, the BRCA1 and BRCA2 genes are each about 80,000 nucleotides long. If just exons are counted, the BRCA1 gene is only about 5,500 nucleotides long; for the BRCA2 gene, that number is about 10,200. Knowledge of the location of the BRCA1 and BRCA2 genes allowed Myriad to determine their typical nucleotide sequence. That information, in turn, enabled Myriad to develop medical tests that are useful for detecting mutations in a patient's BRCA1 and BRCA2 genes and thereby assessing whether the patient has an increased risk of cancer.

Once it found the location and sequence of the BRCA1 and BRCA2 genes, Myriad sought and obtained a number of patents. Nine composition claims from three of those patents are at issue in this case. Claims 1, 2, 5, and 6 from [U.S. Patent 5,747,282] are representative. The first claim asserts a patent on "[a]n isolated DNA coding for a BRCA1 polypeptide," which has "the amino acid sequence set forth in SEQ ID NO:2." App. 822. SEQ ID NO:2 sets forth a list of 1,863 amino acids that the typical BRCA1 gene encodes. See id., at 785–790. Put differently, claim 1 asserts a patent claim on the DNA code that tells a cell to produce the string of BRCA1 amino acids listed in SEQ ID NO:2.

Claim 2 of the '282 patent operates similarly. It claims "[t]he isolated DNA of claim 1, wherein said DNA has the nucleotide sequence set forth in SEQ ID NO:1." Like SEQ ID NO:2, SEQ ID NO:1 sets forth a long list of data, in this instance the sequence of cDNA that codes for the BRCA1 amino acids listed in claim 1. Importantly, SEQ ID NO:1 lists only the cDNA exons in the BRCA1 gene, rather than a full DNA sequence containing both exons and introns. As a result, the Federal Circuit recognized that claim 2 asserts a patent on the cDNA nucleotide sequence listed in SEQ ID NO:1, which codes for the typical BRCA1 gene.

Claim 5 of the '282 patent claims a subset of the data in claim 1. In particular, it claims "[a]n isolated DNA having at least 15 nucleotides of the DNA of claim 1." App. 822. The practical effect of claim 5 is to assert a patent on any series of 15 nucleotides that exist in the typical BRCA1 gene. Because the BRCA1 gene is thousands of nucleotides long, even BRCA1 genes with substantial mutations are likely to contain at least one segment of 15 nucleotides that correspond to the typical BRCA1 gene. Similarly, claim 6 of the '282 patent claims "[a]n isolated DNA having at least 15 nucleotides of the DNA of claim 2." *Ibid.* This claim operates similarly to claim 5, except that it references the cDNA-based claim 2. The remaining claims at issue are similar, though several list common mutations rather than typical BRCA1 and BRCA2 sequences. *See ibid.* (claim 7 of the '282 patent); *id.*, at 930 (claim 1 of the '473 patent); *id.*, at 1028 (claims 1, 6, and 7 of the '492 patent).

C

Myriad's patents would, if valid, give it the exclusive right to isolate an individual's BRCA1 and BRCA2 genes (or any strand of 15 or more nucleotides within the genes) by breaking the covalent bonds that connect the DNA to the rest of the individual's genome. The patents would also give Myriad the exclusive right to synthetically create BRCA cDNA.

But isolation is necessary to conduct genetic testing, and Myriad was not the only entity to offer BRCA testing after it discovered the genes. The University of Pennsylvania's Genetic Diagnostic Laboratory (GDL) and others provided genetic testing services to women. Petitioner Dr. Harry Ostrer, then a researcher at New York University School of Medicine, routinely sent his patients' DNA samples to GDL for testing. After learning of GDL's testing and Ostrer's activities, Myriad sent letters to them asserting that the genetic testing infringed Myriad's patents. App. 94–95 (Ostrer letter). In response, GDL agreed to stop testing and informed Ostrer that it would no longer accept patient samples. Myriad also filed patent infringement suits against other entities that performed BRCA testing, resulting in settlements in which the defendants agreed to cease all allegedly infringing activity. Myriad, thus, solidified its position as the only entity providing BRCA testing.

Some years later, petitioner Ostrer, along with medical patients, advocacy groups, and other doctors, filed this lawsuit seeking a declaration that Myriad's patents are invalid under 35 U.S.C. §101. The District Court . . . granted summary judgment to petitioners on the composition claims at issue in this case based on its conclusion that Myriad's claims, including claims related to cDNA, were invalid because they covered products of nature. The Federal Circuit reversed, and this Court granted the petition for certiorari, vacated the judgment, and remanded the case in light of *Mayo Collaborative Services v. Prometheus Laboratories, Inc.*, 566 U.S. 66 (2012).

II

A

Section 101 of the Patent Act provides:

"Whoever invents or discovers any new and useful . . . composition of matter, or any new and useful improvement thereof, may obtain a patent therefor, subject to the conditions and requirements of this title."

35 U.S.C. §101.

We have "long held that this provision contains an important implicit exception[:] Laws of nature, natural phenomena, and abstract ideas are not patentable." *Mayo*, 566 U.S., at 70. Rather, "'they are the basic tools of scientific and technological work'" that lie beyond the domain of patent protection. As the Court has explained, without this exception, there would be considerable danger that the grant of patents would "tie up" the use of such tools and thereby "inhibit future innovation premised upon them." This would be at odds with the very point of patents, which exist to promote creation.

The rule against patents on naturally occurring things is not without limits, however, for "all inventions at some level embody, use, reflect, rest upon, or apply laws of nature, natural phenomena, or abstract ideas," and "too broad an interpretation of this exclusionary principle could eviscerate patent law." 566 U.S., at 71. As we have recognized before, patent protection strikes a delicate balance between creating "incentives that lead to creation, invention, and discovery" and "imped[ing] the flow of information that might permit, indeed spur, invention." *Id.*, at 92. We must apply this well-established standard to determine whether Myriad's patents claim any "new and useful . . . composition of matter," §101, or instead claim naturally occurring phenomena.

B

It is undisputed that Myriad did not create or alter any of the genetic information encoded in the BRCA1 and BRCA2 genes. The location and order of the nucleotides existed in nature before Myriad found them. Nor did Myriad create or alter the genetic structure of DNA. Instead, Myriad's principal contribution was uncovering the precise location and genetic sequence of the BRCA1 and BRCA2 genes within chromosomes 17 and 13. The question is whether this renders the genes patentable.

Myriad recognizes that our decision in [*Diamond v.*] *Chakrabarty*, 447 U.S. 303 (1980)] is central to this inquiry. In *Chakrabarty*, scientists added four plasmids to a bacterium, which enabled it to break down various components of crude oil. 447 U.S., at 305, and n.1. The Court held that the modified bacterium was patentable. The *Chakrabarty* bacterium was new "with markedly different characteristics from any found in nature," 447 U.S., at 310, due to the additional plasmids and resultant "capacity for degrading oil." *Id.*, at 305, n.1. In this case, by contrast, Myriad did not create anything. To be sure, it found an important and useful gene, but separating that gene from its surrounding genetic material is not an act of invention.

Groundbreaking, innovative, or even brilliant discovery does not by itself satisfy the §101 inquiry. In *Funk Brothers Seed Co. v. Kalo Inoculant Co.*, 333 U.S. 127 (1948), this Court considered a composition patent that claimed a mixture of naturally occurring strains of bacteria that helped leguminous plants take nitrogen from the air and fix it in the soil. The Court held that the composition was not patent eligible because the patent holder did not alter the bacteria in any way. His patent claim thus fell squarely within the law of nature exception. So do Myriad's. Myriad found the location of the BRCA1 and BRCA2 genes, but that discovery, by itself, does not render the BRCA genes "new . . . composition[s] of matter," §101, that are patent eligible.

Indeed, Myriad's patent descriptions highlight the problem with its claims. For example, a section of the '282 patent's Detailed Description of the Invention indicates that Myriad found the location of a gene associated with increased risk of breast cancer and identified mutations of that gene that increase the risk. In subsequent language Myriad explains that the location of the gene was unknown until Myriad found it among the approximately eight million nucleotide pairs contained in a subpart of chromosome 17. Many of Myriad's patent descriptions simply detail the "iterative process" of discovery by which Myriad narrowed the possible locations for the gene sequences that it sought. Myriad seeks to import these extensive research efforts into the §101 patent-eligibility inquiry. But extensive effort alone is insufficient to satisfy the demands of §101.

Nor are Myriad's claims saved by the fact that isolating DNA from the human genome severs chemical bonds and thereby creates a nonnaturally occurring molecule. Myriad's claims are simply not expressed in terms of chemical composition, nor do they rely in any way on the chemical changes that result from the isolation of a particular section of DNA. Instead, the claims understandably focus on the genetic information encoded in the BRCA1 and BRCA2 genes. If the patents depended upon the creation of a unique molecule, then a would-be infringer could arguably avoid at least Myriad's patent claims on entire genes (such as claims 1 and 2 of the '282 patent) by isolating a DNA sequence that included both the BRCA1 or BRCA2 gene and one additional nucleotide pair. Such a molecule would not be chemically identical to the molecule "invented" by Myriad. But Myriad obviously would resist that outcome because its claim is concerned primarily with the information contained in the genetic sequence, not with the specific chemical composition of a particular molecule.

Finally, Myriad argues that the PTO's past practice of awarding gene patents is entitled to deference, citing *J.E.M. Ag Supply, Inc. v. Pioneer Hi-Bred Int'l, Inc.*, 534 U.S. 124 (2001). We disagree. Congress has not endorsed the views of the PTO in subsequent legislation.

Further undercutting the PTO's practice, the United States argued in the Federal Circuit and in this Court that isolated DNA was not patent eligible under §101, Brief for United States as Amicus Curiae 20-33, and that the PTO's practice was not "a sufficient reason to hold that isolated DNA is patent-eligible." *Id.*, at 26. *See also id.*, at 28–29. These concessions weigh against deferring to the PTO's determination.

C

cDNA does not present the same obstacles to patentability as naturally occurring, isolated DNA segments. As already explained, creation of a cDNA sequence from mRNA results in an exons-only molecule that is not naturally occurring. Petitioners concede that cDNA differs from natural DNA in that "the non-coding regions have been removed." They nevertheless argue that cDNA is not patent eligible because "[t]he nucleotide sequence of cDNA is dictated by nature, not by the lab technician." That may be so, but the lab technician unquestionably creates something new when cDNA is made. cDNA retains the naturally occurring exons of DNA, but it is distinct from the DNA from which it was derived. As a result, cDNA is not a "product of nature" and is patent eligible under §101, except insofar as very short series of DNA may have no intervening introns to remove when creating cDNA. In that situation, a short strand of cDNA may be indistinguishable from natural DNA.

III

It is important to note what is not implicated by this decision. First, there are no method claims before this Court. Had Myriad created an innovative method of manipulating genes while searching for the BRCA1 and BRCA2 genes, it could possibly have sought a method patent. But the processes used by Myriad to isolate DNA were well understood by geneticists at the time of Myriad's patents [and so method claims were not available].

Similarly, this case does not involve patents on new applications of knowledge about the BRCA1 and BRCA2 genes. Judge Bryson aptly noted that, "[a]s the first party with knowledge of the [BRCA1 and BRCA2] sequences, Myriad was in an excellent position to claim applications of that knowledge. Many of its unchallenged claims are limited to such applications." 689 F.3d, at 1349.

Nor do we consider the patentability of DNA in which the order of the naturally occurring nucleotides has been altered. Scientific alteration of the genetic code presents a different inquiry, and we express no opinion about the application of §101 to such endeavors. We merely hold that genes and the information they encode are not patent eligible under §101 simply because they have been isolated from the surrounding genetic material.

COMMENTS AND QUESTIONS

1. In invalidating Myriad's isolated DNA claims, the Court noted that the isolated DNA contained the same genetic information as naturally occurring genomic DNA and that Myriad did not create or alter this information. The Court also noted that "[a]s the first party with knowledge of the [BRCA1] sequences, Myriad was in an excellent position to claim applications of that knowledge." One very useful application is sequencing BRCA1 DNA for mutations to diagnose or prognose breast cancer. Should the patentee's identification of the function of the sequence and listing the sequence mean that the sequence is patentable? How about a method claim limited to the use of the sequence to diagnose susceptibility to breast cancer?

2. The Court affirmed the validity of Myriad's BRCA1 cDNA claims on the ground that BRCA1 cDNA was not naturally occurring and therefore not drawn to a judicial exception: "the lab technician unquestionably creates something new when cDNA is made." cDNA, however, contains the same genetic information as naturally occurring mRNA and Myriad did not create or alter this information. The act of reverse-transcribing natural mRNA into cDNA was known, routine, and conventional when the Myriad patents were filed in 1994. *See* Jeffrey A. Lefstin, *The Three Faces of Prometheus: A Post-*Alice *Jurisprudence of Abstractions*, 16 N.C. J.L. & TECH. 647, 678–79 (2015). Are the chemical differences between cDNA and mRNA sufficient to make cDNA patentable? Would your answer change if you were presented evidence that isolated DNA is similarly chemically different from genomic DNA? (This was in fact an emphasis in some of the Federal Circuit opinions in *Myriad*.) How can the conventional (non-inventive) application of an unpatentable product of nature (genomic DNA) result in a patentable composition (cDNA)? Note that the Court does not mention *Mayo* and the "inventive concept" test in distinguishing cDNA from gDNA.

Lower courts have not read *Myriad*'s discussion of cDNA expansively. They have refused to patent human gene sequences modified with other standard but non-naturally-occurring material like primers. *In re BRCA1- and BRCA2-Based Heredity Cancer Test Patent Litig.*, 774 F.3d 755 (Fed. Cir. 2014).

3. Justice Scalia concurred in part and concurred in the judgment. Here is the entirety of his opinion:

> I join the judgment of the Court, and all of its opinion except Part I-A and some portions of the rest of the opinion going into fine details of molecular biology. I am unable to affirm those details on my own knowledge or even my own belief. It suffices for me to affirm, having studied the opinions below and the expert briefs presented here, that the portion of DNA isolated from its natural state sought to be patented is identical to that portion of the DNA in its natural state; and that complementary DNA (cDNA) is a synthetic creation not normally present in nature.

Is Justice Scalia concerned that his colleagues on the Court lack the capacity to resolve patent cases involving advanced scientific issues? As just noted, arguably he was right to be so concerned. The majority did not appear to understand the simplicity of the relationship between gDNA and cDNA or how easy it is to make cDNA. It is notable that Judge Learned Hand, widely considered one of the most accomplished intellectual property jurists, voiced a similar sentiment in the concluding paragraph of the *Parke-Davis* opinion.

> I cannot stop without calling attention to the extraordinary condition of the law which makes it possible for a man without any knowledge of even the rudiments of chemistry to pass upon such questions as these. The inordinate expense of time is the least of the resulting evils, for only a trained chemist is really capable of passing upon such facts . . . In Germany, where the national spirit eagerly seeks for all the assistance it can get from the whole range of human knowledge, they do quite differently. The court summons technical judges to whom technical questions are submitted and who can intelligently pass upon the issues without blindly groping among testimony upon matters wholly out of their ken. How long we shall continue to blunder along without the aid of unpartisan and authoritative scientific assistance in the administration of justice, no one knows; but all fair persons not conventionalized by provincial legal habits of mind ought, I should think, unite to effect some such advance.

Parke-Davis & Co. v. H.K. Mulford Co., 189 F. 95, 115 (C.C.S.D.N.Y 1911). Germany uses a three-judge panel, including a technical expert, on its patent cases. What are the benefits and drawbacks of employing technically trained judges instead of generalists to adjudicate patent cases?

4. Courts and the PTO considered DNA compositions to be patent-eligible (subject to meeting the separate utility requirement, which we will turn to in Chapter III(B)(5)) beginning in the 1980s. By the time *Myriad* was decided, the era of new human gene patents was effectively over; the human genome had been sequenced more than a decade before. In what ways do you think the history of the BRCA1 discovery might have been different if isolated DNA was not considered patent-eligible subject matter in the 1990s? What about the development of genetic tests for breast cancer?

PROBLEM

Problem III-10. Expectant parents have long sought to know about the health of their fetus. Through amniocentesis, doctors have been able to extract fluid from the amniotic sac surrounding the developing fetus to conduct various tests to determine genetic disorders, such as Down syndrome. Amniocentesis is usually done when a woman is between fourteen and sixteen weeks pregnant. The procedure is typically limited to women who have an elevated risk for genetic or chromosomal problems. The test is invasive and poses small but significant risks to the fetus and mother, such as miscarriage, needle injury to the fetus, and transmission of infection such as HIV or hepatitis C from an infected mother to fetus.

In 1996, Drs. Dennis Lo and James Wainscoat discovered cell-free fetal DNA ("cffDNA") in maternal plasma and serum. cffDNA is non-cellular fetal DNA that circulates freely in a pregnant woman's blood. Drs. Lo and Wainscoat implemented a method for detecting the small fraction of paternally inherited cffDNA in maternal plasma or serum to determine fetal characteristics, such as gender and genetic abnormalities. The invention, commercialized by Sequenom as its MaterniT21 test, created a non-invasive alternative technique to analyze fetal DNA that avoids the risks of amniocentesis.

In 1999, they filed a patent application that claimed these non-invasive prenatal diagnosis methods:

> 1. A method for detecting a paternally inherited nucleic acid of fetal origin performed on a maternal serum or plasma sample from a pregnant female, which method comprises amplifying a paternally inherited nucleic acid from the serum or plasma sample and detecting the presence of a paternally inherited nucleic acid of fetal origin in the sample.

The specification provides, in pertinent part:

SUMMARY AND OBJECTS OF THE INVENTION

> It has now been discovered that foetal DNA is detectable in maternal serum or plasma samples. This is a surprising and unexpected finding; maternal plasma is the very material that is routinely discarded by investigators studying noninvasive prenatal diagnosis using foetal cells in maternal blood.

DETAILED DESCRIPTION OF THE PREFERRED EMBODIMENTS

> The preparation of serum or plasma from the maternal blood sample is carried out by standard techniques. . . . Standard nucleic acid amplification systems can be used, including PCR [polymerase chain reaction], the ligase chain reaction, nucleic acid sequence based amplification (NASBA), branched DNA methods, and so on.

> [O]ne skilled in the art is aware of a variety of techniques which might be used to detect different nucleic acid species. . . . These techniques are a matter of routine for one skilled in the art for the analysis of DNA.

The PTO granted Drs. Lo and Wainscoat U.S. Patent No. 6,258,540 in 2001. When Sequenom learned that Ariosa Diagnostics was offering non-invasive fetal diagnostic testing, it threatened to sue. Ariosa filed a declaratory relief action seeking to invalidate the '540 patent under §101. How should this case be decided under the applicable Supreme Court decisions?

iv.   *Reassessing Patent Eligibility*

The role of Section 101 of the Patent Act has undergone convulsive change through judicial interpretation over the past two decades. From the Federal Circuit's dismantling of eligibility limitations in *State Street Bank* to the Supreme Court's revival and expansion of eligibility limitations in *Mayo* and *Alice* to the Federal Circuit's latest pronouncements in *Berkheimer* and *Vanda*, inventors, venture capitalists, and patent attorneys have weathered an unremitting storm. It remains to be seen how this battleground will ultimately play out.

Berkheimer v. HP Inc.
United States Court of Appeals, Federal Circuit
890 F.3d 1369 (2018)

LOURIE, CIRCUIT JUDGE, with whom NEWMAN, CIRCUIT JUDGE, joins, concurring in the denial of the petition for rehearing en banc.

. . . I believe the law needs clarification by higher authority, perhaps by Congress, to work its way out of what so many in the innovation field consider are §101 problems. Individual cases, whether heard by this court or the Supreme Court, are imperfect vehicles for enunciating broad principles because they are limited to the facts presented. Section 101 issues certainly require attention beyond the power of this court.

We started from the statute that provides for patents on "any new and useful process, machine, manufacture, or composition of matter." 35 U.S.C. §101. The Supreme Court put a gloss on this provision by excluding laws of nature, natural phenomena, and abstract ideas. *Le Roy v. Tatham*, 55 U.S. (14 How.) 156, 174–75 (1852) ("[A] principle is not patentable. A principle, in the abstract, is a fundamental truth; an original cause; a motive; these cannot be patented, as no one can claim in either of them an exclusive right."); *Diamond v. Chakrabarty*, 447 U.S. 303, 309 (1980) ("The laws of nature, physical phenomena, and abstract ideas have been held not patentable."). So far, so good. Laws of nature (Ohm's Law, Boyle's Law, the equivalence of matter and energy), properly construed, should not be eligible for patent. Nor should natural phenomena (lightning, earthquakes, rain, gravity, sunlight) or natural products, per se (blood, brain, skin). Of course, the latter are also unpatentable as lacking novelty under §102.

But it's in the details that problems and uncertainties have arisen. The Court held in *Mayo Collaborative Services v. Prometheus Laboratories, Inc.*, that the claim at issue "set forth laws of nature" and was ineligible under §101 as "a drafting effort designed to monopolize the law of nature itself." 566 U.S. 66, 77 (2012). That claim recited "[a] method of optimizing therapeutic efficacy for treatment of an immune-mediated gastrointestinal disorder, comprising" administering a drug and then measuring the level of a metabolite of the drug. *Id.* at 74–75.

The Supreme Court whittled away at the §101 statute in *Mayo* by analyzing abstract ideas and natural phenomena with a two-step test, including looking for an "inventive concept" at step two, thereby bringing aspects of §§102 and 103 into the eligibility analysis. *Id.* at 72–73, 90. The decision we now decide not to rehear en banc holds that step two of the two-step analysis may involve the type of fact-finding that underlies §§102 and 103, further complicating what used to be a fairly simple analysis of patent eligibility under §101. We now are interpreting what began, when it rarely arose, as a simple §101 analysis, as a complicated multiple-step consideration of inventiveness ("something more"), with the result that an increasing amount of inventive research is no longer subject to patent. For example, because the Mayo analysis forecloses identifying any "inventive concept" in the discovery of natural phenomena, we have held as ineligible subject matter even meritorious inventions that "combined and utilized man-made tools of biotechnology in a way that revolutionized prenatal care." *Ariosa Diagnostics, Inc. v. Sequenom, Inc.*, 788 F.3d 1371, 1379 (Fed. Cir. 2015) (internal quotation marks omitted).

The case before us involves the abstract idea exception to the statute. Abstract ideas indeed should not be subject to patent. They are products of the mind, mental steps, not capable of being controlled by others, regardless what a statute or patent claim might say. *Gottschalk v. Benson*, 409 U.S. 63, 67 (1972) ("[M]ental processes, and abstract intellectual concepts are not patentable, as they are the basic tools of scientific and technological work."). No one should be inhibited from thinking by a patent. *See* Letter from Thomas Jefferson to Isaac McPherson (Aug. 13, 1813) ("[I]f nature has made any one thing less susceptible, than all others, of exclusive property, it is the action of the thinking power called an Idea."). Thus, many brilliant and unconventional ideas must be beyond patenting simply because they are "only" ideas, which cannot be monopolized. Moreover such a patent would be unenforceable. Who knows what people are thinking?

But why should there be a step two in an abstract idea analysis at all? If a method is entirely abstract, is it no less abstract because it contains an inventive step? And, if a claim recites "something more," an "inventive" physical or technological step, it is not an abstract idea, and can be examined under established patentability provisions such as §§102 and 103. Step two's prohibition on identifying the something more from "computer functions [that] are 'well-understood, routine, conventional activit[ies]' previously known to the industry," *Alice Corp. Pty. Ltd. v. CLS Bank Int'l*, 134 S.Ct. 2347, 2359 (2014) (alteration in original) (quoting *Mayo*, 566 U.S. at 73), is essentially a §§102 and 103 inquiry. Section 101 does not need a two-step analysis to determine whether an idea is abstract.

I therefore believe that §101 requires further authoritative treatment. Thinking further concerning §101, but beyond these cases, steps that utilize natural processes, as all mechanical, chemical, and biological steps do, should be patent-eligible, provided they meet the other tests of the statute, including novelty, nonobviousness, and written description. A claim to a natural process itself should not be patentable, not least because it lacks novelty, but also because natural processes should be available to all. But claims to using such processes should not be barred at the threshold of a patentability analysis by being considered natural laws, as a method that utilizes a natural law is not itself a natural law.

The Supreme Court also held in *Association for Molecular Pathology v. Myriad Genetics, Inc.*, that claims to isolated natural products were ineligible for claiming "naturally occurring phenomena." 569 U.S. 576, 590 (2013). The Court concluded that those claims "are not patent eligible simply because they have been isolated from the surrounding genetic material." *Id.* at 596.

However, finding, isolating, and purifying such products are genuine acts of inventiveness, which should be incentivized and rewarded by patents. We are all aware of the need for new antibiotics because bacteria have become resistant to our existing products. Nature, including soil and plants, is a fertile possible source of new antibiotics, but there will be much scientific work to be done to find or discover, isolate, and purify any such products before they can be useful to us. Industry should not be deprived of the incentive to develop such products that a patent creates. But, while they are part of the same patent-eligibility problems we face, these specific issues are not in the cases before us.

Accordingly, I concur in the decision of the court not to rehear this §101 case en banc. Even if it was decided wrongly, which I doubt, it would not work us out of the current §101 dilemma. In fact, it digs the hole deeper by further complicating the §101 analysis. Resolution of patent-eligibility issues requires higher intervention, hopefully with ideas reflective of the best thinking that can be brought to bear on the subject.

COMMENTS AND QUESTIONS

1. Do you agree with Judge Lourie's assessment of §101? Does the Supreme Court's *Mayo/Alice* framework conflate §101 with §§102 and 103? Does the Court's preemption rationale improperly bring §112 patent scope considerations into §101 analysis? Has the Supreme Court read "discovery" out of the Patent Act?

2. Should Congress intervene? If so, how? *See generally* Jeffrey A. Lefstin, Peter S. Menell, & David O. Taylor, *Final Report of the Berkeley Center for Law & Technology Section 101 Workshop: Addressing Patent Eligibility Challenges*, 33 BERKELEY TECH. L.J. 551 (2018). §

PROBLEM III-11

The "Patent Eligibility Restoration Act of 2023," introduced by Senators Tillis and Coons, "finds" that efforts of district court, Federal Circuit, and PTO examiners to apply the judicial exceptions to patent eligbility (laws of nature, physical phenomena, and abstract ideas) have led to "extensive confusion and a lack of consistency." As a corrective, the bill's authors propose to eliminate the judicial exceptions while expressing excluding particular categories from patent eligibility. The revised provision would provide:

§101. Patent eligibility

(a) In General.—Whoever invents or discovers any useful process, machine, manufacture, or composition of matter, or any useful improvement thereof, may obtain a patent therefor, subject only to the exclusions in subsection (b) and to the further conditions and requirements of this title.

(b) Eligibility Exclusions.—

(1) In General.—Subject to paragraph (2), a person may not obtain a patent for any of the following, if claimed as such:

(A) A mathematical formula that is not part of a claimed invention in a category described in subsection (a).

(B)(i) Subject to clause (ii), a process that is substantially economic, financial, business, social, cultural, or artistic, even though not less than 1 step in

the process refers to a machine or manufacture.
            (ii) The process described in clause (i) shall not be excluded from eligibility for a patent if the process cannot practically be performed without the use of a machine or manufacture.
        (C) A process that—
            (i) is a mental process performed solely in the human mind; or
            (ii) occurs in nature wholly independent of, and prior to, any human activity.
        (D) An unmodified human gene, as that gene exists in the human body.
        (E) An unmodified natural material, as that material exists in nature.
    (2) Conditions.—For the purposes of subparagraphs (D) and (E) of paragraph (1), a human gene or natural material shall not be considered to be unmodified if the gene or material, as applicable, is—
        (A) isolated, purified, enriched, or otherwise altered by human activity; or
        (B) otherwise employed in a useful invention or discovery.

What, if anything, would be unpatentable subject matter under this bill? Would patent law extend to a new song played on a guitar? to a process for dividing one number by another that involves writing the numbers on paper? to a naturally-occurring metal that must be excavated from surrounding rock?

Would this reform improve the patent system? How might this legislation be improved?

C. INVENTORSHIP

U.S. patent law requires that patents be issued in the name of the "inventor" or "inventors." §115(a) ("Naming the Inventor; Inventor's Oath or Declaration"). This requirement derives from the U.S. Constitution—which grants power to Congress to "secure for limited times to . . . *inventors* the exclusive rights to their . . . discoveries," U.S. CONST. ART. 1, §8, CL. 8 (emphasis added)—although not necessarily so. As we will see in Chapter IV, U.S. copyright law authorizes corporations to obtain copyrights in their own name under the work-made-for-hire doctrine. *See* Chapter IV(D)(1)(i). Nonetheless, the Patent Act specifies that inventors are "individuals." §100(f).

Inventorship is distinct from assignments of patents. Patent applications must properly name the inventor or inventors. They can also identify the assignee of the patent.

The inventorship requirement and its associated doctrines have long served a significant role in U.S. patent law. As set forth in §102(f) of the 1952 Act, a patent filed by someone other than the true inventor is invalid. The AIA carries forward this principle through its "derivation proceedings" to resolve claims that a patent applicant stole the invention from another. *See* §135. The Patent Act authorizes both the PTO (§116) and the courts (§256) to correct inventorship.

Scientists often work in teams, with different people collaborating on different parts of a new project. While the norm in science is to list everyone who worked on the project as a co-author on academic papers, patent law has a different and more restrictive view of inventorship. It is the act of conceiving the idea, not the actual work of reducing that idea to practice, that the courts call invention:

> The arguments of both Barr and Novopharm are directed to when the inventors conceived the invention. Burroughs Wellcome says it was before they learned the results of the NIH tests; Barr and Novopharm say that confirmation of the inventions' operability, which came from the NIH tests, was an essential part of the inventive process. If Burroughs Wellcome is right, then the patents name the proper inventors, they are not invalid, and the appellants are liable for infringement. If Barr and Novopharm are correct, then Broder, Mitsuya, and Yarchoan should have been named as joint inventors and the resolution of Burroughs Wellcome's infringement suits is premature.
>
> . . .
>
> Conception is the touchstone of inventorship, the completion of the mental part of invention. *Sewall v. Walters,* 21 F.3d 411, 415 (Fed. Cir. 1994). It is 'the formation in the mind of the inventor, of a definite and permanent idea of the complete and operative invention, as it is hereafter to be applied in practice.' *Hybritech Inc. v. Monoclonal Antibodies, Inc.,* 802 F.2d 1367, 1376 (Fed. Cir. 1986) (citation omitted). Conception is complete only when the idea is so clearly defined in the inventor's mind that only ordinary skill would be necessary to reduce the invention to practice, without extensive research or experimentation. *Sewall,* 21 F.3d at 415; *see also Coleman v. Dines,* 754 F.2d 353, 359 (Fed. Cir. 1985) (conception must include every feature of claimed invention). Because it is a mental act, courts require corroborating evidence of a contemporaneous disclosure that would enable one skilled in the art to make the invention. *Coleman v. Dines,* 754 F.2d at 359.
>
> Thus, the test for conception is whether the inventor had an idea that was definite and permanent enough that one skilled in the art could understand the invention; the inventor must prove his conception by corroborating evidence, preferably by showing a contemporaneous disclosure. An idea is definite and permanent when the inventor has a specific, settled idea, a particular solution to the problem at hand, not just a general goal or research plan he hopes to pursue. *See Fiers v. Revel,* 984 F.2d 1164, 1169 (Fed. Cir. 1993); *Amgen, Inc. v. Chugai Pharmaceutical Co.,* 927 F.2d 1200, 1206 (Fed. Cir. 1991) (no conception of chemical compound based solely on its biological activity). The conception analysis necessarily turns on the inventor's ability to describe his invention with particularity. Until he can do so, he cannot prove possession of the complete mental picture of the invention. These rules ensure that patent rights attach only when an idea is so far developed that the inventor can point to a definite, particular invention.
>
> But an inventor need not know that his invention will work for conception to be complete. *Applegate v. Scherer,* 332 F.2d 571, 573 (CCPA 1964). He need only show that he had the idea; the discovery that an invention actually works

is part of its reduction to practice. *Id.; see also Oka v. Youssefyeh,* 849 F.2d 581, 584 n. 1 (Fed. Cir. 1988).

Barr and Novopharm suggest that the inventor's definite and permanent idea must include a reasonable expectation that the invention will work for its intended purpose. They argue that this expectation is of paramount importance when the invention deals with uncertain or experimental disciplines, where the inventor cannot reasonably believe an idea will be operable until some result supports that conclusion. Without some experimental confirmation, they suggest, the inventor has only a hope or an expectation, and has not yet conceived the invention in sufficiently definite and permanent form. But this is not the law. An inventor's belief that his invention will work or his reasons for choosing a particular approach are irrelevant to conception. *MacMillan v. Moffett,* 432 F.2d 1237, 1239 (CCPA 1970).

Burroughs Wellcome v. Barr Labs, 40 F.3d 1223, 1227-28 (Fed. Cir. 1994). The court in *Burroughs* held that the scientists who came up AZT, an early treatment for HIV, were the sole inventors of the patent even though they didn't know the drug would work until other scientists at the National Institutes of Health tested the drug. The idea of the drug was the mental act of invention; determining that it worked for its intended purpose was simply part of reduction to practice.

Merely having an idea, however, is typically not enough to make one an inventor. Conception requires a definite and firm idea of the complete and operative invention that ultimately results. While some ideas are so simple that they can spring fully formed in the inventor's mind, many require significant work towards reduction to practice before the idea is fully formed. And if the invention changes during the process of making it work, the idea wasn't complete when it was first formulated. Indeed, some inventions, including accidental ones, cannot be conceived until they are actually reduced to practice.

The principles of conception and reduction to practice come from the law of priority, which as we have seen, *see* Section B(1)(vi), determined who was the first to invent under the 1952 Act. Now that we have moved to a "first inventor to file" regime, the statutory anchor for this standard for inventorship no longer exists. Should it still govern inventorship? On what legal basis?

The inventorship determination can be complicated when multiple individuals contribute to the invention or particular claims of the patent:

A joint invention is the product of a collaboration between two or more persons working together to solve the problem addressed. People may be joint inventors even though they do not physically work on the invention together or at the same time, and even though each does not make the same type or amount of contribution. 35 U.S.C. §116. The statute does not set forth the minimum quality or quantity of contribution required for joint inventorship.

Burroughs Wellcome Co. v. Barr Lab., Inc., 40 F.3d 1223, 1227 (Fed. Cir. 1994). It is enough for one to contribute conception to a single claim to be considered a joint inventor. *See SmithKline Diagnostics, Inc. v. Helena Lab. Corp.*, 859 F.2d 878, 888 (Fed. Cir. 1988). Nonetheless, one does not qualify as a joint inventor by merely assisting the true inventor after conception of the claimed invention. *See Sewall v. Walters*, 21 F.3d 411 (Fed. Cir. 1994).

Due to the collaborative, uncertain, and evolutionary nature of many inventive activities, joint inventorship cases are often complex, fact-specific, and, at times, highly technical. "To show co-inventorship, the alleged co-inventor or co-inventors must prove their contribution to the conception of the claims by clear and convincing evidence." *See Ethicon, Inc. v. United States Surgical Corp.*, 135 F.3d 1456, 1461 (Fed. Cir. 1998). "[A]n inventor's testimony respecting the facts surrounding a claim of derivation or priority of invention cannot, standing alone, rise to the level of clear and convincing proof." *Price v. Symsek*, 988 F.2d 1187, 1194 (Fed. Cir. 1993). Thus, an alleged co-inventor must supply evidence to corroborate his testimony.

A patent filed by someone other than the true inventor is invalid. That was established by §102(f) in the 1952 Act, which barred patenting by someone who "derived" the invention from the true inventor. The AIA carries forward that principle through "derivation proceedings," which resolve allegations that a patent applicant "derived" the invention from another. *See* §135.

Patent law provides that both the PTO (§116) and the courts (§256) can correct inventorship, and that the patent is not invalid if inventorship can be corrected. Correction is even possible when it involves a complete substitution of inventors. That is, if *A* steals an invention from *B* and patents it in their own name, *B* may be able to have inventorship corrected so that the patent is still valid but now *B* is the sole inventor. *B* may have other claims as well based on the theft. *See Univ. of Colorado Found. v. American Cyanamid Co.*, 196 F.3d 1366 (Fed. Cir. 2003) (awarding damages for fraud and unjust enrichment against company that stole invention and patented it in its own name).

Before the AIA, the ability to correct inventorship depended on the good faith of the parties involved. Under current law, correction is possible even if the original misjoinder of inventors was fraud rather than error. That makes correction substantially easier, and should make it more common, though the Federal Circuit has been careful to require corroboration to police opportunistic claims of invention.

Inventorship does not only matter for ownership; it also affects prior art. An inventor's own acts cannot count as prior art under §102(a) of the 1952 Act, and are subject to the grace period under the AIA. But that is true only if the individual or group of individuals who created the prior art are the same as the individuals that apply for a patent. Prior conduct by an overlapping but not identical group can be prior art that bars the group from obtaining a patent. Thus, in *Google LLC v. IPA Techs. Inc.*, 34 F.4th 1081 (Fed. Cir. 2022), the court held that a paper by three individuals could be prior art against a patent on the same invention later filed only by two of them. Congress has limited the effects of this rule by providing that inventions that are obvious in view of each other are not prior art if the inventions are all required to be assigned to the same company anyway. §103(c).

As the following case illustrates, the advent of generative artificial intelligence raises a host of novel inventorship questions.

Thaler v. Vidal
United States Court of Appeals, Federal Circuit
43 F.4th 1207 (2022)

STARK, CIRCUIT JUDGE.

This case presents the question of who, or what, can be an inventor. Specifically, we are asked to decide if an artificial intelligence (AI) software system can be listed as the inventor on a patent application. At first, it might seem that resolving this issue would involve an abstract inquiry into the nature of invention or the rights, if any, of AI systems. In fact, however, we do not need to ponder these metaphysical matters. Instead, our task begins—and ends—with consideration of the applicable definition in the relevant statute.

The United States Patent and Trademark Office (PTO) undertook the same analysis and concluded that the Patent Act defines "inventor" as limited to natural persons; that is, human beings. Accordingly, the PTO denied Stephen Thaler's patent applications, which failed to list any human as an inventor. . . .

I

Thaler represents that he develops and runs AI systems that generate patentable inventions. One such system is his "Device for the Autonomous Bootstrapping of Unified Science," which Thaler calls "DABUS." Thaler has described DABUS as "a collection of source code or programming and a software program."

In July 2019, Thaler sought patent protection for two of DABUS' putative inventions by filing two patent applications with the PTO: U.S. Application Nos. 16/524,350 (teaching a "Neural Flame") and 16/524,532 (teaching a "Fractal Container"). He listed DABUS as the sole inventor on both applications. Thaler maintains that he did not contribute to the conception of these inventions and that any person having skill in the art could have taken DABUS' output and reduced the ideas in the applications to practice.

In lieu of an inventor's last name, Thaler wrote on the applications that "the invention [was] generated by artificial intelligence." . . . Thaler filed a document purporting to assign himself all of DABUS' rights as an inventor.

. . . The PTO denied Thaler's petitions on the ground that "a machine does not qualify as an inventor." . . .

II

. . . Challenges to PTO petition decisions are governed by the APA and pertinent administrative law standards. Thus, we may set aside the judgment resulting from an administrative adjudication only if the agency's decision is "arbitrary, capricious, an abuse of discretion, or otherwise not in accordance with law" or if the agency's actions are "in excess of statutory jurisdiction, authority, or limitations." 5 U.S.C. §706. "Statutory interpretation is an issue of law that we review de novo."

A

The sole issue on appeal is whether an AI software system can be an "inventor" under the Patent Act. In resolving disputes of statutory interpretation, we "begin[ ] with the statutory text, and end[ ] there as well if the text is unambiguous." Here, there is no ambiguity: the Patent Act requires that inventors must be natural persons; that is, human beings.

The Patent Act expressly provides that inventors are "individuals." Since 2011, with the passage of the Leahy-Smith America Invents Act, the Patent Act has defined an "inventor" as "the *individual* or, if a joint invention, the *individuals* collectively who invented or discovered the subject matter of the invention." 35 U.S.C. §100(f) (emphasis added). The Act similarly defines "joint inventor" and "coinventor" as "any 1 of the *individuals* who invented or discovered the subject matter of a joint invention." §100(g) (emphasis added). In describing the statements required of an inventor when applying for a patent, the statute consistently refers to inventors and co-inventors as "individuals." *See* §115.

The Patent Act does not define "individual." However, as the Supreme Court has explained, when used "[a]s a noun, 'individual' ordinarily means a human being, a person." *Mohamad v. Palestinian Auth.*, 566 U.S. 449, 454 (2012) (internal alteration and quotation marks omitted). This is in accord with "how we use the word in everyday parlance": "We say 'the individual went to the store,' 'the individual left the room,' and 'the individual took the car,' each time referring unmistakably to a natural person." *Id.* Dictionaries confirm that this is the common understanding of the word. *See, e.g., Individual*, Oxford English Dictionary (2022) (giving first definition of "individual" as "[a] single human being"); *Individual*, Dictionary.com (last visited July 11, 2022), https://www.dictionary.com/browse/individual (giving "a single human being, as distinguished from a group" as first definition for "individual"). So, too, does the Dictionary Act, which provides that legislative use of the words "person" and "whoever" broadly include ("unless the context indicates otherwise") "corporations, companies, associations, firms, partnerships, societies, and joint stock companies, *as well as individuals*." 1 U.S.C. §1 (emphasis added). "With the phrase 'as well as,' the definition marks 'individual' as distinct from the list of artificial entities that precedes it," showing that Congress understands "individual" to indicate natural persons unless otherwise noted. *Mohamad*, 566 U.S. at 454.

Consequently, the Supreme Court has held that, when used in statutes, the word "individual" refers to human beings unless there is "some indication Congress intended" a different reading. *Id.* at 455 (emphasis omitted). Nothing in the Patent Act indicates Congress intended to deviate from the default meaning. To the contrary, the rest of the Patent Act supports the conclusion that "individual" in the Act refers to human beings.

. . . The Patent Act also requires inventors (unless deceased, incapacitated, or unavailable) to submit an oath or declaration. *See* [§115(b)(2)] (requiring oath or declaration from inventor that "such individual believes himself or herself to be the original inventor or an original joint inventor of a claimed invention in the application"). While we do not decide whether an AI system can form beliefs, nothing in our record shows that one can, as reflected in the fact that Thaler submitted the requisite statements himself, purportedly on DABUS' behalf.

Thaler directs us to several provisions of the Patent Act as supposed support for his position that "inventor" should be broadly read to include AI software, but each fails to persuade. First, Thaler points to the use of "whoever" in 35 U.S.C. §§101 and 271. Section 101 provides that "[w]hoever invents or discovers any new and useful process, machine, manufacture, or composition of matter, or any new and useful improvement thereof, may obtain a patent therefor, subject to the conditions and requirements of this title." As this very section makes clear, however, patents must satisfy the "conditions and requirements of" Title 35 of the U.S. Code, including its definition of "inventor." Section 271, in setting out what constitutes infringement, repeatedly uses "whoever" to include corporations and other non-human entities. That non-humans may infringe patents does not tell us anything about whether non-humans may also be inventors of patents. The question before us inevitably leads back to the Patent Act's definition of "inventor," which uses the word "individual"—and does not use "whoever." Furthermore, as we noted already, the Dictionary Act establishes that Congress uses "whoever" as a much broader term than "individual." *See* 1 U.S.C. §1.

Second, Thaler contends that AI software programs must qualify as inventors because otherwise patentability would depend on "the manner in which the invention was made," in contravention of 35 U.S.C. §103. Section 103 is not about inventorship. Instead, it provides, in relevant part, that inventions may still be nonobvious even if they are discovered during "routine" testing or experimentation. *See Honeywell Int'l Inc. v. Mexichem Amanco Holding S.A. de C.V.*, 865 F.3d 1348, 1356 (Fed. Cir. 2017); *see also Graham v. John Deere Co.*, 383 U.S. 1, 15 (1966) (explaining that second sentence of §103 was intended to clarify that "flash of creative genius" is unnecessary for patentability). This statutory provision relates to how an invention is made and does not trump a provision that specifically addresses who may be an inventor.

Third, Thaler emphasizes that the term "inventor" must be interpreted with attention to the "context in which that language is used[ ] and the broader context of the statute as a whole." Yates v. United States, 574 U.S. 528, 537 (2015) (internal quotation marks omitted). We have undertaken precisely this task. For the reasons explained above, the Patent Act, when considered in its entirety, confirms that "inventors" must be human beings.

B

Our holding today that an "inventor" must be a human being is supported by our own precedent. *See Univ. of Utah v. Max-Planck-Gesellschaft zur Forderung der Wissenschaften E.V.*, 734 F.3d 1315, 1323 (Fed. Cir. 2013) ("[I]nventors must be *natural* persons and cannot be corporations or sovereigns.") (emphasis added); *Beech Aircraft Corp. v. EDO Corp.*, 990 F.2d 1237, 1248 (Fed. Cir. 1993) ("[O]nly natural persons can be 'inventors.' "). While these opinions addressed different questions—

concluding that neither corporations nor sovereigns can be inventors—our reasoning did not depend on the fact that institutions are collective entities. The two cases confirm that the plain meaning of "inventor" in the Patent Act is limited to natural persons.

. . .

III

We briefly address Thaler's additional arguments.

Thaler argues that inventions generated by AI should be patentable in order to encourage innovation and public disclosure. Thaler's policy arguments are speculative and lack a basis in the text of the Patent Act and in the record. . . . Moreover, we are not confronted today with the question of whether inventions made by human beings with the assistance of AI are eligible for patent protection.

Thaler invokes the canon of constitutional avoidance. In Thaler's view, permitting AI programs to be inventors would support the constitutional purpose of patents "[t]o promote the progress of science and the useful arts." U.S. Const. art. I, §8, cl. 8. It follows, Thaler continues, that not recognizing AI as an inventor undermines such progress, raising potential constitutional concerns we should be careful to avoid. Thaler is incorrect. The constitutional provision he cites is a grant of legislative power to Congress; Congress has chosen to act pursuant to that power by passing the Patent Act. Thaler does not (and cannot) argue that limiting inventorship to human beings is unconstitutional. Therefore, the canon of constitutional avoidance is simply inapplicable. . . .

Thaler also notes that South Africa has granted patents with DABUS as an inventor. This foreign patent office was not interpreting our Patent Act. Its determination does not alter our conclusion. . . .

IV

When a statute unambiguously and directly answers the question before us, our analysis does not stray beyond the plain text. Here, Congress has determined that only a natural person can be an inventor, so AI cannot be. Accordingly, the decision of the district court is affirmed.

AFFIRMED

COMMENTS AND QUESTIONS

1. Neither the drafters of the U.S. Constitution nor the drafters of the patent statutes considered the possibility of AI-generated inventions and discoveries. Does the court's textual analysis make sense in resolving the patentability of AI inventions? Could the court have analogized artificial intelligence to human intelligence?

2. *Joint Human-AI Inventorship*? Although *Thaler* forecloses AI machines as sole inventors, it leaves open the patentability of inventions in which humans use machines to co-invent and co-discover new and useful processes, machines, manufactures, and compositions of matter. Humans have long used machines, including computers, in the process of inventing and discovering. They are increasingly using AI technology as part of the inventive process, resulting in a rising tide of AI-assisted patent applications. The

Patent Office is currently considering how to examine inventions and discoveries made with the new generation of generative artificial intelligence technology. How should the Patent Office assess these applications? Is it enough for humans to pose insightful prompts to Large Language Models (LLMs) such as OpenAI's GPT series or Google's BERT? *See* Yuan Hao, *The Rise of "Centaur" Inventors: How Patent Law Should Adapt to the Challenge to Inventorship Doctrine by Human-AI Inventing Synergies* (August 10, 2022), available at https://ssrn.com/abstract=4186684 (suggesting the concept of "constructive conception" when AI software assists a human inventor in conceiving of a patentable invention).

3. Richard Thaler asserted that the patenting of AI-generated inventions would promote progress. Do you agree? Consider the utilitarian framework introduced in Chapter 1, as well the potential for a proliferation of patents generated by increasingly "intelligent" machines. Does generative AI require rethinking of the patent system?

D. ADMINISTRATIVE PATENT REVIEW

In 1980, Congress established the *ex parte* reexamination process to enable patent owners and third parties to request the PTO to review the validity of issued patents. *See* J. Steven Baughman, *Reexamination Reexaminations: A Fresh Look at the Ex Parte and Inter Partes Mechanisms for Reviewing Issued Patents*, 89 J. PAT & TRADEMARK OFF. SOC'Y 349 (2007); §303(a); PTO Ex Parte Reexamination Rules, 37 C.F.R. §1.515(a). The review process was limited to novelty and nonobviousness and a limited range of prior art (patents and printed publications). The process was conducted *ex parte*—i.e., only the patent owner participated. And the process could and often did take years to complete. Courts were reluctant to stay enforcement proceedings pending completion of reexamination. Most accused infringers did not consider *ex parte* reexamination to be a viable alternative to litigation. As a result, the ex parte reexamination was only sparsely utilized.

In 1999, Congress established a more balanced *inter partes* reexamination procedure which allowed third party challengers to comment on patent owner responses. This procedure also failed to gain much traction. The process was slow and barred challengers from raising any ground that could have been raised during the reexamination during subsequent civil litigation. In 2005, the PTO established the Central Reexamination Unit ("CRU"), which expedited reexaminations and resulted in greater usage of the reexamination. Nonetheless, district courts were still reluctant to stay parallel cases, leading to costly duplication.

As the patent reform efforts gained traction in the post dot-com period, momentum increased for the US to follow the logic of a more robust administrative review process paralleling patent oppositions in the European Patent Office, Patent Review Board (PRB) proceedings in the Chinese Patent Office (SIPO), and similar proceedings around the world. *See* Joseph Farrell and Robert P. Merges, *Incentives to Challenge and Defend Patents: Why Litigation Won't Reliably Fix Patent Office Errors and Why Administrative Patent Review Might Help*, 19 BERKELEY TECH. L.J. 9430 (2004). Much of the AIA focused on expanding and expediting review.

The AIA established three principal review procedures: (1) *inter partes* review (IPR)—*inter partes* reexamination was phased out and folded into IPR, §§311–19; (2) covered business method review (CBMR)—a transitional review proceeding focused on weeding out dubious business method patents, AIA §18; and (3) post-grant review (PGR), §§321–29. The AIA left *ex parte* reexamination in place. *See* §§301–07; Jonathan Tamimi, *Breaking Bad Patents: The Formula for Quick, Inexpensive Resolution of Patent Validity*, 29 BERKELEY TECH. L.J. 587 (2014). CBMR expired in September 2020. The following table compares the key characteristics of the remaining AIA review systems.

Administrative Patent Review Proceedings

AIA Review	IPR	PGR
Evidentiary Standard	Petitioner to prove invalidity by the preponderance of the evidence	
Grounds for Review	§102, §103	Any defense relating to invalidity
Prior Art Limited to:	Patents and printed publications	No Limits
Threshold to Institute Review	Reasonable likelihood that one or more claims is invalid	More likely than not at least one claim is unpatentable, or petition raises a novel legal question of patentability
Time to Institution	More than 9 months after issue/reissue or after PGR	w/i 9 months of issue/ reissue date
Time to Decision	Maximum of 12–18 months from institution decision	
Claim Amendments	Patent owner may cancel claims, or propose a reasonable number of substitute claims; Presumption that only one substitute claim will be required for each challenged claim	
Claim Construction	*Phillips* standard: "ordinary and customary meaning to a person of ordinary skill in the art at the time of the invention"	
Stay Considerations:	1) Stay simplify issues and streamline trial? 2) Is Discovery complete, trial date set? 3) Stay tactically advantage moving party or unduly burden nonmoving party?	
Estoppel in Subsequent Civil Action	Any ground raised or reasonably could have been raised	
Effect of Settlement	Estoppel provisions do not apply	

1. Post-Grant Review

The AIA's new Post-Grant Review (PGR) procedure parallels the European-style "patent oppositions." A PGR permits anyone to challenge the validity of a patent within nine months of its issuance (or nine months of a patent reissue). The challenger—or "petitioner," in the words of the statute—may "request to cancel as unpatentable [one] or more claims of a patent on any ground that could be raised" in a district court proceeding. *See* §321, citing §282(b) (relating to grounds for invalidity). Unlike pre-AIA reexamination procedures, which were focused on prior art in the form of patents and printed publications, PGR significantly widens the grounds for challenge, creating in effect a mini-trial on patent validity. A PGR permits evidence of on-sale activities, public uses, prior-filed but not-yet-issued patents, and other types of disclosures, as well as issues such as enablement. *See, e.g., Grunenthal Gmbh v. Antecip Bioventures II LLC*, Case PGR2017–00008, 2017 WL 2901321 (P.T.A.B. July 7, 2017) (agreeing to institute PGR challenge based on written description and enablement for a pharmaceutical patent, U.S. Pat. No. 9,283,239).

PGRs (as well as other review proceedings) are heard by three administrative patent judge (APJ) panels of the Patent Trial and Appeal Board (PTAB), successor to the pre-AIA Board of Patent Appeals and Interferences.

Congress expressed its hope that the PGR proceeding would come to be seen as a viable alternative to traditional ex parte reexaminations, and to district court litigation as well:

> The initial reexamination statute [in 1980] had several limitations that later proved to make it a less viable alternative to litigation for evaluating patent validity than Congress intended. First, a reexamination request could only be based on prior art, and could not be based on prior public use or prior sales. Moreover, the requestor could not raise any challenge based on §101 (utility, eligibility) or §112 (indefiniteness, enablement, written description, best mode). A third party alleging a patent is invalid, therefore, had fewer challenges it could raise in the proceeding and, therefore, may instead opt to risk infringement and litigate the validity of the patent in court. Second, in the original reexamination system, the third-party challenger had no role once the proceeding was initiated, while the patent holder had significant input throughout the entire process. Third, a challenger that lost at the USPTO under reexamination had no right to appeal an examiner's, or the Patent Board's, decision either administratively or in court. Restrictions such as these made reexamination a much less favored avenue to challenge questionable patents than litigation. Reexamination proceedings are also often costly, taking several years to complete, . . . and are first conducted by examiners and, if the patent is rejected, then by Patent Board judges. Thus, many patents must go through two rounds of administrative review (one by the examiner, and a second by the Patent Board) adding to the length of the proceeding.

Committee on the Judiciary, U.S. Cong., America Invents Act, H.R. REP. NO 112-98, 112th Cong., 1st Sess., at 45 (June 1, 2011). The House Report goes on to say:

The Committee believes that this new, early-stage process for challenging patent validity and its clear procedures for submission of art will make the patent system more efficient and improve the quality of patents and the patent system. This new, but time-limited, post-grant review procedure will provide a meaningful opportunity to improve patent quality and restore confidence in the presumption of validity that comes with issued patents in court.

Id. at 48.

i.   *Timing and Sequencing*

PGR requests must be filed within a statutory nine-month "window" after the patent issues. §321(c). The PTO's regulations accompanying the AIA provide a timeline for PGR proceedings. In general, these proceedings are expected to move quickly in keeping with the notion that a PGR is intended to be a streamlined, cheaper alternative to district court litigation for assessing patent validity.

The PGR process begins with a request from a petitioner.

[T]he petition [must] identify each claim being challenged, the specific grounds on which each claim is challenged, how the claims are to be construed, how the claims as construed are unpatentable, why the claims as construed are unpatentable under the identified grounds, and . . . [citations to] evidence relied upon . . . to support the challenge.

USPTO, Notice of Proposed Rulemaking, Changes to Implement Post-Grant Review Proceedings, 77 Fed. Reg. 7060, 7064 (Feb. 10, 2012) (proposing new provision to be codified at 37 C.F.R. §42.204(b)).

The patent owner then has two months to respond. The patent owner may set forth reasons why the PGR should not be instituted, but cannot at this point present new evidence of patentability such as expert declarations. After this filing, the PTO has three months to decide if a PGR is warranted. §324(c).

The Director may not authorize a post-grant review to be instituted unless the Director determines that the information presented in the petition filed under section 321, if such information is not rebutted, would demonstrate that it is more likely than not that at least [one] of the claims challenged in the petition is unpatentable.

An additional criterion is described in §324(b): "The determination required under subsection (a) may also be satisfied by a showing that the petition raises a novel or unsettled legal question that is important to other patents or patent applications." Under §324(e), the PTO Commissioner's decision whether or not to institute a PGR proceeding is final and non-appealable.

Once a PGR is instituted, the PTO can, by regulation, require the "patent owner [to] file with [a PGR] response, through affidavits or declarations, any additional factual evidence and expert opinions on which the patent owner relies in support of the response." §326(a)(8). The patent owner can respond in a number of ways, including the filing of substituted or amended claims, as long as the new claims (1) find support in the originally filed specification, (2) respond in some way to the ground for the PGR request, and (3) do not broaden the scope of coverage of the original claims. *See* Proposed Rules to be codified at 37 C.F.R. §§42.220(b) and (c), 77 Fed. Reg. 7060, 7066. The AIA envisions a focused discovery process in connection with PGR proceedings; "such discovery shall be limited to evidence directly related to factual assertions advanced by either party in the proceeding," and these limits are backed by sanctions "should a party to a PGR misuse discovery to harass or to cause unnecessary delay or an unnecessary increase in the cost of the proceeding. . . ." §326(a)(5) and (6).

The limits on discovery are one way that the drafters of the AIA hoped to make PGRs effective but efficient. In general, the goal is for the PTO to reach a final decision in a PGR proceeding within one year of deciding the PGR may proceed. There is the possibility of a six-month extension "for good cause." 77 Fed. Reg. 7060, 7064.

ii.   *Coordination with Other Proceedings*

The AIA reduces the burden of parallel proceedings by barring PGR proceedings if a requestor has already filed a civil action. §325(a)(1) If a civil action is filed after a PGR petition, that action will be stayed until the patent owner requests that the stay be lifted or the patent owner files a counterclaim. Furthermore, the AIA authorizes the PTAB to streamline and coordinate different administrative proceedings by consolidating diverse challenges involving a single patent into one proceeding. §315(d). Pursuant to the AIA's estoppel provisions, any issue that was raised or could reasonably have been raised in a PGR may not be further contested in another PTO proceeding (such as an Inter Partes Review) or in a district court or ITC proceeding. *See* §§325(e)(1) and (2). In these ways, the AIA PGR process discourages duplicative proceedings and channels validity determinations issues toward the PGR process in the first instance.

Final PGR decisions can be appealed to the Federal Circuit. §329. (PGR institution decisions are not appealable. §324(e)). It should be noted that even with a very efficient Federal Circuit disposition, a PGR could well run three years through appeal, which is a long time in light of the stated goal of providing an efficient procedure for weeding out weak patent claims.

2.   Inter Partes Review: Successor to Inter Partes Reexaminations

The new Inter Partes Review (IPR) procedure replaces the Inter Partes Reexamination system. As of September 16, 2012, anyone other than the patent owner may request a review of an issued patent. The requestor must show that there is "a reasonable likelihood that the requester would prevail with respect to at least [one] of the claims challenged in the request." The new IPR system replaces only existing *inter partes reexaminations*—not the parallel system of *ex parte reexamination*. Existing ex parte reexamination rules provide a different threshold for initiating a proceeding;[12]

---

[12] Section 303(a), which applies to ex parte reexaminations, says in part: "[T]he [PTO] Director will determine whether a substantial new question of patentability affecting any claim of the patent concerned is raised by the request," and if so, a reexamination will be instituted. The "substantial new question of patentability" standard is lower than the "reasonable likelihood that the requestor would prevail" standard under the AIA's IPR procedure, which means it should be easier to initiate a reexamination than an IPR.

require the proceeding to be conducted by an examiner with a right of appeal to the PTAB; and allow for limited participation by third parties. These ex parte reexaminations were left essentially intact; the new IPR system will run in conjunction with them.

IPRs have become an important part of the patent landscape. By late 2020, there had been over 12,000 IPR petitions filed. Of these, over 3,400 had been instituted and resulted in a Final Written Decision (FWD). At the same time, appeals from PTAB trials at the PTO have quickly become a significant portion of the Federal Circuit's workload. Court data shows that 38% of current Federal Circuit cases are Patent Office appeals. This does include examiner appeals, remaining (pre-AIA) interferences, etc., but the largest portion is appeals from IPRs. For the first time, the U.S. patent system includes an effective and widely-employed post-issuance administrative patent validity hearing, independent from patent infringement litigation in the federal courts. This brings the U.S. into line with other major patent systems. *See* ROBERT P. MERGES AND HAIYAN SEAGULL SONG, TRANSNATIONAL INTELLECTUAL PROPERTY LAW 146-153 (2018) (illustrating Patent Review Board cases and their review by Chinese courts); *id.*, at 36-37 (overview of European Patent Office oppositions); Colleen Chien, Christian Helmers, and Alfred Spigarelli, *Inter Partes Reviews and the Design of Post-Grant Patent Reviews*, 33 BERKELEY TECH. L.J. 817 (2018) (comparing U.S. IPRs with EPO oppositions and German national court revocation proceedings).

An IPR proceeding is subject to the same limits as to prior art that apply in current reexamination proceedings: only patents and printed publications can be cited to initiate an IPR. *See* §311(b). The AIA, in §316(a)(9), permits the patent owner to submit substitute claims, or to cancel claims, in light of an IPR proceeding.

Unlike the PGR process, which can raise any invalidity ground, IPRs may only challenge lack of novelty or obviousness and only on the basis of prior patents or printed publications.

Patents challenged in an IPR proceeding are not subject to the strong presumption of validity that requires clear and convincing evidence to invalidate a patent in court, but benefit only from the lesser preponderance of the evidence standard.

i. *Timing and Sequencing*

The PTAB has plenary authority to decide whether to institute an IPR, precluding an appeal of the decision whether to institute an IPR. Its decision is final and unreviewable. *See Thryv v. Click-to-Call Techs.*, 140 S.Ct. 1367 (2020).

The IPR process was designed to dovetail with the PGR process. Therefore, IPRs cannot be filed until after the PGR filing period (nine months after patent issuance) has passed or until after a PGR proceeding has been completed. Thus, an IPR can follow directly after an unsuccessful PGR request, although it is unlikely such a petition will be successful. §311(c).

ii. Coordination with Other Proceedings

An accused infringer who has been sued by the patentee for patent infringement must file a request to initiate an IPR within one year after the patentee files an infringement action. §315(b). One additional point to note: though anyone can file an IPR request, a losing party at the PTAB must establish Article III (constitutional) standing in order to challenge a PTAB decision in the Federal Circuit. *See, e.g., AVX Corp. v. Presidio Components, Inc.*, 923 F.3d 1357 (Fed. Cir. 2019) (IPR challenger failed to show injury in fact, and thus lacked standing to appeal PTAB decision; even though the decision to uphold the challenged claims reduced challenger's ability to compete with patent owner, the challenger had no present or non-speculative interest in engaging in conduct even arguably covered by patent claims at issue, and so lacked standing).

IPRs were intended to be a more focused and efficient alternative to district court litigation. Liberal IPR filing rules have permitted some patent challengers—including loose coalitions of independent companies, all of whom are threatened by a single "target" patent—to file numerous IPRs against a single patent. This multiplicity of validity proceedings has proven to be a burden to some patent owners, and has sparked calls for PTO and legislative reforms.

For example, Genentech's patent on "Method for Making Humanized Antibodies," U.S. Patent 6,407,213 (Jun. 12, 2002), has been challenged in no fewer than 16 separate actions. *See* Spencer J. Johnson, Rothwell Figg's Biosimilar Law Bulletin, Dec. 11, 2018, avail. at https://www.biosimilarsip.com/2018/12/11/claims-of-genentechs-carter-213-patent-found-unpatentable/ (describing two successful IPRs that led to cancellation of 18 claims of the '213 patent, plus another IPR that had just been instituted). Although there is a case to be made that any additional challenge to a patent has social benefit, there is also a need to recognize that the marginal value of a fifteenth or twentieth challenge to a patent may be low. The private costs of defending all these challenges might provide strategic leverage to patent challengers, but all this expense might not add much value to society overall. There is value, also, in promoting "title security" for patent owners. That's because many patents are the basis of elaborate contracts and business dealing. Business often engage in patent-based licensing, funding, collaboration, and the like – meaning that "security of title" helps form the foundation for many value-increasing private arrangements. Unlimited patent challenges may undermine these arrangements, adding a hidden social cost to the private burden of defending against fifteen or twenty IPRs. *See* ROBERT P. MERGES AND JOHN F. DUFFY, PATENT LAW AND POLICY Ch.8(B)(3)(c) (8th ed., 2021) (discussing the notion of patent incontestability).

The AIA seeks to avoid duplicative litigation by estopping an IPR requestor from challenging a patent claim in district court or an ITC enforcement action on the basis of "any ground that the petitioner raised or reasonably could have raised during that inter partes review." §315(e)(2). Similarly, the requestor may not file a second IPR or pursue any other administrative proceeding on any ground that was raised or could have been raised in the IPR. §315(e)(1). And courts have even barred other proceedings, like ex parte reexamination, if they were duplicative of IPR proceedings. *In re Vivint*, 14 F.4th 1342 (Fed. Cir. 2021).

To facilitate efficiency, the Patent Act permits a court to grant a stay motion, postponing district court litigation while the PTAB decides a parallel IPR. District courts retain substantial discretion over case management. To avoid duplicative proceedings, the PTAB has increasingly refused to institute IPRs if the district court is nearing trial. *See, e.g.*, *Apple Inc. v. Fintiv, Inc.*, No. IPR2020-00019, 2020 WL 2486683, at *5 (P.T.A.B. May 13, 2020) (denying institution "[b]ecause the currently scheduled District Court trial [in the Eastern District of Texas] is scheduled to begin two months before our deadline to reach a final decision, this factor weighs somewhat in favor of discretionary denial in this case.").

The *Fintiv* approach, however, has led to its own form of gaming. Some district courts, apparently eager to attract patent litigation to their courtroom and district, frequently deny a motion to stay pending IPR petitions. One rationale is that a court which is set up for rapid hearings on validity might finish its work before the IPR is resolved. *See, e.g.*, *NHK Spring Co., Ltd. v. Intri-Plex Techs., Inc.*, No. IPR2018-00752, 2018 WL 4373643, at *4 (P.T.A.B. Sept. 12, 2018) (denying IPR institution because a parallel district court case had set an early trial date, making the IPR perhaps duplicative). The *NHK Spring* decision has encouraged patent owners to file infringement cases in a "rocket docket" (such as the Western District of Texas), and fend off an IPR stay request by citing NHK. This gamesmanship arguably causes inefficiency and unfairness by channeling invalidity determinations to the more expensive institution, promoting forum shopping, and pressuring defendants to settle by removing IPR invalidation from the table.

3. Derivation Proceeding

By shifting from a first-to-invent to a modified first-to-file priority system, the AIA eliminates the interference proceedings for patents filed after March 15, 2013. Nevertheless, due to concern that unscrupulous claimants might steal an invention and beat the true inventor to the Patent Office by filing first, Congress established a special administrative proceeding to sort out claims that the applicant stole or "derived" an invention from another.

Under AIA §135, a Derivation Proceeding begins when a petitioner alleges that "an inventor named in an earlier application derived the claimed invention from an inventor named in the petitioner's application and, without authorization, the earlier application claiming such invention was filed." AIA §135. The challenge must be brought within one year of the publication of the claim to the invention that the petitioner says was derived (i.e., one year after patent publication, or one year after patent issuance if the application was never published under §122).

COMMENTS AND QUESTIONS

1. The IPR procedures have proven very popular among accused infringers and district judges. The PTAB hired more than 200 APJs to handle this considerable workload.

2. *Constitutionality of IPR.* The Supreme Court rejected a constitutional challenge to the IPR proceeding in *Oil States Energy Servs. v. Greene's Energy*, 138 S.Ct. 1365 (2018). It emphasized that patents were public franchises that implicated public rights, and that the administrative agency that granted those patents should have the power to revoke them.

3. *Constitutionality of Appointments Process for PTAB Judges.* The Supreme Court ruled in *United States v. Arthrex*, 141 S.Ct. 1970 (2021), that the AIA's designation of PTAB APJs as inferior "Officers" whose decisions are not reviewable by the Executive branch was unconstitutional. The Court corrected this constitutional defect by holding that the PTO Director "may review final PTAB and, upon review, may issue decisions" on behalf of the Board.

E. CLAIMS AND CLAIM CONSTRUCTION

Patent claims define a patent owner's legal rights; they have been analogized to the "metes and bounds" of a real property deed. The meaning of words in the claim determine the claim boundaries. As we saw in our analysis of the novelty requirement, a claim is anticipated if the claim limitations "read on" a prior art reference. As we will see in Chapter III(F)(1), direct infringement analysis is the mirror image of novelty analysis: an accused device or process that "reads on" the claimed invention infringes the patent.

Thus, claim boundaries are critical to patent validity and infringement determinations. They are also critical to patent law's notice function. In the words of the late Federal Circuit Judge Giles Rich, one of the most influential patent lawyers (he co-drafted the 1952 Patent Act) and jurists of the 20th century, "the name of the game is the claim." Giles S. Rich, *Extent of Protection and Interpretation of Claims—American Perspectives*, 21 INT'L REV. INDUS. PROP. & COPYRIGHT L. 497, 499 (1990).

Linguistically minor variations in phraseology and meaning can be the difference between a finding of infringement (and thus exclusion of the competitor, and perhaps damages) and non-infringement (and thus open entry in at least part of the patentee's market). To the hard-headed businessperson, claim interpretation defines the intangible real estate that belongs exclusively to a patentee. To a patent lawyer, precision (or a lack of precision, in some cases) is a tool of the trade. The typical businessperson looks straight to the bottom line: can the patentee exclude a competitor (expanding the reach of its exclusive legal franchise) or will it have to share shelf space and profits? That validity pushes in the opposite direction from infringement makes the analysis even more complex: a broader claim is easier to invalidate since it encompasses more potential prior art. As Judge Rich put it: "the stronger a patent the weaker it is and the weaker a patent the stronger it is." Giles S. Rich, *The Proposed Patent Legislation: Some Comments*, 35 GEO. WASH. L. REV. 641, 644 (1967).

This section begins with an overview of patent claiming and claim formats. It then examines claim construction jurisprudence. We then explore functional claiming. We conclude with the claim indefiniteness doctrine.

1. Patent Claiming and Claim Formats

i. *The Evolution of Patent Claiming: From Central Claims to Peripheral Claims*

The practice of claiming inventions, as opposed to merely describing them, traces back to the early nineteenth century. *See* J. Jonas Anderson & Peter S. Menell, *Informal Deference: A Historical, Empirical, and Normative Analysis of Patent Claim Construction*, 108 NW. U. L. REV. 1, 8–21 (2014). Historians credit Robert Fulton, developer of the first commercially successful steamboat, with "inventing" the patent claim. *See* Karl B. Lutz, *Evolution of the Claims of U.S. Patents*, 20 J. PAT. OFF. SOC'Y 134, 137 (1938). His 1811 patent stated:

> Having been the first to demonstrate the superior advantages of a water wheel or wheels, I claim as my exclusive right, the use of two wheels, one over each side of the boat to take the purchase on the water . . . .

See also Camilla A. Hrdy, *State Patent Laws in the Age of Laissez Faire*, 28 BERKELEY TECH. L.J. 45, 78 (2013) (describing patent-like right granted to Fulton by New York State, and subsequent litigation). Although there were sporadic examples in the first two decades of the nineteenth century of patents expressly claiming inventions, such explicit claiming was not the general practice.

Justice Joseph Story, who would emerge as the leading patent jurist of the first half of the nineteenth century, immediately came to see the problems with vague and conclusory descriptions of inventions. Sitting in his first patent case (and the first case to focus on the question of distinguishing a patented invention from the prior art), he noted the "intrinsic difficulty . . . to ascertain . . . the exact boundaries between what was known and used before, and what is new." *See Whittemore v. Cutter*, 29 F. Cas. 1123, 1124 (C.C.D. Mass. 1813) (No. 17,601); *see also Odiorne v. Winkley*, 18 F. Cas. 581, 582 (C.C.D. Mass. 1814) (No. 10,432) (noting the "intrinsic difficulty"). Justice Story explicated this principle more fully four years later, charging the jury that:

> A patent is grantable only for a new and useful invention; and, unless it be distinctly stated, in what that invention specifically consists, it is impossible to say, whether it ought to be patented or not; and it is equally difficult to know, whether the public infringe upon or violate the exclusive right secured by the patent.

Lowell v. Lewis, 15 F. Cas. 1018, 1020 (C.C.D. Mass. 1817) (No. 8568).

In 1828, the Superintendent of the Patent Office instructed applicants that many patents had been vacated for failure to claim what is new and is the invention or discovery:

> In the specification it is perfectly proper to describe an entire machine, although most parts of it may have been long known and used, as, otherwise, it may be difficult to make known the improvements; but after doing this, the patentee should distinctly set forth what he claims as new; and this is best done in a separate paragraph, at the end of the specification . . . .

Thomas P. Jones, *Information to Persons Applying for Patents, or Transacting Other Business at the Patent Office*, 6 FRANKLIN J. & AM. MECHANICS' MAG. 332, 334 (1828).

Thus, by the late 1820s, it had become common practice for patent applicants to include a formal designation of the claimed invention in a separate paragraph at the end of the specification. The 1836 Patent Act, which reinstituted patent examination, required applicants to "particularly specify and point out the part, improvement, or combination, which he claims as his own invention or discovery." Patent Act of 1836, ch. 357, §6.

The form of patent claiming that emerged during this period—which has come to be known as "central" claiming—differs substantially from the "peripheral" format in common usage today. Central claiming was directed at identifying the thing the patentee built as the invention—a "sign post" indicating that this, and things sufficiently similar to it, were protected by patent. *See* Dan L. Burk & Mark A. Lemley, *Fence Posts or Sign Posts? Rethinking Patent Claim Construction*, 157 U. PA. L. REV. 1743 (2009).

Even before the 1836 Act, some applicants began using a more radical claiming format that would come to be known as "peripheral" claiming. These claims used linguistic formulations, rather than references to specific improvements, to delineate the metes and bounds of the claimed invention. If central claims were sign posts, peripheral claims are "fence posts" that attempt to define the outer bounds of the patent right. Burk & Lemley, *supra*. In a series of pamphlets issued in the 1860s, the Patent Office pushed applicants toward the use of peripheral claiming. The Patent Office permitted "genus claiming," and signaled receptivity to multiple claims in stating that "claims in different forms . . . prevent misconstructions." *See Ex parte Perry & Lay*, 1869 Dec. Comm'r Pat. 1, 1.

The courts also played a critical role in the shift toward peripheral claiming. In two 1877 Supreme Court decisions—*Merrill v. Yeomans*, 94 U.S. 568, 573–74 (1876) and *Keystone Bridge Co. v. Phoenix Iron Co.*, 95 U.S. 274, 278 (1877)—the Supreme Court embraced patent law's public notice function by linking the scope of patent protection to the metes and bounds set forth in patent claims. This contributed to the decline of central claiming and eventually made claim construction an essential step in infringement analysis. In a watershed passage in *Merrill*, the Court explained the critical role of clearly identifiable patent boundaries for technological and economic advance:

> The genius of the inventor, constantly making improvements in existing patents -- a process which gives to the patent system its greatest value, -- should not be restrained by vague and indefinite descriptions of claims in existing patents from the salutary and necessary right of improving on that which has already been invented. It seems to us that nothing can be more just and fair, both to the patentee and to the public, than that the former should understand, and correctly describe, just what he has invented, and for what he claims a patent.

The patent claim thereafter quickly emerged as the defining feature of the patent. *See Burns v. Meyer*, 100 U.S. 671, 672 (1879) ("The courts, therefore, should be careful not to enlarge, by construction, the claim which the Patent Office has admitted, and which the patentee has acquiesced in, beyond the fair interpretation of its terms."). In his seminal 1890 treatise, William C. Robinson characterized it as "the office of the Claim to define the limits of that exclusive use which is secured to the inventor by the patent"; "[t]he Claim is thus the life of the patent so far as the rights of the inventor are concerned." 2 WILLIAM C. ROBINSON, THE LAW OF PATENTS FOR USEFUL INVENTIONS §§504, 505 (1890). This shift brought claim construction to a prominent role in patent litigation. As Robinson explained, "The paramount importance of the Claim, and the necessity for such exactness and completeness in its statements as will precisely define the invention to be protected by the patent, have led to the establishment of numerous rules for framing it." *Id.* at §507.

ii. Claim Formats

The challenge in drafting patent claims is to make them as broad as the prior art and other patent doctrines will allow. Because of this, and because drafting claims is time-consuming and expensive, patent drafters are always on the lookout for convenient ways to broadly cover the elements of inventions. Section 112(b)–(f) guide the drafting of patent claims:

(b) CONCLUSION.—The specification shall conclude with one or more claims particularly pointing out and distinctly claiming the subject matter which the inventor or a joint inventor regards as the invention.

(c) FORM.—A claim may be written in independent or, if the nature of the case admits, in dependent or multiple dependent form.

(d) REFERENCE IN DEPENDENT FORMS.—Subject to subsection (e), a claim in dependent form shall contain a reference to a claim previously set forth and then specify a further limitation of the subject matter claimed. A claim in dependent form shall be construed to incorporate by reference all the limitations of the claim to which it refers.

(e) REFERENCE IN MULTIPLE DEPENDENT FORM.—A claim in multiple dependent form shall contain a reference, in the alternative only, to more than one claim previously set forth and then specify a further limitation of the subject matter claimed. A multiple dependent claim shall not serve as a basis for any other multiple dependent claim. A multiple dependent claim shall be construed to incorporate by reference all the limitations of the particular claim in relation to which it is being considered.

(f) ELEMENT IN CLAIM FOR A COMBINATION.—An element in a claim for a combination may be expressed as a means or step for performing a specified function without the recital of structure, material, or acts in support thereof, and such claim shall be construed to cover the corresponding structure, material, or acts described in the specification and equivalents thereof.

These provisions establish formatting rules to avoid confusion and promote clarity. We will be focusing on §§112(b) and (f) in subsections 4 and 3 respectively. Before doing so, it will be useful to review the basic principles of patent claim construction.

2.   Judicial Claim Construction

The construction of patent claims plays a critical role in nearly every patent case. It is central to the evaluation of infringement and validity, and can affect or determine the outcome of other significant issues such as unenforceability, enablement, and remedies. The process by which courts interpret patent claims represents one of the most distinctive aspects of patent litigation.

In patent cases, as elsewhere, the distinction between questions of law and fact is an important issue. As we have seen so far, patent cases often center on scientific or technical details such as how an invention differs from the prior art, or how it works compared to a competitor's product. Whether a judge or a jury decides these key issues may make a significant difference in the outcome of a patent infringement case.

For most of the twentieth century judges, not juries, heard nearly all patent cases. Mark A. Lemley, *Why Do Juries Decide If Patents Are Valid?*, 99 VA. L. REV. 1673 (2013). By 1995, though, approximately 75% of patent cases were tried to juries—partly a result of the shift in patent litigation from specialized patent boutique firms to general trial-oriented law firms. *See* ROBERT P. MERGES, AMERICAN PATENT LAW: A BUSINESS AND ECONOMIC HISTORY, 1790-PRESENT, Ch. 6 (forthcoming 2021). Many courts gave the question of the scope of the patent claim to the jury. One effect of this practice was to shroud the jury's claim construction in the black box of jury deliberations, making patent decisions especially difficult to review. Federal Circuit Judge Paul Michel lamented that "[w]hen the court delegates both construction and infringement to the jury's discretion, the jury is free to do almost anything it wishes." *See* Paul R. Michel, *The Challenge Ahead: Increasing Predictability in Federal Circuit Jurisprudence for the New Century*, 43 AM. U. L. REV. 1231, 1239 (1994). The question of who should determine the meaning of patent claims came before the Supreme Court in the seminal case of *Markman v. Westview Instruments*, 517 U.S. 370 (1996).

Markman sued Westview Instruments for infringement of its patent on a system for tracking articles of clothing in a dry-cleaning operation. After a jury found infringement, Westview Instruments moved for judgment as a matter of law on the ground that the patent and its prosecution history made it clear that the patent claims at issue did not extend to the Westview's accused device. The trial court granted the motion based on its examination of the relevant documentation. On appeal, the patentee asserted that the trial court's judgment violated its Seventh Amendment right to a jury trial on claim construction. Markman stressed that it had introduced expert testimony on the issue. Based largely on functional considerations, the Supreme Court held that claim construction is a matter for the court and hence beyond the province of the jury. The Court emphasized that judges are better equipped than juries to construe the meaning of patent claim terms, given their training and experience interpreting written instruments (such as contracts and statutes). Even though cases may arise in which the credibility of competing experts affects the determination of claim meaning "in the main," the Court anticipated that claim construction determinations will be "subsumed within the necessarily sophisticated analysis of the whole document, required by the standard construction rule that a term can be defined only in a way that comports with the instrument as a whole." *Id.* at 389. The Court also emphasized that judges can better promote uniformity and certainty in claim construction.

The *Markman* decision ushered in a new era and quickly led to the emergence of pre-trial "Markman hearings" to construe disputed claim terms. Following the lead of the Northern District of California, many of the most patent-intensive districts have adopted Patent Local Rules providing for joint, sequenced, staged, and timely disclosure of claim construction and other contentions, paving the way to a claim construction hearing within about eight months of the first case management conference. *See generally* PETER S. MENELL, ET AL., PATENT CASE MANAGEMENT JUDICIAL GUIDE, chs. 2 and 5 (Federal Judicial Center) (3rd ed. 2016). Most courts conduct a separate Markman hearing and issue a claim construction order before trial. Such hearings are often held in conjunction with a technology tutorial provided by the attorneys or technical experts. In many cases, such rulings provide the basis for summary judgment determinations on issues of validity and infringement.

Another effect of the *Markman* ruling was to bring claim construction out into the open. This has produced voluminous jurisprudence on how to construe claims. Within a few years, many litigants, lower court judges, scholars, and even some Federal Circuit jurists perceived claim construction law to be in chaos. Between 2000 and 2005, the reversal rate for district court claim constructions hovered in the mid-40 percent range. *See* J. Jonas Anderson & Peter S. Menell, *Informal Deference: A Historical, Empirical, and Normative Analysis of Patent Claim Construction*, 108 NW. U. L. REV. 1, 40–41 (2014). A respected district court judge observed that given such a high reversal rate, "you might as well throw darts." *See* Anandashankar Mazumdar, *Federal District Courts Need Experts that Are Good 'Teachers,' Judges Tell Bar*, 70 PAT. TRADEMARK & COPYRIGHT J. (BNA) 536, 537 (Sept. 16, 2005) (quoting Judge Marsha J. Pechman of the U.S. District Court of Western Washington).

During this period, many perceived the outcome of claim construction decisions to be highly panel-specific. *See* R. Polk Wagner & Lee Petherbridge, *Is the Federal Circuit Succeeding? An Empirical Assessment of Judicial Performance*, 152 U. PA. L. REV. 1105 (2004). "Proceduralist" jurists on the Federal Circuit gave primary weight to the claim language, focusing on ordinary meaning derived from dictionaries. "Holistic" jurists drew upon the full range of interpretive tools—claim language, specification, prosecution history, dictionaries, and expert testimony.

The Federal Circuit granted en banc review in the following case to clarify and harmonize claim construction jurisprudence.

Phillips v. AWH Corporation
United States Court of Appeals for the Federal Circuit
415 F.3d 1303 (Fed. Cir. 2005) (en banc)

BRYSON, CIRCUIT JUDGE:

Edward H. Phillips invented modular, steel-shell panels that can be welded together to form vandalism-resistant walls. The panels are especially useful in building prisons because they are load-bearing and impact-resistant, while also insulating against fire and noise. Mr. Phillips obtained a patent on the invention, U.S. Patent No. 4,677,798 ("the '798 patent"). . . .

In February 1997, Mr. Phillips brought suit in the United States District Court for the District of Colorado charging AWH with . . . infringement. . . .

[In deciding] the patent infringement issue, the district court focused on the language of claim 1, which recites "further means disposed inside the shell for increasing its load bearing capacity comprising internal steel baffles extending inwardly from the steel shell walls." . . . [Finding that the accused product did not contain "baffles" as that term is used in claim 1,] the district court granted summary judgment of non-infringement.

Mr. Phillips appealed [and a divided] panel of this court affirmed. *Phillips v. AWH Corp.*, 363 F.3d 1207 (Fed. Cir. 2004). The majority [Judge Lourie, joined by Judge Newman] sustained the district court's summary judgment of noninfringement, although on different grounds. The dissenting judge [Judge Dyk] would have reversed the summary judgment of noninfringement . . . .

[T]he [original Federal Circuit] panel concluded that the patent uses the term "baffles" in a restrictive manner. Based on the patent's written description, the panel held that the claim term "baffles" excludes structures that extend at a 90 degree angle from the walls. The panel noted that the specification repeatedly refers to the ability of the claimed baffles to deflect projectiles and that it describes the baffles as being "disposed at such angles that bullets which might penetrate the outer steel panels are deflected." '798 patent, col. 2, ll. 13–15; *see also id.* at col. 5, ll. 17–19 (baffles are "disposed at angles which tend to deflect the bullets"). In addition, the panel observed that nowhere in the patent is there any disclosure of a baffle projecting from the wall at a right angle and that baffles oriented at 90 degrees to the wall were found in the prior art. Based on "the specification's explicit descriptions," the panel concluded "that the patentee regarded his invention as panels providing impact or projectile resistance and that the baffles must be oriented at angles other than 90 [degrees]." *Phillips*, 363 F.3d at 1213. The panel added that the patent specification "is intended to support and inform the claims, and here it makes it unmistakably clear that the invention involves baffles angled at other than 90 [degrees]." The panel therefore upheld the district court's summary judgment of noninfringement.

The dissenting judge argued that the panel had improperly limited the claims to the particular embodiment of the invention disclosed in the specification, rather than adopting the "plain meaning" of the term "baffles." [T]he dissenting judge contended, the specification "merely identifies impact resistance as one of several objectives of the invention." In sum, the dissent concluded that "there is no reason to supplement the plain meaning of the claim language with a limitation from the preferred embodiment." Consequently, the dissenting judge argued that the court should have adopted the general purpose dictionary definition of the term baffle, i.e., "something for deflecting, checking, or otherwise regulating flow," and therefore should have reversed the summary judgment of noninfringement.

This court agreed to rehear the appeal en banc and vacated the judgment of the panel. We now . . . reverse the portion of the court's judgment addressed to the issue of infringement.

I

Claim 1 of the '798 patent is representative of the asserted claims with respect to the use of the term "baffles." It recites:

Building modules adapted to fit together for construction of fire, sound and impact resistant security barriers and rooms for use in securing records and persons, comprising in combination, an outer shell . . ., sealant means . . . and further means disposed inside the shell for increasing its load bearing capacity comprising internal steel baffles extending inwardly from the steel shell walls. . . .

II

The first paragraph of section 112 of the Patent Act states that the specification shall contain a written description of the invention, and of the manner and process of making and using it, in such full, clear, concise, and exact terms as to enable any person skilled in the art to which it pertains . . . to make and use the same. . . .

The second paragraph of section 112 provides that the specification shall conclude with one or more claims particularly pointing out and distinctly claiming the subject matter which the applicant regards as his invention.

Those two paragraphs of section 112 frame the issue of claim interpretation for us. The second paragraph requires us to look to the language of the claims to determine what "the applicant regards as his invention." On the other hand, the first paragraph requires that the specification describe the invention set forth in the claims. The principal question that this case presents to us is the extent to which we should resort to and rely on a patent's specification in seeking to ascertain the proper scope of its claims. . . .

A

It is a "bedrock principle" of patent law that "the claims of a patent define the invention to which the patentee is entitled the right to exclude." *Innova[/Pure Water, Inc. v. Safari Water Filtration Systems, Inc.*, 381 F.3d 1111 (Fed. Cir. 2004)], at 1115. That principle has been recognized since at least 1836, when Congress first required that the specification include a portion in which the inventor "shall particularly specify and point out the part, improvement, or combination, which he claims as his own invention or discovery." Act of July 4, 1836, ch. 357, §6, 5 Stat. 117, 119. In the following years, the Supreme Court made clear that the claims are "of primary importance, in the effort to ascertain precisely what it is that is patented." *Merrill v. Yeomans*, 94 U.S. 568, 570 (1876). . . . We have frequently stated that the words of a claim "are generally given their ordinary and customary meaning." *Vitronics [Corp. v. Conceptronic, Inc.*, 90 F.3d 1576 (Fed. Cir. 1996)], at 1582. We have made clear, moreover, that the ordinary and customary meaning of a claim term is the meaning that the term would have to a person of ordinary skill in the art in question at the time of the invention, i.e., as of the effective filing date of the patent application.

The inquiry into how a person of ordinary skill in the art understands a claim term provides an objective baseline from which to begin claim interpretation. . . . That starting point is based on the well-settled understanding that inventors are typically persons skilled in the field of the invention and that patents are addressed to and intended to be read by others of skill in the pertinent art.

Importantly, the person of ordinary skill in the art is deemed to read the claim term not only in the context of the particular claim in which the disputed term appears, but in the context of the entire patent, including the specification.

B

In some cases, the ordinary meaning of claim language as understood by a person of skill in the art may be readily apparent even to lay judges, and claim construction in such cases involves little more than the application of the widely accepted meaning of commonly understood words. *See Brown v. 3M*, 265 F.3d 1349, 1352 (Fed Cir. 2001) (holding that the claims did "not require elaborate interpretation"). In such circumstances, general purpose dictionaries may be helpful. In many cases that give rise to litigation, however, determining the ordinary and customary meaning of the claim requires examination of terms that have a particular meaning in a field of art. Because the meaning of a claim term as understood by persons of skill in the art is often not immediately apparent, and because patentees frequently use terms idiosyncratically, the court looks to "those sources available to the public that show what a person of skill in the art would have understood disputed claim language to mean." *Innova*, 381 F.3d at 1116. Those sources include "the words of the claims themselves, the remainder of the specification, the prosecution history, and extrinsic evidence concerning relevant scientific principles, the meaning of technical terms, and the state of the art." *Id.* . . .

1

Quite apart from the written description and the prosecution history, the claims themselves provide substantial guidance as to the meaning of particular claim terms. *See Vitronics*, 90 F.3d at 1582.

To begin with, the context in which a term is used in the asserted claim can be highly instructive. To take a simple example, the claim in this case refers to "steel baffles," which strongly implies that the term "baffles" does not inherently mean objects made of steel. . . .

Other claims of the patent in question, both asserted and unasserted, can also be valuable sources of enlightenment as to the meaning of a claim term. *Vitronics*, 90 F.3d at 1582. Because claim terms are normally used consistently throughout the patent, the usage of a term in one claim can often illuminate the meaning of the same term in other claims. . . . Differences among claims can also be a useful guide in understanding the meaning of particular claim terms. . . . For example, the presence of a dependent claim that adds a particular limitation gives rise to a presumption that the limitation in question is not present in the independent claim. *See Liebel-Flarsheim Co. v. Medrad, Inc.*, 358 F.3d 898, 910 (Fed. Cir. 2004).

2

The claims, of course, do not stand alone. Rather, they are part of "a fully integrated written instrument," *Markman*, 52 F.3d at 978, consisting principally of a specification that concludes with the claims. For that reason, claims "must be read in view of the specification, of which they are a part." *Id.* at 979. As we stated in *Vitronics*, the specification "is always highly relevant to the claim construction analysis. Usually, it is dispositive; it is the single best guide to the meaning of a disputed term." 90 F.3d at 1582.

This court and its predecessors have long emphasized the importance of the specification in claim construction. In *Autogiro Co. of America v. United States*, 384 F.2d 391, 397–98 (Ct. Cl. 1967*)*, the Court of Claims characterized the specification as "a concordance for the claims," based on the statutory requirement that the specification "describe the manner and process of making and using" the patented invention. . . . That principle has a long pedigree in Supreme Court decisions as well. [Citations omitted.]

3

In addition to consulting the specification, we have held that a court "should also consider the patent's prosecution history, if it is in evidence." *Markman*, 52 F.3d at 980. Like the specification, the prosecution history provides evidence of how the PTO and the inventor understood the patent. Furthermore, like the specification, the prosecution history was created by the patentee in attempting to explain and obtain the patent. Yet because the prosecution history represents an ongoing negotiation between the PTO and the applicant, rather than the final product of that negotiation, it often lacks the clarity of the specification and thus is less useful for claim construction purposes. Nonetheless, the prosecution history can often inform the meaning of the claim language by demonstrating how the inventor understood the invention and whether the inventor limited the invention in the course of prosecution, making the claim scope narrower than it would otherwise be.

C

Although we have emphasized the importance of intrinsic evidence in claim construction, we have also authorized district courts to rely on extrinsic evidence, which "consists of all evidence external to the patent and prosecution history, including expert and inventor testimony, dictionaries, and learned treatises." *Markman*, 52 F.3d at 980, citing *Seymour v. Osborne*, 78 U.S. (11 Wall.) 516, 546 (1870). However, while extrinsic evidence "can shed useful light on the relevant art," we have explained that it is "less significant than the intrinsic record in determining 'the legally operative meaning of claim language.' " *C.R. Bard, Inc. v. U.S. Surgical Corp.*, 388 F.3d 858, 862 (Fed.Cir. 2004)).

Within the class of extrinsic evidence, the court has observed that dictionaries and treatises can be useful in claim construction. . . . We have especially noted the help that technical dictionaries may provide to a court "to better understand the underlying technology" and the way in which one of skill in the art might use the claim terms. *Vitronics*, 90 F.3d at 1584 n.6. Because dictionaries, and especially technical dictionaries, endeavor to collect the accepted meanings of terms used in various fields of science and technology, those resources have been properly recognized as among the many tools that can assist the court in determining the meaning of particular terminology to those of skill in the art of the invention.

We have also held that extrinsic evidence in the form of expert testimony can be useful to a court for a variety of purposes, such as to provide background on the technology at issue, to explain how an invention works, to ensure that the court's understanding of the technical aspects of the patent is consistent with that of a person of skill in the art, or to establish that a particular term in the patent or the prior art has a particular meaning in the pertinent field. . . . However, conclusory, unsupported assertions by experts as to the definition of a claim term are not useful to a court. . . .

[U]ndue reliance on extrinsic evidence poses the risk that it will be used to change the meaning of claims in derogation of the "indisputable public records consisting of the claims, the specification and the prosecution history," thereby undermining the public notice function of patents. *Southwall Techs.[, Inc. v. Cardinal IG Co.,]* 54 F.3d [1570] at 1578 [Fed. Cir. 1995].

III

Although the principles outlined above have been articulated on numerous occasions, some of this court's cases have suggested a somewhat different approach to claim construction, in which the court has given greater emphasis to dictionary definitions of claim terms and has assigned a less prominent role to the specification and the prosecution history. The leading case in this line is *Texas Digital Systems, Inc. v. Telegenix, Inc.*, 308 F.3d 1193 (Fed. Cir. 2002).

A

In *Texas Digital*, the court noted that "dictionaries, encyclopedias and treatises are particularly useful resources to assist the court in determining the ordinary and customary meanings of claim terms." 308 F.3d at 1202. Those texts, the court explained, are "objective resources that serve as reliable sources of information on the established meanings that would have been attributed to the terms of the claims by those of skill in the art," and they "deserve no less fealty in the context of claim construction" than in any other area of law. *Id.* at 1203. The court added that because words often have multiple dictionary meanings, the intrinsic record must be consulted to determine which of the different possible dictionary meanings is most consistent with the use of the term in question by the inventor. If more than one dictionary definition is consistent with the use of the words in the intrinsic record, the court stated, "the claim terms may be construed to encompass all such consistent meanings." *Id.*

The *Texas Digital* court further explained that the patent's specification and prosecution history must be consulted to determine if the patentee has used "the words [of the claim] in a manner clearly inconsistent with the ordinary meaning reflected, for example, in a dictionary definition." 308 F.3d at 1204. The court identified two circumstances in which such an inconsistency may be found. First, the court stated, "the presumption in favor of a dictionary definition will be overcome where the patentee, acting as his or her own lexicographer, has clearly set forth an explicit definition of the term different from its ordinary meaning." Second, "the presumption also will be rebutted if the inventor has disavowed or disclaimed scope of coverage, by using words or expressions of manifest exclusion or restriction, representing a clear disavowal of claim scope."

The court concluded that it is improper to consult "the written description and prosecution history as a threshold step in the claim construction process, before any effort is made to discern the ordinary and customary meanings attributed to the words themselves." *Texas Digital*, 308 F.3d at 1204. To do so, the court reasoned, "invites a violation of our precedent counseling against importing limitations into the claims." *Id.*

B

Although the concern expressed by the court in *Texas Digital* was valid, the methodology it adopted placed too much reliance on extrinsic sources such as dictionaries, treatises, and encyclopedias and too little on intrinsic sources, in particular the specification and prosecution history. In effect, the *Texas Digital* approach limits the role of the specification in claim construction to serving as a check on the dictionary meaning of a claim term. . . . That approach, in our view, improperly restricts the role of the specification in claim construction.

Assigning such a limited role to the specification, and in particular requiring that any definition of claim language in the specification be express, is inconsistent with our rulings that the specification is "the single best guide to the meaning of a disputed term," and that the specification "acts as a dictionary when it expressly defines terms used in the claims or when it defines terms by implication." *Vitronics*, 90 F.3d at 1582.

The main problem with elevating the dictionary to such prominence is that it focuses the inquiry on the abstract meaning of words rather than on the meaning of claim terms within the context of the patent. Properly viewed, the "ordinary meaning" of a claim term is its meaning to the ordinary artisan after reading the entire patent. Yet heavy reliance on the dictionary divorced from the intrinsic evidence risks transforming the meaning of the claim term to the artisan into the meaning of the term in the abstract, out of its particular context, which is the specification. Thus, there may be a disconnect between the patentee's responsibility to describe and claim his invention, and the dictionary editors' objective of aggregating all possible definitions for particular words.

The problem is that if the district court starts with the broad dictionary definition in every case and fails to fully appreciate how the specification implicitly limits that definition, the error will systematically cause the construction of the claim to be unduly expansive. The risk of systematic overbreadth is greatly reduced if the court instead focuses at the outset on how the patentee used the claim term in the claims, specification, and prosecution history, rather than starting with a broad definition and whittling it down.

Thus, the use of the dictionary may extend patent protection beyond what should properly be afforded by the inventor's patent. . . .

Even technical dictionaries or treatises, under certain circumstances, may suffer from some of these deficiencies. There is no guarantee that a term is used in the same way in a treatise as it would be by the patentee. In fact, discrepancies between the patent and treatises are apt to be common because the patent by its nature describes something novel.

Moreover, different dictionaries may contain somewhat different sets of definitions for the same words. A claim should not rise or fall based upon the preferences of a particular dictionary editor, or the court's independent decision, uninformed by the specification, to rely on one dictionary rather than another. Finally, the authors of dictionaries or treatises may simplify ideas to communicate them most effectively to the public and may thus choose a meaning that is not pertinent to the understanding of particular claim language. The resulting definitions therefore do not necessarily reflect the inventor's goal of distinctly setting forth his invention as a person of ordinary skill in that particular art would understand it.

As we have noted above, however, we do not intend to preclude the appropriate use of dictionaries. Dictionaries or comparable sources are often useful to assist in understanding the commonly understood meaning of words and have been used both by our court and the Supreme Court in claim interpretation. . . .

We also acknowledge that the purpose underlying the *Texas Digital* line of cases—to avoid the danger of reading limitations from the specification into the claim—is sound. Moreover, we recognize that the distinction between using the specification to interpret the meaning of a claim and importing limitations from the specification into the claim can be a difficult one to apply in practice. *See Comark Communic'ns, Inc. v. Harris Corp.*, 156 F.3d 1182, 1186–87 (Fed. Cir. 1998) ("there is sometimes a fine line between reading a claim in light of the specification, and reading a limitation into the claim from the specification"). However, the line between construing terms and importing limitations can be discerned with reasonable certainty and predictability if the court's focus remains on understanding how a person of ordinary skill in the art would understand the claim terms. For instance, although the specification often describes very specific embodiments of the invention, we have repeatedly warned against confining the claims to those embodiments. *See, e.g., Nazomi Communic'ns, Inc. v. ARM Holdings, PLC*, 403 F.3d 1364, 1369 (Fed. Cir. 2005) (claims may embrace "different subject matter than is illustrated in the specific embodiments in the specification). In particular, we have expressly rejected the contention that if a patent describes only a single embodiment, the claims of the patent must be construed as being limited to that embodiment. That is not just because section 112 of the Patent Act requires that the claims themselves set forth the limits of the patent grant, but also because persons of ordinary skill in the art rarely would confine their definitions of terms to the exact representations depicted in the embodiments.

To avoid importing limitations from the specification into the claims, it is important to keep in mind that the purposes of the specification are to teach and enable those of skill in the art to make and use the invention and to provide a best mode for doing so. . . . One of the best ways to teach a person of ordinary skill in the art how to make and use the invention is to provide an example of how to practice the invention in a particular case. Much of the time, upon reading the specification in that context, it will become clear whether the patentee is setting out specific examples of the invention to accomplish those goals, or whether the patentee instead intends for the claims and the embodiments in the specification to be strictly coextensive. . . . The manner in which the patentee uses a term within the specification and claims usually will make the distinction apparent. . . .

In the end, there will still remain some cases in which it will be hard to determine whether a person of skill in the art would understand the embodiments to define the outer limits of the claim term or merely to be exemplary in nature. While that task may present difficulties in some cases, we nonetheless believe that attempting to resolve that problem in the context of the particular patent is likely to capture the scope of the actual invention more accurately than either strictly limiting the scope of the claims to the embodiments disclosed in the specification or divorcing the claim language from the specification.

In *Vitronics*, we did not attempt to provide a rigid algorithm for claim construction, but simply attempted to explain why, in general, certain types of evidence are more valuable than others. Today, we adhere to that approach and reaffirm the approach to claim construction outlined in that case, in *Markman*, and in *Innova*. We now turn to the application of those principles to the case at bar.

IV

A

The critical language of claim 1 of the '798 patent—"further means disposed inside the shell for increasing its load bearing capacity comprising internal steel baffles extending inwardly from the steel shell walls"—imposes three clear requirements with respect to the baffles. First, the baffles must be made of steel. Second, they must be part of the load-bearing means for the wall section. Third, they must be pointed inward from the walls. Both parties, stipulating to a dictionary definition, also conceded that the term "baffles" refers to objects that check, impede, or obstruct the flow of something. The intrinsic evidence confirms that a person of skill in the art would understand that the term "baffles," as used in the '798 patent, would have that generic meaning.

The other claims of the '798 patent specify particular functions to be served by the baffles. For example, dependent claim 2 states that the baffles may be "oriented with the panel sections disposed at angles for deflecting projectiles such as bullets able to penetrate the steel plates." The inclusion of such a specific limitation on the term "baffles" in claim 2 makes it likely that the patentee did not contemplate that the term "baffles" already contained that limitation. *See Dow Chem. Co. v. United States*, 226 F.3d 1334, 1341–42 (Fed. Cir. 2000) (concluding that an independent claim should be given broader scope than a dependent claim to avoid rendering the dependent claim redundant). Independent claim 17 further supports that proposition. It states that baffles are placed "projecting inwardly from the outer shell at angles tending to deflect projectiles that penetrate the outer shell." That limitation would be unnecessary if persons of skill in the art understood that the baffles inherently served such a function. . . . Dependent claim 6 provides an additional requirement for the baffles, stating that "the internal baffles of both outer panel sections overlap and interlock at angles providing deflector panels extending from one end of the module to the other." If the baffles recited in claim 1 were inherently placed at specific angles, or interlocked to form an intermediate barrier, claim 6 would be redundant.

The specification further supports the conclusion that persons of ordinary skill in the art would understand the baffles recited in the '798 patent to be load-bearing objects that serve to check, impede, or obstruct flow. At several points, the specification discusses positioning the baffles so as to deflect projectiles. *See* '798 patent, col. 2, ll. 13–15; *id.*, col. 5, ll. 17–19. The patent states that one advantage of the invention over the prior art is that "there have not been effective ways of dealing with these powerful impact weapons with inexpensive housing." *Id.*, col. 3, ll. 28–30. While that statement makes clear the invention envisions baffles that serve that function, it does not imply that in order to qualify as baffles within the meaning of the claims, the internal support structures must serve the projectile-deflecting function in all the embodiments of all the claims. The specification must teach and enable all the claims, and the section of the written description discussing the use of baffles to deflect projectiles serves that purpose for claims 2, 6, 17, and 23, which specifically claim baffles that deflect projectiles. . . .

The specification discusses several other purposes served by the baffles. For example, the baffles are described as providing structural support. The patent states that one way to increase load-bearing capacity is to use "at least in part inwardly directed steel baffles 15, 16." '798 patent, col. 4, ll. 14–15. The baffle 16 is described as a "strengthening triangular baffle." *Id.*, col. 4, line 37. Importantly, Figures 4 and 6 do not show the baffles as part of an "intermediate interlocking, but not solid, internal barrier." In those figures, the baffle 16 simply provides structural support for one of the walls, as depicted below:

FIG. 4

FIG. 6

Other uses for the baffles are listed in the specification as well. In Figure 7, the overlapping flanges "provide for overlapping and interlocking the baffles to produce substantially an intermediate barrier wall between the opposite [wall] faces":

FIG. 7

'798 patent, col. 5, ll. 26–29. Those baffles thus create small compartments that can be filled with either sound and thermal insulation or rock and gravel to stop projectiles. *Id.,* col. 5, ll. 29–34. By separating the interwall area into compartments (*See, e.g.,* compartment 55 in Figure 7), the user of the modules can choose different types of material for each compartment, so that the module can be "easily custom tailored for the specific needs of each installation." *Id.,* col. 5, ll. 36–37. When material is placed into the wall during installation, the baffles obstruct the flow of material from one compartment to another so that this "custom tailoring" is possible.

The fact that the written description of the '798 patent sets forth multiple objectives to be served by the baffles recited in the claims confirms that the term "baffles" should not be read restrictively to require that the baffles in each case serve all of the recited functions. We have held that "the fact that a patent asserts that an invention achieves several objectives does not require that each of the claims be construed as limited to structures that are capable of achieving all of the objectives." *Liebel-Flarsheim,* 358 F.3d at 908. . . . Although deflecting projectiles is one of the advantages of the baffles of the '798 patent, the patent does not require that the inward extending structures always be capable of performing that function. Accordingly, we conclude that a person of skill in the art would not interpret the disclosure and claims of the '798 patent to mean that a structure extending inward from one of the wall faces is a "baffle" if it is at an acute or obtuse angle, but is not a "baffle" if it is disposed at a right angle.

B

Invoking the principle that "claims should be so construed, if possible, as to sustain their validity," *Rhine v. Casio*, Inc., 183 F.3d 1342, 1345 (Fed. Cir. 1999), AWH argues that the term "baffles" should be given a restrictive meaning because if the term is not construed restrictively, the asserted claims would be invalid.

While we have acknowledged the maxim that claims should be construed to preserve their validity, we have not applied that principle broadly, and we have certainly not endorsed a regime in which validity analysis is a regular component of claim construction. . . . Instead, we have limited the maxim to cases in which "the court concludes, after applying all the available tools of claim construction, that the claim is still ambiguous." *Liebel-Flarsheim*, 358 F.3d at 911. In such cases, we have looked to whether it is reasonable to infer that the PTO would not have issued an invalid patent, and that the ambiguity in the claim language should therefore be resolved in a manner that would preserve the patent's validity.

In this case . . . the claim term at issue is not ambiguous. Thus, it can be construed without the need to consider whether one possible construction would render the claim invalid while the other would not. The doctrine of construing claims to preserve their validity, a doctrine of limited utility in any event, therefore has no applicability here.

In sum, we reject AWH's arguments in favor of a restrictive definition of the term "baffles." Because we disagree with the district court's claim construction, we reverse the summary judgment of noninfringement. In light of our decision on claim construction, it is necessary to remand the infringement claims to the district court for further proceedings.

MAYER, Circuit Judge, with whom NEWMAN, Circuit Judge, joins, dissenting.

Now more than ever I am convinced of the futility, indeed the absurdity, of this court's persistence in adhering to the falsehood that claim construction is a matter of law devoid of any factual component. Because any attempt to fashion a coherent standard under this regime is pointless, as illustrated by our many failed attempts to do so, I dissent.

This court was created for the purpose of bringing consistency to the patent field. *See* H.R. REP. NO 312, 97th Cong., 1st Sess. 20–23 (1981). Instead, we have taken this noble mandate, to reinvigorate the patent and introduce predictability to the field, and focused inappropriate power in this court. In our quest to elevate our importance, we have, however, disregarded our role as an appellate court; the resulting mayhem has seriously undermined the legitimacy of the process, if not the integrity of the institution.

In the name of uniformity, *Cybor Corp. v. FAS Technologies, Inc.*, 138 F.3d 1448 (Fed. Cir. 1998) (en banc), held that claim construction does not involve subsidiary or underlying questions of fact and that we are, therefore, unbridled by either the expertise or efforts of the district court. What we have wrought, instead, is the substitution of a black box, as it so pejoratively has been said of the jury, with the black hole of this court. Out of this void we emit "legal" pronouncements by way of "interpretive necromancy"; these rulings resemble reality, if at all, only by chance. Regardless, and with a blind eye to the consequences, we continue to struggle under this irrational and reckless regime, trying every alternative—dictionaries first, dictionaries second, never dictionaries, etc., etc., etc.

Again today we vainly attempt to establish standards by which this court will interpret claims. But after proposing no fewer than seven questions, receiving more than thirty amici curiae briefs, and whipping the bar into a frenzy of expectation, we say nothing new, but merely restate what has become the practice over the last ten years— that we will decide cases according to whatever mode or method results in the outcome we desire, or at least allows us a seemingly plausible way out of the case. I am not surprised by this. Indeed, there can be no workable standards by which this court will interpret claims so long as we are blind to the factual component of the task.

While this court may persist in the delusion that claim construction is a purely legal determination, unaffected by underlying facts, it is plainly not the case. Claim construction is, or should be, made in context: a claim should be interpreted both from the perspective of one of ordinary skill in the art and in view of the state of the art at the time of invention. . . . These questions, which are critical to the correct interpretation of a claim, are inherently factual. They are hotly contested by the parties, not by resort to case law as one would expect for legal issues, but based on testimony and documentary evidence. During so called *Markman* "hearings," which are often longer than jury trials, parties battle over experts offering conflicting evidence regarding who qualifies as one of ordinary skill in the art; the meaning of patent terms to that person; the state of the art at the time of the invention; contradictory dictionary definitions and [specifically] which [particular dictionary to use, when more than one was available at the time] would be consulted by the skilled artisan; the scope of specialized terms; the problem a patent was solving; what is related or pertinent art; whether a construction was disallowed during prosecution; how one of skill in the art would understand statements during prosecution; and on and on. In order to reconcile the parties' inconsistent submissions and arrive at a sound interpretation, the district court is required to sift through and weigh volumes of evidence. While this court treats the district court as an intake clerk, whose only role is to collect, shuffle and collate evidence, the reality, as revealed by conventional practice, is far different.

* * *

If we persist in deciding the subsidiary factual components of claim construction without deference, there is no reason why litigants should be required to parade their evidence before the district courts or for district courts to waste time and resources evaluating such evidence. . . . If the proceedings before the district court are merely a "tryout on the road," [citation omitted] . . . as they are under our current regimen, it is wasteful to require such proceedings at all. Instead, all patent cases could be filed in this court; we would determine whether claim construction is necessary, and, if so, the meaning of the claims. Those few cases in which claim construction is not dispositive can be remanded to the district court for trial. In this way, we would at least eliminate the time and expense of the charade currently played out before the district court.

Eloquent words can mask much mischief. The court's opinion today is akin to rearranging the deck chairs on the Titanic—the orchestra is playing as if nothing is amiss, but the ship is still heading for Davey Jones' locker.

COMMENTS AND QUESTIONS

1. *Clarifying Claim Construction Standards.* The *Phillips* case represents the most comprehensive statement of claim construction principles:

Perspective: Claims are construed from the standpoint of the PHOSITA.
Time Period: Claims are construed as of the time of the invention (or the effective filing date; the court treats the two dates as interchangeable, although they are not)
Evidentiary Sources:
• *Intrinsic Evidence* (claims, specification and prosecution history) shall be the principal basis for construing claims
• *Extrinsic Evidence* (expert testimony, dictionaries) are permissible sources, but cannot contradict intrinsic evidence
• There is no presumption in favor of dictionary definitions
• There is no heavy presumption in favor of ordinary meaning

2. *Are Embodiments Merely Examples or Limitations?* In many construction disputes, including Phillips, the dispute boils down to whether the claimed invention is limited to the embodiments (i.e., the examples set forth in the specification) or are those embodiments merely illustrative. While recognizing that "[t]here is sometimes a fine line between reading a claim in light of the specification, and reading a limitation into the claim from the specification," the court nonetheless observes that "[m]uch of the time, upon reading the specification [from the perspective of a PHOSITA], it will become clear whether the patentee is setting out specific examples of the invention to [teach how to make and use the invention], or whether the patentee instead intends for the claims and the embodiments in the specification to be strictly coextensive. The manner in which the patentee uses a term within the specification and claims usually will make the distinction apparent." In reality, however, patent drafters are often intentionally vague about this issue so as to leave flexibility to argue either that the claim should not be limited so to ensnare the alleged infringer or should be limited to the embodiments to avoid prior art.

The *Phillips* court emphasized that "although the specification often describes very specific embodiments of the invention, we have repeatedly warned against confining the claims to those embodiments. In particular, we have expressly rejected the contention that if a patent describes only a single embodiment, the claims of the patent must be construed as being limited to that embodiment."

3. *Meaning and Certainty.* Federal Circuit cases have had to decide plausible disagreements over the meanings of the words "a," *North American Vaccine, Inc. v. American Cyanamid Co.*, 7 F.3d 1571, 1581 (Fed. Cir. 1993); *contra Traxcell Techs., LLC v. Nokia Solutions*, 15 F.4th 1136 (Fed. Cir. 2021); "or," *Kustom Signals, Inc. v. Applied Concepts, Inc.*, 264 F.3d 1326 (Fed. Cir. 2001) "to," *Cybor Corp. v. FAS*

Technologies, Inc., 138 F.3d 1448, 1459 (Fed. Cir. 1998); "including," *Toro Co. v. White Consolidated Industries, Inc.*, 199 F.3d 1295 (Fed. Cir. 1999); and "through," *Sage Products, Inc. v. Devon Industries, Inc.*, 126 F.3d 1420 (Fed. Cir. 1997), to name but a few, suggesting that even words we think have clear meanings may be subject to interpretation.

Given this, does the focus on the words of the claim make sense at all? Some scholars have argued that the claim construction process is irretrievably broken because it focuses on malleable words chosen by lawyers rather than on what the patentee actually invented. *See* Dan L. Burk & Mark A. Lemley, *Fence Posts or Sign Posts? Rethinking Patent Claim Construction*, 157 U. PA. L. REV. 1743 (2009).

4. *Does a Court Have to Construe Each and Every Word in a Disputed Claim?* The answer has traditionally been no. *See U.S. Surgical Corp. v. Ethicon, Inc.*, 103 F.3d 1554, 1568 (Fed. Cir. 1997) ("Claim construction is a matter of resolution of disputed meanings and technical scope, to clarify and when necessary to explain what the patentee covered by the claims, for use in the determination of infringement. It is not an obligatory exercise in redundancy."); *Acumed LLC v. Stryker Corp.*, 483 F.3d 800, 806 (Fed. Cir. 2007) ("[A] sound claim construction need not always purge every shred of ambiguity. The resolution of some line-drawing problems—especially easy ones like this one—is properly left to the trier of fact."). Federal judges regularly limit the number of disputed terms they will construe. *See* PETER S. MENELL, ET AL., PATENT CASE MANAGEMENT JUDICIAL GUIDE §5.1.2. (Federal Judicial Center) (3rd ed. 2016) (discussing mechanisms for limiting the number of claim terms to construe).

Increasingly, however, the Federal Circuit has emphasized that when the parties have a dispute over the scope of the claim, it is the district court, not the jury, that must resolve that dispute. *See O2 Micro Int'l v. Beyond Innovation Tech. Co.,* 521 F.3d 1351, 1362 (Fed. Cir. 2008) (although "district courts are not (and should not be) required to construe every limitation present in a patent's asserted claims," the court must interpret the scope of any claim term for which the parties have presented a "fundamental dispute"); *EON IP Corp. v. Silver Spring Networks*, 815 F.3d 1314 (Fed. Cir. 2016) (reversing district court for failing to construe the terms "mobile" and "portable" when it was evident the parties gave those terms different meanings).

Does it make sense to construe ordinary English terms, as opposed to technical terms a jury might not be expected to understand? Does construing non-technical terms encroach upon the jury's prerogative to determine infringement?

5. *Meaning as of When?* At what point in time should a court consider the meaning of a claim term—when the claim was filed in a patent application, at the time the infringement took place, or some other time? *PC Connector Solutions LLC v. SmartDisk Corp.*, 406 F.3d 1359 (Fed. Cir. 2005), holds that the claim words "conventional," "traditional," and "standard" should be interpreted as being temporally limited to the conventions, traditions, and standards that existed at the time when the patent was filed. The patent at issue covered a device for connecting peripheral devices to a computer via the computer's disk drive. Claim 1 of the patent is representative:

1. In combination a computer having a diskette drive, an end user computer peripheral device having an input/output port normally connectible to a *conventional* computer input/output port, and a coupler which couples the computer with the end user computer peripheral device without using a *conventional* computer input/output port: said coupler being sized and shaped for insertion within the diskette drive of the computer ... whereby data is transferred from said computer to said end user computer peripheral device via said read/write head of said computer, said coupler, and said input/output port of said end user computer peripheral device.

The accused devices in the case were couplers to link peripheral devices through a computer disk drive, but the couplers were designed to handle a particular class of peripheral devices—flash memories and smart cards that have flat, planar surface contact electrodes as their normal connecting elements (connectors radically different from the sort of multi-pronged connectors conventional in 1988). The court held that the accused devices could not infringe the patent because the relevant claim language limited the invention to an adapter for peripheral devices having 1988-style connectors:

We find nothing in the written description that amounts to a clear attempt by the patentee to impart any special meaning to the words "normally," "conventional," "traditionally," or "standard." Likewise, in the prosecution history, we do not read the patentability arguments that were made specifically to distinguish a test fixture as having effected the particular redefinition now advanced on appeal. As a consequence, the terms "normally," "conventional," "traditionally," and "standard" are governed by their ordinary and customary meanings, and that, in view of their implicit time-dependence, the district court did not err in construing the literal scope of the claim limitations qualified by those terms as being limited to technologies existing at the time of the invention.

PC Connector's argument that the dictionary definitions of "normally," "conventional," "traditionally," and "standard" contain no explicit reference to a time limitation is not persuasive, as their time-related significance is implicit from their ordinary usage—just as other words are implicitly not time-related. A comparison of the words "conventional" and "dedicated" is instructive in this regard, as PC Connector's briefs appear to treat them as interchangeable and coterminous in claim scope, when, in fact, they are not. To illustrate, a present-day USB port may be described as a "dedicated" I/O port within the ordinary meaning of "dedicated" as that word would be used to characterize the I/O ports found on a computer built in 1988, yet it would not be considered "conventional" back then, even though it is "conventional" today. Thus, unlike the word "dedicated," the word "conventional" necessarily has a meaning specific to the time of filing.

406 F.3d at 1363–64. Do these words have "implicit" time-related significance? Why did the patentee invite this discussion by limiting the claim to an adapter for peripherals having "conventional" connectors? For more on this important issue, *see* Mark A. Lemley, *The Changing Meaning of Patent Claim Terms*, 104 MICH. L. REV. 101 (2005)

(arguing that patent claim terms should have a fixed meaning throughout time, and that that meaning should be fixed at the time the patent application is first filed).

6. *Two Standards of Claim Construction.* During patent prosecution, the PTO applies "the broadest reasonable interpretation" (BRI) in construing claims, not the normal rules of claim construction just discussed. The rationale for using this standard, as opposed to the meaning that a PHOSITA would give a claim term (as articulated in *Phillips*), is that it facilitates the exploration of the "metes and bounds to which the applicant may be entitled, and thus to aid in sharpening and clarifying the claims during the application stage, when claims are readily changed." *See In re Skvorecz*, 580 F.3d 1262, 1267 (Fed. Cir. 2009); U.S. PATENT AND TRADEMARK OFFICE, MANUAL OF PATENT EXAMINING PROCEDURE §2111 (9th ed. Mar. 2014). The applicant has wide latitude to amend claims during examination.

The Supreme Court upheld the use of BRI in IPR proceedings as a reasonable exercise of the PTO's rulemaking authority under the AIA. *See Cuozzo Speed Techs., LLC, v. Lee*, 136 S.Ct. 2131 (2016). The PTO has nonetheless abandoned BRI for IPRs, using the normal rules of claim construction instead.

7. *Standard of Appellate Review.* One of the most controversial issues briefed, but not resolved, in *Phillips* was whether the Federal Circuit should review district court decisions de novo, i.e., without deference to underlying factual findings. Judge Mayer's dissent took the issue up, but did not bring along enough of his colleagues.

The deference issue continued to reverberate in the Federal Circuit after the *Phillips* decision. Even though the claim construction reversal rate dropped significantly, *see* J. Jonas Anderson & Peter S. Menell, *Informal Deference: A Historical, Empirical, and Normative Analysis of Patent Claim Construction*, 108 NW. U. L. REV. 1, 41–42, 48–56 (2014), judges within the circuit remained split on the proper standard of review. The Supreme Court finally resolved the controversy in *Teva Pharmaceuticals USA, Inc. v. Sandoz, Inc.*, 135 S.Ct. 831 (2015). The Court held that claim construction can entail fact-finding and restored the fundamental juridical principle—reflected in Federal Rule of Civil Procedure 52(a)(6)—that the Federal Circuit, like other appellate courts, must "give due regard to the trial court's opportunity to judge the witnesses' credibility" and defer to the trial court's factual determinations unless "clearly erroneous." Nonetheless, the Court recognized the primacy of the intrinsic evidence. Thus, while factual determinations underlying claim construction rulings are subject to the "clearly erroneous" (or "abuse of discretion") standard of review, the Federal Circuit exercises *de novo* review over the ultimate claim construction decision. In this manner, district judges can use their distinctive vantage point and evidentiary tools to ferret out factual underpinnings while the Federal Circuit can operate as a check on fidelity to the patent instrument.

As a practical matter, however, very little has changed since *Teva*. Courts overwhelmingly focus on intrinsic evidence, following *Phillips*, and so the Federal Circuit has not had occasion to defer to district court factfinding on claim construction. This may change if district judges begin to hold evidentiary hearings as part of claim construction and make formal factual findings as to the meaning of disputed claim terms. *See* J. Jonas Anderson & Peter S. Menell, *Restoring the Fact/Law Distinction in Patent Claim Construction*, 109 Nw. U. L. REV. ONLINE 187 (2015).

3. Canons of Claim Construction

Courts have established a set of rules, or canons, of interpretation to help guide the claim construction process. *See generally* Peter S. Menell, Matthew D. Powers, & Steven C. Carlson, *Patent Claim Construction: A Modern Synthesis and Structured Framework*, 25 BERKELEY TECH. L.J. 711 (2010).

i. *Ordinary vs. Contextual or "Particular" Meaning*

Reliance on context is actually a collection of rules and sub-doctrines, rather than a single canon. The general issue is this: claims are skeletal, employing as few words as possible. (Remember that in general the fewer the words, the broader the claim.) Specifications, by contrast, are written to put flesh on these bones—to provide background and depth to explain how an invention works. The goal in drafting a specification is to satisfy the enablement and written description requirements of §112—to tell people in the art how to "make and use" the invention. Often a word used in a claim will also be used in the specification—in context. These contrasting uses provide the grist for many a hard-fought contest over claim interpretation.

As a starting point, the Federal Circuit has often stated its presumption that the meaning of words in a claim is the "ordinary," i.e., non-contextual, meaning that would be assigned to those words. *Phillips v. AWH Corp.* 415 F.3d 1303, 1312–13 (Fed. Cir. 2005) (en banc).

Despite starting with ordinary meaning, most claim interpretation cases turn on contextual (or, as the *Phillips* court called them, "particular") meanings. The dispute in *Nystrom v. TREX Co., Inc.*, 424 F.3d 1136 (Fed. Cir. 2005), concerned the term "board." Nystrom, the patentee, claimed "[a] board for use in constructing a flooring surface for exterior use. . . ." The question was whether "boards" was limited to *wooden* boards. The accused infringer, TREX, sold exterior decking planks made from composites of wood fibers and recycled plastic. Nystrom argued for the plain or ordinary meaning of "board" and cited various dictionary definitions to prove that the "ordinary" or "plain" meaning of "board" is not limited to a thing made of wood. Nystrom's specification, however, consistently described his decking invention with respect to *wooden* boards. The court limited Nystrom to the context and background of the specification to flesh out—and hence limit—the meaning of the word in the claim.

ii. *"Lexicographer" Rule*

The "ordinary meaning" approach has a further limitation: patentees are free to be their own lexicographers—i.e., to define claim terms in any way they wish. *Phillips v. AWH Corp.*, 415 F.3d 1303, 1316 (Fed. Cir. 2005) (en banc) ("[O]ur cases recognize that the specification may reveal a special definition given to a claim term by the patentee that differs from the meaning it would otherwise possess. In such cases, the inventor's lexicography governs."); *Jack Guttman, Inc. v. Kopykake Enterprises, Inc.*, 302 F.3d 1352 (Fed. Cir. 2002) (an example of a patentee expressly defining a term).

Jack Gutman Enterprises is a very rare case: the vast majority of cases that cite the "lexicographer rule" do *not* involve an explicit definition.

Definitions, however, need not be explicit. Because of this, the "lexicographer rule" is very often invoked in service of the routine search for contextual or "particular" meaning, as described above. In *AstraZeneca AB, Inc. v. Mutual*, 384 F.3d 1333 (Fed. Cir. 2004), the principal claim in the key patent at issue reads as follows:

> 1. A solid preparation providing extended release of an active compound with very low solubility in water comprising a solution or dispersion of an effective amount of the active compound in a semi-solid or liquid nonionic solubilizer, wherein the amount by weight of the solubilizer is at least equal to the amount by weight of the active compound, and a release controlling system to provide extended release.

The dispute centered on the term "solubilizer." The Federal Circuit observed that "[t]he parties agree that as a general matter, artisans would understand the term 'solubilizer' to embrace three distinct types of chemicals: (1) surface active agents (also known as "surfactants"), (2) co-solvents, and (3) complexation agents." *Id.* at 1336 (footnote omitted). The district court, looking to "ordinary meaning," held that "solubilizer" comprised three types of chemicals noted above based on a dictionary definition. The Federal Circuit reversed on the ground that the patentee had specifically "disavowed" the latter two categories of chemicals.

> [W]e hold that the inventors deliberately acted as their own lexicographers. The 'Description of the Invention' states that '[t]he solubilizers suitable according to the invention *are defined below*' (emphasis added), and two paragraphs later, states that '[t]he solubilizers suitable for the preparations according to the invention are semi-solid or liquid non-ionic *surface active agents*' (emphasis added). Astrazeneca maintains that these statements simply refer to preferred embodiments of 'suitable' solubilizers. We might agree if the specification stated, for example, '*a solubilizer* suitable for the preparations according to the invention,' but in fact, the specification definitively states '*the solubilizers* suitable for the preparations according to the invention' (emphasis added). Astrazeneca seems to suggest that lexicography requires a statement in the form 'I define _____ to mean _____,' but such rigid formalism is not required. . . Certainly the '081 specification's statement that '[t]he solubilizers suitable according to the invention are defined below' provides a strong signal of lexicography.

Id. at 1340.

In an effort to promote claim clarity, the PTO instituted a pilot program to encourage applicants to provide glossaries by offering accelerated examination. The program ended as a result of the relatively low participation. *See* USPTO, Glossary Initiative, http://www.uspto.gov/patent/initiatives/glossary-initiative.

iii.   Disclaimer of Subject Matter

Accused infringers often contend that language in a patent's specification forms a special contextual meaning for a word used in a patent claim. At times, "meaning through context" involves the more specific argument that a patentee has affirmatively *disclaimed* a certain meaning. This can arise through language in the specification or, commonly, statements made during patent prosecution. If successful, this argument establishes that certain interpretations of claim language are foreclosed by the patentee's own explicit statements. *AstraZeneca AB, Inc. v. Mutual*, 384 F.3d 1333 (Fed. Cir. 2004), is once again instructive:

> Second, we hold the specification clearly disavows nonsurfactant solubilizers. The inventors' lexicography alone works an implicit disavowal of nonsurfactant solubilizers, but the rest of the specification goes further. The 'Description of the Invention' twice describes micelle structures as a feature of the novel formulation structure conceived by the inventors. . . . It is undisputed that surfactants are the only solubilizers believed to form micelle structures in watery environments. Indeed, immediately after the reference to the 'micelle-structure formed by the solubilizer' of the invention, the specification criticizes other types of solubilizers—and specifically co-solvents—as leading to undesirable precipitation. . . . AstraZeneca contends that these statements in the specification simply address the features of preferred embodiments. Astrazeneca seems to suggest that clear disavowal requires an 'expression of manifest exclusion or restriction' in the form of 'my invention does not include _____.' But again, such rigid formalism is not required: Where the general summary or description of the invention describes a feature of the invention (here, micelles formed by the solubilizer) and criticizes other products (here, other solubilizers, including co-solvents) that lack that same feature, this operates as a clear disavowal of these other products (and processes using these products).

Id. at at 1340.

The Federal Circuit requires that any such disavowal be "clear and unambiguous" to alter claim scope. *See Microsoft Corp. v. Multi-Tech Sys., Inc.*, 357 F.3d 1340 (Fed. Cir. 2004). It regularly resists efforts to change the ordinary meaning of claim terms through disclaimer, particularly when it is based on the prosecution history rather than the specification. For a debated example, see *Astrazeneca AB v. Mylan Pharms.*, 19 F.4th 1325 (Fed. Cir. 2021) (construing the term "0.001%" to mean exactly or nearly 0.001%; the ordinary meaning (and the dissent's reading) would include rounding up from 0.0005% and down from 0.0014%, but here the patentee distinguished its invention from one at 0.0005%).

iv.   "Claim Differentiation": Contextual Meaning from Other Claims

The doctrine of claim differentiation is the patent law version of a general principle of legal interpretation: the non-redundancy principle. *See, e.g., Bailey v. United States*,

516 U.S. 137, 146 (1995) ("We assume that Congress used two terms because it intended each term to have a particular, nonsuperfluous meaning."); *Reiter v. Sonotone Corp.*, 442 U.S. 330, 339 (1979) ("In construing a statute we are obliged to give effect, if possible, to every word Congress used."); *Colautti v. Franklin*, 439 U.S. 379, 392 (1979) (explaining that an "elementary canon of construction [is] that a statute should be interpreted so as not to render one part inoperative"). The court relied on the claim differentiation doctrine in *Phillips*. Do you agree with its analysis?

Recall that the issue in *Nystrom* was the meaning of the word "board." The accused infringer, TREX, wanted to limit the meaning of the claim to "wooden boards," so as to exclude TREX's composite boards from the definition and therefore from legal liability for infringement. Nystrom argued that the meaning of "board" in claim 1 could not logically be limited to "wooden boards," because claim 16 of the Nystrom patent specifically claimed "a wooden board." Interpreting "board" in claim 1 as implicitly meaning "wooden board" would render meaningless the language of claim 16. If "board" in this patent means "wooden board," claim 16 would mean "wooden wooden board"—a ridiculous proposition. Why might that argument not have prevailed? *Cf.* Mark A. Lemley, *The Limits of Claim Differentiation*, 22 BERKELEY TECH. L.J. 1389 (2007) (arguing that claim differentiation should be applied with caution because patent drafters are often aiming for redundancy).

v. *Purpose or Goal of the Invention*

One contextual clue that courts have used to supply meaning for a claim term is the purpose or goal of an invention. In *Minnesota Mining & Manufacturing Co. v. Johnson & Johnson Orthopaedics, Inc.,* 976 F.2d 1559 (Fed. Cir. 1992), Minnesota Mining held a series of patents related to orthopedic casting tapes and, more specifically, to resin-based casting systems which have replaced the old-fashioned plaster casts. The claimed casts were formed from curable sheets of material. Several key claims required that each sheet have a "lubricant" or be "pre-lubricated." Polyethylene and silicon were identified in the patent as effective lubricants. This posed a problem, given that certain references in the prior art disclosed identical lubricants, but those lubricants were said to be directed to other functions, and when used they resulted in a "tacky" surface that would not serve the purpose of making a smooth orthopedic cast. The Federal Circuit interpreted the claims at issue so as to find no anticipation. The district court had found that the lubricants disclosed in the patent specification were designed to make the sheet's resin slippery when activated. The Federal Circuit held that it was absolutely correct to "use the specification . . . to determine what the inventor meant by terms and phrases in the claims." And, more importantly: "The fundamental purpose and significance of the [patented] invention is to produce a non-sticky or non-tacky resin (i.e., a slippery resin) to permit smoothing and forming of the casting tapes, thereby overcoming the 'tacky resin' problem of the prior art. . . . This is evident throughout the patent specification."

Related to this idea is the canon that a construction that excludes the patentee's preferred embodiment is ordinarily improper. *Vitronics Corp. v. Conceptronic, Inc.,* 90

F.3d 1576, 1578 (Fed. Cir. 1996) ("Such an interpretation is rarely, if ever, correct and would require highly persuasive evidentiary support.").

vi. *Construing Claims to Preserve Their Validity*

A traditional maxim of claim construction was that claims should be construed, where possible, to preserve their validity. *See, e.g., Rhine v. Casio, Inc.*, 183 F.3d 1342, 1345 (Fed. Cir. 1999) ("claims should be so construed, if possible, as to sustain their validity"). This canon too has its roots in statutory interpretation—the rule that statutes are to be construed where possible to avoid raising constitutional questions. Similarly, courts sought to construe claims to avoid raising questions of validity. Almost always, that maxim counseled in favor of construing those claims narrowly.

Since *Markman*, however, courts have shied away from applying this doctrine. In part the problem is procedural: a court construing patent claims pretrial cannot know how a jury will rule on the question of validity. *Phillips* was dismissive of the canon, and it has fallen into general disuse in the wake of that opinion. The courts have warned that this canon is "a last resort, not a first principle." *MBO Labs., Inc. v. Becton, Dickinson & Co.*, 474 F.3d 1323, 1331 (Fed. Cir. 2007). And in any event, patent claim drafters should not rely on courts to save their patents from inadvertent drafting errors. This was the sad lesson of the drafter in *Chef America, Inc. v. Lamb-Weston, Inc.*, 358 F.3d 1371, 1371 (Fed. Cir. 2004), who made the mistake of claiming that its cookie dough product should be baked "to" a temperature of 450–800 degrees Fahrenheit. Although the drafter undoubtedly intended to claim a process of baking that involved heating *the oven* to this temperature, and then baking for a brief time, the court would not change the clearly stated claim language; so the inventor ended up with a patent that covered only charred hunks of dough.

vii. *A Tiebreaker: Narrow Construction Preferred*

Some have suggested, drawing upon the *contra proferentem* contract law principle, that the claims should be interpreted against the draftsperson, i.e., the patentee. *See 3M Innovative Properties Cos. v. Tredegar Corp.*, 725 F.3d 1315, 1336 (Fed. Cir. 2013). Does this analogy make sense? Should it matter whether (as is normally true) the patentee wants the claim construed broadly or whether (as is sometimes the case) it is the accused infringer who wants the broad construction? The final canon of construction may be expressed as a tie-breaker rule: when two interpretations are equally plausible, choose the narrower interpretation. Hence, the rule is to be deployed sparingly, only in cases that remain close after all other interpretive resources have been exhausted. But sometimes after all the rules are applied, two equally plausible interpretations of a claim—one broader, one narrower—are possible. In such a case, the Federal Circuit has held that the "notice function" of claims requires that the narrower interpretation prevail. *See Athletic Alternatives, Inc. v. Prince Manufacturing, Inc.*, 73 F.3d 1573, 1581 (Fed. Cir. 1996).

An argument can be made that the *contra proferentem* rule ought to be applied routinely to encourage more clarity and less opportunism by patent drafters. *See* Peter

S. Menell & Michael J. Meurer, *Notice Failure and Notice Externalities*, 5 J. LEGAL ANALYSIS 1 (2013).

The following chart summarizes the principal claim construction principles and canons:

FOUNDATIONAL PRINCIPLES

- Construe from perspective of one of ordinary skill in the art
- Construe from time period of invention (i.e., effective filing date)
- Interpret claim terms by reference to patent and prosecution history as a whole
- Appropriate to consider extrinsic evidence, but it cannot contradict intrinsic evidence
    - No "presumption in favor of dictionary definition"
    - No "heavy presumption" of ordinary meaning

ORDINARY MEANING

FACTORS THAT FAVOR NARROWER CONSTRUCTION

DESCRIPTION OF INVENTION

- Characterization of "the present invention"
- Distinctions over the prior art
- Consistent usage of claim terms in patent and prosecution history

PROSECUTION DISCLAIMER

- Surrendering claim scope during prosecution narrows claim interpretation
- "Clear and unmistakable disavowal" required for prosecution disclaimer

SPECIAL CASES

- Inventors may expressly define terms differently than ordinary meaning
- Specification may disclaim coverage to embodiments
- Ambiguity in claim term may permit limiting scope to preferred embodiment
- Means-plus-function terms are limited to structures in specification, and equivalents

FACTORS THAT FAVOR BROADER CONSTRUCTION

CLAIM DIFFERENTIATION

- "Pure" claim differentiation creates a presumption that independent claims are broader than dependent claims
- Presumption may be rebutted based on specification or prosecution history, or where §112, ¶6 involved

PREFERRED EMBODIMENT GENERALLY NOT LIMITING

PETER S. MENELL, ET AL., PATENT CASE MANAGEMENT JUDICIAL GUIDE §5.2.3.2.1 (FEDERAL JUDICIAL CENTER) (3RD ED. 2016).

PROBLEMS

Problem III-12. Pizza King holds U.S. Patent No. 4,498,686 pertaining to a "package saver" invention.

Abstract

A temperature resistant molded plastic device is described for use in boxes or packages such as pizza boxes where there is a tendency of large cover portions to sag downwardly to damage the soft pizza or other packaged products. In use, the saver is positioned near the center of the package to support the box cover for protecting the contents.

Background of the Invention

[T]he invention relates to such a package saver which is molded from plastic to have minimal size, weight, and cost and which is suitable for supporting large carton covers such as those used for pizza pies. The molded plastic saver is positioned centrally of the completed pie or other product to support the cover during storage and delivery. * * *

[A]n object of the present invention is to provide an easily manufactured, relatively inexpensive, lightweight article which is placed on the pie or cake within the package to support the central portion of the package cover during delivery.

Description of the Preferred Embodiment

To provide a lightweight and inexpensive device for the purpose discussed above, the saver is preferably molded as a unitary device from one of the plastics which is heat resistant such as the thermo set plastics and which will resist temperatures of as high as about 500° F.

In its preferred form, as illustrated, the saver 1 has spaced vertical legs 2 connected to a cover support 3. The lower portions of the legs 4 have a minimal cross section to minimize any marking of the protected article 5 and they are also made thin for minimizing the volume of plastic required. The cover support 3 of the saver 1 also preferably has a minimum volume by consisting of a spoke-like arrangement of radially oriented leg supports 6 molded to extend from a central portion 7.

This construction of portion support 3 provides a suitable broad and stable support for box 8 cover 9 which is of minimal volume and thus has minimal cost. A disposable saver 1 is provided which may be used in the boxes or cartons without damage to the packaged pizza pie or other product.

As various changes may be made in the form, construction and arrangement of the invention and without departing from the spirit and scope of the invention, and without sacrificing any of its advantages, it is to be understood that all matters herein is to be interpreted as illustrative and not in a limiting sense.

Claims

Having thus described my invention, I claim:

1. in combination a package having a flexible cover, a food article packaged therein and spaced downwardly from the cover, a unitary molded plastic package saving device for positioning between the cover and the article for supporting the package cover thereby preventing damage to the packaged food article by the cover, said device comprising the combination of three or more spaced legs, each leg having one relatively flat end adapted for engaging the packaged article and having its opposite end attached to a device cover portion.

2. The combination as claimed in claim 1 in which said device cover portion comprises a number of flat cover sections radiating from a common flat central portion.

3. The combination as claimed in claim 1 wherein said device is formed of heat resistant plastic.

4. The combination as claimed in claim 1 wherein said device is formed of thermo-setting plastic.

* * * * *

Giuseppe's Pizza develops its own package saver device by fusing together two plastic pieces.

Pizza King sues for patent infringement. The court schedules a Markman hearing to construe the patent claim. What is Giuseppe's best claim construction? What is Pizza King's best response? On what do you base the argument and counter-argument? If you were the judge, what would you decide?

Problem III-13. Lonnie Jackson operates a hair salon. She has struggled over the years to deal with clogged drains. To keep her plumbing costs under control, Lonnie invented the Hair Hook:

It works by threading the elongated end into the clogged drain, fishing for hair, and then removing the device.

The Patent Office grants Jackson the following claim:

1. Apparatus for removing hair from a drain, comprising:

    (a) an elongate, flexible Strip;

    (b) the elongate, flexible Strip having a plurality of barbed portions, the barbed portions being adapted to grip hair in the drain, wherein the barbed portions are oriented at an acute angle to the axis of the elongate Strip, wherein the vertex of the angle points away from the handle; and

    (c) a handle, wherein the handle is a distinct structural element from the elongate, flexible Strip.

After Drain Declogger (DD) starts selling a product that is identical to the claimed invention, Jackson sues for patent infringement. DD responds that the Hair Hook patent is invalid based on the '789 patent (issued more than 20 years ago) which discloses "resilient flat strip of metal capable of being extended and consisting normally of a series of concentric coils, one end of said strip being provided with a sharp spear-point."

Fig. 1.

Fig. 3.

What claim term(s) require(s) construction in sorting out this invalidity defense? How should a court resolve the claim construction? How should the court resolve the invalidity defense?

4.   The Special Case (and Problems) of Functional Claims – §112(f)

Patent scope plays a critical role in patent law. Beginning in the middle of the nineteenth century, inventors sought greater breadth in the boundaries of their invention by attempting to define their invention at a higher level of abstraction. Rather than claiming the device they actually built or described, inventors sought to identify the inventive contribution and to claim any device that incorporated that inventive contribution, even if it was not identical to the patentee's device. These patentees were using claim language to define a conceptual area rather than identify specific patent boundaries. *See* Mark A. Lemley, *Software Patents and the Return of Functional Claiming*, 2013 WIS. L. REV. 905. An inventor of a new chemical might, for instance, claim a group of related chemicals—a genus—rather than specify each of the species.

The Wright Brothers, for instance, invented only a particular improvement to flying machines, albeit a critical one: they came up with a way of warping a wing to control the direction of flight while turning a rear rudder to counterbalance the effect of bending the wing, maintaining the stability of the plane. JOHN ANDERSON, JR., INVENTING FLIGHT: THE WRIGHT BROTHERS AND THEIR PREDECESSORS 101 (2004). The Wrights solved the stability problem by having a single cable warp the wing and turn the rudder at the same time. Their patent, however, was written using functional language, claiming "means for simultaneously moving the lateral portions [of a wing] into different angular relations" and "means whereby said rudder is caused to present to the wind that side thereof . . . having the smaller angle of incidence." U.S. Patent No. 821,393 claim 7 (filed Mar. 23, 1903). Glenn Curtiss improved the design of the wing by using ailerons, movable portions of the wing. Ailerons could be moved independently of the rudder by the pilot; the two were not connected, as they were in the Wright's design. But the Wright Brothers nonetheless successfully asserted the patent against subsequent inventors such as Glenn Curtiss. Judge Learned Hand held that the ailerons under separate control were literally within the scope of the patent. *Wright Co. v. Paulhan*, 177 F. 261, 264 (C.C.S.D.N.Y. 1910) (holding the Wrights' patent to be pioneering and so entitled to broad scope). A frustrated Curtiss was reported to have said that the Wright brothers believed their patent was so broad that anyone who jumped up and down and flapped their arms infringed it. The Wrights successfully enforced their patent to defeat all alternative aircraft, including many that surpassed the technical achievement of the Wrights.

By the 1940s, functional claiming of this sort had become widespread. The Supreme Court rejected the practice in 1946 in *Halliburton Oil Well Cementing Co. v. Walker*, 329 U.S. 1 (1946); *cf. Funk Bros. Seed Co. v. Kalo Inoculant Co.*, 333 U.S. 127, 133 (1948) (Frankfurter, J., concurring) (arguing that claims to groups of bacteria that are "not identified and are identifiable only by their compatibility" should be rejected because similar efforts to claim by function in other areas are impermissible). In *Halliburton*, the patentee had drafted its claim entirely in functional terms, referring to "means for" performing various functions. The Court held that the patent claim was indefinite because it did not specify how the patent performed the function or limited the invention to the particular means the patentee actually invented. Substituting broad functional language at the very point of novelty, the Court said, did not sufficiently put the world on notice of what the patentee was removing from the world.

Patent lawyers took their case to Congress. When Congress passed the Patent Act of 1952 six years after *Halliburton*, it overruled Halliburton insofar as that decision had prevented functional claiming at the point of novelty. Patentees could once again use functional language such as "means for processing data" even if the data processing means was the novel part of the invention. Nonetheless, Congress limited the scope of "means-plus-function" claim elements. Section 112(f) provides:

> An element in a claim for a combination may be expressed as a means or step for performing a specified function without the recital of structure, material, or acts in support thereof, and such claim shall be construed to cover the corresponding structure, material, or acts described in the specification and equivalents thereof.

This "means-plus-function" claiming represents a significant departure from the normal rules of patent claim construction. Patent claim construction starts with the plain meaning of the claim language. While the description of the invention can be read to help understand what the claims mean, the fundamental rule of patent claim construction is that the claim terms are not to be narrowed by reference to what the patentee actually invented or described. A patentee can, for example, claim a group of chemicals without having described, much less tested, all or even many of the chemicals in the group. Similarly, a patent claim to a "chair comprising a seat, legs, and a back" would cover a nearly infinite array of chairs, regardless of how many legs it has, whether it has wheels on the legs, and whether it is made of wood, metal, plastic, or upholstery. *See* Jeffrey A. Lefstin, *The Formal Structure of Patent Law and the Limits of Enablement*, 23 BERKELEY TECH. L.J. 1141, 1169–70 (2008). Further, if the patentee uses the magic word "comprising" (and virtually all do) the patent claim must include the listed elements but is not limited to those elements; adding additional elements (such as arms) will not avoid infringement.

Against this backdrop, §112(f) actually represents a significant narrowing of claim scope. While the 1952 Act rejected *Halliburton* and permitted functional claiming, in fact the sort of functional claiming the statutory text allows is far different from the functional claiming that was the norm in 1940. A means-plus-function claim element is not interpreted to cover every means of performing the function. Instead, the courts apply a different rule of claim construction, limiting the scope of these claims by reading in the particular technologies described in the patent specification.

To take an example, suppose that the patent claim includes as an element a "means for processing data." Read literally, without reference to §112(f), this language would encompass any possible means for processing data, including any computer, but also a calculator, an abacus, pencil and paper, and perhaps even the human brain. Section 112(f) permits the use of such functional language but doesn't permit it to cover any means of performing the data-processing function. Instead, the claim would be limited to the particular "means for processing data" actually described in the patent specification (say, an iPad) "and equivalents thereof."

While the last phrase in the statute—"and equivalents thereof"—permits some broadening of both means-plus-function and step-plus-function claims, such equivalents must have been known as of the time of the invention. (As we will see in (D)(1)(a)(ii), *infra*, the doctrine of equivalents can provide an additional stretch to "equivalents" based on after-arising advances, i.e., based on technologies that emerge after the time of the invention claimed using functional language.) The first stage in the analysis is whether the term in question is "mean-plus-function." *See DePuy Spine, Inc. v. Medtronic Sofamor Danek, Inc.*, 469 F.3d 1005, 1023 (Fed. Cir. 2006) (Means-plus-function claiming applies only to "purely functional limitations that do not provide the structure that performs the recited function."). The Federal Circuit applied a rebuttable presumption that §112(f) applies "[i]f the word 'means' appears in a claim element in association with a function." *Callicrate v. Wadsworth Mfg., Inc.*, 427 F.3d 1361, 1368 (Fed. Cir. 2005). As illustrated in *Phillips*, however, the presumption is rebutted where the claim language itself provides the structure that performs the recited function.

This presumption against construing such limitations under §112(f) used to be characterized as a "strong" presumption. *See Inventio AG v. ThyssenKrupp Elevator Americas Corp.*, 649 F.3d 1350, 1358 (Fed. Cir. 2011). To rein in vague claims, the Federal Circuit revoked this characterization of the presumption as "strong" in *Williamson v. Citrix Online LLC*, 792 F.3d 1339 (Fed. Cir. 2015) (en banc): a term lacking "means" will nonetheless be construed under §112(f) if the "challenger demonstrates that the claim fails to recite sufficiently definite structure or else recites function without reciting sufficient structure for performing that function." The focus is on the claim language as a whole, not just the isolated term that is akin to "means." Generic terms such as "mechanism," "element," "device" and other such terms that do not connote sufficiently definite structure in the context of the overall claim are tantamount to stating "means," and therefore may be construed pursuant to §112(f) if nothing else in the claim provides sufficient structure. The Federal Circuit referred to such "black box" words as "nonce" words. *But see Dyfan, LLC v. Target Corp.*, 28 F.4th 1360 (Fed. Cir. 2022) (concluding that the term "code" provided sufficient structure). The focus should remain on whether the term, in the context of the claim as a whole, connotes a class (even a broad class) of specific structures. If so, then the term should not be construed under §112(f).

Once it is determined that §112(f) applies, then the court proceeds through three steps: (1) identifying the function of the term based upon claim term language (but not embodiments); (2) identifying the corresponding structure, material, or act based on disclosed embodiments; and (3) at the infringement stage, the fact-finder determines whether the accused device falls within "equivalents thereof" as of the time of patent issuance. *See* PETER S. MENELL, ET AL., PATENT CASE MANAGEMENT JUDICIAL GUIDE, §5.2.3.5 (Federal Judicial Center 3rd ed. 2016).

PROBLEM III-14

Ernest Kahlert obtained a patent for in-line skates in 1953. His breakthrough related to cushioning the wheels. To avoid cluttering his apparatus claim with detailed explanation of the upper portion of the device, he began his claim as follows: "An in-line roller skate, comprising an upper portion adapted to receive the skater's foot, a means for fastening said upper portion . . ." His specification notes that "[t]he upper portion of the roller blade can be fastened with laces, zippers, buckles, and snaps."

Unbeknownst to Kahlert, a Swiss electrical engineer George de Mestral had been experimenting with a new method of fastening. While walking in the woods, he wondered if the burrs that clung to his trousers—and dog—could be turned into something useful. This led him to develop a hook and loop fastener, which he patented in 1955. The fastener consisted of two components: a lineal fabric strip with tiny hooks that could "mate" with another fabric strip with smaller loops, attaching temporarily, until pulled apart. The early prototypes were made of cotton, which proved impractical. He eventually landed on the idea of using nylon and polyester, which became a great success. De Mestral gave the name Velcro, combining the French words *velours* ("velvet"), and *crochet* ("hook").

In 1958, Rollerglide introduced an inline skate that had all of the elements of Kahlert's claimed invention except that it used a compression strap combined with a buckle as well as Velcro (duly licensed) to fasten the upper portion of the shoe. The compression strap/buckle and Velcro fasteners held the foot snugly, while providing flexibility. Inline skate enthusiasts loved it and it quickly displaced sales of Kaglert's product. Kahlert seeks your advice on whether Rollerglide's product falls within the scope of Kahlert's claim. Does Rollerglide's product come within Kahlert's claim? Explain how you reached this conclusion.

5. Claim Indefiniteness

Nautilus, Inc. v. Biosig Instruments, Inc.
Supreme Court of the United States
572 U.S. 898 (2014)

JUSTICE GINSBURG delivered the opinion of the Court.

The Patent Act requires that a patent specification "conclude with one or more claims *particularly pointing out and distinctly claiming* the subject matter which the applicant regards as [the] invention." 35 U.S.C. §112[(b)] (emphasis added). This case, involving a heart-rate monitor used with exercise equipment, concerns the proper reading of the statute's clarity and precision demand. According to the Federal Circuit, a patent claim passes the §112[(b)] threshold so long as the claim is "amenable to construction," and the claim, as construed, is not "insolubly ambiguous." 715 F.3d 891, 898–899 (2013). We conclude that the Federal Circuit's formulation, which tolerates some ambiguous claims but not others, does not satisfy the statute's definiteness requirement. In place of the "insolubly ambiguous" standard, we hold that a patent is invalid for indefiniteness if its claims, read in light of the specification delineating the patent, and the prosecution history, fail to inform, with reasonable certainty, those skilled in the art about the scope of the invention. Expressing no opinion on the validity of the patent-in-suit, we remand, instructing the Federal Circuit to decide the case employing the standard we have prescribed.

I

Authorized by the Constitution "[t]o promote the Progress of Science and useful Arts, by securing for limited Times to . . . Inventors the exclusive Right to their . . . Discoveries," Art. I, §8, cl. 8, Congress has enacted patent laws rewarding inventors with a limited monopoly. "Th[at] monopoly is a property right," and "like any property right, its boundaries should be clear." *Festo Corp. v. Shoketsu Kinzoku Kogyo Kabushiki Co.*, 535 U.S. 722, 730 (2002). *See* also *Markman v. Westview Instruments, Inc.*, 517 U.S. 370, 373 (1996) ("It has long been understood that a patent must describe the exact scope of an invention and its manufacture. . . ."). Thus, when Congress enacted the first Patent Act in 1790, it directed that patent grantees file a written specification "containing a description . . . of the thing or things . . . invented or discovered," which "shall be so particular" as to "distinguish the invention or discovery from other things before known and used." Act of Apr. 10, 1790, §2, 1 Stat. 110.

The patent laws have retained this requirement of definiteness even as the focus of patent construction has shifted. Under early patent practice in the United States, we have recounted, it was the written specification that "represented the key to the patent." *Markman*, 517 U.S., at 379. Eventually, however, patent applicants began to set out the invention's scope in a separate section known as the "claim." *See* generally 1 R. MOY, WALKER ON PATENTS §4.2, pp. 4–17 to 4–20 (4th ed. 2012). The Patent Act of 1870 expressly conditioned the receipt of a patent on the inventor's inclusion of one or more such claims, described with particularity and distinctness. *See* Act of July 8, 1870, §26, 16 Stat. 201 (to obtain a patent, the inventor must "particularly point out and distinctly claim the part, improvement, or combination which [the inventor] claims as his invention or discovery").

The 1870 Act's definiteness requirement survives today, largely unaltered. Section 112 of the Patent Act of 1952, applicable to this case, requires the patent applicant to conclude the specification with "one or more claims particularly pointing out and distinctly claiming the subject matter which the applicant regards as his invention." 35 U.S.C. §112[(b)]. A lack of definiteness renders invalid "the patent or any claim in suit." §282, ¶2(3).

II

A

The patent in dispute, U.S. Patent No. 5,337,753 ('753 patent), issued to Dr. Gregory Lekhtman in 1994 and assigned to respondent Biosig Instruments, Inc., concerns a heart-rate monitor for use during exercise. Previous heart-rate monitors, the patent asserts, were often inaccurate in measuring the electrical signals accompanying each heartbeat (electrocardiograph or ECG signals). The inaccuracy was caused by electrical signals of a different sort, known as electromyogram or EMG signals, generated by an exerciser's skeletal muscles when, for example, she moves her arm, or grips an exercise monitor with her hand. These EMG signals can "mask" ECG signals and thereby impede their detection.

Dr. Lekhtman's invention claims to improve on prior art by eliminating that impediment. The invention focuses on a key difference between EMG and ECG waveforms: while ECG signals detected from a user's left hand have a polarity opposite to that of the signals detected from her right hand,[2] EMG signals from each hand have the same polarity. The patented device works by measuring equalized EMG signals detected at each hand and then using circuitry to subtract the identical EMG signals from each other, thus filtering out the EMG interference.

---

[2] This difference in polarity occurs because the heart is not aligned vertically in relation to the center of the body; the organ tilts leftward from apex to bottom.

As relevant here, the '753 patent describes a heart-rate monitor contained in a hollow cylindrical bar that a user grips with both hands, such that each hand comes into contact with two electrodes, one "live" and one "common." The device is illustrated in figure 1 of the patent, *id.*, at 41, reproduced [at the end of] this opinion.

Claim 1 of the '753 patent, which contains the limitations critical to this dispute, refers to a "heart rate monitor for use by a user in association with exercise apparatus and/or exercise procedures." *Id.*, at 61. The claim "comprise[s]," among other elements, an "elongate member" (cylindrical bar) with a display device; "electronic circuitry including a difference amplifier"; and, on each half of the cylindrical bar, a live electrode and a common electrode "mounted . . . in spaced relationship with each other." *Ibid.* [In Figure 1 from the patent, the live electrodes are identified by numbers 9 and 13, and the common electrodes, by 11 and 15. The spaced relationship is the area between 9 and 11 on the left side and between 11 and 15 on the right side of the elongate member.]

The claim sets forth additional elements, including that the cylindrical bar is to be held in such a way that each of the user's hands "contact[s]" both electrodes on each side of the bar. Further, the EMG signals detected by the two electrode pairs are to be "of substantially equal magnitude and phase" so that the difference amplifier will "produce a substantially zero [EMG] signal" upon subtracting the [EMG from the ECG] signals.

B

The dispute between the parties arose in the 1990s, when Biosig allegedly disclosed the patented technology to StairMaster Sports Medical Products, Inc. According to Biosig, StairMaster, without ever obtaining a license, sold exercise machines that included Biosig's patented technology, and petitioner Nautilus, Inc., continued to do so after acquiring the StairMaster brand. In 2004, based on these allegations, Biosig brought a patent infringement suit against Nautilus in the U.S. District Court for the Southern District of New York.

With Biosig's lawsuit launched, Nautilus asked the U.S. Patent and Trademark Office (PTO) to reexamine the '753 patent. The reexamination proceedings centered on whether the patent was anticipated or rendered obvious by prior art—principally, a patent issued in 1984 to an inventor named Fujisaki, which similarly disclosed a heart-rate monitor using two pairs of electrodes and a difference amplifier. Endeavoring to distinguish the '753 patent from prior art, Biosig submitted a declaration from Dr. Lekhtman. The declaration attested, among other things, that the '753 patent sufficiently informed a person skilled in the art how to configure the detecting electrodes so as "to produce equal EMG [signals] from the left and right hands." *Id.*, at 160. Although the electrodes' design variables—including spacing, shape, size, and material—cannot be standardized across all exercise machines, Dr. Lekhtman explained, a skilled artisan could undertake a "trial and error" process of equalization. This would entail experimentation with different electrode configurations in order to optimize EMG signal cancellation. [Dr. Lekhtman's declaration also referred to an expert report prepared by Dr. Henrietta Galiana, Chair of the Department of Biomedical Engineering at McGill University, for use in the infringement litigation. That report described how Dr. Galiana's laboratory technician, equipped with a wooden dowel, wire, metal foil, glue, electrical tape, and the drawings from the '753 patent, was able in two hours to build a monitor that "worked just as described in the . . . patent." *Id.*, at 226.] In 2010, the PTO issued a determination confirming the patentability of the '753 patent's claims.

* * * In 2011, the District Court conducted a hearing to determine the proper construction of the patent's claims, *see Markman v. Westview Instruments, Inc.*, 517 U.S. 370 (1996) (claim construction is a matter of law reserved for court decision), including the claim term "in spaced relationship with each other." According to Biosig, that "spaced relationship" referred to the distance between the live electrode and the common electrode in each electrode pair. Nautilus, seizing on Biosig's submissions to the PTO during the reexamination, maintained that the "spaced relationship" must be a distance "greater than the width of each electrode." The District Court ultimately construed the term to mean "there is a defined relationship between the live electrode and the common electrode on one side of the cylindrical bar and the same or a different defined relationship between the live electrode and the common electrode on the other side of the cylindrical bar," without any reference to the electrodes' width. . . .

III

A

Although the parties here disagree on the dispositive question—does the '753 patent withstand definiteness scrutiny—they are in accord on several aspects of the §112[(b)] inquiry. First, definiteness is to be evaluated from the perspective of someone skilled in the relevant art. *See, e.g., General Elec. Co. v. Wabash Appliance Corp.*, 304 U.S. 364, 371 (1938). *See also* §112[(a)] (patent's specification "shall contain a written description of the invention, and of the manner and process of making and using it, in such full, clear, concise, and exact terms as to enable *any person skilled in the art* to which it pertains, or with which it is most nearly connected, to make and use the same" (emphasis added)). Second, in assessing definiteness, claims are to be read in light of the patent's specification and prosecution history. *See, e.g., United States v. Adams*, 383 U.S. 39, 48–49 (1966) (specification); *Festo Corp. v. Shoketsu Kinzoku Kogyo Kabushiki Co.*, 535 U.S. 722, 741 (2002) (prosecution history). Third, "[d]efiniteness is measured from the viewpoint of a person skilled in [the] art *at the time the patent was filed.*" Brief for Respondent 55 (emphasis added).

The parties differ, however, in their articulations of just how much imprecision §112[(b)] tolerates. In Nautilus' view, a patent is invalid when a claim is "ambiguous, such that readers could reasonably interpret the claim's scope differently." Biosig and the Solicitor General would require only that the patent provide reasonable notice of the scope of the claimed invention.

Section 112, we have said, entails a "delicate balance." *Festo*, 535 U.S., at 731. On the one hand, the definiteness requirement must take into account the inherent limitations of language. Some modicum of uncertainty, the Court has recognized, is the "price of ensuring the appropriate incentives for innovation." *Id.* at 732. One must bear in mind, moreover, that patents are "not addressed to lawyers, or even to the public generally," but rather to those skilled in the relevant art. *Carnegie Steel Co. v. Cambria Iron Co.*, 185 U.S. 403, 437 (1902) (also stating that "any description which is sufficient to apprise [steel manufacturers] in the language of the art of the definite feature of the invention, and to serve as a warning to others of what the patent claims as a monopoly, is sufficiently definite to sustain the patent").

At the same time, a patent must be precise enough to afford clear notice of what is claimed, thereby "'appris[ing] the public of what is still open to them.'" *Markman*, 517 U.S., at 373 (quoting *McClain v. Ortmayer*, 141 U.S. 419, 424 (1891)). Otherwise there would be "[a] zone of uncertainty which enterprise and experimentation may enter only at the risk of infringement claims." *United Carbon Co. v. Binney & Smith Co.*, 317 U.S. 228, 236 (1942). And absent a meaningful definiteness check, we are told, patent applicants face powerful incentives to inject ambiguity into their claims. *See* Brief for Petitioner 30—32 (citing patent treatises and drafting guides). *See also* FEDERAL TRADE COMMISSION, THE EVOLVING IP MARKETPLACE: ALIGNING PATENT NOTICE AND REMEDIES WITH COMPETITION 85 (2011) (quoting testimony that patent system fosters "an incentive to be as vague and ambiguous as you can with your claims" and "defer clarity at all costs"). Eliminating that temptation is in order, and "the patent drafter is in the best position to resolve the ambiguity in . . . patent claims." *Halliburton Energy Servs., Inc. v. M-I LLC*, 514 F.3d 1244, 1255 (C.A. Fed. 2008). *See also Hormone Research Foundation, Inc. v. Genentech, Inc.*, 904 F.2d 1558, 1563 (C.A. Fed. 1990) ("It is a well-established axiom in patent law that a patentee is free to be his or her own lexicographer. . . .").

To determine the proper office of the definiteness command, therefore, we must reconcile concerns that tug in opposite directions. Cognizant of the competing concerns, we read §112[(b)] to require that a patent's claims, viewed in light of the specification and prosecution history, inform those skilled in the art about the scope of the invention with reasonable certainty. The definiteness requirement, so understood, mandates clarity, while recognizing that absolute precision is unattainable. The standard we adopt accords with opinions of this Court stating that "the certainty which the law requires in patents is not greater than is reasonable, having regard to their subject-matter." *Minerals Separation, Ltd. v. Hyde*, 242 U.S. 261, 270 (1916). *See also United Carbon*, 317 U.S., at 236 ("claims must be reasonably clear-cut"); *Markman*, 517 U.S., at 389 (claim construction calls for "the necessarily sophisticated analysis of the whole document," and may turn on evaluations of expert testimony).

B

In resolving Nautilus' definiteness challenge, the Federal Circuit asked whether the '753 patent's claims were "amenable to construction" or "insolubly ambiguous." Those formulations can breed lower court confusion,[8] for they lack the precision §112[(b)] demands. It cannot be sufficient that a court can ascribe some meaning to a patent's claims; the definiteness inquiry trains on the understanding of a skilled artisan at the time of the patent application, not that of a court viewing matters post hoc. To tolerate imprecision just short of that rendering a claim "insolubly ambiguous" would diminish the definiteness requirement's public-notice function and foster the innovation-discouraging "zone of uncertainty," *United Carbon*, 317 U.S. at 236, against which this Court has warned.

Appreciating that "terms like 'insolubly ambiguous' may not be felicitous," Brief for Respondent 34, Biosig argues the phrase is a shorthand label for a more probing inquiry that the Federal Circuit applies in practice. The Federal Circuit's fuller explications of the term "insolubly ambiguous," we recognize, may come closer to tracking the statutory prescription. *See, e.g.*, 715 F.3d, at 898 (case below) ("[I]f reasonable efforts at claim construction result in a definition that does not provide sufficient particularity and clarity to inform skilled artisans of the bounds of the claim, the claim is insolubly ambiguous and invalid for indefiniteness." (internal quotation marks omitted)). But although this Court does not "micromanag[e] the Federal Circuit's particular word choice" in applying patent-law doctrines, we must ensure that the Federal Circuit's test is at least "probative of the essential inquiry." *Warner-Jenkinson Co. v. Hilton Davis Chemical Co.*, 520 U.S. 17, 40 (1997). Falling short in that regard, the expressions "insolubly ambiguous" and "amenable to construction" permeate the Federal Circuit's recent decisions concerning §112[(b)]'s requirement. We agree with Nautilus and its amici that such terminology can leave courts and the patent bar at sea without a reliable compass.

The parties nonetheless dispute whether factual findings subsidiary to the ultimate issue of definiteness trigger the clear-and-convincing-evidence standard and, relatedly, whether deference is due to the PTO's resolution of disputed issues of fact. We leave these questions for another day. The court below treated definiteness as "a legal issue [the] court reviews without deference," 715 F.3d at 897, and Biosig has not called our attention to any contested factual matter—or PTO determination thereof—pertinent to its infringement claims.

---

[8] *See, e.g., Every Penny Counts, Inc. v. Wells Fargo Bank, N.A.*, 4 F. Supp. 3d 1286, 1292 (M.D. Fla. 2014) (finding that "the account," as used in claim, "lacks definiteness," because it might mean several different things and "no informed and confident choice is available among the contending definitions," but that "the extent of the indefiniteness . . . falls far short of the 'insoluble ambiguity' required to invalidate the claim").

IV

Both here and in the courts below, the parties have advanced conflicting arguments as to the definiteness of the claims in the '753 patent. Nautilus maintains that the claim term "spaced relationship" is open to multiple interpretations reflecting markedly different understandings of the patent's scope, as exemplified by the disagreement among the members of the Federal Circuit panel.

Notably, however, all three panel members found Nautilus' arguments unavailing.

Biosig responds that "spaced relationship," read in light of the specification and as illustrated in the accompanying drawings, delineates the permissible spacing with sufficient precision.

"[M]indful that we are a court of review, not of first view," *Cutter v. Wilkinson*, 544 U.S. 709, 718, n.7 (2005), we decline to apply the standard we have announced to the controversy between Nautilus and Biosig. As we have explained, the Federal Circuit invoked a standard more amorphous than the statutory definiteness requirement allows. We therefore follow our ordinary practice of remanding so that the Court of Appeals can reconsider, under the proper standard, whether the relevant claims in the '753 patent are sufficiently definite.

* * *

For the reasons stated, we vacate the judgment of the United States Court of Appeals for the Federal Circuit and remand the case for further proceedings consistent with this opinion.

It is so ordered.

COMMENTS AND QUESTIONS

1. *Interaction with Claim Construction.* Given its close connection to claim construction, the claim indefiniteness issue typically arises in conjunction with claim construction. As a result, we present it here, rather than with the rest of the §112 validity doctrines.

2. The Court states the new test for indefiniteness: a claim is indefinite if it "fail[s] to inform, with reasonable certainty, those skilled in the art about the scope of the invention." It is left to the Federal Circuit to apply the new test to the patent at issue in this case. Does the claim term "spaced relationship" fail to inform about the scope of the invention? What about the evidence regarding what this term would mean to one skilled in the art, discussed especially by the Federal Circuit judges in their opinions below? How much should the stated purpose of the invention bear on the question of reasonable certainty regarding claim scope?

3. *Terms of Degree.* In footnote 5 of the opinion (omitted in the excerpt above), the Court mentions some cases involving the common issue of claims that include terms of degree:

> *See also Eibel Process Co. v. Minnesota & Ontario Paper Co.*, 261 U.S. 45, 58, 65–66 (1923) (upholding as definite a patent for an improvement to a paper-making machine, which provided that a wire be placed at a "high" or

"substantial elevation," where "readers . . . skilled in the art of paper making and versed in the use of the . . . machine" would have "no difficulty . . . in determining . . . the substantial [elevation] needed" for the machine to operate as specified).

572 U.S. at 909, n.5. It is important to remember, as the Court emphasizes in *Nautilus*, that definiteness is to be viewed from the PHOSITA's perspective. Hence the "reasonable certainty" required by the opinion is the reasonable certainty of an expert in the field. This may render many terms of approximation definite, because knowledge of the field may often supply implicit parameters in areas where the layperson would be quite uncertain about claim scope.

4. *Nautilus Remand.* The Federal Circuit upheld the patent under the Supreme Court's indefiniteness standard, but suggested somewhat cynically that "we may now steer by the bright star of 'reasonable certainty,' rather than the unreliable compass of 'insoluble ambiguity.'" *Biosig Instruments, Inc.v. Nautilus, Inc.*, 783 F.3d 1374, 1379 (Fed. Cir. 2015). It remains to be seen whether the Supreme Court's intervention will alter the stringency of the indefiniteness standard. It does perhaps send a message to district courts that they have a greater role to play in policing the clarity of patent claims.

5. *Interaction with Presumption of Validity.* In footnote 10 (omitted), the Court says:

The Federal Circuit suggests that a permissive definiteness standard "'accord[s] respect to the statutory presumption of patent validity.'" 715 F.3d 891, 902 (2013) (quoting Exxon Research, 265 F.3d, at 1375). *See also* §282, ¶1 ("[a] patent shall be presumed valid," and "[t]he burden of establishing invalidity of a patent or any claim thereof shall rest on the party asserting such invalidity"); *Microsoft Corp. v. i4i Ltd. Partnership*, 131 S.Ct. 2238, 2242 (2011) (invalidity defenses must be proved by "clear and convincing evidence"). As the parties appear to agree, however, this presumption of validity does not alter the degree of clarity that §112[(b)] demands from patent applicants; to the contrary, it incorporates that definiteness requirement by reference. *See* §282, ¶2(3) (defenses to infringement actions include "[i]nvalidity of the patent or any claim in suit for failure to comply with . . . any requirement of [§112]").

572 U.S. at 912, n.10. It is worth pondering how one attacking a patent for indefiniteness can go about establishing the invalidity case. How does one establish a lack of reasonable certainty regarding claim scope, in clear and convincing terms, so as to overcome the statutory presumption of validity? Does that standard even apply, since indefiniteness is theoretically a question of law based on interpretation of the document? *See* J. Jonas Anderson & Peter S. Menell, *Restoring the Fact/Law Distinction in Patent Claim Construction*, 109 NW. U. L. REV. ONLINE 187, 198–200 (2015) (challenging the court's characterization of indefiniteness as a pure question of law after *Teva*). In view of the Supreme Court's rejection of *Cybor*'s *de novo* standard of review of patent claim construction in *Teva*, there is good reason to believe that a district judge's determination of claim indefiniteness would also fall within the Rule 52(a)(6) framework on which the Supreme Court relied. The same functional considerations that led the Court to place

claim construction within the province of the court apply to indefiniteness. Therefore, even if claim indefiniteness ought not be characterized as a pure question of law, it nonetheless likely falls exclusively "within the province of the court." In any event, the Federal Circuit does not hesitate to reverse district courts on indefiniteness. *See, e.g., Eidos Display, LLC v. AU Optronics Corp.*, 779 F.3d 1360 (Fed. Cir. 2015) (reversing district court invalidation of patent on indefiniteness grounds).

F.   INFRINGEMENT

Infringement of a patent is a tort. Section 271 sets forth the basic standards for patent infringement.

There are several kinds of infringement. We begin with the most basic type: direct infringement. For infringement to occur, there must be at least one act of direct infringement. After exploring this terrain, we examine various forms of indirect infringement.

1.   Direct Infringement

Direct infringement can occur literally—where a person squarely carries out all of the elements of the claimed invention—as well as non-literally.

i.   *Literal Infringement*

Section 271(a) provides that "whoever without authority makes, uses, offers to sell, or sells any patented invention, within the United States or imports into the United States any patented invention during the term of the patent therefor, infringes the patent." To prove literal infringement, the patent owner must prove that the alleged infringer carries out all of the elements of the claimed invention. This is essentially the mirror image of novelty analysis. If what comes before the patent filing would anticipate the patent claim, it infringes the claim if it comes after the invention date. The analysis often boils down to a dispute over claim interpretation.

 Larami Corp. v. Amron
United States District Court for the Eastern District of Pennsylvania
27 U.S.P.Q.2d 1280 (E.D. Pa. 1993)

REED, J.

This is a patent case concerning toy water guns manufactured by plaintiff Larami Corporation ("Larami"). [The patent claim by defendant appears to have grown out of a counterclaim to plaintiff's action for various Lanham Act and state law violations, predicated on threats made by defendants to various of plaintiff's customers and business associates.] Currently before me is Larami's motion for partial summary judgment of noninfringement of [defendant's] United States Patent No. 4,239,129 ("the '129 patent"). . . .

For the reasons discussed below, the motion will be granted.

I. Background

Larami manufactures a line of toy water guns called "SUPER SOAKERS." This line includes five models: SUPER SOAKER 20, SUPER SOAKER 30, SUPER SOAKER 50, SUPER SOAKER 100, and SUPER SOAKER 200. All use a hand-operated air pump to pressurize water and a "pinch trigger" valve mechanism for controlling the ejection of the pressurized water. All feature detachable water reservoirs prominently situated outside and above the barrel of the gun. . . .

Defendants Alan Amron and Talk To Me Products, Inc. (hereinafter referred to collectively as "TTMP") claim that the SUPER SOAKER guns infringe on the '129 patent which TTMP obtained by assignment from Gary Esposito ("Esposito"), the inventor. The '129 patent covers a water gun which, like the SUPER SOAKERS, operates by pressurizing water housed in a tank with an air pump. In the '129 patent, the pressure enables the water to travel out of the tank through a trigger-operated valve into an outlet tube and to squirt through a nozzle. Unlike the SUPER SOAKERS, the '129 patent also contains various electrical features to illuminate the water stream and create noises. Also, the water tank in the '129 patent is not detachable, but is contained within a housing in the body of the water gun.

The "Background of the Invention" contained in the '129 patent reads as follows:

> Children of all ages, especially boys, through the years have exhibited a fascination for water, lights and noise and the subject invention deals with these factors embodied in a toy simulating a pistol.

An appreciable number of U.S. patents have been issued which are directed to water pistols but none appear to disclose a unique assembly of components which can be utilized to simultaneously produce a jet or stream of water, means for illuminating the stream and a noise, or if so desired, one which can be operated without employing the noise and stream illuminating means. A reciprocal pump is employed to obtain sufficient pressure whereby the pistol can eject a stream an appreciable distance in the neighborhood of thirty feet and this stream can be illuminated to more or less simulate a lazer [sic] beam. . . .

Larami has moved for partial summary judgment of noninfringement of the '129 patent. . . .

II. Discussion

. . .

B. Infringement and Claim Interpretation

A patent owner's right to exclude others from making, using or selling the patented invention is defined and limited by the language in that patent's claims. *Corning Glass Works v. Sumitomo Electric U.S.A., Inc.*, 868 F.2d 1251, 1257 (Fed. Cir. 1989). Thus, establishing infringement requires the interpretation of the "elements" or "limitations" of the claim and a comparison of the accused product with those elements as so interpreted. Because claim interpretation is a question of law, it is amenable to summary judgment.

The words in a claim should be given their "ordinary or accustomed" meaning. *Senmed, Inc. v. Richard-Allan Medical Industries, Inc.*, 888 F.2d 815, 819 & n.8 (Fed.

Cir. 1989). An inventor's interpretations of words in a claim that are proffered after the patent has issued for purposes of litigation are given no weight. . . .

A patent holder can seek to establish patent infringement in either of two ways: by demonstrating that every element of a claim (1) is literally infringed or (2) is infringed under the doctrine of equivalents. To put it a different way, because every element of a claim is essential and material to that claim, a patent owner must, to meet the burden of establishing infringement, "show the presence of every element or its substantial equivalent in the accused device." If even one element of a patent's claim is missing from the accused product, then "[t]here can be no infringement as a matter of law." . . . *London v. Carson Pirie Scott & Co.*, 946 F.2d 1534, 1538–39 (Fed. Cir. 1991).

Larami contends, and TTMP does not dispute, that twenty-eight (28) of the thirty-five (35) claims in the '129 patent are directed to the electrical components that create the light and noise. Larami's SUPER SOAKER water guns have no light or noise components. Larami also contends, again with no rebuttal from TTMP, that claim 28 relates to a "poppet valve" mechanism for controlling the flow of water that is entirely different from Larami's "pinch trigger" mechanism. Thus, according to Larami, the six remaining claims (claims 1, 5, 10, 11, 12 and 16) are the only ones in dispute. Larami admits that these six claims address the one thing that the SUPER SOAKERS and the '129 patent have in common—the use of air pressure created by a hand pump to dispense liquid. Larami argues, however, that the SUPER SOAKERS and the '129 patent go about this task in such fundamentally different ways that no claim of patent infringement is sustainable as a matter of law.

1. Literal Infringement of Claim 1

TTMP claims that SUPER SOAKER 20 literally infringes claim 1 of the '129 patent. Claim 1 describes the water gun as:

> [a] toy comprising an elongated housing [case] having a chamber therein for a liquid [tank], a pump including a piston having an exposed rod [piston rod] and extending rearwardly of said toy facilitating manual operation for building up an appreciable amount of pressure in said chamber for ejecting a stream of liquid therefrom an appreciable distance substantially forwardly of said toy, and means for controlling the ejection.

Patent drawing showing the preferred embodiment of TTMP's water pistol and/or flash light structure. (Figure 5 in the '129 patent)

Claim 1 requires, among other things, that the toy gun have "an elongated housing having a chamber therein for a liquid." The SUPER SOAKER 20 water gun, in contrast, has an external water reservoir (chamber) that is detachable from the gun housing, and not contained within the housing. TTMP argues that SUPER SOAKER 20 contains a "chamber therein for a liquid" as well as a detachable water reservoir. It is difficult to discern from TTMP's memorandum of law exactly where it contends the "chamber therein" is located in SUPER SOAKER 20. Furthermore, after having examined SUPER SOAKER 20 . . . , I find that it is plain that there is no "chamber" for liquid contained within the housing of the water gun. The only element of SUPER SOAKER 20 which could be described as a "chamber" for liquid is the external water reservoir located atop the housing. Indeed, liquid is located within the housing only when the trigger causes the liquid to pass from the external water reservoir through the tubing in the housing and out of the nozzle at the front end of the barrel. SUPER SOAKER 20 itself shows that such a transitory avenue for the release of liquid is clearly not a "chamber therein for liquid." Therefore, because the absence of even one element of a patent's claim from the accused product means there can be no finding of literal infringement, London, 946 F.2d at 1538–39, I find that SUPER SOAKER 20 does not infringe claim 1 of the '129 patent as a matter of law. . . .

Accordingly, I conclude that the SUPER SOAKER 20 water gun does not literally infringe claim 1 of the '129 patent.

2. Infringement by Equivalents of Claim 10

[The court further found that defendants TTMP failed to produce evidence which would support a finding that there was a genuine issue of material fact as to whether the Super Soaker guns infringed claim 10 under the doctrine of equivalents. The court began its analysis by noting that successful use of the doctrine to show infringement requires the patent owner to prove that the accused product has the "substantial equivalent" of every limitation or element of a patent claim. Additionally, Super Soaker's use of an external, detachable water reservoir was found to be such a dramatic improvement over the traditional design—benefiting both the manufacturer and user—that it could not be held to be the "substantial equivalent" of the claim 10 requirement of "a tank in the barrel for a liquid."]

III. Conclusion

In patent cases, summary judgment is appropriate where the accused product does not literally infringe the patent and where the patent owner does not muster evidence that is "sufficient to satisfy the legal standard for infringement under the doctrine of equivalents." *London*, 946 F.2d at 1538. Thus, and for the foregoing reasons, Larami's motion for partial summary judgment of noninfringement of the '129 patent will be granted.

COMMENTS AND QUESTIONS

1. Suppose TTMP had drafted claim 1 using the following phrase: "an elongated housing having a chamber for a liquid." If the specification failed to attach any special meaning to this term, would the court's holding regarding literal infringement of claim 1 have been affected?

2. As in Comment 1, assume that the specification did not discuss further the phrase "having a chamber for a liquid." But suppose that Larami discovers that claim 1 was originally rejected by an examiner because a prior art reference showed a squirt gun with an oversized chamber on top of the body of the gun. The patent applicant successfully overcame this rejection by pointing out that in the invention the chamber is inside the housing of the gun. The face of the '129 patent would not, however, give a clue to potential infringers such as Larami as to the potentially narrower definition of the claim language conceded during the prosecution history. To find out what the inventor argued during prosecution, one would need to obtain the prosecution history for the patent.

3. The elements of a patent claim are of considerable importance in determining its scope. For an accused product to literally infringe a patent, *every* element contained in the patent claim must also be present in the accused product or device. If a claimed apparatus has five parts, or "elements," and the allegedly infringing apparatus has only four of those five, it does not literally infringe. This is true even though the defendant may have copied the four elements exactly, and regardless of how significant or insignificant the missing element is.

What happens if an alleged infringer *adds* elements? The outcome then depends on the wording of the patentee's claim. If the patentee has drafted an "open" claim, usually indicated by the term "comprising," the additional elements do not circumvent the claim. *See, e.g., Genentech, Inc. v. Chiron Corp.*, 112 F.3d 495, 501 (Fed. Cir. 1997) ("'Comprising' is a term of art used in claim language which means that the named elements are essential, but other elements may be added and still form a construct within the scope of the claim."). But if the claim stated "consisting of," then the alleged infringer would not literally infringe. *See Norian Corp. v. Stryker Corp.*, 363 F.3d 1321 (Fed. Cir. 2004) (claims to dental repair kit "consisting of" certain chemicals not infringed by infringer's kit, which also included mixing spatula).

This rule has an important consequence for the process of innovation. Patentees who have properly claimed a fundamental technology can assert their patent against anyone who uses that technology, even if the defendants have improved it or put it to different use. A broad basic patent therefore gives its owner a great deal of control not only over potential direct competitors, but over a number of derivative or ancillary markets during the term of the patent.

ii.   Infringement Under the Doctrine of Equivalents

If competitors could circumvent patents through insubstantial changes in the design of a product, then many patents would lose their value, and patent drafters would expend unreasonable efforts trying to include every possible variation. Patent claims are supposed to describe the "metes and bounds" of the invention, just as deeds do for real property. But unlike geophysical measurement, the English language lacks numerical precision. The doctrine of equivalents exists to prevent defendants from taking the essence of the patented invention while skirting the literal language of the claims.

Graver Tank & Mfg. Co. v. Linde Air Products Co.
Supreme Court of the United States
339 U.S. 605 (1950)

MR. JUSTICE JACKSON delivered the opinion of the Court.

Linde Air Products Co., owner of the Jones patent for an electric welding process and for fluxes to be used therewith, brought an action for infringement against Lincoln and the two Graver companies. . . .

In determining whether an accused device or composition infringes a valid patent, resort must be had in the first instance to the words of the claim. If accused matter falls clearly within the claim, infringement is made out and that is the end of it.

But courts have also recognized that to permit imitation of a patented invention which does not copy every literal detail would be to convert the protection of the patent grant into a hollow and useless thing. Such a limitation would leave room for—indeed encourage—the unscrupulous copyist to make unimportant and insubstantial changes and substitutions in the patent which, though adding nothing, would be enough to take the copied matter outside the claim, and hence outside the reach of law. One who seeks to pirate an invention, like one who seeks to pirate a copyrighted book or play, may be expected to introduce minor variations to conceal and shelter the piracy. Outright and forthright duplication is a dull and very rare type of infringement. To prohibit no other would place the inventor at the mercy of verbalism and would be subordinating substance to form. It would deprive him of the benefit of his invention and would foster concealment rather than disclosure of inventions, which is one of the primary purposes of the patent system.

The doctrine of equivalents evolved in response to this experience. The essence of the doctrine is that one may not practice a fraud on a patent. Originating almost a century ago in the case of *Winans v. Denmead*, 15 How. 330 [(1853)], it has been consistently applied by this Court and the lower federal courts, and continues today ready and available for utilization when the proper circumstances for its application arise. "To temper unsparing logic and prevent an infringer from stealing the benefit of the invention" a patentee may invoke this doctrine to proceed against the producer of a device "if it performs substantially the same function in substantially the same way to obtain the same result." *Sanitary Refrigerator Co. v. Winters*, 280 U.S. 30, 42 [(1929)]. The theory on which it is founded is that "if two devices do the same work in substantially the same way, and accomplish substantially the same result, they are the same, even though they differ in name, form or shape." *Union Paper-Bag Machine Co. v. Murphy*, 97 U.S. 120, 125 [(1877)]. The doctrine operates not only in favor of the patentee of a pioneer or primary invention, but also for the patentee of a secondary invention consisting of a combination of old ingredients which produce new and useful results, although the area of equivalence may vary under the circumstances. The wholesome realism of this doctrine is not always applied in favor of a patentee but is sometimes used against him. Thus, where a device is so far changed in principle from a patented article that it performs the same or a similar function in a substantially different way, but nevertheless falls within the literal words of the claim, the doctrine of equivalents may be used to restrict the claim and defeat the patentee's action for infringement. *Westinghouse v. Boyden Power Brake Co.*, 170 U.S. 537, 568 [(1898)]. . . .

What constitutes equivalency must be determined against the context of the patent, the prior art, and the particular circumstances of the case. Equivalence, in the patent law, is not the prisoner of a formula and is not an absolute to be considered in a vacuum. It does not require complete identity for every purpose and in every respect. In determining equivalents, things equal to the same thing may not be equal to each other and, by the same token, things for most purposes different may sometimes be equivalents. Consideration must be given to the purpose for which an ingredient is used in a patent, the qualities it has when combined with the other ingredients, and the function which it is intended to perform. An important factor is whether persons reasonably skilled in the art would have known of the interchangeability of an ingredient not contained in the patent with one that was. . . .

In the case before us, we have two electric welding compositions or fluxes: the patented composition, Unionmelt Grade 20, and the accused composition, Lincolnweld 660. The patent under which Unionmelt is made claims essentially a combination of alkaline earth metal silicate and calcium fluoride; Unionmelt actually contains, however, silicates of calcium and magnesium, two alkaline earth metal silicates. Lincolnweld's composition is similar to Unionmelt's, except that it substitutes silicates of calcium and manganese—the latter not an alkaline earth metal—for silicates of calcium and magnesium. In all other respects, the two compositions are alike. The mechanical methods in which these compositions are employed are similar. They are identical in operation and produce the same kind and quality of weld.

The question which thus emerges is whether the substitution of the manganese which is not an alkaline earth metal for the magnesium which is, under the circumstances of this case, and in view of the technology and the prior art, is a change of such substance as to make the doctrine of equivalents inapplicable; or conversely, whether under the circumstances the change was so insubstantial that the trial court's invocation of the doctrine of equivalents was justified.

Without attempting to be all-inclusive, we note the following evidence in the record: Chemists familiar with the two fluxes testified that manganese and magnesium were similar in many of their reactions. There is testimony by a metallurgist that alkaline earth metals are often found in manganese ores in their natural state and that they serve the same purpose in the fluxes; and a chemist testified that "in the sense of the patent" manganese could be included as an alkaline earth metal. Much of this testimony was corroborated by reference to recognized texts on inorganic chemistry. Particularly important, in addition, were the disclosures of the prior art, also contained in the record. The Miller patent, No. 1,754,566, which preceded the patent in suit, taught the use of manganese silicate in welding fluxes. Manganese was similarly disclosed in the Armor patent, No. 1,467,825, which also described a welding composition. And the record contains no evidence of any kind to show that Lincolnweld was developed as the result of independent research or experiments.

It is not for this Court to even essay an independent evaluation of this evidence. This is the function of the trial court. . . .

The trial judge found on the evidence before him that the Lincolnweld flux and the composition of the patent in suit are substantially identical in operation and in result. He found also that Lincolnweld is in all respects equivalent to Unionmelt for welding purposes. And he concluded that "for all practical purposes, manganese silicate can be efficiently and effectively substituted for calcium and magnesium silicates as the major constituent of the welding composition." These conclusions are adequately supported by the record; certainly they are not clearly erroneous.

It is difficult to conceive of a case more appropriate for application of the doctrine of equivalents. The disclosures of the prior art made clear that manganese silicate was a useful ingredient in welding compositions. Specialists familiar with the problems of welding compositions understood that manganese was equivalent to and could be substituted for magnesium in the composition of the patented flux and their observations were confirmed by the literature of chemistry. Without some explanation or indication that Lincolnweld was developed by independent research, the trial court could properly infer that the accused flux is the result of imitation rather than experimentation or invention. Though infringement was not literal, the changes which avoid literal infringement are colorable only. We conclude that the trial court's judgment of infringement respecting the four flux claims was proper, and we adhere to our prior decision on this aspect of the case.

Affirmed.

MR. JUSTICE BLACK, with whom MR. JUSTICE DOUGLAS concurs, dissenting.

I heartily agree with the Court that "fraud" is bad, "piracy" is evil, and "stealing" is reprehensible. But in this case, where petitioners are not charged with any such malevolence, these lofty principles do not justify the Court's sterilization of Acts of Congress and prior decisions, none of which are even mentioned in today's opinion. . . .

[The Patent Act] provides that an applicant "shall particularly point out and distinctly claim the part, improvement, or combination which he claims as his invention or discovery." . . . "[I]t is the claim which measures the grant to the patentee." What is not specifically claimed is dedicated to the public. *See, e.g., Miller v. Brass Co.*, 104 U.S. 350, 352 [(1881)]. . . . Today the Court tacitly rejects those cases. It departs from the underlying principle which, as the Court pointed out in *White v. Dunbar*, 119 U.S. 47, 51 [(1886)], forbids treating a patent claim "like a nose of wax, which may be turned and twisted in any direction, by merely referring to the specification, so as to make it include something more than, or something different from, what its words express." . . .

Giving this patentee the benefit of a grant that it did not precisely claim is no less "unjust to the public" and no less an evasion of [the Patent Act] merely because done in the name of the "doctrine of equivalents."

In seeking to justify its emasculation of [the Patent Act] by parading potential hardships which literal enforcement might conceivably impose on patentees who had for some reason failed to claim complete protection for their discoveries, the Court fails even to mention the program for alleviation of such hardships which Congress itself has provided [for reissue of patents due to certain errors arising from "inadvertence, accident, or mistake" of the patentee.] . . .

MR. JUSTICE DOUGLAS, dissenting.

The Court applies the doctrine of equivalents in a way which subverts the constitutional and statutory scheme for the grant and use of patents.

The claims of the patent are limited to a flux "containing a major proportion of alkaline earth metal silicate." Manganese silicate, the flux which is held to infringe, is not an alkaline earth metal silicate. It was disclosed in the application and then excluded from the claims. It therefore became public property. *See Mahn v. Harwood*, 112 U.S. 354, 361 [(1884)]. It was, to be sure, mentioned in the specifications. But the measure of the grant is to be found in the claims, not in the specifications. The specifications can be used to limit but never to expand the claim.

The Court now allows the doctrine of equivalents to erase those time-honored rules. Moreover, a doctrine which is said to protect against practicing "a fraud on a patent" is used to extend a patent to a composition which could not be patented. For manganese silicate had been covered by prior patents, now expired. Thus we end with a strange anomaly: a monopoly is obtained on an unpatented and unpatentable article.

COMMENTS AND QUESTIONS

1. *Fair Reward vs. Public Notice.* Justice Black complains that the DOE undermines the disclosure requirement. He notes that the patentee could have sought re-issuance of the patent to expand coverage, but broadening reissues may only be obtained within two years of patent issuance. *See* §251(d). Who should bear the risk of failing to do so—the patentee or the public? Do you read the dissents to be questioning the DOE or just the majority's application of the DOE to this case?

2. *Subject Matter Disclosed but Not Claimed/Dedication to the Public.* Justice Douglas rebukes the majority for overriding a venerable doctrine that bars reclaiming of knowledge that has fallen into the public domain. He notes that the patentee disclosed both magnesium and manganese silicates in its specification, yet only claimed magnesium silicates were claimed. (He also notes manganese silicates were in the prior art.) Do you find his criticism persuasive?

The Federal Circuit revisited this question in *Johnson & Johnston Associates Inc. v. R.E. Service Co., Inc.*, 285 F.3d 1046 (Fed. Cir. 2002) (en banc) and sided with Justice Douglas. The court squarely held that the DOE cannot be used to reach subject matter that was disclosed but not claimed. The only option for the patentee is to reclaim that matter through reissuance of the patent within two years of the patent's issuance. The Federal Circuit emphasized the importance of public notice.

3. *Prior Art Rule.* A patentee may not use the doctrine of equivalents to obtain coverage of subject matter in the prior art, i.e., "coverage which he could not lawfully have obtained from the USPTO by literal claims." *Wilson Sporting Goods Co. v. David Geoffrey & Assocs.*, 904 F.2d 677, 683–84 (Fed. Cir. 1990). Accordingly, an accused infringer who merely practices the prior art cannot infringe under the doctrine of equivalents. This principle is applied by constructing a hypothetical claim based on the accused technology. If the PTO could have allowed the hypothetical claim over the prior art (i.e., if the prior art did not anticipate or render the hypothetical claim obvious, *Abbott Labs v. Dey, L.P.*, 287 F.3d 1097, 1105–06 (Fed. Cir. 2002)), the prior art does not preclude infringement under the doctrine of equivalents.

4. *All-Elements Rule.* In *Warner-Jenkinson v. Hilton Davis Chemical Co.*, 520 U.S. 17 (1997), the Supreme Court revisited the doctrine of equivalents for the first time since *Graver Tank. Warner-Jenkinson* involved a claim to a process for purifying dyes. The claim had three key limitations: (1) the pore diameter of the filtration screen; (2) a pressure range under which the filtration took place; and (3) a requirement that the filtration take place in an aqueous solution having a pH range "from approximately 6.0 to 9.0." Limitation (3), the pH range, was added by the patentee during the prosecution of the patent. The accused infringer, Warner-Jenkinson, used a filtration process that met the first two limitations, but operated at a pH of 5.0.

The Supreme Court first affirmed the continued viability of the doctrine of equivalents, as it had in *Graver Tank*. Next, it laid down some basic principles regarding the doctrine. The Court did not reject the venerable "triple identity" test of *Graver Tank*—i.e., that equivalence may be found where the accused product performs substantially the same function, in substantially the same way, to achieve substantially the same result as the device of the patent claim. But it noted that this test might be more suitable to mechanical inventions than to chemical processes such as the one in this case. On the ultimate question of the proper standard in a doctrine of equivalents case, the Court held:

> In our view, the particular linguistic framework used is less important than whether the test is probative of the essential inquiry: Does the accused product or process contain elements identical or equivalent to each claimed element of the patented invention? Different linguistic frameworks may be more suitable to different cases, depending on their particular facts. A focus on individual elements and a special vigilance against allowing the concept of equivalence to eliminate completely any such elements should reduce considerably the imprecision of whatever language is used. An analysis of the role played by each element in the context of the specific patent claim will thus inform the inquiry as to whether a substitute element matches the function, way, and result of the claimed element, or whether the substitute element plays a role substantially different from the claimed element.

520 U.S. at 40. This approach is known as the "all elements rule." A corollary of the rule states that an accused device cannot be infringing if it would effectively vitiate (or eliminate) any claim limitation. *See Freedman Seating Co. v. Am. Seating Co.*, 420 F.3d 1350, 1358 (Fed. Cir. 2005).

5. *Prosecution History Estoppel.* Another central issue in *Warner-Jenkinson* was the addition of the pH limit to the claim during prosecution of the patent. This triggered application of the doctrine of "prosecution history estoppel." The accused infringer argued that that doctrine prevented the patentee from arguing infringement under the doctrine of equivalents because the patentee had surrendered coverage for any pH under 6.0 when the "6.0 to 9.0" range was added to the claim during prosecution. The Court in *Warner-Jenkinson* created a presumption under these circumstances that the claim had been amended to avoid prior art, and thus that prosecution history estoppel did indeed apply. 520 U.S. at 33. But it permitted the patentee to rebut this presumption with evidence that the claim had been amended for some other purpose, unrelated to avoiding the prior art. The status of this presumption, and the doctrine of prosecution history estoppel generally, was the key issue in *Festo Corp. v. Shoketsu Kinzoku Kogyo Kabushiki Co., Ltd.*, 535 U.S. 722 (2002).

Recognizing both the difficulties faced by patentees of anticipating unimportant and insubstantial substitutes for elements of their invention as well as the need for clear public notice, the Supreme Court adopted a rebuttable presumption that amendments made to narrow a claim limitation foreclose later stretching of that limitation to reach an accused technology under the doctrine of equivalents. The patentee can rebut this presumption under three scenarios: (1) the equivalent was unforeseeable to a person having ordinary skill in the art at the time of the amendment; (2) the rationale for the amendment was no more than tangentially related to the equivalent at issue; or (3) another reason suggesting that the patentee could not reasonably be expected to have described the alleged equivalent.

If the Court sought to encourage public notice optimally, why not limit the DOE to unforeseeable equivalents—i.e., after-arising technology? Isn't the patentee the least-cost-avoider? Isn't such a foreseeability rule consistent with the *contra proferentem* (interpret against the draftsperson) doctrine?

6. *§112(f) Equivalents and the Doctrine of Equivalents: After-Arising Technology.* Recall in Problem III-14 (in-line skates) and the Rollerglide's use of Velcro to secure the shoe portion of its in-line skate. As that problem explained, Velcro was not invented until after the patentee's in-line skate invention. Therefore, the use of Velcro as a fastening method could not be equivalent to the corresponding structure, material, or acts described in the specification as of time of the in-line skate invention. But could it be equivalent under the DOE? Can a means-plus-function claim that is not literally infringed be infringed under the doctrine of equivalents?

The cases say yes, but only in two limited circumstances. Specifically, the Federal Circuit has found separate ground for the doctrine of equivalents in §112(f) cases where the *function* (as opposed to the corresponding structure) was equivalent but not identical, and where the accused device contained *after-arising technology* that was equivalent to the patented structure, but was not known at the time the patent application was filed. *See WMS Gaming, Inc. v. International Game Technology*, 184 F.3d 1339 (Fed. Cir. 1999).

7. *Reverse Doctrine of Equivalents*. The majority in *Graver Tank* notes that the DOE also works in reverse: "where a device is so far changed in principle from a patented article that it performs the same or a similar function in a substantially different way, but nevertheless falls within the literal words of the claim, the doctrine of equivalents may be used to restrict the claim and defeat the patentee's action for infringement." The Court cites *Westinghouse v. Boyden Power Brake Co.*, 170 U.S. 537, 568 (1898) which has never been overruled, but largely stands alone as a case of literal infringement for which liability did not attach.

The case traces back to a time when trains were the most important overland transportation system. In 1869, George Westinghouse invented a train brake that used a central reservoir of compressed air for stopping power. Further advances in his design, primarily the addition of an air reservoir in each brake cylinder, resulted in a brake that was patented in 1887. An improvement on this 1887 brake, invented by George Boyden, added an ingenious mechanism for pushing compressed air into the brake piston both from the central reservoir *and* from a local reservoir in each brake cylinder. (Westinghouse's brake required a complicated series of passageways to supply air from the two sources.) With the added stopping power of the Boyden brake, engineers could safely operate the increasingly long trains of the late nineteenth century.

The Westinghouse patent included a claim for "the combination of a main air-pipe, an auxiliary reservoir, a brake-cylinder, a triple valve [the device that coordinated the airflows from the main reservoir and the individual brake reservoir] and an auxiliary-valve device, actuated by the piston of the triple-valve . . . for admitting air in the application of the brake." The Court noted that the literal wording of the Westinghouse patent could be read to cover Boyden's brake, since it included what could be described as a "triple valve." But it refused to find infringement, on the ground that Boyden's was a significant contribution that took the invention outside the equitable bounds of the patent:

> We are induced to look with more favor upon this device, not only because it is a novel one and a manifest departure from the principle of the Westinghouse patent, but because it solved at once in the simplest manner the problem of quick [braking] action, whereas the Westinghouse patent did not prove to be a success until certain additional members had been incorporated in it.

Id. at 572.

According to the Federal Circuit, "because products on which patent claims are readable word for word often are in fact the same, perform the same function in the same way, and achieve the same result, as the claimed invention, a defense based on the reverse doctrine of equivalents is rarely offered." *SRI Int'l v. Matsushita Electric Corp. of America*, 775 F.2d 1107, 1123 n.19 (Fed. Cir. 1985); *see also Tate Access Floors,*

Inc. v. Interface Architectural Resources, Inc., 279 F.3d 1357 (Fed. Cir. 2002) (coming close to sounding the death knell for the reverse DOE).

The Federal Circuit has, however, applied the doctrine to reverse a finding of infringement in *Scripps Clinic & Research Foundation v. Genentech, Inc.*, 927 F.2d 1565 (Fed. Cir. 1991), a case typical of an early wave of biotechnology patent actions. Genentech invented and patented the recombinant DNA form of the blood protein Factor VIII:C, a blood clotting agent made by the body and useful in treating patients with clotting disorders. Scripps had previously obtained a patent on purified Factor VIII:C, which it made by isolating and purifying the protein from raw human blood. Scripps sued Genentech for infringement of its product patent, citing the conventional rule that a product patent covers the product no matter how it is made. After attempting to distinguish its recombinant version from Scripps' purified natural protein, Genentech ultimately relied on a pragmatic defense: that the recombinant version was by far cheaper to make, and therefore ought not to be deemed an infringement. The Federal Circuit remanded the case for a determination whether the reverse doctrine of equivalents applied in these circumstances. Since *Tate Access,* the Federal Circuit has gone out of its way on several occasions to make it clear that the reverse doctrine of equivalents, while rare, does still have viability. *See, e.g., Amgen, Inc. v. Hoechst Marion Roussel,* 314 F.3d 1313, 1351 (Fed. Cir. 2003); *Plant Genetic Systems, N.V. v. DeKalb Genetics Corp.,* 315 F.3d 1335, 1341 (Fed. Cir. 2003) ("[T]he judicially-developed 'reverse doctrine of equivalents,' requiring interpretation of claims in light of the specification, may be safely relied upon to preclude improper enforcement against later developers.").

Summary: Non-Literal Infringement

Limiting Principles
- **The All-Elements (All-Limitations) Rule**
- **Prosecution History Estoppel**
  - *Festo* Rebuttable Presumption: amendments made to narrow a claim limitation foreclose application of the DOE unless:
    1. Unforeseeable Equivalents—principally after-arising art
    2. Tangential Amendments
    3. Amendments for "Other Reasons"
- **Prior Art Rule** (*Wilson Sporting Goods*)
- **The Public Dedication Rule** (*Johnson & Johnston*)

Means-Plus-Function Claims (applies to after-arising art)
The Reverse Doctrine of Equivalents

PROBLEMS

Problem III-15. Mike Molar, a production engineer for Tasty Toothpaste Corp. (Tasty) hit upon a way to make a sanitary, cheap, and small disposable toothbrush. The problem he had been running into was how to keep the toothbrush small while still providing a feature he thought necessary to make it attractive—a built-in supply of toothpaste. The solution: a small reservoir for holding toothpaste in the handle of the toothbrush. Then the user could squeeze the toothpaste from the reservoir to the brush bristles.

He quickly built a prototype of the invention. To build it, he bought a fountain pen, pulled out the ink cartridge and other parts from the interior, tore the bristles off a toothbrush and glued them onto a hollow tube, poked two holes in the top of the tube between two rows of bristles, fitted up a plastic plunger that slid in and out at the back of the fountain pen body, pulled the plunger all the way out, filled the tube with toothpaste, glued the tube inside the fountain pen body, and pushed the plunger. Voilà! Toothpaste came out of the holes more or less onto the bristles, ready for brushing. It worked! He drafted a patent specification that included this passage:

It is one important object of the present invention to provide a portable toothbrush which is easily carried in the pocket and which is thus available whenever it is required for brushing teeth.

The open end of the device includes a reduced section portion which carries the bristles. The cylindrical body shaft includes an interior passage that extends into the reduced section end (i.e., the one with the bristles). The passage includes two termination openings which are in the area at the base of the toothbrush bristles.

An open space for placing toothpaste is provided within the interior passage, and a movable plunger is provided for forcing the toothpaste from this space through the narrow part of the passage and out through the termination openings into the toothpaste bristles for use.

In the preferred embodiment, the body shaft is made of plastic. The invention may be made so as to be disposable. Various means for filling the space with toothpaste are envisioned, including pressure-injection through a small hole in the top of the body, which hole can then be sealed. This would make the toothbrush usable only once; it would then be disposed.

He concluded with the following claim.

1. A pocket toothbrush having an exterior structure resembling a traditional fountain pen case comprising

    a. a removable cylindrical end cap cover,

    b. a main cylindrical body shaft over at least one end of which said end cap cover fits and having means for engaging the interior of said end cap cover to retain said end cap cover,

    c. said cylindrical body shaft having one end which contains toothbrush bristles [the "bristle end"] extending transversely and capable of being confined within said end cap,

    d. said cylindrical body shaft including an interior passage extending into said bristle end and having at least one termination opening in the area at the base of said bristles,

    e. a movable plunger extending into said cylindrical body shaft in said main cylindrical body shaft,

    f. said body shaft including an interior space for the accommodation of a charge of toothpaste to be fed to said bristles by the operation of said movable plunger, said space being at least big enough to hold a charge for a single application of toothpaste.

Once the patent issued, Tasty began selling a disposable, portable toothbrush that garnered a loyal following. Soon competitors entered the market. One, KopyCat Industries, Inc. (KCI), began selling a portable toothbrush that included a replaceable toothpaste cartridge so that the brush housing could be reused. The cartridges have a weak plastic closure that easily breaks when the plunger is pushed against the cartridge. This keeps the toothpaste from hardening in the openings to the bristles. Also, instead of a cap, the KCI design has a telescoping retractable cover that remains attached to the non-bristle end of the brush. The cover is collapsed down, the brush used, and then the cover is pulled back into place. The retractable cover is attached very firmly with two tiny screws. The screws can be taken out and the cover removed, but it takes a tiny jeweler screwdriver and is difficult.

Tasty threatens to sue KCI for infringement of the Molar patent. KCI has come to you for advice. Does KCI run a serious risk of being found liable for infringing the Molar patent, either literally or under the doctrine of equivalents? What changes might KCI make in its product to avoid a future infringement action by Tasty?

Problem III-16. In the early 1960s, Hughes Aircraft invented an apparatus for maintaining a satellite in geosynchronous orbit (i.e., maintaining a constant position relative to a location on earth). Claim 1 of its 1964 patent application claimed an apparatus comprising:

a. a body adapted to spin about an axis;

b. fluid supply means associated with said body;

c. a valve connected to said fluid supply means;

d. fluid expulsion means disposed on said body and coupled with said valve and oriented to expel said fluid substantially along a line parallel to said axis and separated therefrom;

e. means disposed on said body for providing an indication to a location external to said body of the instantaneous spin angle position of said body about said axis and the orientation of said axis with reference to a fixed external coordinate system;

f. and means disposed on said body for receiving from said location control signals synchronized with said indication;

g. said valve being coupled to said last-named means and responsive to said control signals for applying fluid to said fluid expulsion means in synchronism therewith for precessing said body to orient said axis in a predetermined desired relationship with said fixed external coordinate system.

Step e refers to "means disposed on said body for providing an indication to a location external to said body of the instantaneous spin angle position." Step f refers to "means disposed on said body for receiving from said location control signals synchronized with said indication." At the time that the invention was made, computer technology was relatively primitive. Consequently, it needed to perform the complex calculations necessary to maintain geosynchronous orbit using a mainframe computer located on earth. The patent issued in 1973.

By that time, microprocessor technology had advanced to the point that computers could be substantially reduced in size. NASA developed a satellite that utilized key elements of the Hughes Aircraft system –i.e., taking "instantaneous spin angle position of said body about said axis and the orientation of said axis with reference to a fixed external coordinate system"—and determining the necessary precession of jets to maintain geosynchronous orbit. But due to advances in microprocessor technology, it could do the entire position adjustment process on board the satellite, i.e., it did not need to send positional information to the earth and receive the adjustment information. Hughes sued for infringement. Under modern infringement doctrines, what are NASA's best arguments to defeat the infringement claim? What are Hughes best counterarguments? How should the judge/jury resolve the case?

2. Indirect Infringement

Tort law principles have long extended liability beyond those who directly commit a tort to those who aid, abet, contribute, and induce violations of property and personal interests. Since patent law traces its infringement principles to tort law, inducement and contributory infringement evolved to address infringing activity that lacked the element of a direct making, using, or selling of the patented invention. These doctrines were codified in the 1952 Act, yet they still retain a common law character. They bring into play the mental state—knowledge and intent—of the alleged infringer.

i. Inducement

Section 271(b) provides that "Whoever actively induces infringement of a patent shall be liable as an infringer." Inducement involves behavior that omits any direct making, using, or selling of the patented invention but that nevertheless amounts to an attempt to appropriate the value of an invention. It is often described as activity that "aids and abets" infringement. Although inducing infringement commonly involves instructing another to violate a patent, this branch of liability is broad enough to ensnare a host of diverse activities.

Global-Tech Appliances, Inc. v. SEB S.A.
Supreme Court of the United States
563 U.S. 754 (2011)

JUSTICE ALITO delivered the opinion of the Court.

We consider whether a party who "actively induces infringement of a patent" under 35 U.S.C. §271(b) must know that the induced acts constitute patent infringement.

I

This case concerns a patent for an innovative deep fryer designed by respondent SEB S.A., a French maker of home appliances. In the late 1980's, SEB invented a "cool-touch" deep fryer, that is, a deep fryer for home use with external surfaces that remain cool during the frying process. The cool-touch deep fryer consisted of a metal frying pot surrounded by a plastic outer housing. Attached to the housing was a ring that suspended the metal pot and insulated the housing from heat by separating it from the pot, creating air space between the two components. SEB obtained a U.S. patent for its design in 1991, and sometime later, SEB started manufacturing the cool-touch fryer and selling it in this country under its well-known "T-Fal" brand. Superior to other products in the American market at the time, SEB's fryer was a commercial success.

In 1997, Sunbeam Products, Inc., a U.S. competitor of SEB, asked petitioner Pentalpha Enterprises, Ltd., to supply it with deep fryers meeting certain specifications. Pentalpha is a Hong Kong maker of home appliances and a wholly owned subsidiary of petitioner Global-Tech Appliances, Inc.

In order to develop a deep fryer for Sunbeam, Pentalpha purchased an SEB fryer in Hong Kong and copied all but its cosmetic features. Because the SEB fryer bought in Hong Kong was made for sale in a foreign market, it bore no U.S. patent markings. After copying SEB's design, Pentalpha retained an attorney to conduct a right-to-use study, but Pentalpha refrained from telling the attorney that its design was copied directly from SEB's.

The attorney failed to locate SEB's patent, and in August 1997 he issued an opinion letter stating that Pentalpha's deep fryer did not infringe any of the patents that he had found. That same month, Pentalpha started selling its deep fryers to Sunbeam, which resold them in the United States under its trademarks. By obtaining its product from a manufacturer with lower production costs, Sunbeam was able to undercut SEB in the U.S. market.

After SEB's customers started defecting to Sunbeam, SEB sued Sunbeam in March 1998, alleging that Sunbeam's sales infringed SEB's patent. Sunbeam notified Pentalpha of the lawsuit the following month. Undeterred, Pentalpha went on to sell deep fryers to Fingerhut Corp. and Montgomery Ward & Co., both of which resold them in the United States under their respective trademarks. . . .

II

Pentalpha argues that active inducement liability under §271(b) requires more than deliberate indifference to a known risk that the induced acts may violate an existing patent. Instead, Pentalpha maintains, actual knowledge of the patent is needed.

A

In assessing Pentalpha's argument, we begin with the text of §271(b)—which is short, simple, and, with respect to the question presented in this case, inconclusive. Section 271(b) states: "Whoever actively induces infringement of a patent shall be liable as an infringer."

Although the text of §271(b) makes no mention of intent, we infer that at least some intent is required. The term "induce" means "[t]o lead on; to influence; to prevail on; to move by persuasion or influence." WEBSTER'S NEW INTERNATIONAL DICTIONARY 1269 (2d ed.1945). The addition of the adverb "actively" suggests that the inducement must involve the taking of affirmative steps to bring about the desired result, *see id.*, at 27.

When a person actively induces another to take some action, the inducer obviously knows the action that he or she wishes to bring about. If a used car salesman induces a customer to buy a car, the salesman knows that the desired result is the purchase of the car. But what if it is said that the salesman induced the customer to buy a damaged car? Does this mean merely that the salesman induced the customer to purchase a car that happened to be damaged, a fact of which the salesman may have been unaware? Or does this mean that the salesman knew that the car was damaged? The statement that the salesman induced the customer to buy a damaged car is ambiguous.

1

So is §271(b). In referring to a party that "induces infringement," this provision may require merely that the inducer lead another to engage in conduct that happens to amount to infringement, i.e., the making, using, offering to sell, selling, or importing of a patented invention. *See* §271(a).[2] On the other hand, the reference to a party that "induces infringement" may also be read to mean that the inducer must persuade another to engage in conduct that the inducer knows is infringement. Both readings are possible. . . .

While both the language of §271(b) and the pre-1952 case law that this provision was meant to codify are susceptible to conflicting interpretations, our decision in [*Aro Mfg. Co. v. Convertible Top Replacement Co.*, 377 U.S. 476 (1964) (*Aro II*)] resolves the question in this case. In *Aro II*, a majority held that a violator of §271(c) must know "that the combination for which his component was especially designed was both patented and infringing," 377 U.S., at 488, and as we explain below, that conclusion compels this same knowledge for liability under §271(b).

C

As noted above, induced infringement was not considered a separate theory of indirect liability in the pre-1952 case law. Rather, it was treated as evidence of "contributory infringement," that is, the aiding and abetting of direct infringement by another party. *See* Lemley, *Inducing Patent Infringement*, 39 U.C.D. L. REV. 225, 227 (2005). When Congress enacted §271, it separated what had previously been regarded as contributory infringement into two categories, one covered by §271(b) and the other covered by §271(c).

Aro II concerned §271(c), which states in relevant part:

> "Whoever offers to sell or sells . . . a component of a patented [invention] . . . , constituting a material part of the invention, knowing the same to be especially made or especially adapted for use in an infringement of such patent, and not a staple article or commodity of commerce suitable for substantial

---

[2] Direct infringement has long been understood to require no more than the unauthorized use of a patented invention. *See Aro Mfg. Co. v. Convertible Top Replacement Co.*, 377 U.S. 476, 484 (1964); 3 A. DELLER, WALKER ON PATENTS §453, p. 1684 (1937). Thus, a direct infringer's knowledge or intent is irrelevant.

noninfringing use, shall be liable as a contributory infringer." (Emphasis added.)

This language contains exactly the same ambiguity as §271(b). The phrase "knowing [a component] to be especially made or especially adapted for use in an infringement" may be read to mean that a violator must know that the component is "especially adapted for use" in a product that happens to infringe a patent. Or the phrase may be read to require, in addition, knowledge of the patent's existence.

This question closely divided the *Aro II* Court. In a badly fractured decision, a majority concluded that knowledge of the patent was needed. 377 U.S., at 488, and n. 8 (White, J., concurring); *id.*, at 524–527 (Black, J., dissenting). Justice Black's opinion, which explained the basis for the majority's view, concluded that the language of §271(c) supported this interpretation. *See id.*, at 525. His opinion also relied on an amendment to this language that was adopted when the bill was in committee. *Id.*, at 525–527.

Four Justices disagreed with this interpretation and would have held that a violator of §271(c) need know only that the component is specially adapted for use in a product that happens to infringe a patent. *See id.*, at 488–490, n. 8. These Justices thought that this reading was supported by the language of §271(c) and the pre–1952 case law, and they disagreed with the inference drawn by the majority from the amendment of §271(c)'s language. *Ibid.*

While there is much to be said in favor of both views expressed in Aro II, the "holding in Aro II has become a fixture in the law of contributory infringement under [section] 271(c)," 5 R. MOY, WALKER ON PATENTS §15:20, p. 15–131 (4th ed.2009)— so much so that SEB has not asked us to overrule it. Nor has Congress seen fit to alter §271(c)'s intent requirement in the nearly half a century since Aro II was decided. In light of the "'special force'" of the doctrine of stare decisis with regard to questions of statutory interpretation, *see John R. Sand & Gravel Co. v. United States*, 552 U.S. 130, 139 (2008), we proceed on the premise that §271(c) requires knowledge of the existence of the patent that is infringed.

Based on this premise, it follows that the same knowledge is needed for induced infringement under §271(b). As noted, the two provisions have a common origin in the pre–1952 understanding of contributory infringement, and the language of the two provisions creates the same difficult interpretive choice. It would thus be strange to hold that knowledge of the relevant patent is needed under §271(c) but not under §271(b).

2

Accordingly, we now hold that induced infringement under §271(b) requires knowledge that the induced acts constitute patent infringement.

III

Returning to Pentalpha's principal challenge, we agree that deliberate indifference to a known risk that a patent exists is not the appropriate standard under §271(b). We nevertheless affirm the judgment of the Court of Appeals because the evidence in this case was plainly sufficient to support a finding of Pentalpha's knowledge under the doctrine of willful blindness.

A

The doctrine of willful blindness is well established in criminal law. Many criminal statutes require proof that a defendant acted knowingly or willfully, and courts applying the doctrine of willful blindness hold that defendants cannot escape the reach of these statutes by deliberately shielding themselves from clear evidence of critical facts that are strongly suggested by the circumstances. The traditional rationale for this doctrine is that defendants who behave in this manner are just as culpable as those who have actual knowledge. Edwards, *The Criminal Degrees of Knowledge*, 17 MOD. L. REV. 294, 302 (1954) (hereinafter Edwards) (observing on the basis of English authorities that "up to the present day, no real doubt has been cast on the proposition that [willful blindness] is as culpable as actual knowledge"). It is also said that persons who know enough to blind themselves to direct proof of critical facts in effect have actual knowledge of those facts. *See United States v. Jewell*, 532 F.2d 697, 700 (C.A.9 1976) (en banc).

This Court's opinion more than a century ago in *Spurr v. United States*, 174 U.S. 728 (1899), while not using the term "willful blindness," endorsed a similar concept. . . . Following our decision in *Spurr*, several federal prosecutions in the first half of the 20th century invoked the doctrine of willful blindness. Later, a 1962 proposed draft of the Model Penal Code, which has since become official, attempted to incorporate the doctrine by defining "knowledge of the existence of a particular fact" to include a situation in which "a person is aware of a high probability of [the fact's] existence, unless he actually believes that it does not exist." ALI, MODEL PENAL CODE §2.02(7) (Proposed Official Draft 1962). . . .

Given the long history of willful blindness and its wide acceptance in the Federal Judiciary, we can see no reason why the doctrine should not apply in civil lawsuits for induced patent infringement under 35 U.S.C. §271(b). . . .

B

. . .

3

While the Courts of Appeals articulate the doctrine of willful blindness in slightly different ways, all appear to agree on two basic requirements: (1) the defendant must subjectively believe that there is a high probability that a fact exists and (2) the defendant must take deliberate actions to avoid learning of that fact. We think these requirements give willful blindness an appropriately limited scope that surpasses recklessness and negligence. Under this formulation, a willfully blind defendant is one who takes deliberate actions to avoid confirming a high probability of wrongdoing and who can almost be said to have actually known the critical facts. *See* G. WILLIAMS, CRIMINAL LAW §57, p. 159 (2d ed. 1961) ("A court can properly find wilful blindness only where it can almost be said that the defendant actually knew"). By contrast, a reckless defendant is one who merely knows of a substantial and unjustified risk of such wrongdoing, *see* ALI, MODEL PENAL CODE §2.02(2)(c) (1985), and a negligent defendant is one who should have known of a similar risk but, in fact, did not, *see* §2.02(2)(d).

The test applied by the Federal Circuit in this case departs from the proper willful blindness standard in two important respects. First, it permits a finding of knowledge when there is merely a "known risk" that the induced acts are infringing. Second, in demanding only "deliberate indifference" to that risk, the Federal Circuit's test does not require active efforts by an inducer to avoid knowing about the infringing nature of the activities.

4

In spite of these flaws, we believe that the evidence when viewed in the light most favorable to the verdict for SEB is sufficient under the correct standard. The jury could have easily found that before April 1998 Pentalpha willfully blinded itself to the infringing nature of the sales it encouraged Sunbeam to make.

SEB's cool-touch fryer was an innovation in the U.S. market when Pentalpha copied it. As one would expect with any superior product, sales of SEB's fryer had been growing for some time. Pentalpha knew all of this, for its CEO and president, John Sham, testified that, in developing a product for Sunbeam, Pentalpha performed "market research" and "gather[ed] information as much as possible." Pentalpha's belief that SEB's fryer embodied advanced technology that would be valuable in the U.S. market is evidenced by its decision to copy all but the cosmetic features of SEB's fryer.

Also revealing is Pentalpha's decision to copy an overseas model of SEB's fryer. Pentalpha knew that the product it was designing was for the U.S. market, and Sham—himself a named inventor on numerous U.S. patents—was well aware that products made for overseas markets usually do not bear U.S. patent markings. Even more telling is Sham's decision not to inform the attorney from whom Pentalpha sought a right-to-use opinion that the product to be evaluated was simply a knockoff of SEB's deep fryer. On the facts of this case, we cannot fathom what motive Sham could have had for withholding this information other than to manufacture a claim of plausible deniability in the event that his company was later accused of patent infringement. Nor does Sham's testimony on this subject provide any reason to doubt that inference. Asked whether the attorney would have fared better had he known of SEB's design, Sham was nonresponsive. All he could say was that a patent search is not an "easy job" and that is why he hired attorneys to perform them.

Taken together, this evidence was more than sufficient for a jury to find that Pentalpha subjectively believed there was a high probability that SEB's fryer was patented, that Pentalpha took deliberate steps to avoid knowing that fact, and that it therefore willfully blinded itself to the infringing nature of Sunbeam's sales.

* * *

The judgment of the United States Court of Appeals for the Federal Circuit is *Affirmed.*

COMMENTS AND QUESTIONS

1. Inducement, like contributory infringement, requires direct patent infringement by another. Someone must actually "make, use, sell, offer for sale, or import" under §271(a). The inducer is "indirectly liable" for encouraging, aiding, and abetting the direct infringer. Because the alleged inducer is not a direct infringer, it may be liable for acts that do not themselves directly violate the patent statute. This explains why some level of knowledge or intent is required: only if the inducer did what it did with the aim and plan of causing an infringing act is it reasonable to find the inducer liable under the patent statute. (There is no knowledge or intent requirement for a direct infringer; this is why an innocent independent inventor can still be liable for patent infringement. *See* Robert P. Merges, *A Few Kind Words for Absolute Infringement Liability in Patent Law*, 31 BERKELEY TECH. L. J. 1 (2016)).

Who were the direct infringers in the Globaltech case? Why did SEB, the patentee, not sue them? If they were foreign manufacturers, perhaps no one "made" an infringing product within the U.S. Hence, such entities would not be liable under U.S. patent law due to the patent law's territoriality limits. How about the retailers selling the infringing fryers in stores in the U.S.? Perhaps SEB did not want to antagonize them, hoping they would sell its fryers at some point. The point is that sometimes, the party the patentee may want to sue is not itself a direct infringer. This means that a complex interplay of strategy and legal principles may be involved. Perhaps SEB wanted to go after the design company that prepared the plans for the infringing fryer – this potential defendant was reachable in the U.S., and perhaps SEB wanted to send a warning not to copy future SEB designs. Whatever the motivation, the point is that by choosing to sue an indirect infringer SEB brought issues of knowledge and intent into the case that are not a problem when suit is brought against a direct infringer.

2. This case illustrates both the similarities and the differences between indirect liability in patent law and tort law. Although the Court begins with the terse statutory standard as well as a dictionary definition, it draws heavily upon the knowledge/intent standards in tort and criminal law in developing the mental state requirement for active inducement under patent law. At the same time, the focus of intent is different. In patent law, unlike tort law, the defendant must know its act is unlawful. Why the difference?

3. *Imputed Knowledge*. Notwithstanding the Court's conclusion that patent inducement "requires knowledge that the induced acts constitute patent infringement," the court nonetheless opens up a broad inquiry by considering willful blindness to establish such knowledge. In dissent, Justice Kennedy contends that "[w]illful blindness is not knowledge; and judges should not broaden a legislative proscription by analogy." *Global-Tech*, 131 S.Ct. at 2072 (Kennedy, J., dissenting). He concludes by noting that "[i]f willful blindness is as close to knowledge and as far from the 'knew or should have known' jury instruction provided in this case as the Court suggests, then reviewing the record becomes all the more difficult. I would leave that task to the Court of Appeals in the first instance on remand." *Id.* at 2074.

4. *Belief of Invalidity Not a Defense to Inducement*. Since the *Global-Tech* Court concluded that "induced infringement . . . requires knowledge that the induced acts

constitute patent infringement," it could reasonably be inferred that a good faith belief that the patent is invalid would negate the requisite intent for inducement liability. After all, how could one have an intent to infringe an invalid patent? Cisco Systems made this argument in defending Commil USA's induced infringement claim. The Supreme Court, in a decision authored by Justice Kennedy, the lone dissenter in Global-Tech, held that a defendant's belief as to validity does not have any bearing on induced infringement. *Commil USA, LLC v. Cisco Systems, Inc.*, 135 S.Ct. 1920 (2015). The Court reasoned

> The scienter element for induced infringement concerns infringement; that is a different issue than validity. Section 271(b) requires that the defendant "actively induce[d] infringement." That language requires intent to "bring about the desired result," which is infringement. And because infringement and validity are separate issues under the Act, belief regarding validity cannot negate the scienter required under §271(b).

> When infringement is the issue, the validity of the patent is not the question to be confronted. . . .

> Indeed, the issues of infringement and validity appear in separate parts of the Patent Act. . . . Further, noninfringement and invalidity are listed as two separate defenses . . . .

> Allowing this new defense would also undermine [patent law's presumption of validity]. . . .

Id. at 1928. Does this make sense to you? Justice Scalia was not persuaded: "[i]nfringing a patent means invading a patentee's exclusive right to practice his claimed invention. Only valid patents confer exclusivity—invalid patents do not. It follows, as night the day, that only valid patents can be infringed. To talk of infringing an invalid patent is to talk nonsense." *Id.* at 1931 (Scalia, J. dissenting).

ii.   *Contributory Infringement*

Section 271(c) provides that

> Whoever offers to sell or sells within the United States or imports into the United States a component of a patented machine, manufacture, combination or composition, or a material or apparatus for use in practicing a patented process, constituting a material part of the invention, knowing the same to be especially made or especially adapted for use in an infringement of such patent, and not a staple article or commodity of commerce suitable for substantial noninfringing use, shall be liable as a contributory infringer.

C.R. Bard, Inc. v. Advanced Cardiovascular Systems, Inc.
United States Court of Appeals for the Federal Circuit
911 F.2d 670 (Fed. Cir. 1990)

PLAGER, CIRCUIT JUDGE.

This is a case of claimed infringement of a method patent for a medical treatment. Defendant-Appellant Advanced Cardiovascular Systems, Inc. (ACS) was marketing [a] perfusion catheter for use in coronary angioplasty. Plaintiff-Appellee C.R. Bard, Inc. (Bard) sued ACS for alleged infringement of U.S. Patent No. 4,581,017 ('017), which Bard had purchased all rights to as of December 31, 1986. The '017 patent relates to a method for using a catheter in coronary angioplasty. The district court granted plaintiff Bard summary judgment against ACS, finding infringement of claim 1 of the '017 patent. We reverse the grant of summary judgment and remand the case for further proceedings.

Plaintiff Bard alleges that the ACS catheter is especially adapted for use by a surgeon in the course of administering a coronary angioplasty in a manner that infringes claim 1 of the '017 patent, that therefore ACS is a contributory infringer, and that ACS actively induces infringement. Of course, a finding of induced or contributory infringement must be predicated on a direct infringement of claim 1 by the users of the ACS catheter.

For purposes of this case, the statute requires that ACS sell a catheter for use in practicing the '017 process, which use constitutes a material part of the invention, knowing that the catheter is especially made or adapted for use in infringing the patent, and that the catheter is not a staple article or commodity of commerce suitable for substantial noninfringing use.

In asserting ACS's contributory infringement of claim 1, Bard seeks to establish the requisite direct infringement by arguing that there is no evidence that any angioplasty procedures using the ACS catheter would be noninfringing. Testing this assertion requires a two step analysis. First is a determination of the scope of the claim at issue. Second is an examination of the evidence before the court to ascertain whether, under §271(c), use of the ACS catheter would infringe the claim as interpreted.

Bard argues that [a] prior art patent teaches the use of the catheter with the inlets (side openings) where the blood enters the tube placed only in the aorta, whereas the '017 method in suit involves insertion of the catheter into the coronary artery in such a manner that the openings "immediately adjacent [the] balloon fluidly connect locations within [the] coronary artery surrounding [the] proximal and distal portions of [the] tube." Thus, Bard argues, a surgeon, inserting the ACS catheter into a coronary artery to a point where an inlet at the catheter's proximal end draws blood from the artery, infringes the '017 patent.

[The aorta is the large blood vessel on top; the coronary artery, labeled 63, is below it.]

[I]t is important to note that the ACS catheter has a series of ten openings in the tube near, and at the proximal end of, the balloon. The first of these openings—the one closest to the balloon [42b in Figure 2 below]—is approximately six millimeters (less than one inch) from the edge of the proximal end of the balloon. The remainder are located along the main lumen at intervals, the furthest from the balloon being 6.3 centimeters (approximately 2½ inches) away [past 40b in Figure 2].

It would appear that three possible fact patterns may arise in the course of using the ACS catheter. The first pattern involves positioning the catheter such that all of its side openings are located only in the aorta. This is clearly contemplated by the prior art '725 patent cited by the examiner. In the second of the possible fact patterns, all of the side openings are located within the coronary artery. This situation appears to have been contemplated by the '017 patent, the method patent at issue. In the third fact pattern, some of the side openings are located in the aorta and some are located in the artery.

There is evidence in the record that 40 to 60 percent of the stenoses that require angioplasty are located less than three centimeters from the entrance to the coronary artery. ACS argues that therefore the ACS catheter may be used in such a way that all of the openings are located in the aorta. Even assuming that the trial judge's conclusion is correct that claim 1 is applicable to the third of the fact patterns, it remains true that on this record a reasonable jury could find that, pursuant to the procedure described in the first of the fact patterns (a noninfringing procedure), there are substantial noninfringing uses for the ACS catheter.

Whether the ACS catheter "has no use except through practice of the patented method," *Dawson Chemical Co. v. Rohm & Haas Co.*, is thus a critical issue to be decided in this case. As the Supreme Court recently noted, "[w]hen a charge of contributory infringement is predicated entirely on the sale of an article of commerce that is used by the purchaser [allegedly] to infringe a patent, the public interest in access to that article of commerce is necessarily implicated." *Sony Corp. v. Universal City Studios, Inc.*, 464 U.S. 417, 440 (198[4]) [declining to find contributory copyright infringement in sale of video cassette recorders]. Viewing the evidence in this case in a light most favorable to the nonmoving party, and resolving reasonable inferences in ACS's favor, it cannot be said that Bard is entitled to judgment as a matter of law. The grant of summary judgment finding ACS a contributory infringer under §271(c) is not appropriate.

. . .

COMMENTS AND QUESTIONS

1. While Bard sued ACS, a competing manufacturer of catheters, the "real" infringer in this case is the doctor who completed the catheterization under circumstances that violated Bard's patent. What should doctors do in such a situation? Refuse to perform procedures that infringe a patent? Seek a license? In 1996, Congress amended the patent laws to exempt doctors who perform medical processes from liability for infringement, rendering this problem moot. However, Congress left device manufacturers liable for contributory infringement of such patents. *See* §287.

2. A classic example of inducement/contributory infringement is the sale of device components or "replacement parts" for a patented device, even though the parts themselves constitute less than the complete device and hence do not directly infringe. Contributory infringement is often used to attack sellers of parts where the actual ultimate infringers are end-users who replace parts or assemble components. The law draws a line between repair of an existing patented product, which is permissible, and reconstruction of the product, which isn't. *See, e.g., Aro Mfg. Corp. v. Convertible Top Co.*, 377 U.S. 176 (1964); *Husky Injection Molding Systems, Ltd. v. R&D Tool Engineering Co.*, 291 F.3d 780 (Fed. Cir. 2002). Another example is the sale of products with instructions that assist buyers in employing a process that infringes a process patent. *See Dawson Chem. Co. v. Rohm & Haas, Inc.*, 448 U.S. 176 (1980).

3. If an unpatented product has no other use except in conjunction with the patented machine, process or product, is it reasonable automatically to presume that making, using or selling the *unpatented* product is contributory infringement? Or should companies be allowed to compete in the market for non-staple products that work with the patented invention? For a discussion of these issues, *see Dawson Chem. Co. v. Rohm & Haas, Inc.*, 448 U.S. 176 (1980); *Husky Injection Molding Systems, Ltd. v. R&D Tool Engineering Co.*, 291 F.3d 780 (Fed. Cir. 2002). Section 271(c) says that whoever sells

or imports a component "constituting a material part of the invention, knowing the same to be especially made or especially adapted for use in an infringement of such patent, and not a staple article or commodity of commerce suitable for substantial noninfringing use" will be an infringer. Notice how this parallels the knowledge or intent requirement for inducement, which was the subject of the *Globaltech* case.

iii.   Joint Infringement

How does patent law handle situations where no single person or entity performs all the acts required to infringe a claim? In *BMC Resources, Inc. v. Paymentech, L.P.*, 498 F.3d 1373 (Fed. Cir. 2007), the patent owner brought suit for infringement of its patented method for processing debit transactions without a personal identification number (PIN). The accused infringer, Paymentech, showed that the claimed process involved performance of the following steps:

1. The customer calls a merchant to pay a bill;
2. The merchant collects payment information from the customer and sends it to Paymentech;
3. Paymentech routes the information to a participating debit network;
4. The debit network forwards the information to an affiliated financial institution;
5. The financial institution authorizes or declines the transaction, and if authorized, charges the customer's account according to the payment information collected by the merchant; and
6. Information regarding the status of the transaction moves from the financial institution to the debit network and then, through Paymentech, to the merchant who informs the customer of the status of the transaction.

Because some of these steps were neither performed by Paymentech nor with its active guidance or control, no single entity performed all the steps of the claim. Therefore, no direct infringement occurred. The court pointed out that more attentive claim drafting might have produced a claim that was infringed by a single entity such as Paymentech, *see* Mark A. Lemley, David O'Brien, Ryan M. Kent, Ashok Ramani, & Robert Van Nast, *Divided Infringement Claims*, 33 AIPLA Q.J. 255, 272–75 (2005), although not all inventions involving multiple actions can feasibly be confined to a single actor. The court further observed that if a single "mastermind" had centrally coordinated all the infringing steps among multiple actors, that mastermind would be liable for inducement under vicarious liability principles. 498 F.3d at 1381.

The next year, another Federal Circuit panel held that when multiple actors belonging to distinct enterprises collectively practice the steps of a process patent, there is no infringement liability unless one organization controls, directly or via contract, the actions of the others. Furthermore, a mere relationship between parties—such as providing access to a system and instructing users on the system's use—cannot establish "control or direction" required for inducement. *Muniauction, Inc. v. Thomson Corp.*, 532 F.3d 1318 (Fed. Cir. 2008).

This standard for liability did not sit well with several members of the Federal Circuit. In 2012, the court reconsidered this rule en banc and concluded that an actor could be held liable for *inducing* infringement even if all of the steps in a patented process were not committed by a single entity. *See Akamai Technologies, Inc. v. Limelight Networks, Inc.*, 692 F.3d 1301 (Fed. Cir. 2012) (per curiam) (en banc). The majority based its analysis on legislative history of the 1952 Act, quoting testimony by Giles Rich, one of the principal drafters:

> Improvements in such arts as radio communication, television, etc., sometimes involve the new combinations of elements which in use are normally owned by different persons. Thus, a new method of radio communication may involve a change in the transmitter and a corresponding change in the receiver. To describe such an invention in patent claims, it is necessary either to specify *a new method which involves both transmitting and receiving*, or a new combination of an element in the receiver and an element in the transmitter. There are patents with such claims covering television inventions of importance.
>
> The recent decisions of the Supreme Court [the cases targeted by the statutory changes] appear to make it impossible to enforce such patents in the usual case where a radio transmitter and a radio receiver are owned and operated by different persons, *for, while there is obvious infringement of the patent, there is no direct infringer of the patent but only two contributory infringers.*

CONTRIBUTORY INFRINGEMENT OF PATENTS: HEARINGS BEFORE THE SUBCOMM. ON PATENTS, TRADE-MARKS, AND COPYRIGHTS OF THE H. COMM. ON THE JUDICIARY, 80th Cong. 5 (1948) (statement of G. Rich on behalf of the New York Patent Law Association) (emphasis added) (quoted in *Akamai*, 692. F.4d at 1310). Mr. (later Judge) Rich's statement indicates that "the 'obvious infringement' should be remediable, even though 'there is no direct infringer' of the patent." *Akamai*, 692. F.3d at 1311.

Judge Linn, joined by three colleagues, accused the majority of "assum[ing] the mantle of policy maker." The dissenters emphasized that both the Patent Act and Supreme Court precedent—*Aro Mfg. Co. v. Convertible Top Replacement Co.*, 365 U.S. 336, 341 (1961); *Deepsouth Packing Co. v. Laitram Corp.*, 406 U.S. 518, 526 (1972)— clearly establish that there can be no indirect liability of a patent without direct infringement. "Section 271, paragraph (a), is *a declaration of what constitutes infringement,*" H.R. REP. NO. 82–1923, at 9 (1952) (emphasis added), and § 271(b) and (c) liability is built on that foundation. *Akamai*, 692. F.3d at 1338 (Linn, J., dissenting). It also criticized the majority for reading the term "infringement" to mean two different things in two different subsections of the statute.

This split prompted the Supreme Court to weigh in. The Supreme Court reversed the Federal Circuit for the reasons articulated by Judge Linn. *See Limelight Networks, Inc. v. Akamai Technologies, Inc.*, 572 U.S. 915 (2014). Nonetheless, the Court noted that the "problem" sought to be resolved by the Federal Circuit's en banc opinion in *Akamai* was created by the Federal Circuit in its decision in *Muniauction*—the rule that when multiple actors belonging to distinct enterprises collectively practice the steps of a process patent, there is no infringement liability unless one organization exercises direct supervisory or contractual control direct supervisory or contractual control over the actions of the other actor(s).

On remand, the full court, *sua sponte*, issued the following opinion.

Akamai Technologies, Inc. v. Limelight Networks, Inc.,
Court of Appeals for the Federal Circuit
797 F.3d 1020 (Fed. Cir. 2015) (en banc)

PER CURIAM.

This case was returned to us by the United States Supreme Court, noting "the possibility that [we] erred by too narrowly circumscribing the scope of §271(a)" and suggesting that we "will have the opportunity to revisit the §271(a) question. . . ." We hereby avail ourselves of that opportunity.

Sitting en banc, we unanimously set forth the law of divided infringement under 35 U.S.C. §271(a). We conclude that, in this case, substantial evidence supports the jury's finding that Limelight Networks, Inc. ("Limelight") directly infringes U.S. Patent 6,108,703 (the "'703 patent") under §271(a). We therefore reverse the district court's grant of judgment of noninfringement as a matter of law.

I. DIVIDED INFRINGEMENT

Direct infringement under §271(a) occurs where all steps of a claimed method are performed by or attributable to a single entity. *See BMC Res., Inc. v. Paymentech, L.P.*, 498 F.3d 1373, 1379–81 (Fed. Cir. 2007). Where more than one actor is involved in practicing the steps, a court must determine whether the acts of one are attributable to the other such that a single entity is responsible for the infringement. We will hold an entity responsible for others' performance of method steps in two sets of circumstances: (1) where that entity directs or controls others' performance, and (2) where the actors form a joint enterprise.

To determine if a single entity directs or controls the acts of another, we continue to consider general principles of vicarious liability. In the past, we have held that an actor is liable for infringement under §271(a) if it acts through an agent (applying traditional agency principles) or contracts with another to perform one or more steps of a claimed method. *See BMC*, 498 F.3d at 1380–81. We conclude, on the facts of this case, that liability under §271(a) can also be found when an alleged infringer conditions participation in an activity or receipt of a benefit upon performance of a step or steps of a patented method and establishes the manner or timing of that performance. *Cf. Metro-Goldwyn-Mayer Studios Inc. v. Grokster, Ltd.*, 545 U.S. 913, 930 (2005) (stating that an actor "infringes vicariously by profiting from direct infringement" if that actor has the right and ability to stop or limit the infringement). In those instances, the third party's actions are attributed to the alleged infringer such that the alleged infringer becomes the single actor chargeable with direct infringement. Whether a single actor directed or controlled the acts of one or more third parties is a question of fact, reviewable on appeal for substantial evidence, when tried to a jury.

Alternatively, where two or more actors form a joint enterprise, all can be charged with the acts of the other, rendering each liable for the steps performed by the other as if each is a single actor. *See* RESTATEMENT (SECOND) OF TORTS §491 cmt. b ("The law . . . considers that each is the agent or servant of the others, and that the act of any one within the scope of the enterprise is to be charged vicariously against the rest."). A joint enterprise requires proof of four elements:

(1) an agreement, express or implied, among the members of the group;

(2) a common purpose to be carried out by the group;

(3) a community of pecuniary interest in that purpose, among the members; and

(4) an equal right to a voice in the direction of the enterprise, which gives an equal right of control.

Id. §491 cmt. c. As with direction or control, whether actors entered into a joint enterprise is a question of fact, reviewable on appeal for substantial evidence. *Id.* ("Whether these elements exist is frequently a question for the jury, under proper direction from the court.").

We believe these approaches to be most consistent with the text of §271(a), the statutory context in which it appears, the legislative purpose behind the Patent Act, and our past case law. Section 271(a) is not limited solely to principal-agent relationships, contractual arrangements, and joint enterprise, as the vacated panel decision held. Rather, to determine direct infringement, we consider whether all method steps can be attributed to a single entity.

II. APPLICATION TO THE FACTS OF THIS CASE

Today we outline the governing legal framework for direct infringement and address the facts presented by this case. In the future, other factual scenarios may arise which warrant attributing others' performance of method steps to a single actor. Going forward, principles of attribution are to be considered in the context of the particular facts presented.

. . . In 2006, Akamai Technologies, Inc. ("Akamai") filed a patent infringement action against Limelight alleging infringement of several patents, including the '703 patent, which claims methods for delivering content over the Internet.

[Claim 34 provides:

A content delivery method, comprising:

distributing a set of page objects across a network of content servers managed by a domain other than a content provider domain, wherein the network of content servers are organized into a set of regions;

for a given page normally served from the content provider domain, tagging at least some of the embedded objects of the page so that requests for the objects resolve to the domain instead of the content provider domain;

in response to a client request for an embedded object of the page:

resolving the client request as a function of a location of the client machine making the request and current Internet traffic conditions to identify a given region; and

returning to the client an IP address of a given one of the content servers within the given region that is likely to host the embedded object and that is not overloaded.

Figure 3

The case proceeded to trial, at which the parties agreed that Limelight's customers—not Limelight—perform the "tagging" and "serving" steps in the claimed methods. For example, as for claim 34 of the '703 patent, Limelight performs every step save the "tagging" step, in which Limelight's customers tag the content to be hosted and delivered by Limelight's content delivery network. After the close of evidence, the district judge instructed the jury that Limelight is responsible for its customers' performance of the tagging and serving method steps if Limelight directs or controls its customers' activities. The jury found that Limelight infringed claims 19, 20, 21, and 34 of the '703 patent. Following post-trial motions, the district court first denied Limelight's motion for judgment of noninfringement as a matter of law, ruling that Akamai had presented substantial evidence that Limelight directed or controlled its customers. After we decided *Muniauction, Inc. v. Thomson Corp.*, 532 F.3d 1318 (Fed. Cir. 2008), the district court granted Limelight's motion for reconsideration, holding as a matter of law that there could be no liability.

We reverse and reinstate the jury verdict. The jury heard substantial evidence from which it could find that Limelight directs or controls its customers' performance of each remaining method step, such that all steps of the method are attributable to Limelight. Specifically, Akamai presented substantial evidence demonstrating that Limelight conditions its customers' use of its content delivery network upon its customers' performance of the tagging and serving steps, and that Limelight establishes the manner or timing of its customers' performance. We review the evidence supporting "conditioning use of the content delivery network" and "establishing the manner or timing of performance" in turn.

First, the jury heard evidence that Limelight requires all of its customers to sign a standard contract. The contract delineates the steps customers must perform if they use the Limelight service. These steps include tagging and serving content. As to tagging, Limelight's form contract provides: "Customer shall be responsible for identifying via the then current [Limelight] process all [URLs] of the Customer Content to enable such Customer Content to be delivered by the [Limelight network]." In addition, the contract requires that Limelight's customers "provide [Limelight] with all cooperation and information reasonably necessary for [Limelight] to implement the [Content Delivery Service]." As for the serving step, the form contract states that Limelight is not responsible for failures in its content delivery network caused by its customers' failure to serve content. If a customer's server is down, Limelight's content delivery network need not perform. Thus, if Limelight's customers wish to use Limelight's product, they must tag and serve content. Accordingly, substantial evidence indicates that Limelight conditions customers' use of its content delivery network upon its customers' performance of the tagging and serving method steps.

Substantial evidence also supports finding that Limelight established the manner or timing of its customers' performance. Upon completing a deal with Limelight, Limelight sends its customer a welcome letter instructing the customer how to use Limelight's service. In particular, the welcome letter tells the customer that a Technical Account Manager employed by Limelight will lead the implementation of Limelight's services. The welcome letter also contains a hostname assigned by Limelight that the customer "integrate[s] into [its] webpages." This integration process includes the tagging step. Moreover, Limelight provides step-by-step instructions to its customers telling them how to integrate Limelight's hostname into its webpages if the customer wants to act as the origin for content. If Limelights customers do not follow these precise steps, Limelight's service will not be available. Limelight's Installation Guidelines give Limelight customers further information on tagging content. Lastly, the jury heard evidence that Limelight's engineers continuously engage with customers' activities. Initially, Limelight's engineers assist with installation and perform quality assurance testing. The engineers remain available if the customer experiences any problems. In sum, Limelight's customers do not merely take Limelight's guidance and act independently on their own. Rather, Limelight establishes the manner and timing of its customers' performance so that customers can only avail themselves of the service upon their performance of the method steps.

We conclude that the facts Akamai presented at trial constitute substantial evidence from which a jury could find that Limelight directed or controlled its customers' performance of each remaining method step. As such, substantial evidence supports the jury's verdict that all steps of the claimed methods were performed by or attributable to Limelight. Therefore, Limelight is liable for direct infringement.

. . .

COMMENTS AND QUESTIONS

1. Does this standard fundamentally change the law to allow joint infringement theories, or merely broaden the scope of §271(a) to ensnare a relatively small subset of joint enterprises? The new joint enterprise theory of vicarious infringement attaches liability "when an alleged infringer conditions participation in an activity or receipt of a benefit upon performance of a [method step] and establishes the manner or timing of that performance." This is a looser type of control than the more rigid tests rejected by the Federal Circuit on remand from the Supreme Court. *See* Olajumoke Obayanju, *What Next? Exploring the Federal Circuit's Expansion of Direct Infringement Liability Post-Akamai v. Limelight and the Process It Took to Get There*, 25 FED. CIRCUIT B.J. 319, 332 (2016). Because of the looser standard, more product sellers and service providers may be liable than under the previous test. Is there any way for these parties and their clients to contractually allocate the risk of infringement?

2. Suppose the contract had been silent on what the customers would do. Would the result change? Should it? What if the software were designed so that the customer had no choice; the software "pulled" information on tagged objects directly from the customer. Would the customer's assent to the overall service constitute acceptance of the service provider's control over the "manner and timing of performance"?

PROBLEM III-17

Nichols, a scientist who enjoys puzzles, designs a "rotating cube" puzzle in which each face of the cube is composed of a number of smaller cubes, each face is initially of a different color, and the object of the puzzle is to restore the original color scheme once it has been disturbed. Nichols obtains a patent on a method of solving this puzzle, but not on the physical puzzle itself.

Rubik builds and sells puzzles similar to the ones Nichols has designed. Has Rubik infringed the Nichols patent, either directly or indirectly? Does it matter whether Nichols's patent covers the only known solution to the puzzle, or only one among many possible solutions? What if Rubik's product includes a "cheat" sheet advising buyers how to solve the puzzle using a number of methods, including Nichols's? What if Rubik includes a copy of the Nichols patent with each cube sold, ostensibly to advise users how to avoid infringement, but arguably with the intent of encouraging them to use the Nichols method?

Patent drawing for Rubik's cube

G. DEFENSES

Section 282(b) of the Patent Act provides for the following defenses:

(1) Noninfringement, absence of liability for infringement or unenforceability;

(2) Invalidity of the patent or any claim in suit on any ground specified in part II [of the Patent Act] as a condition for patentability;

(3) Invalidity of the patent or any claim in suit for failure to comply with—

(A) any requirement of section 112, except that the failure to disclose the best mode shall not be a basis on which any claim of a patent may be canceled or held invalid or otherwise unenforceable; or

(B) any requirement of section 251 [relating to reissue of defective patents];

(4) Any other fact or act made a defense by [the Patent Act].

In addition to these statutory defenses, courts have recognized a variety of other defenses, including experimental use, inequitable conduct, patent misuse, and equitable estoppel.

1.   Invalidity and the Presumption of Validity

In a conventional patent enforcement action, where a patent owner seeks to hold an alleged infringer liable, the patent owner does not have to prove the validity of the patent. Under §282(a), a patent is presumed valid. We discussed the grounds for invalidity in Chapter III(B). They are the same whether the PTO or the courts are considering validity. Once a patent has issued, though, "[t]he burden of establishing invalidity . . . rest[s] on the party asserting such invalidity." *Id.* This presumption aims to secure the patentee's quasi-property right and reflects the role of the PTO in examining the application. The party disputing the patent's validity must prove invalidity by "clear and convincing evidence," a higher standard than the typical civil law standard—preponderance of the evidence.

COMMENTS AND QUESTIONS

1. Should this standard apply where the alleged infringer brings forth prior art that the Patent Office did not consider during examination? The Supreme Court noted in *KSR Int'l Co. v. Teleflex Inc.*, 550 U.S. 398, 426 (2007) "the rationale underlying the presumption—that the PTO, in its expertise, has approved the claim—seems much diminished." Yet the Court ruled in *Microsoft Corp. v. i4i Ltd.*, 564 U.S. 91 (2011), that the presumption still applies, but "the challenger's burden to persuade the jury of its invalidity defense by clear and convincing evidence may be easier to sustain. . . . [T]he jury may be instructed to consider that it has heard evidence that the PTO had no opportunity to evaluate before granting the patent."

2. *Assignor Estoppel.* Based on norms of equitable dealing and the property doctrine of estoppel by deed—which prohibits a property grantor from challenging the validity of a grant—courts have long barred the assignor of a patent or patent application from attacking the validity of that patent in a subsequent patent infringement litigation absent exceptional circumstances. *See Mentor Graphics Corp. v. Quickturn Design Systems,*

Inc., 150 F.3d 1374, 1378 (Fed. Cir. 1998); *Westinghouse Elec. & Mfg. Co. v. Formica Insulation Co.*, 266 U.S. 342, 348–49 (1924). The Federal Circuit had interpreted the doctrine broadly to bar inventors who later move to a competing company or start one of their own from challenging patents that they had assigned to a prior employer, even if they did not sell the patent to its current owner but simply signed an employment agreement assigning all rights in their inventions. Scholars have questioned the breadth of this interpretation. *See* Mark A. Lemley, *Rethinking Assignor Estoppel*, 54 HOUS. L. REV. 513 (2016).

In *Minerva Surgical, Inv., v. Hologic, Inc.*, 141 S.Ct. 2298 (2021), the Supreme Court substantially cabined the assignor estoppel doctrine in holding that there is no unfairness where a patent assignor who has not explicitly or implicitly represented the validity of an assigned patent asserts an invalidity defense. The Court specifically noted that this circumstance arises where: (1) an employee assigns future inventions to an employer as part of a standard invention assignment agreement. patent rights in any future inventions he may develop during his employment; (2) a later legal development renders irrelevant the warranty given at the time of assignment; (3) a post-assignment change in patent claims removes the rationale for applying assignor estoppel; and (4) when an inventor assigns a patent application, rather than an issued patent. In the latter situation, the assignee may return to the PTO to enlarge the patent's claims. Assuming that the new claims are materially broader than the old ones, the assignor did not warrant to the new claims' validity. And if the assignor made no such representation, then assignor estoppel does not prevent the assignor from challenging the new claims in litigation. Absent "an explicit or implicit representation made in assigning patent rights," "an invalidity defense raises no concern of fair dealing—so assignor estoppel has no place." Three dissenters, led by Justice Barrett, would have done away with the doctrine altogether.

3. No Licensee Estoppel. Under traditional contract and property principles, "one receiving bargained-for benefits under a contract may not question the consideration he has received." *See* Robert B. Orr, Note, *The Doctrine of Licensee Repudiation in Patent Law*, 63 YALE L.J. 125 (1953). Courts have applied this doctrine to bar patent licensees from challenging the validity of the patents supporting their bargain since the mid-19th century. *See Automatic Radio Manufacturing Co. v. Hazeltine Research, Inc.*, 339 U.S. 827, 836 (1950). In a break from this tradition, the Supreme Court ruled in *Lear, Inc. v. Adkins*, 395 U.S. 653 (1969) looked to "the strong federal policy favoring free competition in ideas which do not merit patent protection" reflected in these cases in refusing to honor contractual restrictions on licensees challenging patent validity. The Court emphasized

> Licensees may often be the only individuals with enough economic incentive to challenge the patentability of an inventor's discovery. If they are muzzled, the public may continually be required to pay tribute to would-be monopolists without need or justification. We think it plain that the technical requirements of contract doctrine must give way before the demands of the

public interest in the typical situation involving the negotiation of a license after a patent has issued.

Id. at 670–71. Can you think of any circumstances in which it might be economically efficient to allow parties to restrict licensee patent challenges? If licensees are free to challenge patents for public policy reasons, why not inventors? *See generally* Rochelle Cooper Dreyfuss, *Dethroning Lear: Licensee Estoppel and the Incentive to Innovate*, 72 VA. L. REV. 677, 694–95 (1986); Rochelle Cooper Dreyfuss & Lawrence S. Pope, *Dethroning Lear? Incentives to Innovate After Medimmune*, 24 BERKELEY TECH. L.J. 971, 1007 (2009).

2. "With Authority"

Recall that §271(a) (Infringement of patent) refers to "whoever without authority makes, sells, . . ." (emphasis added). Thus, an important set of defenses to infringement relate to authorization—either through agreement or by operation of law. Patent licenses can be express or implied.

i. *Express or Implied License*

Obviously, an express license to practice a patented invention would preclude a patent suit, since the defendant was using the invention "with authority" from the patent owner. An implied license arises by acquiescence, conduct, equitable estoppel, or legal estoppel. *Wang Labs., Inc. v. Mitsubishi Elecs. Am., Inc.*, 103 F.3d 1571, 1580 (Fed. Cir. 1997). Such licenses are generally revocable. The existence and scope of licenses are generally governed by state contract law.

ii. *The Exhaustion Principle/First Sale Doctrine*

Under the exhaustion principle (also referred to as the first sale doctrine), the first unrestricted sale of a patented product exhausts the patentee's control over that product and it can be resold and repaired without implicating the patent owner's rights. The doctrine traces back to the nineteenth century. "[T]he patentee or his assignee having in the act of sale received all the royalty or consideration which he claims for the use of his invention in that particular machine or instrument, it is open to the use of the purchaser without further restriction on account of the monopoly of the patentees." *Adams v. Burke*, 84 U.S. 453 (1873); *see Aro Mfg. Co. v. Convertible Top Replacement Co.*, 377 U.S. 476, 484 (1964) (stating that "it is fundamental that sale of a patented article by the patentee . . . carries with it an 'implied license to use.'").

The Supreme Court reaffirmed the principle of exhaustion in *Quanta Computer, Inc. v. LG Electronics, Inc.*, 533 U.S. 617 (2008). It strongly suggested that once a patentee sold or authorized the sale of a product in this country, its control over that particular product ended, at least as a matter of patent law. It acknowledged that parties could contract for post-sale restrictions, but noted that those restrictions would be evaluated and enforced as a matter of contract, not patent, law. *Id.* n.7.

The Supreme Court confirmed that conclusion in *Impression Prods. v. Lexmark Int'l*, 137 S.Ct. 1523 (2017). The case involved a defendant that refilled and refurbished printer toner cartridges in spite of a "single use only" label on the cartridges. Such a "label license" pushes hard against the line that separates a bilateral contract from a unilateral restriction on personal property that purports to "run with the goods," i.e., a restriction that applies to all subsequent transferees who receive notice of the restriction. Such "personal property servitudes" have traditionally been disfavored, on the theory that they gum up free flowing markets for goods. The Court reaffirmed that rule, holding that a patent owner could not assert patent claims against the use or resale of a particular good once it had entered the stream of commerce, whether in the United States or abroad. The patent owner having been paid once, its rights were exhausted. The Court noted that if the patentee entered into a contract limiting the use of the products it sold, that contract might be enforceable—but only under contract, not patent, law.

COMMENTS AND QUESTIONS

1. *Method Claims.* The doctrine of patent exhaustion applies to method claims and the method patent is exhausted by sale of the item that embodies the method. *See Quanta Computer, Inc. v. LG Electronics, Inc.*, 533 U.S. 617 (2008). Although repair of a patented product that has been sold is permissible, reconstruction of the patented technology crosses the line into the patentee's "make" right.

2. *Permissible Repair/Impermissible Reconstruction Doctrine.* The line between permitted repair and impermissible reconstruction is not easily determined, resulting in vague, context-specific rulings. *See, e.g., Hewlett-Packard Co. v. Repeat-O-Type Stencil Mfg. Co.*, 123 F.3d 1445 (Fed. Cir. 1997) (dealing with refilling of printer cartridges). Such issues frequently arise in the context of contributory infringement claims, where the alleged infringer is providing specialized replacement parts. *See, e.g., Everpure v. Cuno, Inc.*, 875 F.3d 300 (Fed. Cir. 1989) ("Here it is the combination that is protected. The cartridge is not. . . . A purchaser of [Everpure's] filter unit is free to replace the worn out filter cartridge and the fact that it requires a particular cartridge configuration to mate it to the head does not alter the legal principle."). Contractual restrictions on resale or reuse can provoke patent misuse allegations and antitrust counterclaims.

3. *Policy Rationale.* The exhaustion doctrine has been criticized for interfering with freedom of contract. *See* Richard A. Epstein, *The Disintegration of Intellectual Property? A Classical Liberal Response to a Premature Obituary*, 62 STAN. L. REV. 455, 502–09 (2010). Professor Glen Robinson contends that

> the traditional hostility to use and resale restraints on personal property is misguided in both the common law and intellectual property contexts. While there may be legitimate reasons for limiting an owner's right to impose post-transfer restrictions on use and resale, those reasons are more exceptional than has been commonly assumed. Moreover, in the new digital world where servitude-type restrictions can be engineered into the architecture of the property itself, public policy restrictions on contractual 'servitudes' may prove to be ineffectual, creating a new reason to take a fresh look at old conceptions of personal property servitudes.

Glen O. Robinson, *Personal Property Servitudes,* 71 U. CHI. L. REV. 1449 (2004).

Other scholars (and the Supreme Court, in the copyright context) worry that contractual restrictions on the use of personal property, like non-possessory interests in real property, can greatly complicate the use of resources over time. *See Kirtsaeng v. John S. Wiley & Sons*, 568 U.S. 519 (2013); Molly Shaffer Van Houweling, *The New Servitudes*, 96 GEO. L.J. 885 (2007); Zechariah Chafee, Jr., *Equitable Servitudes on Chattels*, 41 HARV. L. REV. 945 (1928); *see generally* MICHAEL HELLER, THE GRIDLOCK ECONOMY: HOW TOO MUCH OWNERSHIP WRECKS MARKETS, STOPS INNOVATION, AND COSTS LIVES (2008). Others have suggested that the issue turns on the optimal standardization of legal regimes. *See* Thomas W. Merrill & Henry E. Smith, *Optimal Standardization in the Law of Property: The* Numerus Clausus *Principle*, 110 YALE L.J. 1 (2000).

4. *Territoriality, Price Discrimination/Gray Goods/Parallel Imports, and International Exhaustion.* Patent protection is territorial. Suppose that a patentee decides to sell its patented widget for a high price in the United States and a lower price in Asia. Drug companies often follow this model, with lower prices in lesser developed nations.

Economists refer to this phenomenon as price discrimination. Although it sounds evil, it has various virtues. First, it ensures that the patented good reaches a larger population, thereby reducing the deadweight loss of a single monopoly price. Second, it facilitates companies to provide different levels of services in different regions.

Does the Patent Act bar the authorized purchaser of a U.S. patented good in Asia from importing it to the United States without authorization—i.e., does the sale abroad exhaust the patent rights in the U.S.? As we will see in Chapter IV, the Supreme Court has interpreted the Copyright Act to hold that such a foreign sale does exhaust copyright protection and such good can lawfully be imported into the United States even though the copyright owner has not authorized importation of the good into the United States. *See Kirtsaeng v. John Wiley & Sons, Inc.*, 568 U.S. 519 (2013). In *Impression Prods. v. Lexmark Int'l*, 137 S.Ct. 1523 (2017), the Supreme Court extended the international exhaustion principle from copyright to patent protection.

What should a patent owner do if it wants to sell the same product in both rich and poor countries? Is price discrimination now impossible? Or could contracts achieve that goal?

PROBLEM III-18

Big Soya, Inc. is a large agricultural chemicals firm that sells a widely used herbicide named WEEDAWAY. Beginning in the 1980s, Big Soya began investing heavily in agricultural biotechnology research, with an eye toward developing advanced herbicides and related products. One of the problems that Big Soya faces, like all herbicide firms, is "selectivity": designing products that kill weeds, but do little or no damage to farm crops. In the mid-1990s, Big Soya researchers hit on the idea of developing a genetically engineered strain of soybeans that is particularly immune to the effects of the popular WEEDAWAY herbicide. By the late 1990s, they had perfected—and patented—special strains of soybean seeds with just these properties, which they called "WEEDAWAY-PROOF" seeds. As part of its strategy to protect the market for its proprietary seeds, Big Soya asks farmers using the seeds to sign a contract restricting the farmers' activities in a number of ways. Specifically, the farmers agree: (1) To use the seed containing Big Soya gene technologies for planting a commercial crop only in a single season; (2) Not to supply any of the seed to any other person or entity for planting, and to not save any crop produced from this seed for replanting, or supply saved seed to anyone for replanting; (3) Not to use the seed or provide it to anyone for crop breeding, research, generation of herbicide registration data, or seed production. The farmers' agreement also contains a clause specifying damages in the event of breach by the farmer:

In the event that the Grower saves, supplies, sells or acquires seed for replant in violation of this Agreement and license restriction, in addition to other remedies available to the technology provider(s), the Grower agrees that damages will include a claim for liquidated damages, which will be based on 120 times the applicable Technology Fee.

In a lawsuit brought against a farmer, Betty Overall, Big Soya alleges that Betty saved seeds from a batch of WEEDAWAY-PROOF soybeans, and used them again the next season. Betty argues that she bought the seeds outright, despite having signed the agreement (which she claims neither to have read nor understood); that farmers have traditionally had the right to plant "saved seed" from the previous year's crops, and that the Plant Variety Protection Act (see below) even enshrines that tradition in a "saved seed" exemption. Betty argues that Big Soya's farmers' agreement and the assertion of its patents against farmers such as Betty is patent misuse. Do you agree? How would you argue the case, based on Motion Picture and the other materials in this chapter?

3. The "Experimental Use" Defense

Notwithstanding the absolute language of §271(a), there is a judicially created exception to infringement that is commonly known as the "experimental use" exception. The doctrine had its origins in Justice Joseph Story's opinion in *Whittemore v. Cutter*, 29 F. Cas. 1120 (C.C.D. Mass. 1813) (No. 17,600). In that case, the defendant appealed a jury instruction to the effect that the "making of a machine . . . with a design to use it for profit" constituted infringement. Justice Story upheld the trial judge's instruction and stated that "it could never have been the intention of the legislature to punish a man, who constructed such a machine merely for philosophical experiments, or for the purpose of ascertaining the sufficiency of the machine to produce its described effects." 29 F. Cas. at 1121.

Madey v. Duke University
United States Court of Appeals for the Federal Circuit
307 F.3d 1351 (Fed. Cir. 2002)

GAJARSA, CIRCUIT JUDGE.

* * *

BACKGROUND

In the mid–1980s Madey was a tenured research professor at Stanford University. At Stanford, he had an innovative laser research program, which was highly regarded in the scientific community. An opportunity arose for Madey to consider leaving Stanford and take a tenured position at Duke. Duke recruited Madey, and in 1988 he left Stanford for a position in Duke's physics department. In 1989 Madey moved his free electron laser ("FEL") research lab from Stanford to Duke. The FEL lab contained substantial equipment, requiring Duke to build an addition to its physics building to house the lab. In addition, during his time at Stanford, Madey had obtained sole ownership of two patents practiced by some of the equipment in the FEL lab.

At Duke, Madey served for almost a decade as director of the FEL lab. During that time the lab continued to achieve success in both research funding and scientific breakthroughs. However, a dispute arose between Madey and Duke. Duke contends that, despite his scientific prowess, Madey ineffectively managed the lab. Madey contends that Duke sought to use the lab's equipment for research areas outside the allocated scope of certain government funding, and that when he objected, Duke sought to remove him as lab director. Duke eventually did remove Madey as director of the lab in 1997. The removal is not at issue in this appeal, however, it is the genesis of this unique patent infringement case. As a result of the removal, Madey resigned from Duke in 1998. Duke, however, continued to operate some of the equipment in the lab. Madey then sued Duke for patent infringement of his two patents, and brought a variety of other claims. . . .

II. DISCUSSION

. . .

The Experimental Use Defense

. . . Madey contends that the Supreme Court's opinion in *Warner-Jenkinson Co. v. Hilton Davis Chem. Co.*, 520 U.S. 17 (1997) eliminates the experimental use defense. The Supreme Court held in *Warner-Jenkinson* that intent plays no role in the application of the doctrine of equivalents. *Warner-Jenkinson*, 520 U.S. at 36. Madey implicitly argues that the experimental use defense necessarily incorporates an intent inquiry, and thus is inconsistent with *Warner-Jenkinson*. . . . [W]e do not view such an inconsistency as inescapable, and conclude the experimental use defense persists albeit in the very narrow form articulated by this court in *Embrex* [*v. Service Engineering Corp.*], 216 F.3d [1343, 1349 [(Fed. Cir. 2000)].

The District Court Improperly Shifted the Burden to Madey

As a precursor to the burden-shifting issue, Madey argues that the experimental use defense is an affirmative defense that Duke must plead or lose. We disagree. Madey points to no source of authority for its assertion that experimental use is an affirmative defense. Indeed, we have referred to the defense in a variety of ways. *See Roche* [*Products, Inc. v. Bolar Pharmaceutical Co., Inc.*, 733 F.2d 858, 862, 221 (Fed. Cir. 1984)] (referring to experimental use as both an exception and a defense). Given this lack of precise treatment in the precedent, Madey has no basis to support its affirmative defense argument. . . .

The district court held that in order for Madey to overcome his burden to establish actionable infringement, he must establish that Duke did not use the patent-covered free electron laser equipment solely for experimental or other non-profit purposes. Madey argues that this improperly shifts the burden to the patentee and conflates the experimental use defense with the initial infringement inquiry.

We agree with Madey that the district court improperly shifted the burden to him. The district court folded the experimental use defense into the baseline assessment as to whether Duke infringed the patents. . . . [The district court] erroneously required Madey to show as a part of his initial claim that Duke's use was not experimental. The defense, if available at all, must be established by Duke.

The District Court's Overly Broad Conception of Experimental Use

Madey argues, and we agree, that the district court had an overly broad conception of the very narrow and strictly limited experimental use defense. The district court stated that the experimental use defense inoculated uses that "were solely for research, academic, or experimental purposes," and that the defense covered use that "is made for experimental, non-profit purposes only." Both formulations are too broad and stand in sharp contrast to our admonitions in *Embrex* and *Roche* that the experimental use defense is very narrow and strictly limited. In *Embrex*, we followed the teachings of *Roche* and *Pitcairn* [*v. United States*, 212 Ct. Cl. 168, 547 F.2d 1106 (1976)) to hold that the defense was very narrow and limited to actions performed "for amusement, to satisfy idle curiosity, or for strictly philosophical inquiry." *Embrex*, 216 F.3d at 1349. Further, use does not qualify for the experimental use defense when it is undertaken in the "guise of scientific inquiry" but has "definite, cognizable, and not insubstantial commercial purposes." *Id.* (quoting *Roche*, 733 F.2d at 863). The concurring opinion in *Embrex* expresses a similar view: use is disqualified from the defense if it has the "slightest commercial implication." *Id.* at 1353. Moreover, use in keeping with the legitimate business of the alleged infringer does not qualify for the experimental use defense. *See Pitcairn*, 547 F.2d at 1125–26. The district court supported its conclusion with a citation to *Ruth v. Stearns-Roger Mfg. Co.*, 13 F. Supp. 697, 713 (D.Colo. 1935), a case that is not binding precedent for this court.

The *Ruth* case represents the conceptual dilemma that may have led the district court astray. Cases evaluating the experimental use defense are few, and those involving non-profit, educational alleged infringers are even fewer. In *Ruth*, the court concluded that a manufacturer of equipment covered by patents was not liable for contributory infringement because the end-user purchaser was the Colorado School of Mines, which used the equipment in furtherance of its educational purpose. Thus, the combination of apparent lack of commerciality, with the non-profit status of an educational institution, prompted the court in *Ruth*, without any detailed analysis of the character, nature and effect of the use, to hold that the experimental use defense applied. This is not consistent with the binding precedent of our case law postulated by *Embrex*, *Roche* and *Pitcairn*.

Our precedent clearly does not immunize use that is in any way commercial in nature. Similarly, our precedent does not immunize any conduct that is in keeping with the alleged infringer's legitimate business, regardless of commercial implications. For example, major research universities, such as Duke, often sanction and fund research projects with arguably no commercial application whatsoever. However, these projects unmistakably further the institution's legitimate business objectives, including educating and enlightening students and faculty participating in these projects. These projects also serve, for example, to increase the status of the institution and lure lucrative research grants, students and faculty.

In short, regardless of whether a particular institution or entity is engaged in an endeavor for commercial gain, so long as the act is in furtherance of the alleged infringer's legitimate business and is not solely for amusement, to satisfy idle curiosity, or for strictly philosophical inquiry, the act does not qualify for the very narrow and strictly limited experimental use defense. Moreover, the profit or non-profit status of the user is not determinative.

In the present case, the district court attached too great a weight to the non-profit, educational status of Duke, effectively suppressing the fact that Duke's acts appear to be in accordance with any reasonable interpretation of Duke's legitimate business objectives.[7] On remand, the district court will have to significantly narrow and limit its conception of the experimental use defense. The correct focus should not be on the non-profit status of Duke but on the legitimate business Duke is involved in and whether or not the use was solely for amusement, to satisfy idle curiosity, or for strictly philosophical inquiry. . . .

COMMENTS AND QUESTIONS

1. *Is the Ivory Tower Just Another Office Building*? Do the aggressive patent acquisition, licensing, and enforcement activities of universities undermine the legitimacy of their claims to "special treatment" under the research exemption? *See* DEREK BOK, UNIVERSITIES IN THE MARKETPLACE: THE COMMERCIALIZATION OF HIGHER EDUCATION 201 (2003) ("Universities may not yet be willing to trade all of their values for money, but they have proceeded much further down that road than they are generally willing to acknowledge."); Mark A. Lemley, *Are Universities Patent Trolls?*, 16 FORDHAM INTELL. PROP., MEDIA, & ENT. L.J. 611 (2008).

2. *Scope of Experimental Use.* Do you think that experimental use should be broader? Note that the Patent Act permits patents on "improvements thereof."

Based on the history and rationale of the experimental use doctrine, Professor Rebecca Eisenberg contends that research to check the adequacy of the specification and the validity of the patent holder's claims about the invention should be exempt from

---

[7] Duke's patent and licensing policy may support its primary function as an educational institution. *See Duke University Policy on Inventions, Patents, and Technology Transfer* (1996), available at http://www.ors.duke.edu/policies/patpol.htm (last visited Oct. 3, 2002). Duke, however, like other major research institutions of higher learning, is not shy in pursuing an aggressive patent licensing program from which it derives a not insubstantial revenue stream.

infringement liability. Rebecca Eisenberg, *Patents and the Progress of Science: Exclusive Rights and Experimental Use*, 56 U. CHI. L. REV. 1017 (1989). By contrast, research use of a patented invention with a primary or significant market among research users should not be exempt from infringement liability when the research user is an ordinary consumer of the patented invention.

Professor Eisenberg argues for a middle ground where a researcher uses a patented invention in a way that could potentially lead to improvements in the patented technology or to the development of alternative means of achieving the same purpose. In those scenarios, it might be appropriate to award a reasonable royalty after the fact to be sure that the patent holder receives an adequate return on the initial investment in developing the patented invention. The patent holder should not, however, be entitled to enjoin the use of a patented invention in such efforts to improve upon the patented technology. How would you go about setting the reasonable royalty in a case where a subsequent improver infringed a patent in the course of developing a superior alternative that destroys the patentee's market?

3. The European Patent Convention provides that patent protection "does not extend to acts done for experimental purposes relating to the subject matter of the patented invention." Art. 27(b), European Patent Convention (implemented in all EU states except Austria). *See also* Patent Act of the People's Republic of China, Article 69(4) (shall not be patent infringement "(4) Any person uses the relevant patent specially for the purpose of scientific research and experimentation"). Would these provisions have immunized Duke University?

4. *Use of Patented Technology for Drug Testing.* Generic drug companies would like to enter the market as soon as a patent expires. This is also valuable for drug consumers who benefit from competitive pricing. To be ready to hit the ground running, however, the generic company needs FDA approval to market the drug. In *Roche Products, Inc. v. Bolar Pharmaceutical Co.*, 733 F.2d 858 (Fed. Cir. 1984), the Federal Circuit held that the experimental use exception did not include "the limited use of a patented drug for testing and investigation strictly related to FDA drug approval requirements.... Bolar may intend to perform "experiments," but unlicensed experiments conducted with a view to the adaption of the patented invention to the experimentor's business are a violation of the rights of the patentee to exclude others from using his patented invention."733 F.2d at 861, 863.

5. *Bolar Amendment: Statutory Experimental Use Exception for Drug Testing.* Congress passed the Drug Price Competition and Patent Term Restoration Act, Pub. L. 98–417 (1984), informally known as the Hatch-Waxman Act. The Act establishes an Abbreviated New Drug Application (ANDA) process to speed entry of generic drugs onto the marketplace after a patent expires. Congress overturned the *Bolar* decision by enacting §271(e)(1):

> it shall not be an act of infringement to make, use, offer to sell, or sell within the United States or import into the United States a patented invention . . . solely for uses reasonably related to the development and submission of information

under a Federal law which regulates the manufacture, use, or sale of drugs or veterinary biological products.

The Supreme Court held in *Merck KGaA v. Integra Life Sciences I Ltd.*, 545 U.S. 193 (2005), that the exemption broadly protects any pre-clinical testing of patented compounds that is reasonably related to the submission of information to a regulatory agency, and not just late-stage safety and efficacy testing in human subjects. Integra owned five patents to "RGD peptides," small proteins that attach tightly to certain binding sites on the surfaces of blood vessel cells. Researchers working in cooperation with Merck discovered that RGD peptides could be used to block receptors active during the proliferation of blood vessel cells. Because this has the effect of slowing down blood vessel growth, it is an effective way to inhibit the growth of tumors. Merck and its research collaborators used RGD peptides in two different ways: (1) to test them directly as tumor-inhibiting agents; and (2) as "benchmarks" against which to measure other compounds they were developing for tumor inhibition.

The Supreme Court held that the Bolar Amendment immunized Merck's use of Integra's patents:

> Congress did not limit §271(e)(1)'s safe harbor to the development of information for inclusion in a submission to the FDA; nor did it create an exemption applicable only to the research relevant to filing an ANDA for approval of a generic drug. Rather, it exempted from infringement all uses of patented compounds "reasonably related" to the process of developing information for submission under any federal law regulating the manufacture, use, or distribution of drugs. We decline to read the "reasonable relation" requirement so narrowly as to render §271(e)(1)'s stated protection of activities leading to FDA approval for all drugs illusory. Properly construed, §271(e)(1) leaves adequate space for experimentation and failure on the road to regulatory approval: At least where a drugmaker has a reasonable basis for believing that a patented compound may work, through a particular biological process, to produce a particular physiological effect, and uses the compound in research that, if successful, would be appropriate to include in a submission to the FDA, that use is "reasonably related" to the "development and submission of information under . . . Federal law."

545 U.S. 206–07. Some have suggested that this result discourages pharmaceutical companies from disclosing their research. *See* Lawrence B. Ebert, *In Favor of the Federal Circuit Position in* Merck v. Integra, 87 J. PAT. & TRADEMARK OFF. SOC'Y 321, 339–40 (2005).

4. Prior User Rights

Congress established the §273 prior user defense as a safe harbor for the financial community in 1999 following *State St. Bank v. Signature Fin. Grp.*, 149 F.3d 1368 (Fed. Cir. 1998), the controversial decision opening the way for business method patents. Congress expanded the prior user defense significantly in the AIA to include "subject matter consisting of a process, or consisting of a machine, manufacture, or composition of matter used in a manufacturing or other commercial process." §273(a). One who secures a prior user right does not invalidate the patent at issue; the right is a personal defense that shields only this one party from liability. For this defense to apply, the invention must have been used commercially in the U.S. by the party asserting the defense at least one year before the earlier of either: (1) the effective filing date, or (2) the date of the first public disclosure of the claimed invention. The prior use defense must be established by clear and convincing evidence. This defense is subject to various limitations and exceptions, including that it may not be asserted against "an institution of higher education . . . or technology transfer organization whose primary purpose is to facilitate the commercialization of technologies developed by one or more such institutions of higher education." §273(e)(5). It is also restricted to continued use at the same plant or facility, significantly limiting the growth of the prior user.

5. Inequitable Conduct

Where a patent applicant breaches the duty to prosecute a patent application in good faith and candor, it may result in a finding of inequitable conduct. *See* 37 C.F.R. §1.56 (2013); *Purdue Pharma L.P. v. Endo Pharm. Inc.*, 410 F.3d 690, 695 (Fed. Cir. 2005). Inequitable conduct may "arise from an affirmative misrepresentation of a material fact, failure to disclose material information, or submission of false material information, coupled with an intent to deceive or mislead the USPTO." *Id.* A determination that inequitable conduct occurred in relation to one or more claims will render the entire patent unenforceable. *Kingsdown Med. Consultants, Ltd. v. Hollister, Inc.*, 863 F.2d 867, 877 (Fed. Cir. 1988) (en banc in relevant part).

This doctrine came under scrutiny as defendants routinely alleged inequitable conduct in the hopes that they could uncover some shred of evidence casting doubt on the patentee's candor during prosecution. Such allegations provided a basis for costly and time-consuming discovery. Well-funded defendants could use the cost and delay as leverage in settling patent litigation. The threat of inequitable conduct also contributed to patentees flooding the PTO with prior art references out of concern that any article in their files could be used as part of a future inequitable conduct defense.

Therasense, Inc. v. Becton-Dickinson, Inc.
United States Court of Appeals for the Federal Circuit
649 F.3d 1276 (Fed. Cir. 2011) (en banc)

RADER, CHIEF JUDGE.

[Therasense, a subsidiary of Abbott Laboratories, obtained several patents on disposable glucose test strips for diabetes management. Becton-Dickinson sued for a declaratory judgment that Abbott's patents were invalid. Abbott countersued Becton and Bayer Healthcare LLC for infringement. After the cases were consolidated for trial in the Northern District of California, the district court held all of the litigated patent claims either invalid or not infringed. The court also held one of the patents, U.S. Patent No. 5,820,551 ("the '551 patent"), unenforceable due to inequitable conduct. On appeal, a panel of the Federal Circuit unanimously affirmed all of the district court's holdings of noninfringement and invalidity, including the district court's ruling that all litigated claims in the '551 patent were invalid for obviousness. The panel also affirmed the district court's holding that the '551 patent was unenforceable due to inequitable conduct, but the panel was divided on that issue. The full court granted rehearing en banc solely on the inequitable conduct issue.]

The '551 patent claims a test strip with an electrochemical sensor . . . *"configured to be exposed to said whole blood sample without an intervening membrane or other whole blood filtering member . . . ."* '551 patent [claim 1] (emphasis added). "Whole blood," an important term in the claim, means blood that contains all of its components, including red blood cells.

In the prior art, some sensors employed diffusion-limiting membranes to control the flow of glucose to the electrode because the slower mediators of the time could not deal with a rapid in-flux of glucose. Other prior art sensors used protective membranes to prevent "fouling." Fouling occurs when red blood cells stick to the active electrode and interfere with electron transfer to the electrode. Protective membranes permit glucose molecules to pass, but not red blood cells.

Abbott filed the original application leading to the '551 patent in 1984. Over thirteen years, that original application saw multiple rejections for anticipation and obviousness, including repeated rejections over U.S. Patent No. 4,545,382 ("the '382 patent"), another patent owned by Abbott. The '382 patent specification discussed protective membranes in the following terms: "Optionally, but preferably when being used on live blood, a protective membrane surrounds both the enzyme and the mediator layers, permeable to water and glucose molecules." Col.4 ll.63–66. "Live blood" refers to blood within a body.

In 1997, Lawrence Pope, Abbott's patent attorney, and Dr. Gordon Sanghera, Abbott's Director of Research and Development, studied the novel features of their application and decided to present a new reason for a patent. Pope presented new claims to the examiner based on a new sensor that did not require a protective membrane for whole blood. Pope asserted that this distinction would overcome the prior art '382 patent, whose electrodes allegedly required a protective membrane. The examiner requested an affidavit to show that the prior art required a membrane for whole blood at the time of the invention.

To meet this evidentiary request, Dr. Sanghera submitted a declaration to the U.S. Patent and Trademark Office ("PTO") stating:

> [O]ne skilled in the art would have felt that an active electrode comprising an enzyme and a mediator would require a protective membrane if it were to be used with a whole blood sample. . . .

J.A. 7637. Pope, in submitting Sanghera's affidavit, represented:

> The art continued to believe [following the '382 patent] that a barrier layer for [a] whole blood sample was necessary. . . .
>
> [O]ne skilled in the art would *not* read lines 63 to 65 of column 4 of U.S. Patent No. 4,545,382 to teach that the use of a protective membrane with a

whole blood sample is optionally or merely preferred. One skilled in the art would not have read the disclosure of the ['382 patent] as teaching that the use of a protective membrane with whole blood samples was optional. He would not, especially in view of the working examples, have read the "optionally, but preferably" language at line 63 of column [4] as a technical teaching but rather mere patent phraseology. . . .

There is no teaching or suggestion of unprotected active electrodes for use with whole blood specimens in [the '382 patent]. . . .

J.A. 7645–46.

Several years earlier, while prosecuting the European counterpart to the '382 patent, European Patent EP 0 078 636 ("EP '636"), Abbott made representations to the European Patent Office ("EPO") regarding the same "optionally, but preferably" language in the European specification. On January 12, 1994, to distinguish a German reference labeled D1, which required a diffusion-limiting membrane, Abbott's European patent counsel argued that their invention did not require a diffusion-limiting membrane:

Contrary to the semipermeable membrane of D1, the protective membrane optionally utilized with the glucose sensor of the patent is [sic] suit is not controlling the permeability of the substrate . . . Rather, in accordance with column 5, lines 30 to 33 of the patent in suit:

> "Optionally, but preferably when being used on live blood, a protective membrane surrounds both the enzyme and the mediator layers, permeable to water and glucose molecules."

See also claim 10 of the patent in suit as granted according to which the sensor electrode has an outermost protective membrane (11) permeable to water and glucose molecules. . . . Accordingly, *the purpose of the protective membrane of the patent in suit, preferably to be used with in vivo measurements, is a safety measurement to prevent any course [sic] particles coming off during use but not a permeability control for the substrate.*

J.A. 6530–31 (emphases added).

On May 23, 1995, Abbott's European patent counsel submitted another explanation about the D1 reference and EP '636.

> "Optionally, but preferably when being used on live blood, a protective membrane surrounds both the enzyme and the mediator layers, permeable to water and glucose molecules."

It is submitted that this disclosure is unequivocally clear. The protective membrane is optional, however, it is preferred when used on live blood in order to prevent the larger constituents of the blood, in particular erythrocytes from interfering with the electrode sensor. Furthermore it is said, that said protective membrane should not prevent the glucose molecules from penetration, the membrane is "permeable" to glucose molecules. This teaches the skilled artisan that, whereas the [D1 membrane] must . . . control the permeability of the glucose . . . the purpose of the protective membrane in the patent in suit is not to control the permeation of the glucose molecules. For this very reason *the sensor electrode as claimed does not have (and must not have) a semipermeable membrane in the sense of D1.*

J.A. 6585 (first and third emphases added).

III

Inequitable conduct is an equitable defense to patent infringement that, if proved, bars enforcement of a patent. This judge-made doctrine evolved from a trio of Supreme Court cases that applied the doctrine of unclean hands to dismiss patent cases involving egregious misconduct: *Keystone Driller Co. v. General Excavator Co.*, 290 U.S. 240, 54 (1933). . . .

Keystone involved the manufacture and suppression of evidence. The patentee knew of "a possible prior use" by a third party prior to filing a patent application but did not inform the PTO. After the issuance of the patent, the patentee paid the prior user to sign a false affidavit stating that his use was an abandoned experiment and bought his agreement to keep secret the details of the prior use and to suppress evidence. With these preparations in place, the patentee then asserted this patent, along with two other patents, against Byers Machine Co. ("Byers"). *Keystone Driller Co. v. Byers Mach. Co.*, 4 F. Supp. 159 (N.D. Ohio 1929). Unaware of the prior use and of the cover-up, the court held the patents valid and infringed and granted an injunction.

The patentee then asserted the same patents against General Excavator Co. and Osgood Co. and sought a temporary injunction based on the decree in the previous Byers case. *Keystone*, 290 U.S. at 242. The district court denied the injunctions but made the defendants post bonds. The defendants discovered and introduced evidence of the corrupt transaction between the patentee and the prior user. The district court declined to dismiss these cases for unclean hands. On appeal, the Sixth Circuit reversed and remanded with instructions to dismiss the complaints. The Supreme Court affirmed.

The Supreme Court explained that if the corrupt transaction between the patentee and the prior user had been discovered in the previous *Byers* case, "the court undoubtedly would have been warranted in holding it sufficient to require dismissal of the cause of action." *Id.* at 246. Because the patentee used the *Byers* decree to seek an injunction in the cases against General Excavator Co. and Osgood Co., it did not come to the court with clean hands, and dismissal of these cases was appropriate.

[The Federal Circuit then summarized similar facts from subsequent Supreme Court cases, *Hazel-Atlas Glass Co. v. Hartford-Empire Co.*, 322 U.S. 238 (1944), *overruled on other grounds by Standard Oil Co. v. United States*, 429 U.S. 17 (1976), and *Precision Instrument Manufacturing Co. v. Automotive Maintenance Machinery Co.*, 324 U.S. 806 (1945).]

IV

The unclean hands cases of *Keystone, Hazel-Atlas*, and *Precision* formed the basis for a new doctrine of inequitable conduct that developed and evolved over time. As the inequitable conduct doctrine evolved from these unclean hands cases, it came to embrace a broader scope of misconduct, including not only egregious affirmative acts of misconduct intended to deceive both the PTO and the courts but also the mere nondisclosure of information to the PTO. Inequitable conduct also diverged from the doctrine of unclean hands by adopting a different and more potent remedy—unenforceability of the entire patent rather than mere dismissal of the instant suit.

In line with this wider scope and stronger remedy, inequitable conduct came to require a finding of both intent to deceive and materiality. *Star Scientific Inc. v. R.J. Reynolds Tobacco Co.*, 537 F.3d 1357, 1365 (Fed. Cir. 2008). To prevail on the defense of inequitable conduct, the accused infringer must prove that the applicant misrepresented or omitted material information with the specific intent to deceive the PTO. *Id.* The accused infringer must prove both elements—intent and materiality—by clear and convincing evidence. *Id.* If the accused infringer meets its burden, then the district court must weigh the equities to determine whether the applicant's conduct before the PTO warrants rendering the entire patent unenforceable. *Id.*

This court recognizes that the early unclean hands cases do not present any standard for materiality. Needless to say, this court's development of a materiality requirement for inequitable conduct does not (and cannot) supplant Supreme Court precedent. Though inequitable conduct developed from these cases, the unclean hands doctrine remains available to supply a remedy for egregious misconduct like that in the Supreme Court cases.

As inequitable conduct emerged from unclean hands, the standards for intent to deceive and materiality have fluctuated over time. In the past, this court has espoused low standards for meeting the intent requirement, finding it satisfied based on gross negligence or even negligence. This court has also previously adopted a broad view of materiality, using a "reasonable examiner" standard based on the PTO's 1977 amendment to Rule 56. *See Am. Hoist & Derrick Co. v. Sowa & Sons, Inc.*, 725 F.2d 1350, 1362 (Fed. Cir. 1984); *see also* 37 C.F.R. §1.56 (1977) (a reference is material if "there is a substantial likelihood that a reasonable examiner would consider it important in deciding whether to allow the application to issue as a patent"). Further weakening the showing needed to establish inequitable conduct, this court then placed intent and materiality together on a "sliding scale." *Am. Hoist*, 725 F.2d at 1362. This modification to the inequitable conduct doctrine held patents unenforceable based on a reduced showing of intent if the record contained a strong showing of materiality, and vice versa. In effect, this change conflated, and diluted, the standards for both intent and materiality.

Perhaps most importantly, the remedy for inequitable conduct is the "atomic bomb" of patent law. *Aventis Pharma S.A. v. Amphastar Pharm., Inc.*, 525 F.3d 1334, 1349 (Fed. Cir. 2008) (Rader, J., dissenting). Unlike validity defenses, which are claim specific, *see* 35 U.S.C. §288, inequitable conduct regarding any single claim renders the entire patent unenforceable. *Kingsdown Med. Consultants, Ltd. v. Hollister Inc.*, 863 F.2d 867, 877 (Fed. Cir. 1988). Unlike other deficiencies, inequitable conduct cannot be cured by reissue or reexamination. Moreover, the taint of a finding of inequitable conduct can spread from a single patent to render unenforceable other related patents and applications in the same technology family. Thus, a finding of inequitable conduct may endanger a substantial portion of a company's patent portfolio. . . .

A finding of inequitable conduct may also spawn antitrust and unfair competition claims. Further, prevailing on a claim of inequitable conduct often makes a case "exceptional," leading potentially to an award of attorneys' fees under 35 U.S.C. §285. A finding of inequitable conduct may also prove the crime or fraud exception to the attorney-client privilege.

With these far-reaching consequences, it is no wonder that charging inequitable conduct has become a common litigation tactic. One study estimated that eighty percent of patent infringement cases included allegations of inequitable conduct. Committee Position Paper[, *The Doctrine of Inequitable Conduct and the Duty of Candor in Patent Prosecution: Its Current Adverse Impact on the Operation of the United States Patent System*, 16 AIPLA Q.J. 74, 75 (1988)]; *see also* Christian Mammen, *Controlling the "Plague": Reforming the Doctrine of Inequitable Conduct*, 24 BERKELEY TECH. L.J. 1329, 1358 (2009). Inequitable conduct "has been overplayed, is appearing in nearly every patent suit, and is cluttering up the patent system." *Kimberly-Clark Corp. v. Johnson & Johnson*, 745 F.2d 1437, 1454 (Fed. Cir. 1984). "[T]he habit of charging inequitable conduct in almost every major patent case has become an absolute plague. Reputable lawyers seem to feel compelled to make the charge against other reputable lawyers on the slenderest grounds, to represent their client's interests adequately, perhaps." *Burlington Indus., Inc. v. Dayco Corp.*, 849 F.2d 1418, 1422 (Fed. Cir. 1988).

Left unfettered, the inequitable conduct doctrine has plagued not only the courts but also the entire patent system. Because allegations of inequitable conduct are routinely brought on "the slenderest grounds," *Burlington Indus.*, 849 F.2d at 1422, patent prosecutors constantly confront the specter of inequitable conduct charges. With inequitable conduct casting the shadow of a hangman's noose, it is unsurprising that patent prosecutors regularly bury PTO examiners with a deluge of prior art references, most of which have marginal value. *See* Brief for the United States as Amicus Curiae at 17 (submission of nine hundred references without any indication which ones were most relevant); Brief of the Biotechnology Industry Organization as Amicus Curiae at 7 (submission of eighteen pages of cited references, including five pages listing references to claims, office actions, declarations, amendments, interview summaries, and other communications in related applications). "Applicants disclose too much prior art for the PTO to meaningfully consider, and do not explain its significance, all out of fear that to do otherwise risks a claim of inequitable conduct." ABA Section of Intellectual Property Law, *A Section White Paper: Agenda for 21st Century Patent Reform* 2 (2009). This tidal wave of disclosure makes identifying the most relevant prior art more difficult. *See* Brief for the United States as Amicus Curiae at 1 (submission of "large numbers of prior art references of questionable materiality . . . harms the effectiveness of the examination process"). "This flood of information strains the agency's examining resources and directly contributes to the backlog." *Id.* at 17–18.

While honesty at the PTO is essential, low standards for intent and materiality have inadvertently led to many unintended consequences, among them, increased adjudication cost and complexity, reduced likelihood of settlement, burdened courts, strained PTO resources, increased PTO backlog, and impaired patent quality. This court now tightens the standards for finding both intent and materiality in order to redirect a doctrine that has been overused to the detriment of the public.

V

To prevail on a claim of inequitable conduct, the accused infringer must prove that the patentee acted with the specific intent to deceive the PTO. A finding that the misrepresentation or omission amounts to gross negligence or negligence under a "should have known" standard does not satisfy this intent requirement. *Kingsdown*, 863 F.2d at 876. In other words, the accused infringer must prove by clear and convincing evidence that the applicant knew of the reference, knew that it was material, and made a deliberate decision to withhold it. . . .

Intent and materiality are separate requirements. *Hoffmann-La Roche, Inc. v. Promega Corp.*, 323 F.3d 1354, 1359 (Fed. Cir. 2003). A district court should not use a "sliding scale," where a weak showing of intent may be found sufficient based on a strong showing of materiality, and vice versa. Moreover, a district court may not infer intent solely from materiality. Instead, a court must weigh the evidence of intent to deceive independent of its analysis of materiality. Proving that the applicant knew of a reference, should have known of its materiality, and decided not to submit it to the PTO does not prove specific intent to deceive.

Because direct evidence of deceptive intent is rare, a district court may infer intent from indirect and circumstantial evidence. *Larson Mfg. Co. of S.D., Inc. v. Aluminart Prods. Ltd.*, 559 F.3d 1317, 1340 (Fed. Cir. 2009). However, to meet the clear and convincing evidence standard, the specific intent to deceive must be "the single most reasonable inference able to be drawn from the evidence." *Star*, 537 F.3d at 1366. Indeed, the evidence "must be sufficient to *require* a finding of deceitful intent in the light of all the circumstances." *Kingsdown*, 863 F.2d at 873 (emphasis added). Hence, when there are multiple reasonable inferences that may be drawn, intent to deceive cannot be found. This court reviews the district court's factual findings regarding what reasonable inferences may be drawn from the evidence for clear error.

VI

This court holds that, as a general matter, the materiality required to establish inequitable conduct is but-for materiality. When an applicant fails to disclose prior art to the PTO, that prior art is but-for material if the PTO would not have allowed a claim had it been aware of the undisclosed prior art. Hence, in assessing the materiality of a withheld reference, the court must determine whether the PTO would have allowed the claim if it had been aware of the undisclosed reference. In making this patentability determination, the court should apply the preponderance of the evidence standard and give claims their broadest reasonable construction. *See* MANUAL OF PATENT EXAMINING PROCEDURE ("MPEP") §§706, 2111 (8th ed. Rev.8, July 2010). Often the patentability of a claim will be congruent with the validity determination—if a claim is properly invalidated in district court based on the deliberately withheld reference, then that reference is necessarily material because a finding of invalidity in a district court requires clear and convincing evidence, a higher evidentiary burden than that used in prosecution at the PTO. However, even if a district court does not invalidate a claim based on a deliberately withheld reference, the reference may be material if it would have blocked patent issuance under the PTO's different evidentiary standards.

Because inequitable conduct renders an entire patent (or even a patent family) unenforceable, as a general rule, this doctrine should only be applied in instances where the patentee's misconduct resulted in the unfair benefit of receiving an unwarranted claim.

After all, the patentee obtains no advantage from misconduct if the patent would have issued anyway. Moreover, enforcement of an otherwise valid patent does not injure the public merely because of misconduct, lurking somewhere in patent prosecution, that was immaterial to the patent's issuance.

Although but-for materiality generally must be proved to satisfy the materiality prong of inequitable conduct, this court recognizes an exception in cases of affirmative egregious misconduct. When the patentee has engaged in affirmative acts of egregious misconduct, such as the filing of an unmistakably false affidavit, the misconduct is material. *See Rohm & Haas Co. v. Crystal Chem. Co.*, 722 F.2d 1556, 1571 (Fed. Cir. 1983) ("there is no room to argue that submission of false affidavits is not material"). After all, a patentee is unlikely to go to great lengths to deceive the PTO with a falsehood unless it believes that the falsehood will affect issuance of the patent. . . .

[T]he general rule requiring but-for materiality provides clear guidance to patent practitioners and courts, while the egregious misconduct exception gives the test sufficient flexibility to capture extraordinary circumstances. Thus, not only is this court's approach sensitive to varied facts and equitable considerations, it is also consistent with the early unclean hands cases—all of which dealt with egregious misconduct.

VII

On remand, the district court should determine whether the PTO would not have granted the patent but for Abbott's failure to disclose the EPO briefs. In particular, the district court must determine whether the PTO would have found Sanghera's declaration and Pope's accompanying submission unpersuasive in overcoming the obviousness rejection over the '382 patent if Abbott had disclosed the EPO briefs. Because the district court did not find intent to deceive under the knowing and deliberate standard set forth in this opinion, this court vacates the district court's findings of intent. On remand, the district court should determine whether there is clear and convincing evidence demonstrating that Sanghera or Pope knew of the EPO briefs, knew of their materiality, and made the conscious decision not to disclose them in order to deceive the PTO.

COMMENTS AND QUESTIONS

1. Judge Bryson, joinied by Judges Gajarsa, Dyk, and Prost dissented. *See Therasense, Inc. v. Becton, Dickinson and Co.*, 649 F.3d 1276, 1302-20 (Fed. Cir. 2011) (Bryson, J., dissenting). While acknowledging that the law of inequitable conduct was

in an unsatisfactory state and needs adjustment, the dissenters considered the majority's solution too restrictive to serve the doctrine's purposes. They instead advocated: (1) requiring proof, by clear and convincing evidence, that the applicant or attorney intended to mislead the PTO with respect to a material matter; (2) measuring materiality by the PTO's disclosure standards (*see* 37 C.F.R. §1.56 Duty to Disclose Information Material to Patentability (requiring proof that the information at issue either established, by itself or in combination with other information, a prima facie case of unpatentability, or was inconsistent with a position taken by the applicant before the PTO with respect to patentability)); and (3) requiring intent to mislead and materiality to be proved separately, i.e., without a sliding scale.

In a partial concurrence emphasizing the equitable nature of the inequitable conduct doctrine, Judge O'Malley urged affording district courts greater flexibility than either the majority or the dissent in applying the doctrine. *See Therasense, Inc. v. Becton, Dickinson and Co.*, 649 F.3d 1296- (Fed. Cir. 2011) (O'Malley, J., concurring in part and dissenting in part). She agreed with the majority's holding that a district court must find that the conduct at issue is of "sufficient culpability to require a finding of intent to deceive." *Kingsdown Med. Consultants, Ltd. v. Hollister Inc.*, 863 F.2d 867, 876 (Fed.Cir.1988). In making this determination, intent to deceive and materiality must be found separately. District courts may not employ a "sliding scale," nor may they infer intent from materiality alone. They may, however, infer intent from indirect and circumstantial evidence, but only where it is "the single most reasonable inference able to be drawn from the evidence."

Which approach—majority, dissent, or partial concurrence—do you find most persuasive?

2. Notwithstanding the majority's effort to tighten the inequitable conduct doctrine, the district court on remand in *Therasense* once again found inequitable conduct under the new standard. Based on the facts provided, does that decision comport with the Federal Circuit's standard?

After *Therasense*, allegations of inequitable conduct dropped significantly. *See* Robert Swanson, *The* Exergen *and* Therasense *Effects*, 66 STAN. L. REV. 695 (2014). But the Federal Circuit continues to find inequitable conduct in some circumstances. In *Belcher Pharms. v. Hospira, Inc.*, 11 F.4th 1345 (Fed. Cir. 2021), for example, the patentee told the FDA that its reformulated epinephrine with a pH of 2.8-3.3 was "old" and "a very minor change." But it told the PTO that reducing the pH to that range was its critical invention, and didn't disclose its contrary statement to the FDA. The Federal Circuit found an intent to deceive the only reasonable inference, particularly because the same person made both representations. *See id.* at 1353-54.

3. Why is the penalty for inequitable conduct stronger than the penalty for invalidity—rendering the patent as a whole unenforceable rather than just the tainted claim? Who has more information about the inventor's work and the precise prior art it relates to—the examiner or the inventor? Who has more to gain from the issuance (or rejection) of a patent?

How harsh is unenforceability really? If a patentee knows their application will be rejected in its entirety if they disclose a key piece of prior art, are they any worse off with unenforceability than if they had never obtained the patent in the first place? *See* Tun-Jen Chiang, *The Upside-Down Inequitable Conduct Doctrine*, 107 NW. U. L. REV. 1243 (2013) (arguing that inequitable conduct under-deters the most egregious cases of abuse while overdeterring marginal ones).

4. Many inequitable conduct cases involve suppressing a key prior art reference. It is important to note, however, that only prior art that was *known* by the inventor or the patent lawyer gives rise to a duty of disclosure. This rule is embodied not only in the doctrine of inequitable conduct in the courts, but also in Rule 56 of the rules of the patent practice, pertaining to the duty of patent applicants during prosecution. *See* 37 C.F.R. §1.56(a) ("Each individual associated with the filing and prosecution of a patent application has a duty of candor and good faith in dealing with the [patent] office, which includes a duty to disclose to the office all information *known to that individual* to be material to patentability . . .") (emphasis added). Note that this means that patentees do *not* have to conduct a prior art search. But if they know about prior art, it must be disclosed. Do you think it should matter whether (1) the reference was in a class or group that the Examiner should have searched? (2) that it was disclosed, but in a long "string cite" of less relevant prior art? (3) that the patentee didn't know of the key reference, but should have?

5. *Supplemental Examination*. Patent owners have long sought to reduce the impact of the inequitable conduct defense. The AIA provides another procedure for doing so. According to the House Report accompanying the AIA:

> The Act addresses the inequitable conduct doctrine by authorizing supplemental examination of a patent to correct errors or omissions in proceedings before the Office. Under this new procedure, information that was not considered or was inadequately considered or was incorrect can be presented to the Office. If the Office determines that the information does not present a substantial new question of patentability or that the patent is still valid, that information cannot later be used to hold the patent unenforceable or invalid on the basis for an inequitable-conduct attack in civil litigation.

Committee on the Judiciary, U.S. Cong., "America Invents Act," H.R. REP. NO 112-98, 112th Cong., 1st Sess., at 50 (June 1, 2011). Section 257(c)(1) provides that

> A patent shall not be held unenforceable on the basis of conduct relating to information that had not been considered, was inadequately considered, or was incorrect in a prior examination of the patent if the information was considered, reconsidered, or corrected during a supplemental examination of the patent.

If the PTO decides that the newly submitted information in supplemental examination presents a substantial new question of patentability with respect to one or more of the petitioner's claims, it may order a reexamination of those claims.

6. Prosecution Laches

The practice of "submarine patenting"—deliberately keeping a secret patent application pending for years in the PTO, only to spring it on an unsuspecting industry—has periodically been challenged under a variety of patent law doctrines. Submarine patenting has survived charges of inequitable conduct in some notable district court cases. *See Ford Motor Co. v. Lemelson*, 42 U.S.P.Q.2d 1706 (D. Nev. 1997); *Advanced Cardiovascular Sys. v. Medtronic Inc.*, 1996 WL 467293 (N.D. Cal. 1996) (both rejecting inequitable conduct claims). But one court has held that allegations of submarine patenting may state an *antitrust* claim against the patentee. *See Discovision Assocs. v. Disc Mfg. Inc.*, 42 U.S.P.Q.2d 1749 (D. Del. 1997).

In *Symbol Technologies v. Lemelson*, 277 F.3d 1361 (Fed. Cir. 2002), the Federal Circuit adopted a theory of "prosecution laches" under which excessive delay in prosecuting a patent could preclude its enforcement against an unsuspecting industry. *Symbol Technologies* involved notorious submarine patentee Jerome Lemelson, who had amassed well over 1,000 paper patents and had kept some applications pending for over 40 years. The Federal Circuit concluded that unreasonable and unexplained delay in prosecuting a patent could be grounds to bar enforcement of that patent. For subsequent opinions after remand, *see* 301 F. Supp. 2d 1147 (D. Nev. 2004), *aff'd*, 422 F.3d 1378 (Fed. Cir. 2005). Judge Newman, dissenting in the original opinion, argued that because Lemelson had followed the rules for filing continuation applications set out in the patent statute, he should not be barred from enforcing his long-pending patents. *See also In re Bogese*, 303 F.3d 1362 (Fed. Cir. 2002) (upholding examiner's final rejection of patent due to applicant's unreasonable delay). On the problem of successive continuations in patent applications, *see* Mark A. Lemley & Kimberly Moore, *Ending Abuse of Patent Continuations*, 84 B.U. L. REV. 63 (2004).

Does *Symbol Technologies* solve the problem of submarine patents by effectively discouraging strategic refiling? Would a bright-line rule serve this purpose better than a reasonableness standard? How can the courts distinguish between delay caused by the patentee and delay that is the fault of the PTO? *See Hyatt v. Hirshfeld*, 998 F.3d 1347 (Fed. Cir. 2021) (applying prosecution laches against inventor who filed 115,000 claims and kept them pending for 25 years because the inventor caused significant delay, even if the PTO was partially responsible for that delay); *Personalized Media Comm'ns., LLC v. Apple Inc.*, 57 F.4th 1346 (Fed. Cir. 2023) (applying doctrine to patentee who kept applications pending for nearly thirty years and expanded its draft claims from one to 20,000).

7. Laches, Statute of Limitations, and Equitable Estoppel

The common law defense of laches bars suit where a plaintiff unreasonably delays in pursuing legal recourse and such delay materially prejudices the defendant. This defense had long been recognized in patent law. *See A.C. Aukerman Co. v. R.L. Chaides Construction Co.*, 960 F.2d 1020 (Fed. Cir. 1992). In *SCA Hygiene Products Aktiebolag v. First Quality Baby Products, LLC*, 137 S.Ct. 954 (2017), the Supreme Court held that because of the Patent Act's statute of limitations (§286), the common law defense of laches cannot preclude a claim for damages incurred within the six-year limitations period. At the same time, the Supreme Court recognized the continued viability of equitable estoppel. Equitable estoppel arises where a patentee misleads an alleged infringer into believing that she would not be sued for using the patented technology. The defense may bar all relief on an infringement claim. *See A.C. Aukerman Co. v. R.L. Chaides Constr. Co.*, 960 F.2d 1020, 1041 (Fed. Cir. 1992) (en banc). Three elements must be established to prove equitable estoppel:

(1) The actor, who usually must have knowledge of the true facts, communicates something in a misleading way, either by words, conduct or silence.

(2) The other relies upon that communication.

(3) And the other would be harmed materially if the actor is later permitted to assert any claim inconsistent with his earlier conduct.

Id. (quoting D.B. DOBBS, HANDBOOK ON THE LAW OF REMEDIES §2.3, at 42 (1973)). In the patent infringement context, the "something" communicated is that the plaintiff will not bring an infringement claim against the accused infringer. Accordingly, the defendant must not only be aware of the patentee and/or his patent but also know or reasonably be able to infer that the patentee has been aware of the accused infringer's acts for some time. A plaintiff's inaction may give rise to the inference that the infringement claim was abandoned based on other facts regarding the parties' relationship or contracts with each other. Regarding the third factor, material harm may include a change of economic position or loss of evidence.

Even where the defendant proves all three elements of the estoppel defense, the court must consider "any other evidence and facts respecting the equities of the parties in exercising its discretion and deciding whether to allow the defense of equitable estoppel to bar the suit." *Id.* at 1043. The defense does not require an unreasonable delay in filing suit. However, such a delay may be evidence relevant to determining whether the plaintiff's conduct was misleading.

8. Patent Misuse

Patent misuse is a judicially created doctrine that bars patentees from enforcing their patent against infringers when they have "misused" the patent. It was first adopted by the Supreme Court in 1917.

Motion Picture Patents Co. v. Universal Film Manufacturing Co. et al.
Supreme Court of the United States
243 U.S. 502 (1917)

MR. JUSTICE CLARKE delivered the opinion of the court.

In this suit relief is sought against three defendant corporations as joint infringers of claim number seven of United States letters patent No. 707,934 granted to Woodville Latham, assignor, on August 26, 1902, for improvements in Projecting-Kinetoscopes. It is sufficient description of the patent to say that it covers a part of the mechanism used in motion picture exhibiting machines for feeding a film through the machine with a regular, uniform and accurate movement and so as not to expose the film to excessive strain or wear.

The defendants in a joint answer do not dispute the title of the plaintiff to the patent but they deny the validity of it, deny infringement, and claim an implied license to use the patented machine.

Evidence which is undisputed shows that the plaintiff on June 20, 1912, in a paper styled "License Agreement" granted to The Precision Machine Company a right and license to manufacture and sell machines embodying the inventions described and claimed in the patent in suit, and in other patents, throughout the United States, its territories and possessions. This agreement contains a covenant on the part of the grantee that every machine sold by it, except those for export, shall be sold "under the restriction and condition that such exhibiting or projecting machines shall be used solely for exhibiting or projecting motion pictures containing the inventions of reissued letters patent No. 12,192, leased by a licensee of the licensor while it owns said patents, and upon other terms to be fixed by the licensor and complied with by the user while the said machine is in use and while the licensor owns said patents (which other terms shall only be the payment of a royalty or rental to the licensor while in use)." . . .

The agreement further provides that the grantee shall not sell any machine at less than the plaintiff's list price, except to jobbers and others for purposes of resale and that it will require such jobbers and others to sell at not less than plaintiff's list price. . . .

It was admitted at the bar that 40,000 of the plaintiff's machines are now in use in this country and that the mechanism covered by the patent in suit is the only one with which motion picture films can be used successfully.

This state of facts presents two questions for decision: . . .

Second. May the assignee of a patent, which has licensed another to make and sell the machine covered by it, by a mere notice attached to such machine, limit the use of it by the purchaser or by the purchaser's lessee to terms not stated in the notice but which are to be fixed, after sale, by such assignee in its discretion? . . .

Since *Pennock v. Dialogue*, 2 Pet. 1, was decided in 1829 this court has consistently held that the primary purpose of our patent laws is not the creation of private fortunes for the owners of patents but is "to promote the progress of science and useful arts" (Constitution, Art. I, §8). . . .

Plainly, this language of the statute and the established rules to which we have referred restrict the patent granted on a machine, such as we have in this case, to the mechanism described in the patent as necessary to produce the described results. It is not concerned with and has nothing to do with the materials with which or on which the machine operates. The grant is of the exclusive right to use the mechanism to produce the result with any appropriate material, and the materials with which the machine is operated are no part of the patented machine or of the combination which produces the patented result. The difference is clear and vital between the exclusive right to use the machine which the law gives to the inventor and the right to use it exclusively with prescribed materials to which such a license notice as we have here seeks to restrict it. . . . Both in form and in substance the notice attempts a restriction upon the use of the supplies only and it cannot with any regard to propriety in the use of language be termed a restriction upon the use of the machine itself.

Whatever right the owner may have to control by restriction the materials to be used in operating the machine must be derived through the general law from the ownership of the property in the machine and it cannot be derived from or protected by the patent law. . . .

This construction gives to the inventor the exclusive use of just what his inventive genius has discovered. It is all that the statute provides shall be given to him and it is all that he should receive, for it is the fair as well as the statutory measure of his reward for his contribution to the public stock of knowledge. If his discovery is an important one his reward under such a construction of the law will be large, as experience has abundantly proved, and if it be unimportant he should not be permitted by legal devices to impose an unjust charge upon the public in return for the use of it. For more than a century this plain meaning of the statute was accepted as its technical meaning, and that it afforded ample incentive to exertion by inventive genius is proved by the fact that under it the greatest inventions of our time, teeming with inventions, were made. . . .

The construction of the patent law which justifies as valid the restriction of patented machines, by notice, to use with unpatented supplies necessary in the operation of them, but which are no part of them, is believed to have originated in *Heaton-Peninsular Button-Fastener Co. v. Eureka Specialty Co.*, 77 Fed. Rep. 288 (which has come to be widely referred to as the *Button-Fastener Case*), decided by the Circuit Court of Appeals of the Sixth Circuit in 1896. In this case the court, recognizing the pioneer character of the decision it was rendering, speaks of the "novel restrictions" which it is considering and says that it is called upon "to mark another boundary line around the patentee's monopoly, which will debar him from engrossing the market for an article not the subject of a patent," which it declined to do.

This decision proceeds upon the argument that, since the patentee may withhold his patent altogether from public use he must logically and necessarily be permitted to impose any conditions which he chooses upon any use which he may allow of it. The defect in this thinking springs from the substituting of inference and argument for the language of the statute and from failure to distinguish between the rights which are given to the inventor by the patent law and which he may assert against all the world through an infringement proceeding and rights which he may create for himself by private contract which, however, are subject to the rules of general as distinguished from those of the patent law. While it is true that under the statutes as they were (and now are) a patentee might withhold his patented machine from public use, yet if he consented to use it himself or through others, such use immediately fell within the terms of the statute and as we have seen he is thereby restricted to the use of the invention as it is described in the claims of his patent and not as it may be expanded by limitations as to materials and supplies necessary to the operation of it imposed by mere notice to the public.

. . .The perfect instrument of favoritism and oppression which such a system of doing business, if valid, would put into the control of the owner of such a patent should make courts astute, if need be, to defeat its operation. If these restrictions were sustained plainly the plaintiff might, for its own profit or that of its favorites, by the obviously simple expedient of varying its royalty charge, ruin anyone unfortunate enough to be dependent upon its confessedly important improvements for the doing of business.

. . . [F]ollowing the decision of the *Button-Fastener Case,* it was widely contended as obviously sound, that the right existed in the owner of a patent to fix a price at which the patented article might be sold and resold under penalty of patent infringement. But this court, when the question came before it in *Bauer v. O'Donnell*, 229 U.S. 1, . . . decided that the owner of a patent is not authorized by either the letter or the purpose of the law to fix, by notice, the price at which a patented article must be sold after the first sale of it, declaring that the right to vend is exhausted by a single, unconditional sale, the article sold being thereby carried outside the monopoly of the patent law and rendered free of every restriction which the vendor may attempt to put upon it. The statutory authority to grant the exclusive right to "use" a patented machine is not greater, indeed it is precisely the same, as the authority to grant the exclusive right to "vend," and, looking to that authority, for the reasons stated in this opinion we are convinced that the exclusive right granted in every patent must be limited to the invention described in the claims of the patent and that it is not competent for the owner of a patent by notice attached to its machine to, in effect, extend the scope of its patent monopoly by restricting the use of it to materials necessary in its operation but which are no part of the patented invention, or to send its machines forth into the channels of trade of the country subject to conditions as to use or royalty to be paid to be imposed thereafter at the discretion of such patent owner. The patent law furnishes no warrant for such a practice and the cost, inconvenience and annoyance to the public which the opposite conclusion would occasion forbid it.

It is argued as a merit of this system of sale under a license notice that the public is benefitted by the sale of the machine at what is practically its cost and by the fact that the owner of the patent makes its entire profit from the sale of the supplies with which it is operated. This fact, if it be a fact, instead of commending, is the clearest possible condemnation of, the practice adopted, for it proves that under color of its patent the owner intends to and does derive its profit, not from the invention on which the law gives it a monopoly but from the unpatented supplies with which it is used and which are wholly without the scope of the patent monopoly, thus in effect extending the power to the owner of the patent to fix the price to the public of the unpatented supplies as effectively as he may fix the price on the patented machine. . . .

Coming now to the terms of the notice attached to the machine sold to the Seventy-Second Street Amusement Company under the license of the plaintiff and to the first question as we have stated it.

This notice first provides that the machine, which was sold to and paid for by the Amusement Company may be used only with moving picture films containing the invention of reissued patent No. 12,192, so long as the plaintiff continues to own this reissued patent.

Such a restriction is invalid because such a film is obviously not any part of the invention of the patent in suit; because it is an attempt, without statutory warrant, to continue the patent monopoly in this particular character of film after it has expired, and because to enforce it would be to create a monopoly in the manufacture and use of moving picture films, wholly outside of the patent in suit and of the patent law as we have interpreted it. . . .

A restriction which would give to the plaintiff such a potential power for evil over an industry which must be recognized as an important element in the amusement life of the nation, under the conclusions we have stated in this opinion, is plainly void, because wholly without the scope and purpose of our patent laws and because, if sustained, it would be gravely injurious to that public interest, which we have seen is more a favorite of the law than is the promotion of private fortunes. . . .

Mr. Justice HOLMES, dissenting.

I suppose that a patentee has no less property in his patented machine than any other owner, and that in addition to keeping the machine to himself the patent gives him the further right to forbid the rest of the world from making others like it. In short, for whatever motive, he may keep his device wholly out of use. *Continental Paper Bag Co. v. Eastern Paper Bag Co.*, 210 U.S. 405, 422. So much being undisputed, I cannot understand why he may not keep it out of use unless the licensee, or, for the matter of that, the buyer, will use some unpatented thing in connection with it. Generally speaking the measure of a condition is the consequence of a breach, and if that consequence is one that the owner may impose unconditionally, he may impose it conditionally upon a certain event. *Ashley v. Ryan*, 153 U.S. 436, 443. *Lloyd v. Dollison*, 194 U.S. 445, 449. . . .

No doubt this principle might be limited or excluded in cases where the condition tends to bring about a state of things that there is a predominant public interest to prevent. But there is no predominant public interest to prevent a patented tea pot or film feeder from being kept from the public, because, as I have said, the patentee may keep them tied up at will while his patent lasts. Neither is there any such interest to prevent the purchase of the tea or films that is made the condition of the use of the machine. The supposed contravention of public interest sometimes is stated as an attempt to extend the patent law to unpatented articles, which of course it is not, and more accurately as a possible domination to be established by such means. But the domination is one only to the extent of the desire for the tea pot or film feeder, and if the owner prefers to keep the pot or the feeder unless you will buy his tea or films, I cannot see in allowing him the right to do so anything more than an ordinary incident of ownership, or at most, a consequence of the *Paper Bag Case,* on which, as it seems to me, this case ought to turn. *See Grant v. Raymond*, 6 Pet. 218, 242. . . .

COMMENTS AND QUESTIONS

1. The asserted justification for the patent misuse doctrine lies in the public policy underpinning the patent laws. It is no coincidence, however, that the doctrine first developed around 1900, shortly after the antitrust laws were passed. Patent misuse and

antitrust are strikingly similar in the sorts of conduct they prohibit. For example, in *Motion Picture,* the conduct at issue was (among other things) resale price maintenance, which is *per se* illegal under the antitrust laws. Patent misuse as originally conceived, however, was broader than the antitrust laws. Neither market power nor actual effect on competition need be proven to show patent misuse, as they would to prove an antitrust violation.

2. The Court continually expanded the scope of the patent misuse doctrine in the decades that followed *Motion Picture.* That expansion culminated in the cases of *Mercoid Corp. v. Mid-Continent Inv. Co.,* 320 U.S. 661 (1944) and *Carbice Corp. v. American Patents Dev. Corp.,* 283 U.S. 27 (1931). *Mercoid* held that it was patent misuse to tie a non-staple product to a patented product. A staple product has an existing market beyond use with the patent. A non-staple product has no substantial commercial use except in connection with the patent. *Carbice* held that a showing of patent misuse (which does not require proof of market power or impact) was prima facie evidence of an antitrust violation.

Both of these rules were short-lived. Congress amended the patent laws in 1952 by adding the following provisions:

35 U.S.C. §271. Infringement of Patent

. . .

(c) Whoever offers to sell or sells within the United States or imports into the United States a component of a patented machine, manufacture, combination or composition, or a material or apparatus for use in practicing a patented process, constituting a material part of the invention, knowing the same to be especially made or especially adapted for use in an infringement of such patent, and *not a staple article or commodity of commerce suitable for substantial noninfringing use,* shall be liable as a contributory infringer.

(d) No patent owner otherwise entitled to relief for infringement or contributory infringement of a patent shall be denied relief or deemed guilty of misuse or illegal extension of the patent right by reason of his having done one or more of the following:

(1) derived revenue from acts which if performed by another without his consent would constitute contributory infringement of the patent;

(2) licensed or authorized another to perform acts which if performed without his consent would constitute contributory infringement of the patent;

(3) sought to enforce his patent rights against infringement or contributory infringement;

(emphasis added). The Supreme Court explicated the importance of this statutory limit on the patent misuse doctrine in *Dawson Chem. Co. v. Rohm & Haas Co.,* 448 U.S. 176, 200–01 (1980):

Section 271(c) identifies the basic dividing line between contributory infringement and patent misuse. It adopts a restrictive definition of contributory infringement that distinguishes between staple and nonstaple articles of commerce. It also defines the class of nonstaple items narrowly. In essence, this provision places materials like the dry ice of the *Carbice* case outside the scope of the contributory infringement doctrine. As a result, it is no longer necessary to resort to the doctrine of patent misuse in order to deny patentees control over staple goods used in their inventions.

The limitations on contributory infringement written into §271(c) are counterbalanced by limitations on patent misuse in §271(d). Three species of conduct by patentees are expressly excluded from characterization as misuse. First, the patentee may "deriv[e] revenue" from acts that "would constitute contributory infringement" if "performed by another without his consent." This provision clearly signifies that a patentee may make and sell nonstaple goods used in connection with his invention. Second, the patentee may "licens[e] or authoriz[e] another to perform acts" which without such authorization would constitute contributory infringement. This provision's use in the disjunctive of the term "authoriz[e]" suggests that more than explicit licensing agreements is contemplated. Finally, the patentee may "enforce his patent rights against . . . contributory infringement." This provision plainly means that the patentee may bring suit without fear that his doing so will be regarded as an unlawful attempt to suppress competition. The statute explicitly states that a patentee may do "one or more" of these permitted acts, and it does not state that he must do any of them.

In our view, the provisions of §271(d) effectively confer upon the patentee, as a lawful adjunct of his patent rights, a limited power to exclude others from competition in nonstaple goods. A patentee may sell a nonstaple article himself while enjoining others from marketing that same good without his authorization. By doing so, he is able to eliminate competitors and thereby to control the market for that product. Moreover, his power to demand royalties from others for the privilege of selling the nonstaple item itself implies that the patentee may control the market for the nonstaple good; otherwise, his "right" to sell licenses for the marketing of the nonstaple good would be meaningless, since no one would be willing to pay him for a superfluous authorization.

3. Congress has shown continued dissatisfaction with the scope of the patent misuse doctrine. In 1988, it passed the Patent Misuse Reform Act, which added an additional limitation on the patent misuse doctrine.

§271(d) No patent owner otherwise entitled to relief for infringement or contributory infringement of a patent shall be denied relief or deemed guilty of misuse or illegal extension of the patent right by reason of his having done one or more of the following: . . . (4) refused to license or use any rights to the patent; or (5) conditioned the license of any rights to the patent or the sale of the patented product on the acquisition of a license to rights in another patent or purchase of a separate product, unless, in view of the circumstances, the patent owner has market power in the relevant market for the patent or patented product on which the license or sale is conditioned.

There is obviously a great deal of overlap between the policies of the patent misuse doctrine and those underlying the antitrust laws. If misuse claims are not tested by conventional antitrust principles, what principles apply?

4. *Differences in Patent Misuse and Conventional Antitrust Doctrines.* Patent misuse extends (or may extend) to a number of practices that do not fall within the antitrust laws at all. Here are the principal contexts:

- *Nonmetered Licenses.* Patentees are entitled to charge royalties on the patents they license to others. What form may those license payments take? Hazeltine Research, a consumer electronics patent consortium, charged a royalty based on a flat percentage of a purchaser's sales, regardless of how many patents the purchaser needed or how important they were to the end product. The Court upheld this arrangement in 1950 in *Automatic Radio Mfg. Co. v. Hazeltine Research, Inc.*, 339 U.S. 827, 833–34 (1950). But in *Zenith Radio Corp. v. Hazeltine Research, Inc.*, 395 U.S. 100 (1969), the Court struck down the royalty provision: "We also think patent misuse inheres in a patentee's insistence on a percentage-of-sales royalty, regardless of use, and his rejection of licensee proposals to pay only for actual use. Unquestionably, a licensee must pay if he uses the patent. . . . There is nothing in the right granted the patentee to keep others from using, selling, or manufacturing his invention which empowers him to insist on payment not only for use but also for producing products which do not employ his discoveries at all."

  What is wrong with nonmetered royalties? *See* ROBERT BORK, THE ANTITRUST PARADOX (1978); RICHARD A. POSNER, ANTITRUST LAW: AN ECONOMIC PERSPECTIVE (1976). If a licensee is only willing to pay a fixed amount for a license, should it matter how that amount is collected? Certainly the "percentage of sales" formula is not itself anticompetitive, and it may be far more convenient than more exact measures of how much a licensee uses a patent. Should the transaction costs of royalty accounting come into play in deciding whether a practice amounts to misuse? One problem with agreements requiring licensees to pay a percentage of all sales is that they also provide an effective source of information for policing a cartel.

- *Grantback Clauses.* As a condition to a license agreement, a patentee will sometimes require the licensee to grant him rights to any "improvement patents" the licensee is issued while using the licensed patent. Courts have been fairly lenient with respect to such "grantback clauses." *See Transparent-Wrap Mach. Corp. v. Stokes & Smith Co.*, 329 U.S. 637 (1947). But grantbacks may sometimes run afoul of the patent misuse doctrine. Grantbacks are common in agreements among independent patent holders to bundle their patents together for "one stop licensing"—an arrangement called a patent pool. Because pools constitute agreements amongst would-be competitors, they have traditionally been suspect under antitrust law, though a fair number have been approved. For a discussion of pool formation, and the proper way to determine whether they are useful or anticompetitive, *see* Robert P. Merges and Michael Mattioli, *Measuring the Costs and Benefits of Patent Pools*, 78 OHIO ST. L.J. 281 (2017).

- *Field-of-Use Restrictions.* Most patent licenses contain some sort of restriction on how the patent may be used by the licensee. Restrictions that attempt to control the price at which the licensee sells products made using the patented process or equipment are illegal per se under Sherman Act §1. Other restrictions, however, control not the price but the geographic or product market in which the licensee sells. These agreements have generally been upheld, unless they are part of a tying arrangement.

- *Post-Expiration Royalties.* The Supreme Court held in *Brulotte v. Thys Co.*, 379 U.S. 29, 32 (1964), that license agreements providing for payment of patent royalties beyond the expiration of a patent are per se patent unlawful. The Supreme Court reaffirmed that decision in *Kimble v. Marvel Entertainment, LLC*, 135 S.Ct. 2401 (2015).

H. REMEDIES

1. Injunctions

As we have seen, the rights conferred by a patent are different from those that grow out of real property rights. On the other hand, there are a number of similarities between patent law and real property law. With patents, as with most other legal entitlements that share the label "property," the traditional rule has been that the owner of the property right may obtain an injunction to prevent ongoing "trespasses." Indeed, in one important conceptual framework used to describe many types of legal entitlements, it is the injunctive remedy that distinguishes the property right from other entitlements. *See* Guido Calabresi & A. Douglas Melamed, *Property Rules, Liability Rules, and Inalienability: One View of the Cathedral*, 85 HARV. L. REV. 1089 (1972).

According to Calabresi and Melamed, the extent and nature of transaction costs in a particular case dictate whether one of the parties ought to have an absolute property right or simply the right to collect damages caused by the other party's encroachment. Within this framework, several factors point toward a property rule: few parties, difficult valuation problems, and otherwise low transaction costs. Other factors indicate that a liability rule might better effectuate the bargain: many parties (especially where any one has the power to "hold up" the whole enterprise), likelihood of strategic bargaining, and otherwise high transaction costs.

The holder of a legal entitlement other than a property right can obtain compensation when the right is violated but cannot prevent violations. Because those who violate such a right must pay damages, this form of entitlement is referred to as a *liability rule.* Classic examples of liability rule entitlements (which we will call "liability rights") are the rights of tort victims, parties facing a breach of an ordinary commercial contract, and landowners whose parcels are taken by the government for public use pursuant to eminent domain.

Comparing patent rights to contract rights illuminates the challenges of compensating patentees for infringement. Take, for example, a contract for delivery of 100 bushels of wheat at $5.00 per bushel. If the seller breaches, contract law provides the buyer the difference between the contract price and the market price at the time of breach. Since wheat is a standard commodity, the market price can be easily determined based on commodity exchanges at the time.

By contrast, patent infringement poses a valuation challenge: Patent rights are unique. A patent might not be co-extensive with a particular product (e.g., a smartphone comprises many patented technologies). Infringing activity can affect the trajectory of the patentee's business over the remaining life of the patent.

The effect of injunctive remedies goes beyond allowing the rightholder to prevent activities of the infringer. To the extent that a rightholder will consider negotiating a license with the infringer, the threat of an injunction will heavily influence the *terms* of the license. Specifically, it allows the rightholder to set her own price for the injury. In intellectual property cases, it allows the rightholder, and not a court, to set the terms of a license agreement settling the infringement litigation. This is assumed to be the efficient result, as a court called on to set the terms of the exchange would have a difficult time doing so quickly and cheaply given the specialized nature of the assets and the varied and complex business environments in which they are deployed. Hence the parties are left to make their own deal.

On the other hand, a property right is a potent weapon. Sometimes this causes problems. Especially where courts may have a difficult time determining how much of a composite product's value is attributable to a (perhaps small) patented component, the availability of a property right may lead to what economists call a "holdup problem"—an entitlement holder who uses his rights strategically to extract more than the fair market value of his or her asset. *See* Mark A. Lemley & Philip J. Weiser, *Should Property or Liability Rules Govern Information?*, 85 TEX. L. REV. 783 (2007). A classic example is the owner of the last of many parcels being assembled for a large real estate project. Should injunctions be readily available when holdup is a potential problem? Calabresi and Melamed suggest not; their framework calls for a liability rule, not a property rule, in that situation. For a general discussion of the desirability of adjusting property rights when economic conditions give rightholders "undue leverage" (i.e., make those rights more valuable than their intrinsic worth), *see* ROBERT P. MERGES, JUSTIFYING INTELLECTUAL PROPERTY ch. 6 (2011).

The Supreme Court confronted this issue in 2006. But it did not limit its decision to holdup situations.

eBay, Inc. v. MercExchange, LLC
Supreme Court of the United States
547 U.S. 388 (2006)

JUSTICE THOMAS delivered the opinion of the Court.

Ordinarily, a federal court considering whether to award permanent injunctive relief to a prevailing plaintiff applies the four-factor test historically employed by courts of equity. Petitioner[] eBay Inc. argue[s] that this traditional test applies to disputes arising under the Patent Act. We agree and, accordingly, vacate the judgment of the Court of Appeals.

I

Petitioner eBay operates a popular Internet Web site that allows private sellers to list goods they wish to sell, either through an auction or at a fixed price. . . . Respondent MercExchange, L.L.C., holds a number of patents, including a business method patent for an electronic market designed to facilitate the sale of goods between private individuals by establishing a central authority to promote trust among participants. *See* U.S. Patent No. 5,845,265. MercExchange sought to license its patent to eBay . . . , as it had previously done with other companies, but the parties failed to reach an agreement. MercExchange subsequently filed a patent infringement suit against eBay . . . A jury found that MercExchange's patent was valid, that eBay . . . had infringed that patent, and that an award of damages was appropriate.

Following the jury verdict, the District Court denied MercExchange's motion for permanent injunctive relief. The Court of Appeals for the Federal Circuit reversed, applying its "general rule that courts will issue permanent injunctions against patent infringement absent exceptional circumstances." We granted certiorari to determine the appropriateness of this general rule.

II

According to well-established principles of equity, a plaintiff seeking a permanent injunction must satisfy a four-factor test before a court may grant such relief. A plaintiff must demonstrate: (1) that it has suffered an irreparable injury; (2) that remedies available at law, such as monetary damages, are inadequate to compensate for that injury; (3) that, considering the balance of hardships between the plaintiff and defendant, a remedy in equity is warranted; and (4) that the public interest would not be disserved by a permanent injunction. *See, e.g., Weinberger v. Romero-Barcelo*, 456 U.S. 305, 311–313 (1982); *Amoco Production Co. v. Gambell*, 480 U.S. 531, 542, (1987). The decision to grant or deny permanent injunctive relief is an act of equitable discretion by the district court, reviewable on appeal for abuse of discretion. *See, e.g., Romero-Barcelo*, 456 U.S., at 320.

These familiar principles apply with equal force to disputes arising under the Patent Act. As this Court has long recognized, "a major departure from the long tradition of equity practice should not be lightly implied." *Ibid.* Nothing in the Patent Act indicates that Congress intended such a departure. To the contrary, the Patent Act expressly provides that injunctions "may" issue "in accordance with the principles of equity." 35 U.S.C. §283.

To be sure, the Patent Act also declares that "patents shall have the attributes of personal property," §261, including "the right to exclude others from making, using, offering for sale, or selling the invention," §154(a)(1). According to the Court of Appeals, this statutory right to exclude alone justifies its general rule in favor of permanent injunctive relief. But the creation of a right is distinct from the provision of remedies for violations of that right. Indeed, the Patent Act itself indicates that patents shall have the attributes of personal property "[s]ubject to the provisions of this title," 35 U.S.C. §261, including, presumably, the provision that injunctive relief "may" issue only "in accordance with the principles of equity," §283.

This approach is consistent with our treatment of injunctions under the Copyright Act. Like a patent owner, a copyright holder possesses "the right to exclude others from using his property." *Fox Film Corp. v. Doyal*, 286 U.S. 123, 127 (1932); *see also id.*, at 127–128, 52 S.Ct. 546 ("A copyright, like a patent, is at once the equivalent given by the public for benefits bestowed by the genius and meditations and skill of individuals, and the incentive to further efforts for the same important objects" (internal quotation marks omitted)). Like the Patent Act, the Copyright Act provides that courts "may" grant injunctive relief "on such terms as it may deem reasonable to prevent or restrain infringement of a copyright." 17 U.S.C. §502(a). And as in our decision today, this Court has consistently rejected invitations to replace traditional equitable considerations with a rule that an injunction automatically follows a determination that a copyright has been infringed. *See, e.g., New York Times Co. v. Tasini*, 533 U.S. 483, 505 (2001) (citing *Campbell v. Acuff-Rose Music, Inc.*, 510 U.S. 569, 578 n. 10 (1994)); *Dun v. Lumbermen's Credit Ass'n*, 209 U.S. 20, 23–24 (1908).

Neither the District Court nor the Court of Appeals below fairly applied these traditional equitable principles in deciding respondent's motion for a permanent injunction. Although the District Court recited the traditional four-factor test, it appeared to adopt certain expansive principles suggesting that injunctive relief could not issue in a broad swath of cases. Most notably, it concluded that a "plaintiff's willingness to license its patents" and "its lack of commercial activity in practicing the patents" would be sufficient to establish that the patent holder would not suffer irreparable harm if an injunction did not issue. But traditional equitable principles do not permit such broad classifications. For example, some patent holders, such as university researchers or self-made inventors, might reasonably prefer to license their patents, rather than undertake efforts to secure the financing necessary to bring their works to market themselves. Such patent holders may be able to satisfy the traditional four-factor test, and we see no basis for categorically denying them the opportunity to do so. To the extent that the District Court adopted such a categorical rule, then, its analysis cannot be squared with the principles of equity adopted by Congress. The court's categorical rule is also in tension with *Continental Paper Bag Co. v. Eastern Paper Bag Co.*, 210 U.S. 405, 422–430 (1908), which rejected the contention that a court of equity has no jurisdiction to grant injunctive relief to a patent holder who has unreasonably declined to use the patent.

In reversing the District Court, the Court of Appeals departed in the opposite direction from the four-factor test. The court articulated a "general rule," unique to patent disputes, "that a permanent injunction will issue once infringement and validity have been adjudged." The court further indicated that injunctions should be denied only in the "unusual" case, under "exceptional circumstances" and "'in rare instances . . . to protect the public interest.'" Just as the District Court erred in its categorical denial of injunctive relief, the Court of Appeals erred in its categorical grant of such relief. *Cf. Roche Products v. Bolar Pharmaceutical Co.*, 733 F.2d 858, 865 (C.A. Fed. 1984) (recognizing the "considerable discretion" district courts have "in determining whether the facts of a situation require it to issue an injunction").

Because we conclude that neither court below correctly applied the traditional four-factor framework that governs the award of injunctive relief, we vacate the judgment of the Court of Appeals, so that the District Court may apply that framework in the first instance. In doing so, we take no position on whether permanent injunctive relief should or should not issue in this particular case, or indeed in any number of other disputes arising under the Patent Act. We hold only that the decision whether to grant or deny injunctive relief rests within the equitable discretion of the district courts, and that such discretion must be exercised consistent with traditional principles of equity, in patent disputes no less than in other cases governed by such standards.

Accordingly, we vacate the judgment of the Court of Appeals, and remand for further proceedings consistent with this opinion.

It is so ordered.

CHIEF JUSTICE ROBERTS, with whom JUSTICE SCALIA and JUSTICE GINSBURG join, concurring.

I agree with the Court's holding that "the decision whether to grant or deny injunctive relief rests within the equitable discretion of the district courts, and that such discretion must be exercised consistent with traditional principles of equity, in patent disputes no less than in other cases governed by such standards," and I join the opinion of the Court. That opinion rightly rests on the proposition that "a major departure from the long tradition of equity practice should not be lightly implied." *Weinberger v. Romero-Barcelo*, 456 U.S. 305, 320 (1982).

From at least the early 19th century, courts have granted injunctive relief upon a finding of infringement in the vast majority of patent cases. This "long tradition of equity practice" is not surprising, given the difficulty of protecting a right to exclude through monetary remedies that allow an infringer to use an invention against the patentee's wishes—a difficulty that often implicates the first two factors of the traditional four-factor test. This historical practice, as the Court holds, does not entitle a patentee to a permanent injunction or justify a general rule that such injunctions should issue. The Federal Circuit itself so recognized in *Roche Products, Inc. v. Bolar Pharmaceutical Co.*, 733 F.2d 858, 865–867 (1984). At the same time, there is a difference between exercising equitable discretion pursuant to the established four-factor test and writing on an entirely clean slate. "Discretion is not whim, and limiting discretion according to legal standards helps promote the basic principle of justice that like cases should be decided alike." *Martin v. Franklin Capital Corp.*, 546 U.S. 132, 139 (2005). When it comes to discerning and applying those standards, in this area as others, "a page of history is worth a volume of logic." *New York Trust Co. v. Eisner*, 256 U.S. 345, 349 (1921) (opinion for the Court by Holmes, J.).

JUSTICE KENNEDY, with whom JUSTICE STEVENS, JUSTICE SOUTER, and JUSTICE BREYER join, concurring.

The Court is correct, in my view, to hold that courts should apply the well-established, four-factor test—without resort to categorical rules—in deciding whether to grant injunctive relief in patent cases. The Chief Justice is also correct that history may be instructive in applying this test. (concurring opinion). The traditional practice of issuing injunctions against patent infringers, however, does not seem to rest on "the difficulty of protecting a right to exclude through monetary remedies that allow an infringer to use an invention against the patentee's wishes." (Roberts, C.J., concurring). Both the terms of the Patent Act and the traditional view of injunctive relief accept that the existence of a right to exclude does not dictate the remedy for a violation of that right. To the extent earlier cases establish a pattern of granting an injunction against patent infringers almost as a matter of course, this pattern simply illustrates the result of the four-factor test in the contexts then prevalent. The lesson of the historical practice, therefore, is most helpful and instructive when the circumstances of a case bear substantial parallels to litigation the courts have confronted before.

In cases now arising trial courts should bear in mind that in many instances the nature of the patent being enforced and the economic function of the patent holder present considerations quite unlike earlier cases. An industry has developed in which firms use patents not as a basis for producing and selling goods but, instead, primarily for obtaining licensing fees. *See* FTC, TO PROMOTE INNOVATION: THE PROPER BALANCE OF COMPETITION AND PATENT LAW AND POLICY, ch. 3, pp. 38–39 (Oct. 2003). For these firms, an injunction, and the potentially serious sanctions arising from its violation, can be employed as a bargaining tool to charge exorbitant fees to companies that seek to buy licenses to practice the patent. *See ibid.* When the patented invention is but a small component of the product the companies seek to produce and the threat of an injunction is employed simply for undue leverage in negotiations, legal damages may well be sufficient to compensate for the infringement and an injunction may not serve the public interest. In addition injunctive relief may have different consequences for the burgeoning number of patents over business methods, which were not of much economic and legal significance in earlier times. The potential vagueness and suspect validity of some of these patents may affect the calculus under the four-factor test.

The equitable discretion over injunctions, granted by the Patent Act, is well suited to allow courts to adapt to the rapid technological and legal developments in the patent system. For these reasons it should be recognized that district courts must determine whether past practice fits the circumstances of the cases before them. With these observations, I join the opinion of the Court.

COMMENTS AND QUESTIONS

1. This Supreme Court ruling has had an immediate and profound impact on patent litigation. *See* Christopher B. Seaman, *Permanent Injunctions in Patent Litigation After eBay: An Empirical Study*, 101 IOWA L. REV. 1949 (2016) (noting that non-practicing entities are much less likely to obtain injunctions after *eBay*.)

2. Leading remedies scholars question whether the Supreme Court's *eBay* test comports with long-standing remedial standards for *permanent* injunctions. Their research indicates that the Supreme Court aligns more closely with the test for *preliminary* injunctions, a judgment which is rendered before the violation has been conclusively established. *See* Mark P. Gergen, John M. Golden & Henry E. Smith, *The Supreme Court's Accidental Revolution? The Test for Permanent Injunctions*, 112 COLUM. L. REV. 203, 208 (2012). While there was no explicit four-factor test for permanent injunctions, each of the factors the Court relies on is a factor courts have regularly applied in deciding whether to grant injunctions.

3. Should the availability of injunctions depend on whether the patentee manufactures the patented product or is simply in the business of licensing (and litigating) patents? What if the plaintiff has as its business model the acquisition of third-party patents, strictly with an eye toward maximizing patent-related revenue by suing as many actual manufacturers as possible? As patents have become more valuable, these and related issues are finding their way into legal arguments regarding the desirability of injunctions and other remedies. Most lower court decisions have split along these lines, granting injunctive relief to patentees who participate in the market but denying injunctive relief to non-practicing entities because they cannot satisfy *eBay*'s four-factor test.

4. *Ongoing Royalties*. In *Paice LLC v. Toyota Motor Corp.*, 609 F. Supp. 2d 620 (E.D. Tex. 2009), the court found that Toyota's hybrid automobiles infringed Paice's patent on a microprocessor and controllable torque transfer unit that accepts input from both an internal combustion engine and an electric motor. The court determined that a permanent injunction is not warranted and awarded a running royalty of $98 per vehicle, nearly four times the award of past damages. Does it make sense to deny an injunction but at the same time punish the defendant by charging a higher royalty rate going forward? *See* Mark A. Lemley, *The Ongoing Confusion Over Ongoing Royalties*, 76 MO. L. REV. (2011) (no).

2. Damages

Section 284 of the Patent Act provides:

> Upon finding for the claimant the court shall award the claimant damages adequate to compensate for the infringement but in no event less than a reasonable royalty for the use made of the invention by the infringer, together with interest and costs as fixed by the court.

When the damages are not found by a jury, the court shall assess them. In either event the court may increase the damages up to three times the amount found or assessed. Increased damages under this paragraph shall not apply to provisional rights under section 154(d) of this title.

The court may receive expert testimony as an aid to the determination of damages or of what royalty would be reasonable under the circumstances.

Section 286 establishes a six-year statute of limitations, barring patentees from recovering damages for any infringing acts committed more than six years prior to the filing of the complaint or counterclaim for infringement.

Courts apply two principal approaches for measuring damages "adequate to compensate" for a defendant's infringement: lost profits and reasonable royalties.

i.   *Lost Profits*

Courts have struggled with the problem of setting appropriate measures of damages for past infringement. In *Panduit Corp. v. Stahlin Bros. Fibre Works, Inc.*, 575 F.2d 1152, 1158 n.5 (6th Cir. 1978), the court adopted an oft-used four-factor test for determining lost profits:

To obtain as damages the profits on sales he would have made absent the infringement, i.e., the sales made by the infringer, a patent owner must prove:

(1) demand for the patented product,

(2) absence of acceptable noninfringing substitutes,

(3) his manufacturing and marketing capability to exploit the demand, and

(4) the amount of the profit he would have made.

Non-practicing entities cannot satisfy this test. Thus, they are limited to a reasonable royalty, which we discuss below.

Price Erosion. The per-unit profit that the patentee would have earned can be difficult to estimate because the infringer's activity has created competition that would not have otherwise occurred in the market. Consequently, the patentee may also recover additional lost profits damages under a price erosion theory. *See Crystal Semiconductor Corp. v. TriTech Microelectronics Int'l, Inc.*, 246 F.3d 1336, 1357 (Fed. Cir. 2001). To recover for price erosion damages, a patentee is required to prove that "but for" the infringement, she would have sold her patented invention at a higher price. Furthermore, the patentee must prove the number of products she would have sold at this price. Accordingly, "the patentee's price erosion theory must account for the nature, or definition, of the market, similarities between any benchmark market and the market in which price erosion is alleged, and the effect of the hypothetically increased price on the likely number of sales at that price in that market."

What assumption does this theory make about the demand for the patentee's product? Wouldn't you expect the number of units sold to decline as the price increases?

Market-Share Rule. When more than two sellers share a market and at least one seller is a non-infringing competitor of the patentee, it would appear that one element in the *Panduit* test is missing: the absence of noninfringing substitutes. Courts can, however, inquire into what would have happened if the infringer had not been in the market. Under this theory, the court is asked to assume that the patentee's market share relative to the noninfringer would have remained the same in the absence of the infringer. Consequently, it is assumed that the patentee would have made the same percentage of the infringer's sales as the patentee made in the overall market. *See, e.g.,* *State Indus. v. Mor-Flo, Inc.*, 883 F.2d 1573 (Fed. Cir. 1988); Roy J. Epstein, *The Market Share Rule with Price Erosion: Patent Infringement Lost Profits Damages After Crystal*, 31 AIPLA Q.J. 1 (2003).

Lost Sales of Unpatented Components or Products. A patentee may also recover for lost profits on unpatented components sold with a patented product, so-called "convoyed sales." *See Rite-Hite Corp. v. Kelley Co.*, 56 F.3d 1538, 1546 (Fed. Cir. 1995) (en banc) ("[i]f a particular injury was or should have been reasonably foreseeable by an infringing competitor in the relevant market, broadly defined, that injury is generally compensable absent a persuasive reason to the contrary.")

COMMENTS AND QUESTIONS

1. The Federal Circuit decision in *Grain Processing Corp. v. American Maize Products Co.*, 185 F.3d 1341 (Fed. Cir. 1999) elucidates the requirement that there be no acceptable noninfringing substitutes. Plaintiff Grain Processing was the holder of a patent on a form of maltodextrin, a food additive used in frostings, syrups, drinks, cereals, and frozen foods. After finding infringement, Judge Frank Easterbrook of the Seventh Circuit (sitting by designation on the district court) denied the patentee lost profits damages. Judge Easterbrook found that although the infringer did not in fact sell a noninfringing alternative during the damages period, it easily *could have.* The Federal Circuit affirmed, opening the way for accused infringers to argue more freely about hypothetical scenarios that might have played out if they had known they were infringing.

> In summary, this court requires reliable economic proof of the market that establishes an accurate context to project the likely results "but for" the infringement. The availability of substitutes invariably will influence the market forces defining this "but for" marketplace, as it did in this case. Moreover, a substitute need not be openly on sale to exert this influence. Thus, with proper economic proof of availability, as American Maize provided the district court in this case, an acceptable substitute not on the market during the infringement may nonetheless become part of the lost profits calculus and therefore limit or preclude those damages.

185 F.3d at 1356.

It should be noted that the facts in *Grain Processing* made it particularly easy to make a persuasive case that the noninfringing substitute would very likely have been employed by the infringer. The technology was well understood—so much so that the infringer switched to a noninfringing version of the product within two weeks of being ordered to do so by the district court; buyers and consumers of maltodextrin did not value the features of the claimed product in a way that set it apart from other versions, making other versions good substitutes; and the accused infringer had especially convincing proof that it could easily have ramped up production of the noninfringing alternative.

The Federal Circuit reaffirmed and applied *Grain Processing* in *Crystal Semiconductor Corp. v. Tritech Microelectronics Int'l, Inc.*, 246 F.3d 1336, 1358–60 (Fed. Cir. 2001) (affirming trial court findings and emphasizing need to analyze market reaction to patented technology). But the court also made clear in a subsequent case that it was serious about the need for the infringer to prove that the noninfringing substitute was *readily* available. *See Micro Chemical, Inc. v. Lextron, Inc.*, 318 F.3d 1119, 1123 (Fed. Cir. 2003) (reversing a trial court finding of ready availability under *Grain Processing*); John W. Schlicher, *Measuring Patent Damages by the Market Value of Inventions—The* Grain Processing, Rite-Hite, *and* Aro *Rules*, 82 J. PAT. & TRADEMARK OFF. SOC'Y 503 (2000).

2. *Lost Foreign Profits*. After the Supreme Court held that there could be no liability for shipping the components of a patented device outside of the United States for purposes of assembly abroad, see *Deepsouth Packing Co. v. Laitram Corp.*, 406 U.S. 518 (1972), Congress added §271(f) to extend liability for supplying unassembled "components" from the United States for "combination" outside the United States where the same combination would infringe a patent if it occurred within the United States. The two prongs of infringement under §271(f) are similar to active inducement and contributory infringement found in §§271(b), (c). In *WesternGeco LLC v. ION Geophysical Corp.*, 138 S.Ct. 2129 (2018), the Supreme Court held that the presumption that federal statutes "apply only within the territorial jurisdiction of the United States" did not bar award of lost *foreign* profits where the defendant (ION Geophysical) manufactured components in the United States that it shipped to customers abroad for assembly of an infringing system (an undersea surveying device). Justice Thomas reasoned that because §284 provides "damages adequate to compensate for the infringement," the focus of this statute is "the infringement." The Court viewed the supplying of the components, which occurred in the United States, as the infringement even though the profits from that domestic act were earned abroad. The Court left open the possibility that the exterritorial reach of the statute could be limited by proximate cause.

ii. *Reasonable Royalty*

a. *The Basic Inquiry*

Section 284 provides that the patent owner is entitled to "damages adequate to compensate for the infringement, but in no event less than a reasonable royalty for the use made of the invention by the infringer." Thus, when lost profits cannot be proved, the patent owner is entitled to a reasonable royalty. A reasonable royalty is an amount "which a person, desiring to manufacture and sell a patented article, as a business proposition, would be willing to pay as a royalty and yet be able to make and sell the patented article, in the market, at a reasonable profit." *Goodyear Tire and Rubber Co. v. Overman Cushion Tire Co.*, 95 F.2d 978 at 984 (6th Cir. 1937) (citing *Rockwood v.*

General Fire Extinguisher Co., 37 F.2d 62 at 66 (2d Cir. 1930)), *appeal dismissed,* 306 U.S. 665 (1938).

"A "reasonable royalty" contemplates a hypothetical negotiation between the patentee and the infringer at a time before the infringement began. [T]his analysis necessarily involves some approximation of the market as it would have hypothetically developed absent infringement. This analysis, in turn, requires sound economic and factual predicates." *Riles v. Shell Exploration and Production Co.*, 298 F.3d 1302, 1311 (Fed. Cir. 2002). "In a normal negotiation, the potential licensee has three basic choices: forgo all use of the invention; pay an agreed royalty; infringe the patent and risk litigation." *Fromson v. Western Litho Plate and Supply Co.*, 853 F.2d 1568, 1576 (Fed. Cir. 1988). In a hypothetical negotiation, however, the factfinder "presumes that the licensee has made the second choice, when in fact it made the third." *Id.* Commentators—and some courts—have noted that this standard would disadvantage a patentee if a court were "to pretend that the infringement never happened." *TWM Mfg. Co. v. Dura Corp.*, 789 F.2d 895, 900 (Fed. Cir. 1986). As a consequence, courts keep in mind that the hypothetical negotiation approach "must be flexibly applied as a device in the aid of justice." *Id.* (internal quotations omitted).

In practice, however, the choice is only rarely between infringing and taking a license. Most patent defendants are not copiers but independent inventors. Had they been aware of the patent when they developed their product, these independent inventors might have had another choice: pick an alternative way of implementing the invention that is not subject to the patent. For that reason, the reasonable royalty should logically be limited by the value of the patent over the available noninfringing alternatives, just as those alternatives constrain the ability to recover lost profits. *See Grain Processing Corp. v. American Maize-Prods. Co.*, 185 F.3d 1341 (Fed. Cir. 1999).

This means that courts walk a fine line when awarding reasonable royalties: between undercompensating the patentee by resort to a purely fictional negotiation which takes place outside the shadow of any actual infringement and awarding damages far in excess of industry standards, the negotiating positions of the parties, and other real world constraints. In addition, although the cases sometimes hint at a quasi-punitive component in a reasonable royalty calculation, the statute provides for an explicit "multiplier" *only* in the case of willful infringement.

A number of commentators and industry representatives have argued that the problem is not undercompensation, but overcompensation, particularly where a patentee owns a patent on a small component but can measure damages based on the sale of a large, multi-component product. *See* Mark A. Lemley & Carl Shapiro, *Patent Holdup and Royalty Stacking*, 85 TEX. L. REV. 1991 (2007). Indeed, if the right measure of royalty is based on the value of the patented invention over the available noninfringing alternatives, the true value of the invention might be zero in many cases. *See* Daniel L. Brean, *Ending Unreasonable Royalties: Why Nominal Damages are Adequate to Compensate Patent Assertion Entities for Infringement*, 39 VT. L. REV. 867 (2015). Nevertheless, courts almost always award some royalty, *Apple Corp. v. Motorola, Inc.*, 757 F.3d 1286 (Fed. Cir. 2014), and they have been unsympathetic to infringers who argue that the patentee's proposed royalty would have meant that the infringer would have lost money on sales of the product. *See, e.g., Golight, Inc. v. Wal-Mart Stores, Inc.*, 355 F.3d 1327, 1338 (Fed. Cir. 2004); *Monsanto Co. v. Ralph*, 382 F.3d 1374, 1384 (Fed. Cir. 2004) ("[T]he law does not require that an infringer be permitted to make a profit. And, where, as here, a patentee is unwilling to grant an unlimited license, the hypothetical negotiation process has its limits.").

Several problems have emerged in determining a reasonably royalty. The principal methodology relies on a broad and open-ended set of factors. Beyond these factors, courts have struggled with apportioning value within patented products. A third issue relates to valuation of patents that are part of a pool of patents governed by fair, reasonable, and non-discriminatory (FRAND) licensing agreements. We discuss each in the sections that follow.

b.   *The Georgia-Pacific Factors*

Setting reasonable royalties entails a detailed review of the technology at issue, the bargaining positions of the parties, and other factors that might have been relevant if the hypothetical negotiation had actually taken place. The district court in *Georgia-Pacific v. U.S. Plywood Corp.*, 318 F. Supp. 1116, 1120 (S.D.N.Y. 1970), enumerated a broad, nonexclusive list of factors that has been widely followed:

1. The royalties received by the patentee for the licensing of the patent in suit, proving or tending to prove an established royalty.

2. The rates paid by the licensee for the use of other patents comparable to the patent in suit.

3. The nature and scope of the license, as exclusive or non-exclusive; or as restricted or non-restricted in terms of territory or with respect to whom the manufactured product may be sold.

4. The licensor's established policy and marketing program to maintain his patent monopoly by not licensing others to use the invention or by granting licenses under special conditions designed to preserve that monopoly.

5. The commercial relationship between the licensor and licensee, such as, whether they are competitors in the same territory in the same line of business; or whether they are inventor and promoter.

6. The effect of selling the patented specialty in promoting sales of other products of the licensee; that existing value of the invention to the licensor as a generator of sales of his non-patented items; and the extent of such derivative or convoyed sales.

7. The duration of the patent and the term of the license.

8. The established profitability of the product made under the patent, its commercial success, and its current popularity.

9. The utility and advantages of the patent property over the old modes or devices, if any, that had been used for working out similar results.

10. The nature of the patented invention, the character of the commercial embodiment of it as owned and produced by the licensor, and the benefits to those who have used the invention.

11. The extent to which the infringer has made use of the invention, and any evidence probative of the value of that use.

12. The portion of the profit or of the selling price that may be customary in the particular business or in comparable businesses to allow for the use of the invention or analogous inventions.

13. The portion of the realizable profit that should be credited to the invention as distinguished from non-patented elements, the manufacturing process, business risks, or significant features or improvements added by the infringer.

14. The opinion testimony of qualified experts.

15. The amount that a licensor (such as the patentee) and a licensee (such as the infringer) would have agreed upon (at the time the infringement began) if both had been reasonably and voluntarily trying to reach an agreement; that is, the amount which a prudent licensee—who desired, as a business proposition, to obtain a license to manufacture and sell a particular article embodying the patented invention—would have been willing to pay as a royalty and yet be able to make a reasonable profit and which amount would have been acceptable by a prudent patentee who was willing to grant a license.

Id. at 1120.

COMMENTS AND QUESTIONS

1. *Circularity of Reasonable Royalty?* While it seems to make sense to base a royalty on what other parties were negotiating for similar rights, those license negotiations themselves will be driven by what the parties think will happen if they don't come to terms and the dispute goes to court, not what parties would have agreed to under the assumption that the patent was valid and infringed. *See* Jonathan Masur, *The Use and Misuse of Patent Licenses*, 110 Nw. U. L. Rev. 1115 (2015).

2. *Reliability of Expert Testimony.* The *Daubert* test for reliability of scientific expert testimony applies to economic expert evidence on damages. *See Lucent Techs., Inc. v. Gateway, Inc.*, 580 F.3d 1301 (Fed. Cir. 2009). The *Lucent* case involved a patent on a minor component (the pop-up calendar, or "date picker" function) of a complex software product (Microsoft's Outlook email scheduling and calendaring program). The jury had awarded over $500 million in damages, in part on the basis of licensing agreements from the computer industry that bore little relationship to the hypothetical license negotiation that served as the foundation of the damages award in the case. The Federal Circuit reversed the trial court's denial of a post-trial motion to reject the jury verdict. Henceforth, the court instructed, judges must actively supervise the introduction of "comparable licensing" evidence so that it is truly comparable, and therefore capable of grounding a truly reasonable royalty finding.

While estimating a reasonable royalty is not an "exact science" in that there may be more than one reliable method, *Apple Inc. v. Motorola, Inc.*, 757 F.3d 1286, 1315 (Fed. Cir. 2014), the Federal Circuit has enhanced the judge's gatekeeping role to prevent excessive awards. Recent decisions have sought to align the royalty base to the patented component of a product, exclude unreliable damage theories, scrutinize the admissibility of various forms of evidence, and provide limiting jury instructions.

Courts seek to ensure that the royalty rate is based on sound economic methodology and grounded in reliable and pertinent evidence. Using the construct of the hypothetical negotiation between a willing licensor and licensee, experts use the *Georgia-Pacific* factors to determine a license rate that would have been agreed upon just before the infringement began (and based on the assumption that the patent was valid, infringed, and enforceable). The proof of an appropriate royalty rate using this method allows for necessary "approximation and uncertainty." *Aqua Shield v. Inter Pool Cover Team*, 774 F.3d 766, 771 (Fed. Cir. 2014). Nevertheless, it must be supported by substantial evidence, which usually will be based on the application of the relevant subset of the *Georgia-Pacific* factors. *See WhitServe, LLC, v. Computer Packages, Inc.*, 694 F.3d 10, 31–32 (Fed. Cir. 2012).

The open-ended *Georgia-Pacific* framework affords economic experts substantial leeway in determining a royalty rate. The most pertinent evidence usually comprises past licenses to the infringing or comparable technology, the value of comparable features in the marketplace, an estimate of the value of the benefit provided by the infringed features by comparison to non-infringing alternatives, or an estimate of the cost to design around the patent. *See, e.g., Ericsson*, 773 F.3d at 1227 (citing *Monsanto Co. v. McFarling*, 488 F.3d 973, 978 (Fed. Cir. 2007) ("An established royalty is usually the best measure of a 'reasonable' royalty for a given use of an invention . . . ."). However, license agreements that are unrelated to the claimed invention cannot form the basis of a reasonable royalty calculation. *See, e.g., Lucent*, 580 F.3d at 1327; *see also ResQNet*, 594 F.3d at 869 ("Any evidence unrelated to the claimed invention does not support compensation for infringement but punishes beyond the reach of the statute."). The Federal Circuit has observed that licenses arising out of litigation might be reliable in certain circumstances, but has cautioned that "litigation itself can skew the results of the hypothetical negotiation." *ResQNet*, 594 F.3d at 872.

In many cases, the technology either has not been previously licensed or the licenses cover a broader range of technologies than the patented invention and/or multiple product or product components. As an alternative or shortcut to considering the *Georgia-Pacific* factors, some patentees have put forward general royalty theories such as the 25% "rule of thumb" and the Nash Bargaining Solution (50% split of net product value). The Federal Circuit has rejected the application of these generalized "rules of thumb." *See Apple*, 757 F.3d at 1324–25; *VirnetX*, 767 F.3d at 1331–34 (rejecting the Nash Bargaining Solution); *Uniloc*, 632 F.3d at 1312 (rejecting the "25% Rule"). Such evidence is inadmissible.

3. *Multiplicity of Factors*. The Georgia-Pacific factors are so numerous, complex, and mind-numbing that jurors have difficulty understanding how to juggle so many

considerations. The Federal Circuit Bar Association's January 2016 Model Jury Instructions have boiled down the factors:

6.7 Reasonable Royalty—Relevant Factors

In determining the reasonable royalty, you should consider all the facts known and available to the parties at the time the infringement began. Some of the kinds of factors that you may consider in making your determination are:

(1) The value that the claimed invention contributes to the accused product.

(2) The value that factors other than the claimed invention contribute to [the accused product].

(3) Comparable license agreements, such as those covering the use of the claimed invention or similar technology.

This concise and focused instruction provides a more balanced and comprehensible set of considerations than the *Georgia-Pacific* laundry list. Does it leave any important considerations out? *Cf.* Norman Siebrasse and Thomas Cotter, *A New Framework for Determining Reasonable Royalties in Patent Litigation*, FLA. L. REV. (forthcoming 2016); William Lee and A. Douglas Melamed, *Breaking the Vicious Cycle of Patent Damages*, 101 CORNELL L. REV. 385 (2016); David O. Taylor, *Using Reasonable Royalties to Value Patented Technology*, 49 GA. L. REV. 79 (2014); Daralyn J. Durie & Mark A. Lemley, *A Structured Approach to Calculating Reasonable Royalties*, 14 LEWIS & CLARK L. REV. 627 (2010) (suggesting that these three factors can explain royalty calculations).

c. *Royalty Base and Apportionment*

A reasonable royalty calculation will typically require determining the royalty base and the royalty rate. The determination is relatively straightforward where the demand for a final product comprises a single patented technology, such as a drug with a patented active ingredient. The most sensible royalty base in that case would typically be total sales revenue for the final product. *See Fonar Corp. v. Gen. Elec. Co.*, 107 F.3d 1543, 1552 (Fed. Cir. 1997) (citing *Rite-Hite Corp. v. Kelley Co.*, 56 F.3d 1538, 1549 (Fed. Cir. 1995) (en banc)). The royalty rate would account for alternative treatments (of which there may be few), marketing costs, and manufacturing costs to determine what percentage of that base is attributable to the patent.

Patent law has long struggled to deal with apportioning patent value where a patent covers only one component of a larger product. *See Cincinnati Car Co. v. New York Rapid Transit Corp.*, 66 F.2d 592, 593 (2d Cir. 1933) (Learned Hand, J.) (observing that the allocation of profits among multiple components "is in its nature unanswerable"). The problem has become particularly acute in modern patent litigation as a result of the growing use of juries called upon to apportion value based on complex and often widely divergent economic expert analyses.

In theory, a wide range of royalty bases can be appropriate with an appropriated calibrated royalty rate to account for the myriad factors affecting consumer demand. In practice, however, the open-ended nature of the *Georgia-Pacific* framework can lead to wildly divergent royalty calculations by expert economists. Especially in a jury trial, such testimony can produce outsized damage awards. As the Supreme Court recognized long ago, it would be "very grave error to instruct a jury 'that as to the measure of damages the same rule is to govern, whether the patent covers an entire machine or an improvement on a machine.'" *Seymore v. McCormick*, 57 U.S. 480, 491 (1853); *see also Westinghouse Elec. & Mfg. Co. v. Wagner Co.*, 225 U.S. 604, 614–15 (1912) ("[The] invention may have been used in combination with valuable improvements made, or other patents appropriated by the infringer, and each may have jointly, but unequally contributed to the profits. In such case, if plaintiff's patent only created a part of the profits, he is only entitled to recover that part of the net gains."); *Garretson v. Clark*, 111 U.S. 120, 121 (1884) ("When a patent is for an improvement, and not for an entirely new machine or contrivance, the patentee must show in what particulars his improvement has added to the usefulness of the machine or contrivance.)

In general, a patent holder seeking a reasonable royalty must provide substantial evidence supporting both its choice of royalty base and royalty rate. "[W]here multi-component products are involved, the governing rule is that the ultimate combination of royalty base and royalty rate must reflect the value attributable to the infringing features of the product, and no more." *Ericsson, Inc., v. D-Link Sys., Inc.*, 773 F.3d 1201, 1226 (Fed. Cir. 2014) (citing *VirnetX, Inc. v. Cisco Sys., Inc.*, 767 F.3d 1308 (Fed. Cir. 2014)).

As the Federal Circuit has warned, "reliance on the entire market value might mislead the jury, who may be less equipped to understand the extent to which the royalty rate would need to do the work in such instances." *Ericsson*, 773 F.3d at 1227 (citing *LaserDynamics, Inc. v. Quanta Computer, Inc.*, 694 F.3d 51, 67, 68 (Fed. Cir. 2012) (barring the use of too high a royalty base—even if mathematically offset by a "'low enough royalty rate'"—because such a base "carries a considerable risk" of misleading a jury into overcompensating, stating that such a base "'cannot help but skew the damages horizon for the jury'" and "make a patentee's proffered damages amount appear modest by comparison" (quoting *Uniloc USA, Inc. v. Microsoft Corp.*, 632 F.3d 1292, 1320 (Fed. Cir. 2011))).

To cabin the risk of outsize awards in multi-component cases, the Federal Circuit has pushed the royalty base toward the smallest salable patent practicing unit or "SSPPU." *See Cornell Univ. v. Hewlett-Packard Co.*, 609 F. Supp. 2d 279 (N.D.N.Y. 2009) (Rader, J., sitting by designation). The Federal Circuit embraced the SSPPU framework in *LaserDynamics Inc. v. Quanta Computer, Inc.*, 694 F.3d 51 (Fed. Cir. 2012), holding that "it is generally required that royalties be based not on the entire product, but instead on the 'smallest salable patent-practicing unit.' . . . The entire market value rule is a narrow exception to this general rule." *Id.* at 67; *see also VirnetX, Inc., v. Cisco Sys., Inc.*, 767 F.3d 1308, 1328–29 (Fed. Cir. 2014); *LaserDynamics, Inc., v. Quanta Comput., Inc.*, 694 F.3d 51, 66–70 (Fed. Cir. 2012); *Uniloc USA, Inc. v. Microsoft Corp.*, 632 F.3d 1292, 1320 (Fed. Cir. 2011); *Lucent Techs., Inc. v. Gateway, Inc.*, 580 F.3d 1301, 1336 (Fed. Cir. 2009).

Damages experts have begun to deploy consumer surveys to allocate value within multi-component patented products. *See* Zelin Yang, Note, *Damaging Royalties: An*

Overview of Reasonable Royalty Damages, 29 BERKELEY TECH. L.J. 647, 664 (2014); S. Christian Platt & Bob Chen, *Recent Trends and Approaches in Calculating Patent Damages: Nash Bargaining Solution and Conjoint Surveys*, 86 PATENT, TRADEMARK & COPYRIGHT J. (BNA) 909 (Aug. 30, 2013). Marketing researchers have long used "conjoint analysis" to differentiate value within product configurations. *See* Paul E. Green, Abba M. Krieger & Yoram Wind, *Thirty Years of Conjoint Analysis: Reflections and Prospects*, 31 INTERFACES 56 (2001); Paul E. Green & V. Srinivasan, *Conjoint Analysis in Marketing: New Developments with Implications for Research and Practice*, 54(4) J. OF MARKETING 3 (1990). Conjoint analysis draws upon consumer ranking of products with different features. Researchers use statistical methods to estimate consumers' willingness to pay for particular attributes. While these methods provide a logical framework for differentiating value, the technique can be limited in practice. *See* Patricia Dyck, *Beyond Confusion—Survey Evidence of Consumer Demand and the Entire Market Value Rule*, 4 HASTINGS SCI. & TECH. L.J. 209, 226 (2012) (noting sensitivity to data collection methods and algorithms and the problem of combinatorial explosion); Lisa Cameron, Michael Cragg & Daniel McFadden, *The Role of Conjoint Surveys in Reasonable Royalty Cases*, LAW360 (Oct. 16, 2013).

Courts have been cautiously receptive to conjoint analysis. *See Oracle Am., Inc. v. Google, Inc.*, No. C 10-03571 WHA, 2012 WL 850705, at *10-*14 (N.D. Cal. Mar. 13, 2012)(rejecting some of Oracle's expert's conjoint analysis as unreliable while allowing some of it to be admitted); *TV Interactive Data Corp. v. Sony Corp.*, 929 F. Supp. 2d 1006, 1019-25 (N.D. Cal. 2013) (holding the patentee's expert testimony using conjoint analysis to be admissible).

One limitation on the apportionment principle is that a sufficiently comparable prior license may dispense with the need to engage in apportionment at all. *See Pavo Solutions LLC v. Kingston Tech. Co.*, 35 F.4th 1367 (Fed. Cir. 2022). The theory is that if prior parties negotiated over this particular patent in the context of very similar technology, they probably took apportionment into account in setting the license royalty rate.

d. FRAND Licenses

A growing number of technologies arise within the context of network industries in which standard protocols and interfaces promote technological innovation and greater consumer value. Industry standard-setting organizations such as the Institute of Electrical Electronics Engineers (IEEE) and the International Telecommunication Union (ITU) bring together company representatives to develop industry standards. To ensure that the industry standards reflect the best technologies while avoiding (or at least postponing) licensing disputes, the participants typically commit to license standard-essential patents (SEPs) on "reasonable and non-discriminatory" (RAND) or "fair, reasonable and non-discriminatory" (FRAND) terms. The standard-setting organizations have typically left the parameters for determining FRAND license terms undefined, *see* Mark A. Lemley, *Intellectual Property Rights and Standard-Setting Organizations*, 90 CAL. L. REV. 1889, 1906 (2002), leaving courts with the difficult task of determining licensing rates for highly complex products involving potentially hundreds of patents.

The valuation of SEPs presents distinct problems. Industry standards can encompass hundreds of patented technologies of varying significance. Not surprisingly, owners of patents within a SEP pool often see their patents as particularly valuable, thereby risking hold-up and undue royalty stacking. The challenge lies in separating the value of the particular technology from the often-tremendous value from standardization. Once consumers adopt a product, they become locked into the standard to varying degrees. This could provide the patentee tremendous leverage in a negotiation. With potentially hundreds of SEPs and dozens of patent owners, the problem becomes intractable if patent owners stake out aggressive positions or refuse to propose licensing terms.

In a series of recent cases, courts have surmounted this challenge by interpreting the principal goal of standard-setting agreements to be widespread adoption of the standard, thereby barring FRAND licensors from capturing the coordination and network value of the standard. *See Microsoft Corp. v. Motorola, Inc.*, No. C10-1823JLR, 2013 U.S. Dist. LEXIS 60233, 2013 WL 2111217 (W.D. Wash. Apr. 25, 2013); *see also Ericsson*, 773 F.3d at 1229–35; *In re Innovatio IP Ventures LLC Patent Litig.*, No. 11 C 9308, 2013 U.S. Dist. LEXIS 144061, 2013 WL 5593609 (N.D. Ill. Oct. 3, 2013). The courts have adapted the *Georgia-Pacific* factors to serve the standard-setting context. Professor Robert Merges and Professor Jeffery Kuhn have suggested that the estoppel concept ought to be extended to situations where the holder of a standard-essential patent leads third parties into adopting a standard with promises of non-enforcement, and then enforces vigorously when those parties are "locked in" to the standard. *See* Robert P. Merges and Jeffery M. Kuhn, *An Estoppel Doctrine for Patented Standards*, 97 CAL. L. REV. 1 (2009).

3. Enhanced Damages

Halo Electronics, Inc. v. Pulse Electronics, Inc.
Stryker Corp. v. Zimmer, Inc.
Supreme Court of the United States
579 U.S. 93 (2016)

CHIEF JUSTICE ROBERTS delivered the opinion of the Court.

Section 284 of the Patent Act provides that, in a case of infringement, courts "may increase the damages up to three times the amount found or assessed." 35 U.S.C. §284. In *In re Seagate Technology, LLC*, 497 F. 3d 1360 (2007) (en banc), the United States Court of Appeals for the Federal Circuit adopted a two-part test for determining when a district court may increase damages pursuant to §284. Under *Seagate*, a patent owner must first "show by clear and convincing evidence that the infringer acted despite an objectively high likelihood that its actions constituted infringement of a valid patent." *Id.*, at 1371. Second, the patentee must demonstrate, again by clear and convincing evidence, that the risk of infringement "was either known or so obvious that it should have been known to the accused infringer." *Ibid.* The question before us is whether this test is consistent with §284. We hold that it is not.

I

A

Enhanced damages are as old as U.S. patent law. The Patent Act of 1793 mandated treble damages in any successful infringement suit. *See* Patent Act of 1793, §5, 1 Stat. 322. In the Patent Act of 1836, however, Congress changed course and made enhanced damages discretionary, specifying that "it shall be in the power of the court to render judgment for any sum above the amount found by [the] verdict . . . not exceeding three times the amount thereof, according to the circumstances of the case." Patent Act of 1836, §14, 5 Stat. 123. In construing that new provision, this Court explained that the change was prompted by the "injustice" of subjecting a "defendant who acted in ignorance or good faith" to the same treatment as the "wanton and malicious pirate." *Seymour* v. *McCormick*, 16 How. 480, 488 (1854). There "is no good reason," we observed, "why taking a man's property in an invention should be trebly punished, while the measure of damages as to other property is single and actual damages." *Id.*, at 488–489. But "where the injury is wanton or malicious, a jury may inflict vindictive or exemplary damages, not to recompense the plaintiff, but to punish the defendant." *Id.*, at 489. . . .

In 1870, Congress amended the Patent Act, but preserved district court discretion to award up to treble damages "according to the circumstances of the case." Patent Act of 1870, §59, 16 Stat. 207. We continued to describe enhanced damages as "vindictive or punitive," which the court may "inflict" when "the circumstances of the case appear to require it." *Tilghman* v. *Proctor*, 125 U.S. 136, 143–144 (1888); *Topliff* v. *Topliff*, 145 U.S. 156, 174 (1892) (infringer knowingly sold copied technology of his former employer). At the same time, we reiterated that there was no basis for increased damages where "[t]here is no pretence of any wanton and wilful breach" and "nothing that suggests punitive damages, or that shows wherein the defendant was damnified other than by the loss of the profits which the plaintiff received." *Cincinnati Siemens-Lungren Gas Illuminating Co.* v. *Western Siemens-Lungren Co.*, 152 U.S. 200, 204 (1894). . . .

Some early decisions did suggest that enhanced damages might serve to compensate patentees as well as to punish infringers. *See, e.g., Clark* v. *Wooster*, 119 U.S. 322, 326 (1886) (noting that "[t]here may be damages beyond" licensing fees "but these are more properly the subjects" of enhanced damage awards). Such statements, however, were not for the ages, in part because the merger of law and equity removed certain procedural obstacles to full compensation absent enhancement. *See generally* 7 CHISUM ON PATENTS §20.03[4][b][iii] (2011). In the main, moreover, the references to compensation concerned costs attendant to litigation. *See Clark*, 119 U.S., at 326 (identifying enhanced damages as compensation for "the expense and trouble the plaintiff has been put to"). That concern dissipated with the enactment in 1952 of 35 U.S.C. §285, which authorized district courts to award reasonable attorney's fees to prevailing parties in "exceptional cases" under the Patent Act. *See Octane Fitness, LLC* v. *ICON Health & Fitness Inc.*, 572 U.S. 545, 549 (2014).

It is against this backdrop that Congress, in the 1952 codification of the Patent Act, enacted §284. "The stated purpose" of the 1952 revision "was merely reorganization in language to clarify the statement of the statutes." *Aro Mfg. Co.* v. *Convertible Top Replacement Co.*, 377 U.S. 476, 505, n.20 (1964) (internal quotation marks omitted). This Court accordingly described §284—consistent with the history of enhanced damages under the Patent Act—as providing that "punitive or 'increased' damages" could be recovered "in a case of willful or bad-faith infringement." *Id.,* at 508; *see also Dowling* v. *United States,* 473 U.S. 207, 227, n.19 (1985) ("willful infringement"); *Florida Prepaid Postsecondary Ed. Expense Bd.* v. *College Savings Bank,* 527 U.S. 627, 648, n. 11 (1999) (describing §284 damages as "punitive").

B

In 2007, the Federal Circuit decided *Seagate* and fashioned the test for enhanced damages now before us. Under *Seagate,* a plaintiff seeking enhanced damages must show that the infringement of his patent was "willful." 497 F. 3d, at 1368. The Federal Circuit announced a two-part test to establish such willfulness: First, "a patentee must show by clear and convincing evidence that the infringer acted despite an objectively high likelihood that its actions constituted infringement of a valid patent," without regard to "[t]he state of mind of the accused infringer." *Id.,* at 1371. This objectively defined risk is to be "determined by the record developed in the infringement proceedings." *Ibid.* "Objective recklessness will not be found" at this first step if the accused infringer, during the infringement proceedings, "raise[s] a 'substantial question' as to the validity or noninfringement of the patent." *Bard Peripheral Vascular, Inc.* v. *W. L. Gore & Assoc., Inc.,* 776 F. 3d 837, 844 (CA Fed. 2015). That categorical bar applies even if the defendant was unaware of the arguable defense when he acted. *See Seagate,* 497 F. 3d, at 1371.

Second, after establishing objective recklessness, a patentee must show—again by clear and convincing evidence—that the risk of infringement "was either known or so obvious that it should have been known to the accused infringer." *Seagate,* 497 F. 3d, at 1371. Only when both steps have been satisfied can the district court proceed to consider whether to exercise its discretion to award enhanced damages. *Ibid.*

Under Federal Circuit precedent, an award of enhanced damages is subject to trifurcated appellate review. The first step of *Seagate*—objective recklessness—is reviewed *de novo*; the second—subjective knowledge—for substantial evidence; and the ultimate decision—whether to award enhanced damages—for abuse of discretion. *See Bard Peripheral Vascular, Inc.* v. *W. L. Gore & Assoc., Inc.,* 682 F. 3d 1003, 1005, 1008 (CA Fed. 2012).

C

1

Petitioner Halo Electronics, Inc., and respondents Pulse Electronics, Inc. supply electronic components. 769 F. 3d 1371, 1374–1375 (CA Fed. 2014). Halo alleges that Pulse infringed its patents for electronic packages containing transformers designed to be mounted to the surface of circuit boards. *Id.,* at 1374. In 2002, Halo sent Pulse two letters offering to license Halo's patents. *Id.,* at 1376. After one of its engineers concluded that Halo's patents were invalid, Pulse continued to sell the allegedly infringing products. *Ibid.*

In 2007, Halo sued Pulse. *Ibid.* The jury found that Pulse had infringed Halo's patents, and that there was a high probability it had done so willfully. *Ibid.* The District Court, however, declined to award enhanced damages under §284, after determining that Pulse had at trial presented a defense that "was not objectively baseless, or a 'sham.'" App. to Pet. for Cert. in No. 14–1513, p. 64a (quoting *Bard*, 682 F. 3d, at 1007). Thus, the court concluded, Halo had failed to show objective recklessness under the first step of *Seagate*. The Federal Circuit affirmed.

2

Petitioners Stryker Corporation, Stryker Puerto Rico, Ltd., and Stryker Sales Corporation (collectively, Stryker) and respondents Zimmer, Inc., and Zimmer Surgical, Inc. (collectively, Zimmer), compete in the market for orthopedic pulsed lavage devices. A pulsed lavage device is a combination spray gun and suction tube, used to clean tissue during surgery. In 2010, Stryker sued Zimmer for patent infringement. The jury found that Zimmer had willfully infringed Stryker's patents and awarded Stryker $70 million in lost profits. The District Court added $6.1 million in supplemental damages and then trebled the total sum under §284, resulting in an award of over $228 million.

Specifically, the District Court noted, the jury had heard testimony that Zimmer had "all-but instructed its design team to copy Stryker's products," and had chosen a "high-risk/high-reward strategy of competing immediately and aggressively in the pulsed lavage market," while "opt[ing] to worry about the potential legal consequences later." "[T]reble damages [were] appropriate," the District Court concluded, "[g]iven the one-sidedness of the case and the flagrancy and scope of Zimmer's infringement."

The Federal Circuit affirmed the judgment of infringement but vacated the award of treble damages. 782 F. 3d, at 662. Applying *de novo* review, the court concluded that enhanced damages were unavailable because Zimmer had asserted "reasonable defenses" at trial. We granted certiorari in both cases and now vacate and remand.

II

A

The pertinent text of §284 provides simply that "the court may increase the damages up to three times the amount found or assessed." 35 U.S.C. §284. That language contains no explicit limit or condition, and we have emphasized that the "word 'may' clearly connotes discretion." *Martin* v. *Franklin Capital Corp.*, 546 U.S. 132, 136 (2005) (quoting *Fogerty* v. *Fantasy, Inc.*, 510 U.S. 517, 533 (1994)).

At the same time, "[d]iscretion is not whim." *Martin*, 546 U.S., at 139. "[I]n a system of laws discretion is rarely without limits," even when the statute "does not specify any limits upon the district courts' discretion." *Flight Attendants* v. *Zipes*, 491 U.S. 754, 758 (1989). "[A] motion to a court's discretion is a motion, not to its inclination, but to its judgment; and its judgment is to be guided by sound legal principles." *Martin,* 546 U S., at 139 (quoting *United States* v. *Burr*, 25 F. Cas. 30, 35

(No. 14,692d) (CC Va. 1807) (Marshall, C. J.); alteration omitted). Thus, although there is "no precise rule or formula" for awarding damages under §284, a district court's "discretion should be exercised in light of the considerations" underlying the grant of that discretion. *Octane Fitness,* 572 U.S., at 554 (quoting *Fogerty,* 510 U.S., at 534).

Awards of enhanced damages under the Patent Act over the past 180 years establish that they are not to be meted out in a typical infringement case, but are instead designed as a "punitive" or "vindictive" sanction for egregious infringement behavior. The sort of conduct warranting enhanced damages has been variously described in our cases as willful, wanton, malicious, bad-faith, deliberate, consciously wrongful, flagrant, or—indeed—characteristic of a pirate. District courts enjoy discretion in deciding whether to award enhanced damages, and in what amount. But through nearly two centuries of discretionary awards and review by appellate tribunals, "the channel of discretion ha[s] narrowed," Friendly, *Indiscretion About Discretion,* 31 EMORY L.J. 747, 772 (1982), so that such damages are generally reserved for egregious cases of culpable behavior.

B

The *Seagate* test reflects, in many respects, a sound recognition that enhanced damages are generally appropriate under §284 only in egregious cases. That test, however, "is unduly rigid, and it impermissibly encumbers the statutory grant of discretion to district courts." *Octane Fitness,* 572 U.S., at 553 (construing §285 of the Patent Act). In particular, it can have the effect of insulating some of the worst patent infringers from any liability for enhanced damages.

1

The principal problem with *Seagate*'s two-part test is that it requires a finding of objective recklessness in every case before district courts may award enhanced damages. Such a threshold requirement excludes from discretionary punishment many of the most culpable offenders, such as the "wanton and malicious pirate" who intentionally infringes another's patent—with no doubts about its validity or any notion of a defense—for no purpose other than to steal the patentee's business. *Seymour,* 16 How. at 488. Under *Seagate*, a district court may not even consider enhanced damages for such a pirate, unless the court first determines that his infringement was "objectively" reckless. In the context of such deliberate wrongdoing, however, it is not clear why an independent showing of objective recklessness—by clear and convincing evidence, no less—should be a prerequisite to enhanced damages. Our recent decision in *Octane Fitness* arose in a different context but points in the same direction. In that case we considered §285 of the Patent Act, which allows district courts to award attorney's fees to prevailing parties in "exceptional" cases. 35 U.S.C. §285. The Federal Circuit had adopted a two-part test for determining when a case qualified as exceptional, requiring that the claim asserted be both objectively baseless and brought in subjective bad faith. We rejected that test on the ground that a case presenting "subjective bad faith" alone could "sufficiently set itself apart from mine-run cases to warrant a fee award." 572 U.S., at 555. So too here. The subjective willfulness of a patent infringer, intentional or knowing, may warrant enhanced damages, without regard to whether his infringement was objectively reckless.

The *Seagate* test aggravates the problem by making dispositive the ability of the infringer to muster a reasonable (even though unsuccessful) defense at the infringement trial. The existence of such a defense insulates the infringer from enhanced damages, even if he did not act on the basis of the defense or was even aware of it. Under that standard, someone who plunders a patent—infringing it without any reason to suppose his conduct is arguably defensible—can nevertheless escape any come-uppance under §284 solely on the strength of his attorney's ingenuity.

But culpability is generally measured against the knowledge of the actor at the time of the challenged conduct. *See generally* RESTATEMENT (SECOND) OF TORTS §8A (1965) ("intent" denotes state of mind in which "the actor desires to cause consequences of his act" or "believes" them to be "substantially certain to result from it"); W. KEETON, D. DOBBS, R. KEETON, & D. OWEN, PROSSER AND KEETON ON LAW OF TORTS §34, p. 212 (5th ed. 1984) (describing willful, wanton, and reckless as "look[ing] to the actor's real or supposed state of mind"); *see also Kolstad* v. *American Dental Assn.*, 527 U.S. 526, 538 (1999) ("Most often . . . eligibility for punitive awards is characterized in terms of a defendant's motive or intent"). In *Safeco Ins. Co. of America* v. *Burr*, 551 U.S. 47 (2007), we stated that a person is reckless if he acts "*knowing* or *having reason to know* of facts which would lead a reasonable man to realize" his actions are unreasonably risky. *Id.*, at 69 (emphasis added and internal quotation marks omitted). The Court found that the defendant had not recklessly violated the Fair Credit Reporting Act because the defendant's interpretation had "a foundation in the statutory text" and the defendant lacked "the benefit of guidance from the courts of appeals or the Federal Trade Commission" that "might have warned it away from the view it took." *Id.*, at 69–70. Nothing in *Safeco* suggests that we should look to facts that the defendant neither knew nor had reason to know at the time he acted.*

Section 284 allows district courts to punish the full range of culpable behavior. Yet none of this is to say that enhanced damages must follow a finding of egregious misconduct. As with any exercise of discretion, courts should continue to take into account the particular circumstances of each case in deciding whether to award damages, and in what amount. Section 284 permits district courts to exercise their discretion in a manner free from the inelastic constraints of the *Seagate* test. Consistent with nearly two centuries of enhanced damages under patent law, however, such punishment should generally be reserved for egregious cases typified by willful misconduct.

2

---

* Respondents invoke a footnote in *Safeco* where we explained that in considering whether there had been a knowing or reckless violation of the Fair Credit Reporting Act, a showing of bad faith was not relevant absent a showing of objective recklessness. *See* 551 U.S., at 70, n. 20. But our precedents make clear that "bad-faith infringement" *is* an independent basis for enhancing patent damages. *Aro Mfg. Co.* v. *Convertible Top Replacement Co.*, 377 U.S. 476, 508 (1964); *see supra,* at 2–5, 9–10; *see also Safeco*, 551 U.S., at 57 (noting that "'willfully' is a word of many meanings whose construction is often dependent on the context in which it appears" (some internal quotation marks omitted)).

The *Seagate* test is also inconsistent with §284 because it requires clear and convincing evidence to prove recklessness. On this point *Octane Fitness* is again instructive. There too the Federal Circuit had adopted a clear and convincing standard of proof, for awards of attorney's fees under §285 of the Patent Act. Because that provision supplied no basis for imposing such a heightened standard of proof, we rejected it. See *Octane Fitness,* 572 U.S., at 553. We do so here as well. Like §285, §284 "imposes no specific evidentiary burden, much less such a high one." *Ibid.* And the fact that Congress expressly erected a higher standard of proof elsewhere in the Patent Act, *see* 35 U.S.C. §273(b), but not in §284, is telling. Furthermore, nothing in historical practice supports a heightened standard. As we explained in *Octane Fitness,* "patent-infringement litigation has always been governed by a preponderance of the evidence standard." 572 U.S., at 558-559. Enhanced damages are no exception.

3

Finally, because we eschew any rigid formula for awarding enhanced damages under §284, we likewise reject the Federal Circuit's tripartite framework for appellate review. In *Highmark Inc.* v. *Allcare Health Management System, Inc.,* 572 U.S. 559 (2014), we built on our *Octane Fitness* holding to reject a similar multipart standard of review. Because *Octane Fitness* confirmed district court discretion to award attorney fees, we concluded that such decisions should be reviewed for abuse of discretion. *Highmark,* 572 U.S., at563.

The same conclusion follows naturally from our holding here. Section 284 gives district courts discretion in meting out enhanced damages. It "commits the determination" whether enhanced damages are appropriate "to the discretion of the district court" and "that decision is to be reviewed on appeal for abuse of discretion." *Id.,* at 563.

That standard allows for review of district court decisions informed by "the considerations we have identified." *Octane Fitness,* 572 U.S., at 554. The appellate review framework adopted by the Federal Circuit reflects a concern that district courts may award enhanced damages too readily, and distort the balance between the protection of patent rights and the interest in technological innovation. Nearly two centuries of exercising discretion in awarding enhanced damages in patent cases, however, has given substance to the notion that there are limits to that discretion. The Federal Circuit should review such exercises of discretion in light of the longstanding considerations we have identified as having guided both Congress and the courts.

III

. . . . [R]espondents' main argument for retaining the *Seagate* test comes down to a matter of policy. Respondents and their *amici* are concerned that allowing district courts unlimited discretion to award up to treble damages in infringement cases will impede innovation as companies steer well clear of any possible interference with patent rights. They also worry that the ready availability of such damages will embolden "trolls." Trolls, in the patois of the patent community, are entities that hold patents for the primary purpose of enforcing them against alleged infringers, often exacting outsized licensing fees on threat of litigation.

Respondents are correct that patent law reflects "a careful balance between the need to promote innovation" through patent protection, and the importance of facilitating the "imitation and refinement through imitation" that are "necessary to invention itself and the very lifeblood of a competitive economy." *Bonito Boats, Inc.* v. *Thunder Craft Boats, Inc.*, 489 U.S. 141, 146 (1989). That balance can indeed be disrupted if enhanced damages are awarded in garden-variety cases. As we have explained, however, they should not be. The seriousness of respondents' policy concerns cannot justify imposing an artificial construct such as the *Seagate* test on the discretion conferred under §284. . . .

COMMENTS AND QUESTIONS

1. What types of conduct fall within the enhanced damages ambit? Is willfulness still required? Could other conduct give rise to an enhancement? What kinds of conduct?

Justice Breyer, joined by Justices Alito and Kennedy, concurred in the unanimous *Halo* decision but wrote separately to emphasize that "willful misconduct" does "not mean that a court may award enhanced damages simply because the evidence shows that the infringer knew about the patent and nothing more." They expressed the view that the Court's opinion should be read to mean that enhanced damages are appropriate "only in egregious cases"—characterized by bad-faith infringement, malicious piracy, or objective recklessness. They note that the owner of a small firm, or a scientist, engineer, or technician working there, could, "without being 'wanton' or 'reckless,' reasonably determine that its product does not infringe a particular patent, or that that patent is probably invalid." They further highlight that the proliferation of demand letters by patent assertion entities ought not to impose undue investigative burdens on the many businesses, hospitals, and individuals targeted.

The Federal Circuit picked up on that concurrence in its articulation of the willfulness standard and the allocation of decisionmaking authority between the jury and judge. *See SRI Int'l v. Cisco Sys.*, 14 F.4th 1323 (Fed. Cir. 2021). It holds that only intent to infringe or willful blindness is required for a jury to find willful infringement. But willful infringement alone is not enough to enhance damages. If a jury finds willfulness, the decision whether to enhance damages is left to the district judge's discretion. The judge may consider the willfulness finding, but to enhance damages must also conclude that the defendant engaged in "egregious conduct" such as "wanton, malicious, and bad faith" behavior.

2. The *Seagate* two-part test reduced the need for companies to obtain opinion letters because they could rely instead on a plausible, although ultimately unsuccessful, legal defense. Does *Halo* make such letters more important? Justice Breyer sought to downplay the need for such letters, but is that a prudent approach?

3. The *Seagate* "objective reasonableness" prong afforded district judges greater leeway to reject enhanced damages at the summary judgment stage and to limit wide-ranging discovery into the defendant's intent. Will *Halo* re-open that discovery

Pandora's Box and make it difficult to resolve willfulness prior to trial? Might a hasty or unduly cautious email create treble exposure?

4. A common critique of willfulness doctrine pre-*Seagate* was that it created a disincentive for research and development staff to read competitors' patents. (It was thought that this practice would establish a company's knowledge of a patented invention, leading to a finding of willful infringement and the attendant increased damages.) *See, e.g.*, Note, *The Disclosure Function of the Patent System (Or Lack Thereof)*, 118 HARV. L. REV. 2007 (2005). *Seagate* reduced that concern. Does *Halo* exacerbate it?

5. Do we need a doctrine of willful infringement? Is there a risk that without some sort of damages enhancement infringers will just copy patented inventions with impunity, secure in the knowledge that they will only have to pay a reasonable royalty? Or does the risk of being enjoined mid-production serve as an adequate deterrent? *See* generally ROGER D. BLAIR & THOMAS F. COTTER, INTELLECTUAL PROPERTY: ECONOMIC AND LEGAL DIMENSIONS OF RIGHTS AND REMEDIES 42–66 (2005) (modeling compensation and deterrence in patent cases, and discussing doctrinal implications).

4. Attorney Fees

Section 285 provides that the "court in exceptional cases may award reasonable attorney fees to the prevailing party." The Supreme Court has interpreted this standard to afford district judges discretion to award attorney fees where it finds that the case "simply . . . stands out from others with respect to the substantive strength of a party's litigating position . . . or the unreasonable manner in which the case was litigated." *Octane Fitness LLC v. Icon Health & Fitness Inc.*, 134 S.Ct. 1749, 1755–76 (2014) (rejecting the Federal Circuit's rule that a defendant may only be awarded fees where it demonstrates that the patentee litigated with subjective bad faith and that the suit was objectively baseless). The Court directed district courts to consider the totality of the circumstances. Such determinations are reviewable for abuse of discretion. *Highmark Inc. v. Allcare Health Mgmt. Sys., Inc.*, 134 S.Ct. 1744, 1749 (2014).

I. DESIGN PATENTS

As the industrial revolution unfolded in the early 19th century, advances in iron casting and other production processes paved the way for mass producing decorative goods (such as stoves, radiators, and other cast-iron consumer goods). *See* Jason J. Du Mont & Mark D. Janis, *The Origins of American Design Patent Protection*, 88 INDIANA L.J. 837, 849-51 (2013). These advances shifted competition toward the decorative elements for consumer goods. Relatedly, the growth of the textile industries during the industrial revolution spawned piracy of popular and attractive rug designs, clothing, and other imprinted goods.Such ornamentation of useful articles did not, however, fit easily within utility patent or copyright protection. Although advances in the production processes and casting machinery were eligible for utility patents, the particular *designs* resulting from such processes and machinery did not qualify for utility patent protection.

And copyright protection extended only to books, maps, charts, prints, engravings, and musical compositions, not to three-dimensional works.

England's more developed manufacturing economy had already confronted these issues through the enactment of copyright-based design protection regimes. *See* An Act to secure to Proprietors of Designs for Articles of Manufacture the Copyright of such Designs for a limited Time, 2 Vict., c. 17 (1839) (Eng.); An Act for the Encouragement of the Arts of designing and printing Linens, Cottons, Callicoes, and Muslins, by vesting the Properties thereof in the Designers, Printers, and Proprietors, for a limited Time, 27 Geo. 3, c. 38, §1 (1787) (Eng.).

Drawing on England's precedent, Jordan L. Mott, a successful American stove manufacturer, along with other industrialists and designers, petitioned Congress to enact design protection. Senator John Ruggles of Maine, former chair of the Senate's Committee on Patents and the Patent Office, presented Mott's petition. The bill proposed a "sole and exclusive copy-right" for the proprietor of any "new and original design" for specified articles of manufacture, including iron products and textiles. The copyright protection was for three years for metal designs and one year for articles other than metals.

Senator Ruggles's proposed bill passed the Senate Committee but was not enacted during that legislative session. Following Ruggles failed reelection, the design protection mantle was taken up by Patent Commissioner Henry Ellsworth, which resulted in an unfortunate drafting twist. *See* Peter S. Menell & Ella Corren, *Design Patent Law's Identity Crisis* 36 BERKELEY TECH. L.J. 1, 9-10 (2021). In his 1841 COMMISSIONER'S REPORT TO CONGRESS, Commissioner Ellsworth called upon Congress to establish a design protection regime under his authority at the Patent Office.

In 1842, Congress extended patent protection to "new and original designs for articles of manufacture." Although largely tracking the original *copyright* proposal, Commissioner Ellsworth's bill shifted the proposal to a patent rubric while retaining copyright language lifted from the British copyright law. The intent of the statute was to "give encouragement to the decorative arts." *Gorham Mfg. Co. v. White*, 81 U.S. (14 Wall.) 511, 524–25 (1871).

Beyond affording copyright-type protection for ornamental features of useful articles, design patents also became a form of protection for graphic trademarks. By the mid-18th century, commerce was rapidly expanding in the United States and Congress had not yet enacted federal trademark protection. Enterprising businesses began to use design patents as a means to obtain exclusive rights for distinctive labels for their products. Between 1842 and 1870, the Patent Office granted more than 200 graphic trademark design patents.

U.S. Design Patent No. 1163 (Nov. 1, 1859)

The use of design patents to protect trademarks rapidly declined with the passage of federal trademark protection in 1870.

Congress tweaked the duration and categories of design patent protection in 1861 and 1870. It afforded design patentees a disgorgement remedy in 1887. In 1902, Congress deleted the word "useful" from the design patent statute and replaced it with "ornamental." It also consolidated the classes of eligible works into a single class: "article of manufacture."

Congress augmented protection for designs through expansion of copyright law to protect sculpture and artistic designs in 1870. During the late 19th century, design patents focused on industrial designs and copyright focused on fine arts. That distinction gradually eroded. In 1954, the Supreme Court ruled that design patent protection and copyright protection are not mutually exclusive. *See Mazer v. Stein*, 347 U.S. 201, 218 (1954). We further explore the interplay of design patent protection and copyright protection for useful articles in Chapter IV(C)(2)(ii); and the interplay of design patent protection and trade dress protection in Chapter V(C)(1)(v).

The modern design patent provisions, codified in 35 U.S.C. §§171–73, carry over the 1887 and 1902 amendments without substantive change. The modern Patent Act allows an applicant to obtain a design patent for "any new, original and ornamental design for an article of manufacture" and provides that most provisions relating to utility patents for inventions also apply to design patents. §171. Design patents now receive a 15-year patent term.[13] A design may consist of surface ornamentation, configuration, or a combination of both.

---

[13] Patents issued from design applications filed before May 13, 2015 have a 14-year term from the date of grant.

1. Requirements for Patentability

A design for an article of manufacture is patentable if it is novel, original, ornamental, and nonobvious. The PTO defines a design as "the visual characteristics or aspects displayed by the object. It is the appearance presented by the object which creates a visual impact upon the mind of the observer." U.S. PATENT AND TRADEMARK OFFICE, MANUAL OF PATENT EXAMINING PROCEDURE, §1502.

Courts have interpreted "article of manufacture" broadly. The Court of Customs and Patent Appeals held that "a manufacture is anything 'made by the hands of man' from raw materials whether literally by hand or by machinery or by art" and found that a design created by the flow of water in a fountain was patentable. *In re Hruby*, 373 F.2d 997, 1000 (C.C.P.A. 1967); *see, e.g., Gorham Mfg. Co. v. White*, 81 U.S. (14 Wall.) 511 (1871) (silverware); *In re Koehring*, 37 F.2d 421 (C.C.P.A. 1930) (cement mixers); *In re Rosen*, 673 F.2d 388 (C.C.P.A. 1982) (furniture); *Unette Corp. v. Unit Pack Co.*, 785 F.2d 1026 (Fed. Cir. 1986) (containers). While the patented design must be embodied in an article of manufacture, a design patent may be obtained for only part of an article. *In re Zahn*, 617 F.2d 261 (C.C.P.A. 1980) (holding that the shank of a drill bit was patentable under §171); *but see* Sarah Burstein, *The Article of Manufacture in 1887*, 32 BERKELEY TECH. L.J. 1 (2017) (tracing the legislative history of the term "article of manufacture" and finding that it was a term of art that referred to a tangible item made by humans, other than a machine or composition of matter, that had a unitary structure and was complete in itself for use or for sale). Thus, the subject matter of a design patent is not limited to designs for discrete articles.

i. *Claim Requirements*

Like utility patents and unlike copyrights, design patents are examined and not merely registered. *See* USPTO, MANUAL OF PATENT EXAMINING PROCEDURE, part 1500 *et seq*. The examination is significantly less searching than for utility patents, however, and the overwhelming majority of design patent applications are approved. The §112 requirements of adequate disclosure and definite claiming also apply to design patents. *See In re Owens*, 710 F.3d 1362 (Fed. Cir. 2013). In the case of design patents, both disclosure and definiteness are accomplished through the drawings. Only one claim is permitted in design patent applications. This claim takes the form of "the ornamental design of the specified article as shown." Although only one claim is permitted, a design application may illustrate multiple embodiments of a design if they involve a single inventive concept. *See In re Rubenfield*, 270 F.2d 391 (C.C.P.A. 1959).

The USPTO requires an applicant to "designate the particular article" for which a design patent is sought, although the patent need not depict the article and can represent it generically (as in the case of surface ornamentation). In *In re SurgiSil*, 14 F.4th 1380, 1382 (Fed. Cir. 2021), the Federal Circuit ruled that "[a] design claim is limited to the article of manufacture identified in the claim; it does not broadly cover a design in the abstract." Consequently, the design patent title (e.g., "ornamental design for a lip implant") limits the range of anticipatory prior art as well as the scope of infringing articles of manufacture.

The degree of specificity with which an applicant must describe and claim the article is not straightforward. For designs of "an ornament, impression, print or picture to be applied to an article of manufacture," an applicant may make a broad claim to the use of the ornament on more than one article. *See In re Schnell*, 46 F.2d 203 (C.C.P.A. 1931). In this case, the applicant must teach the manner of applying the design to show reduction to practice. For designs that consist of a shape or configuration for an article of manufacture, the claim and specification must be narrower. *Id.*

Drawings must contain a "sufficient number of views to constitute a complete disclosure of the appearance of the design." 37 C.F.R. §1.152(a) (2014). If the drawings are insufficient, a patent may be declared invalid under §112. The solid lines of a drawing define the scope of the claimed invention. The dotted or dashed lines merely provide context; they do not limit the scope of the claimed design. The illustration below reflects a typical design patent:

US Patent No. D517,789

ii.   Novelty

Novelty is established if no prior art shows exactly the same design. *OddzOn Prod., Inc. v. Just Toys, Inc.*, 122 F.3d 1396, 1404 (Fed. Cir. 1997). A design is novel if the "ordinary observer," viewing the new design as a whole, would consider it to be distinct from, rather than a modification of, an already existing design. *See, e.g., Clark Equip. Co. v. Keller*, 570 F.2d 778, 799 (8th Cir. 1978).

The claim is compared to the design disclosed in the allegedly anticipatory prior art reference, assuming that reference has qualified as prior art under the applicable provisions of §102. If the claimed design and the alleged prior art design are substantially the same, the alleged prior art design anticipates the claimed design. Designs are "substantially the same" when their resemblance is deceptive to the extent that it would induce the ordinary observer to purchase an article, supposing it to be the other. *Door-Master Corp. v. Yorktowne, Inc.*, 256 F.3d 1308, 1313 (Fed. Cir. 2001). Once identity is established, a prior design will anticipate even though it is an article of different use or is in a non-analogous art. *See In re Glavas*, 230 F. 2d 447, 450 (C.C.P.A. 1956).

The experimental use exception to the §102(b) "public use" and "on sale" bars has limited application to design patents. An ornamental design alone for an article of manufacture cannot qualify under the experimental use exception. *In re Mann*, 861 F.2d 1581 (Fed. Cir. 1988) ("obtaining the reactions of people to a design, whether they like it or not, is not experimentation"). However, where experimentation is directed to the functional features of an article, the use may fall within the experimental use exception. *See Tone Bros., Inc. v. Sysco Corp.*, 28 F.3d 1192 (Fed. Cir. 1994).

iii.   Nonobviousness

Like utility patents, design patents must also meet the non-obviousness requirement of §103. *See Titan Tire Corp. v. Case New Holland, Inc.*, 566 F.3d 1372, 1380 (Fed. Cir. 2009). Challenges to a design patent under §103 may include evidence from one skilled in the art regarding prior art references and whether and how those references would be combined to form a design that compares to the claimed design. The test for obviousness is different from the test for infringement and anticipation. Whereas the comparison of the claimed design to an accused article or potentially anticipatory prior art is seen through the eyes of the "ordinary observer," the comparison of the claimed design to the prior art for obviousness purposes is seen through the eyes of the "ordinary designer." *High Point Design LLC v. Buyers Direct, Inc.*, 730 F. 3d 1301, 1311 (Fed. Cir. 2013); *Apple, Inc. v. Samsung Elecs. Co.*, 678 F.3d 1314, 1324 (Fed. Cir. 2012) ("In addressing a claim of obviousness in a design patent, the ultimate inquiry is whether the claimed design would have been obvious to a designer of ordinary skill who designs articles of the type involved.").

Federal Circuit decisions set forth a two-step process for the obviousness inquiry, which includes a "primary reference" requirement. In the first step, one must find a single prior art reference that has design characteristics "basically the same as the claimed design" (the "primary reference"). In the second step, "other references may be used to modify it to create a design that has the same overall visual appearance as the claimed design." *High Point*, 730 F. 3d at 1311 (quoting *Durling v. Spectrum Furniture Co.*, 101 F.3d 100, 103 (Fed. Cir. 1996)) (internal quotations omitted). The pertinent references sought to be combined to show obviousness need not be analogous arts in the mechanical sense, but must be so related that the "appearance of certain ornamental features in one would suggest the application of those features to another." *In re Glavas*, 230 F.2d 447 (C.C.P.A. 1956). "The undisputed commercial success of the patented design, and Appellants' copying thereof, are also relevant to analysis of the obviousness of a design." *L.A. Gear, Inc. v. Thom McAn Shoe Co.*, 988 F.2d 1117, 1124 (Fed. Cir. 1993).

Judges have long recognized the subjective quality of non-obviousness determinations in design patent cases. *See, e.g., In re Nalbandian*, 661 F.2d 1214, 1219 (CCPA 1981) (Rich, J. concurring) (noting the "impossible issue of obviousness in design patentability cases").

2.   Ornamentality/Non-functionality

From the mid 19th century until the turn of the 20th century, the Patent Office and the courts vacillated on whether design patents could extend to functional design elements. *See* Peter S. Menell & Ella Corren, *The Design Patent Identity Crisis*, 36

BERKELEY TECH. L.J.1 (2021). Lacking clear resolution of the scope of design patent protection, the Patent Office eventually pushed Congress to restore design patent law to its original limited purpose of protecting ornamental features of articles of manufacture. *See* S. Rep. No. 57-1139, at 1 (1902). Against the backdrop of confusion and disarray, Congress deleted the word "useful" from the design patent statute and replaced it with "ornamental." Act of May 9, 1902, ch. 783, §4929, 32 Stat. 193 (1902). Under the new Act, "Any person who has invented any new, original, and ornamental design for an article of manufacture" could apply for a design patent. These changes aimed to shift the focus of design patents to appearances and ornamentality and differentiate them from the domain of utility patents.

The 1902 legislation clarified Congress's intent to reinforce the *channeling principle* between design and utility patents through deletion of the word "useful" and insertion of the "ornamental" rubric. This change sought to limit design patents to original *ornamental* features and channel functional advances to the utility patent regime. In the first few decades following the 1902 Act, courts sought to evaluate the question of ornamentality directly, focusing on whether the design in question manifested artistic beauty and aesthetic appeal or by addressing the question of visibility of the design, namely, the "matter of concern" test. *See e.g.*, *In re Stimpson*, 24 F.2d 1012, 1012 (C.A.D.C. 1928) (invalidating a design patent because it was "lacking in symmetry, wanting in grace, and destitute of any appeal to the senses or emotions"). This approach, however, put judges in the uncomfortable role of art critic. As an alternative, courts shifted their focus to the question of functionality—which became the prevalent test.

The Second Circuit's decision in *Baker v. Hughes-Evans Co.*, 270 F. 97 (2d Cir. 1920), confronted the interplay of the utility and design patent regimes. The patentee sought to enforce both a utility and a design patent for an inset soap dish wall receptacle with a protruding lip that could be used as a handle.

Baker Soap Receptacle Patents

Utility Patent No. 1,239,076   **Design Patent No. 50,291**

In ruling that the design was ineligible for a design patent, the court explained that

> the lip receptacle is open to the criticism that its desirable features are functional rather than ornamental. *Weisgerber v. Clowney* (C.C.) 131 Fed. 477. It is true, as pointed out in *Bayley, etc., Co. v. Standart, etc., Co.*, 249 Fed. 478, 161 C.C.A. 436, that the same device or article may exhibit patentable mechanical invention and a patentable design; *but it is not true that the design can ever be used to appropriate (per se) the mechanical function. The two inventions must be separable; otherwise, it would be a contradiction in terms to grant two patents for them.*

Baker v. Hughes-Evans Co., 270 F. 99 (citation omitted).

The court's recognition that a design patent can *never* be used to appropriate a mechanical function aligns with the Supreme Court's fundamental insight in *Baker v. Selden*, 101 U.S. 99 (1879), that it would be a "surprise and fraud upon the public" to grant the author of a book "an exclusive property in the art described." *Id.* at 102. Such is the exclusive province of the utility patent regime. Furthermore, the Second Circuit's recognition in *Baker v. Hughes-Evans Co.* that the functional and ornamental features must be *separable* anticipates the essential limitation on the scope of copyright protection for useful articles. *See* 17 U.S.C. §101 (limiting protection of "Pictorial, graphic, and sculptural works" to "artistic craftsmanship" . . . only to the extent that such design incorporates . . . features that can be identified *separately* from, and are capable of existing independently of, the utilitarian aspects of the article." (emphasis added)). We explore this doctrine in Chapter IV(C)(2)(ii).

In another early case, the Second Circuit observed in a relatively straightforward case invalidating a design patent that the design "does not seem to us to have been dictated by other than utilitarian considerations." *Strause Gas Iron Co. v. William M. Crane Co.*, 235 F. 126, 131 (2d Cir. 1916). The plaintiff asserted both a utility patent and a design patent claiming mechanical and gas means for supplying air and gas for heating the solid ("sad") iron efficiently. The design patent application, filed two years after the utility patent application, claimed the outer shape of the iron. In affirming invalidation of the design patent, Judge Learned Hand explained:

> If there be any room at all in the subject-matter for a design patent, the patentees have not found it. [The court described several similar prior art design patents.] *The modification of these forms into the design patent does not seem to us to have been dictated by other than utilitarian considerations*. To suppose that any inventive effort was necessarily addressed towards pleasing even a most rudimentary aesthetic susceptibility appears to us far-fetched. . . . We believe that any one starting to design sad irons with the art before him, and *governed only by considerations of proportion and plan*, would have had no difficulty in making the plaintiff's iron.

235 F. at 130-31 (emphasis added).

Other courts also found the "dictated by functionality" or "primarily functional" label to be a useful way of resolving easy design patent cases. *See* Menell & Corren, 36 Berkeley Tech. L.J. at 35-53. None of these cases, however, stated or implied that a design that was partially based on functional considerations or in which ornamental elements were inextricably intertwined with functional features was eligible for protection. They simply concluded that a design patent claim that was dictated by functionality or was primarily functional was clearly invalid.

Later cases, without referring back to the clear intent and logic of the 1902 Act, allowed this language to drift into a doctrine that liberalized design patent eligibility, extending protection to features that were both functional and ornamental. In *In re Garbo*, the CCPA reviewed an appeal from the decision of the Board of Appeals of the Patent Office which rejected an application for a design patent on obviousness grounds. The CCPA noted that

> *a design may embody functional features and still be patentable*, but in order to attain this legal status under these circumstances, the design must have an *unobvious appearance* distinct from that dictated *solely* by functional considerations. We do not find this situation here.

In re Garbo, 287 F.2d 192, 193 (C.C.P.A. 1961) (emphases added). The CCPA's terse statement left room for doubt as to the scope of design patent eligibility. What did it mean to say that a design patent "may embody functional features"? Did the CCPA imply that a design patent could extend to functional features so long as they were not "dictated solely by functional considerations"? Could a design that inextricably intertwined aesthetic and functional elements be eligible for a design patent? The regional appellate courts decisions were far more circumspect in communicating that design patents could not monopolize functional elements. *See, e.g., Strause Gas Iron Co.*, 235 F. at 130-31; *Applied Arts Corp. v. Grand Rapids Metalcraft Corp.*, 67 F.2d 428, 430 (6th Cir. 1933) (expressing concern about monopolizing conventional designs through design patent protection); *Circle S Prods. Co. v. Powell Prods.*, 174 F.2d 562, 564 (7th Cir. 1949).

In 1980, the District of Minnesota in *Bergstrom v. Sears, Roebuck & Co.* 496 F. Supp. 476 (D. Minn. 1980), applied an especially lax new test of design patent eligibility: whether "there are numerous possible design solutions" for the article of manufacture. The design patent claimed a series of side-by-side C-shaped tubes that function as both a fireplace grate and a heater. The design heats the ambient air by drawing cool air from the room into the tubes, which is then heated by the fire and then propelling the warm air from the top of the tubes. The court cited no authority for this test, yet it would soon gain favor at the Federal Circuit, which was established two years later and became the exclusive appellate tribunal for utility and design patent cases.

L.A. Gear, Inc. v. Thom McAn Shoe Co.
United States Court of Appeals for the Federal Circuit
988 F.2d 1117 (Fed. Cir. 2008)

NEWMAN, CIRCUIT JUDGE.

Thom McAn Shoe Company appeal[s] the decision of the United States District Court for the Southern District of New York holding [it] liable for design patent infringement . . .

Background

In 1987 L.A. Gear designed a line of women's and girls' athletic shoes identified as the L.A. Gear's "Hot Shots" shoes. United States Design Patent No. 299,081 was granted on December 27, 1988 ("the '081 patent"). Figure 4 of the patent is shown:

. . .

In the summer and fall of 1987 L.A. Gear exhibited the Hot Shots line of shoes to retailers at trade shows, and announced that these shoes had been selected as L.A. Gear's "hero" or featured shoe line, on which major promotion and advertising would be focused for the ensuing year.

Designers employed by [McAn] used the L.A. Gear shoes as models for the shoes accused of infringement: a women's high top shoe sold in Thom McAn stores . . .

Functionality

[McAn] asserted at trial, and argues on appeal, that the design of the '081 patent is "functional" and that the patent is therefore invalid. . . .

A design patent is directed to the appearance of an article of manufacture. An article of manufacture necessarily serves a utilitarian purpose, and the design of a useful article is deemed to be functional when the appearance of the claimed design is "dictated by" the use or purpose of the article. *In re Carletti*, 328 F.2d 1020, 1022, 140 USPQ 653, 654 (CCPA 1964); *Power Controls Corp. v. Hybrinetics, Inc.*, 806 F.2d 234, 238, 231 USPQ 774, 777 (Fed.Cir.1986) (patented design must be primarily ornamental). If the particular design is essential to the use of the article, it can not be the subject of a design patent.

[McAn] argues that each element comprising the '081 design has a utilitarian purpose: that is, the delta wing provides support for the foot and reinforces the shoelace eyelets; the mesh on the side of the shoe also provides support; the moustache at the back of the shoe provides cushioning for the Achilles tendon and reinforcement for the rear of the shoe; and the position of each of these elements on the shoe is due to its function. However, the utility of each of the various elements that comprise the design is not the relevant inquiry with respect to a design patent. In determining whether a design is primarily functional or primarily ornamental the claimed design is viewed in its entirety, for the ultimate question is not the functional or decorative aspect of each separate feature, but the overall appearance of the article, in determining whether the claimed design is dictated by the utilitarian purpose of the article.

That elements of the '081 design, such as the delta wing or the side mesh, also provide support for the foot does not mean that the specific design of each element, and the combination of these elements into the patented design, is dictated by primarily functional considerations. The elements of the design may indeed serve a utilitarian purpose, but it is the ornamental aspect that is the basis of the design patent. *Carletti*, 328 F.2d at 1022.

The district court remarked on the existence of a myriad of athletic shoe designs in which each of the functions identified by [McAn] as performed by the '081 design elements was achieved in a way other than by the design of the '081 patent. When there are several ways to achieve the function of an article of manufacture, the design of the article is more likely to serve a primarily ornamental purpose. *See Avia Group International, Inc. v. L.A. Gear California, Inc.*, 853 F.2d 1557, 1563 (Fed.Cir.1988). It was not disputed that there were other ways of designing athletic shoes to perform the functions of the elements of the '081 design. In today's marketplace, the primacy of appearance in the design of shoes can not be ignored when analyzing functionality.

The district court found that the '081 design was primarily ornamental, and that the patent was not invalid on the ground of functionality. Clear error has not been shown in this ruling, which is affirmed.

COMMENTS AND QUESTIONS

1. What is the Federal Circuit's ornamentality/non-functionality test? Does it exclude a design that inextricably intertwines decorative and functional elements? Why isn't "the utility of each of the various elements that comprise the design" a key clue to the question of design patent functionality? What if an expert were to show that this combination of elements is synergistic and effective in achieving optimal support and performance for an athletic shoe? Does the court give adequate consideration to the functionality of the composite design?

2. Doesn't the "availability of alternative designs" test ensure that almost all designs that comprise a combination of elements will be eligible for design patent protection? *See* Peter S. Menell & Ella Corren, *The Design Patent Emperor Wears No Clothes: Responding to Advocates of Design Patent Protection for Functionality*, 36 BERKELEY TECH. L.J. 231(2021); Christopher Buccafusco & Mark A. Lemley, *Functionality*

Screens, 103 VA. L. REV. 1293 (2017) (making this claim and arguing that the court has whittled functionality away to the vanishing point); *cf. Ezaki Glico Kabushiki Kaisha v. Lotte Int'l*, 986 F.3d 250, 260 (3d Cir. 2021) (observing that the availability of alternative designs does not make a design non-functional under trademark law).

3. *Fidelity to the 1902 Act?* Does the Federal Circuit's test for ornamentality/non-functionality comport with Congress's intention to ensure that functional advances are channeled exclusively to the utility patent regime? *See generally*, Peter S. Menell & Ella Corren, *Design Patent Law's Identity Crisis* 36 BERKELEY TECH. L.J. 1 (2021) (tracing the history of the ornamentality/non-functionality jurisprudence and highlighting that the Federal Circuit has never expressly considered the 1902 Act and its legislative history).

4. *Interaction with Other Laws.* As we will see, both copyright and trademark law also have rules that restriction protection for functional elements. But the modern design patent rule reads functionality so narrowly that the Federal Circuit has held the very same design elements to be functional under trademark law but nonfunctional under design patent law. *Apple Corp. v. Samsung Elecs., Inc.*, 786 F.3d 983 (Fed. Cir. 2015). Does it make sense to treat functionality differently in different legal regimes?

3. Infringement

Egyptian Goddess, Inc. v. Swisa, Inc.
United States Court of Appeals for the Federal Circuit
543 F.3d 665 (Fed. Cir. 2008) (en banc)

BRYSON, CIRCUIT JUDGE.

We granted rehearing en banc in this design patent case to address the appropriate legal standard to be used in assessing claims of design patent infringement.

Appellant Egyptian Goddess, Inc., ("EGI") brought this action . . . alleging that Swisa, Inc., had infringed EGI's U.S. Design Patent No. 467,389 ("the '389 patent"). The patent claimed a design for a nail buffer, consisting of a rectangular, hollow tube having a generally square cross-section and featuring buffer surfaces on three of its four sides. Swisa's accused product consists of a rectangular, hollow tube having a square cross-section, but featuring buffer surfaces on all four of its sides.

The district court first issued an order construing the claim of the '389 patent. In so doing, the district court sought to describe in words the design set forth in Figure 1 of the patent, which is depicted below:

Upon study of the claimed design, the court described it as follows:

A hollow tubular frame of generally square cross section, where the square has sides of length S, the frame has a length of approximately 3S, and the frame has a thickness of approximately $T = 0.1S$; the corners of the cross section are rounded, with the outer corner of the cross section rounded on a 90 degree radius of approximately 1.25T, and the inner corner of the cross section rounded on a 90 degree radius of approximately 0.25T; and with rectangular abrasive pads of thickness T affixed to three of the sides of the frame, covering the flat portion of the sides while leaving the curved radius uncovered, with the fourth side of the frame bare.

In the same order, the district court ruled that "Swisa has not shown that the appearance of the Buffer Patent is dictated by its utilitarian purpose." The court therefore held that the patent is not invalid on the ground that the design was governed solely by function.

Swisa then moved for summary judgment of noninfringement. The district court granted the motion. Citing precedent of this court, the district court stated that the plaintiff in a design patent case must prove both (1) that the accused device is "substantially similar" to the claimed design under what is referred to as the "ordinary observer" test, and (2) that the accused device contains "substantially the same points of novelty that distinguished the patented design from the prior art. After comparing the claimed design and the accused product, the court held that Swisa's allegedly infringing product did not incorporate the "point of novelty" of the '389 patent, which the court identified as "a fourth, bare side to the buffer."

The district court noted that the parties disagreed as to the points of novelty in the '389 patent. EGI identified four elements in its design, and for each element it identified prior art that did not embody that element. EGI therefore contended that the point of novelty of the '389 patent is the combination of those four elements. The district court, however, declined to address the question whether the point of novelty could be found in the combination of elements not present in various prior art references, because the court found that a single prior art reference, United States Design Patent No. 416,648 ("the Nailco patent"), contained all but one of the elements of the '389 design. The court described the Nailco Patent as disclosing "a nail buffer with an open and hollow body, raised rectangular pads, and open corners." The only element of the '389 patent design that was not present in the Nailco patent, according to the district court, was "the addition of the fourth side without a pad, thereby transforming the equilateral triangular cross-section into a square." Because the Swisa product does not incorporate the point of novelty of the '389 patent—a fourth side without a pad—the court concluded that there was no infringement.

EGI appealed, and a panel of this court affirmed. . . .

This court granted rehearing en banc and asked the parties to address several questions, including whether the "point of novelty" test should continue to be used as a test for infringement of a design patent; whether the court should adopt the "non-trivial advance test" as a means of determining whether a particular design feature qualifies as a point of novelty; how the point of novelty test should be administered, particularly when numerous features of the design differ from certain prior art designs; and whether district courts should perform formal claim construction in design patent cases.

I

The starting point for any discussion of the law of design patents is the Supreme Court's decision in *Gorham Co. v. White*, 14 Wall. 511 (1871). That case involved a design patent for the handles of tablespoons and forks. In its analysis of claim infringement, the Court stated that the test of identity of design "must be sameness of appearance, and mere difference of lines in the drawing or sketch . . . or slight variances in configuration . . . will not destroy the substantial identity." *Id.* at 526–27. Identity of appearance, the Court explained, or "sameness of effect upon the eye, is the main test of substantial identity of design"; the two need not be the same "to the eye of an expert," because if that were the test, "[t]here never could be piracy of a patented design, for human ingenuity has never yet produced a design, in all its details, exactly like another, so like, that an expert could not distinguish them." *Id.* at 527.

The Gorham Court then set forth the test that has been cited in many subsequent cases: "[I]f, in the eye of an ordinary observer, giving such attention as a purchaser usually gives, two designs are substantially the same, if the resemblance is such as to deceive such an observer, inducing him to purchase one supposing it to be the other, the first one patented is infringed by the other." 81 U.S. at 528. In the case before it, the Court concluded that "whatever differences there may be between the plaintiffs' design and those of the defendant in details of ornament, they are still the same in general appearance and effect, so much alike that in the market and with purchasers they would pass for the same thing—so much alike that even persons in the trade would be in danger of being deceived." *Id.* at 531.

Since the decision in Gorham, the test articulated by the Court in that case has been referred to as the "ordinary observer" test and has been recognized by lower courts, including both of this court's predecessors, as the proper standard for determining design patent infringement. . . .

II

EGI argues that this court should no longer recognize the point of novelty test as a second part of the test for design patent infringement, distinct from the ordinary observer test established in Gorham. Instead of requiring the fact-finder to identify one or more points of novelty in the patented design and then determining whether the accused design has appropriated some or all of those points of novelty, EGI contends that the ordinary observer test can fulfill the purposes for which the point of novelty test was designed, but with less risk of confusion. As long as the ordinary observer test focuses on the "appearance that distinguishes the patented design from the prior art," EGI contends that it will enable the fact-finder to address the proper inquiry, i.e., whether an ordinary observer, familiar with the prior art, would be deceived into thinking that the accused design was the same as the patented design. Relatedly, EGI argues that if the ordinary observer test is performed from the perspective of an ordinary observer who is familiar with the prior art, there is no need for a separate "non-trivial advance" test, because the attention of an ordinary observer familiar with prior art designs will naturally be drawn to the features of the claimed and accused designs that render them distinct from the prior art.

Several of the amici make essentially the same point, referring to the proper approach as calling for a three-way visual comparison between the patented design, the accused design, and the closest prior art. . . .

Swisa counters that this court may not, and should not, abandon the point of novelty test. According to Swisa, the point of novelty test was adopted by the Supreme Court in *Smith v. Whitman Saddle Co.*, 148 U.S. 674 (1893). . . .

We disagree with Swisa's submission. A close reading of Whitman Saddle and subsequent authorities indicates that the Supreme Court did not adopt a separate point of novelty test for design patent infringement cases. In fact, a study of the development of design patent law in the years after Gorham shows that the point of novelty test, in its current form, is of quite recent vintage. After a review of those authorities, which we examine in some detail below, we conclude that the point of novelty test, as a second and free-standing requirement for proof of design patent infringement, is inconsistent with the ordinary observer test laid down in *Gorham*, is not mandated by *Whitman Saddle* or precedent from other courts, and is not needed to protect against unduly broad assertions of design patent rights. . . .

[T]his court has cited *Litton Systems* for the proposition that the point of novelty test is separate from the ordinary observer test and requires the patentee to point out the point of novelty in the claimed design that has been appropriated by the accused design. We think, however, that Litton and the predecessor cases on which it relied are more properly read as applying a version of the ordinary observer test in which the ordinary observer is deemed to view the differences between the patented design and the accused product in the context of the prior art. When the differences between the claimed and accused design are viewed in light of the prior art, the attention of the hypothetical ordinary observer will be drawn to those aspects of the claimed design that differ from the prior art. And when the claimed design is close to the prior art designs, small differences between the accused design and the claimed design are likely to be important to the eye of the hypothetical ordinary observer. It was for that reason that the Supreme Court in *Whitman Saddle* focused on the one feature of the patented saddle design that departed from the prior art—the sharp drop at the rear of the pommel. To an observer familiar with the multitude of prior art saddle designs, including the design incorporating the Granger pommel and the Jenifer cantle, "an addition frequently made," 148 U.S. at 682, the sharp drop at the rear of the pommel would be important to the overall appearance of the design and would serve to distinguish the accused design, which did not possess that feature, from the claimed design. . . .

Not only is this approach consistent with the precedents discussed above, but it makes sense as a matter of logic as well. Particularly in close cases, it can be difficult to answer the question whether one thing is like another without being given a frame of reference. The context in which the claimed and accused designs are compared, i.e., the background prior art, provides such a frame of reference and is therefore often useful in the process of comparison. Where the frame of reference consists of numerous similar prior art designs, those designs can highlight the distinctions between the claimed design and the accused design as viewed by the ordinary observer.

Applying the ordinary observer test with reference to prior art designs also avoids some of the problems created by the separate point of novelty test. One such problem is that the point of novelty test has proved difficult to apply in cases in which there are several different features that can be argued to be points of novelty in the claimed design. In such cases, the outcome of the case can turn on which of the several candidate points of novelty the court or fact-finder focuses on. The attention of the court may therefore be focused on whether the accused design has appropriated a single specified feature of the claimed design, rather than on the proper inquiry, i.e., whether the accused design has appropriated the claimed design as a whole.

In addition, the more novel the design, and the more points of novelty that are identified, the more opportunities there are for a defendant to argue that its design does not infringe because it does not copy all of the points of novelty, even though it may copy most of them and even though it may give the overall appearance of being identical to the claimed design. In such cases, a test that asks how an ordinary observer with knowledge of the prior art designs would view the differences between the claimed and accused designs is likely to produce results more in line with the purposes of design patent protection.

This court has characterized the purpose of the point of novelty test as being "to focus on those aspects of a design which render the design different from prior art designs." *Sun Hill Indus., Inc.*, 48 F.3d at 1197, quoting *Winner Int'l Corp. v. Wolo Mfg. Corp.*, 905 F.2d 375, 376 (Fed. Cir. 1990). That purpose can be equally well served, however, by applying the ordinary observer test through the eyes of an observer familiar with the prior art. If the accused design has copied a particular feature of the claimed design that departs conspicuously from the prior art, the accused design is naturally more likely to be regarded as deceptively similar to the claimed design, and thus infringing. At the same time, unlike the point of novelty test, the ordinary observer test does not present the risk of assigning exaggerated importance to small differences between the claimed and accused designs relating to an insignificant feature simply because that feature can be characterized as a point of novelty.

This approach also has the advantage of avoiding the debate over the extent to which a combination of old design features can serve as a point of novelty under the point of novelty test. An ordinary observer, comparing the claimed and accused designs in light of the prior art, will attach importance to differences between the claimed design and the prior art depending on the overall effect of those differences on the design. If the claimed design consists of a combination of old features that creates an appearance deceptively similar to the accused design, even to an observer familiar with similar prior art designs, a finding of infringement would be justified. Otherwise, infringement would not be found.

One function that has been served by the point of novelty test, according to Swisa and its supporting amici, is to cabin unduly broad assertions of design patent scope by ensuring that a design that merely embodies or is substantially similar to prior art designs is not found to infringe. Again, however, we believe that the preferable way to achieve that purpose is to do so directly, by relying on the ordinary observer test, conducted in light of the prior art. Our rejection of the point of novelty test does not mean, of course, that the differences between the claimed design and prior art designs are irrelevant. To the contrary, examining the novel features of the claimed design can be an important component of the comparison of the claimed design with the accused design and the prior art. But the comparison of the designs, including the examination of any novel features, must be conducted as part of the ordinary observer test, not as part of a separate test focusing on particular points of novelty that are designated only in the course of litigation.

On the basis of the foregoing analysis, we hold that the "point of novelty" test should no longer be used in the analysis of a claim of design patent infringement. Because we reject the "point of novelty" test, we also do not adopt the "non-trivial advance" test, which is a refinement of the "point of novelty" test. Instead, in accordance with *Gorham* and subsequent decisions, we hold that the "ordinary observer" test should be the sole test for determining whether a design patent has been infringed. Under that test, as this court has sometimes described it, infringement will not be found unless the accused article "embod[ies] the patented design or any colorable imitation thereof." *Goodyear Tire & Rubber Co.*, 162 F.3d at 1116–17.

In some instances, the claimed design and the accused design will be sufficiently distinct that it will be clear without more that the patentee has not met its burden of proving the two designs would appear "substantially the same" to the ordinary observer, as required by Gorham. In other instances, when the claimed and accused designs are not plainly dissimilar, resolution of the question whether the ordinary observer would consider the two designs to be substantially the same will benefit from a comparison of the claimed and accused designs with the prior art, as in many of the cases discussed above and in the case at bar. Where there are many examples of similar prior art designs, as in a case such as *Whitman Saddle*, differences between the claimed and accused designs that might not be noticeable in the abstract can become significant to the hypothetical ordinary observer who is conversant with the prior art.

We emphasize that although the approach we adopt will frequently involve comparisons between the claimed design and the prior art, it is not a test for determining validity, but is designed solely as a test of infringement. Thus, as is always the case, the burden of proof as to infringement remains on the patentee. However, if the accused infringer elects to rely on the comparison prior art as part of its defense against the claim of infringement, the burden of production of that prior art is on the accused infringer. To be sure, we have stated that the burden to introduce prior art under the point of novelty test falls on the patentee. Under the ordinary observer test, however, it makes sense to impose the burden of production as to any comparison prior art on the accused infringer. The accused infringer is the party with the motivation to point out close prior art, and in particular to call to the court's attention the prior art that an ordinary observer is most likely to regard as highlighting the differences between the claimed and accused design. Regardless of whether the accused infringer elects to present prior art that it considers pertinent to the comparison between the claimed and accused design, however, the patentee bears the ultimate burden of proof to demonstrate infringement by a preponderance of the evidence. . . .

III

One of the issues raised by this court in its order granting en banc review was whether trial courts should conduct claim construction in design patent cases. While this court has held that trial courts have a duty to conduct claim construction in design patent cases, as in utility patent cases, the court has not prescribed any particular form that the claim construction must take. To the contrary, the court has recognized that design patents "typically are claimed as shown in drawings," and that claim construction "is adapted accordingly." *Arminak & Assocs., Inc.*, 501 F.3d at 1319. For that reason, this court has not required that the trial court attempt to provide a detailed verbal description of the claimed design, as is typically done in the case of utility patents. *See Contessa Food Prods., Inc.* [*v. Conagra, Inc.*, 282 F.3d 1370, 1377 (Fed. Cir.2002)] (approving district court's construction of the asserted claim as meaning "a tray of a certain design as shown in Figures 1–3").[1]

As the Supreme Court has recognized, a design is better represented by an illustration "than it could be by any description and a description would probably not be intelligible without the illustration." *Dobson v. Dornan*, 118 U.S. 10, 14 (1886). The Patent and Trademark Office has made the same observation. MANUAL OF PATENT EXAMINING PROCEDURE §1503.01 (8th ed. 2006) ("[A]s a rule the illustration in the drawing views is its own best description."). Given the recognized difficulties entailed in trying to describe a design in words, the preferable course ordinarily will be for a district court not to attempt to "construe" a design patent claim by providing a detailed verbal description of the claimed design.

With that said, it is important to emphasize that a district court's decision regarding the level of detail to be used in describing the claimed design is a matter within the court's discretion, and absent a showing of prejudice, the court's decision to issue a relatively detailed claim construction will not be reversible error. At the same time, it should be clear that the court is not obligated to issue a detailed verbal description of the design if it does not regard verbal elaboration as necessary or helpful. In addition, in deciding whether to attempt a verbal description of the claimed design, the court should recognize the risks entailed in such a description, such as the risk of placing

---

[1] This court has required that in determining obviousness, a district court must attempt to "translate [the] visual descriptions into words" in order to communicate the reasoning behind the court's decision and to enable "the parties and appellate courts TTT to discern the internal reasoning employed by the trial court." *Durling v. Spectrum Furniture Co.*, 101 F.3d 100, 102 (Fed. Cir.1996). Requiring such an explanation of a legal ruling as to invalidity is quite different from requiring an elaborate verbal claim construction to guide the finder of fact in conducting the infringement inquiry.

undue emphasis on particular features of the design and the risk that a finder of fact will focus on each individual described feature in the verbal description rather than on the design as a whole. In this case, for example, the district court came up with a detailed verbal description of the claimed design. We see no inaccuracy in the court's description, and neither party has pointed to any prejudice resulting from the court's interpretation. Yet it is not clear that the considerable effort needed to fashion the verbal description contributed enough to the process of analyzing the case to justify the effort.

While it may be unwise to attempt a full description of the claimed design, a court may find it helpful to point out, either for a jury or in the case of a bench trial by way of describing the court's own analysis, various features of the claimed design as they relate to the accused design and the prior art. . . .

. . . We therefore leave the question of verbal characterization of the claimed designs to the discretion of trial judges, with the proviso that as a general matter, those courts should not treat the process of claim construction as requiring a detailed verbal description of the claimed design, as would typically be true in the case of utility patents.

IV

We now turn to the facts of this case. It is agreed that the general shape of the accused nail buffer at issue in this case is the same as that of the patented buffer design. The difference between the two is that the accused buffer has raised buffing pads on all four sides, while the patented buffer has buffing pads on only three sides. The two closest prior art nail buffers before the court were the Falley nail buffer, which has a solid, rectangular cross section with slightly raised buffers on all sides, and the Nailco patent, which shows a nail buffer design having a triangular shape and a hollow cross section, and in which raised buffing pads are located on all three sides. The four nail buffers are pictured below:

Falley Buffer Block   Nailco Patent   Swisa Buffer   '389 patent

The question before this court under the standard we have set forth above is whether an ordinary observer, familiar with the prior art Falley and Nailco designs, would be deceived into believing the Swisa buffer is the same as the patented buffer. EGI argues that such an observer would notice a difference between the prior art and the '389 patent, consisting of "the hollow tube that is square in cross section and that has raised pads with exposed gaps at the corners." To support that contention, EGI invokes the declaration of its expert witness, Kathleen Eaton. After viewing the patented, accused, and Nailco buffers, Ms. Eaton concluded that the patented and accused designs would "confuse an ordinary observer into purchasing the accused buffer thinking it to be the patented buffer design." She reached that conclusion, she explained, because "the substantially similar appearance [between the accused and patented designs] results from both designs having a hollow tube, square in cross section and rectangular in length, with multiple raised rectangular pads mounted on the sides, and that do not cover the corners of the tube." While recognizing that the accused buffer has pads on all four sides and that the claimed design has buffer pads on only three sides, she stated that "I do not believe that, to an ordinary observer and purchaser of nail buffers, the presence of one more buffer pad[s] greatly alters the ornamental effect and appearance of the whole design as compared to the whole patented design."

Swisa counters that the '389 patent closely tracks the design of the Nailco nail buffer, except that it "add[s] a fourth side without an abrasive pad, resulting in square ends." In light of the close prior art buffers, including a number having square cross-sections, Swisa argues that an ordinary observer would notice the difference between the claimed and accused designs. To support that contention, Swisa cites the declaration of its expert, Steve Falley. Mr. Falley addressed the differences among the prior art designs, the accused design, and patented design, and he concluded that

> you could simply add to the Nailco Buffer a fourth side without an abrasive on it. This merely takes the Nailco Buffer to the block shape of the original Falley Buffer Block, while keeping the hollow aspect of the Nailco Buffer. As there had already been on the market for a long time 3-way buffer blocks that had no abrasive on one side, it was also obvious after the Nailco Buffer that you could have a three way hollow buffer that had four sides but with no abrasive on one side.

Mr. Falley added that "four-way" nail buffers having four different abrasive surfaces have been made since 1985, and that four-sided "buffer blocks" have been on the market since 1987. He pointed to catalogs showing three-sided and four-sided buffer blocks that have been offered for sale since at least 1994, and in light of his knowledge of the industry, he stated that the "number of sides with abrasive surface on them would be important to purchasers because it determines whether a buffer is a 'three way buffer' or a 'four way buffer.'" Accordingly, he concluded:

> The difference between a buffer with abrasive on three sides—a "three-way buffer"—and a buffer with abrasive on four sides—a "four-way buffer"—is immediately apparent to any consumer used to buying nail buffers. Even if such a consumer did not have a preference for either three-way or four-way buffers (although they almost always do), they would at a glance be able to tell that a buffer with abrasive on only three sides had abrasive on three sides, and was a three-way buffer, while a buffer with abrasive on four sides had abrasive on all four sides, and was a four-way buffer. I cannot imagine consumers would buy buffers with abrasive on four sides thinking that they were buying buffers with abrasive on three sides.

The problem with Ms. Eaton's declaration is that she characterized the accused and patented designs as similar because they both have square cross sections and "multiple" raised buffer pads, without directly acknowledging that the patented design has three pads while the accused design has four, one on each side. She also failed to address the fact that the design of the Nailco patent is identical to the accused device except that the Nailco design has three sides rather than four. Thus, she could as easily have said that the Nailco buffer design "is like the accused design because both designs have a hollow tube, have multiple rectangular sides with raised rectangular pads mounted on each side that do not cover the corners of the tube," in which case the Nailco prior art buffer would be seen to closely resemble the accused design. Nothing about Ms. Eaton's declaration explains why an ordinary observer would regard the accused design as being closer to the claimed design than to the Nailco prior art patent. In fact, Ms. Eaton's reference to the prior art buffers is limited to the single, and conclusory, comment that an ordinary observer and purchaser of nail buffers would consider the patented design and the accused buffer to be substantially similar, "particularly in light of other nail buffers, such as a solid block buffer and the hollow triangular Nailco buffer."

In light of the similarity of the prior art buffers to the accused buffer, we conclude that no reasonable fact-finder could find that EGI met its burden of showing, by a preponderance of the evidence, that an ordinary observer, taking into account the prior art, would believe the accused design to be the same as the patented design. In concluding that a reasonable fact-finder could not find infringement in this case, we reach the same conclusion that the district court reached, and for many of the same reasons. Although we do so by using the ordinary observer test as informed by the prior art, rather than by applying the point of novelty test, our analysis largely tracks that of the district court. After analyzing the Nailco patent and the claimed design, as they related to the accused design, the district court concluded that "in the context of nail buffers, a fourth side without a pad is not substantially the same as a fourth side with a pad." While the district court focused on the differences in the particular feature at issue rather than the effect of those differences on the appearance of the design as a whole, we are satisfied that the difference on which the district court focused is important, viewed in the context of the prior art. . . .

AFFIRMED.

COMMENTS AND QUESTIONS

1. *Point of Novelty.* The court dismissed the point of novelty inquiry. Does that make sense to you? Consider the following objection to *Egyptian Goddess*:

[S]ubsequent Federal Circuit cases have used *Egyptian Goddess* as precedent in concluding that point of novelty is no longer the test for the invalidity of a design patent either.

Think about this for a minute. It is no longer the law that the defendant must incorporate the very thing that makes the patented invention patentable. As long as an ordinary observer would confuse the two products, the fact that that confusion arises from similarities that already exist in the prior art doesn't defeat a finding of infringement. It might or might not create a defense that the patent is invalid for anticipation, though again that seems to depend on what an ordinary observer would think when comparing the patented design and the prior art. Translated for a moment into terms of utility patents, it is as though we granted a patent on a car having an intermittent windshield wiper as the novel feature and then allowed the patentee to sue a car maker that didn't include that feature because the cars otherwise had the same elements. That can't possibly be the right rule.

. . . [O]ne reasonable reading of the case is that the court intended not to make the point of novelty irrelevant but simply to change the burden of proof on whether the defendant appropriated the novelty of the patentee's invention. . . . But if avoiding burden-shifting was the court's goal, it didn't do a very good job of achieving it. Whatever the legal standard, we don't want patentees suing defendants who do no more than practice the prior art. Such suits can't succeed in utility patent law because of the requirement that each element be present in the accused device. If the defendant is merely practicing the prior art and the patent is construed so broadly that it covers what the defendant is doing, the patent will be invalid. So to infringe a utility patent, the defendant must include the thing that makes the invention patentable. But after *Egyptian Goddess*, there is no longer such a requirement in design patent law. A design patent can now be infringed even by a product that lacks the new feature encompassed by the patent as long as an ordinary observer would think the two were substantially the same.

Mark A. Lemley, *Point of Novelty*, 105 Nw. U. L. Rev. 1253, 1271–72 (2012).

2. *Claim Construction.* How does claim construction of design patents compare with claim construction of utility patent claims? Does it make sense to try to compare drawings of three-dimensional objects with verbal descriptions?

3. *Relevance of Consumer Confusion?* The court's infringement standard references "consumer confusion," a concept that will be the focus of analysis in the trademark chapter. Why is this relevant to design patent infringement?

This appears to be a relic of the mid-19th century when design patents served, in part, to protect product labels before federal trademark law emerged. We see such trademark-like language dating back to that era.

4. *Interplay of Infringement, Nonobviousness, and Functionality Analysis.* Is it possible to conduct the infringement comparison without considering originality and functionality? To what extent does the "three-way" test incorporate these considerations? We will revisit these issues when we get to copyright and trademark infringement analysis.

Richardson v. Stanley Works, Inc.
United States Court of Appeals for the Federal Circuit
597 F.3d 1288 (Fed. Cir. 2010)

LOURIE, CIRCUIT JUDGE.

David Richardson appeals from a final decision of the United States District Court for the District of Arizona. After a bench trial, the district court found that Stanley Works, Inc. ("Stanley") did not infringe U.S. Patent D507,167 ("the '167 patent"). Because the court correctly construed the claim at issue and correctly determined that the patent was not infringed, we affirm.

BACKGROUND

Richardson owns the '167 patent, a design patent that claims the design for a multi-function carpentry tool that combines a conventional hammer with a stud climbing tool and a crowbar. The tool is known as the "Stepclaw." The only claim of the '167 patent claims the ornamental design of the tool as depicted in figures 1 and 2 of the patent:

FIG.1

FIG.2

Stanley manufactures and sells construction tools. In 2005, Stanley introduced into the U.S. market a product line of tools by the series name "Fubar." The Fubar is sold in five different versions and is useful in carpentry, demolition, and construction work. Stanley successfully applied for and obtained U.S. Patent D562,101 ("the '101 patent") on the basic Fubar design. All five versions of the tool are built around that same basic Fubar design. Figures 1 and 5 of the '101 patent are illustrative of the Fubar design:

Figure 1

Figure 5

Richardson filed a complaint against Stanley . . . alleging that the Fubar tools infringed his '167 patent. . . . [Following a bench trial,] the court . . . entered judgment of noninfringement in favor of Stanley. In its order, the court first distinguished, as part of its claim construction, the ornamental aspects from the functional aspects of Richardson's design and then determined that an ordinary observer, after discounting the functional elements of Richardson's design, would not be deceived into thinking that any of the Fubar tools were the same as Richardson's Stepclaw. The court therefore concluded that the overall visual effect of the Fubar was not substantially similar to that of the Stepclaw, and that the '167 patent had not been infringed. . . .

DISCUSSION

A. *Claim Construction*

Richardson argues that the district court's approach to evaluating infringement of a design patent was incorrect. Richardson primarily argues that the district court erred in its claim construction by separating the functional aspects of the design from the ornamental ones, rather than considering the design as a whole. Richardson argues that our *Egyptian Goddess* decision requires that the patented design be compared in its entirety with the accused design, and that the comparison be made from the perspective of an ordinary observer. *See Egyptian Goddess, Inc. v. Swisa, Inc.,* 543 F.3d 665 (Fed.Cir.2008) (en banc). A claim construction such as the one performed by the district court, Richardson argues, is necessary only for designs that contain "purely functional" elements. According to Richardson, a design element is purely functional only when the function encompassed by that element cannot be performed by any other design. Richardson contends that the overall design of the '167 patent is not dictated by the useful elements found in the tool, and that the functional parts of its design remain relevant to the scope of the patented claim.

. . . We disagree with Richardson that the district court erred in its claim construction by separating the functional and ornamental aspects of the '167 patent design. In *OddzOn,* we affirmed a district court's claim construction wherein the court had carefully distinguished the ornamental features of the patented design from the overall "rocket-like" appearance of the design of a football-shaped foam ball with a tail and fin structure. *OddzOn Prods., Inc. v. Just Toys, Inc.,* 122 F.3d 1396, 1405 (Fed.Cir.1997). We held that "[w]here a design contains both functional and non-functional elements, the scope of the claim must be construed in order to identify the non-functional aspects of the design as shown in the patent." *Id.*

The issue before us is not very different from that in *OddzOn,* and we are not persuaded by Richardson's argument that our holding in *Egyptian Goddess* mandates a different result here. In *Egyptian Goddess,* we abandoned the point of novelty test for design patent infringement and held that the ordinary observer test should serve as the sole test for infringement. 543 F.3d at 679. Although we proposed that the preferable course ordinarily will be for a district court not to attempt to construe a design patent claim, *id.,* we also emphasized that there are a number of claim scope issues on which a court's guidance would be useful to the fact finder. *Id.* at 680. Among them, we specifically noted, is the distinction between the functional and ornamental aspects of a design. *Id.* (citing *OddzOn,* 122 F.3d at 1405).

The district court here properly factored out the functional aspects of Richardson's design as part of its claim construction. By definition, the patented design is for a multi-function tool that has several functional components, and we have made clear that a design patent, unlike a utility patent, limits protection to the ornamental design of the article. *Lee v. Dayton–Hudson Corp.,* 838 F.2d 1186, 1188 (Fed.Cir.1988) (citing 35 U.S.C. §171). If the patented design is primarily functional rather than ornamental, the patent is invalid. *Id.* However, when the design also contains ornamental aspects, it is entitled to a design patent whose scope is limited to those aspects alone and does not extend to any functional elements of the claimed article. *See L.A. Gear, Inc. v. Thom McAn Shoe Co.,* 988 F.2d 1117, 1123 (Fed.Cir.1993) ("The elements of the design may indeed serve a utilitarian purpose, but it is the ornamental aspect that is the basis of the design patent.").

Richardson's multi-function tool comprises several elements that are driven purely by utility. As the district court noted, elements such as the handle, the hammerhead, the jaw, and the crowbar are dictated by their functional purpose. The jaw, for example, has to be located on the opposite end of the hammer head such that the tool can be used as a step. The crowbar, by definition, needs to be on the end of the longer handle such that it can reach into narrow spaces. The handle has to be the longest arm of the tool to allow for maximum leverage. The hammer-head has to be flat on its end to effectively deliver force to the object being struck. As demonstrated by the prior art, those are purely functional elements whose utility has been known and used in the art for well over a century.

Richardson's argument that the court erred in separating out functional aspects of his design essentially is an argument for a claim scope that includes the utilitarian elements of his multi-function tool. We agree with the district court that it would indeed be improper to allow Richardson to do so. The '167 patent specifically claims "the ornamental design" for the multi-function tool shown in the drawings. A claim to a design containing numerous functional elements, such as here, necessarily mandates a narrow construction. Nothing in our *en banc Egyptian Goddess* opinion compels a different outcome. . . .

B. *Infringement*

Richardson argues that the district court failed to analyze infringement of the '167 patent by Stanley's tools under an ordinary observer test. According to Richardson, had the court conducted a three-way comparison between the prior art, the patented design and the accused products, it would have found the accused product design to be substantially the same as the patented one.

Stanley responds that, having identified the ornamental aspects of Richardson's patented design, the court properly found that the only similarities between the patented Stepclaw and the accused Fubar tools were those of unprotectable functional elements.

Stanley argues that when those utilitarian aspects are ignored, none of the accused Fubar products looks even remotely like Richardson's patented design.

We agree with the court's finding of noninfringement. Design patent infringement is a question of fact, which a patentee must prove by a preponderance of the evidence. In *Egyptian Goddess,* we held that "the 'ordinary observer' test should be the sole test for determining whether a design patent has been infringed." 543 F.3d at 678. The patentee must establish that an ordinary observer, familiar with the prior art designs, would be deceived into believing that the accused product is the same as the patented design. In our recent *Crocs* decision, we set out in detail how an ordinary observer analysis could be conducted to determine infringement. *See Crocs,* 598 F.3d at 1303–06. In analyzing whether a design patent on footwear was infringed, noting the various differences that could be found between the two pieces of footwear in question, we compared their overall effect on the designs. We looked to ornamental elements such as the curves in the design, the strap assembly, and the base portion of the footwear. We concluded that both the claimed design and the accused designs contained those overall ornamental effects, thereby allowing for market confusion.

The ordinary observer test similarly applies in cases where the patented design incorporates numerous functional elements. *See Amini Innovation Corp. v. Anthony Cal., Inc.,* 439 F.3d 1365, 1372 (Fed.Cir.2006) (holding that while it is proper to factor out the functional aspects of various design elements, that discounting of functional elements must not convert the overall infringement test to an element-by-element comparison). In evaluating infringement, we determine whether "the deception that arises is a result of the similarities in the overall design, not of similarities in ornamental features in isolation." *Amini Innovation,* 439 F.3d at 1371. . . .

We . . . agree that, ignoring the functional elements of the tools, the two designs are indeed different. Each of the Fubar tools has a streamlined visual theme that runs throughout the design including elements such as a tapered hammer-head, a streamlined crow-bar, a triangular neck with rounded surfaces, and a smoothly contoured handled. In a side-by-side comparison with the '167 patent design, the overall effect of this streamlined theme makes the Fubar tools significantly different from Richardson's design. Overall, the accused products clearly have a more rounded appearance and fewer blunt edges than the patented design. The court therefore was not clearly erroneous in concluding that the accused products embody an overall effect that cannot be found in the '167 patent design and hence cannot cause market confusion. *See Egyptian Goddess,* 543 F.3d at 681 (infringement cannot be found unless the accused product creates an appearance deceptively similar to the claimed design).

CONCLUSION

We have considered Richardson's remaining arguments and do not find them persuasive. Accordingly, the judgment of the district court is

AFFIRMED.

COMMENTS AND QUESTIONS

1. *Claim Construction and Functionality.* Wouldn't it be more appropriate for the court to use claim construction to dissect the claimed design and assess the extent to which functional features are separable or inextricably intertwined with ornamental attributes? The court instead poses a subjective question: Is the claimed design "primarily functional" or "primarily ornamental"? Yet the "primarily functional"/"primarily ornamental" framework is neither in the statute nor supported by the legislative history. *See* Peter S. Menell & Ella Corren, *Design Patent Law's Identity Crisis* 36 BERKELEY TECH. L.J. 1, 24-28, 54-59, 126-27 (2021). Congress sought to channel functional advances to the utility patent system alone. Courts cannot achieve that purpose unless they dissect the work and specifically identify the functional features that lie outside of the design patent regime. *See* Peter S. Menell, *Economic Analysis of Intellectual Property Notice and Disclosure*, in BEN DEPOORTER & PETER S. MENELL (EDS.), ECONOMICS OF INTELLECTUAL PROPERTY LAW, VOLUME I: THEORY 462-65 (2019).

2. *Eligibility vs. Infringement Analysis.* As we saw with regard to trade secret law (is there a trade secret?) and utility patent law (is the claim patent-eligible?), and we will see in the copyright and trademark chapters, the complexities of intellectual property law afford courts several stages for winnowing and resolving infringement disputes. Stanley had a strong argument that Richardson's design patent on a multi-purpose construction tool was ineligible based on its minimalist, functional design. Yet the court pushed the issue into an infringement trial.

3. *Infringement Analysis: Copyright Law Preview.* The court brings the narrow scope of the design patent into the infringement inquiry by factoring out the unprotectable, i.e., functional, elements and then framing the infringement inquiry as whether accused product infringes the protectable elements. This parallels the abstraction-filtration-comparison framework used in copyright law. *See Computer Associates Int'l v. Altai, Inc.*, 982 F.2d 693 (2d Cir. 1992); *Nichols v. Universal Pictures Corp.*, 45 F.2d 119 (2d Cir. 1930). Both cases are covered in Chapter IV(E)(1). Yet the Federal Circuit muddies the discounting of functional features by adhering to the notion that the design must be analyzed as a whole.Does this narrowing effectively address the concerns expressed in the notes after *Egyptian Goddess* that the ordinary observer standard could effectively give design patent owners control over designs in the prior art?

4. Remedies

i. *Injunctive Relief*

A design patent plaintiff must satisfy the *eBay* test for preliminary or permanent injunctive relief, just as in a utility patent case. Because the analysis focuses on the *ornamental design* depicted in the patent, the patentee must make a slightly different factual showing with respect to the first *eBay* factor, irreparable injury: the design patentee must show "some causal nexus between" the defendant's *design* and the plaintiff's alleged injury. *Apple, Inc. v. Samsung Elecs. Co.*, 678 F.3d 1314, 1324 (Fed.

Cir. 2012). It also is possible to demonstrate irreparable harm by showing "design dilution," meaning that the presence of similar substitutes diminishes the value of the patented design. *Id.* at 1325 (noting, however, that the lower court properly had not found design dilution in the case at bar).

ii.   Damages

After the Supreme Court ruled in *Dobson v. Hartford Carpet Co.*, 114 U.S. 439 (1885), that the rug design patentee was entitled to just 6 cents in damages, Congress added a disgorgement remedy for design patent infringement. The modern provision, largely unchanged since the 1887 legislation, provides:

> Whoever during the term of a patent for a design, without license of the owner, (1) applies the patented design, or any colorable imitation thereof, to any article of manufacture for the purpose of sale, or (2) sells or exposes for sale any article of manufacture to which such design or colorable imitation has been applied shall be liable to the owner to the extent of his *total* profit, but not less than $250, recoverable in any United States district court having jurisdiction of the parties.
>
> Nothing in this section shall prevent, lessen, or impeach any other remedy which an owner of an infringed patent has under the provisions of this title, but he shall not twice recover the profit made from the infringement.

§289 (emphasis added). Thus, a design patent owner can obtain the infringer's *total* profits for sale of an article to which the infringing design has been applied, but no less than $250.

To establish profits under §289, the patentee need only demonstrate the defendant's total sales. The defendant typically then demonstrates what portion of those sales is not attributable to the infringing design. Importantly, §289(2) applies to any entity that "sells or exposes for sale any article of manufacture to which such design or colorable imitation has been applied." This means that distributors and retailers can be liable for *their* total profit, which likely far exceeds the manufacturer's total profit. Thus, design patent cases often give rise to indemnity disputes between manufacturers and retailers, because the possible total exposure for accused items with significant retail markups can easily surpass the manufacturer's total revenue, to say nothing of its total profit.

While §289 is an additional remedy available to design patent holders, a design patentee cannot "twice recover" an infringer's profits. *See* §289 ("Nothing in this section shall prevent, lessen, or impeach any other remedy which an owner of an infringed patent has under the provisions of this title, but he shall not twice recover the profit made from the infringement."). For example, a patentee is not entitled to both a reasonable royalty *and* the infringer's profits. *See Catalina Lighting, Inc. v. Lamps Plus, Inc.*, 295 F.3d 1277, 1291 (Fed. Cir. 2002). Similarly, when a utility patent and a design patent are asserted against the same accused product, a patentee can only recover damages for the single infringing act. *See id.* at 1292.

In *Samsung Electronics Co. v. Apple Inc.*, 137 S.Ct. 429 (2016), the Supreme Court tempered the disgorgement remedy by holding that ownership of a design patent on the rounded rectangular shape of an iPhone did not necessarily entitle Apple to Samsung's entire profit from the sale of competing phones embodying the patented design. The Court opened up the possibility that the physical shell of Apple's iPhone was a different "article of manufacture" than the software or hardware in the phone.

On remand, Judge Koh instructed the jury to identify the articles of manufacture to which Samsung applied Apple's patented designs based on the following factors:

> (1) The scope of the design claimed in Apple's patent, including the drawing and written description; (2) The relative prominence of the design within the product as a whole; (3) Whether the design is conceptually distinct from the product as a whole; and (4) The physical relationship between the patented design and the rest of the product, including whether the design pertains to a component that a user or seller can physically separate from the product as a whole, and whether the design is embodied in a component that is manufactured separately from the rest of the product, or if the component can be sold separately.

Final Jury Instruction No. 29, Design Patent Damages—Article of Manufacture, *Apple Inc. v. Samsung Electronics Co.*, U.S. District Court, No. 11-CV-01846-LHK, 2017 WL 4776443, at *19 (N.D. Cal. Oct. 22, 2017). Apple contended that the articles of manufacture to which Samsung applied Apple's patented designs were the whole phones. Samsung contended that the articles of manufacture are a component or collection of components of each phone. Specifically, for the D618,677 patent, Samsung contended that the article of manufacture was a phone's round-cornered, black glass front face. For the D593,087 patent, Samsung contended the article of manufacture was a phone's round-cornered, glass front face and surrounding rim or bezel. For the D604,305 patent, Samsung contended that the article of manufacture was a phone's display screen.

The jury awarded Apple $533 million for infringement of the design patents and $5.3 million for infringement of the utility patents, approximately 20% *more* than the verdict that Samsung appealed to the Supreme Court. The parties settled their seven-year smart phone patent battle before a further appeal.

COMMENTS AND QUESTIONS

For most of the history of design patents, the articles of manufacture protected were generic products with decorative ornamentation. Many of the early design patterns covered area rugs and cast iron radiators and stoves. The ornamental design is what separated products in the marketplace. By contrast, some modern design patents cover complex, multi-component, technological goods, such as smartphones. Does it make sense to award the "total profit" for infringing articles? *See* Mark P. Gergen & Pamela Samuelson, *The Disgorgement Remedy of Design Patent Law*, 108 CAL. L. REV. 183 (2020) (contending that the fragmentation of design patents creates substantial risk that disgorgement of "total profits" will yield grossly excessive awards); Mark A. Lemley, *A Rational System of Design Patent Remedies*, 17 STAN. TECH. L. REV. 219 (2013) (arguing for reform of §289 to allow for apportionment). Note however that even though products such as mobile phones involve many components, and many design elements, the overall impression of the product is often largely a function of its design. Thus, even if some form of apportionment is reinstated, the value of design elements may prove to be substantial. For this reason, some commentators believe that the traditional "total profits" rule of §289 still makes sense. *See* Jason J. Du Mont & Mark D. Janis, *The Origins of American Design Patent Protection*, 88 IND. L.J. 837 (2013).

PROBLEM III-19

Apple Corp. obtained US D504,889 on March 17, 2004 on an "Electronic Device."

FIG. 1

FIG. 8

Samsung has entered the electronic tablet marketplace with a similar looking device.

We have discovered the following prior art references. The 1994 Fidler tablet is a tablet newspaper reader.

In 2002, Compaq introduced the TC1000 tablet.

Can Apple succeed in a design patent infringement against Samsung? If so, what remedies could it obtain?

J.   INTERNATIONAL PATENT LAW

To obtain international protection for patented technology, lawyers and businesspeople must ultimately rely on the domestic patent law of each country. In two respects, however, international treaties do come into play. First, a number of international conventions streamline the procedures under which patents originating outside the host country are prosecuted. Second, certain international treaties provide a uniform substantive floor of protection, a minimum set of rights below which treaty signatories must not fall in conferring patents. Chief among these is the Trade-Related Aspects of Intellectual Property (TRIPs) Agreement, part of the 1994 Uruguay Round of GATT revisions, which are discussed later in this section.

1.   Procedural Rules

The most important set of international procedural rules for patentees involve filing and priority dates. To understand them, however, one must first recognize that in practice they interact with elements of each country's domestic law. Recall, in this regard, the crucial divergence between U.S. and foreign priority rules. Until March 15, 2013, the U.S. judged novelty based on the complex 1952 Act first-to-invent regime. Although those rules still apply to applications files up until that date, the U.S. has moved to a first-to-file system, although it uses a unique grace period. All other countries, with trivial exceptions, establish priority based on a "first-to-file" system. If an inventor has an interest in securing patent protection overseas—whether in addition to U.S. protection or in place of it—he or she must file there *as soon after invention as possible.*

i.   *Coordinating International Prosecution*

Patent lawyers face two problems in coordinating the prosecution of a series of national patents. First, a common priority date must be obtained to ensure that protection will be uniform and unaffected by prior art published (or otherwise having an effective date) before one or more of the national patent applications. Also, a common date will ensure that prosecution of a patent in country *A* does not somehow compromise the patentability of the invention in Country *B*. Second, the patent lawyer has to deal with the logistics of international protection; she must oversee multiple filings in diverse languages in numerous countries. The wide variations in national practices and the high cost of conducting a large-scale application barrage make multiple filings one of the more challenging professional tasks in patent law.

Fortunately, two international agreements make these tasks a bit more tolerable. First is the Paris Convention, a longstanding international organization created by treaty in 1886 whose primary function is to guarantee a uniform worldwide priority date across all member countries. An applicant may file in any member country of the Convention up to one year after an initial (typically home-country) filing, without losing the priority date of the initial filing. (This treatment is provided under United States law in 35 U.S.C. §119.) The second international agreement is the Patent Cooperation Treaty (PCT), which streamlines the filing of multiple national patent applications. Each agreement in its own way is an indispensable tool of the patent trade. Although detailed discussion of the agreements would take up too much room for this volume, a few words about the essential features of each is in order.

ii.   *The Paris Convention*

The Paris Convention was signed in 1883, a product of the first true "internationalization" wave in the field of patent law. Paris Convention for the Protection of Industrial Property, as last revised, July 14, 1967, 21 U.S.T. 1583, T.I.A.S. No. 6295, 828 U.N.T.S. 305 (the last revision, sometimes referred to as the "Stockholm" revision, entered into force April 26, 1970). Its primary function is to define a common priority date so that one may file an application in one member state and have the benefit of that same filing date when filing later in another member state. One purpose of this is to prevent interlopers from copying patents applied for or issued in one state and claiming them as their own in another, before the legitimate owner has time to file in the other country.

The key provision in the Convention as regards priority is Article 4. The relevant portions read as follows:

Article 4

A(1) Any person who has duly filed an application for a patent, or for the registration of a utility model, or of an industrial design, or of a trademark, in one of the countries of the Union, or his successor in title, shall enjoy, for the purpose of filing in the other countries, a right of priority in the periods hereinafter fixed.

(2) Any filing that is equivalent to a regular national filing under the domestic legislation of any country of the Union or under bilateral or multilateral treaties concluded between countries of the Union shall be recognized as giving rise to the right of priority.

(3) By a regular national filing is meant any filing that is adequate to establish the date on which the application was filed in the country concerned, whatever may be the subsequent fate of the application.

B. Consequently, any subsequent filing in any of the other countries of the Union before the expiration of the periods referred to above shall not be invalidated by reason of any acts accomplished in the interval, in particular, another filing, the publication or exploitation of the invention, the putting on sale of copies of the design, or the use of the mark, and such acts cannot give rise to any third-party right or any right of personal possession. Rights acquired by third parties before the date of the first application that serves as the basis for the right of priority are reserved in accordance with the domestic legislation of each country of the Union.

C(1) The periods of priority referred to above shall be twelve months for patents and utility models, and six months for industrial designs and trademarks.

Thus filing in one country that is a signatory to the Paris convention gives an applicant some "breathing room"—12 months in which to prepare to file in other signatory nations.

iii.   The Patent Cooperation Treaty (PCT)

The PCT was signed in 1970. The Patent Cooperation Treaty, opened for signature June 19, 1970, 28 U.S.T. 7645, T.I.A.S. No. 8733 (entered into force Jan. 24, 1978). Its major purpose is to streamline the early prosecution stages of patent applications filed in numerous countries. It is often described as a clearinghouse for international patent applications. As a practical matter, its major advantage is that it gives an inventor (and her patent lawyer) more time, a precious commodity in the prosecution of an application destined for many countries. The signatories to the PCT have agreed to permit an applicant to wait for up to 30 months after the initial filing of a patent application in one country to begin the in-depth prosecution of the application in other countries. This allows the inventor more time, compared to non-PCT prosecution, in which to test the product, decide which countries' protection is worthwhile, and pay the patent office filing fees in the various countries.

There are two main parts of the PCT. Chapter 1 provides that an applicant who files in a national patent office may elect within 12 months to add a PCT filing. The PCT filing is simply an additional filing in any national patent office designated in the PCT. In this case, the applicant has up to 20 months from the initial filing to request that the PCT preliminary prosecution procedure be initiated. At that time, the applicant must also select the PCT member nations in which the applicant wishes to prosecute the patent. Note that Chapter 1 preserves the applicant's priority date (in PCT member countries), without having to begin active prosecution, for eight months longer than the simple Paris Convention priority period.

Chapter 2 of the PCT extends the election period to 30 months. To qualify under Chapter 2, the applicant must make her PCT filing at most five months after the first national filing. Chapter 2 gives an inventor 18 extra months, compared to the Paris Convention, to select countries for coverage and initiate multiple national prosecutions. In other words, so-called "Chapter Two" PCT filings give the inventor up to 30 months to make his or her "national elections."

The extra time is a substantial advantage. Besides simply delaying the expenditure of filing and examination fees, the PCT allows an inventor a significant extra period to assess the technical merits and commercial potential of the invention. This extra time helps the inventor save wasted filing fees for inventions that fail to blossom; for those that show great promise, the various patent applications that grow out of the PCT filing can be tailored to reflect the commercially significant embodiments that have emerged from the extensive testing.

2.   Substantive Harmonization and GATT-TRIPs

As noted earlier, the lasting impact of the Paris Convention was primarily procedural, especially with respect to the uniform, worldwide priority date it made possible. The Paris Convention did, however, contain some minimum substantive standards of protection, as described earlier. Even so, further efforts at harmonizing worldwide standards of patentability, patentees' rights, and infringement bore little fruit for most of the twentieth century.

Harmonization proceeded slowly because the international business community had little interest in parsing the detailed, esoteric issues that harmonization requires. Although it was cumbersome to deal with the divergent standards held by the world's many individual domestic patent jurisdictions, some level of effective protection was available in most of the commercially important countries. Furthermore, patent law harmonization was the domain of a highly specialized affiliate of the United Nations, the World Intellectual Property Organization (WIPO), a forum not thought to be particularly friendly to Western business interests.

Things were changing by the mid-1980s, however. For one thing, the perceived value of intellectual property was increasing; it was beginning to take on a more central role in business planning and strategy. Of special concern was the increasing importance to U.S. businesses of overseas markets in developing countries—countries that had traditionally opposed strong intellectual property protection. Businesses in the United States and Europe, aware both of the increasing importance of intellectual property and of WIPO's slow progress in harmonization, were thus on the lookout for an alternative forum in which to pursue harmonization. The search ended with the announcement of the Uruguay Round of negotiations to revise the main international trade agreement/organization, the General Agreement on Tariffs and Trade (GATT).

In addition to proposed reforms to the core function and structure of the GATT, the early Uruguay Round agenda soon grew to encompass negotiations on the "Trade-Related Aspects of Intellectual Property," or TRIPs, as it became known. The reference in the title to "Trade-Related" issues was a concession to those who doubted the relevance of intellectual property to the basic GATT mission; it soon became clear, however, that most of the basic elements of intellectual property protection would be up for discussion and potential harmonization in the TRIPs negotiations. By the time the GATT round ended in late 1993, TRIPs had become one of the principal components in the overall package of changes. *See* Robert P. Merges, *National Sovereignty and International Patent Law*, MICH. ST. L. REV. (forthcoming 2020) (comparing the Paris Convention and TRIPs)..

Although the post-TRIPs amendments to U.S. law are important, they pale in contrast to the revolutionary changes the agreement makes to the intellectual property regimes of many developing countries. To summarize the highlights, all signatories of the Uruguay Round treaty (who, under the agreement, become members of the World Trade Organization (WTO)) must now:

- Include virtually all important commercial fields within the ambit of patentable subject matter, a major change for countries that, for example, have traditionally refused to enforce pharmaceutical patents on public health/access grounds.

- Test patent applications for (a) the presence of an inventive step, which is defined as precisely synonymous with nonobviousness under §103 of the U.S. Patent Act, and for (b) "industrial application," similarly defined as coextensive with the U.S. utility requirement.
- Include in the patentees' bundle of exclusive rights the right to control the market for imports of the patented products.
- Eliminate or severely curtail the practice of granting compulsory licenses for patented technology.

See Final Act Embodying the Results of the Uruguay Round of Multilateral Trade Negotiations, Apr. 15, 1994 2–3 (GATT Secretariat 1994); Annex 1C: Agreement on Trade-Related Aspects of Intellectual Property Rights, *id.* at 6–19, 365–403. For implementation in the United States, Uruguay Round Agreements Act, Pub. L. No. 103-465 (H.R. 5110), Dec. 8, 1994. *See also* J.H. Reichman, *Universal Minimum Standards of Intellectual Property Protection Under the TRIPs Component of the WTO Agreement*, 29 INT'L LAW. 345 (1995) (able summary of provisions and open questions).

The most important GATT-related changes to U.S. law were:

- Changing the U.S. patent term to 20 years, measured from the date the patent application is filed, rather than 17 years from the date the patent was issued by the Patent Office. §154. (Under certain circumstances, such as interferences and appealed rejections, this term may be extended for up to five years. Id.).
- Opening up the U.S. "first-to-invent" system by allowing members of the WTO to introduce evidence of inventive acts in their home country for purposes of establishing priority. §104.
- Expanding the definition of infringement to include acts of unauthorized offering for sale and importing. §271.
- Adding a new procedure for filing "provisional applications," §111, which must satisfy §112 but need not include claims. Such an application does not begin the 20-year clock for the applicant's patent term.
- Requiring publication of U.S. patent applications covering inventions also claimed in foreign applications. §122(b).

These changes furthered the substantive harmonization of world patent law by bringing the United States into line with the rest of the world on a number of important issues. The AIA further harmonized U.S. patent law with patent law in many other nations. So long as patent applicants must file and prosecute (and pay fees) in each country in which they require protection, however, the impact of substantive harmonization will be limited.

In addition to worldwide harmonization, Europe has also taken significant steps to harmonize its patent law, with mixed results. European countries have for decades been able to file a single patent application at the European Patent Office instead of filing in member state patent offices. European patents may also someday be enforced in a Europe-wide patent court, a vision that has not yet come to fruition. In both instances, however, the pan-European system supplements rather than replaces the national systems of prosecution and enforcement, leaving a hodgepodge of national and EU-level rights.

K. FEDERAL PREEMPTION

The term "preemption" arises in two distinct contexts in intellectual property law. One context derives from economic analysis. Economists use the term to refer to the extent to which exclusive rights bar or "preempt" others, in the absence of a license, from pursuing research or entering a field governed by a patent (or, as we will see in later chapters, other forms of intellectual property). The higher upstream or broad is the patent—e.g., laws of nature, abstract ideas—the greater the preemptive effect.

The U.S. Constitution speaks to a different form of preemption. The Supremacy Clause of the U.S. CONSTITUTION provides that

> This Constitution, and the Laws of the United States which shall be made in Pursuance thereof; and all Treaties made, or which shall be made, under the Authority of the United States, shall be the supreme Law of the Land; and the Judges in every State shall be bound thereby, any Thing [sic] in the Constitution or Laws of any State to the Contrary notwithstanding

U.S. CONSTITUTION, ART. VI, CL. 2. Thus, the Supremacy Clause preempts or nullifies state law attempts to duplicate or interfere with federal intellectual property protection. More difficult cases involve state laws that do not directly conflict with federal authority but instead address interstitial gaps within the federal regime. Courts must grapple with whether Congress intended to leave such gaps unfilled, thereby precluding state protection, or simply allowed state law to fill these voids. This logical structure—which involves a search for the intent behind uncovered cases, sometimes in cases where technology has outpaced legislative foresight—makes preemption particularly challenging. The doctrinal distinctions are subtle and elusive.

Bonito Boats, Inc. v. Thunder Craft Boats, Inc.
Supreme Court of the United States
489 U.S. 141 (1989)

JUSTICE O'CONNOR delivered the opinion of the Court. . . .

I.

In September 1976, petitioner Bonito Boats, Inc., a Florida corporation, developed a hull design for a fiberglass recreational boat which it marketed under the trade name Bonito Boat Model 5VBR. Designing the boat hull required substantial effort on the part of Bonito. A set of engineering drawings was prepared, from which a hardwood model was created. The hardwood model was then sprayed with fiberglass to create a mold, which then served to produce the finished fiberglass boats for sale. The 5VBR was placed on the market sometime in September 1976. There is no indication in the record that a patent application was ever filed for protection of the utilitarian or design aspects of the hull, or for the process by which the hull was manufactured. The 5VBR was favorably received by the boating public, and "a broad interstate market" developed for its sale.

In May 1983, after the Bonito 5VBR had been available to the public for over six years, the Florida Legislature enacted Fla. Stat. §559.94 (1987). The statute makes "it . . . unlawful for any person to use the direct molding process to duplicate for the purpose of sale any manufactured vessel hull or component part of a vessel made by another without the written permission of that other person." §559.94(2). The statute also makes it unlawful for a person to "knowingly sell a vessel hull or component part of a vessel duplicated in violation of subsection (2)." §559.94(3). Damages, injunctive relief, and attorney's fees are made available to "any person who suffers injury or damage as the result of a violation" of the statute. §559.94(4). The statute was made applicable to vessel hulls or component parts duplicated through the use of direct molding after July 1, 1983. §559.94(5).

On December 21, 1984, Bonito filed this action in the Circuit Court of Orange County, Florida. The complaint alleged that respondent here, Thunder Craft Boats, Inc., a Tennessee corporation, had violated the Florida statute by using the direct molding process to duplicate the Bonito 5VBR fiberglass hull, and had knowingly sold such duplicates in violation of the Florida statute. . . .

III.

We believe that the Florida statute at issue in this case so substantially impedes the public use of the otherwise unprotected design and utilitarian ideas embodied in unpatented boat hulls as to run afoul of the teaching of our decisions in *Sears* and *Compco*. It is readily apparent that the Florida statute does not operate to prohibit "unfair competition" in the usual sense that the term is understood. The law of unfair competition has its roots in the common-law tort of deceit: its general concern is with protecting *consumers* from confusion as to source. . . .

In contrast to the operation of unfair competition law, the Florida statute is aimed directly at preventing the exploitation of the design and utilitarian conceptions embodied in the product itself. The sparse legislative history surrounding its enactment indicates that it was intended to create an inducement for the improvement of boat hull designs. *See* Tr. of Meeting of Transportation Committee, Florida House of Representatives, May 3, 1983 ("There is no inducement for [a] quality boat manufacturer to improve these designs and secondly, if he does, it is immediately copied. This would prevent that and allow him recourse in circuit court"). To accomplish this goal, the Florida statute endows the original boat hull manufacturer with rights against the world, similar in scope and operation to the rights accorded a federal patentee. Like the patentee, the beneficiary of the Florida statute may prevent a competitor from "making" the product in what is evidently the most efficient manner available and from "selling" the product when it is produced in that fashion. Compare 35 U.S.C. §154. The Florida scheme offers this protection for an unlimited number of years to all boat hulls and their component parts, without regard to their ornamental or technological merit. Protection is available for subject matter for which patent protection has been denied or has expired, as well as for designs which have been freely revealed to the consuming public by their creators. That the Florida statute does not remove all means of reproduction and sale does not eliminate the conflict with the federal scheme. See *Kellogg*, 305 U.S., at 122. In essence, the Florida law prohibits the entire public from engaging in a form of reverse engineering of a product in the public domain. This is clearly one of the rights vested in the federal patent holder, but has never been a part of state protection under the law of unfair competition or trade secrets. . . .

Moreover, as we noted in *Kewanee*, the competitive reality of reverse engineering may act as a spur to the inventor, creating an incentive to develop inventions that meet the rigorous requirements of patentability. 416 U.S., at 489–490. The Florida statute substantially reduces this competitive incentive, thus eroding the general rule of free competition upon which the attractiveness of the federal patent bargain depends. . . . The Florida statute is aimed directly at the promotion of intellectual creation by substantially restricting the public's ability to exploit ideas that the patent system mandates shall be free for all to use. Like the interpretation of Illinois unfair competition law in *Sears* and *Compco*, the Florida statute represents a break with the tradition of peaceful coexistence between state market regulation and federal patent policy. The Florida law substantially restricts the public's ability to exploit an unpatented design in general circulation, raising the specter of state-created monopolies in a host of useful shapes and processes for which patent protection has been denied or is otherwise unobtainable. It thus enters a field of regulation which the patent laws have reserved to Congress. The patent statute's careful balance between public right and private monopoly to promote certain creative activity is a "scheme of federal regulation . . . so pervasive as to make reasonable the inference that Congress left no room for the States to supplement it." *Rice v. Santa Fe Elevator Corp.*, 331 U.S. 218, 230 (1947). . . .

COMMENTS AND QUESTIONS

1. Does this result make sense? Is it consistent with *Kewanee Oil Co. v. Bicron Corp.*, 416 U.S. 470 (1974) (excerpted in Chapter II(H))? *Bonito Boats* can be reconciled with trade secrets statutes if one accepts the reverse engineering rationale described above. Whatever one thinks of the *Bonito* result, the last sentence remains troubling. Characterizing patent law as "pervasive federal regulation" suggests that it might preempt the field, automatically striking down all state laws that attempt to regulate intellectual property. If taken seriously, that approach would leave no room at all for state protection of inventions.

2. Note the similarity between the statutes struck down in *Sears* and *Bonito Boats*. In both cases, what was prohibited was the direct copying of a competitor's design. The *Bonito Boats* statute is more limited than that in *Sears*, since it prohibits only one particular method of copying. Nonetheless, the Court struck it down. Why should the courts be concerned about these comparatively narrow statutes when they allowed the far broader statute in *Kewanee* to pass muster?

3. The *Bonito Boats* decision has been criticized. *See* John S. Wiley, Jr., *Bonito Boats: Uninformed but Mandatory Federal Innovation Policy*, 1989 SUP. CT. REV. 283. *Cf.* Symposium, *Product Simulation: A Right or a Wrong?*, 64 COLUM. L. REV. 1178

(1964) (articles criticizing the analogous decisions in *Sears* and *Compco*). Does this criticism make sense? Or is *Bonito Boats* a needed barrier to the creation of state laws that would undo the balance struck by Congress?

As part of the Digital Millenium Copyright Act, Congress created a new federal intellectual property right protecting "original" boat hull designs. 17 U.S.C. §§1301 et seq., discussed in Chapter IV. Can Congress lawfully accomplish here what the states cannot? Does *Bonito Boats* suggest some sort of constitutional limitation on any form of protection (state or federal) in this area?

4. Some lawyers have tried to apply *Bonito Boats* in contexts beyond the patent-like legislation actually considered in the case. This has not met with much success, however; like other broad preemption decisions before it, *Bonito Boats* has been hemmed in by subsequent qualifications. In *Waits v. Frito-Lay, Inc.*, 978 F.2d 1093 (9th Cir. 1992), a right of publicity case based on an advertising campaign imitating Tom Waits' distinctive vocal qualities, the Ninth Circuit had the following to say about *Bonito Boats:*

Bonito Boats involved a Florida statute giving perpetual patent-like protection to boat hull designs already on the market, a class of manufactured articles expressly excluded from federal patent protection. The Court ruled that the Florida statute was preempted by federal patent law because it directly conflicted with the comprehensive federal patent scheme. In reaching this conclusion, the Court cited its earlier decisions in *Sears Roebuck & Co. v. Stiffel Co.*, 376 U.S. 225 (1964), and *Compco Corp. v. Day-Brite Lighting*, 376 U.S. 234 (1964), for the proposition that "publicly known design and utilitarian ideas which were unprotected by patent occupied much the same position as the subject matter of an expired patent," i.e., they are expressly unprotected. *Bonito Boats*, 489 U.S. at 152.

The defendants seize upon this citation to *Sears* and *Compco* as a reaffirmation of the sweeping preemption principles for which these cases were once read to stand. They argue that *Midler* [*v. Ford Motor Co.*, 849 F.2d 460 (9th Cir. 1988) (another sound-alike right of publicity case that is reproduced in Chapter VI(D)] was wrongly decided because it ignores these two decisions, an omission that the defendants say indicates an erroneous assumption that *Sears* and *Compco* have been "relegated to the constitutional junkyard." Thus, the defendants go on to reason, earlier cases that rejected entertainers' challenges to imitations of their performances based on federal copyright preemption, were correctly decided because they relied on *Sears* and *Compco*. *See Sinatra v. Goodyear Tire & Rubber Co.*, 435 F.2d 711, 716–18 (9th Cir. 1970), *cert. denied*, 402 U.S. 906 (1971); *Booth v. Colgate-Palmolive Co.*, 362 F. Supp. 343, 348 (S.D.N.Y. 1973); *Davis v. Trans World Airlines*, 297 F. Supp. 1145, 1147 (C.D. Cal. 1969). This reasoning suffers from a number of flaws.

Bonito Boats itself cautions against reading *Sears* and *Compco* for a "broad pre-emptive principle" and cites subsequent Supreme Court decisions retreating from such a sweeping interpretation. "[T]he Patent and Copyright Clauses do not, by their own force or by negative implication, deprive the States of the power to adopt rules for the promotion of intellectual creation." *Bonito Boats*, 489 U.S. at 165 (citing, inter alia, *Goldstein v. California*, 412 U.S. 546, 552–61 (1973) and *Kewanee Oil Co. v. Bicron Corp.*, 416 U.S. 470, 478–79 (1974)). Instead, the Court reaffirmed the right of states to "place limited regulations on the use of unpatented designs in order to prevent consumer confusion as to source." *Id. Bonito Boats* thus cannot be read as endorsing or resurrecting the broad reading of *Compco* and *Sears* urged by the defendants, under which Waits' state tort claim arguably would be preempted.

Moreover, the Court itself recognized the authority of states to protect entertainers' "right of publicity" in *Zacchini v. Scripps-Howard Broadcasting Co.*, 433 U.S. 562 (1977). In *Zacchini*, the Court endorsed a state right-of-publicity law as in harmony with federal patent and copyright law, holding that an unconsented-to television news broadcast of a commercial entertainer's performance was not protected by the First Amendment. *Id.* at 573, 576–78. The cases *Frito* asserts were "rightly decided" all predate *Zacchini* and other Supreme Court precedent narrowing *Sears'* and *Compco's* sweeping preemption principles. In sum, our holding in *Midler*, upon which Waits' voice misappropriation claim rests, has not been eroded by subsequent authority.

Waits v. Frito-Lay, Inc., 978 F.2d 1099–1100.

The Federal Circuit has allowed state claims that tread on patent law, particularly where the claims are made against patent owners rather than in an effort to create a new form of intellectual property protection. *See, e.g., Dow Chemical v. Exxon Corp.*, 139 F.3d 1470 (Fed. Cir. 1998) (unfair competition claims by accused infringer based on alleged inequitable conduct not preempted); *Univ. of Colorado Found. v. American Cyanamid, Inc.*, 196 F.3d 1366 (Fed. Cir. 1999) (state claims of fraud and unjust enrichment against patentee who stole invention from plaintiff not preempted). The court has, however, required that state claims that touch on areas of federal patent interest be judged by federal, not state, standards, so that they do not upset the balance struck by patent law. *See Univ. of Colorado, supra; Midwest Industries v. Karavan Trailers*, 175 F.3d 1356 (Fed. Cir. 1999). Is this a reasonable compromise?

5. In a number of cases, restrictions on the content of licensing contracts are said to raise preemption issues. One might question whether contracts are equivalent to state statutes for preemption purposes. On at least one occasion, the Supreme Court has suggested that protection of unpatentable goods (which would be prohibited under state misappropriation statutes) is permissible under contract law. *See, e.g., Aronson v. Quick Point Pencil*, 440 U.S. 257 (1979). On the other hand, there are a variety of circumstances in which federal patent policy precludes the parties from contracting to the contrary. *See, e.g., Brulotte v. Thys Co.*, 379 U.S. 29 (1964) (holding unenforceable patent licensed in agreement that extends beyond patent term); *Kimble v. Marvel Entertainment, LLC*, 135 S.Ct. 2401 (2015) (upholding *Brulotte*); *Lear, Inc. v. Adkins*, 395 U.S. 653 (1969) (contracts estopping licensee from challenging the validity of a patent are void); *Everex Systems Inc. v. Cadtrak Corp.*, 89 F.3d 673 (9th Cir. 1996)

(federal policy precluding assignment of nonexclusive patent licenses prevailed over state doctrine permitting such assignments). Note that in some of these cases, such as *Everex*, federal preemption actually works to the benefit of the intellectual property owner.

Regardless of the particular limitations federal law imposes on licensing agreements, patent licensing in general is a question of state (not federal) law. *See Gjerlov v. Schuyler Labs. Inc.*, 131 F.3d 1016 (Fed. Cir. 1997).

6. State laws providing a remedy when patentees send threatening "demand letters" without adequate research raise preemption concerns. These laws aim to address fair trade or consumer protection concerns, but have the potential to affect the enforcement powers of federal patentees. *See* Robin Feldman, *Federalism, First Amendment & Patents: The Fraud Fallacy*, 17 COLUM. SCI. & TECH. L. REV. 30, 32 (2015); Paul R. Gugliuzza, *Patent Trolls and Preemption*, 101 VA. L. REV. 1579, 1580 (2015).